introduction
to
social
welfare

FOURTH EDITION

Walter A. Friedlander
Robert Z. Apte

University of California at Berkeley

PRENTICE-HALL, INC., Englewood Cliffs, New Jersey

Library of Congress Cataloging in Publication Data

FRIEDLANDER, WALTER A
  Introduction to social welfare.

  (Prentice-Hall sociology series)
  Includes bibliographies.
  1. Public welfare—United States. 2. Charities—United States. 3. Social service—United States.
I. Apte, Robert Z., joint author. II. Title.
HV91.F7 1974   362'.973   73–15573
ISBN 0-13-497016-0

Prentice-Hall Sociology Series
Herbert Blumer, Editor

Printed in the United States of America

10 9 8 7 6 5 4 3 2 1

PRENTICE-HALL INTERNATIONAL, INC., *London*
PRENTICE-HALL OF AUSTRALIA, PTY. LTD., *Sydney*
PRENTICE-HALL OF CANADA, LTD., *Toronto*
PRENTICE-HALL OF INDIA PRIVATE LIMITED, *New Delhi*
PRENTICE-HALL OF JAPAN, INC., *Tokyo*

contents

foreword

Beginning with its first edition in 1955, *Introduction to Social Welfare* has established itself as the most outstanding and widely used introductory textbook in the field of social welfare. This position of eminence attests to its scholarly soundness and pedagogical excellence. Dr. Walter Friedlander, the sole author of the preceding editions, has shown himself a scholarly craftsman of high order. He has a profound knowledge of the history of social welfare, is keenly sensitive to contemporaneous developments in the field, and has developed a comprehensive and studious familiarity with social welfare thought and practice. These scholarly qualifications have enabled him to treat the field of social welfare with admirable thoroughness and thoughtfulness. In addition, Dr. Friedlander has shown high pedagogical talent and skill. He is clearly the type of writer who can put himself effectively in the position of his audience, grasping the direction of interest of its members, understanding the level of their intellectual preparation, and sensing how topics should be presented to stimulate and guide intelligent comprehension. On the side of exposition, Dr. Friedlander is obviously gifted in converting his rich scholarly knowledge into a well organized, coherent, and lucid presentation. His selection and organization of topics have provided fine coverage of the field. His language is simple and clear, his explanations readily grasped; he has great skill in guiding readers over difficult terrain. These pedagogical talents have contributed significantly to the continuing success of the book.

With the collaboration of a gifted younger scholar, Dr. Robert Apte, Dr. Friedlander has prepared a new edition of *Introduction to Social Welfare*. Their task was not easy, because the field of social welfare has undergone profound changes within the last few years. Drs. Friedlander and Apte could not merely bring the book "up to date" by introducing new statistical data and research findings; they confronted a much more challenging task set by the transformations and stresses now in play in the field of social welfare. These transformations and stresses are not merely minor increases or decreases in pre-existing lines of development. They are mutational, more in the nature of a critical recasting of the field of social welfare, of its premises, its philosophy, its problems, and the modes of attack on the problems. To appreciate what Drs. Friedlander and Apte have done in revising this book, let us designate and discuss briefly several of the changes that have been twisting the field of social welfare out of its customary shape.

One of the lines of development is the increasing incorporation of welfare activities into the national political process. This has affected the structure and functioning of social welfare in several ways. Of particular importance is the increasing responsibility devolving on the government for the provision of social welfare. Acceptance of this responsibility, whether willing or otherwise, by the State creates exasperating problems of social policy and perhaps even more disturbing problems of bureaucracy. In large measure it removes the field of social welfare from the direction of social welfare professionals and subjects it to a significant degree to political pressures. This momentous shift strikes at the center of social welfare organization and practice.

The elevation of social welfare to a major government enterprise and its emergence as a political issue have brought the field of social welfare much more under the influence of public attitudes and opinions. As political forces, such attitudes can profoundly affect the content and delivery of social welfare. Professionals and other workers in social welfare must give careful attention to trends in public sentiment as they relate to social welfare. One such long-term trend is the growing recognition that certain forms of welfare assistance are a citizen's indigenous right. The public also takes short-run stances as a consequence of political conflicts over welfare issues, and those stances are all too frequently confused by inadequate knowledge.

Another line of development which is particularly stressful to professional social welfare workers is a change in the position and posture of clients or recipients of social welfare. Recently social welfare clients and recipients in several areas have asserted strongly their right to share in the determination of welfare services. On occasion, this pressure has led to the achievement of local control by the ostensible recipients of aid; in other instances, assertiveness has led to bitter struggles among rival local groups or between recipients and professionals. The significant changes in clients' views of their position and claims create unusual problems for the structure of social welfare.

Finally, professional social workers are viewing their field, their mission, and themselves differently. A fair number of social welfare professionals are beginning to believe that the problems which programs of social welfare seek to address can be solved only through extensive changes in the economic and social structure of society, not by conventional programs of social welfare. The consequences of this belief are obviously profound. Other professionals are coming to rely on vast, complex, monolithically directed programs, in line with what are seen as the large-scale organizational tendencies of modern society. Others are disposed toward the traditional image of close relations between the professional and the client, but wish to guide this relation by new sets of principles. These are but a few of the new self-conceptions and conceptions of the field of social welfare that are appearing among professional social welfare workers. Of course, social welfare professionals have always had diverging conceptions of their task and how to carry it out. Yet there seems now to be a much greater and more profound questioning by social welfare workers of their field and their traditional role in it.

The four lines of development we have discussed suggest the situation of rather profound change in which the field of social welfare is presently caught. The challenge confronting Drs. Friedlander and Apte in preparing the fourth edition of *Introduction to Social Welfare* was to see the field of social welfare in its new dimensions, to identify and describe the new lines along which social welfare is moving, to analyze the emerging social welfare problems, and always to emphasize what is central and viable in this complex scene. The authors have responded most admirably to this challenging task. Readers will find in this revised edition a discriminating and judicious treatment of the field of social welfare as it is taking shape today.

The same high level of scholarship and pedagogical skill that marked earlier editions is present in the fourth edition. In the important chapters which he has contributed, Dr. Apte has shown himself to have the same talents of craftsmanship as Dr. Friedlander. Their collaboration bodes well for the present work.

HERBERT BLUMER
University of California

preface

The fourth edition of *Introduction to Social Welfare* is written in the context of a rapidly changing national and international environment which strongly influences the practice of social work and the field of social welfare. Social welfare concerns and activities have expanded to touch the lives of more and more groups of human beings, and to involve our major social systems—the family, the neighborhood, the schools, the health system, the church, occupations, and the law. As the scope of social welfare activities widens, the various philosophies, theories, and concepts of social welfare also change. Fundamental premises of social work theory and practice are being challenged, partly because of extensive involvement of government in the operation of various social welfare programs, and partly because of profound changes in our social values. New social policies affect the funding and delivery of human health and welfare services. These new policies reflect the questions of economic and political equality, legal rights, institutional and other forms of racism and sexism, consumer activism, ecology, crime prevention, the needs of special population groups, and the need for more effective manpower use in the social services.

It is important that the student of social welfare be aware of changing policies which aim to ameliorate social problems and to improve the condition of the poor, the disadvantaged minorities, the disenfranchised, and those who suffer from various handicaps. What appears to be a new approach to a social problem is often only a reshuffling of limited resources, resulting in only minor, limited change. The field of social welfare is concerned with helping human beings in need by redistributing enough of the resources of our society to solve social problems. Such a redistribution, however, will take place only after a basic change in our beliefs and values regarding our responsibility toward our fellow human beings.

The book has three major sections. Part I deals with the concepts of social welfare and social work and their history in Europe, their effect on Colonial America, and their development in the United States up to the post-Vietnam period. Part II discusses briefly various social work methods employed in carrying out social welfare programs, including case and group work with individuals and families, and community organization and social welfare planning. Part III, Chapters 8 through 18, covers the range of social welfare programs. Chapters 9 through 18 discuss four fields of practice: economic security and employment opportunity (Chapters 9 and 10), social environment and housing services (Chapter 11), personal and developmental services (Chapters 12, 13, 17, and 18), and health promotion and health care services (Chapters 14, 15, and 16). These groupings should facilitate the reader's approach to the subject by linking the main social problem areas with the systems of social welfare and health services. Chapter 19 focuses on professional aspects of social work and education for social services.

The book is aimed particularly at serving the following groups: undergraduate and graduate students of social work, psychology, sociology, criminology, public health, and related human sciences; persons working in public assistance, health and mental health services, community services, social insurance, employment, and correctional services; persons working or planning to work in human services of various types who want to gain broader perspectives for their work; indigenous workers in various public and private services who seek insight into the changing system of human services in our society; and citizens planning to participate as volunteers in one of the many new opportunities in welfare and health services.

The authors are indebted to Dr. Herbert Blumer, General Editor of the Prentice-Hall Sociology Series and Professor Emeritus of the University of California, Berkeley; to Edward H. Stanford, Prentice-Hall Sociology Editor; to R. James Mullen, Prentice-Hall Field Editor; and to Carolyn Davidson, Production Editor, for their encouragement, advice, and assistance; and to the authors and publishers of professional publications quoted within this work, although the authors alone are responsible for the concepts and content of this book.

the concept and the historical development of social welfare

1

the concept
of
social welfare
and
social work

The concept and the term *social welfare* in the sense of a scientific program have developed only in connection with the social problems of industrial society. Poverty, sickness, suffering, and social disorganization have existed throughout mankind's history. But the rising industrial society of the nineteenth and twentieth centuries had to face so many new social problems that the older human institutions—family, neighborhood, churches, and local community—could no longer adequately meet them. The need for a broader system of social services resulted. In the following chapters we shall briefly analyze how human society attempts to deal with destitution, maladjustment, and physical and mental ills and how family, community, church, private philanthropy, and public agencies, under the influence of humanitarianism, in turn assume some of the responsibility for satisfying human needs.

The magnitude of social problems in our present society makes it necessary to organize, under public and private initiative, social services for people in need. Government is taking an increasingly larger responsibility for citizens' well-being. Recently, international organizations have also shared to some extent the responsibility for meeting larger health and social problems. At the same time as humanitarian ideas developed about our responsibility to assist those who need help, progress in the biological and social sciences and in modern technology have provided new tools for investigating the causes of human suffering, poverty, deficiencies, and dissatisfaction, opening ways to alleviate or cure certain social and individual problems. Still, social welfare and social work never pretend to be able to solve all human and social problems.

Although numerous studies have tried to establish a concise terminology for the concepts of "social welfare," "social work," "social services," and "social security," no universally accepted definitions exist. In this study we shall use the definitions that follow.

Social welfare is a system of laws, programs, benefits, and services which strengthen or assure provisions for meeting social needs recognized as basic for the welfare of the population and for the functioning of the social order. The system is undergoing rapid transformation in response to the transition of our society from scarcity to relative abundance and to the revolution of rising expectations.[1]

Social work is a professional service, based on scientific knowledge and skill in human relations, which helps individuals, groups, or communities obtain social or personal satisfaction and independence. While professional social work was first performed by private or public agencies, it is now also carried on in private practice, by various counseling services, and in other settings. The term *social welfare* has a broader meaning than professional social work. In the definition accepted by the United Nations, it includes organized activities aimed at helping individuals or communities to meet their basic needs, and at promoting their well-being in harmony with the interests of their families and communities.[2] Education, labor legislation,

---

[1] Elizabeth Wickenden, *Social Welfare in a Changing World* (Washington, D.C.: Department of Health, Education and Welfare, 1965), p. vii; John M. Romanyshyn, *Social Welfare: Charity to Justice* (New York: Random House, 1971), pp. 3, 5. See also Ralph Pumphrey, "Social Welfare: History," in *Encyclopedia of Social Work, 1971* (hereinafter called *Encyclopedia 1971*) (New York: National Association of Social Workers), p. 1446.

[2] *The Development of National Social Welfare Programmes* (New York: United Nations, 1959). Harold Wilensky and Charles Lebeaux define social welfare as "the organized system of agencies, institutions, and programs which function to

and recreation contribute to the well-being of the population, but we do not include them in our discussion of social welfare.

We shall, however, discuss the structure and function of *social services* administered by public and private organizations. The objective of these services is to secure for each human being, as much as possible, the economic and social necessities: a decent standard of health and living conditions, equal opportunities, and the highest possible degree of self-respect, dignity, and freedom of thought and action without interfering with the same rights of others.

Social security is a program of protection provided by social legislation against sickness, unemployment, death of wage-earner, old-age or disability dependency, and accidents—contingencies against which the individual cannot be expected to protect himself.[3] As a rule, protection is secured by various forms of social insurance, public assistance, and health and welfare services. In the strict sense the term *social security* does not include private, voluntary social services or industrial or cooperative activities, but in many countries these play an important role.

The philosophy underlying our system of social welfare is an essential cultural characteristic of modern society. In the following chapters we shall trace its essential elements to comprehend the present aspects of social welfare and the attitude of the public toward its problems. This book does not attempt to teach the methods of professional social work. They are based on a knowledge of human behavior and motivations; the dynamics of human relationships; the sociological, economic, and political conditions of our society; the community and its social services; and the practical application of social work techniques. Instead, this study will analyze both the evolving structure and functions of social welfare and the underlying social philosophy.[4]

Social work, like other professions, is both a science and an art. Its functions and methods will be discussed in Part Two, its major programs and practices in Part Three. Social work draws scientific knowledge and

---

maintain or improve the economic conditions, health or interpersonal competence of a population," and social work as "an occupation or profession with more or less specific training and skills who occupy along with other groups key positions in the provision of welfare services" (*Industrial Society and Social Welfare* [New York: Russell Sage Foundation, 1958], p. 17).

[3] Charles I. Schottland, *The Social Security Program in the United States* (New York: Appleton-Century-Crofts, 1963), pp. 1–6; Maurice Stack, "The Meaning of Social Security," in *Readings in Social Security*, eds. William Haber and Wilbur J. Cohen (Englewood Cliffs, N.J.: Prentice-Hall, 1948), pp. 41–45; Wilbur J. Cohen, "Social Insurance," *Encyclopedia 1971*, p. 1277.

[4] For valuable information on this development and on current theory and practice of social welfare, see the *Encyclopedia of Social Work, 1971* (particularly James Leiby, "Social Welfare: History," pp. 1461–77), and the references listed at the end of this chapter.

insight from several disciplines—sociology, economics, political science, psychology, psychiatry, anthropology, biology, history, law, education, and philosophy—but it has synthesized them into a unique science. Social work as a profession depends on the body of knowledge of these other sciences, but also on the specific structure and functions of the social services and the skill and responsibility of professional social workers.

We live in a period of rapid change in which fundamental values, legislation, and institutions are not stable. Therefore, we suggest that in addition to studying this book, the reader keep up with professional literature in the field of social welfare to be informed of new ideas, experiments, and developments.

SELECTED BIBLIOGRAPHY

ABBOTT, EDITH, *Social Welfare and Professional Education,* 2nd ed. Chicago: University of Chicago Press, 1942.

BISNO, HERBERT, *The Philosophy of Social Work.* Washington, D.C.: Public Affairs Press, 1952.

COHEN, NATHAN E., ed., *Social Work and Social Problems.* New York: National Association of Social Workers, 1964.

————, *Social Work in the American Tradition.* New York: Holt, Rinehart and Winston, 1958.

CRAMPTON, HELEN M., and KENNETH K. KEISER, *Social Welfare: Institution and Process.* New York: Random House, 1970.

DAVIS, F. JAMES, *Social Problems: Enduring Major Issues and Social Change.* New York: Free Press, 1970.

FERGUSON, ELIZABETH, *Social Work: An Introduction.* Philadelphia: J. B. Lippincott, 1963.

FINK, ARTHUR E., EVERETT E. WILSON, and MERRILL B. CONOVER, *The Field of Social Work,* 5th ed. New York: Holt, Rinehart and Winston, 1968.

FRIEDLANDER, WALTER A., HENRY S. MAAS, GISELA KONOPKA, and GENEVIEVE CARTER, *Concepts and Methods of Social Work.* Englewood Cliffs, N.J.: Prentice-Hall, 1958.

HERAUD, BRYAN J., *Sociology and Social Work: Perspectives and Problems.* Elmsford, N.Y.: Pergamon Press, 1970.

KAHN, ALFRED J., ed., *Issues in American Social Work.* New York: Columbia University Press, 1959.

KLENK, ROBERT W., and ROBERT M. RYAN, *The Practice of Social Work.* Belmont, Ca.: Wadsworth, 1970.

KONOPKA, GISELA, *Eduard C. Lindeman and Social Work Philosophy.* Minneapolis: University of Minnesota Press, 1958.

LUBOVE, ROY, *The Struggle for Social Security.* Cambridge, Mass.: Harvard University Press, 1968.

MENDES, RICHARD H. P., et al., *Social Welfare as a Social Institution.* New York: Council on Social Work Education, 1969.

NORDHAUS, WILLIAM D., *Invention, Growth and Welfare: A Theoretical Treatment of Technological Change.* Cambridge, Mass.: M.I.T. Press, 1969.

PUMPHREY, RALPH E., and MURIEL W. PUMPHREY, eds., *The Heritage of American Social Work.* New York: Columbia University Press, 1961.

REYNOLDS, BERTHA C., *Social Work and Social Living—Explorations in Philosophy and Practice.* New York: Citadel Press, 1951.

ROMANYSHYN, JOHN M., *Social Welfare: Charity to Justice.* New York: Random House and Council on Social Work Education, 1971.

SCHOTTLAND, CHARLES I., *The Social Security Program in the United States.* New York: Appleton-Century-Crofts, 1963.

SKIDMORE, REX A., and MILTON G. THACKARY, *Introduction to Social Work.* New York: Appleton-Century-Crofts, 1964.

SMITH, EDMUND A., *Social Welfare: Principles and Concepts.* New York: Association Press, 1965.

TURNER, JOHN B., "In Response to Change: Social Work at the Crossroads," *Social Work,* 13, No. 3 (July 1968), 7–15.

WEINBERGER, PAUL E., ed., *Perspectives on Social Welfare: An Introductory Anthology.* Toronto: Macmillan, 1969.

WICKENDEN, ELIZABETH, *Social Welfare in a Changing World.* Washington, D.C.: Department of Health, Education and Welfare, 1965.

WILCOX, CLAIR, *Toward Social Welfare.* Homewood, Ill.: Richard D. Irwin, 1969.

WITMER, HELEN L., *Social Work: An Analysis of a Social Institution.* New York: Farrar & Roinehart, 1942.

2

old world background

SOCIAL PROBLEMS

Modern anthropology and sociology have shown that with the beginning of human society the feeling of belonging, and the readiness to provide mutual protection, were just as influential as the selfish desire to dominate weaker human beings. Dating from this early phase of human development, mutual assistance can be called one of man's fundamental drives. Mutual aid served as the means of protection for family or tribe against the hostile world. The role of the head or chief was mainly that of protector against human enemies as well as against wild animals.

With the growth of tribes and the beginnings of religion, priests assumed leadership in providing protection for the helpless, widows and orphans, and the sick. Religious devotion became the most powerful incentive for benevolence and charity. We find this motive in ancient religions, the Vendidad and Hindu philosophy, in Assyrian, Babylonian, and Egyptian codes, in Greek and Roman customs—particularly, however, in Jewish and Christian religious teachings.[1] Charity was motivated primarily by the desire to receive the grace of God or to secure the merits of good deeds for eternal life, but a genuine feeling of pity for the widows and orphans may well have been a reason that the churches' demands for the relief of the poor were willingly followed. To relieve the distress of the unfortunate became, in Jewish and Christian concepts, an important religious duty. It was essential to the church as a moral force, to the giver as a means of satisfaction and hope, to the destitute and to the community as a welcome aid. The teaching of the prophets in Israel and of St. Paul, St. Augustine, St. Francis, and St. Thomas Aquinas in the Christian church gave the recipient of alms dignity, whereas almsgiving ennobled the generous donor. Early Christians helped one another when facing poverty and persecution but the medieval church entrusted the administration of charity to the bishops, the local priest, and the deacons. With the growing influence of the church and the acceptance of Christianity as state religion, institutions for the poor were established in the monasteries, serving as orphanages, as homes for the old, the sick, and the handicapped, and as refuge for the homeless, continuing the tradition of the Greek *xenodochia* (guest houses). Particularly active in distributing alms to the poor were the Franciscans, founded by Saint Francis d'Assisi, and the Hospitallers, established by Guy de Montpelliers. They devoted their main activity to missionary preaching, collecting alms, and distributing relief to the destitute.[2] Under these circumstances mendicancy grew throughout Europe, since asking for alms was not only an easy way of making a living but was also socially respected because it was shared with the missionaries and monks, with students of the universities, and with the Crusaders on their way to the Holy Land. Although the church praised charity and almsgiving, the state did not take the same attitude. Beginning with the statute of Charlemagne in 800, secular authorities threatened to prohibit mendicancy and fined citizens who gave alms to able-bodied beg-

[1] Frank T. Bruno, "New Light on Oriental and Classical Charity in the Pre-Christian Era," *Family*, 25 (November 1944), 260–265; Amos G. Warner, *American Charities*, 3rd ed. (New York: Crowell, 1919), pp. 4–6; Stuart A. Queen, *Social Work in the Light of History* (Philadelphia: J.B. Lippincott, 1922), pp. 267–307; and Gisela Konopka, *Eduard C. Lindeman and Social Work Philosophy* (Minneapolis: University of Minnesota Press, 1958), pp. 84–88.

[2] Charles A. Henderson, *Modern Methods of Charity* (*hôtels-Dieu*) (New York: Macmillan, 1904), pp. 513 ff.; Blanche D. Coll, *Perspectives in Public Welfare: A History* (Washington, D.C.: HEW, 1970), pp. 1–3.

gars. These decrees aimed to force serfs and rural laborers to stay on the manors and to protect peasants and travelers against robbery by vagrant beggars. This conflict between church and state existed until the end of the Middle Ages.[3]

The older church institutions in which charity was rendered—monasteries, abbeys, and convents—were partly replaced by the "hospitals" (hôtels-Dieu) which administered to old and sick persons, orphans, abandoned children, and pregnant women. They became the main agency of medieval charity. Hospitals were founded with the help of donations from kings, dukes, and members of the aristocracy. However, only some of the destitute found shelter and refuge in these institutions; many wandering beggars remained on the roads, a curse with which local and state governments were unable to cope. The difference in ideology regarding beggars was not the only conflict between the church and the secular authorities in the field of charity. Another conflict arose over mismanagement of church institutions and hospitals and the abuse of funds, which led to criticism, measures of control, and the setting up of boards of supervision by the states. To stop vagrancy and mendicancy, many European states enacted repressive statutes imposing brutal penalties, but none really succeeded in wiping out vagabondage.

The conflict between church and state became still more violent in the sixteenth century during the period of the Reformation. In Germany Martin Luther appealed in an open address, "Appeal to the Christian Nobility of the German Nation" (1520), to the princes to forbid begging and to organize in all parishes a "common chest" for the receipt of money, food, and clothes for the needy. Luther requested that regular contributions in addition to voluntary gifts be made to these chests. A similar plan for relief was carried out in Zurich, Switzerland, by the Protestant Reformator Ulrich Zwingli in 1525. France, Austria, and the Scandinavian countries developed programs which resembled the Lutheran concept; the responsibility for the collection of funds and the distribution of relief to destitute, sick, and orphans was assumed by local authorities, but the church wardens played the leading role in relief administration.[4]

Although such methods recognized the legal responsibility of the community for the maintenance of the poor, they did little to change the social conditions of destitute families. The idea that the fate of the individual poor deserved attention was first conceived by the Spanish philosopher Juan

[3] Walter A. Friedlander, Individualism and Social Welfare (New York: Free Press, 1962), pp. 1–25.

[4] Karl de Schweinitz, England's Road to Social Security, 1349 to 1947, 3rd rev. ed. (Philadelphia: University of Pennsylvania Press, 1947), pp. 36–38; Coll, Perspectives in Public Welfare, pp. 6–8; Wilbur K. Jordan, Philanthropy in England 1480–1660 (New York: Russell Sage Foundation, 1959).

Luis Vives in the sixteenth century. Vives was educated in Paris and lived most of his life in Belgium. A friend of Erasmus of Rotterdam and of Sir Thomas More, he was one of the noted scientists of his time. He developed a concise program of poor relief for the Consuls and the Senate of the city of Bruges in Flanders under the title *"De Subventione Pauperum."*[5] He proposed dividing the city into parish quarters, assigning two senators with a secretary to each quarter to investigate the social conditions of every pauper family, and providing for aid through vocational training, employment, and rehabilitation instead of the customary distribution of alms. For the aged and unemployable Vives asked commitment to a hospital (almshouse).

Not until two and one-half centuries later were the foresighted methods of Vives' plan applied in practice in continental Europe. This was done in Hamburg in 1788, where a reform of poor relief introduced a district system of investigation and distribution of relief to individual paupers through volunteer committees appointed by the Senate. The city was divided into sixty quarters following a plan suggested by Professor Busch, city senator and commissioner of public relief. Each quarter had about the same number of poor families. Each commission consisted of three respectable citizens who served without compensation. The investigations were directed by regulations of a central board composed of five senators and ten other citizens. The sixty commissions acted at the same time as agents of the "central poor house," interviewed the poor, inquired about their health, earnings, and morals, and determined the individual needs of each family. Children and adolescents were trained in elementary courses and in an industrial school attached to the central orphan asylum.[6]

A similar system of relief was inaugurated by an American Tory, Benjamin Thompson, later Count of Rumford, in Munich in 1790. To prevent sturdy paupers from begging, he founded a "military workhouse" which manufactured clothing for the army. With the help of volunteer district commissions, able-bodied beggars were recruited for this workhouse; there they, their families, and other destitutes were given a free meal. It also provided raw materials for home industry to poor people who wanted to earn their living. Both the Hamburg and the Munich relief systems were financed by taxation and by collections of voluntary gifts. The city of Elberfeld introduced the same plan in 1853 and financed it exclusively

[5] Juan Luis Vives, *Concerning the Relief of the Poor or Concerning Human Need*, A Letter Addressed to the Senate of Bruges, trans. Margaret M. Sherwood, New York School of Philanthropy, 1927; Thomas F. Graham, *Medieval Minds: Mental Health in the Middle Ages* (London: Allen & Unwin, 1967).

[6] De Schweinitz, *England's Road to Social Security*, pp. 91–99; and Walter A. Friedlander and Earl Dewey Myers, *Child Welfare in Germany Before and After Naziism* (Chicago: University of Chicago Press, 1940), pp. 39–44.

from public taxation. The volunteers of the Elberfeld commissions lived in the same quarter as the poor whom they supervised, and thus were acquainted with their conditions. Later a large number of other European cities adopted this program.[7] Although the system was actually used first in Hamburg, it was called the *Elberfeld system.*

The most important reformer of the charities of the Catholic Church was Father Vincent de Paul in France, who was active during the seventeenth century.[8] This young priest had been captured by Tunisian pirates and sold as a galley slave. Sharing for a number of years the fate of the most unfortunate, he devoted his life after his escape to the improvement of charities, especially for prisoners and their families, orphans, illegitimate children, and the sick and hungry. He succeeded in arousing interest among the aristocracy and at the royal court, and obtained large foundations for the establishment of hospitals, orphanages, and foundling asylums. Not satisfied with such spectacular success, he persuaded the ladies of the court to devote themselves to personal services for the destitute and sick. He organized a lay order, the "Ladies of Charity," whose members visited the poor in their homes, distributing food and clothes. To improve the methods of nursing the sick and handicapped, in 1633 Father Vincent founded another order, the "Daughters of Charity," composed of young peasant women who wanted to devote themselves to charitable work. They were trained in nursing the poor and became the forerunners of the social worker. The ideas of Father Vincent caused important reforms to be made in the entire charity program under Catholic auspices, not only in France, but also in other countries.

EARLY CHARITIES IN ENGLAND

In medieval England, care of the poor was an activity of the church. To give alms to the destitute, blind, and lame was a religious duty and a means of salvation from the threat of divine punishment after death. Since the main motive for almsgiving was the salvation of the soul of the donor, he usually had little concern for the human being who received his charity. Beginning in the fourteenth century, however, some distinction was made between two classes of the poor: the able-bodied poor who could earn their living, and the impotent poor who were unable to work—the blind, the lame, the aged, the sick, young children, and pregnant women. For the care of the poor the church devoted from one-fourth to one-third of the tithes and offerings collected from its parishioners.

Relief to the destitute was first distributed by the priest of the parish,

[7] De Schweinitz, *England's Road to Social Security,* pp. 148–50.
[8] Friedlander, *Individualism and Social Welfare,* pp. 6–8.

with the help of the churchwardens and deacons. In the thirteenth and fourteenth centuries, religious orders and church institutions relieved the parish churches from most of the duties of caring for the poor. In the fifteenth century more than a thousand monasteries, convents, hospitals, and abbeys provided shelter, clothes, food, and alms for the poor and for wandering beggars. Many institutions were maintained by endowments donated for charitable purposes by members of the royal house and the aristocracy. Although daily distributions of food were made at the convent gate and shelter was granted to the homeless, little was done to change the social conditions of the poor so that they might become self-supporting again.

Although the church was by far the most important charitable institution of this period, its work was supplemented from the twelfth to the fifteenth century by the relief activities of the guilds. Craft and merchant guilds, rural fraternities, and social or church guilds were organized primarily for mutual self-help, brotherhood, and fellowship. They first supported sick or needy members, and their widows and orphans, but they also organized charities for the poor of the town. Particularly in times of drought and famine, they distributed barley and corn to the destitute, fed them on certain feast days, and offered free lodging to poor travelers.

Until the fourteenth century the king and Parliament did not concern themselves with the charities of the church and the guilds. Under the feudal system the serf and his family were fed and clad by the lord and cared for by the lady when they were old or sick. With the disappearance of feudalism and the rise of a new order which freed the serfs and employed agricultural labor for wages, the king and his nobles faced the problem of how to maintain order among the laborers and prevent vagrancy and crime. Emancipation gave the laborer and his family the freedom to wander, but it deprived him of his former security. In times of unemployment, sickness, old age, and invalidity, he was forced to go begging. At the beginning of the Industrial Revolution the manufacture of wood opened some work to the laborer, but resident workers were hired first. During the summer workers migrated from one part of the country to another to harvest the crops. Soldiers returning from the wars in France often preferred to live in the towns rather than to go back to their hard, low-paid work and dependency on the manor. These social conditions increased the danger of poverty.

The first poor law in England was based on a national catastrophe.[9] In 1348 the plague or "Black Death," brought in from the Levant on ships carrying infected rats, killed two-thirds of the English population within

---

[9] We recommend the description of the development of social welfare in England presented in de Schweinitz, *England's Road to Social Security*, for further study. See also Brian Tiernay, *Medieval Poor Law* (Berkeley: University of California Press, 1959); Ralph Arnold, *A Social History of England: 55 B.C. to 1215 A.D.* (New York: Barnes & Noble, 1967).

two years. It caused a severe shortage of labor on the manors and resulted in a steep rise in wages.[10] Urged by the landed gentry, King Edward III issued the *Statute of Laborers* of 1349. It ordered that able-bodied laborers without means must accept employment from any master willing to hire them and it forbade them to leave their parish. Citizens were not allowed to give alms to able-bodied beggars. The Statute of Laborers became the first of many laws in the development of the "Erastian State" in which secular power replaced clerical authority. It was designed to prevent vagrancy and begging, and to force the rural worker to stay on the land. Cruel punishment such as being put into the stocks, whipped, branded, mutilated by cutting off the ears and the nose, condemned to the galleys, or even hanged was ordered for beggars and vagrants. When the expanding woolen industry made sheep raising more profitable for the gentry than growing grain crops, tilled land was converted into pasture. Only a small number of shepherds was needed to replace the large numbers of rural laborers, and the unemployed families joined the ranks of former soldiers and sailors unable to find work.

The first constructive measure taken by government for relief of the poor was the statute of Henry VIII in 1531. It provided that mayors and justices of the peace should investigate applications of the aged and paupers unable to work who were maintained by the parish. They were to be registered and licensed to beg in an assigned area. This law was the beginning of a recognition of public responsibility for the poor, but it still threatened brutal punishment for other beggars and vagrants.

The Reformation brought a fundamental change in the system of charities and relief for the poor in England. One of its features was the secularization of the monasteries and hospitals which had been the primary source for the relief of the destitute. The influence of the guilds had vanished during the fifteenth century. Other benevolent foundations which had provided aid to needy groups no longer did so, and with the confiscation of church property by Henry VIII it became necessary to provide otherwise for the care of the poor. Therefore, the *Statute of 1536* established the first plan of public relief under the auspices of the government in England. It ruled that paupers could be registered in their parishes only after they had resided for three years in the county. The parish had to maintain the "impotent poor" from voluntary contributions of the parishioners through church collections. Able-bodied beggars were forced to work, and idle children from five to fourteen years of age were taken away from their parents and indentured. In 1562 the *Statute of Artificers* was issued to regulate wages and hours of labor and to increase the skill of artisans by an appren-

---

[10] Eugene and Fanchon Mead, *Man Among Men* (Englewood Cliffs, N.J.: Prentice-Hall, 1965), pp. 341–42; Brian Rodgers, *From Pauperism to Human Rights* (New York: Humanities Press, 1966).

tice system. It required that vagrants and vagabonds be forced to hard labor and that unemployed beggars between twelve and sixty years of age be hired out as servants. However, voluntary collections proved to be insufficient for the support of the poor. Their ranks had been swelled by disbanded monks and nuns and by thousands of families formerly sheltered or employed in monasteries and convents. As work became scarce and the price of food rose, vagrancy and begging increased. In 1563 Parliament had to adopt compulsory measures to finance parish poor relief. Each householder was compelled by law to make a weekly contribution based on property and income.

In 1572 Queen Elizabeth signed a statute of Parliament that introduced a general tax to provide funds for poor relief and established overseers of the poor to administer the new law. The *Statute of 1572* marked the final recognition that the government was responsible for providing aid to people who could not maintain themselves. In 1576 "houses of correction," supplied with wool, hemp, flax, and iron, were established in which the able-bodied poor, particularly young persons, were forced to work.

The *Statute of 1597* confirmed that the churchwardens and four substantial householders were to be appointed as overseers of the poor by the justices of the peace. Almshouses should be erected for the impotent poor, the old, the blind, the lame, and those unable to work, and parents and children were made liable for each other's maintenance.

THE ELIZABETHAN POOR LAW OF 1601

The *Poor Law of 1601,* often referred to as "43 Elizabeth," was a codification of the preceding poor relief legislation. Its only new feature was the establishment of liability for support to grandparents as well as to parents in need. The statute represented the final form of poor law legislation in England after three generations in which public opinion had been greatly excited about the necessary provisions for the poor in a period of political, religious, and economic changes that required government action.[11] The law confirmed the responsibility of the parish—the local community—for the maintenance of the poor who were not supported by their relatives. The parish's responsibility to the destitute was limited to persons who had been born there or who had lived in the parish for at least three years. This question of residence or settlement right as one of the important requirements for the receipt of public relief has remained a vital issue in public assistance.

[11] De Schweinitz, *England's Road to Social Security,* pp. 20–29; W. K. Jordan, *Philanthropy in England: 1480–1660* (New York: Russell Sage Foundation, 1959); Coll, *Perspectives in Public Welfare,* pp. 3–10.

The Poor Law of 1601 did not permit a person to register as being in need of charity whenever his relatives, husband or wife, parents or children were able to support him. The principle of relatives' responsibility or family responsibility means that relatives must assume the primary obligation for supporting the poor, and that public relief authorities aid the destitute only if the family cannot maintain him. This question of family responsibility also has persisted as a serious problem in public assistance. The law distinguished three classes of the poor:

(1) *The able-bodied poor* were called "sturdy beggars" and were forced to work in the house of correction or workhouse. Citizens were forbidden to give them alms, and paupers who arrived from other parishes were returned to the place where they had last dwelt for a year. A beggar or "valiant vagabond" who refused to work in the house of correction was put in the stocks or in jail.

(2) *The impotent poor* were people unable to work—the sick, the old, the blind, the deaf-mute, the lame, the demented, and mothers with young children. They were to be placed in the almshouse where they were to help within the limits of their capacities. If the impotent poor had a place to live and it seemed less expensive to maintain them there, the overseers of the poor could grant them "outdoor relief," usually "in kind," sending food, clothes, and fuel to their homes.

(3) *Dependent children* were orphans, foundlings, and children who had been deserted by their parents or whose parents were so poor that they could not support them. These children were to be placed out to any citizen who was willing to take them without a charge. If no such "free home" was available, the child was to be given to the lowest bidder. Children eight years and older able to do some domestic and other work were indentured with a townsman. Boys were taught the trade of their master and had to serve until their twenty-fourth birthday. Girls were brought up as domestic servants and remained in indenture until they were twenty-one years of age or married.

The overseers of the poor administered the poor law in the parish. They were appointed by the justices of the peace or the magistrates. Their function was to receive the application of the poor person for relief, to investigate his condition, and to decide whether he was eligible for relief. The overseers decided whether the applicant and his family should be placed in the workhouse or almshouse, should be "sold out," or should receive aid in their home. As a rule, an old unused building served as almshouse and workhouse. In the workhouse the inmates were forced to do hard labor, under the supervision of a superintendent appointed by the overseers of the poor. The overseers had to collect the poor tax assessed on land, houses, and tithes of all inhabitants, and to register assessment and payments. The poor tax was the main source for the financing of poor relief.

It was supplemented by private donations and bequests, and by the use of fines for the violation of certain statutes.

The Poor Law of 1601 set the pattern of public relief under governmental responsibility for Great Britain for 300 years. It established the principle that the local community—the parish—had to organize and finance poor relief for its residents and provide sustenance to the unemployable and children and work to the able-bodied. It still maintained many of the earlier features of repression and disdain for the destitute, but it also accepted an obligation for the aid of people who could not provide for themselves. The fundamental provisions of the Elizabethan Poor Law were incorporated into the laws of the American colonies and have remained an important element even in present concepts of public assistance and in the considerations of the public in regard to social legislation.

The Settlement Act of 1662

Because each parish was responsible for the maintenance of its poor, it wanted to protect itself against an additional burden created by poor persons moving in from other communities who might ask for relief. The gentry, however, were anxious to retain on the land rural laborers who were needed for the cultivation of their estates. Following the pressure of both the parishes and the gentry, Charles II enacted in 1662 the *Law of Settlement*. It empowered the justices of the peace to return to his former residence any newcomer who, in the opinion of the overseers of the poor, might at some future date become a public charge. Within forty days after arrival, the overseers had to investigate and might request from the justice of peace that the newcomer be expelled. However, if the newcomer was able to rent property for ten pounds sterling a year or to deposit this sum, he was exempted from the threat of removal.

This statute was the expression of an extreme parochialism. It discriminated against the common laborer who could not afford a deposit or a rent of ten pounds sterling a year. It represented a postfeudal attempt to force the rural workers to stay in their villages, although the industrial development of the towns offered greater promise for them. Difficulties arose in some towns when the overseers, eager to get rid of paupers, offered them bribes to go clandestinely to another parish. Therefore, in 1686 King James II ruled that the prescribed forty days for investigation should be counted only from the date on which the newcomer sent a written report on his abode and his family to the overseers or the churchwardens. A few years later, in 1691, King William III required that an announcement of the arrival of newcomers be posted in the church. Despite these legal amendments, frequent disputes arose between townships over the question of whether laborers had gained settlement in a parish. Litigation before the courts and useless transportation of families and witnesses cost the country a great deal of money. Furthermore, the statute prevented workers from going during harvest time to other counties where they were badly needed. These economic conditions made necessary further changes in the administration of the settlement law. Mobility of labor was finally achieved by the introduction of the "certificate," a document issued by the parish authorities which guaranteed that the township would pay the cost of maintenance of the bearer if he should be in need. Thereafter, each community requested such a certificate from newcomers. Not until 1795 was the Act of 1662 amended so that a newcomer could not be sent back to his former residence until he had actually applied for relief. Even so vagabonds, "disorderly persons," and unmarried pregnant women could still be forcibly expelled immediately.

Workhouses and Outdoor Relief

During the second half of the seventeenth century, the English were in fierce commercial competition with the Dutch, who had succeeded in developing an efficient industry and trade. English economists admired the absence of beggars in the streets and the productive operation of the Dutch almshouses, in which inmates manufactured goods for export. The desire to keep raw materials, wool, and mining iron in England and to produce finished goods for export led to the training of the English poor for industry. Following the *Workhouse Act of 1696,* workhouses in Bristol and other cities instructed the inmates, adults and children, in spinning, knitting, linen weaving, lace work, and in the manufacture of nets and sails. However, these experiments had no economic success since the unemployed poor had no particular training and could not compete with workshops employing skilled foremen and laborers. In 1722 the overseers were authorized to make contracts with private manufacturers who employed the paupers, and relief was refused to any person not willing to enter the workhouse. This "workhouse test" forced families to give up their homes and to live in the workhouse as in a prison, the men separated from their wives and children. Many paupers preferred to live in utmost poverty with their families rather than to move to the workhouse or "house of correction." Workhouses conducted by private contractors attempted to make profits by spending as little as possible for equipment and repair and for the food and clothing of the inmates, but the work of the tired and hungry inhabitants was so inadequate that the contractors still operated at a loss. The mistreatment of the inmates, the lack of fresh air and proper sanitation, and the immorality in the overcrowded wards aroused serious criticism from ministers and social reformers such as Jonas Hanway, Joseph Townsend, Richard Burn, John Scott, and Thomas Gilbert. The first of the crusaders for a reform of the workhouse, Jonas Hanway, spent several years studying these institutions. He exposed the appalling rate of infant mortality in the workhouses where sometimes 82 percent of all babies under one year of age died. In 1761, on the incentive of Hanway, Parliament attempted to improve these conditions by the registration of all infants in workhouses, and in 1767 the removal from the workhouse of all children under six years and their placement with foster families was ruled.

One of the most persistent reformers of the workhouse was Thomas Gilbert. As a magistrate he knew of the failures of the poor laws, but as member of the House of Commons he could appraise them with more effect. The *Poor Law Amendment of 1782,* known as the "Gilbert Act," abolished the contractor system of the workhouse, replaced the honorary overseers of the poor by salaried "guardians of the poor," and reversed the principle of indoor relief by providing that persons able and willing to work should be maintained in their homes until employment was procured.

Economic changes in England, however, were a continuous source of increasing poverty. For centuries the poor man had used the "common" of the village. He had grown vegetables, potatoes, barley, and wheat for his family, had grazed his sheep, geese, pigs, or cows, and had thus supplemented the meager earnings from his small field or from working as a tenant farmer. The "enclosure movement" which began in the fourteenth century enlarged the holdings of the landed aristocracy, but took away from the poor peasant the livestock and products that had enabled him to maintain his family. Moreover, many peasants lived on the common land and thought they owned it. With the enclosure they became "squatters," landless poor, and were forced to move. In industry, the invention of power machinery driven by wind or water transferred production from villages and small towns to larger cities where water transportation was available. The place of manufacture shifted from the home of the craftsman to the larger workshop and mill. The growth of industry tended to increase the number of workers, but the new machinery in the mills replaced many of the hand weavers, creating unemployed paupers and vagrants.

Partial Relief

The war with France from 1793 to 1815, following the French Revolution, increased the cost of living. Disabled war veterans refused to go to the poorhouse with their families and insisted on receiving poor relief in their homes. Magistrates and guardians became concerned with the suffering of the poor and considered means to increase wages or to secure a minimum wage. In May 1795 a conference of poor-law officials of Berkshire County at Speenhamland decided to establish a "table of universal practice," which determined the amount of relief on the basis of the local cost of bread needed for the sustenance of the family. This so-called "bread scale" was also to be used to supplement wages of laborers whose earnings were less than this minimum subsistence. The new practice spread to other places and was approved by Parliament by the *Speenhamland Act of 1795*. The statute authorized relief allowances in the homes of the poor, according to the size of the family, either for their support or to supplement low wages. It led to widespread use of outdoor relief for old, infirm, and handicapped persons.[12]

As a result of these measures, wages and the general standard of living were lowered. More and more persons received full or partial relief and therefore contributed to the need for higher poor-tax rates. Employers became accustomed to paying substandard wages and to referring workers to the guardians of the poor. Relief destroyed the workers' incentive to do a good job and tended to keep wages at the bread scale.

It is not difficult to understand why such a system was severely criticized. The opposition centered on the granting of relief to persons in their homes, that is, "outdoor relief." This practice was held responsible for the economic and moral failure of the program. In reality, it was not the method of "direct" or "outdoor" relief which caused undesirable effects, but rather the failure to secure minimum wages that would maintain the worker, and the lack of administrative ability for constructive use of poor relief. With the increasing cost of the poor rate, dissatisfaction among taxpayers was aggravated by the uneven distribution of this burden. Communities with a large number of paupers frequently had few wealthy merchants, which meant that the poor tax had to be collected from householders of modest income.

Another criticism of poor-law practice was based on the economic theory of laissez-faire, as presented in Adam Smith's *Wealth of Nations*.[13] It postulated that the state should not interfere with private economy so that the manufacturer could reap the profits of production. Supporters of Smith's doctrine, such as Jeremy Bentham and the Reverend Joseph Townsend, suggested a gradual decrease and, finally, the elimination of public poor relief. The most influential representative of this theory was another clergyman, Thomas R. Malthus. In his famous *Essay on Population*, which appeared in 1798, he explained that while the food supply increased only in arithmetic progression, the population grew in geometric progression, and

12 See Walter Elder, "Speenhamland Revisited," *Social Service Review*, 38, No. 3 (September 1964), 204–302; Mark Blany, "The Poor Law Report Re-examined," *Journal of Economic History*, 24 (June 1964), 229–45; Karl Polanyi, *The Great Transformation* (New York: Rinehart, 1944), Chap. 8; and Michael E. Rose, *The English Poor Law 1780–1930* (New York: Barnes & Noble, 1971). In the United States the suggestions of President Nixon's "family assistance plan" (see Chapter 10) have aroused renewed interest in this English example.

13 *An Inquiry into the Nature and Causes of the Wealth of Nations*, published in 1776.

that agriculture, therefore, was unable to feed a steadily increasing population—a situation, he claimed, that made war, famine, and pestilence necessary to stem this dangerous growth. Malthus disapproved of poor relief because it tended to encourage paupers to have more children to get relief for them, and tended to raise the price of food, which again impoverished the entire working class.

Although the opposition of the classical economists to public relief had a theoretical, financial, and commercial basis, the objection of others, such as John Stuart Mill, to the poor law practices was founded on humanitarian and moral considerations.[14] Reverend Thomas Chalmers (1780–1847), a parish minister in the small community of Kilmany, Scotland, organized a program of private charity on the principle of neighborly aid. An eloquent preacher, he was called to Glasgow in 1814 and found there an expensive system of poor relief financed from public taxes and church collections. Chalmers opposed the impersonal character and inefficiency of this charity. At Kilmany he had visited each home of the parish, and he resumed this custom at the large Tron parish in Glasgow with its 11,000 members. His visits revealed numerous personal and health problems which had been unknown before. After four successful years, Chalmers was called to organize the St. John parish in a very poor section of Glasgow. He accepted on condition that he would be given full control over the administration of relief. He divided this parish into twenty-five districts with about 400 parishioners each, under the guidance of a deacon who investigated relief applications. The surprising result was that during four years only twenty new applicants, from a parish population of 8,000, were found in need.

Based on this experience, Chalmers proclaimed that the prevalent practice of public and church relief was wasteful, demoralized the pauper, destroyed his will to support himself; that it eliminated the will of his relatives, friends, and neighbors to help; and that it failed to use the readiness of philanthropists to aid the poor. Chalmers suggested the following procedure: (1) each case of distress be carefully investigated, the cause of destitution determined, and the possibilities of self-maintenance of the pauper developed; (2) if self-support was not possible, relatives, friends, and neighbors be encouraged to care for orphans, the aged, the sick and handicapped; (3) if the need of the family could not thus be met, wealthy citizens be found to maintain the family; (4) only if none of these measures succeeded, the deacon of the district should ask for the help of the congregation.[15]

---

14 Abram L. Harris, "John Stuart Mill: Government and Economy," *Social Service Review*, 37, No. 2 (June 1963), 134–53.

15 Thomas Chalmers, *The Four Fountains of Charity* (Edinburgh: Sutherland & Knox, 1823) and *The Parochial System Without a Poor Rate* (Edinburgh: Sutherland & Knox, 1848); Ralph Pumphrey and Muriel Pumphrey, eds., *The Heritage of American Social Work* (New York: Columbia University Press, 1961, pp. 67–70).

Chalmers's important contribution to the field of charity was his philosophy of personal, parochial relief. He developed the principle of investigating each case of destitution individually and of attempting a solution of the cause of distress.[16] Chalmers, like his contemporaries, considered personal failures as the main cause of poverty and overlooked the economic and social factors outside the power of the individual. Nevertheless, his concept that a personal interest in the fate of the destitute is essential was important to the progress of relief work. Fifty years after Chalmers's pioneer work, the London Charity Organization Society organized a program of relief that was, in the main, based on Thomas Chalmers's ideas. They laid the first foundation for the individual approach in social work which today we call "casework."

POOR LAW REFORM OF 1834

Severe opposition to the poor law practice, the rising flood of pauperism, and the heavy increase in the poor-tax burden led in 1832 to the appointment of a "Royal Commission for Inquiring into the Administration and Practical Operation of the Poor Laws." Its chairman became Professor Nassau W. Senior, a noted economist, and its secretary Edwin Chadwick, a brilliant young lawyer who had studied under Jeremy Bentham. The commission undertook for two years in every county of England an extensive survey of poor-law administration and rendered its report in 1834. The report emphasized that the prevailing practice of poor relief had failed to bring children and able-bodied adults to work and had made them "permanent paupers" instead of self-supporting citizens, particularly through the introduction of "partial relief." Poor-tax rates were used as subsidies to farmers, landlords, storekeepers, and manufacturers. The six main recommendations of the report were (1) to abolish partial relief as provided under the Speenhamland system; (2) to place all able-bodied applicants for relief in the workhouse; (3) to grant outdoor relief only to the sick, the old, the invalid, and widows with young children; (4) to coordinate the administration of relief of several parishes into a "poor law union"; (5) to make the conditions of poor relief recipients less desirable than those of the lowest paid worker in the community (*Principle of "Less Eligibility"*); and (6) to establish a central board of control to be appointed by the king. These recommendations were enacted August 14, 1834, in a statute known in England for one hundred years as "The New Poor Law."

"Poor Law Unions" were formed by neighboring parishes. They were administered by a Board of Guardians, composed of representatives of each parish with a paid staff, and managed a common workhouse and almshouse.

---

[16] Thomas Chalmers, *The Christian and Civic Economy of Large Towns* (Glasgow, 1821).

To develop a uniform poor-law policy, a Permanent Royal Poor Law Commission was appointed with three commissioners; Edwin Chadwick was its first secretary. Assistant commissioners visited poor law unions, attended meetings of the boards of guardians, and inspected workhouses and alms-houses.

The application of the legal principle of "less eligibility" meant that poor relief was granted to the destitute in such a meager amount and in such a derogatory way that its receipt put the poor in a condition less desirable than that of the lowest paid laborer in the community. By maintaining this principle the boards of guardians thought to force relief applicants to accept any type of labor rather than ask for public support. This concept has persisted in public assistance in many parts of the world. The public is afraid that destitute persons prefer receiving poor relief to exerting themselves in unpleasant manual work; the amount of assistance, therefore, should be less than the wage earned by a low paid worker and should not provide a higher standard of living than can be earned by work. In large families, however, the maintenance of the children might require a higher amount than some underpaid workers earn, and for this reason the old idea of less eligibility is still controversial.

From the point of view of financial economy, the reform of 1834 was a success. It reduced the cost of poor relief between 1834 and 1837 by more than one-third; 200 workhouses were constructed and old institutions improved. Able-bodied poor were forced to go to the workhouse with their families as a test of their economic need. No separate buildings for alms-houses and workhouses were established, however, as had been recommended by the commission in 1834. Old and young people, sturdy and ill, feeble-minded, insane, and cripples were placed in the same institution. Families were broken up, because women, young boys and girls, the aged, crippled, and infirm were assigned to separate wards of the workhouse. Mothers were permitted to care for their young children in the so-called "nursery" only at prescribed hours. Under rigid discipline, inmates were forced to hard labor as much as their physical strength permitted and were treated not differently from convicts. No wonder that the workhouse was very unpopular, and hated by the working class.[17] Disraeli said in a famous address that the reform bill of 1834 pronounced that "to be poor in England was a crime."

The reform of 1834 meant a resumption of the rigid, repressive measures of the Poor Law of 1601. It reduced the expenditures for poor relief, but made life in the workhouse so unbearable that the poor asked for relief

17 Polanyi, *The Great Transformation*, Chap. 8; Blany, "The Poor Law Report Re-examined"; G. M. Trevelyan, *English Social History*, 3rd ed. (New York: Barnes & Noble, 1946); Roy Lubove, ed., *Social Welfare in Transition: Selected English Documents, 1834–1909* (Pittsburgh: University of Pittsburgh Press, 1966).

only when there was no other way to survive. These methods did not consider the danger of mass poverty in periods of unemployment and economic depression. Therefore, some poor law unions introduced "a work test outside the workhouse," and permitted the poor to receive outdoor relief in their homes. To maintain uniform practices, the *Outdoor Relief Regulation Order of 1852* upheld the principle of less eligibility. These measures were violently resented by the working class, who called the workhouse the "bastille." Interest in the poor was awakened by humanitarians such as Charles Dickens, who published *Oliver Twist* with its description of workhouse life in 1837 and 1838, and by members of Parliament who disliked the power entrusted to the poor-law commissioners. The Poor Law Commission also had internal difficulties. Edwin Chadwick was an energetic, aggressive reformer, not content with the cautious actions of the commissioners. In 1847 the commission was replaced by a Poor Law Board whose president had a seat in the House of Commons. The four other members of the board were appointed by the crown. Edwin Chadwick became General Commissioner of the Poor and supervised investigations into the causes of poverty and the means of effective social reform.

Earlier surveys made by the poor-law commissioners with the assistance of medical inspectors, especially Dr. Southwood Smith, had revealed that widespread prevalence of disease among the lower classes was a major cause of destitution. Disease deprived the laborer and his family of the means of livelihood and made them dependent on public relief. Disease among the poor was caused mainly by unhealthy housing and living conditions and by malnutrition. In urban slums people lived in overcrowded quarters, and often adolescents and children of both sexes slept in one bed. This led to promiscuity, quarrels, delinquency, immorality, and rapid spread of contagious diseases. Many workingmen-boarders lived with families in the same room. Often seven to ten used one sleeping room, or lived in damp, dark cellars without any ventilation. All over England the poorer quarters were without water supply and drainage; drinking water was often polluted in rivers or deficient pipelines. There were usually no outside toilets and no sewers in the streets. Refuse was thrown into the public gutter, and there existed no scavenger service or regular street cleaning, although this was occasionally done by inmates of the workhouse. Another cause of epidemics was the failure to bury the dead, among the poor, until the poor-law guardians assumed the cost of the funeral.

On the initiative of Edwin Chadwick, the Poor Law Board brought these conditions to the attention of Parliament. Chadwick thus became the first pioneer of public hygiene. He developed a program of protection against contagious disease by sanitary provisions for water systems, sewage, and drainage. He also advocated the establishment of parks and flower gardens for public recreation. At his insistence, free public vaccination against cholera, typhus, and smallpox was introduced in 1840. The *Public Health Act* of August 31, 1848 established a General Board of Health, and Edwin Chadwick served as one of its members. The board supported local authorities in the fight against epidemics, in the improvement of housing conditions in the slums, and in the establishment of sanitation. Despite his devoted service, Edwin Chadwick again found severe opposition. After six years he was dismissed because the House of Commons felt that he entrusted too much power to a central health authority, and because the physicians complained that he infringed on vested interests of the medical profession. Undertakers and water-supply companies also complained that their profits were curtailed by the regulations of the Board of Health. But less than a decade later, Florence Nightingale, denouncing the miserable status of the army medical service, aroused public opinion and started single-handed a reform of nursing, hospitals, and medical practice.

Chadwick was far ahead of his contemporaries. It took many decades before his vision of a system of government providing under central direction decent aid to the poor, sound public health protection, adequate housing, recreation, and public schools for the entire population became an accepted concept of society.[18]

CHILD LABOR AND FACTORY LEGISLATION

Until the beginning of the nineteenth century, social policy in England had been used to suppress the laboring classes in the interest of the land owners, the manufacturers, and the merchants. Pauper children were set to work by "selling" them to farmers, by indenture to craftsmen, or by hard labor in almshouses. The development of the textile mills in the nineteenth century, however, offered an unprecedented opportunity to use the poorhouse children. They were offered to textile manufacturers as cheap labor. The fate of these children became deplorable. Some were as young as four years of age, and there was no legal limitation of their working hours. "Slappers" kept them awake by whipping them when they fell asleep. Typically such poor children leased out to a textile mill got up at four or five in the morning. The younger ones had to pick up cotton waste from the factory floor all day. Children of six or seven years were put to the spinning wheel or to the loom where their small, deft, flexible fingers could throw the thread quicker than adults. The children usually had half an hour for a frugal breakfast and an hour for a lunch of similar quality. During work-

[18] See Jeanne L. Brand, *Doctors and the State: The British Medical Profession and Government. Action in Public Health, 1870–1912* (Baltimore: Johns Hopkins Press, 1965); and Dorsey D. Jones, *Edwin Chadwick and the Early Public Health Movement in England* (Iowa City: University of Iowa Press, 1931).

ing hours they had to stand and were not allowed to leave their work place, outside of the meals, to go to the toilet or to get a drink of water. If he had to leave his station, the hapless child was brutally punished by whipping. As a rule, the child's labor was completed after five or six in the evening, often hours later, so that the working day was sometimes sixteen to eighteen hours long. The lack of sleep, of fresh air and sunshine, of rest, and of any vacation made many of these children undernourished, weak, and sick. Many died in their teens, when they had worked themselves to death.[19]

The first step in the direction of their protection was the *Health and Morals Act of 1802*, passed on the initiative of Sir Robert Peel, who objected to the use of young children in labor camps at the textile mills. The statute of 1802 restricted the working hours of "pauper apprentices" to twelve hours a day, and forbade night work for children. The law applied, however, only to pauper children leased out from the poor houses. Cotton-mill owners, however, hired children directly from their parents and continued to exploit them without any limit of working hours.

Concerned about these conditions, Peel, Robert Owen, John Wood, and John Fielden pursued the demand for protection of working children against mistreatment and overwork which was so destructive to their health. In Parliament Michael Sadler, Anthony Ashley Cooper (later the Earl of Shaftesbury), R. Cobden, and James Graham became the advocates of child labor legislation. This movement led to the enactment of the *Factory Act of 1833*, which prohibited the employment of children under nine in the textile industry and limited daily working hours for children. At the suggestion of Edwin Chadwick, the law introduced the appointment of factory inspectors under a central national office. An amendment of the *Factory Act of 1847* ordered a daily maximum of ten working hours for women and children under eighteen years.

The industrial development of England and the economic crises which accompanied the introduction of modern machinery led to several periods of unemployment. Local boards of guardians were forced to borrow money to maintain the workhouses or to provide public works in times of widespread unemployment. Even so, conditions in numerous workhouses were unbearable. Most workhouses had inadequate sanitary facilities, poor ventilation, and no medical and nursing care for the sick and the aged. Beds were so short that inmates were unable to sleep well. Above all, superintendents and attendants were, as a rule, ignorant and callous. Legislative reforms led to an expansion of the supervisory powers of the Poor Law Board. In 1871 the Local Government Board was founded to take over the

---

[19] Grace Abbott, *The Child and the State*, Vol. I (Chicago: University of Chicago Press, 1938), pp. 138–52; De Schweinitz, *England's Road to Social Security*, pp. 166–70; G. H. Feinstein, ed., *Socialism, Capitalism, and Economic Growth* (Cambridge: Cambridge University Press, 1967).

functions of the Board of Health and the Poor Law Board. The new board maintained the policy of advocating the workhouse test and of warning the boards of guardians against a liberal granting of outdoor relief. The Local Government Board failed to recognize that such stern treatment usually fell on broken-down, depressed, and feeble persons who could not obtain employment and needed encouragement and help.

PRISON REFORM

Since the Middle Ages, prisons had been a place of severe human suffering. Medieval dungeons, often situated without light and air in the deep, humid cellars of old castles, were not much different from the prisons used during the seventeenth to the nineteenth century. Convicts suffered from hunger, cold, neglect, and brutal beatings. The prison population consisted not only of offenders convicted for crime but also persons who could not pay their civil debts. Nevertheless, all inmates were forced to pay the jailer for their upkeep; he and his assistants lived off the money they extorted from the prisoners and their families and friends. Some charitable donations provided prisoners with bread, beef, and broth on Sundays and holidays but did not change the miserable conditions in the prisons and on the floating jail-hulks on the Thames.

In 1681 Thomas Firmin began to free hundreds of unfortunate debtors from prison by paying their small debts and the jailers' fees, and other philanthropists followed his example. In 1700 a meeting of the Society for Promoting Christian Knowledge advocated that jailers found guilty of extortion and mistreatment should be dismissed.

The demand for prison reform was rising throughout the eighteenth century. Among the early reformers who became deeply concerned about the inhuman treatment of the victims of penal institutions was General James Oglethorpe. One of his friends, a young architect named Castell, had been imprisoned for debt in the London Fleet prison in 1728; after he was forced to spend all his money for his upkeep, he was sent to the "sponging house" despite his plea that he would die there because it was infected with smallpox. His fear proved justified; he contracted the disease and died. The House of Commons appointed a committee of inquiry with Oglethorpe as chairman. The investigation led to some improvements, especially the prohibition of sale of liquors in prisons.

The work of prison reform found its strongest advocate in another philanthropist, John Howard. Born in 1726 as the son of a well-to-do London tradesman, he was of delicate health, a quiet, self-enclosed, deeply religious young man without ambitions for honors and conformity. The death of his father left him at the age of sixteen heir to a considerable fortune. He traveled through France and Italy and became interested in the relief of the people of Lisbon, which had been destroyed in the earthquake of 1755. He decided to sail to Lisbon to organize a relief action. The ship on which he was sailing was captured by a privateer, and together with the other passengers and the crew he was brought to Brest and confined to a filthy, dark dungeon as a prisoner of war. During the following months, Howard and his companions were dragged through several other prisons along the French coast; everywhere the conditions were the same—unhealthy, cold quarters without light and air, insufficient food, no bedding, and brutal treatment. Howard finally succeeded in being released under his pledge to find an exchange in England. There he began telling of his horrible adversities. This experience became the root of Howard's life work for prison reform. During the following decade he improved housing conditions of tenants on his estate, whom he encouraged by low rent and active support to reconstruct their homes, to educate their children, and to participate in church and recreational activities. After making studies of prisons in France, Italy, Switzerland, and Holland, Howard was nominated Sheriff of Bedford in 1773. In general, the office was a post of honor, but Howard took his assignment seriously and devoted his time to its duties. He sat in the courts during trials and visited all prisoners in the county jails. His conscience was aroused when defendants accused of crimes, but not found guilty, were often dragged back to jail, after already having suffered months of unjust imprisonment before trial, because they could not pay the fees to the jailer. In surrounding counties Howard found the same prison conditions that had shocked him when he was incarcerated in France. Debtors who could not pay their debts were treated like felons who had committed serious crimes, and men were hanged as certainly for stealing a pair of shoes as for arson or murder. The job of feeding the prisoners was farmed out to the lowest bidder. Tap-selling of beer and liquor induced the jail-keeper to encourage drunkenness and orgies. Because separation between the sexes was not properly secured, temptation and vice were prevalent. The prisoners were kept in idleness, whereas in continental countries prison inmates were put to work. The jailers and their helpers were coarse and ignorant men, selected for their brutality and insensibility to human suffering. The decayed, insecure buildings led to the use of irons, clubs, and whipping to prevent escape.[20]

Many prisons had no water supply, and the excrements of a large mass of prisoners accumulated in heaps of poisonous feculence within the precincts. The prisoners were forced to sleep on muddy floors and a rotten mass of litter in their cells while the stench of the manure oozed into them.

20 H. W. Bellows, *John Howard: His Life, Character and Service* (Chicago: Howard Association, 1948); Eris M. O'Brien, *The Foundation of Australia (1786–1800): A Study in English Criminal Practice and Penal Colonization* (Sydney, 1950).

No wonder that prisoners died from cold and from the "gaol-fever." No ventilation or light was available in the overcrowded cells. The prisoners did not receive religious or moral comfort, since most of the prison chaplains were rough, idle men who preferred to drink and gamble with the debtors. John Howard's sense of justice was aroused, and he recorded his distressing observations with the conclusion that a more searching investigation was necessary. In the House of Commons, Howard was invited to speak as an expert on prison questions. He continued his studies on travels to the European continent and published, in 1777, his work, *On the State of the Prisons in England and Wales, with Preliminary Observations and an Account of Some Foreign Prisons and Hospitals,* written with the aid of his friends the Reverend Densham and Dr. Price. The book was received with unusual interest by the public and was highly praised. Although it led to improvements in English prisons, to better food and ventilation, to the cleaning of cells, to the supply of bedding and blankets, and to medical care in cases of "gaol-fever," Howard was not satisfied. He continued his travels to the European countries and the Near East to help other countries in prison reform. On such a journey he died in Russia, in 1789.

Another pioneer in prison reform was Elizabeth Fry (1780–1845). As a Quaker she followed her religious inspiration to visit the infamous Newgate prison, known as "hell upon earth." Using the influence of her wealthy banker husband, she succeeded in starting a school for the children in the prison and in employing one of the women convicts as teacher. She then introduced, for the adult women, knitting and lace embroidery work, which improved their morale and gave them new hope. Her interest in the personal fate of the inmates brought a new spirit of order, industry, and religion into their habits. Her methods inspired other philanthropists to make similar attempts in other penal institutions in England.[21]

Despite some improvements brought about by the reformers, jails and prisons remained backward in England as long as they were under local administration. Not until 1877, when the *Prison Act* transferred the administration of penal institutions to a central organization—the National Prison Commission—did reform of the entire correctional system start. Until this time most jails and prisons did not separate young offenders from hardened criminals. As a result, prisons became "schools of vice" where the youngsters as novices were introduced into the skills of crime. The lack of segregation and of protection by the jailers had often calloused the young delinquent against the feeling of responsibility for his fellow men, while his greed for

---

21 Kathleen Bell, *Tribunals in the Social Service* (London: Routledge & Kegan Paul, 1969); F. E. Emery, *Freedom and Justice Within Walls* (London: Tavistock Publications, 1970); Tony Parker, *The Frying Pan: A Prison and Its Prisoners* (New York: Basic Books, 1970); Janet Whitney, *Elizabeth Fry, Quaker Heroine* (London: Harrap, 1937).

money and his drives for violence and lust were developed. In 1894 a parliamentary committee investigated the penal institutions and requested the separation of young offenders from older convicts, and their special treatment with vocational training. One of the committee members, Sir Evelyn Ruggles-Brise, visited the United States in 1897 and studied the youth reformatory at Elmira, New York. Stimulated by his observations, the first separate institution for the treatment of young delinquents in England was established at the Rochester Prison near Borstal. From this school the entire new program of special correction of young offenders received the name "Borstal System."

The Courts of Chancery in England long had jurisdiction over neglected and dependent children. In criminal cases, however, children over seven years of age were treated as adults. The first legal protection for delinquent children was created by the *Juvenile Offenders Act of 1847,* which limited the criminal persecution of children under fourteen years of age and of adolescents under sixteen years to specific cases of crime. Special children's courts which replaced the criminal courts were introduced in England only in 1912, after the previous experience of juvenile courts in the United States had been studied.

SOCIAL REFORM AND CHARITY ORGANIZATION

Three main factors influenced the social philosophy and practice of poor relief in England during the nineteenth century: the social reform movements, the Charity Organization Societies, and social research. These three developments were possible through the initiative of individuals deeply devoted to philanthropy and human progress.

Social Reform

Important elements in the development of social reform caused by the rapid industrialization of England were the Chartist, Christian Socialist, and the trade-union movements.

At the turn of the century, the *Combination Laws of 1799 and 1800* prohibited workers, under the threat of severe penalties, from forming trade unions to obtain higher wages or better working conditions. Not until 1824, on the initiative of Francis Place, was this legislation repealed. Even with this advance, however, political discrimination against the working class remained effective. Laborers were excluded from suffrage when this civic privilege, in 1832, was extended to the middle class and the professions. The Chartist movement, beginning in the 1830s as the political voice of labor, attempted to obtain suffrage and secret vote by ballot for all citizens, but it failed in spite of riots and petitions to Parliament with millions of signatures. Thereafter, the disappointed workers turned their interest from political aims to methods of improving their economic conditions. In 1844 the Chartists opened the first cooperative store owned by the workers themselves at Rochdale. The example for consumers' cooperatives had been presented by the philanthropist Robert Owen in his textile mills at New Lanark. Owen started his career as a poor boy, but gained a large fortune as a manufacturer in the textile industry. He recognized that decent wages and sanitary working conditions attracted the best workers and made the industry profitable. He established a model industrial community, providing low-cost housing with gardens, sanitation, and playgrounds, cooperative stores selling at cost, and a library and recreation facilities for workers and their families. Several other manufacturers in various parts of England followed the example of Robert Owen.[22]

Another approach to the improvement of social conditions of the workers was taken when trade unions began to organize mutual benefit plans for their members, providing aid in case of sickness, accidents, unemployment, invalidism, and old age. The success of cooperative and mutual aid enterprises led to the establishment of the Trades Union Congress as a national federation. Under the leadership of Richard Cobden and John Bright, the congress campaigned for the extension of suffrage to laborers, which was granted to urban workers by Parliament through the *Reform Bill of 1867*. An amendment to the *Poor Law of 1894* made elected officers the members of the boards of guardians which administered poor relief. Women as well as labor representatives became eligible for membership. The influence of the social reform movement freed workers from the continuous threat of destitution, and the trade-union movement made labor a new participating force in government, rather than a mere object of pity and poor relief.

After the collapse of the Chartists in 1848, a group of religious and intellectual reformers under the guidance of Frederick Denison Maurice, Charles Kingsley, and J. M. Ludlow pursued the idea of improving social conditions of the working class through education. They appealed to the church to assist the masses in their desire for cultural and social emancipation. The Christian Socialists sponsored cooperative associations among the workers of various industries, and they developed night classes for adult education for which they found idealistic teachers among clergymen and university faculties. The Christian Socialist movement laid the groundwork for a sympathetic understanding between labor and the church which is

---

[22] T. H. Marshall, *Social Policy in the Twentieth Century* (London: Hutchins University Library, 1970); T. S. Simey, *Social Science and Social Purpose* (New York: Schocken Books, 1969); Mark Hovell, *The Chartist Movement* (Manchester: Manchester University Press, 1925).

still characteristic of England. The "Working Men's College" in East London, founded by F. D. Maurice in 1854, was the most famous of these adult schools.

British socialism had its roots in the ideas of the social reformers, particularly Robert Owen. In addition to his work in connection with his own factories, Owen conceived a general plan to establish cooperative rural communities in which agricultural and industrial products would be exchanged to make their population self-supporting. He proposed that educational and cultural facilities be included in such an organization. Owen appealed to his friends and other wealthy citizens to assist the working class in its attempt to gain self-respect, education, and independence. The socialist philosophy was further developed by Karl Marx and Friedrich Engels, who lived in exile in England. Marx's influence as a theoretical philosopher was profound, but his political and economic ideas were not widely accepted among British labor. Of the groups interested in social reform, the most influential became the Fabian Society, which was founded in 1883. Among its leading members were Bernard Shaw, Sidney and Beatrice Webb,[23] Sidney Olivier, and Graham Wallas. The Fabians did not, in contrast to Marx's philosophy, advocate revolutionary socialist action to achieve a classless society; rather, they embarked on such practical reforms as women's suffrage, wage and hours legislation, housing projects, and education. Their influence on the practice and legal background of poor relief was, however, delayed until the social legislation at the beginning of the twentieth century accepted their basic concepts.

Housing Reform

After the beginning of the nineteenth century, the expanding industries attracted hundreds of thousands of workers and their families to the towns. This rapidly growing urban population could not be housed easily in the cities unless construction was stepped up to increase the housing facilities available to industrial workers. Several philanthropists exposed the serious danger to the health and morale of the working class from unsatisfactory housing conditions. Old mansions left by wealthy owners of mills and factories were split up into tenements with small apartments or single rooms for the workers' families. Near the mills, gardens and open spaces were quickly filled with shoddy constructions, erected without regard to sanitation, ventilation, or security against fire hazards. To maximize profits, builders in new industrial areas were bent on squeezing the largest possible number of dwellings onto every acre of land. In contrast, a few model cot-

---

[23] Kitty Muggeridge and Ruth Adam, *Beatrice Webb: A Life* (New York: Alfred A. Knopf, 1968); Margaret Cole, *Beatrice Webb* (New York: Harcourt, 1946).

tages were established by some philanthropic employers. At their initiative, the Metropolitan Association for Improving the Dwellings of the Industrious Classes was founded in 1842 in London. Following suggestions of Edwin Chadwick, several cities enforced the clearance of the worst slums to avoid the grave danger of cholera and typhus. The interest of the public in housing reform was aroused by the writings of John Stuart Mill, Thomas Carlyle, John Ruskin, and Charles Dickens, who were concerned about the poverty and degradation of working masses. Thus, Parliament also became aware of the need for social reform.

Outstanding in the fight against unhealthy housing and the exploitation of the workers in the slum tenements was Octavia Hill, an admirer of John Frederick Denison Maurice and a member of the Christian Socialists. With the help of her friend, philosopher John Ruskin, Hill started, in 1864, a philanthropic scheme of rebuilding slum tenements in London.[24] She rented sanitary, decent living quarters at low prices to working families who could not afford to pay higher rents. In this project she enlisted a number of ladies as volunteers, who collected the monthly rent from the residents and at the same time advised the families in economical home management and sound leisure time activities. Hill was convinced that the personal influence of these volunteer rent collectors encouraged the workers and their families to better training, self-respect, and an education of their children which would secure them the skills of higher paid trades and regular jobs. In 1865 Octavia Hill was also one of the founders of the Commons Society in London, which began to build recreational facilities, parks, and gardens in various districts of London.[25]

The Charity Organization Society

The *Poor Law Reform of 1834* did not bridge the widening gulf between the growing wealth of the manufacturers and mill owners and the severe pauperization of the steadily increasing masses of industrial workers. Philanthropists became concerned with saving either individuals whom they personally knew or certain groups of the poor, such as the children and the blind, lame, or crippled, from the degradation and cruel treatment of the mixed almshouse.

In periods of economic crisis and unemployment, public concern became particularly strong, and many charitable societies with various purposes

24 See David Owen, *English Philanthropy, 1660–1960* (Cambridge, Mass.: Harvard University Press, 1964); S. E. Finer, *The Life and Times of Sir Edwin Chadwick* (London: Methuen, 1952).

25 For a perceptive analysis of this pioneer work, see Robert H. Bremner, "An Iron Scepter Twined with Roses," *Social Service Review,* 39, No. 2 (June 1965), 222–31.

were endowed and organized. Newspapers solicited donations for the poor, and a large number of philanthropic agencies were established. In the 1860s several business crises occurred, and in London almost all churches and about one hundred charitable agencies distributed alms in money, food, clothes, and fuel tickets. Private charity societies began to face the usual criticism that they were wasting money and that by their alms and gifts they induced people to become beggars. Private charities still considered poverty a personal fault of the poor, as did the boards of guardians in public relief.

To overcome the chaos created by charitable church groups and philanthropic societies, the Reverend Henry Solly recommended in 1868 establishing a board to coordinate the activities of private and public charities. In 1869 the Society for Organizing Charitable Relief and Repressing Mendicity was founded in London, soon to be renamed the Charity Organization Society (frequently abbreviated C.O.S.). The leading spirit of the Society was Sir Charles Stewart Loch, who served from 1875 to 1915 as its secretary.[26] Other well-known members of the Society were the Reverend Richard Green, Edward Denison, Octavia Hill, and the Reverend Samuel Barnett. In its principles the Charity Organization Society was guided by the theories of Thomas Chalmers, that the individual was responsible for his poverty and that acceptance of public relief destroyed the self-respect of the pauper and led him to subsist on alms. The Society also followed Chalmers's thought that the pauper be asked to exert all his abilities for maintaining himself. To carry out these principles, the Charity Organization Society set up an inquiry department where the poor-law guardians, charity societies, and individual philanthropists were given information about an applicant for relief. This innovation caused the unmasking of many "professional beggars" and people who received aid from several relief agencies. The Charity Organization Society used the German method of the "Elberfeld System." It divided the city into small districts, each of which was administered for relief distribution by a group of citizens serving as a volunteer commission. Great confidence was bestowed on the activities of well-to-do volunteers, who would take a strong personal interest in the poor families assigned to them. They were to assist the families with money, clothes, and food, but the main emphasis was placed on their moral influence that would change the way of life of the poor. In larger districts the direction of the work of these volunteers was entrusted to a paid agent of the Charity Organization Society.

26 Charles Loch, *The Charity Organization Society: 1869–1913* (London: Methuen, 1961); Samuel Mencher, "The Influence of Romanticism on Nineteenth Century British Social Work," *Social Service Review,* 38, No. 2 (June 1964), 174–90; Loch, *Charity and Social Life* (London: Macmillan, 1910); E. M. Bell, *The Life of Octavia Hill* (London: Constable, 1938).

The Society was opposed to an extension of public poor relief and supported the tendency among its members to reduce government expenditures for the poor. It encouraged, however, the growth of private charities, the giving of donations and bequests in their behalf, and the initiative among the volunteers for bringing individual aid to families in distress.

The example of the London Charity Organization Society of 1869 was followed in other large cities in England and Scotland, and nine years after the foundation of the Society in London, this movement reached the United States. It developed cooperation between poor relief and private charities, succeeded in eliminating some fraudulent setups, prevented duplication of support, and strengthened the concept of rehabilitation of the poor. It formed the groundwork for casework as individual aid, on the one hand, and for community organization, on the other.

The Settlement House

Among the Christian Socialists, Edward Denison took a new approach in the endeavor to help the underprivileged gain education. As a volunteer of the Society for the Relief of Distress in London, in 1867 he became convinced that the mere distribution of alms was futile. He abandoned his comfortable life and moved to Stepney, a poor quarter in East London, to live with the people in this slum district. There Denison taught Bible classes, history, and economics. The inhabitants of Stepney found him reluctant to give them the customary meat and coal tickets unless he was certain they were in dire need, but he was generous with his time in listening to their personal problems and offered his counsel when he felt they were oppressed.

The idea of living among the people who needed help was most effectively demonstrated by Canon Samuel Augustus Barnett. Born in Bristol in 1844, he had studied theology at Oxford and accepted, in 1873, the post of Vicar of St. Jude's Church in Whitechapel in East London, one of the poorest parishes in the diocese. Barnett was encouraged by his fiancée, Henrietta Rowland, who had worked under Octavia Hill. After their marriage Henrietta became her husband's coworker. In Whitechapel the Barnetts found a great proportion of the 8,000 parishioners unemployed or sick, living in filthy, overcrowded tenements. The Barnetts went to Oxford and Cambridge and discussed with university students the conditions they had encountered in St. Jude's. They invited the students to come to live with them in Whitechapel to study the life of the underprivileged, to help in their education, and to render personal aid. Among those who followed Vicar Barnett's invitation was Arnold Toynbee, an enthusiastic and gifted young Oxford graduate. He was outstanding among his colleagues because of his devotion and the warm, personal contact he established with the families of the parish. Unfortunately he was of poor health, contracted tuberculosis, and died in 1883, before reaching his thirtieth birthday. In his memory, a number of his friends built, in 1884, a university settlement in the Whitechapel district and called it "Toynbee Hall," the first settlement house in the world.

Canon Barnett was elected the first warden of the settlement house. Toynbee Hall had three main objectives: (1) education and cultural development of the poor, (2) information for the students and other residents of the settlement regarding the conditions of the poor and the urgent need for social reforms, and (3) a general awakening of popular interest in social and health problems, and in social legislation. The basic purpose of the settlement was to bring educated men and women into contact with the poor for their mutual benefit, so that by common work and studies they could exercise a cultural influence beyond the teaching of special subjects.[27] Toynbee Hall brought to the people in this quarter heretofore inaccessible educational opportunities. The attitude of a superior "lady bountiful" which still prevailed in charity societies was replaced by cooperation and learning on the part of both instructors and workers attending lectures and discussion groups.

Social Research

Social research was a third important factor that influenced the social philosophy and the practice of poor relief in England. The first of a long series of social studies was undertaken by Edwin Chadwick when he was secretary of the Poor Law Commissioners; it dealt with health and sanitary conditions of the working classes. The report, published in 1842, became the start of the public health movement. Another stimulus to public concern and philanthropic endeavor was found in the articles of Henry Mayhew on "London Labour and the London Poor," published in 1849 in the London *Morning Chronicle*. These articles made a deep impression on such people as Octavia Hill and awakened their social conscience. They contributed as well to the rise of the movement of the Christian Socialists. The most important social survey, however, was made by a wealthy businessman, Charles Booth. In 1886 he hired a staff of interviewers and conducted the research as his private enterprise. The study investigated people by trades, their living and labor conditions, working hours and wages, and unemployment. Booth was determined to get the true facts, and his staff worked systematically and with precision. The study was not limited to destitute

[27] Clarke A. Chambers, *Seedtime of Reform. American Social Service and Social Action, 1918–1933* (Minneapolis: University of Minnesota Press, 1963), pp. 107–50; Henrietta O. Barnett, *Canon Barnett: His Life, Work, and Friends* (London: Murray, 1918, 1921); David Roberts, *Victorian Origins of the British Welfare State* (New Haven, Conn.: Yale University Press, 1960).

people. It covered thousands of employed workers' families. The results of Booth's study, which was published yearly, showed that one-third of the London population was living on, or below, the poverty line. Booth's findings disproved the previous theory of poverty always being the fault of the individual. They also showed that the deterrent features of the poor laws were no solution, and that human suffering from destitution was often created by insufficient wages, environment, inadequate housing, and unhealthy sanitary equipment. The results of this research were supported by another study, *Poverty, A Study of Town Life,* conducted by R. Seebohm Rowntree in the city of York and published in 1901. It revealed that in the small city of York 27.84 percent of the entire population were living in poverty. Through these findings of social research, the necessity of introducing more effective measures of social reform became evident.

THE POOR LAW COMMISSION OF 1905

At the beginning of the twentieth century, the people of England faced the grave threat of unemployment, especially in the coal mining regions. Because of the technical superiority of the United States mines, and more favorable production and transportation conditions in the European continental coal industries, a number of British mines were unable to compete and were forced to discontinue operations. Others needed fewer workers, and some closed because their coal supply was exhausted. As a result, masses of unemployed coal miners and their families asked for relief. However, it was not possible to put entire communities into the workhouse, as required by the Poor Law of 1834. Some mining towns applied to Parliament for aid. Private charities found themselves unable to support tens of thousands of jobless families for unlimited periods, and national emergency funds had to be appropriated. The Liberal Party in 1905 promised a reform of the poor laws and aid to the unemployed. After its victory, the new government embarked on a policy of social reform. A "Royal Commission on the Poor Laws and Relief of Distress," with Lord George Hamilton as chairman, was appointed. Among its eighteen members were Sir Charles Loch, Octavia Hill, and Helen Bosanquet, but only four composed an aggressive minority: Mrs. Beatrice Webb (representing the Fabian Society), George Lansbury (Trade Unions and Labour Party), Francis Chandler (Trade Unions), and the Reverend Prebendary, later Bishop H. Russell Wakefield. In press discussions, the meetings of the Commission were cited as "The Webbs Against the Poor Law." Beatrice Webb was morally supported by her husband, although he was not a member of the commission.

Sidney Webb's father had served on one of the London boards of guardians, and his son inherited from him a concern for the fate of the workers and the poor. From the time he was sixteen years of age, Sidney Webb worked for a living. He became an official with the London City Council and accepted the role of economic analyst with the Fabian Society. His wife, Beatrice Potter Webb, came from a wealthy London business family. During her studies she became interested in economic and political theory. After serving for some time as a visitor for a district committee of the London Charity Organization Society and as a rent collector in a philanthropic housing project, she assisted Charles Booth as an investigator in his study of the conditions of workers at the docks and in the "sweat" industries of London. In 1890 she undertook on her own a study of the cooperative movement and, during its preparation, met Sidney Webb, who advised her in this research. After the completion of the work they decided to study together the trade union movement. They were married in 1892, and completed many studies in the field of labor conditions, economics, political science, and social legislation.

Beatrice Webb insisted, in the Royal Commission, on a critical investigation of the poor law philosophy and its results. The extent of economic distress which the investigation revealed was appalling. The official statistics showed that 928,621 persons were receiving public relief, among them 300,000 children living under most unfavorable conditions.

The Poor Law Commission agreed on the following recommendations: (1) poor law unions and boards of guardians should be replaced by county councils, reducing the number of local relief administrations by three-quarters; (2) the punitive character of poor relief should be abolished in favor of a humane public assistance program; (3) mixed almshouses should be abolished, mentally deficient and mentally ill patients should be treated in hospitals, and children placed in foster homes or residential schools; and (4) national pensions for the aged, free hospital treatment for the poor, gratuitous public employment services, and a program of social insurance with unemployment and invalidity benefits should be introduced.

However, there were fundamental differences of opinion between the majority and minority of the commission. The majority wanted a mild reform of the old poor law and advocated close cooperation with private charities. The minority demanded the abolition of the poor law. As a result of the work of the commission the way for fundamental progress in social legislation was opened. Sidney and Beatrice Webb founded a "Committee for the Prevention of Destitution," which worked with the trade unions for social reform.

Already during the sessions of the Royal Commission social legislation had started. The *Provision of Meals Act of 1906* organized free school lunches in the elementary schools; the *Education Act of 1907* provided medical examinations for school children; the *Old Age Pensions Act of 1908* secured a weekly pension of five shillings for deserving poor persons over seventy years of age.

Employment Services and Social Insurance

Large-scale unemployment forced Parliament to pass the *Unemployed Workmen Act of 1905*. For unemployed workers it provided relief administered by local distress committees which tried to find jobs for them. Following the proposal of the Royal Commission, the *Labor Exchange Act of 1909* empowered the Board of Trade (comparable to the Department of Commerce in the United States) to set up labor exchanges (employment services) to help employers find competent workers, help workers find jobs, and increase the mobility of labor.

In the field of social insurance legislation, the urgent need for protection of injured workers led in 1897 to the enactment of the *Workmen's Compensation Act*.[28] Earlier legislation, the *Fatal Accidents Act of 1846* and the *Employers' Liability Act of 1880,* had proved insufficient to help the injured worker and his family. The statute of 1897 established the legal right of compensation for the injured worker independent of any fault of the employer or his crew. No machinery for public administration, however, was provided. Injured workers and the widows and orphans of those killed in industrial accidents were forced to sue the employer before the courts. This led to long delays and high expenses, which the workers could not afford, or settlements which deprived the injured worker or his survivors of most of his compensation.

The need for protection of the workers in periods of unemployment proved to be an urgent problem. The report of 1909, therefore, proposed the establishment of a system of compulsory unemployment insurance. On a visit to the European continent in 1908, David Lloyd George was impressed with the operation of the German sickness insurance plan, and recommended insurance with unemployment and health benefits. This twofold program was enacted by the *National Insurance Act of 1911,* prepared by Sir Hubert Llewellyn-Smith and William H. Beveridge.

Beveridge was the son of a Scottish judge. Born in India, he studied law and economics at Oxford, where he was a brilliant student. Greatly

---

[28] The first compulsory social insurance legislation had been enacted in Germany. On the initiative of Chancellor Bismarck, who pursued political as well as economic goals, the German Parliament had passed a sickness insurance law in 1883, an industrial accident insurance law (corresponding to workmen's compensation) in 1884, and old age and invalidity insurance in 1889. The German program did not include an unemployment insurance law because the problem of unemployment was not of major importance during the 1880s in Germany. Many other countries in Central and Northern Europe followed the German example. Some of them chose instead of the German system of compulsory insurance the way of voluntary insurance legislation. Denmark enacted in 1891 an old-age pensions act which required contributions neither from the insured workers nor from the employers. See also Helen Bosanquist, *The Poor Law Report of 1909* (London: Macmillan, 1909).

influenced by the work and ideas of Sidney and Beatrice Webb, he left a successful law practice after one year of activity at the London Bar to accept the position as subwarden at Toynbee Hall. There he lived among the East London workers and studied particularly the conditions of the unemployed families. In 1909 he published his first book, *Unemployment—A Problem of Industry*. After the enactment of the *Labor Exchange Act of 1909*, Churchill appointed William Beveridge to organize the labor exchanges. When the National Insurance Act was passed, it was natural that Beveridge was called on to take responsibility for the setup of the unemployment insurance plan.

The National Insurance Act of 1911 established compulsory health insurance for workers of modest income. The program was financed by contributions of the insured workers and their employers, and by grants from Parliament. It was administered by "approved societies," nonprofit organizations established by trade unions, mutual aid societies, employers, or commercial insurance companies. The insurance companies were interested in carrying health insurance because their agents could sell other policies, particularly accident and death insurance, to families when they collected health insurance contributions. The insured worker received only medical treatment from a practitioner who prescribed medicine. The worker received no hospital care or treatment by a medical specialist and no insurance for his family. Cash allowances during the time of sickness were limited to twenty-six weeks; after this period a reduced disablement benefit was paid. Maternity benefit was given at confinement to insured women workers and to the wives of insured men.

In 1925 the *Widows', Orphans' and Old Age Contributory Pensions Act* extended the principle of social insurance to men over sixty-five, women over sixty, and to widows, orphans, and dependent children under fourteen (or under sixteen when in school). Contributions from the insured workers and their employers were collected by the "approved societies," together with health insurance contributions. Local post offices paid the benefits, and the claims were adjudicated by local branch offices of the Ministry of Health. For both contributions and benefits a flat rate system was used so that uniform amounts were paid throughout the country.

The program of social insurance was fundamentally different from poor relief. Its contributions and benefits were determined by law. Payments were made on the arrival of contingencies—old age, sickness, widow- and orphanhood, unemployment—without regard to the financial situation of the insured individual. There was no disgrace in receiving benefits from funds to which the insured himself or the husband or father had contributed. Psychologically, people were stimulated to save money, because they were anxious to have funds in addition to the social insurance benefits which merely covered basic necessities. Thus, the initiative toward economic independence of the insured persons was not suppressed.

Changing Social Policy

World War I absorbed the unemployed and even created a labor shortage. Toward the end of the war, the *Representation of People Act of 1918* abolished the disfranchisement for recipients of poor relief. In 1919 the central poor-law agency, the Local Government Board, was replaced by the Ministry of Health, which administered poor relief, public health, sanitation, and health insurance benefits, as well as public housing and town planning. But after the abolishment of rent protection in 1957, there existed in London a severe exploitation of families with several children in the "colored slums," and regrettable housing conditions.

The *Local Government Act of 1929* led to a fundamental reform of the public relief structure. It abolished the poor law unions and boards of guardians and assigned public relief to the county councils and in metropolitan areas to borough councils, concentrating the administration in 145 counties. Public assistance committees composed of members of the county councils and other citizens were appointed. In each county, a "guardians committee" acted as voluntary investigators of relief applications. The *National Economy Act of 1931* introduced "Unemployment Assistance" payments from the Exchequer (the national treasury) to unemployed persons who had exhausted, or were not eligible for, unemployment insurance benefits. The administration of assistance was placed by the *Unemployment Act of 1934* in the Unemployment Assistance Board.

The *Children and Young Persons Act of 1933* introduced a comprehensive system of child care which, by the amendment of 1948, was supplemented by professional personnel, preventive services, and modern child care methods.

SOCIAL WELFARE DURING WORLD WAR II

At the outbreak of the war in 1939, the Unemployment Assistance Board was charged with payment of war victim allowances and its name was changed to National Assistance Board. The *Old-Age Pensions Act of 1940* provided for additional pensions based on individual need, particularly for medical care.[29]

In the field of health services, the war demand increased efforts for the treatment of tuberculosis, cancer, and venereal diseases. Important changes were made in the coordination of hospital facilities. When the outbreak of the war seemed imminent in 1939, an "Emergency Hospital Scheme" coordinated the voluntary and public hospitals and clinics. Mod-

[29] Richard M. Titmuss, *Essays on the Welfare State* (New Haven, Conn.: Yale University Press, 1959), pp. 75–87; Bentley B. Gilbert, *British Social Policy: 1914–1939* (Ithaca, N.Y.: Cornell University Press, 1970).

ern health treatment centers, consultation services, and rehabilitation clinics were set up. An extension of medical research and an expanded program for training young physicians were undertaken.

Serious problems were created in England during World War II by the necessity of evacuating hundreds of thousands of women, children, and the old, infirm, and sick from the large cities. The population in England found it hard to understand the many regulations regarding air raid protection, rationing, shelters, war damage compensation, family allowances for wives and children of men in the armed forces, rent control, taxes, and evacuation schedules, so that reliable information became necessary. Following London's example, over 1,000 Citizens' Advice Bureaus were established to meet this need, especially for information for servicemen on furlough regarding the whereabouts of their evacuated families. The bureaus gave free advice on war-related questions, gave legal opinion, and issued forms for applications. The Citizens' Advice Bureaus did not dispense assistance but referred applicants for material help to social agencies. Their staff consisted of trained social workers, lawyers, administrative officials, and volunteers borrowed from both public and voluntary social agencies.[30] The services of the Citizens' Advice Bureaus proved so valuable that a large number have been maintained to give community information services.

THE BEVERIDGE REPORT

In June 1941, when in a dramatic hour of the war bombs were continuously falling near Westminster Hall, England began a revolutionary reform of her entire social welfare program. Arthur Greenwood, Labour Minister of Reconstruction, appointed, with the unanimous consent of Parliament, an Interdepartmental Committee on Social Insurance and Allied Services under the chairmanship of Sir William Beveridge, to survey the structure and the efficiency of the British social services and to recommend necessary reforms. After World War I, Beveridge was Director of the London School of Economics, and in 1937 he became Master of the noted University College at Oxford. This explains why the challenging task of a reexamination of the entire social insurance and welfare program was entrusted to him. The Beveridge Committee included representatives of all organizations of public assistance, social insurance, pensions, health, and economic affairs. The committee's investigations included hundreds of hearings of citizens' groups, ranging from chambers of commerce, manufac-

---

[30] See Mildred Zucker, "Citizens' Advice Bureaus: The British Way," *Social Work*, 10, No. 4 (October 1965), 85–91; Pauline Gregg, *The Welfare State: An Economic and Social History of Great Britain from 1945 to the Present Day* (London, Harrys, 1969).

turers' associations, and commercial insurance companies to labor unions, consumers' cooperatives, and the Fabian Society. Sir William's report attempted to find a way to gain freedom from want, taking into consideration that personal and economic suffering in modern industrial society was, as a rule, caused by disruption or loss of earning power. It emphasized that, in addition to want, four other "giants" also prevent human well-being: disease, ignorance, squalor, and idleness.

The Beveridge Report devised a system of social security in which the program of social insurance is only one, although the most important, of several measures. Without losing a bold look into the future, recommendations were based on past experience in England. The goal of social security was to guarantee with his own efforts a basic level of income for every citizen, so that his initiative to secure for himself and his family more than a mere subsistence minimum should not be stifled.

The report inaugurated a comprehensive system of social security based on five programs: (1) a unified, comprehensive, and adequate program of *social insurance;* (2) *public assistance* as a national program for aiding people who were not sufficiently protected through social insurance benefits; (3) *children's allowances* (now called "family allowances") providing a weekly benefit for each child after the first; (4) comprehensive free *health and rehabilitation services* for the entire population; and (5) the *maintenance of full employment* through public works to prevent mass unemployment in economic crises.

The proposal aimed to protect the entire population, not just the working class. It was conceived as a unified plan, to be administered by one national agency (now called Ministry of Pensions and National Insurance) integrating the vast number of uncoordinated, overlapping efforts that had been made in the past. Six basic principles were suggested for the procedure: (1) unified administration, (2) comprehensive coverage, (3) flat rate of contributions, (4) flat rate of benefits, (5) adequacy of all benefits to meet basic needs of the recipients, and (6) classification of the population.[31]

Beveridge emphasized that the underlying social philosophy of his plan was to secure the British people against want and other social evils, and

---

[31] The report suggested six groups: (1) employees; (2) employers and self-employed persons; (3) housewives; (4) adult persons not gainfully employed, for example, cripples, invalids, insane; (5) retired persons above working age; and (6) children below working age. The *National Insurance Act of 1946* (see below) reduced the classification scheme to three groups: (1) employed persons, gainfully occupied in Great Britain under a contract of service; (2) self-employed people, gainfully occupied, but under no control of an employer; and (3) nonemployed persons. See David C. Marsh, *National Insurance and Assistance in Great Britain* (London: Pitman, 1951), p. 83; M. Penelope Hall, *The Social Services of Modern England* (London: Routledge, 1952), pp. 31–38; Samuel Mencher, *Poor Law to Poverty Program: Economic Security Policy in Britain and the United States* (Pittsburgh: University of Pittsburgh Press, 1968).

that social security could be rendered while preserving the personal freedom, enterprise, and responsibility of the individual for his family. The Beveridge Report became the foundation of the modern social welfare legislation of Great Britain and a model for other countries.

ENGLAND'S SOCIAL SECURITY PROGRAM

The structure of the present British social security program follows the recommendations of the Beveridge Report, although certain changes have been made. The Ministry of National Insurance coordinates the program. Its administration comprises two main sections: a comprehensive social insurance scheme for old-age, invalidity, and health insurance (*National Insurance Act of 1946*); and workmen's compensation (*Industrial Injuries Act of 1946*). A system of family allowances was established by the *Family Allowance Act of 1945*. Public assistance is provided according to the *National Assistance Act of 1948* through the National Assistance Board, a division of the Home Office. The Ministry of Public Health administers a broad program of public health services based on the *National Health Service Act of 1946*. The family allowances have been in effect since August 1, 1946, and the other parts of the program since July 5, 1948.[32]

The backbone of the entire social security plan is the *social insurance system*. It includes health insurance, unemployment insurance, old-age (superannuation) and invalidity insurance, workmen's compensation, and special grants for marriage, childbirth, and funeral expenses. It protects over thirty-five million people against the dangers of sickness, unemployment, old age, invalidism, death of the breadwinner, and industrial injuries. The insured population is divided into three categories: employed persons; the self-employed—employers, members of the professions, independent artists, and artisans; and nonemployed people—most married women in their own households.

In the original legislation of 1946, contributions and benefits of the social insurance program were flat rate payments, the same amount for the members of each of the three categories: adult men, adult women, and working boys and girls under eighteen years of age. Benefits were paid in case of retirement, invalidity, unemployment, before and after childbirth, and higher benefits under the industrial accident insurance program to totally or partially disabled workers and their dependents. Supplementary benefits were paid to the wife of the retired worker, to his widow after his

32 Muriel Brown, *Introduction to Social Administration in Great Britain* (New York: Hillory, 1969); David C. Marsch, *An Introduction to the Study of Social Administration* (London: Routledge & Kegan Paul, 1965); Bentley B. Gilbert, *The Origins of the Welfare State* (London: Allen & Unwin, 1966).

death, and to his first child under sixteen years of age, while family allowances were paid to subsequent children in the family.[33]

The *National Insurance Act of 1959* amended this principle of a unified flat rate system of contributions and benefits and introduced an additional graduated program of contributions and benefits for the retirement pensions of workers and employees. These graduated contributions are related to the insured person's remuneration and are paid by the insured worker and by his employer. The graduated contributions, however, do not affect the maternity, sickness, unemployment, and survivor benefits, nor do they apply to self-employed and nonemployed persons who continue to be insured under the original system of flat rate contributions and flat rate benefits. For the last two categories the national treasury pays one-third of the contributions.

Graduated contributions and the corresponding graduated retirement benefits are related to the earnings of insured persons who earn more than £9 up to £15 a week and are covered under the supplementary plan of 1959. They may be "contracted out" to approved private insurance companies or to retirement pension systems for public employees. Private pension plans must meet legal requirements securing the solvency of the companies and must provide retirement payments and the reservation of pension rights equivalent to the official graduated pension benefits under the national insurance program.[34]

Three types of maternity benefits are provided: (1) a *maternity grant* which permits the mother to make the necessary purchases for the baby; and either (2) a weekly *attendance allowance* for four weeks, or (3) a *maternity allowance* for eighteen weeks. An additional *home confinement grant* is paid if no maternity ward was used for the delivery.

After the death of her husband, a widow has a claim to a widow's allowance for an adjustment period of thirteen weeks. After this time, she receives a weekly guardian's benefit for each of her dependent children as long as they are under sixteen years of age. Orphans who have lost both parents receive the same orphan's benefit. Death benefits are given in case of the loss of either husband or wife to the survivor, so that funeral expenses can be met.[35]

---

[33] Richard M. Titmuss, "The Welfare State: Images and Realities," *Social Service Review,* 37, No. 1 (March 1963), 1–11.

[34] The rates of contributions may be reduced or increased by order of the treasury to assist in the maintenance of employment or to combat inflation in accordance with the economic needs of the country. The law provides also for a review every five years to adjust the rates of benefits. See also "New Graduated Retirement Benefits in Great Britain," *Social Security Bulletin,* 23, No. 9 (September 1959), 4–9.

[35] The various grants also are adjusted to changing living standards. A special child's allowance is paid to a divorced mother after the death of her former husband.

The administration of the social insurance benefits is carried out through the Ministry of Pensions and National Insurance and its regional and local offices, with the help of local advisory committees. Medical boards and medical appeal tribunals decide questions of health damage and capacity to work. Independent local appeal tribunals hear grievances of the insured persons. Employees of the National Assistance Board usually are not professionally trained social workers. Private social agencies offer personal counseling to beneficiaries of public assistance and social insurance benefits.

The second part of the British social security system is *family allowances*, paid upon application to every family with two or more children under sixteen years of age, without regard to the financial condition of the family. The allowance is paid to the mother until the year after the child's sixteenth birthday, if he is in school or in apprenticeship. The family allowance is based on the consideration that, in our industrial society, wages are paid for work rendered. For this reason, families with numerous children earn barely enough for a decent living, whereas a single worker might be able to live well on the same earnings. The family allowance represents, therefore, a mutual sharing between society and parents in the expenses for the upbringing, education, and preservation of health of children. The family allowance does not cover the entire cost of rearing the children. All children receive free school lunches or dinners, recreation, and health services, in a free day camp or summer vacation home. Family allowances are financed from national taxation.[36] Although family allowances are free of any kind of behavioral requirements, they are not popular in Britain, partly because they are rather nominal. Critics pointed out that women often spend the allowance on drinks at their favorite pub instead of on food for their children. They questioned whether the allowances should be increased and earmarked for low-income families. Thus, since August 1971 a "family income supplement" has been paid to the working poor who earn small wages, especially widows and divorced and single women. This "children's allowance plan" pays supplements for children up to sixteen years of age in school or vocational training.

The third part of the social security system is *public assistance*. Under the *National Assistance Act of 1948*, public assistance replaced the poor law through two new schemes: (1) financial assistance to persons in economic need, administered by the National Assistance Board and its 12 regional and 350 local offices; and (2) institutional and individual services,

---

[36] Hugh H. R. Vibart, *Family Allowances in Practice* (London: P. King, 1926); United Nations *Statistics of Social Services* (1963); George Hoshino, "Income Security and Personal Social Services," *Social Work*, 16, No. 2 (April 1971), 29; *Social Security Bulletin*, June 1971, 21–22.

administered by the county councils. In urgent cases the local office immediately may grant emergency relief. Old, blind, deaf, crippled, and disabled persons are encouraged in their efforts to earn a part of their living. National assistance is granted according to general regulations, but the applicant's individual conditions are considered. The applicant has a right of appeal against the decision of the local office to the National Assistance Board. The board assumes financial responsibility for vagrants and "casual poor persons" who formerly were supported by the local authorities. In 1966 national assistance benefits were renamed "supplementary benefits" provided by the national government, and the former National Assistance Board is now called the Supplementary Benefits Commission. The commission operates under the Ministry of Social Security.[37]

County councils, as local authorities, provide *welfare services* distinct from financial aid, including old people's homes and hostels for the infirm, blind, deaf, mentally deficient, crippled, and handicapped. Residents pay their board from their income or insurance benefits. If their income is insufficient, the Supplementary Benefits Commission pays the difference, including a small amount for pocket money. The county provides instruction, workshops, vocational training, and cultural and recreational activities, and it employs the staff of the hostels as well as social workers who give casework service to the residents. Private social agencies may be asked by the county to accept old and handicapped people into their institutions and to provide individual care by their social work staffs and volunteers.

Care of orphans and neglected and deserted children remains the responsibility of the county councils. The children are placed either in foster families or in children's institutions. Under the provisions of the *Children Act of 1948,* each county council appoints a Children's Committee as the authority for child care with a Children's Officer as head of its staff. The children remain under the protection of the committee until they are eighteen. The court may appoint the county council to serve as legal guardian of the child. The central supervisory authority for the care of dependent children is the Home Secretary, who is assisted by an Advisory Council on Child Care. Private agencies and children's institutions that receive children or place them in foster homes are registered with the Home Office, and have to meet established standards of care. The amendment of 1963 aims at the strengthening of preventive services by the local authorities, an improvement of the juvenile court procedure by the use of reception centers, prohibition of newspaper, radio, and television publicity about juvenile

[37] George Hoshino, "Simplifications of the Means Test and Its Consequences," The *Social Service Review,* 41, No. 3 (September 1967), 238–41; and "British Cash and Care," *Social Work,* 16, No. 2 (April 1971), 21–23.

offenders during trial, and new public "approved schools" instead of "remand homes."[38]

The "Seebohm Report" of 1968 recommended the establishment of unified local social service departments under local (county) authorities. Following the suggestions of the Seebohm Report, local children's services have since 1971 been integrated into the social welfare departments. Administrative arrangements are flexible enough to consider local conditions and needs.[39]

A Central Training Council in Child Care has organized two types of special training. The first, developed in cooperation with the universities, trains "boarding-out officers"—social workers who explore suitable foster homes and supervise the children placed in these families. The second type, established with the help of local education authorities, prepares house mothers, house fathers, and other resident workers for children's homes.

The county councils use facilities of voluntary social agencies for the accommodation of children and adults who need institutional placement, vocational training, recreation, and skilled social work service. The counties grant subsidies to private organizations which provide welfare services. Each county council has an advisory committee.[40] Adoption was introduced as a legal measure in 1926; the *Adoption Act of 1950* regulates the process of adoption to protect the child, his mother, and the adopting parents.

The *Disabled Persons (Employment) Act of 1944* requires industrial or commercial enterprises with a regular working force of twenty or more workers to employ disabled persons. The quota is assigned annually by the Minister of Labor; it is usually 3 percent of the working force of the plant. No disabled person is forced to register, but the law entitles the registered disabled worker to attend vocational training courses, without charge, to complete his interrupted apprenticeship, and to receive vocational guidance. He also has the right of reemployment in private industry and priority on employment in occupations designated by the Minister of Labor as appropriate for disabled workers, such as car park attendant or electric elevator operator. "Reemploy factories" provide jobs for severely disabled persons

---

[38] Alec Samuels, *Social Service Quarterly* (London, Winter 1963), pp. 112 ff; H. R. Schaffer and Evelyn R. Schaffer, *Child Care and the Family* (London: Bell & Sons, 1968); David Maclay, *Treatment for Children: The Work of a Child Guidance Clinic* (London: Allen & Unwin, 1970); Richard M. Titmuss and Michael Zander, *Unequal Rights* (London: Child Poverty Action Group, 1968).

[39] Richard M. Titmuss, *Commitment to Welfare* (London: Allen & Unwin, 1968), pp. 59–71; John Moss, *The Duties of Local Authorities Under the National Assistance Act* (London: Hadden & Best, 1948); Phyllis Osborn, "The National Assistance Program of Great Britain," *Social Service Review,* 32, No. 3 (March 1958), 24–32.

[40] Margaret Adams, "Social Services for the Mentally Retarded in Great Britain," *Social Work,* 9, No. 1 (January 1964), 69–78; Raymond T. Clarke, ed., *Working with Communities* (London: Council of Social Service, 1963).

under particular legal protection, with safety measures and special production methods. Other factories voluntarily offer employment to registered severely handicapped workers.

Special care is given by the Supplementary Benefits Commission to "persons without a settled way of life." They are divided into two groups: (1) those able to work and (2) the unemployables, particularly the invalid, aged, and sick. Reception centers permit individual observation and diagnosis and separate the unsettled from their habitual life on the road or in the city slums. After the diagnosis has been made, a treatment plan is developed. The treatment is provided in reestablishment centers, which provide the unsettled with the opportunity to adjust to work, to accept vocational training, and to use workshop facilities. The centers combine strict discipline with a sympathetic approach to the individual's problems and attempt to bring him back to normal life and work. The second category, old, sick, and invalid vagabonds, are cared for in casual wards where they receive medical and custodial treatment; many of these wards are affiliated with hospitals.

The Public Health Service

Among modern British social legislation, none has provoked so much attention and heated controversy as the *National Health Service Act of 1946,* which came into force on July 5, 1948 and marks a fundamental change in the attitude toward health.[41] It provides free medical care to all British citizens who apply for it. Already in 1942 the Medical Planning Commission of the British Medical Association had recommended a program of medical care for the entire people. The Churchill government first introduced the plan, which was enacted in 1946 under Prime Minister Atlee.

The National Health Service system is not "socialized medicine." The patient is not compelled to use the service; if he takes advantage of the service, he may choose his family doctor, dentist, hospitals, and specialists. Physicians, dentists, pharmacists, and nurses are not forced to work for the Health Service, either; they may continue private practice. The majority of physicians support the Plan, but their associations fought it.[42] There have been difficulties because of the division of general practitioners and specialists in the hospitals and dissatisfaction of the first group about the heavy load of work and their compensation.

The Health Insurance program secures financial benefits during illness while the patient loses his income. It protects the insured and his family

41 Titmuss, *Essays on the Welfare State,* pp. 133–214.

42 See Harry Eckstein, "The Politics of the British Medical Association," *The Political Quarterly,* 26 (1955), 345–59; Titmuss, *Essays on the Welfare State,* pp. 133–202, and *Commitment to Welfare,* pp. 104–9.

against destitution. Distinguished from the Insurance program, the National Health Service provides medical examination, diagnosis, free treatment in the doctor's office or at the patient's home, and hospitalization. The health service supplies medicines, artificial limbs, and appliances. Services are obtained through the family doctor with whom the patient has registered, if he wants to use the health service. A change of the family physician is possible any time, and the physician also may remove a patient from his list when he no longer wishes to serve him. The family doctor prescribes medicines, hearing aids, and appliances, which the patient receives at the pharmacy.[43] Since the Amendment of 1951, one-half of the cost of dentures and eyeglasses is charged to patients who are able to afford this contribution. Prescriptions for old-age pensioners and ex-servicemen are free of charge. The family physician refers the patient whenever necessary to specialists, hospitals, and clinics. If a patient is taken sick while away from home, he may consult any doctor in the Health Service for free treatment as a "temporary resident."

Dental treatment does not require previous registration. For complicated and expensive dental work, the patient needs an approval by the local Dental Estimate Board. Under the auspices of the local public health authorities, priority in preventive and curative dental clinics is given to expectant mothers and young children.

The Public Health Service Plan is widely used in England. Ninety-seven percent of the population have registered with a family physician in the Service. About 97 percent of all general physicians, over 94 percent of the dentists, and the great majority of medical specialists, opticians, and pharmacists offer their services under the health plan. Among the citizens registered for the Service are, of course, people of means who expect from the family physician the same medical attention which they formerly received as private patients. This will not always be possible, because of the larger number of patients involved, but this fact helps maintain high standards of medical care.

Physicians in the National Health Plan receive a "capitation payment" for each registered patient, determined by the Ministry of Public Health after consultation with the medical association. Supplements are granted to doctors working in difficult and unpopular areas. Dentists, ophthalmologists, opticians, and pharmacists are paid, according to their individual services, on the basis of an approved fee schedule. Medical specialists receive

---

[43] The statute of 1946 did not provide a fee for medicines and appliances. The introduction of a fee, however, was felt necessary in 1949 to avoid the abuse of drugs and medicines and to prevent too heavy expenditures under the health service. It was increased to one shilling for each item on the prescription in 1956. The Minister of Health is authorized to regulate the fees. Patients have to pay for replacement of appliances which have been lost or damaged through carelessness.

their remuneration on a part-time or full-time salary basis, with special awards for qualified professional services. Government grants are available for physicians who attend medical postgraduate refresher courses, who accept young assistant doctors for training, and who are engaged in medical research.

The administration of the National Health Service is organized, according to the three branches of the Service, into: (a) general medical and dental services, (b) hospital and specialist services, and (c) local government services. The general medical and dental services are administered by 138 Executive Councils established by the counties as local health authorities. They review the physicians' lists of patients, allocate patients whom no doctor wants to accept, and refuse in "over-doctored areas" the admission of new general practitioners until there is need for them.

Hospital and consultant physicians' services are administered by fourteen Regional Boards. After consultation with the medical executive councils, the local medical associations, and senior staffs of the hospitals in the area, the regional board appoints management committees to coordinate local hospitals, regional health policies, and public health planning.

Each region is connected with a university medical school which uses one or several "voluntary teaching hospitals" for training medical and dental students. The university teaching hospitals retain their legacies, gifts, and endowments for research and fellowship. Hospital management committees and regional medical boards use a special fund for the development and improvement of hospital facilities, equipment, and research. Under the health plan, about 2,700 hospitals with 500,000 beds are available. Professional and technical improvements and an amalgamation of small and inefficient hospitals were achieved.[44] Two hundred and fifty denominational hospitals have been "disclaimed," and continue to operate under private management. The regional hospital boards negotiate the contracts with specialists (medical consultants).

Local health authorities provide for maternity and child welfare services, midwifery, home nursing, health visiting, and aftercare of the sick. They arrange for domestic help in time of confinement and sickness, for vaccination and immunization, and for ambulance services for emergency transportation to hospitals or clinics. Domestic help under the Home Help Service is free to families who cannot afford to pay for a homemaker; other families pay a moderate weekly charge. In cases of home confinement, free midwife service and a maternity outfit is granted, and in cases of home

---

[44] An increasing number of British hospitals have "almoner's departments," staffed by medical social workers. Mental hospitals and psychiatric clinics employ psychiatric social workers. Two public medical services have not been incorporated: the Schools Medical Service, controlled by the Minister of Education, and the Industrial Medical Service, under the Minister of Labor.

nursing, such articles as crutches and wheel chairs for the sickroom and for convalescence. Tubercular patients receive medical care and public assistance benefits. After the patient returns from the hospital or tuberculosis sanitarium, a social worker or a visiting nurse assumes aftercare. By the establishment of child guidance and mental hygiene clinics, local health authorities help in the prevention of mental diseases.

Special attention is given to expectant and nursing mothers, infants, and young children under five years of age. County maternity and child welfare services provide free prenatal and postnatal care with obstetric and pediatric examination and treatment.

In schools, free medical inspections, dental treatment, and special attention to blind, visually handicapped, epileptic, and crippled children are provided. Some counties employ medical social workers under the title "welfare officer" for services for children, the aged, and the handicapped.

The cost of the National Health Service is high. Funds contributed by the social insurance program to the health service cover about 13 percent of the entire health service budget. The remainder is financed by national and some local taxes. Administrative cost of the National Health Service amounts to only 2.5 to 3 percent of the expenditure.[45]

The final success of the health service depends on the cooperation of the public and the professions. The statute provides for the future establishment of additional health centers by the counties, when financial and technical conditions permit. At these centers family doctors, medical specialists, and dentists have their offices for both the health service and their private practice, with laboratory and pharmaceutical facilities.[46]

The public in England often regards the health service as part of the social insurance plan and as a return for the weekly social insurance contribution. In fact, the health service is available to everyone independent of his coverage under the social insurance program.

MENTAL HEALTH SERVICES

As early as 1879, the Mental After Care Association offered post-hospital services for patients released from hospitals, placing them in private

[45] For a penetrating analysis of the operation of the British National Health Plan, see Titmuss, *Essays on the Welfare State,* pp. 8–10, 133–202. For a description of special care for severely handicapped children suffering from cerebral palsy, see Sheila Hewett, *The Family and the Handicapped Child* (Chicago: Aldine Press, 1970).

[46] See Agnes W. Brewster and Estelle Seldowitz, "Trends in the National Health Service in England and Wales," *Public Health Reports,* 77 (September 1962), 735–44; and David Owen, *A Unified Health Service* (Oxford: Pergamon Press, 1968).

homes of retired personnel of mental institutions. In 1959 the *Mental Health Act* required county authorities to establish hostels or halfway houses for mental patients. These halfway houses were organized to alleviate the burden of the regional mental hospitals, which had been established on the basis of the National Health Service Act of 1946, by placing in the community patients whose health had improved in the hospital.[47] Based on the operations of the Mental Health Act of 1959, broad community mental health services with preventive treatment, outside hospitals and residential homes, have recently been developed. These are closely related to school psychological services.

PRIVATE SOCIAL SERVICES

For centuries England has been noted for the important role that private charities have played in its society as pioneers of the various social services, and for the numerous volunteers active in the field of social work. The recent expansion of public welfare and the social insurances has still left wide opportunities for the activities of private social agencies. The public authorities encourage voluntary agencies to continue their work in personal aid to old, sick, handicapped, and young persons. Characteristic examples of present social services provided under the auspices of voluntary agencies are maternity and old-age homes, health visiting, home nursing, midwives' services, ambulances and transportation aid, care of mothers and babies, clinics and sanitariums for tubercular patients, hostels for mentally retarded children and adults, and aftercare service for the sick. Other activities of private social agencies include probation and parole for juveniles and adults; social clubs for adolescents, the aged, and the unemployed; marriage guidance councils; child guidance clinics; disaster relief; visiting old people in their homes or in institutions; and managing "village halls" (rural cultural and education centers).

The essential functions of private social agencies in England today are: (1) carrying on new experiments and developing new forms of social work which may later be taken over by public agencies when they have proved successful; (2) supplementing public social services when certain persons or particular needs are not covered by public services, limited in funds and by legal provisions, and because individual care and counseling is required; (3) interpreting social work to the public, particularly through citizens' advice bureaus, and by informing legislators and public agencies

---

[47] Elizabeth Jones, *Mental Health and Social Policy* (London: Routledge & Kegan Paul, 1960), pp. 157–58; Robert Z. Apte, *Halfway Houses: A New Dilemma in Institutional Care* (London: Bell, 1968), pp. 11–17; Titmuss, *Commitment to Welfare,* pp. 104–9.

of the special problems which have escaped their attention; and (4) performing social surveys to determine the social and health needs of a community and the quest for social legislation—plus stimulating public authorities to take necessary action.

Volunteers participate in private social agencies in Great Britain, particularly in youth groups, advisory bureaus, and child care work affiliated with the schools, and probation, but they often work under instruction and supervision of trained professional workers. Volunteers are particularly active in work with aged and handicapped persons. Subsidies to private agencies are frequently granted by the counties and the various ministries of the national government. Nearly all voluntary social agencies are represented in the National Council of Social Service, founded in 1919. More than one hundred national organizations are members of the council, among them the Family Welfare Association (successor to the Charity Organization Society). The National Council encourages the setup of local "councils of social services" and "rural community councils" to coordinate the work of local agencies.[48]

The recent extension of public social services has led to a certain duplication of work and overlapping between public and private social work activities. Some private social agencies still maintain a critical attitude toward public social services, arguing that private organizations have a superior social philosophy and practice based on the old principle of voluntary action; at present there is scarcely any proof of this. In the interest of economy and efficiency, it seems desirable to eliminate overlapping services and coordinate public and private activities to meet the social needs of the population.[49]

Recipients of public assistance payments are entitled to be members of advisory councils, grievance committees, and appeal tribunals. The participation of laymen and of recipients of social aid, as well as of professionals, secures their understanding of the social problems these institutions must face in carrying out their objectives. The broad representation of the public on both public and private boards in England secures deeper understanding of the social problems and a democratic interpretation.

Voluntary agencies are now able to concentrate on their real task, the difficult, intangible problems of bringing aid to human beings in need of understanding and encouragement, and, especially, the prevention of juvenile delinquency.[50]

---

[48] Peter Townsend, *The Last Refuge: A Survey of Residential Institutions and Homes for the Aged in England and Wales* (London: Routledge & Kegan Paul, 1962).

[49] John E. Mayer and Noel Timms, *The Client Speaks: Working Class Impressions of Casework* (New York: Atherton, 1970).

[50] Geraldine M. Aves et al., *The Voluntary Worker in the Social Services* (London: Allen & Unwin, 1969); Margaret Brasnett, *Voluntary Social Action* (London: National Council of Social Service, 1969).

BEVERIDGE, SIR WILLIAM, *Social Insurance and Allied Services*. New York: Macmillan, 1942.

BOOTH, CHARLES, *Life and Labour of the People of London* (10 vols.). London: Longmans, 1900–1911.

CARTWRIGHT, ANN, *Parents and Family Planning Services (England and Wales)*. Chicago: Aldine Press, 1971.

CHALMERS, THOMAS, *The Christian and Civic Economy of Large Towns*. New York: Charles Scribner's, 1900.

COLL, BLANCHE, "Perspectives in Public Welfare: The English Heritage," *Welfare in Review*, 4, No. 3 (March 1966), 1–12.

DE SCHWEINITZ, KARL, *England's Road to Social Security, 1349–1947*, 3rd rev. ed. Philadelphia: University of Pennsylvania Press, 1947.

HALL, PENELOPE, *The Social Services of Modern England*. London: Routledge & Kegan Paul, 1952.

HEALEY, WILLIAM, and BENEDICT S. ALPER, *Criminal Youth and the Borstal System*. New York: The Commonwealth Fund, 1941.

HERAUD, BRYAN J., *Sociology and Social Work*. Oxford: Pergamon Press, 1970.

HILL, CLIFFORD, *Immigration and Integration: A Study of the Settlement of Coloured Minorities in Britain*. New York: Pergamon Press, 1970.

JOHNSON, ARLIEN, et al., *Impressions of Social Services in Great Britain*. London: U.S. Educational Commission in the U.K., 1956.

OWEN, DAVID, *English Philanthropy*. Cambridge, Mass.: Harvard University Press, 1964.

RATHBONE, ELEANOR, *Family Allowances*. London: G. Allen, 1949.

ROBSON, WILLIAM A., *Social Security*, 3rd ed. London: G. Allen, 1949.

RODGERS, BRIAN, *Towards a Welfare State*. New York: Humanities Press, 1969.

ROWNTREE, B. SEEBOHM, and G. R. LAVERS, *English Life and Leisure: A Social Study*. London: Longmans, 1951.

TIERNEY, BRIAN, *Medieval Poor Law*. Berkeley: University of California Press, 1959.

TITMUSS, RICHARD M., *Commitment to Welfare*. New York: Pantheon, 1968.

————, *Essays on the Welfare State*. New Haven, Conn.: Yale University Press, 1959.

————, "New Guardians of the Poor in Britain," pp. 151–70 in Shirley Jenkins, ed., *Social Security in International Perspectives*. New York: Columbia University Press, 1969.

————, "Social Policy and Economic Progress," *Social Welfare Forum 1966*, 25–39.

WEBB, BEATRICE, *My Apprenticeship*. London: Longmans, 1928.

WEBB, SIDNEY, *The Break-Up of the Poor Law*. London: Longmans, 1909.

WEBB, SIDNEY, and BEATRICE WEBB, *English Poor Law Policy*. London: Longmans, 1910.

————, *The Prevention of Destitution*. London: Longmans, 1912.

WEST, D. J., *The Young Offender*. New York: International Universities Press, 1967.

WILLIAMS, GERTRUDE, *The Coming of the Welfare State*. London: Allen & Unwin, 1967.

WOODROOFE, KATHERINE, *From Charity to Social Work in England and the United States*. London: Routledge & Kegan Paul, 1962.

YOUNGHUSBAND, DAME EILEEN L., *Community Work and Social Change*. London: Longmans, 1968.

————, *Social Work and Social Change*. London: Allen & Unwin, 1964.

————, *Social Work in Britain*. Edinburgh: Constable, 1951.

3

history of voluntary and public social services in the United States

EARLY DEVELOPMENT: LOCAL CHARITIES

As early as the beginning of the seventeenth century, the colonists (most of them coming from England) brought with them the customs, laws, and institutions of the mother country. In general, they were vigorous persons who came to the New World to find freedom to worship, better economic opportunities, to rule themselves, or to seek adventure. They found a vast land of forests, fertile valleys, an abundance of wild game, and fish in the lakes and rivers. Few of the new settlers had substantial means, but they were willing to work hard for their living as farmers, hunters, or traders.

The isolated settlements of the new frontier were subject to the dangers of Indian assaults, of wild animals, and of natural disasters.

Various cultural backgrounds influenced the colonists' attitude to welfare problems, particularly British Puritan, Scotch, English Catholic, Anglican, Dutch, and French, as well as the Quaker traditions. Most followed a strict code of behavior and disapproved of drinking, gambling, and other vices. They demanded thrift and industrious work which was necessary for the survival of their community, and the test of religiosity was material success. The Puritans had a horror of laziness and poverty because they considered idleness a sin and the source of unhappiness and crime, and poverty a proof of low moral quality. They were also anxious to avoid the heavy taxes common in England, where some parishes spent as much as one-third of their total revenues for poor relief. From the English tradition, the colonists inherited the concept that paupers, beggars, and vagrants were criminals, and this accentuated their contempt for those who asked for support from the parish.

Most paupers were widows and orphans and the sick, old, and invalid. But there was another category of involuntary immigrants that the mother countries, especially England, wanted to be rid of. At the order of English courts, demented and maimed persons and convicted offenders were deported as "involuntary servants" to work for a number of years. Others were kidnapped by traders and sea captains and sold as servants to colonists. Under the apprenticeship laws, dependent children were also deported from the poorhouses to the Colonies. The majority of the involuntary servants became self-supporting, law-abiding citizens, but some of them were weak, sick, or unwilling to work.[1]

In contrast to the thickly populated European countries from which they had emigrated, in America the settlers lived in scattered places, as farmers and hunters, on the ragged edge of existence, and struggled hard to wrench a bare living from the soil and the woods. They were so involved in their own problems of survival that they gave little thought to the needs of those unable to face the hardships of frontier life. Since land was cheap and labor scarce, beggars able to work were not given alms. Still, the aged, the sick, and women with young children needed help. The traditional resources of the mother country, such as church institutions, endowed charities, hospitals, and almshouses, did not exist in the settlements. The local parish had to take care of its destitute. As in England, the colonists

---

[1] See George Soule, *Economic Forces in American History* (New York: Dryden, 1952), 13, 153–55; Gerhard Colm and Theodore Geiger, *The Economy of the American People* (Washington, D.C.: National Planning Association, 1961), pp. 76–80; Gary B. Nash, *Class and Society in Early America* (Englewood Cliffs, N.J.: Prentice-Hall, 1970); Blanche D. Coll, *Perspectives in Public Welfare* (Washington, D.C.: Department of Health, Education and Welfare, 1970), pp. 17–22.

were eager to prevent from entering the settlement those who might become a public charge or who seemed objectionable for religious, political, or moral reasons. Such persons were deported, and the Colonies sometimes even paid their passage back to Europe when the individual settlement could not afford the expense.

When the number of paupers increased to the point that some action had to be taken, overseers or supervisors of the poor were appointed in the parish or township. They had to assess and collect a poor tax, to investigate the resources of relief applicants, and to dispense relief to the paupers. Frequently the overseer held other functions, too, such as councilman or town treasurer; later, in many places, his position became a full township office.

The Colonies adopted the Elizabethan Poor Law, at least in principle. Every town made provision for the maintenance of the poor, supplying food, clothing, firewood, and household essentials. The poor had to be residents for a statutory period, varying between three months and five years. Following English tradition, newcomers often were "warned out," ordered to leave the community unless they could provide security by bond of a resident in good standing. If members of such a family were found begging, they were whipped in the marketplace and forcibly returned to their former residence. Since many immigrants arrived without means, ship masters who brought them over had to deliver passenger lists and to deposit bond that no passenger would become a public charge for five years. Residents responsible for the arrival of paupers had to indemnify the town.[2]

Poor relief was given mainly in two forms: either as "outdoor relief" in kind (food, clothes, fuel), or by "farming out" or "selling out" the pauper to the lowest bidder. A special type of farming out was the placement of widows and infirm and aged paupers, for short periods, from house to house. Older children were "indentured"; the town did not pay for them, as they worked for their maintenance.

The cost of poor relief was met by the poor tax and certain fines imposed for refusal to work at harvest time, for selling bread or butter at short weight, for not attending public worship, or for illegally bringing a pauper into the colony. If a town failed to make appropriations for poor relief, the county courts assessed the town and disposed of the funds.

Whatever the cause of his distress, the pauper was treated as a morally deficient person. He had to swear to the "pauper's oath" and his name was entered on the poor roll exhibited in the city hall or in the marketplace.

[2] Ralph E. Pumphrey and Muriel W. Pumphrey, eds., *The Heritage of American Social Work* (New York: Columbia University Press, 1961), pp. 10–26; S. C. Kohs, *The Roots of Social Work* (New York: Association Press, 1966), pp. 23–29; Frank J. Bruno, "The English Poor Law in America," in Paul Weinberger, ed., *Perspectives on Social Welfare* (Toronto: Collier-Macmillan, 1969), pp. 63–69; Elizabeth Wisner, *Social Welfare in the South from Colonial Times to World War I* (Baton Rouge: Louisiana State University Press, 1970).

Local newspapers published the names of all paupers, with the amount of their relief allowances. In Pennsylvania, paupers had to wear the Roman letter "P" on the shoulder of their right sleeve. Old and invalid indigents who had long resided in the parish were considered "worthy poor," if they complied with the moral standards of the neighborhood; all others, particularly strangers and newcomers, were considered "unworthy poor." Disfranchisement of paupers prevailed everywhere. The repressive, punitive character of poor relief, as it had developed in Europe, was maintained in the New World.

Especially harsh was the treatment of "wanderers" or vagabonds; they were adjudged "rogues" to be "stripped naked from the middle upward, be openly whipt on his or her naked body, not exceeding the number of fifteen stripes"[3] and ordered to leave the parish. Idlers and beggars were often confined to the jail, the "bridewell," or the house of correction. The main purpose of this practice was to spare the citizens of the colony taxes for poor relief.

In Virginia and North Carolina, using the English parish system, churchwardens and vestrymen acted as overseers of the poor, levied pauper taxes, distributed relief, and farmed out the indigent. In 1785 county overseers of the poor were appointed as a consequence of the separation of church and state. In Louisiana, a French colony, religious charities, according to French tradition, took care of the poor. Children were cared for in orphanages, the sick and the aged in hospitals.

Orphaned, abandoned, and illegitimate children remained a major problem of the southern states; many were born to Negro, Indian, and mulatto women and others to white servants who were not permitted to care for the child. In the eighteenth century impoverished Negro slaves and freed mulatto servants became another group requiring poor relief. Illegitimate children and orphans were "bound out" to save poor relief expenses.[4]

There were two fundamental differences between the English and the American poor-law practice in the seventeenth and eighteenth centuries. In England the general method of poor relief was to place the paupers into poorhouses and workhouses; in the Colonies, only in some larger cities were

[3] Marcus W. Jernigan, *Laboring and Dependent Classes in Colonial America, 1607–1783* (Chicago: University of Chicago Press, 1931), p. 201; Jacob A. Riis, *How the Other Half Lives* (New York: Charles Scribner's, 1890); Robert H. Bremner, *From the Depth* (New York: New York University Press, 1956), pp. 68 ff, 142 ff.

[4] Nathan E. Cohen, *Social Work in the American Tradition* (New York: Holt, Rinehart and Winston, 1958), pp. 19–39; Pumphrey, *The Heritage of American Social Work,* pp. 38–44; Ralph Pumphrey, "Social Welfare: History," *Encyclopedia of Social Work 1971* (New York: National Association of Social Workers), pp. 1446–59; Leo Fishman, *Poverty and Affluence* (New Haven, Conn.: Yale University Press, 1966), pp. 6–17.

almshouses and houses of correction established. In England legacies, endowments, and bequests provided substantial funds for the support of the poor in hospitals, asylums, and orphanages; in the Colonies private charities played an insignificant role until the end of the eighteenth century.

The first almshouse was established as early as 1657 at Rensselaerswyck, New York. Plymouth Colony ordered the construction of a workhouse in 1658, and Boston set up an almshouse in 1660. The legislature of Massachusetts ruled in 1699 that vagabonds, beggars, and disorderly persons should be put to work in houses of correction. During the eighteenth century some colonies began to use almshouses and workhouses in large cities, instead of boarding out the paupers with families. Most smaller towns continued, however, to farm out the poor by "auctioning them off" to the lowest bidder. Other towns contracted with a resident to take care of all paupers in town for a stipulated sum. This method secured the taxpayers against unexpected expenses for poor relief but did not protect the poor against brutal treatment, inadequate care, hunger, and exploitation.[5]

Besides public poor relief, church charities during the Colonial period provided some relief but limited their aid to members of the congregation. The minister, his wife, and deacons visited the sick, widows, and orphans. Assistance was denied to people who neglected admonitions of the minister or whose moral behavior, laziness, drinking, or gambling were criticized in the parish. Churches financed their charity by collections among their members, offerings at religious services, and appeals for funds in cases of emergency.

A second characteristic type of private charities in America were the National Benevolent Societies, fraternal orders of various nationality groups. The first was founded in Boston among Scottish immigrants in 1657. Other benevolent societies for the English (St. Andrew's Societies), the Irish, the French, the Dutch, and the Germans were organized in the eighteenth and nineteenth centuries.

A third type of private charity was the philanthropic association, founded for humanitarian motives to aid groups in special need. Examples are the Philadelphia Society for Alleviating the Miseries of Public Prisoners, founded in 1787; the Massachusetts Charitable Fire Society of 1794, for the victims of fire; and the New York Society for the Relief of Poor Widows with Small Children, founded in 1798. Endowments to charities became important during the nineteenth and twentieth centuries. Founders of private charities assigned in their wills the administration of endowed funds to a board of trustees who incorporated the foundation according to state laws.

[5] Lorman Ratner, *Pre–Civil-War Reform* (Englewood Cliffs, N.J.: Prentice-Hall, 1967); Margaret L. Coit, ed., *John C. Calhoun* (Englewood Cliffs, N.J.: Prentice-Hall, 1970).

THE ALMSHOUSE AND THE WAR
BETWEEN THE STATES

The American Revolution was influenced by the people's desire for liberty, by their resentment of British governmental oppression, and by the French equalitarian philosophy of Jean Jacques Rousseau. During the final years of the eighteenth and the early years of the nineteenth century, the ideals of individual freedom and self-help grew in importance and inspired humanitarian movements for the abolition of slavery, for general public education, women's rights, better treatment of the poor and the mentally ill, reform of prisons, and for religious tolerance. An example was an orphanage in Philadelphia founded by the Quaker Stephen Girard in 1830.

During the first decades of the nineteenth century, the parishes and counties complained about rising expenses for poor relief. In Massachusetts and Connecticut, the state governments had at least assumed the cost for those paupers who were "unsettled" or were "warned out." In New York, Laws on the State Poor provided state funds for refugees fleeing the Indians or the British armies. In general, the maintenance of the poor remained the responsibility either of the town or township, or of the county. Some midwestern and western states made the counties responsible for the administration of the poor laws, whereas in New England and the eastern states the township continued to provide poor relief.[6]

The growing burden of the expenses for poor relief on local government resulted from two causes: (1) the number of poor increased with the total increase in population; and (2) in times of failure of crops and lack of suitable employment, other "able-bodied persons" also applied for poor relief, often granted them by the overseer of the poor as a political or personal favor. This "spoil system of poor relief" led to the support of families who might have been able to maintain themselves.

Large cities in the eastern states had established poorhouses and considered them the most economic and effective means to care for the poor. In 1821 the General Court of Massachusetts appointed a committee to investigate the pauper laws of the Commonwealth. Under the chairmanship of Josiah Quincy, the committee suggested to the legislature the adoption of five principles: (1) that outdoor relief was wasteful, expensive, and destructive to the morals of the poor; (2) that almshouses were the most economic mode of relief, because in a "house of industry" each pauper was

---

[6] Pumphrey, *The Heritage of American Social Work*, pp. 53–66; Cohen, *Social Work in the American Tradition*, pp. 43–79; Edith Abbott, *Some Pioneers in Social Welfare* (Chicago: University of Chicago Press, 1937), pp. 77–83; Sidney V. James, *A People Among People: Quaker Benevolence in Eighteenth Century America* (Cambridge, Mass.: Harvard University Press, 1963).

set to work according to his ability, the result being that the able-bodied earned their maintenance and contributed to the support of the impotent group; (3) that the poor be employed in agricultural work; (4) that a board of citizens supervise the almshouse; and (5) that intemperance was considered the most powerful and universal cause of pauperism.

Two years later, in 1823, the New York legislature instructed Secretary of State J. V. N. Yates to collect information on the expense and operation of the poor laws. The Yates Report, rendered in 1824, divided the poor into two classes—those under permanent support and the "temporary poor." Among the first class, 35 percent were unable to work because of age, infirmity, blindness, and physical and mental handicaps; 38 percent were children under fourteen years of age. The remaining 27 percent, however, were considered able to earn their living if proper arrangements were made. The report criticized that sturdy beggars and "profligate vagrants" were encouraged to become "pensioners of public relief" because overseers granted them aid without careful examination. The complicated system of legal settlement led to expensive litigation between towns and counties; paupers suffered by their cruel removal from one town to another; and the "farmed out" paupers were mistreated and "tortured" by their keepers. Education and morals of the children were neglected; they grew up in filth, idleness, ignorance, and disease "to become early candidates for the prison or the grave." No adequate provisions were made for setting the paupers to work. On the basis of these findings, the Yates Report recommended the following measures: (1) to establish in each county a "house of employment," providing a farm for agricultural work and education of the children; (2) to procure a workhouse (or "penitentiary") for sturdy beggars and vagrants, with enforced hard labor; (3) to levy an excise tax on whisky distilleries to raise the funds for poor relief; (4) to rule that one year's residence in a county of New York constitutes a legal settlement; (5) to abolish the "orders of removal" and the appeals in poor-law litigation; (6) to order that no healthy male between eighteen and fifty years of age be placed on the pauper list; and (7) to punish street begging and bringing paupers into the state.[7]

Following the Quincy and Yates Reports, Massachusetts, New York, and most other states of the Union established almshouses and workhouses and placed relief applicants in these institutions. Immediately after the release of the Yates Report, the state of New York passed, in 1824, the *County Poor House Act,* which transferred the management of the almshouse from the township to the county.

The War Beween the States ended with the abolition of slavery

---

[7] For the text of the Quincy and Yates Reports, see Sophonisba P. Breckinridge, *Public Welfare Administration in the United States* (Chicago: University of Chicago Press, 1935), pp. 30–54; see also Coll, *Perspectives in Public Welfare,* pp. 35–39.

through the Thirteenth Amendment; the Constitutional authority of the federal government, which became responsible for the welfare of the people, under the Fifteenth Amendment, was interpreted by the courts and the administration as restricting the federal role.[8]

Unfortunately, the introduction of almshouse care did not have the effect of improving the conditions of the poor, which the legislators had hoped for. The first almshouses had sheltered the old and the sick. Now the poor families who had been supported in their own homes, and persons who were boarded out to families, were forced into the almshouses. There the old and sick were thrown together with tramps and vagabonds, with blind, deaf-mutes, cripples, idiots, epileptics, and insane people. Children, orphans, foundlings, unmarried mothers with their children, prostitutes, and criminals were put in these houses, often without separation of the sexes and age groups. There were no sanitary facilities, and old cots and straw substituted for beds. The almshouse usually was a dilapidated building, bequested to the town or cheaply bought at auction. Its management frequently was assigned to a jobless political supporter of the overseer or to an old farm couple unable to continue regular work and unqualified for the care of children and adults. For the education of the children in the almshouse there were no funds nor personnel able to teach. Sometimes 20 to 25 percent of the inmates were idiots or insane. The almshouses became a human scrap heap and did not fulfill the hope that had been raised in a reform of the care of the poor.[9]

Medical Care for the Poor

From the beginning of American colonial history, the hardships of frontier life, unwholesome situations on immigrant ships, climatic conditions, natural disasters, and battles with Indians caused injuries and illness among the settlers. Because doctors were few and lived long distances from their patients, their services were expensive. Under these circumstances it became necessary for the towns to provide for the medical treatment and maintenance of the indigent sick. Such statutory provisions were enacted in Rhode Island in 1662, in Connecticut in 1673, and in New York in 1687. If a destitute patient needed medical care the overseer of the poor or the justice of peace arranged for the service of a physician. Sometimes an annual contract was made between the overseer and a physician to care for all assigned paupers. In New York, pauper patients were boarded out to families, and

[8] See Victoria Olds, "The Freedmen's Bureau: A Nineteenth Century Federal Welfare Agency," *Social Casework*, 44, No. 5 (May 1963), 247–54.

[9] Henry Steele Commager, *Living Ideas in America* (New York: Harper, 1951), pp. 355–56; Pumphrey, "History," *Encyclopedia of Social Work 1971*, pp. 1448–49.

the city paid for their maintenance and nursing.[10] During the seventeenth century there were no hospitals in the colonies, and not until the second half of the eighteenth century were the first private hospitals built. Because the poor-law authorities were reluctant to spend money for paupers, they assumed the responsibility for payment of surgical treatment for poor patients only after they had approved the expense or had been ordered to do so by the court. In emergencies, especially when the patient's life was endangered, physicians cared for him and later sued the poor-law authorities for their fees.

In some colonies physicians were engaged by the colony, not by the individual towns, to "attend upon the poor generally in the county."[11] Pauper patients had no free choice of a physician. These doctors frequently were not the most competent or the best trained and the contracts granted them rather low compensation.

Mentally disturbed and feeble-minded patients—children as well as adults—were usually left with their families without special care. The violently insane and the deformed were considered to be possessed by the devil. The colonists attempted to drive out the evil spirit by whipping the unfortunate victim, by shackling him to stakes at the marketplace or throwing him into coarse pens, leaving him to hunger and cold. Other mental patients were locked up in attics, basements, and outhouses, were put into strait jackets, chained to a wall of their homes, or confined to the local jail. When the family could not pay for the maintenance of an insane patient, the overseers farmed the "lunatic" out to people willing to take him, just as was done with lame, blind, and crippled indigents.

The first hospitals in the colonies for indigent patients were the infirmaries or sick wards of the almshouses.[12] When the city of New York established, in 1736, its Public Workhouse and House of Correction, a physician was engaged as medical officer for the infirmary. Bellevue Hospital in New York was started in 1794 as a "pesthouse"; a "fever hospital ward" for patients suffering from contagious diseases was added in 1825. When most counties established almshouses during the period following the Quincy and Yates Reports, they also took care of the indigent sick. Only in larger almshouses were the sick paupers separated from other inmates and placed in a "sick bay" or infirmary, and even there medical care was limited to emergency operations and rare visits of the doctor. In general, sick inmates of the almshouse were left to the attention of the matron, or, more often,

[10] David M. Schneider, *History of Public Welfare in New York, 1609–1866* (Chicago: University of Chicago Press, 1938), p. 84.

[11] Edith Abbott, *Public Assistance; American Principles and Policies* (Chicago: University of Chicago Press, 1940), p. 358.

[12] Bernhard J. Stern, *Medical Services by Government* (New York: Commonwealth Fund, 1946), p. 15.

of other inmates. Not until the end of the nineteenth century did Massachusetts and Rhode Island set up "almshouse hospitals," and special wards in almshouses were set aside for the medical care of sick paupers.

The first hospitals were established as private charity institutions, for example, the Almshouse and Infirmary of the Society of Friends in Philadelphia, but after some time it became necessary for cities, counties, or the states to grant subsidies to the hospitals. During the nineteenth century the separation of the hospital from the almshouse became necessary. In Washington, Oregon, Nevada, and California, the lack of almshouses caused counties to set up hospitals. The rapid development of medical and sanitary science in the nineteenth century contributed to the improvement of medical facilities in the county hospitals. An important stimulus to the raising of standards was the beginning awareness of the dangers for the entire community of epidemics and contagious diseases.

Characteristics of Public Poor Relief

The deplorable conditions in the poorhouses led to three major changes in poor relief during the nineteenth century: (1) Private charity societies took the initiative in establishing orphanages and asylums because they objected to the placement of children and helpless invalid and old people in mixed almshouses where they were forced to live with vagrants, rogues, prostitutes, mentally disturbed patients, and criminals. Private relief societies were often affiliated with churches, fraternal orders, or national benevolent associations, and they became the leading, progressive element in American social welfare during the past century. (2) The states themselves assumed responsibility for certain classes of the poor, such as the insane, the feeble-minded, and convicted offenders for whom there were no adequate local facilities. (3) Some local public relief authorities, under the influence of state boards of charity, began to question the old concepts of poor relief with their humiliating, deterrent treatment of the poor. As a whole, however, public poor relief was still following the pattern of the Elizabethan Poor Law.

Changes of the underlying principles and improvements in the practice of poor relief were rather slow and sporadic as a result of sociological and economic factors.

The Practice of Poor Relief

The spirit of the English poor laws dominated most of the colonial laws, whether or not they used degrading terminology in speaking of "paupers." The public, with few exceptions, maintained its resentment against the poor-tax burden and its contempt for people unable to take care of themselves in a society which identified economic prosperity and success with efficiency and virtue under the influence of Herbert Spencer's "Social Darwinism," advocated in this country by William Graham Sumner, the militant defender of a laissez-faire policy and of individualism. Some of the most cruel forms of treatment of the poor, such as the whipping after the "warning out" and the posting of the poor roll at the marketplace, were gradually abandoned, but there remained the spirit of unwillingness to recognize aid for the poor as socially necessary and justified.[13] The abuses of corrupt local politicians to maintain their positions with the help of poor relief did not make it popular with the people. However, indigent families were still subject to such humiliation that they would rather starve than go on relief. An example of this attitude[14] is the case of a Kansas farmer's family. A severe drought that caused a failure of the crop in 1878 forced them to ask for county relief when both husband and wife fell ill. The family with their two children was put into the poor farm. After he recovered from his illness, the husband left to take a job as a farm hand and his wife wtih the two children remained at the poor farm until he could earn money. The superintendent of the poor farm bound out the eight-year-old son of the couple for ten years, against the child's will and without the consent of his parents. When the parents asked for the boy, the courts refused to release him. This treatment of parents and child characterizes the disregard of their human rights and feelings in the practice of the old poor laws.[15]

Inadequate Relief Funds

Because of the principle of local responsibility for general poor relief, the towns, parishes, or counties had to raise from local taxes the funds for the care of the poor. The various states differed in their legislation regarding the tax power of municipalities and counties, but usually the "general property tax" on real estate was the sole source of revenue for local government. Small towns and thinly populated rural counties, therefore, were unwilling and sometimes unable to raise sufficient funds for poor relief.

SOCIAL SERVICES UNDER STATE AUSPICES

The legal principle that the town or county was responsible for poor relief and the development of private charities within the community indi-

---

[13] Cohen, *Social Work in the American Tradition*, pp. 22–32; Coll, "Perspectives in Public Welfare: Colonial Times to 1860," *Welfare in Review*, No. 9 (December 1967), 1–9.

[14] Abbott, *Public Assistance*, pp. 125–79.

[15] Grace Browning and Sophonisba P. Breckinridge, *The Development of Poor Relief Legislation in Kansas* (Chicago: University of Chicago Press, 1935), pp. 130–33.

cate that institutions for relief and charity were local in character. For certain groups of the poor—the insane, the feeble-minded, the blind, the deaf-mute, the criminal, and the delinquent—the resources of the community were insufficient. A more powerful authority had to assume responsibility. The states, therefore, had to establish the necessary provisions for the care and treatment of these people in special institutions. This change occurred gradually during the eighteenth and nineteenth centuries.

The various state institutions were administered by separate boards of directors or trustees, and at first there was no cooperation whatsoever between these boards nor was there a unified plan in using the available facilities. Finally, for financial and practical reasons, the states coordinated the use of their institutions and developed uniform standards of care in hospitals, asylums, and correctional institutions.

The Care of the Insane

Mentally ill or "distraught" persons were, since colonial times, as a rule kept by their families locked or chained in a barred room or jailed with beggars and criminals. The nature of mental illness was not understood.[16] However, since 1732, they had received hospital care in the almshouse of Philadelphia and later, in 1753, in the Pennsylvania Hospital. In Philadelphia Thomas Eddy (1758–1827), a Quaker, was one of the pioneers in the care of the mentally ill. The first institution to be established especially for the mentally ill was the Eastern State Hospital at Williamsburg, Virginia, founded in 1773. With the progress of medicine and natural science, physicians became optimistic about the possibility of curing mental diseases.

Ten years after the opening of the hospital at Williamsburg, the outstanding psychiatrist of this period, Dr. Benjamin Rush, joined the medical staff of the Pennsylvania Hospital in Philadelphia and became a member of the medical faculty of the University of Pennsylvania. Dr. Rush had visited England and France and was greatly impressed by the work of Philippe Pinel at the Bicêtre Hospital in Paris. Instead of the cruel method of chaining the insane to the walls in the dungeon-like basements and the whipping of unruly patients, Pinel advocated their humane treatment, bloodletting, and occupation of the patients in the hospital. Inspired by these ideas, Dr. Rush in 1783 introduced the new methods to the Pennsylvania Hospital and taught them to medical students at the university. In thirty years of devoted service to the mentally ill he won the title of "The Father of American

16 Albert Deutsch, *The Mentally Ill in America,* (New York: Columbia University Press, 1949), pp. 32, 47–48; Milton Greenblatt, et al. eds., *The Patient and the Mental Hospital* (Glencoe, Ill.: Free Press, 1957); Abbott, *Public Assistance,* pp. 50–65; Carl Binger, *Revolutionary Doctor: Benjamin Rush* (New York: Norton, 1967); Gerald N. Grob, *The State and the Mentally Ill* (Chapel Hill: University of North Carolina Press, 1966).

Psychiatry." Recognizing the importance of diseases of the mind, Dr. Rush insisted that mental patients should no longer be considered incapable of human reactions and left in cold, dark, windowless wards. He introduced cold and hot baths, placed the patients in heated and ventilated rooms, assigned them simple work as occupational therapy, and trained male and female attendants to nurse the patients with kindness. He separated the sexes and the violent from the quiet patients, as well as the chronic from acute cases of mental illness. He removed the iron rings which had been used for chaining the patients to the wall, and changed the attitude from giving mere custodial care to giving active cure.

The Eastern State Hospital remained for nearly half a century the only hospital reserved for mental patients. In 1817 the Friends Asylum at Frankford, Pennsylvania was opened as a private institution, and in 1824 the state of Kentucky opened the Eastern Lunatic Asylum at Lexington. Mental hospitals, however, could accommodate only a small fraction of the mentally ill. Many dependent insane and feeble-minded remained neglected, and often poor-law commissioners failed to commit insane paupers to the state hospitals that charged the county higher rates. They preferred to keep the insane who could not remain with their families in local jails, houses of correction, and almshouses.

The great pioneer for the care of the mentally ill was a woman without medical training, Dorothea Dix.[17] Born in 1802, she left her parents after an unhappy childhood to live with her wealthy grandmother in Boston. At the age of fourteen she opened a school at Worcester and, after completing her education, the Dame School (in Boston, in 1821), which became a famous institution for girls. Miss Dix became acquainted with the leading citizens of New England who sent their children to her school. In 1836 her health forced her to take a rest in England. After her return to Boston in 1841, a young divinity student asked her to speak at a Sunday service to women convicts at the East Cambridge jail. Miss Dix was deeply shocked to find the women in their cells, many of them mentally deranged, in bare, filthy, and unheated quarters. This caused her to enlist the help of influential friends—the statesman Charles Sumner and the physician Dr. Samuel Gridley Howe—to investigate the jail with her and to mobilize the Boston press. Her findings aroused her suspicion that conditions in other institutions

---

[17] For a description of Dorothea Dix's life and work, see Edith Abbott, *Some American Pioneers in Social Welfare;* Helen E. Marshall, *Dorothea Dix, Forgotten Samaritan* (Chapel Hill: University of North Carolina Press, 1937); and Francis Tiffany, *Life of Dorothea Lynde Dix* (Boston: Houghton, 1890). Dorothea Dix published several books for children, among them, *Hymns for Children* (Boston: Munroe & Francis, 1825) and *American Moral Tales for Young Persons* (Boston: L. Bowles & Greene, 1832). See also Arthur Mandelbaum, "Mental Health and Retardation," *Encyclopedia of Social Work 1971,* pp. 791–802.

might be similar. Without any public authority, Miss Dix visited every almshouse, workhouse, jail, and prison in Massachusetts. After talking with the inmates and the keepers, she explored possibilities of improvements. On the advice of her friends, Miss Dix submitted in 1843 a memorial to the state legislature in which she described the shocking conditions which she had found. Insane patients and idiots were chained to the walls in cold cellars, beaten with rods, lashed, and confined in cages and pens. One man was in a close stall for seventeen years, and a young girl, naked in a barn, was the prey for the boys of the village. Another patient had been chained in an outhouse in winter and his feet had frozen. Although some politicians and overseers tried to obstruct Miss Dix's survey, public indignation and the influence of Charles Summer, Horace Mann, Dr. Samuel Gridley Howe, and Dr. Luther Bell led the legislature to pass a bill providing for immediate relief of the insane and the enlargement of the state lunatic hospital at Worcester. After this success, Miss Dix decided to continue her investigations of the conditions of the insane and feeble-minded in other states. In Rhode Island she received large donations from two philanthropists, Cyrus Butler and Nicholas Brown, for an asylum. In New Jersey she convinced the legislature of the necessity of building a mental hospital at Trenton. She traveled many thousands of miles and inspected hundreds of almshouses and jails. By her accurate, reliable reports of the suffering of mental patients, she convinced eleven state legislatures of the necessity of constructing or increasing the capacity of mental hospitals. She became the crusader for the mentally ill.

Her observations convinced her that, with the growth of industrialization, mental diseases would increase, and that it would be necessary to obtain federal grants from Congress for the future care of the insane. In 1848 she submitted a memorial to Congress and pleaded that 5,000,000 acres of land be given to the states for the care of indigent insane. When her proposal was rejected, she repeated her request in 1849, suggesting the land grant should be used also for blind and deaf-mute persons. After much delay Congress passed the bill in 1854. The bill provided for 10,000,000 acres of land for care of insane persons and 2,250,000 acres for maintenance and training of blind and deaf-mutes (*12¼ Million Acre Bill*). However, President Pierce vetoed the bill on constitutional grounds because "the power for relief of the needy or otherwise unfortunate members of society" was vested in the states and not conferred upon the federal government. There was bitter debate in Congress, but the veto was not overruled, and it established for eighty years a principle of abstention by the federal government from the field of social welfare. But Dorothea Dix's life work had made the public aware of the sufferings of the mentally disturbed patients and had caused the building of thirty-two hospitals in the United States.

Care for the Mentally Retarded

For a long time the feeble-minded (idiots, imbeciles, and morons) shared the fate of the psychotic (insane). They were kept at home without proper care or were committed to jails or poorhouses whenever their families were unable or unwilling to keep them. The first attempt to educate a feeble-minded child was made in France in 1799, when Dr. Jean Marc Gaspard Itard trained an idiot boy found in the woods by hunters. In 1837 Dr. Edouard Seguin opened a private school for feeble-minded children in Paris. His work found recognition throughout Europe, and in 1848 he followed an invitation to the United States to address legislatures and medical societies in several states. In the meantime, studies of the conditions of the mentally retarded had been made in Massachusetts and New York, and the first state School for Idiots and Feeble-minded Youth was opened in South Boston, Massachusetts in 1848. Dr. Samuel Gridley Howe, who was appointed its director, had studied the treatment of mentally deficient children in Paris.[18] The Massachusetts school under Dr. Walter E. Fernald developed new methods of training feeble-minded children. Other states established mental institutions during the following decades, such as the school for retarded children in Elwyn, Pennsylvania in 1875, under the renowned Quaker physician Dr. Joseph Parrisch, and in 1887 the training school at Vineland, New Jersey under Rev. Stephen O. Garrison. Many private institutions were first supported by state grants, and later were taken over by the state when private funds were insufficient. The *Development Disabilities Service Act* of 1970 provides a state–federal partnership for retarded children and adults not covered by programs of health, education and welfare.

Other provisions for mentally retarded children were the establishment of separate classes in elementary schools and of special schools in larger cities.[19]

[18] For information on Samuel Howe's life and work, see Julia W. Howe, *Reminiscence* (Boston: Houghton, 1900); and Laura E. Richards, *Samuel Gridley Howe* (New York: Appleton, 1935). The problem of mental deficiency is discussed in Richard L. Masland, et al., *Mental Subnormality—Biological, Psychological, and Cultural Factors* (New York: Basic Books, 1958); and Harry Best, *Public Provisions for the Mentally Retarded in the United States* (New York: Crowell, 1965).

[19] Arthur J. Lesser, "Prevention Through Improved Service," *Children*, 11, No. 1 (January–February 1964), 13–18; Harry Best, *Public Provisions for the Mentally Retarded*; Helen L. Beck, *Social Services for the Mentally Retarded* (Springfield, Ill.: Thomas, 1969); and Margaret E. Adams, *Mental Retardation and Its Social Dimensions* (New York: Columbia University Press, 1971). For more detail see Chapter 16.

Care of the Blind

Indigent blind persons had long been the object of private and public charity, and the almshouses sheltered many blind children and adults. The first attempt to educate blind children was made in Paris in 1784 by Valentin Haüy. His school set patterns for other European institutions. A Boston physician, Dr. John D. Fisher, visited the school for the blind in Paris and aroused interest in Boston for an institution for blind children. In 1832 the Massachusetts Asylum for the Blind, under the direction of Dr. Samuel Gridley Howe, was opened.

Samuel G. Howe (1801–1876) graduated from Harvard Medical School in 1824 and joined the Greeks in their fight for independence. Before returning to the United States, Dr. Howe observed in France new methods of teaching the blind and mentally deficient. Before opening the school in Boston, Howe returned to Europe to study the methods of education of the blind in England, France, and Germany and to recruit experienced teachers for the new asylum. The school soon became too small for the growing number of blind students and moved to a mansion donated by Colonel Thomas H. Perkins. The institution later was named Perkins Institute and Massachusetts School for the Blind.

Dr. Howe's outstanding success was Laura Bridgman, a seven-year-old blind and deaf girl. She was brought to Dr. Howe as a hopeless idiot. Howe taught her, with years of patient work, to read, speak, and become an intelligent, thoughtful woman. After Dr. Howe's death she became one of his biographers. Together with his friend Horace Mann, Howe achieved a reform of the Boston school system, the training of teachers, and the education of deaf-mute children.[20]

The Perkins Institute offered training of the blind in academic studies, music, and gymnastics and developed mechanical and domestic skills for vocational preparation. Michael Anagnos established the Howe Memorial Press, a Reference Library on Blindness and the Blind, and a kindergarten for blind children.

In 1832 a second school, the New York Institution for the Blind, was set up under the direction of Dr. John D. Russ, and was later known as The New York Institute for the Education of the Blind. There, in 1863, a modification of the French Braille system of raised print was introduced.

[20] Gabriel Farrell, *The Story of Blindness* (Cambridge, Mass.: Harvard University Press, 1956); Berthold Loewenfeld, *Our Blind Children: Growing and Learning with Them* (Springfield, Ill.: Thomas, 1956); Jacobus Ten Broek and Floyd W. Matson, *Hope Deferred: Public Welfare and the Blind* (Berkeley: University of California Press, 1959); *Blindness in the U.S.* (Hartford, Conn: Travelers' Research Center, 1968).

In day schools blind children are taught together with sighted children, but the blind receive special instruction in reading, writing, and arithmetic. Now all states educate blind children, either in special classes or at home.

The prevention of blindness was first stressed by Dr. Park Lewis in New York. There, the State Commission for the Prevention of Blindness, organized under Miss Louise Schuyler in 1908, was devoted primarily to spreading the knowledge of prophylaxis of ophthalmia neonatorum, an eye infection occurring at childbirth. The commission, now named the National Society for the Prevention of Blindness, extends its program to the entire country, includes other diseases which may lead to blindness, and promotes safety programs in industry for the protection of eyesight.

Before the enactment of the *Social Security Act,* in 1935, twenty-nine states had passed special statutes on blind relief. There were, however, among social workers and among the blind themselves, differences of opinion over whether special relief was undermining the initiative of the blind in their attempt to learn a trade or a profession and thus to become self-reliant citizens. This desire of the blind to be respected as normal human beings deserves recognition, appreciation, and encouragement. The number of blind persons in the United States today is estimated at about 300,000.[21]

The Care of the Deaf and Deaf-Mute

Different from the blind, the deaf and deaf-mute have found in human society less sympathy and help. Their inability to understand the world around them has been a source of irritation or ridicule to others. If the deaf were poor, they were treated as idiots, left to their families, or placed in poorhouses. The first scientific training of deaf-mute children, in the eighteenth century, was undertaken by Jacob Rodriges Pereire of Bordeaux, France. Based on Pereire's method, the first school for deaf-mute children was founded in Paris in 1760 by the Abbé Charles Michel de l'Epée.

An attempt to teach the deaf in the United States was made in New York when, in 1810, Dr. John Stanford, a minister, found a number of deaf children on his visits to the almshouse and offered them religious education.

When at Hartford, Connecticut in 1815 Alice Cogswell, the deaf daughter of a physician, was in need of education, friends of the family took up a collection and sent Dr. Thomas H. Gallaudet to Europe to study

21 See Thomas J. Carroll, *Blindness, What It Is, What It Does, and How to Live with It* (Boston: Little, Brown, 1961); Hector Chevigny and S. Braverman, *Adjustment of the Blind* (New Haven, Conn.: Yale University Press, 1950); Samuel Finestine, ed., *Social Casework and Blindness* (New York: American Foundation for the Blind, 1960); and Alexander F. Handel, "The Blind," *Encyclopedia of Social Work 1965,* pp. 102–7.

the methods of teaching the deaf. In Paris Abbé Sicard, director of the Paris school for the deaf, instructed him in the art of training the deaf. He also sent one of his best teachers, Lautent Clerc, with Dr. Gallaudet to America, where both opened the first American Asylum for the Deaf at Hartford in 1817.

The first public residential school for the deaf was the Central College at Danville, Kentucky, organized in 1823. Other states followed the Kentucky pattern. Private as well as public institutions for the deaf, in their early development, had the character of charities and were primarily devoted to the education of poor deaf children. The first day school for deaf children was opened in New York in 1869. In the beginning sign language was taught; more recently, the oral method and lipreading have been emphasized. Frequently both methods are combined. Of all handicapped groups, the federal government first assumed responsibility for the education of the deaf. Today most states have residential schools for the deaf.

The deaf are no longer treated as charity cases, but as people of normal intelligence, permitted to participate in such occupations as they can perform. There are about 250,000 deaf and 15,000,000 hard-of-hearing persons in the United States. About 3,000 adults are blind and deaf. Emphasis is laid on their education, not on public assistance.[22]

Private societies such as the American Society for the Hard-of-Hearing support the work for the prevention of deafness, procure some hearing aids for people who cannot afford to buy them, and urge the medical examination of preschool children so that medical treatment and education may start early.

The "State Poor"

Since local poor relief was granted only to residents who had acquired legal settlement, towns refused to take care of other paupers who had recently arrived, or who had been "warned out." The urgent need for food and medical care of such unfortunates, however, could not fully be denied. For this reason the colonial legislature of Massachusetts assumed the payment of the necessary expenses for these "state paupers" in 1675. Other

[22] See Harry Best, *Deafness and the Deaf in the United States* (New York: Macmillan, 1943) ; Edna S. Levine, *The Psychology of Deafness* (New York: Columbia University Press, 1960) ; John D. Rainer, ed., *Family and Mental Health Problems in a Deaf Population* (New York: Columbia University Press, 1963) ; Tanya Nash and Emil M. Zabell, "The Deaf and the Hard-of-Hearing," *Encyclopedia of Social Work 1965*, pp. 247–53; Herbert R. Kohl, *Language and Education of the Deaf* (New York: Center for Urban Education, 1966) ; Madeline Shipsey, "Disability and Physical Handicap," *Encyclopedia 1971*, p. 231; Laura L. Knox and Freeman McConnell, "Helping Parents to Help Deaf Children," *Children*, 15, No. 5 (October 1968), 183–87; K. P. Meadow, "Self-Image, Family Climate, and Deafness," *Social Forces*, 47, No. 4 (October 1969), 428–38.

colonies took similar measures, particularly during such emergencies as attacks by Indian tribes, inundations, and other natural disasters. In New York State, relief at the expense of the state treasury was granted refugees from the wars against the Indians and, in 1778, to the survivors of veterans in the War of the Revolution.

The assumption of state responsibility for persons without legal settlement and without an earlier residence to which they could be returned became a necessity, because townships or counties refused to care for such persons in need.[23] The beginning of industrial production in New England attracted agricultural workers from the farms to look for jobs in the towns. If they lost their jobs, the period of legal settlement often had not been attained, so that the number of "state poor" greatly increased during the nineteenth century and sometimes was almost as high as that of the resident poor under township relief.

Another group of needy persons who were considered a responsibility of the colonies and later the states, rather than of local government, were the disabled veterans. Various provisions for the veterans were enacted during the colonial period. Immediately after the Revolution the federal government became the main source of their support, while the states continued to grant veterans and their survivors additional pensions and special privileges. For recent developments in veterans' services, see Chapter 17.

Social Problems of the Black Population

Toward the end of the Civil War, in 1863, "Freedmen's Aid Societies" were founded in the northern states to help in the education and economic adjustment of the liberated Negro slaves. They sent missionaries and teachers to the South, organized schools for the freedmen and their children, and planned to assist them in economic integration. Within three years following the legal abolition of slavery, fourteen institutions of higher education and teacher training seminars had been set up, among them Howard University in Washington, D.C., Fisk University, Morehouse College, and Hampton Institute. They were supported by the George Peabody Fund and the John F. Slaton Fund, later by the Rockefeller General Education Board and the Julius Rosenwald Fund.[24] Since that time, edu-

---

[23] The states paid a lump sum for the relief of these "state poor" to the towns, which delegated it to a contractor. Frequently, both the towns and the contractors wanted to profit from this appropriation so that very meager care resulted for the poor.

[24] Horace Mann Bond, *The Education of the Negro in the American Social Order* (Englewood Cliffs, N.J.: Prentice-Hall, 1934), pp. 22–29; E. Franklin Frazier, *The Negro in the United States* (New York: Macmillan, 1949), pp. 471–73; W. E. B. Du Bois, *Efforts of Social Betterment Among Negro Americans* (Atlanta, Ga.: Atlanta University Press, 1909); John H. Franklin, *From Slavery to Freedom,* 3rd ed. (New York: Alfred A. Knopf, 1967).

cated blacks have found employment as teachers and social workers. As black social workers were mainly employed by "white charities" before the Depression of the 1930s, they often followed the ideas of their white employers. The leading black organization in the field of social work, the National Urban League, grew out of several philanthropic committees of white citizens in northern cities in 1911.[25] The League considers its staff members as "social workers," and it does not have the support of the black masses. On the other hand, the National Association for the Advancement of Colored People (NAACP), founded in 1909, is an activist agency of the blacks.[26] Recently the program against poverty (see Chapter 11) has introduced measures to help in black education, vocational training, and job finding for unemployed black youths. Many administrators under the Office of Economic Opportunity are Negro sociologists, economists, and social workers, and the majority of its clients are blacks and members of other minority groups.[27] Discrimination against all racial minorities, particularly blacks, has become one of the most severe problems facing the United States (see Chapter 17).

Crime and Delinquency

During the Middle Ages and up to the sixteenth century, many crimes were punished by death or exile. Prisoners were detained, usually tortured before sentence, and incarcerated, often for life, in dungeons of castles or

[25] E. Franklin Frazier, *Black Bourgeoisie* (New York: Free Press, 1957), pp. 60–71, 98; Richard B. Sherman, *The Negro and the City* (Englewood Cliffs, N.J.: Prentice-Hall, 1970).

[26] Frazier, *Black Bourgeoisie*, pp. 100, 231; LeRoy Collins, "Civil Rights and a Concerned Community," *Social Welfare Forum* (1965), 35–42; LeRoy Collins and Whitney M. Young, Jr., "Civil Rights and a Militant Profession," *Social Welfare Forum* (1965), 42–54; Andrew Billingsley, *Black Families in White America* (Englewood Cliffs, N.J.: Prentice-Hall, 1968); J. Milton Yinger, "Recent Developments in Minority and Race Relations," *The Annals*, 378 (July 1968), 130–45; Whitney M. Young, Jr., *Beyond Racism: Building an Open Society* (New York: McGraw-Hill, 1969). See also Chapter 17.

[27] Nicholas Babchuck and Ralph V. Thompson, "The Voluntary Associations of Negroes," *American Sociological Review*, 27, No. 3 (October 1962), 647–55; Paul E. Mott, *The Organization of Society* (Englewood Cliffs, N.J.: Prentice-Hall, 1965), pp. 245–60; Charles F. Grosser, "Community Development Programs Serving the Urban Poor," *Social Work*, 10, No. 3 (July 1965), 15–21; Daniel P. Moynihan and Paul Barton, *The Negro Family: The Case for National Action* (Washington, D.C.: Department of Labor, 1965); Talcott Parsons and Kenneth Clark, *The Negro American* (Boston: Houghton Mifflin, 1966); A. H. Passow, *Education of the Disadvantaged* (New York: Holt, Rinehart and Winston, 1967); Michael Banton, *Race Relations* (New York: Basic Books, 1967); Frances M. Beal, "Double Jeopardy: To Be Black and Female," *New Generation*, 51, No. 4 (Fall 1969), 23–28; Milton Rokeach and Seymour Parker, "Values as Social Indicators of Poverty and Race Relations in America," *The Annals*, 388 (March 1970), 97–111; Louis L. Knowles and Kenneth Prewitt, eds., *Institutional Racism in America* (Englewood Cliffs, N.J.: Prentice-Hall, 1969).

towers. No consideration was given to their health, and they lived or died under the worst conditions. In the colonial period a large number of crimes against persons or property was punished by hanging or by banishment from the colony. Persons arrested were held by the sheriff or his deputies in the local jail, which was frequently unsafe because outbreaks of desperate criminals and attacks by gangs of friends of the convicted person were not rare, but no other facilities existed until the latter part of the eighteenth century.[28] The growing population, the deportation of convicts from Australia and England to America, and the changing economic structure of our country led to an increase in serious crimes. However, the influence of French humanitarianism made it difficult to continue the death sentence as punishment for minor crimes. As the number of convicted offenders became larger, the communities began looking to the states for protection. Pennsylvania was the first to establish a state penal institution. In 1790 the legislature decided to convert the local jail at Walnut Street in Philadelphia into a state prison. Since its founding by William Penn, Pennsylvania lived under the influence of the philosophy of the Religious Society of Friends (Quakers). They were convinced that the divine power in every human being could achieve his reformation and that the sinner left to meditation would repent and give up his sin. In accordance with this philosophy, prisoners in the state prison in Philadelphia were segregated into two groups. Those convicted for such serious crimes as murder, arson, adultery, burglary, and manslaughter were confined to solitary cells without communication with other prisoners. Others who had committed minor offenses were lodged in dormitories, where they lived in groups. The new method meant a classification of the prisoners according to the nature of their offense; it was a step toward differentiation of treatment and rehabilitation.[29] Under this "Pennsylvania system" of prisons, which was accepted by other states, more humane treatment and less corporal punishment were exercised. The system was optimistic in hoping for an inner reformation of the convict. The lack of qualified and devoted personnel (due to low wages of the warden and guards), overcrowding of the institutions, idleness of the convicts, lack of sufficient funds for proper management, and political scandals led to a failure of this type of prison management.

A second type of state prison was introduced at Auburn, New York

[28] The typical jail was a "catch-all" for dangerous criminals, minor offenders, debtors, and destitute people. There was no separation of prisoners by crime, age, or sex. Debauchery and promiscuous intercourse were frequent. The jailers demanded fees from all prisoners, regardless of whether they had been acquitted by the court. See Orlando Lewis, *The Development of American Prisons and Prison Customs* (New York: American Prison Association, 1922), p. 13.

[29] Auguste Jorns, *The Quakers as Pioneers in Social Work* (Montclair, N.J.: Patterson-Smith, 1969).

in 1816. It differed from the Pennsylvania plan in that the prisoners were confined only at night to solitary cells, but had to work during the day in congregate prison workshops. The plan of reformation by isolation was abandoned; confinement to a single cell was used only as a disciplinary measure. Following the example of the prison at Ghent (Belgium), the Auburn prison was built in a star shape with cell blocks opening onto a gallery which could be easily watched by one guard in the center of the building at each floor. The Auburn system was widely accepted, and well-known prisons such as Sing Sing in New York (1825) and San Quentin in California (1852) followed its pattern.

Prison reform in the United States, the introduction of more humane treatment of the convicts, and the use of work as a means of rehabilitation were influenced by experiences of the English reformers (particularly John Howard)[30] and by the penal philosophy of Beccaria and Lombroso. It proved important to segregate young offenders from hard-boiled criminals; this resulted in the establishment, in 1876, of a special institution in Elmira, New York. The "reformatory" was used for young convicts between sixteen and thirty years of age, and later also for older first offenders. Its main purpose was to prevent the "habitual criminals" from infecting younger offenders. The first prison for women was established at Sherborn, Massachusetts in 1879, and most states followed by building separate penal institutions for women.

In many prisons and penitentiaries, as well as reformatories, employment in workshops equipped with industrial machinery, and agricultural and road-building work are provided for the prisoners. The present method, therefore, is called the "industrial prison system." The production of goods in prisons or by prison gangs hired by farmers, mill owners, and manufacturers presented serious competition with free labor. Employers, workers, and labor unions objected to this competition, so that federal and state legislation finally limited the use of prison labor. Modern industrial machinery, and the production of goods, is necessary to train the prisoners for useful work (see Chapter 18).

STATE BOARDS OF CHARITIES

The increasing number of state institutions for the handicapped and delinquent in the nineteenth century created a chaotic state of administration. These institutions were based on special state legislation and each placed under the administration of a separate board of directors. Each board annually requested higher appropriations from the legislature. There

---

[30] See Chapter 2, pp. 27–29; Chapter 18; and John Irwin, *The Felon* (Englewood Cliffs, N.J.: Prentice-Hall, 1970), pp. 36–60.

was no uniform policy in principles of management, treatment of inmates, budgets, or personnel standards in institutions, even within the same state. The lack of coordination between the various institutions and of intelligent use of their facilities was strongly felt.

The first state to create a central agency for the supervision of all state charitable institutions was Massachusetts, which organized a State Board of Charities in 1863. The board had an able secretary in Mr. Frank S. Sanborn. Dr. Samuel Gridley Howe served from 1864 for ten years as its president. He initiated a survey of the existing statutes and regulations of the lunatic asylums, state hospitals, almshouses, industrial schools, and charitable institutions for which Massachusetts granted annual subsidies.[31] Dr. Howe recommended methods for humane treatment of the poor in all these institutions and for efficient management; these rules were published in 1866 under the title *Principles of Public Charities*. They emphasized the family system in placing children and adults in the community whenever it was not absolutely necessary to keep them in almshouses, hospitals, or asylums. Members of the Massachusetts Board of Charities inspected not only the state almshouses, lunatic asylums, reform schools, and prisons, but also local almshouses and jails. Information and data collected from the inspections were summarized and submitted to the legislature. In five years the State Board of Charities succeeded in reducing substantially the number of "state paupers," by introducing a plan of classification for all inmates of state institutions, and in establishing order in the administration of state charity institutions. In 1869 a "state visiting agent" was appointed to attend the court trials of juvenile delinquents to assume care for the children who were not committed to reform schools. The state agent became a forerunner of the juvenile probation officer.[32]

The advantages of a central state charity agency were soon recognized in other states. They followed the example of Massachusetts, in that each established its own State Board of Charities and Correction. In the meantime, Massachusetts had added in 1869 an agency of coordination in the field of public health—the State Board of Health. Its example stimulated other states to organize such boards, first California in 1870, the District of Columbia in 1871, and New Jersey in 1874.

The main results of the activities of the state boards of charities were: (1) better care and protection of dependent children whom they removed from the poorhouses and placed in licensed children's asylums or in foster homes with standards set by the state boards; (2) more uniform and efficient administration of local public relief; (3) the decrease of pauperism

---

[31] See *Encyclopedia of Social Work 1971,* p. 1153; and Pumphrey, *The Heritage of American Social Work,* pp. 141–60.

[32] Frank J. Bruno, *Trends in Social Work* (New York: Columbia University Press, 1957), pp. 31–43; and *Encyclopedia of Social Work 1971,* p. 1457.

in industrial districts by the protection of immigrants; and (4) improvement in the care of the mentally ill. The state boards also were instrumental in the foundation of a nationwide organization representing the field of social welfare. In 1865 the American Social Science Association was established, which preceded the Conference of Boards of Public Charities, now the National Conference on Social Welfare.[33]

In the western states the counties, rather than cities and townships, assumed the responsibility for poor relief. In California even counties were unable to meet the problems of the Gold Rush of 1850, when tens of thousands of immigrants arrived after long, strenuous travels. Mining towns had no facilities for medical care nor public relief of any kind. Thus, for the first years of California's statehood, the state government was forced to assume the sole responsibility for the maintenance of the sick and of orphans. Orphanages founded by religious societies were first maintained partly by municipal subsidies, later by the state. In 1853 the counties, under the boards of supervisors, assumed the responsibility for the care of the aged and the sick, which was regulated by a state *Poor Law of 1855.*

Upon the requests of various citizens' groups and social agencies, the California legislature established a State Board of Charities and Corrections in 1903 for the supervision of the charitable, correctional, and penal institutions of the state, counties, and cities. In 1913 "children's agents" in the State Board of Control were appointed to supervise children's institutions and children in foster care for whom state aid was paid; their activities were in 1921 assigned to the Bureau of Children's Aid in the Department of Finance. Finally, in 1925, the functions of supervision and control of state agencies were consolidated in the Department of Public Welfare which was renamed, in 1927, the State Department of Social Welfare. This illustration of the California development is characteristic of the haphazard legislation and slow development of systematic organization of welfare functions in the western states.[34]

PRIVATE SOCIAL AGENCIES AND CHARITY ORGANIZATIONS

The inadequacies of the mixed poorhouses that were harmful to the poor, and especially to children and young people who were forced to live with vagrants, criminal elements, prostitutes, and sick and mentally dis-

[33] Bruno, *Trends in Social Work,* pp. 3–7; Harry L. Lurie, "The Development of Social Welfare Programs," *Social Work Year Book* (1960), 28–29; Ralph Pumphrey, in *Encyclopedia of Social Work 1971,* pp. 1456–57.

[34] For example, see Nathan I. Huggins, *Protestants Against Poverty: Boston Charities, 1870–1900* (Westport, Conn.: Greenwood, 1971); and Raymond Mohl, *Poverty in New York: 1783–1825* (New York: Oxford University Press, 1971).

turbed persons, were the main incentive for the foundation of private social agencies during the nineteenth century. As we have seen, religious charities and philanthropic relief societies were already in existence, but their activities were limited to aid for special local groups. One of the first organizations which attempted to find a constructive remedy for people in economic distress was the New York Society for the Prevention of Pauperism, created in 1817. Its aim was to determine the causes of poverty and to develop means of rehabilitation instead of the mere palliative of financial relief. In a survey made under the auspices of the Society, the following causes of poverty were found: ignorance, idleness, intemperance, lack of thrift, imprudent hasty marriages, lotteries, pawnbrokers, houses of prostitution, gambling, and the large number of charitable institutions. The Society divided New York City into districts and assigned to each district two or three volunteer "visitors of the indigent" as its agents. It introduced bills in the city council to prohibit street begging and to restrict saloons, which were considered a primary cause of destitution. The Society established an employment bureau and a savings bank and encouraged the foundation of mutual aid and mutual life insurance groups to protect their members against economic hazards. It provided supplies for home industrial employment of women. The studies of the Society revealed the lack of cooperation between the various charitable organizations, and the need for rehabilitation of the poor families.

In Boston the Reverend Joseph Tuckerman, a Unitarian minister and city missionary, was appointed by the Massachusetts legislature in 1832 to conduct a survey of the conditions of the poor. His investigations pointed out the influence of low wages and unemployment, which did not permit the unskilled worker and his family to buy the bare necessities of life. He recommended securing better housing facilities for the poor, compulsory school attendance for all children, and providing an individual consideration of the conditions and needs of each family in distress.[35] In 1833 the Seamen's Aid Society of Boston procured work for wives and widows of seamen in clothing workshops, and fought a campaign under the leadership of Sarah J. Hale for decent wages for women workers to protect them from pauperism.

After a severe winter in 1843, which caused large-scale unemployment in New York, the Association for Improving the Condition of the Poor was founded to coordinate the disorganized relief measures of the large number of church and other charitable societies which had been set up to give

---

[35] Daniel T. McColgan, *Joseph Tuckerman, Pioneer in American Social Work* (Washington: Catholic University of America, 1940); Robert H. Bremner, *From the Depths—the Discovery of Poverty in the United States* (New York: New York University Press, 1956); and Pumphery, *The Heritage of American Social Work*, pp. 71–79.

relief. The Association, under the able leadership of Robert Hartley, criticized indiscriminate almsgiving without knowledge of the individual needs of the applicants and the lack of constructive measures to make the poor families self-supporting. The Association requested that each applicant for relief be visited in his home by either a volunteer or an employee of the charity society so that the family could be counseled.[36]

The city was divided into 21 districts with 225 subdistricts, each of them assigned to one "friendly visitor." The Association did not grant money, but the visitor might enlist financial aid from relatives or friends of the poor, or from relief societies. The Association attempted to restrict lotteries, gambling, and drinking, and it organized the foundation of the New York Juvenile Asylum in 1851, the Society for the Relief of the Ruptured and Crippled in 1853, and the New York Children's Aid Society in 1854. Similar associations were established in other cities. These associations had certain success in the line of social reform, but they did not accomplish the desired cooperation between the numerous relief and charity societies. These agencies jealously guarded the favor of wealthy citizens for contributions to their own institutions and refused to cooperate in a systematic plan for relief and rehabilitation.

The Charity Organization Societies

During the economic depression of 1873, the public again became aware of the inadequacy and disorganization of public and private relief, and its interest in the work of the London Charity Organization Society was aroused. The Reverend S. Humphreys Gurteen, who had been in London and was acquainted with the Charity Organization Society, organized in 1877 in Buffalo, New York the first society of this type in the United States. Its aim was to help the poor more effectively and to avoid waste of funds, competition, and duplication of work among the relief societies. Within ten years, twenty-five charity organization societies were founded. Among their leaders were Josephine Shaw Lowell in New York, Robert T. Paine and Zilpha D. Smith in Boston, Amos G. Warner in Baltimore, the Reverend Oscar McCulloch in Indianapolis, and Emily Williamson and Caroline Alexander in New Jersey. The main principles of the Charity Organization Societies (C.O.S.) were (1) cooperation of all local charity agencies under a board of their representatives; (2) a central "confidential register"; and (3) an investigation of the social condition of every applicant by a "friendly

---

[36] Dorothy G. Becker, "The Visitor to the New York City Poor, 1843–1920," *Social Service Review*, 35, No. 4 (December 1961), 382–96, and "Early Adventures in Social Casework, 1880–1910," *Social Casework*, 44, No. 5 (May 1963), 253–61; "Robert Milham Hartley," *Encyclopedia of Social Work 1971*, pp. 489–90.

visitor" to determine the need and the individual measures necessary in each individual case.[37]

The founders of the societies represented the "bourgeois benevolence," wealthy citizens who felt morally obligated to alleviate the suffering of the poor and hoped thus to minimize political unrest and industrial strife. The members of the board, manufacturers, bankers, and merchants, wanted to be respected in their communities as religious and philanthropic benefactors and civic leaders. Their economic and political philosophy influenced the attitude of the visitors. They believed that poverty was caused by personal fault, idleness, negligence, mismanagement, drinking, gambling, and vice. They hoped that by giving friendly advice, by helping in procuring employment or, sometimes, by giving a loan, they could strengthen the moral fiber of the indigent and encourage them to become self-supporting.[38]

Although this doctrine was originally the accepted social philosophy of the C.O.S., the visitors found when they became more intimately acquainted with the conditions of "their families" that there were other factors that caused destitution. They recognized that unhealthy neighborhood and housing conditions prevented the maintenance of health and morals, that low wages did not allow the purchase of adequate food and clothes, even with careful housekeeping and thrift. Jobs were scarce in periods of economic depression, and it was not the fault of the unemployed worker that he could not find a new position. In times of sickness or unemployment, families became the victims of "loan sharks" who caused them to go into debt for years by charging high interest and heartlessly demanding money. Others lost their meager savings by fraud. The practical experiences of the visitors repeated those of the New York Association for Improving the Conditions of the Poor of 1843. They revealed that the concept of individual fault did not stand the test of honest analysis. They began to ask for measures which would fundamentally change those social conditions, and became advocates of social reform. To implement the findings of their members, Charity Organization Societies became active in promoting social legislation for improvement of housing and of penal institutions, clearance of slums, and better enforcement of tenement legislation, as well as in measures for prevention and treatment of tuberculosis, widespread among

[37] Alvin B. Kogut, "The Negro and the C.O.S. in the Progressive Era," *Social Service Review*, 44, No. 1 (March 1970), 11–21; Coll, *Perspectives in Public Welfare*, pp. 44–62.

[38] Robert H. Bremner, "The Rediscovery of Pauperism," *Current Issues in Social Work Seen in Historical Perspective* (New York: Council on Social Work Education, 1962), pp. 10–19. About their religious motivation, see Genevieve C. Weeks, "Religion and Social Work as Exemplified in the Life of Oscar McCulloch," *Social Service Review*, 39, No. 1 (March 1965), 38–52, and ibid., No. 2 (June 1965), 209–21. See also Lilian Brandt, *Growth and Development of AICP and COS: A Preliminary and Exploratory Review* (New York: Community Service Society, 1942).

the poverty-stricken classes. Some societies established employment bureaus, loan societies, workshops, laundries, lumberyards, wayfarers' lodges and shelters, and legal-aid bureaus. Training centers were set up for the rehabilitation of handicapped people, the blind, deaf, and crippled, and for domestic training of girls. Hospitals, dispensaries, and visiting nurses' services, recreation and summer camps, nurseries for young children, fresh-air playgrounds, and related facilities were organized under the auspices of Charity Organization Societies. They supported the movement for child labor legislation, for prison reform, and the organization of special courts for children and adolescents. Many active workers and volunteers of the Charity Organization Societies felt the need for a deeper understanding of the behavior of individuals and of social and economic problems and asked for special training for social work. Such study was first suggested by Anna L. Dawes of Pittsfield, Massachusetts in 1893. Mary Richmond in 1897 formulated the plan for the establishment of the Training School for Applied Philanthropy, which organized the first social work courses in New York in 1898.[39] Out of requests within the Charity Organization Societies grew the recognition of the need of professional education for social work. Another characteristic of the Charity Organization Societies was that their members desired for themselves, and for the public, reliable information on social and health conditions and on the activities of the societies. The result was the publication in New York in 1891, of a magazine, *Charities Review,* which merged in 1910 with several related journals and became one of the leading professional publications under the title *The Survey.* This was published until 1952, and has greatly contributed to the theoretical and practical development of social work. Major concerns of the C.O.S. were health problems and family and children dependency.[40]

The Charity Organization Societies did not attempt to reform public poor relief. They followed Thomas Chalmers's belief that receipt of public poor relief weakened the initiative and moral strength of the indigent. In several cities—Brooklyn, New York, Baltimore, Philadelphia, Washington, St. Louis, Kansas City, Missouri, and San Francisco—the Charity Organiza-

---

[39] Edith Abbott, *Social Welfare and Professional Education,* rev. ed. (Chicago: University of Chicago Press, 1942), pp. 20–21; Bruno, *Trends in Social Work,* pp. 138–44; Arthur S. Link, *American Epoch: A History of the United States Since the 1890's* (New York: Alfred A. Knopf, 1955); Ernest V. Hollis and Alice L. Taylor, *Social Work Education in the United States* (New York: Columbia University Press, 1951), pp. 5–19; Werner W. Boehm, "Education for Social Work," *Encyclopedia of Social Work 1971,* pp. 257–73.

[40] Walter I. Trattner, "Homer Folks and the Public Health Movement," *Social Service Review,* 40, No. 4 (December 1966), 410–28, and *Homer Folks: Pioneer of Social Welfare* (New York: Columbia University Press, 1968); "Homer Folks," *Encyclopedia of Social Work 1971,* pp. 451–53; Clark A. Chambers, *Paul U. Kellogg and the Survey: Voices for Social Welfare and Social Justice* (Minneapolis: University of Minnesota Press, 1971).

tion Societies convinced the city councils that public outdoor relief could be abolished and might be dispensed more efficiently by private relief agencies. Some societies received public subsidies for several years for saving the municipal treasury the expense for public outdoor relief.

In their programs the Charity Organization Societies faced two conflicting tasks. They had been organized to achieve better coordination and integration of the existing relief societies and to improve the health and social resources of the community. However, vested interests among member agencies often resented recommendations for changes of methods of work, so that some societies were forced to establish divisions for service to families in need. These divisions conflicted with the activities of other relief societies, which objected because the C.O.S. had not been founded to set up rival organizations. Therefore, at the suggestion of Francis H. McLean, Director of the Russell Sage Foundation, functions of the Charity Organization Societies were separated. In 1908 in Pittsburgh, Pennsylvania, a Council of Social Agencies was founded as the social welfare coordination and planning body. It was composed of representatives of all member social agencies, and The Associated Charities of Pittsburgh was organized as a family welfare society. This pattern was applied in most of the C.O.S. They assumed the title Council of Social Agencies for their planning and coordinating activities,[41] while United Charities, Federated Charities, and so forth were established as nondenominational family and children's services. The Council of Social Agencies had difficulties in raising its operating funds from the public because administrative functions do not appeal to the donors. Thus, in 1913 in Cleveland, the need for joint financing of all private charity work, including the activities of the Council of Social Agencies, was recognized, leading to the establishment of a Community Chest as the organization for collecting private contributions and donations and for distributing them fairly to the social agencies.

One of the main arguments that C.O.S. had used in their criticism of public relief was that they were able to operate more cheaply than poor-law authorities and would save taxpayers money. Local governments, states, and even Congress had long supported the work of private charities by subsidies for institutions, schools, hospitals, and relief services to children and adults. This practice was widely used throughout the country.[42]

The main point in favor of public subsidies to private relief societies was that they were more economical. They relied on endowments, dona-

---

[41] Councils of similar nature had been set up before in New York City, Rochester, and Elmira, New York (Bruno, *Trends in Social Work*, p. 194; and Pumphrey, *The Heritage of American Social Work*, pp. 168–91). See also Chapter 6.

[42] Amos G. Warner, Stuart A. Queen, and Ernest B. Harper, *American Charities and Social Work* (New York: Crowell, 1930), pp. 185–89; Frank D. Watson, *The Charity Organization Movement in the U.S.* (New York: Macmillan, 1922).

tions, and voluntary contributions, and often had only minor expenses for salaries and wages; this was particularly true of sectarian agencies, which used mainly the service of volunteers and religious orders. Another argument was that private charities had a wholesome moral influence on the clients and were directed by devoted people, not by bureaucrats or political appointees. The spoils system in public service had indeed caused mismanagement and inadequacies in public relief. Some philanthropists also thought that relief from private charities would not burden the poor with the stigma of pauper relief and was therefore less degrading.

However, there were valid arguments against tax-supported subsidies to private charities: the objection that public funds should not be spent for denominational or private purposes; that private charity encouraged pauperism and frequently duplicated public efforts; and, that public subsidies would weaken the willingness of sponsors to contribute to private charities. From the point of social philosophy, the subsidy system had definite weaknesses. American characteristics are self-reliance, pride of independence, and neighborly aid to people in distress. It seemed inconsistent for private charity to ask for the help of the same government that was criticized in its relief administration as corrupt and inefficient.

The concept of public subsidy to private agencies made necessary the introduction of certain safeguards whenever public tax funds were used to subsidize private social work. The formula "public control must go where public money goes" expresses this trend. This principle requires the following measures: (1) the methods and standards of the private agency have to be approved by the public organization granting the subsidy; (2) the private agency and institution have to permit inspections by government representatives; (3) the organization has to keep accounts, has to allow their auditing, and has to render reports; (4) the admission policy of the private institution needs approval by the public subsidizing agency; and (5) the private agency agrees to ask for a uniform rate of subsidy for each needy client or patient per month or day.[43] The general trend seems to be toward limiting the use of public funds to public social welfare activities, leaving the maintenance of private social agencies to their membership, to

[43] For an analysis of the principles involved in public subsidies in social work, see Arlien Johnson, *Public Policy and Private Charities* (Chicago: University of Chicago Press, 1931); see also Wayne McMillen, "Financing Social Welfare Services," *Social Work Year Book* (1957), 260–67; Kenyon Poole, ed., *Fiscal Policies and the American Economy* (Englewood Cliffs, N.J.: Prentice-Hall, 1951); Ida C. Merriam, "Financial Social Welfare Services," *Encyclopedia of Social Work 1965*, 342–48; Arlien Johnson, "Public Funds for Voluntary Agencies," *Social Welfare Forum* (1959), 83–102; Ralph Kramer, "Voluntary Agencies and the Use of Public Funds: Some Policy Issues," *Social Service Review*, 40, No. 1 (March 1966), 15–26; Bernard J. Coughlin, *Church and State in Social Welfare* (New York: Columbia University Press, 1965); William J. Reid, "Sectarian Agencies," *Encyclopedia 1971*, pp. 1154–63.

donations and foundations, and to financial campaigns through Community Chests, United Funds, and national agencies. With the increasing involvement of the churches in social problems, there may well be a resurgence of participation of sectarian agencies in social change.

Youth Services and Settlement Houses

Youth services. Organizations planned to meet the needs of young persons, especially in big cities, began their work in the mid-nineteenth century. The first society of this type was founded in 1844 in England by a draper, George Williams, who attempetd to bring the young drapers of London back to a Christian way of life. With this purpose in mind, he founded the first Young Men's Christian Association (YMCA).

A retired American sea captain, J. V. Sullivan, who had founded the Marine Mission for seamen, was impressed by the success of the London YMCA, gathered together young men, and established in Boston in 1851 the first American YMCA, which spread in a few years to many other cities of the United States. The purpose of this organization was the improvement of the spiritual and mental conditions of young men, the establishment of living quarters at low price with decent, sanitary facilities, particularly for young men who came to the large cities to find work and who could not afford to pay room and board in more expensive homes.

In 1860 the first Boys' Club was founded in Hartford, Connecticut by a church women's group, to give young boys an opportunity to pursue games and sports, music, dancing, and dramatic activities. Other Boys' Clubs spread quickly over the country, frequently under the auspices of church groups or civic organizations which desired to attract the children by games, play, and crafts, rather than leaving them to the doubtful influences of city streets. The Jewish Center movement traced its origin to the "literary societies of young people," in the 1840s, who wanted to get together for lectures and discussions.

The first Young Women's Christian Association (YWCA) in the United States was founded in Boston in 1866, under the leadership of Lucretia Boyd, and in New York in 1867, by Grace Dodge. They provided clean, low-rent housing and a cultural center for girls and young women who came to the cities from other parts of the country to work. Girls found it difficult to rent rooms in a decent neighborhood for prices they could afford to pay.

Following the example of the English foundation of the Boy Scouts by Sir Robert Baden-Powell, the American Boy Scouts were organized in 1910; a few years later a similar movement for girls was created by Juliette Low in 1912 under the title of "Girl Guides." The Campfire Girls were established in 1911 following the planning of a group of educators, under the leadership of Dr. Luther Gulick; their activities were not limited to outings and hiking, but included, as did most of the other youth organizations, games, singing, workshops, and educational and cultural activities in meetings and club discussions. The American Junior Red Cross is composed of nearly 20,000,000 school children engaged in health, safety, and recreational programs. The 4-H Clubs, sponsored by the U.S. Department of Agriculture, state colleges, and counties, develop in rural youth ten to twenty years of age high standards for farming, home skills, and cultural life in the rural community.

The motives for the foundation of these organizations were, of course, different. Frequently, there were religious reasons with the idea of strengthening in children and adults in poor neighborhoods the interest in and devotion to a religious life and of counteracting the demoralizing influences of slums, filth, and crime. Many organizations started with such motivation, but all agencies in this field had also the sincere desire to advance the moral, intellectual, and spiritual, as well as the physical and social, well-being of children, young people, and adults whom they invited to join their activities, to develop a sound body and a healthy character. They wanted to help underprivileged children and young people have social pleasure and recreational advantages which were lacking in their families, and tried to overcome limitations, prejudice, and injustices based on low economic status and difference in race, color, and religion.[44]

The settlement house movement. The development of modern industry brought masses of workers and their families into the cities. They lived in overcrowded quarters, without comfort, sufficient space for their children, and without relatives and friends. Even more forlorn were the large numbers of immigrants arriving in the United States who were needed as industrial labor. They were living in slums in unsanitary surroundings of overcrowded flats or shabby shacks around the factories, railroad yards, docks, or stockyards. Little of promise from an educational or cultural standpoint could be expected in neighborhoods where poverty went hand in hand with sickness and ignorance. There was little mutual understanding among the poor who came from different racial and religious backgrounds and spoke different languages. The need to create a new sense of neighborhood spirit to make good citizens out of underprivileged families in slum conditions had first been felt by Canon Samuel Barnett and his friends at Toynbee Hall in London. Toynbee Hall gave the inspiration to American visitors that

---

[44] Grace Coyle, *Group Work with American Youth* (New York: Harper, 1948); Arthur Hillman, *Neighborhood Centers Today* (New York: National Federation of Settlements, 1960); Jessie Bernard, et al., "Teen-Age Culture," *The Annals,* 338 (November 1961), 1–143; Bernard M. Shiffman, "Youth Services," *Encyclopedia of Social Work 1965,* pp. 843–50; Henry W. Maier, *Three Theories of Child Development* (Erickson, Piaget, Sears) (New York: Harper & Row, 1965), pp. 207–40; Catherine P. Papell, "Youth Service Agencies," *Encyclopedia 1971,* pp. 1548–56.

educated persons living in such a neighborhood together with the poor and sharing life with the underprivileged would be a valiant factor in overcoming dangers of social and spiritual disorganization (see Chapter 2, pp. 35–36). Stanton Coit and Charles B. Stover were the first Americans to transplant the idea of the settlement house to this country. After a study of Toynbee Hall and European experiments, they founded in 1887 the Neighborhood Guild of New York City, later changed to the University Settlement House. One of the most important social settlements in the United States became Hull House in Chicago, founded by Jane Addams and Ellen Gates Starr in 1889.[45]

Jane Addams, one of the great pioneers in American social work, was born in Cedarville, Illinois in 1861. Since her childhood she had wanted to live among the poor. Her travels with Ellen Starr in Europe, the observation of living conditions in Italy and London, and the remarkable success of the Barnetts at Toynbee Hall strengthened Miss Addams's desire to create a similar cultural center in Chicago. They did not plan a new charity, but built the settlement house as a place for the working people (particularly new immigrant groups of various nations and religions), where they might enjoy life in the new country with its opportunities, to develop those higher moral and intellectual qualities on which depend values of living in a democracy. Hull House, the settlement on the west side of Chicago on Halsted Street, was open to large groups of foreign immigrants in the neighborhood: Bohemians, Italians, Germans, Greeks, Polish and Russian Jews, and Irish newcomers. Among the residents who joined Jane Addams in devoted work at Hull House were Florence Kelley, Julia Lathrop, Edith and Grace Abbott, Mrs. J. T. Bowens, Graham Taylor, and Alice Hamilton.[46] Although at first the neighborhood was distrustful of the aims of the newcomers, some people accepted the invitation to visit the settlement house, began to ask for advice, and came to work with the residents. Deserted women, injured workmen, widows, families unable to pay their installments on furniture asked for counsel. To meet the needs of the neigh-

[45] Jane Addams, *Twenty Years at Hull House* (New York: Macmillan, 1910), pp. 121–27; Lorene M. Pacey, *Readings in the Development of Settlement Work* (New York: Association Press, 1950); Clarke A. Chambers, *Seedtime of Reform* (Minneapolis: University of Minnesota Press, 1963), pp. 107–50; Pumphrey, *The Heritage of American Social Work*, pp. 192–201; Allan F. Davis and Mary L. McCree, *Eighty Years at Hull House* (Chicago: Quadrangle, 1969); Coll, *Perspectives in Public Welfare*, pp. 66–74.

[46] In this connection, the leading role of Jane Addams as a pacifist, in the international women's movement, in the fight for women's suffrage and for civil liberty, in foreign relief for children after the end of World War I, for school reform, and for tolerance in religious and racial questions can only be indicated. Among her books are the following: *Democracy and Social Ethics* (1902), *Newer Ideals of Peace* (1907), *The Spirit of Youth and the City Streets* (1909), *Twenty Years at Hull House* (1910), and *The Second Twenty Years at Hull House* (1930). Jane Addams died May 21, 1935.

borhood, a day nursery and kindergarten were established, followed by various clubs for boys and girls and an art gallery. Discussion and study groups, a school of music, dramatics and arts, classes in rhythm and dancing, and workshops for children and adults developed. The residents became active in promoting factory legislation, better housing, adequate wages and working hours, arbitration of labor disputes, free employment services, and other social reforms. Jane Addams and her coworkers lectured to civic groups to convince them of the need of social legislation, child labor protection, prohibition of night work for women and children, juvenile courts, and probation services.

The experiences of Hull House helped in the development of other settlement houses. We might mention here College Settlement for Women in New York, Andover House in Boston (later called South End House), founded by Robert A. Woods,[47] and Chicago Commons, organized by Professor Graham Taylor. Lillian Wald and Mary Brewster founded Henry Street Settlement in New York; Mary Kingsbury Simkhovitch, the Cooperative Social Settlement (later, Greenwich House) in New York; Mary McDowell, the University of Chicago Settlement near the stockyards.[48] Other early settlement houses were Gaylord White Union Settlement attached to Union Theological Seminary, New York; Goodrich House in Cleveland; the Irene Kaufman Settlement, Pittsburgh; Telegraph Hill Neighborhood House, San Francisco; and Flanner House, Indianapolis.

Residents of settlement houses became champions of social reform. Living among the poorest classes of industrial workers and immigrants, they recognized the damage done by unsanitary housing conditions, overcrowded flats, low wages, and night work for women and children. From the settlement houses came the call for slum clearance, for special juvenile courts to deal with young offenders, and for the organization of the Consumers' League to help the housewife and to protect the health of the family. They requested housing legislation, supported the prevention of tuberculosis, and organized child labor committees. Settlement houses attempted to develop among the poor and the low-paid working class a feeling of self-respect; their resident staff let the neighborhood share the advantage

[47] See Eleanor H. Woods, *Robert A. Woods: Champion of Democracy* (Boston: Houghton Mifflin, 1929).

[48] Leah D. Taylor, "Social Settlement and Civic Responsibility: The Life Work of Mary McDowell and Graham Taylor," *Social Service Review,* 28, No. 1 (March 1954), 31–40; Graham Taylor, *Religion and Social Action* (New York: Dodd, 1913); Louise C. Wade, *Graham Taylor: Pioneer for Social Justice, 1851–1938* (Chicago: University of Chicago Press, 1964); Genevieve C. Weeks, "Oscar C. McCullough: Leader in Organized Charity," *Social Service Review,* 39, No. 1 (March 1965), 38–52, and ibid., No. 2 (June 1965), 209–21; Allen F. Davis, "Settlements: History," *Encyclopedia 1971,* pp. 1175–80; Helen Hall, *Unfinished Business in Neighborhood and Nation* (New York: Macmillan, 1971), pp. 219–34, 245–353.

of higher education, culture, and knowledge by living and working together in the settlement house.

Hospitality, friendliness, education, information, and getting acquainted with one another in the neighborhood was the main pattern of their activities. Settlement workers labored in slums and congested areas in an endeavor to demonstrate by life experience their firm belief in democracy, human equality, and dignity. They fought for equal opportunities for the poor and handicapped and for the abolition of prejudice and discrimination against people because of their religion, race, and foreign birth. Important tools in this fight for human values, education, and cultural development of the underprivileged were various activities of the settlement houses: boys' and girls' clubs; playgrounds; kindergartens; adult education classes in languages, economic and legal problems; hygiene; labor relations; handicraft; the study of American history and its institutions; and discussion groups. These activities with children, adolescents, and adults emphasized the need for adjustment of the immigrant groups arriving from many countries. They were organized to acquaint newcomers with their new environment and to help them understand the morals, customs, and laws of the United States. Other informal study groups were devoted to cultural and civic affairs, to economic and health problems, and to the development of creative abilities in art classes and workshops, dramatic and literary groups.

The settlement houses are working to rebuild understanding and cooperation of neighbors in city quarters where there are frequently a lack of good will, hostility, disunity, and bitter competition, aggravated by low wages, poor working conditions, and neglect of sanitary housing facilities.[49] Immigrant groups in these neighborhoods arrive with unrealistic, exaggerated ideas about American opportunities and wealth. They have to go through difficult periods of economic deprivation, discrimination because of their language and foreign background, dangers to their health, and humiliation until they become settled in the new country. The settlement houses help the immigrants through such trying periods by strengthening their feelings of being welcome and accepted in the new country, by maintaining some of their native skills in arts and crafts, and by encouraging their pride in cultural values brought from their homes.

FEDERAL PARTICIPATION IN THE SOCIAL SERVICES

Until the end of the nineteenth century, social services under private and public auspices maintained their local character. Only to a limited extent were statewide systems for a few special groups of people established

---

[49] See Arthur Hillman, "Settlements and Community Centers," *Encyclopedia of Social Work 1965*, pp. 690–95; and Harold H. Weissman, "Settlements and Community Centers," *Encyclopedia 1971*, pp. 1170–75.

(see above). One of the new trends in social welfare in the twentieth century is the recognition of the need to consider problems of social welfare on the national scale, using the experience of local and state organizations to introduce effective measures throughout the country.

This development was not a rapid one. It faced the traditional resistance of local and state interests, which insisted on their autonomy. Until the Depression of the 1930s, federal participation was only half-hearted and partial. The leadership in nationwide organization was taken by private organizations, particularly the National Child Labor Committee (1904), now called the National Committee on Employment of Youth, and the National Consumers' League (1899).

The Constitution of the United States did not contain a specific principle regarding the responsibility of the federal government with respect to social welfare. The power of Congress to provide for the "general welfare of the people" (Article 1, Section 8) was a rather general clause and did not refer especially to the setup of public social services. This fact explains the veto of President Pierce against Dorothea Dix's suggestion of federal land grants to the states for mental hospitals (see page 71). For certain categories of persons, however, the federal government could not refuse to accept responsibility. These five groups are sometimes called the "Federal Wards": Indians, immigrants, passengers and crews of seagoing vessels, veterans, and offenders of federal laws.

Social Services for the Indians

In 1775 the Continental Congress founded departments of Indian affairs to improve relations with the Indian tribes and to protect Indian land against seizure without treaty. In 1789 a Bureau of Indian Affairs was organized in the War Department to regulate treaties for land purchase, schools for Indian children, and some medical care.[50] In 1849, when the Gold Rush in California lured large masses of migrants to the West, the Bureau was reorganized as the Office of Indian Affairs, under the Department of Interior, to placate the Indian tribes. After the War Between the States, a Board of Commissioners arranged for reservations on which the Indians might live without interference from the whites. These reservations would include schools and health facilities. In 1887 the *Allotment Act* provided for a distribution of land to Indian families to be held in trust by the United States so that it could not be sold. Unfortunately, the aims of

---

[50] The *Indian Removal Act of 1830,* however, forced the Indians to leave all their lands east of the Mississippi, although they met in the West hostile native tribes unwilling to let them in. See Clyde Kluckholm and Dorothea Leighton, *The Navaho* (Cambridge, Mass.: Harvard University Press, 1946); Vine Deloria, Jr., et al., "American Indian Youth," in David Gottlieb and Anne Lienhard Heinson, *America's Other Youth—Growing Up Poor* (Englewood Cliffs, N.J.: Prentice-Hall, 1971), pp. 83–114.

the law were not fulfilled. The land was largely "rented" to white men, and the Indians lost nearly 60 percent of their original property. The Indian Service of the Department of the Interior, meanwhile, employed experts on land use to help the Indians in the reservations learn more effective methods of agricultural production and husbandry, and a medical supervisor to improve the health services.

In 1924 all Indians received United States citizenship, but the poverty of the tribes continued with a few exceptions. On the basis of Lewis Meriam's survey in 1928, the appropriations for education of Indian children were increased, and in 1934 the *Indian Reorganization Act* provided protection for the Indian tribes by incorporation of the land and support of agricultural training and production, schools, and medical care. The act attempted to secure the Indians civic and cultural freedom, to restore their management of their affairs, to prevent further depletion of natural resources in the reservations, and to develop a sound economy which would make the Indians independent of outside support. With the help of this program under the Bureau of Indian Affairs, the number of Indians and Eskimos in Alaska is now increasing and has grown from 1933, when it was only 200,000, to more than 400,000. However, the average income of an Indian farm family in most reservations is still only about one-third of that of a white farm family. While tuberculosis and infant death rates have decreased, their living conditions often still are primitive and unsanitary, and their general state of health is about comparable to that of the national population twenty-five years ago. Some tribes, such as the Navahos and Hopis, whose grazing lands were insufficient for their growing population, have suffered severe hardship.

Schools for Indians on the reservations are still not adequate to secure education for all Indian children. The death rate among the Indians is far above the national average. Although the Indians are entitled to receive free medical service, available hospitals, tuberculosis dispensaries, and sanitation and health centers need further expansion. Indian physicians, nurses, laboratory technicians, and social workers are being trained. The funds allocated for relief administered to Indians are too low to meet the need of the many indigent Indians. Social services are rendered in the states through the Indian Agency set up by the Bureau of Indian Affairs for each tribe. The payment of public assistance to the Indians in the states is frequently difficult because their economic need and their legal eligibility are not proved. The lack of adequate appropriations for the Bureau of Indian Affairs makes it difficult to attract well-qualified physicians, teachers, nurses, and social workers needed for medical care, preventive health work, education, and counseling on the reservations. To create self-maintaining Indian tribes, the irrigation of unproductive and arid land, the introduction of productive home industries and other industrial manufacturing, and native crafts will be necessary.[51] Experiences on the reservations prove that with patient education and industrial and technical training, the Indians will be able to become self-supporting and to maintain their native culture and dignity; but as long as the tribes remain on the reservations, special educational, health, and social services will be absolutely needed.[52] For Indians who leave the reservations to live in urban communities, the Bureau of Indian Affairs offers relocation and placement services.

In 1967 the Indian reservations, with a labor force of 131,000, had an unemployment rate of 38 percent, more than ten times the national average. The Economic Opportunity Act emphasized self-determination, and its agency gave grants to Indian tribes, stimulating local initiative and remedial programs under indigenous leadership. In several reservations, legal-aid services, Head Start programs, health services, and business activities were supported.

In contrast to the submissive attitude of most American Indian tribes, a number of Indian organizations cutting across reservation and tribal lines, such as the National Congress of American Indians and many state organizations, attempt to strengthen their control over cultural, economic, and social developments and over the community service programs on the reservations. Their severe criticism of Bureau of Indian Affairs policy on education and health services is leading to some improvements in Indian schools, and the health services have recently been transferred to the United States Public Health Service.

The Immigrants

With regard to new immigrants, the colonies and later the states assumed measures of control primarily to protect their citizens against health and moral dangers and financial burdens which the newcomers might engender. Supplementing many state statutes, the federal *Passenger Act of 1819* required medical inspection of all arriving immigrants, to control their health status. In 1882 the federal government assumed most of the control over immigration (thus replacing the states), introduced a head tax for immi-

---

[51] Voluntary organizations, working in the interest of the Indians, include the Indian Rights Association, the Association on American Indian Affairs, the Institute on Ethnic Affairs, various Indian native organizations, and the American Friends Service Committee.

[52] Alexander Lesser, "Education and the Future of Tribalism in the U.S.," *Social Service Review,* 35, No. 2 (June 1961), 135–43; for a significant case history on the need of cultural consideration in casework with a Navajo family, see Inez M. Tyler and Sophie D. Thompson, "Casework Treatment of a Navajo Mental Patient," *Social Casework,* 46, No. 4 (April 1965), 215–20; Sar A. Levitan, *The Great Society's Poor Law: A New Approach* (Baltimore, Johns Hopkins, 1969), pp. 262–70; Fred R. Harris, "Indian Health and Indian Rights: From Dependency to Self-Determination," *Public Welfare,* 28, No. 4 (October 1970), 362–65, 369–70.

grants, and prohibited the naturalization of foreign-born Orientals. In 1891 the administrative federal agent became the Bureau of Immigration in the Treasury Department, in 1903 the Department of Commerce and Labor, and in 1906 the Bureau of Immigration and Naturalization. Under changing laws and regulations, admission of immigrants became more difficult. Persons considered of immoral character or likely to become public charges, and contract laborers hired abroad were excluded. In 1917 the *Burnett Bill* introduced a literacy test. After the end of World War I, in a period of intense isolationism, the so-called *Quota System Law of 1921* and the *Immigration Act of 1924* were passed. They limited the annual number of immigrants to a total of 153,774. The policy toward immigration was discriminatory and restrictive. Immigrants from England, Ireland, and northern and western Europe were favored over those from southern and eastern Europe, where pressure to emigrate was high. The *Oriental Exclusion Law of 1924* virtually stopped immigration from the Far East until 1968. As a consequence immigration, which in the decade before 1914 had averaged over 1,000,000 per year, fell during the decade preceding World War II to a yearly average of 53,000. In 1940 the Bureau of Immigration and Naturalization was transferred to the Department of Justice under a Commissioner for Immigration and Naturalization.

Federal immigration services have been mainly agencies for legal control of naturalization procedure. When the *Alien Registration Act of 1940* required the registration of all immigrants and alien residents, the Bureau of Immigration and Naturalization developed an Educational Services Division. Most language and citizens' classes are conducted by local boards of education and voluntary social agencies.[53]

Social work for immigrants is rendered by private social agencies, particularly the International Institutes; Protestant, Catholic, and Jewish welfare agencies; the International Social Service; Travelers' Aid Societies; settlement houses; and other voluntary groups.[54] The Department of State and the American Consulates administer immigration procedure abroad.

After World War II, the *Displaced Persons Act of 1948* permitted the admission of refugees and victims of Nazi forced-labor camps. The act

---

[53] F. Campbell Bruce, *The Golden Door: The Irony of Our Immigration Policy* (New York: Random House, 1954); Frank L. Auerbach, *The Immigration and Naturalization Act: A Summary of Its Principal Provisions* (New York: Common Council for American Unity, 1952), pp. 18–23; George M. Stevenson, *History of American Immigration, 1820–1924* (New York: Russell Sage Foundation, 1967); W. J. Bromwell, *History of Immigration to the United States* (New York: Kelly, 1967).

[54] James R. W. Leiby, "How Social Workers Viewed the Immigration Problem, 1880–1930," in *Current Issues in Social Work Seen in Historical Perspective* (New York: Council on Social Work Education, 1962), pp. 30–42.

was severely criticized for its religious and ethnic discrimination, but a 1950 amendment corrected some of its faults. A three-man Displaced Persons Commission administered the act, working closely with accredited voluntary social agencies. Private agencies, through their state and local committees, were providing housing and employment, affidavits of support, and placement with relatives and friends. Several states organized commissions for resettlement of displaced persons, conducted surveys on employment opportunities, and coordinated the resettlement work carried on by public and private agencies.[55]

Recently, immigration authorities have interpreted the provisions of the laws so that displaced persons and other immigrants are not subject to deportation if they become ill, develop a mental disability, lose a job, and are forced to apply for public assistance.

President Truman's Commission on Immigration and Naturalization submitted recommendations in 1953 evaluating the immigration and naturalization policies. The commission expressed its conviction that immigration has given strength to America not only in manpower, new industries, and prosperity, but also in new ideas, inventions, and culture that have enriched our nation.[56] On the basis of these considerations the commission believed that immigration laws flout fundamental American traditions and ideals, display lack of faith in America's future, damage American prestige and position among other nations, and ignore the lessons of the American way of life. It recommended that the immigration law should be completely rewritten. The long-desired reform has been, at least partially, achieved by the *Immigration Law of 1965,* which repealed the Oriental exclusion provisions and terminated the "national origins quota system."

The Immigration Law permits the annual immigration of 170,000 persons, among them 120,000 from Western countries, and establishes a "preference system" for the following groups: (1) unmarried sons and daughters of United States citizens; (2) spouses and unmarried children

---

[55] See Arthur Greenleigh, "Aliens and Foreign Born," *Social Work Year Book* (1957), 105–10; the article explains the controversial nature of our immigration policies. See also Herbert Hill, "Anti-Oriental Agitation and the Rise of Working-Class Racism," *Society,* 10, No. 2 (February 1973), 43–54, for an analysis of the cruel discrimination against Chinese immigrants.

[56] President's Commission on Immigration and Naturalization, *Whom Shall We Welcome?* Vols. 14–15 (Washington, D.C.: Government Printing Office, 1953); William S. Bernard and Arthur Greenleigh, "Aliens and Foreign Born," *Social Work Year Book* (1960), 106–12; Marion T. Bennett, *American Immigration Policies: A History* (Washington, D.C.: Public Affairs Press, 1964); E. P. Hutchinson, "The New Immigration," *The Annals,* 367 (September 1966); J. Milton Yinger, "Recent Developments in Minority and Race Relations," *The Annals,* 378 (July 1968), 130–45; Joseph P. Fitzpatrick, *Puerto Rican Americans: The Meaning of Migration to the Mainland* (Englewood Cliffs, N.J.: Prentice-Hall, 1971).

of aliens residing in the United States; (3) professional persons or people with special talents (including architects, engineers, lawyers, physicians, surgeons, and teachers); (4) married sons and daughters of United States citizens; (5) brothers and sisters of United States citizens; (6) skilled or unskilled laborers who could fill a specified need for labor in the United States; and (7) religious, racial, and political refugees from Communist and Communist-dominated countries who cannot return to their homeland (primarily from Cuba, Poland, and Czechoslovakia) and refugees uprooted by major natural catastrophes.

The main objective of the law is to terminate the undue discrimination against people from Asia and Southern Europe and to reunite families which had been separated by wars, revolutions, natural disasters, and economic circumstances. Epilepsy no longer is a reason for exclusion, but sexual deviation is. Congress receives reports twice a year by the Attorney General concerning immigration.

Federal Public Health Service

The first federal program in the field of public health, the Marine Hospitals Service, in 1798 provided medical care and hospitalization for American seamen. In 1878 foreign quarantine was made a responsibility of the Service. Emergency funds for the prevention of epidemics were appropriated in 1883 and a hygienic laboratory added in 1887. Foreign and interstate quarantine became the full responsibility of the federal service in 1893. Its name was changed to Public Health and Marine Hospital Service in 1902, cooperation with the states and responsibilities of the service were expanded, and the Pan American Sanitary Bureau was established. The research activities of the agency were broadened and the name changed again to United States Public Health Service in 1912. Venereal disease control was added in 1918, two hospitals for narcotic drug addicts and the Mental Hygiene Division in 1930. At the same time the National Institute of Health was developed as an expanded research and laboratory division of the Public Health Service.

Under the *Social Security Act of 1935,* the Public Health Service became, first, a part of the agencies under the Social Security Board. With the establishment of the Federal Security Agency in 1939, the Public Health Service became an independent agency under the Federal Security Administrator and is now a major part of the Department of Health, Education and Welfare. In 1944 the *Public Health Service Act* codified the provisions on federal public health activities, and expanded research and tuberculosis control. Special attention has been given to research and development of facilities for prevention and treatment of mental diseases, cancer, and heart diseases, and for dental care and pollution control. Research activities of the U.S. Public Health Services are conducted through the National Institutes of Health, which now comprise cancer, mental health, heart, dental, experimental biology, and microbiology research.[57]

War Veterans

Already in the New England colonies pensions for war veterans disabled in their military service and for their survivors were an accepted practice. The Continental Congress in 1776 provided pensions for invalid veterans and the widows of soldiers who had died in the Revolutionary War, and the federal government accepted this concept after the adoption of the Constitution. After the War Between the States, benefits granted to the veterans as "federal wards" were limited to pensions, land grants, and the care of severely mutilated veterans in the National Asylum for Disabled Volunteer Soldiers and Sailors. In 1833 the Federal Bureau of Pensions took over veterans' pensions. Under the impact of World War I, benefits to war veterans were supplemented by hospitalization, vocational rehabilitation, and government life insurance after the *War Risk Insurance Act of 1917* established insurance compensation in case of death or disability caused by war injuries. The administration of federal veterans' benefits still was spread among many agencies, which led to red tape and delay in the operations. To create a more efficient organization, the Veterans Bureau was established in 1921, and in 1930 the Veterans Administration, as a further step in the consolidation of federal activities for veterans. The Veterans Administration coordinated the work formerly done by the Bureau of Pensions, the War Risk Insurance Bureau, the Board of Vocational Education, and the National Home for Disabled Volunteer Soldiers.

During World War II a new social philosophy developed regarding the duties of the nation for its veterans. Until this time it was assumed that pensions for the disabled and the survivors of those who lost their lives in the war was the main task. The new concept expanded this program by assisting all veterans to regain a position in the community after their return equal to that which they would have obtained if they had not been absent in military service. Vocational rehabilitation, medical care, and educational benefits were strengthened or newly added for the returning veterans. The

[57] Wilson G. Smilie and Edwin D. Kilbourne, *Preventive Medicine and Public Health*, 3rd ed. (New York: Macmillan, 1963); Berwyn F. Mattison, "Public Health," *Encyclopedia of Social Work* (1965), pp. 606–14; Alfred H. Katz and J. S. Felton, *Health and the Community* (New York: Free Press, 1965); Nancy Anderson, *Comprehensive Health Planning in the States* (Minneapolis: American Rehabilitation Foundation, 1968). See also Chapters 14, 15, and 16.

veterans of the Korean War and the Vietnam War are entitled to privileges similar to those of the two World Wars.[58]

In addition to these federal services for veterans, the states also established benefits for veterans who had been residents of the state for a certain period, and during World War II these supplementary state plans were enlarged.[59]

Offenders Against Federal Laws

Federal wards of a different nature are those persons who violate federal laws and are sentenced to prison by federal courts. Because the federal government first had no facilities for convicted offenders, it committed them to state prisons and penitentiaries for which the federal courts paid. In 1890 the establishment of federal prisons was enacted by Congress. They were expanded and improved after prison riots at Leavenworth in 1919. The United States Department of Justice introduced parole services for discharged prisoners under the *Federal Probation Act of 1925*. In 1930 the Federal Bureau of Prisons was organized; it developed pioneer methods in effective care and rehabilitation of the inmates of the federal prisons, under the leadership of Sanford Bates and his successor, James V. Bennett. Vocational training (with the aim of preparing the prisoner for a job after his release), recreational and educational facilities, medical and dental care, and religious and cultural activities in the federal prisons and penitentiaries became examples for other institutions. The federal penal institutions were classified into penitentiaries for serious crimes with separation of intractable, older offenders from habitual but tractable offenders; reformatories; correctional institutions for short-term offenders; one medical center for mentally and physically maladjusted convicts; the National Training School for Boys; two detention headquarters; and federal prison camps. The United States Probation Systems is attached to the administrative office of the United States Courts. It investigates the social condition and background of an offender appearing before a federal court and supervises offenders selected for probation and persons released from federal correctional institutions on parole or on "conditional release." It also refers juvenile delinquents to local juvenile courts for probation services. Despite modest progress, a fundamental change in the entire criminal justice system is still necessary, because the system is unfit to solve the social problems of our society. Only a comprehensive program of counseling, therapy, medical and psy-

[58] See Margaret Neville, "Veterans' Benefits and Services," *Encyclopedia of Social Work* (1965), 809–16; Delwin M. Anderson, "Veterans Services," *Encyclopedia 1971*, pp. 1513–18.

[59] For more details, see Chapter 17.

chiatric services, education, and rehabilitation are able to prevent and eliminate the causes of crime and drug abuse (see Chapter 18).[60]

THE WHITE HOUSE CONFERENCES

Important evidence of the trend in the social welfare scene in the twentieth century toward recognizing the need for a national policy instead of local efforts and piecemeal state legislation occurred in the field of child welfare. It began in 1909, when President Theodore Roosevelt, at the suggestion of the National Child Labor Committee, the National Consumers' League, and prominent social workers such as Paul Kellogg, Florence Kelley, and Edward Devine, invited leading workers of child welfare agencies from all over the country to the White House for a Conference on the Care of Dependent Children. The conference adopted a platform that children should not be taken from their families for reasons of poverty, and that normal children who had to be removed from their families should be placed in foster homes rather than in children's institutions. If children, for special reasons, had to be placed in orphanages or other children's institutions, these should be operated on the cottage plan with small units for the children instead of the large dormitories often used until this time. Children's agencies should be licensed for their work and should be inspected by state authorities. Two recommendations of the conference were of special importance: first, that the states should enact mothers' pension laws to enable widows and deserted women to care for their children; and second, that the federal government should establish a federal children's agency. The first recommendation led, in 1911, to legislation of mothers' pensions or allowances laws in several states; Illinois was the first to do this.

The second proposal of the Conference of 1909 resulted in the creation of the Children's Bureau by Congress in 1912. This idea had been conceived by Lillian Wald and Florence Kelley and was vigorously endorsed by social agencies and citizens' groups. President Taft nominated Julia Lathrop, prominent social worker and close friend of Jane Addams at Hull House in Chicago, as the first chief of the bureau. The Children's Bureau was the first agency of the federal government active in social welfare (as distinguished from education and public health). The purpose of the agency was to act as a clearinghouse for the entire country, "to investigate and report upon all matters pertaining to the welfare of children and child life

---

[60] Negley K. Teeters and John Otto Reinemann, *The Challenge of Delinquency* (Englewood Cliffs, N.J.: Prentice-Hall, 1950), pp. 627–28; Sophia M. Robison, "Juvenile Delinquency," *Encyclopedia of Social Work* (1965), 429–39; Albert K. Cohen, *Delinquent Boys* (New York: Free Press, 1955); Irving H. Spergel, *Community Problem Solving* (Chicago: University of Chicago Press, 1969).

among all classes of our people," especially the questions of infant mortality, birth rate, orphanages, juvenile courts, child labor, and social legislation on children. The Children's Bureau's investigations greatly influenced the practice of child care and legislation for the protection of children. Since 1969 the Children's Bureau has been a division in the Office of Child Development of the Department of Health, Education and Welfare.

Another suggestion of the White House Conference was the establishment of a voluntary nationwide organization to develop standards for child care and protection. This organization was founded in 1920 under the title Child Welfare League of America. Its membership consists of voluntary and public child welfare agencies and institutions which meet the standards set by the League, and of individual members; it publishes a monthly journal, *Child Welfare.*

The second White House Conference, held in 1919 on the invitation of President Woodrow Wilson, was called The Children's Bureau Conference on Child Welfare Standards. It discussed problems of child labor, juvenile delinquency, and dependent children that had been aggravated by World War I, the health of mothers and young children, needs of the preschool and school child, and child welfare legislation. This conference led to the enactment of the *Maternity and Infancy Act of 1921* and to the setup of child welfare divisions in many states.

The third White House Conference on Child Health and Protection, called by President Herbert Hoover, convened in 1930. It concentrated on the health needs of children, with special emphasis on the physically and mentally handicapped child, education, medical care, and health protection of children. The principles of the conference were announced as "The Children's Charter.[61] For rural children, the conference demanded equal services as for urban children; for blind, deaf, crippled, and mentally handicapped children, special care, treatment and training; and the establishment of necessary health and welfare services.

President Franklin D. Roosevelt called the fourth White House Conference on Children in a Democracy under the theme "Our Concern—Every Child." When the conference met in January 1940, the war in Europe was raging. The conference affirmed the interdependence of social and economic security, tolerance, health education, and opportunity for personal growth for the welfare of children. To follow up its recommendations, the conference formed a voluntary National Citizens Committee, which remained active during World War II for the protection of children.

---

61 Reproduced in Teeters and Reinemann, *The Challenge of Delinquency,* p. 626; see also Zitha R. Turitz and Rebecca Smith, "Child Welfare," *Encyclopedia of Social Work 1965,* 144; Clarke A. Chambers, "Creative Effort in the Age of Normalcy, 1918–33," *Social Welfare Forum* (1961), 252–71; Walter I. Trattner, *Crusade for the Children: A History of the National Child Labor Committee and Child Labor Reform in America* (Chicago: Quadrangle, 1970).

The Midcentury White House Conference on Children and Youth held in December, 1950 was invited by President Harry Truman. The conference, held under the shadow of the Korean War, emphasized the emotional factor in the development of children and the specific aspects of adolescence, rather than those of younger children. It was aware that the child and adolescent should be regarded as a whole personality, not as separate entities. Characteristic of this fifth White House Conference was that young delegates as representatives of youth organizations participated with full rights. The conference expressed its firm belief in the principle of separation of church and state and its opposition to the use of public schools for religious education. Also suggested were expansion of recreation with participation of youth in its planning, extension of social insurance and public assistance, the use of social and psychological knowledge in the treatment of children before courts, and coordination of preventive services for children among private agencies and public authorities.

The sixth White House Conference on Children and Youth was held in Washington March 27 to April 2, 1960 with the focus on the study of children and youth in a changing world.[62] Emphasis was placed on "opportunities for children and youth to realize their full potential for creative life in freedom and dignity." The conference meetings discussed the ideals and values of our civilization, their changes, and the effects of scientific and technical developments, population pressures, and world events on youth. The conference evaluated the influence of the environment in which the young generation grows up and the necessity of improving urban, suburban, and rural communities. It also studied the stages of development with emphasis on the problems of adolescents, of education in response to particular needs for different groups of gifted, retarded, and handicapped children, work facilities, and the responsibilities of young persons as citizens to the community and the nation. Representatives of youth organizations participated actively together with adult members of the conference in its deliberations. The 1970 White House Conference called a separate meeting of youth for developing its own policy. It refused to be guided by federal rules.[63]

THE SOCIAL SERVICES IN THE DEPRESSION OF 1930

The economic depression which started with the crash of the New York Stock Exchange in October 1929 marked a complete change in the

---

[62] Katherine B. Oettinger, "The Growth and Meaning of White House Conferences on Children and Youth," *Children,* 7, No. 1 (January–February 1960), 3–8.

[63] Sidney Rosendorf, "Youth Has Its Say in the Rockies," *Children,* 18, No. 4 (August 1971), 122–126.

principles and practice of American social welfare.[64] Until this time public relief had been managed mainly by political appointees in cities or counties, by overseers, or by supervisors of the poor. They identified poverty with vice or idleness and distributed relief on a starvation level. Only in forty large cities were trained social workers on the staff of public relief agencies. Private family welfare agencies existed in about four hundred larger cities, and self-respecting families in financial need went to voluntary agencies, which "protected them" from the disgrace of applying for "pauper aid." Public expenditures for poor relief had slowly been increased during the two preceding decades, but private agencies emphasized that their methods for preventing destitution and for achieving rehabilitation were more economic and, therefore, justified subsidies from taxation.

When, because of the Depression, the number of unemployed increased from 2,860,000 in the spring of 1929 to over 4,000,000 in January 1930, the public in the larger cities looked to the voluntary welfare agencies as the main source of financial support for the steadily growing mass of unemployed. Local private welfare agencies attempted to aid new applicants who never before had asked for relief. Many unemployed used up their savings whenever they could get payments from the banks that had not closed; others tried to borrow money from relatives, friends, the grocer, and the baker, but credit was quickly exhausted and did not keep the family fed and rent or mortgage paid. In a few months the private social agencies had spent their entire annual budget, exhausted their reserves, or incurred debts to continue their activities. By the spring of 1930 all private agencies (as well as public relief offices) were deeply alarmed. The public expected that the private agencies would meet their obligation, but this trust did not fill the exhausted coffers. The Association of Community Chests and Councils issued frantic appeals to industry and to local Chests to secure the necessary funds by a special emergency campaign. However, the results of this effort were spent in a few months, because unemployment increased in the spring of 1930 to over 4,600,000. Several severe droughts which afflicted Arkansas, Kentucky, Louisiana, Mississippi, Oklahoma, and Texas aggravated economic conditions.[65]

President Hoover refused to consider federal aid to states which applied for help. He thought the American way of handling the emergency, which might be of only short duration, was through private charities, sup-

---

[64] Virginia Robinson, *A Changing Psychology of Social Casework* (Chapel Hill: University of North Carolina Press, 1930); Chambers, "Creative Effort in the Age of Normalcy, 1918–33," *Social Welfare Forum* (1961), 252–71, and *Seedtime of Reform*, pp. 229–45; and Charles I. Schottland, *The Social Security Program in the United States* (New York: Appleton, 1963), pp. 29–39.

[65] Cohen, *Social Work in the American Tradition*, pp. 161–206; and Pumphrey, *The Heritage of American Social Work*, pp. 405–31.

ported by voluntary donations–not by tax money. In August 1930, he called a conference of governors and appointed an Emergency Committee for Employment under the chairmanship of his personal friend, Colonel Arthur Woods. This committee followed Hoover's philosophy and appealed to Community Chests, private industry, and the public to supply money for the support of the unemployed. It also requested free services from hospitals and dispensaries, and that child care and recreation agencies accept more children. These well-meant pleas, however, had as little success as the committee's slogans, "Spread the work" (suggesting that persons should be employed on part-time work) and "Give a job." In April 1931, Colonel Woods resigned; his successor was Fred C. Croxton, an experienced social worker.[66]

During this time the number of unemployed increased; by September 1930 it exceeded 5,000,000, and all over the country municipal and county relief offices had to support a larger and larger amount of unemployed families. Public relief was slowly taken out of its "Cinderella" role and became one of the principal functions of government. Many states were at first reluctant to assume financial responsibility, since their taxes had decreased due to losses in business, tax delinquencies, and lower production. But in 1931 Massachusetts, New York, Oklahoma, California, New Hampshire, and Maryland were forced to provide state unemployment relief to avoid starvation among the unemployed families. In the spring of 1931, the unemployed numbered over 8,000,000, and their number steadily increased. Not only employees and industrial workers lost their jobs; with the decreasing purchasing power of a large proportion of the entire population, over 750,000 farmers went bankrupt between 1930 and 1933, and 54.1 of every 1,000 farms were forcibly sold in 1932 because the farmers were unable to pay their mortgages or tax returns.

President Hoover maintained his belief that private charity should continue in meeting distress, and, encouraged by his pronouncements, private social agencies still hoped that with a decrease in unemployment they would again be able to take care of the unemployed and their families. They stated the emergency required a combination of the resources of private philanthropy, government, and business. Because their hesitancy delayed the urgently needed appropriations for relief from state legislatures eager to avoid higher taxation for relief funds, counties and cities saw no way of accepting more of the responsibility for mass relief in behalf of local government. The Depression, however, grew more severe. The repeated appeals of

[66] Josephine C. Brown, *Public Relief, 1929–1939* (New York: Holt, Rinehart, and Winston, 1940), pp. 63–71; John K. Galbraith, *The Great Crash 1929* (Boston: Houghton Mifflin, 1955); Chambers, *Seedtime of Reform,* pp. 225–50; Edwin E. Witte, *The Development of the Social Security Act* (Madison: University of Wisconsin Press, 1962); Arthur J. Altmeyer, *The Formative Years of Social Security* (Madison: University of Wisconsin Press, 1966); Studs Terkel, *An Oral History of the Great Depression* (New York: Pantheon, 1969).

Community Chests and private charities no longer could raise the funds necessary to maintain the unemployed. In New York the first Temporary Emergency Relief Administration was organized, with Harry L. Hopkins as executive director, a trained social worker with experience in settlement house work, family welfare, Red Cross, and health services. He immediately established uniform policies and standards of relief for the entire state. Other states soon followed the example of New York, so that at the end of 1932 twenty-four states had granted appropriations for disaster relief or emergency relief for the unemployed.[67]

The means of private charities became exhausted. Local and state funds proved inadequate to protect the growing millions of unemployed against hunger, cold, suffering, and despair, and requests for federal action were heard more frequently every month. Families were broken up in the vain, hectic attempt of the husband and father to find work. Disease increased, and sick people did not receive medical care. Children were passed around among neighbors because the parents had no food or were looking for jobs. The number of suicides mounted. Tuberculosis and malnutrition in children grew dangerously, and most savings of the middle class had been lost. In Congress, Senators Edward Costigan and Robert La Follette introduced bills for federal aid to provide emergency relief, and the governors of several states claimed the unemployment problem could not be solved without federal support. But the opposition of the Hoover cabinet, the chambers of commerce, and some citizen's organizations remained firm. Several bills providing federal funds for relief were passed, but vetoed by President Hoover. Finally, he consented to sign the *Emergency Relief and Construction Act of 1932*. It authorized the Reconstruction Finance Corporation (RFC) to loan the states, counties, and cities $300,000,000 for relief and public work relief projects.[68] Numerous applications from states, counties, and cities immediately made it necessary that an expert should determine the real need of the various states. Fred Croxton was therefore appointed head of the Emergency Relief Division of the corporation. Loans were given on an emergency basis, not exceeding the expenses for one month, with the result that neither adequate machinery could be set up nor projects developed to secure employment of large numbers of people out of work or to be of permanent value to the community. The local administrators never knew what funds for work relief would be available for the next month, so that no planning was possible in an operation from hand to mouth, which only supplied bare subsistence to the unemployed.

---

[67] National Resources Planning Board, *Security, Work and Relief Policies* (1942), p. 29; Roy Lubove, *The Struggle for Social Security, 1900–1935* (Cambridge, Mass.: Harvard University Press, 1968).

[68] The loans of the RFC were to be refunded by 1935, but legislation in 1934 and 1938 repealed this provision.

When Franklin D. Roosevelt was elected president in November 1932, the economic depression had reached its depth. People hoped the new president would cope with an unemployment of 15,000,000 workers, which was depriving thousands of families of their homes and farms and forcing them to live on meager relief without a real hope for recovery. In his inaugural address, on March 4, 1933, President Roosevelt analyzed this economic breakdown:

> Values have shrunken to fantastic levels; taxes have risen; our ability to pay has fallen; . . . the withered leaves of industrial enterprise lie on every side; farmers find no market for their produce; the savings of many years in thousands of families are gone.
> More important, a host of unemployed citizens face the grim problems of existence, and an equally great number toil with little return . . . . The only thing we have to fear is fear itself—nameless, unreasoning, unjustified terror which paralyzes needed efforts to convert retreat into advance.

In some states 40 percent of the total population were receiving relief, in some counties even as much as 90 percent.

In this period of despair, the New Deal succeeded in reestablishing new confidence and a balance in the nation's economic system. It replaced profiteering and speculation by stabilization, and enforced essential humanitarian measures for the suffering, deprived masses of the population.[69]

The first major legislation under President Roosevelt in the fight against depression, unemployment, and economic apathy was the *Federal Emergency Relief Act of 1933*. It represented a radical change in federal relief policy. It abolished the principle of short loans to the states and substituted for it a new concept of federal responsibility for human welfare, because, under our economic system, the individual has little control over and influence on the national production in periods of crisis. Federal grants to the states were provided to help the states meet the urgent needs of their citizens.

The administration of the new law was assigned to the Federal Emergency Relief Administration (FERA), and President Roosevelt appointed Harry L. Hopkins its administrator. FERA was an independent agency directly under the president. The initial appropriation of Congress was $500,000,000, one-half of which was to be given as grants to states on a matching basis. The other half was given, without matching provision, to states whose resources were depleted or whose unemployment was so grave

---

[69] Thomas H. Greer, *American Social Reform Movements* (Englewood Cliffs, N.J.: Prentice-Hall, 1949), pp. 266–68; Arthur M. Schlesinger, Jr., *The Coming of the New Deal* (Boston, Houghton Mifflin, 1959); Cohen, *Social Work in the American Tradition*, pp. 163–69; and Chambers, *Seedtime of Reform*, pp. 183–250.

that no matching could be expected. Congress appropriated additional funds later, so that, until the end of FERA in 1936, the amount of $3,088,670,625 was allocated for this program. After October 1933, FERA was authorized to grant the funds to the states without a matching requirement at the discretion of the administrator. The two main functions of FERA were: (1) to administer the grants to the states for unemployment relief which was exclusively distributed by public welfare agencies, and (2) to control proper use of the federal grants and to establish satisfactory relief standards in the interest of the unemployed.[70]

Among the first rules issued by FERA was that all federal grants were to be administered only by public agencies. It was prohibited, therefore, to delegate distribution of federal relief to private charities, a widespread custom before this period. All state plans were carefully reviewed, and the insistence of FERA on employment of trained social workers and qualified personnel helped in an efficient control of the entire program.

The objective of the FERA program was to provide work for the unemployed and to use appropriations exclusively for persons who had lost their jobs because of the Depression. Local authorities attempted to place their unemployables—sick, old, and infirm persons and mothers with young children—on the federal relief rolls, but the surveys of the Research Division revealed this practice and led to the elimination of unemployable people from FERA grants. The standards for relief developed by FERA required that consideration be made of the amount of money that would be needed to pay for adequate living conditions and medical care, and that relief should be given by cash instead of the commissary system, which had been frequently used by local relief offices. Useful public work was considered superior to direct relief, which endangered the self-respect and technical skill of the recipient.

To provide jobs for the unemployed, FERA immediately began to cooperate with the United States Employment Service and the Federal Emergency Public Works Administration. A special National Re-employment Service was organized, supported by FERA funds, to find jobs for as many unemployed as possible. The work relief projects in most states were not too satisfactory and employed only about 1,000,000 (mostly unskilled) workers. To introduce more adequate opportunities for the unemployed, the president created the Civil Works Administration in 1933 as a means of promoting recovery through the employment at regular wages of 4,000,000 unemployed workers. It was thought of as "a shot in the arm" for the economic system that would bring about a rapid increase of purchasing power which would set normal production and consumption again

[70] Cohen, *Social Work in the American Tradition,* pp. 169–72; Chambers, *Seedtime of Reform,* pp. 253–67; Howard Zinn, *New Deal Thought* (Indianapolis: Bobbs-Merrill, 1967).

in motion. The main difference between the FERA and the Civil Works Administration (CWA) was that CWA was exclusively operated by the federal government; it used skilled workers in teaching and supervision, and it paid union wages. The administrator of CWA was also Harry Hopkins, an appointment which guaranteed close cooperation with FERA. One-half of the workers in CWA were taken from the emergency work relief rolls; the other half were people in general need of jobs. The program went into effect with remarkable speed and employed at its peak, in January 1934, 4,260,000 persons. It was so costly that Congress decided to liquidate it only shortly after it had been undertaken. The liquidation was completed in July 1934 after the Civil Works Administration had functioned only four and one-half months. The workers were transferred again to the FERA program, which took over many unfinished projects of the CWA. The period of CWA operation was too short to draw reliable conclusions regarding its economic, social, and psychological effect. In view of the recent "war against poverty" it seems worthwhile to consider an intensive research of the results of the CWA to explore whether a similar large-scale public works program might be necessary to change the unemployment problem in the present economic and industrial development (see Chapter 10).

With the close of the work projects of the Civil Works Administration, the FERA organized the Emergency Work Relief Program, set up to help urban communities, the Rural Rehabilitation Program, to assist farmers to become self-supporting again; and a resettlement plan to relocate landless rural workers, the beginning of a land use program to be continued later under the Department of Agriculture. In addition to these work-relief programs, direct relief was granted to people who could not be employed on work projects.[71]

The administration of this huge unemployment relief program under FERA was extremely difficult. It was carried on as a new venture in a confused and disturbed economic situation in which state and local authorities, as well as private social agencies, had to orient themselves to new principles and methods. It is not surprising, therefore, that severe criticism of the FERA operations was mixed with recognition for its unusually effective policies in the field of public welfare. Its strict separation from the regular activities of state and local public welfare agencies prevented the immediate influence of the new concepts of public responsibility on the policies of cities and counties that social workers had expected. But the acceptance

[71] Edith Abbott, *Public Assistance,* I (Chicago: University of Chicago Press, 1940), pp. 669–90; Donald S. Howard, *The WPA and Federal Relief Policy* (New York: Russell Sage Foundation, 1943); Schlesinger, *The Coming of the New Deal,* Chap. 16; Irving Bernstein, "Unemployment in the Great Depression," *Social Welfare Forum* (1959), 39–48; Charles A. Reich, *The Greening of America* (New York: Random House, 1970), pp. 45–58.

of government responsibility for the relief of economic distress was definitely established as social philosophy during this period, and it was also recognized that people had a right to assistance without thereby losing respect for their dignity and worth as human beings.

THE WORKS PROJECTS ADMINISTRATION

As the FERA had been set up only as a temporary measure and the federal government felt that it should not assume responsibility for direct relief to people unfit for employment, President Roosevelt decided in May 1935 to substitute a work relief program under centralized federal control with the title Works Progress Administration (WPA). Originally it was hoped that private industry and the Public Works Administration would be able to absorb most of the unemployed people, but it soon became evident that the Works Progress Administration (WPA) would have to supply the jobs itself. Its objective was to employ 3,500,000 people on relief. The WPA established the policies, administered the program, approved the projects presented by local and state governments, and reviewed the certifications of workers on the projects to determine whether they were in economic need and employable. The state and local governments selected work projects of value to the communities and provided funds for materials and supervision. The WPA paid the wages of the workers. Congress excluded certain types of projects, such as military production, slum clearance, demolition work, and theater production projects, to avoid competition with private industries.

The wages in WPA were different from the earlier FERA method of family budget; they were a "security wage" without relation to family size and dependents. The wage provided a "minimum security income" which varied according to local standards and the skill of the worker. The restriction that in each family only one member might be employed under WPA was a hardship on large families.

The administration of WPA was assigned to Harry L. Hopkins immediately under the president. In 1939, the agency was renamed Works Projects Administration and was merged with the Federal Works Agency. With exception of some federal projects, WPA projects were prepared and sponsored by cities, counties, and states. During its entire function, WPA furnished jobs for 7,800,000 individuals who had been unemployed.

The WPA projects have contributed greatly to the improvement of economic, health, welfare, and cultural facilities of our country and provided 470,000 miles of highways, bridges, roads and streets, and 90,000 public buildings, among them 132 new, and 1,500 enlarged hospitals, medical and dental clinics, visiting nursing stations, libraries, schools, and museums. Three and one-half million acres of swamp land were drained to eliminate the danger of malaria. A large number of playgrounds and parks, sport fields and swimming pools for recreation, airports for national defense, soil and water conservation works, and flood control and reforestation projects were part of the WPA activities. Unemployed professional persons, artists, sculptors, painters, musicians, teachers, day-nursery teachers, nurses, librarians, and recreation leaders were given jobs in their fields for the benefit of communities. They taught classes and courses which could not otherwise have been offered. The arts projects brought new cultural stimulation, and the theatre and concert projects gave enjoyment to the people. Valuable research projects for unemployed writers and scientists created such books as the *American Guide Series*.[72]

Despite these achievements, the WPA was not able to overcome severe criticism. The great costs of a public works program, the lack of conscientious labor on some projects, and the fact that WPA took away some private business were the main sources of complaint. As WPA never had sufficient funds to give work to all unemployed, those unable to get WPA jobs were among its opponents. Contractors were dissatisfied because they wanted to do construction work themselves; organized labor was uneasy because it feared that the low WPA wages would keep down union wages. The WPA was accused of engaging in political activities, particularly in the plays of the theatre projects and in paintings and murals of some artists. Much of this criticism may have been rather factional and biased, but the legal limitations and the lack of certainty about the continuation and financing of the projects made it impossible to develop the program in an ideal form. After 1940 most projects were devoted to the defense effort, and when industries and production absorbed all available labor, the WPA was closed in 1943.

Social workers in the Works Project Administration program had objected to the punitive policies of the poor-law authorities, which tended to degrade the poor and to create a demoralized pauper class. In the principles of the work program they found an opportunity to treat the applicant with respect, to maintain his human dignity and his feeling of usefulness, and to use the work-relief assignment as a means for his economic rehabilitation.

Work Programs for Unemployed Youth

Even in normal times it is not always easy for youth in a highly industrialized society to obtain work without special education, training, and experience,

---

[72] William F. McDonald, *Federal Relief Administration and the Arts* (Columbus: Ohio State University Press, 1969).

but the Depression aggravated this problem. Under the New Deal two programs were developed to help youth prepare for satisfactory employment and to prevent enforced idleness and unhappiness.[73] The first of these programs was the Civilian Conservation Corps, the other the National Youth Administration.

The law on the Civilian Conservation Corps (CCC) was the first social legislation enacted under President Franklin D. Roosevelt. It authorized the president to establish a nationwide chain of forest camps for unemployed youth. The aim was to supply healthy surroundings, adequate food, training and vocational education, and at the same time to assist in the conservation of our country's national resources. Unemployed youth between the ages of seventeen and twenty-five (later twenty-three), unmarried, in need of work, out of school, and physically and mentally fit for vigorous work could enroll for a CCC camp. War veterans and Indians were entitled to enroll; they were employed in the administration of the camps or in supervision of the work. Campers received thirty dollars a month, of which twenty-five dollars was sent home for the support of their families; in 1939 this compensation was reduced to twenty-two dollars. The camps of wooden barracks and tents were set up in national and state forests and parks. The boys and young men built fire towers and fire breaks, forest nurseries, truck and hiking trails, and emergency airfields. They worked in forest insect and tree disease control and planted over 300,000,000 new trees. They constructed roads in parks and rural areas, built dams to forestall soil erosion, cleared forests from blister rust and tree beetles, cleaned the streams for fish and fowl, and drained mosquito-infested marsh land. They assisted in flood control by constructing irrigation and drainage ditches and dams and helped to create recreational facilities by developing trails, picnic grounds, and vacation camps.[74]

The president appointed Robert Fechner, general vice-president of the International Association of Machinists and lecturer on labor problems at Harvard University, as director of the emergency conservation work. The boys received, in 1,500 camps, medical care and preliminary training conditioning them for forest work, education in subjects from elementary to high school levels, and vocational and technical training. In 1939 the admission requirement of having to be in financial need was abolished, and the Civilian Conservation Corps was placed under the Federal Security Agency.

Among the criticisms voiced against the CCC program were lack of integration with other federal agencies, the secondary role of the educational activities, and that it competed with local training programs better

---

[73] Cohen, *Social Work in the American Tradition*, pp. 175–76.

[74] John D. Guthrie, *Saga of the CCC* (Washington, D.C.: American Forestry Association, 1942), pp. 5–7; John A. Salmond, *The Civilian Conservation Corps, 1933–1942: A New Deal Case Study* (Durham, N.C.: Duke University Press, 1967).

fitted for urban youth. In fact, the corps greatly improved the physical and mental health and the fitness of its members, their education and vocational skill, maturity, morale, and self-confidence. Fourteen thousand Indians were employed on Indian reservations, doing work on drainage and improvement of land. About 260,000 enrollees were war veterans for whom no age limit was imposed. The normal time of enrollment was for six months, with the possibility of reenrollment for up to two years. During the last years of its operation, from 1940 to 1942, the CCC shifted to defense, industrial training, and installation of public utilities. In 1942, contrary to the advice of the president, Congress decided to terminate the CCC program because it was too expensive and rural districts needed young agricultural workers.

The second work program for youth was the National Youth Administration (NYA).[75] When in 1935 almost 3,000,000 young people received emergency relief from public funds, President Roosevelt felt it imperative to establish a special program which would preserve the energy and skill of unemployed young women and men. He created the National Youth Administration in 1935 as an independent unit within the Works Progress Administration. Two main programs were established: (1) a student-aid plan of part-time work with financial assistance to needy high school, college, and graduate students sixteen to twenty-four years of age, to enable them to continue their education, and (2) an out-of-school work program consisting of part-time employment on work projects designed to give experience and training to unemployed youths eighteen to twenty-five. In addition to these two main activities, the NYA established junior guidance and placement services in cooperation with the public employment services, training courses for recreational leaders, some resident projects for experience in cooperative living between rural and urban youth, and health examinations for its members. The work of the NYA led to a sharp increase in high school and college enrollment.

The administration of NYA was headed by Aubrey Williams as executive director, and by a National Advisory Committee representing labor, business, agriculture, education, church, and welfare groups. The organization was decentralized through five regional offices, a state youth administrator in every state with a volunteer advisory committee, and district and local directors and advisory committees to meet local needs. Lyndon B. Johnson was administrator of the Texas program. In 1939 the NYA was transferred to the Federal Security Agency, and in September 1942 to the

[75] Palmer O. Johnson and Oswald L. Harvey, *The National Youth Administration* (Washington, D.C.: Advisory Committee on Education, 1938), pp. 6–7; W. L. Warner, R. J. Havighurst, and Martin Loeb, *Who Shall Be Educated—The Challenge of Unequal Opportunities* (New York: Harper, 1944); Lewis L. Lorwin, *Youth Work Programs: Problems and Policies* (Washington, D.C.: American Council on Education, 1941).

War Manpower Commission. In July 1943 Congress withdrew the appropriations and ordered the liquidation of the NYA. In its eight years, NYA had served 4,800,000 young men and women, helping them continue their education or training them for employment. It discontinued January 1, 1944.

The student-aid program provided 1,514,000 students in secondary schools with monthly allowances to cover carfare, shoes, and incidental expenses. They were selected by the schools on the basis of economic need and scholarship. Their activities in school ranged from maintenance and clerical help to tutoring, library, and research work. The out-of-school program aimed primarily at giving youths between eighteen and twenty-five years of age experience and confidence in their ability to work. It helped 2,700,000 youths. All projects were devised by public authorities, who provided materials, equipment, and supervision. The allocation of federal funds of the NYA was made on the basis of the total youth population of every state.

The main objections to the NYA came from the school authorities, who protested that a federal agency controlled the education program, that the activities of the regular schools were duplicated, and that NYA was too costly. In fact, the funds allocated to NYA were never adequate to meet the need for continued schooling, so that it was forced to limit the allowances to modest supplements. One of the valuable fruits of NYA and CCC work was the introduction of work experience into the educational program of American schools.

Rural Rehabilitation

In rural regions with poor soil, or under the one-crop system, the Depression brought disaster. Farmers lost their part-time jobs in industries, their unemployed children returned from industrial centers, and they could not meet their installment rates or buy feed and seed. Many lost their land to the mortgage holder. The Federal Emergency Relief Administration, following examples in Texas and Alabama, first offered loans to farmers as well as some subsistence homesteads.

In 1935 President Roosevelt established the Resettlement Administration to continue the agricultural program of the FERA,[76] which was succeeded in September 1937 by the Farm Security Administration. It provided two programs, "rehabilitation" and "social services." The first included (1) loans to farmers, tenants, and sharecroppers on easy terms for

[76] U.S. Department of Agriculture, *History of Farm Security Administration* (1940), pp. 2–4; Sidney Baldwin, *Poverty and Politics: The Rise and Decline of the Farm Security Administration* (Chapel Hill: University of North Carolina Press, 1968); Donald H. Grubbs, *Cry from the Cotton: The Southern Tenant Farmers' Union and the New Deal* (Chapel Hill: University of North Carolina Press, 1971).

the purchase of land, farm equipment, seed, feed, and livestock, with counseling on efficient farm management; (2) purchase of farms or homesteads with payment in installments running as long as forty years; (3) setup of farm cooperatives for the joint purchase of tractors, elevators, or purebred sires and for common use of the equipment; and (4) a "debt adjustment service," including legal advice and economic aid. The social services program organized voluntary prepaid medical and dental care at an annual cost, varying from fifteen to forty-five dollars per family. It provided cash grants in emergencies, such as sickness and accidents, and set up migrant camps (partly permanent and partly mobile) with sanitation, medical and dental service. In the national defense program the Farm Security Administration resettled farm families whose land was used for army needs, established emergency housing for war workers in dormitories and trailers, and erected public housing projects in defense areas.

In 1946 the Farmers Home Administration in the United States Department of Agriculture became the successor of the Farm Security Administration. The new agency grants three types of credit to farmers: (1) *farm ownership loans,* amortized over a forty-year period, to enable the farmer to purchase a family-size farm or to improve, enlarge, or repair the farm; (2) *insured mortgages* to guarantee, for a period of forty years, loans of private lenders so that farmers may purchase or improve farms; and (3) *production and subsistence* loans to allow farmers to purchase on reasonable rates and terms seed, livestock, feed, fertilizer, and farm equipment, to refinance debts, and to bolster family subsistence in emergencies. Loans carry no more than 5 percent interest, and veterans and disabled veterans receive preference. The field staff of the Farmers Home Administration still gives individual advice in farm management to farmers who ask for loans or help.

A PERMANENT SOCIAL SECURITY PROGRAM

Although temporary emergency measures for relief and work projects under the FERA were carried on, it became evident that a permanent organization of the welfare system of the country, with the federal government sharing in its expenditures, was necessary. In his message to Congress on June 8, 1934, President Roosevelt announced that a bill would be presented to provide security against the great disturbing factors in life, especially unemployment and old age. On June 29, 1934 he appointed a Committee on Economic Security consisting of Miss Frances Perkins, Secretary of Labor, as chairman and the Secretaries of the Treasury, of Agriculture, the Attorney General, and the Federal Emergency Relief Administrator as members. In the preparation of legislation, the committee enlisted the help of a Technical Board of Economic Security, consisting of government experts in federal, state, and local public agencies, with Arthur J. Altmeyer as chairman. The committee also was aided by an Advisory Council on Economic Security, composed of experts who were not connected with public agencies under the chairmanship of President Frank Graham of the University of North Carolina. He had a professional staff, with Professor Edwin E. Witte as executive director.[77]

On January 15, 1935 the Committee on Economic Security submitted its report to President Roosevelt, who transmitted it, under the title *Economic Security Bill*, to Congress. After certain amendments and changes the *Social Security Act* became law on August 14, 1935. Thus, the fundamental federal law in the field of social welfare in the United States was created.[78] The Social Security Act introduced three main programs: (1) a program of *social insurance*, consisting of a federal old-age insurance system and of a federal-state system of unemployment compensation, (2) a program of *public categorical assistance* supported by federal grants-in-aid for three groups, including Old-Age Assistance, Aid to the Needy Blind, and Aid to Dependent Children, to which a fourth category, Aid to the Permanently and Totally Disabled, was added in 1950, and (3) a program of *health and welfare services*, providing for Maternal and Child Health Services, Services for Crippled Children, Child Welfare Services, Vocational Rehabilitation, and Public Health Services. The last two programs later were based on different legal foundations, the *Vocational Rehabilitation Act of 1943* and the *Public Health Service Act of 1944*.

The Social Security Act placed the federal administration of the three programs under a new agency, the Social Security Board. In 1946 a reorganization of the Federal Security Agency abolished the Social Security Board and replaced it by the Social Security Administration under a single Commissioner for Social Security. Under Presidents Franklin D. Roosevelt and Harry Truman, the change of the Federal Security Agency into a cabinet department was proposed in several bills. In 1953 President Eisenhower established the Department of Health, Education and Welfare with

---

[77] Social Security Board, *Social Security in America* (1937), III–V, pp. 515–17; Wilbur J. Cohen, "The First Twenty Years of the Social Security Act, 1935–1960," *Social Work Year Book* (1960), 49–62; Edwin E. Witte, *The Development of the Social Security Act* (Madison: University of Wisconsin Press, 1962), pp. 3–108; Theron Schlabach, *Edwin E. Witte, Cautious Reformer* (Madison, Wis.: State Historical Society, 1969); Archer Hanlan, "From Social Reform to Social Security," in Paul E. Weinberger, ed., *Perspectives on Social Welfare: An Introductory Anthology* (Toronto: Macmillan, 1969), pp. 107–18.

[78] Pumphrey, *The Heritage of American Social Work*, pp. 432–50; Cohen, *Social Work in the American Tradition*, pp. 176–83; Eveline M. Burns, *The American Social Security System* (Boston: Houghton Mifflin, 1949), pp. 44–62; Charles E. Hawkins, "Welfare and Child Health Provisions of the 'Medicare' Act," *Welfare in Review*, 3, No. 8 (August 1965), 1–13; Ralph Pumphrey, "Social Welfare History," *Encyclopedia 1971*, pp. 1450–51.

that department's secretary as a member of the Cabinet. The Social Security Administration, the Public Health Services, the Office of Education, and the Office of Vocational Rehabilitation are branches of the department.

The amendments to the Social Security Act, particularly those of 1950, 1952, 1954, 1956, 1958, 1963, and especially 1965, increased the numbers of people eligible for old-age and survivors' insurance and unemployment compensation. These amendments strengthened the operations of the public assistance programs and the various health and welfare services, and indicated society's increasing recognition of responsibility for the preservation of the welfare of all people.[79]

The New Deal succeeded in solving the breakdown of the American economy during the Great Depression and in starting a program of serious social reform. But because of congressional unwillingness to carry out some of the relevant aims of the New Deal, especially a redistribution of wealth to eliminate the poverty of the lower classes, minority groups, and landless rural workers, the New Deal failed to improve permanently the quality of life for all Americans, which President Roosevelt had announced as his goal in the reform.[80]

New Developments

The amendment of July 30, 1965 represented essential improvements in the provisions of the Old-Age, Survivors, and Disability Insurance Program as well as in Public Assistance, and the Maternal, Child Health, and Child Welfare Services. Above all, the amendment established for the first time two coordinated health insurance programs for the aged.

In the general social insurance area, the benefits for old-age, survivors, and disability allowances were increased by 7 percent. The definitions of disability and of the retirement test were liberalized. Children aged eighteen to twenty-one years were made eligible for benefits while attending school. Widows could receive benefits at age sixty, although at a reduced rate. Physicians are covered under the law. Persons over seventy-two years are eligible under liberalized conditions. Recent major changes in the field of social security and welfare services are discussed in Chapters 9, 10, and 11.[81]

---

[79] Wilbur J. Cohen and Robert M. Ball, "Social Security Amendments of 1965," *Social Security Bulletin,* 28, No. 9 (September 1965), 3–24; Paul A. Brinker, *Econo-Insecurity and Social Security* (New York: Appleton, 1968); Joseph A. Pechman, et al., *Social Security: Perspectives for Reform* (Washington, D.C.: Brookings Institution, 1968); Maurice B. Hamovitch, "History of the Movement for Compulsory Health Insurance in the United States," *Social Service Review,* 27, No. 3 (September 1953), 281–99.

[80] This failure is clearly demonstrated in Charles A. Reich, *The Greening of America,* pp. 45–58.

[81] On deficiencies in health care, see Beth Kupper and Alfred D. Klinger, M.D., "Who Cares for the Sick Poor?" *Public Welfare,* 28, No. 4 (October 1970), 356–79.

Health insurance for the aged is provided by two programs: Medicare, a Basic Hospital Insurance Plan covering the costs of hospitalization and related care, and Medicaid, Supplemental Voluntary Medical Insurance Plan, assuming the payment for those physicians' services and other medical and health treatments not covered under the hospital insurance plan.

PRIVATE SOCIAL AGENCIES

The role of private social agencies changed fundamentally during the Depression. At the start of the Depression, private agencies soon exhausted all their funds and were forced to abandon the dispensation of economic aid that was considered, until this date, one of their main functions. Public welfare departments in cities and counties took over the main responsibility for relief of the financially distressed. Private social agencies still are granting some economic aid to persons who are not eligible for public assistance, and if it is necessary to make casework and counseling services effective, they are rendering such financial help as cannot be given by public agencies. The basic distinction between the present functions of public and private agencies is that private social agencies emphasize casework services for personal and behavior questions, adjustment in family and environmental problems, and the providing of group work and recreational facilities not supplied by public authorities. Private agencies no longer assume the main responsibility for economic support of people in financial need, but supplement the assistance given by public welfare agencies. Private agencies still engage in health services for tuberculosis, cancer, venereal diseases, heart ailments, infantile paralysis, and rheumatic fever and in children's services, particularly for adoption and child placement, institutional care for children and adults, vocational guidance, and training. Often, these services are coordinated with those offered under public auspices.[82]

WAR PROBLEMS

The main problems which social services faced during World War II and in some aspects also in the Vietnam War were family separation caused by the absence of husbands, fathers, and fiancés in the armed services or in war industries, and children left without proper care and supervision by working mothers. There also were general health and moral difficulties caused by mass living in military training locations and inadequate condi-

[82] James Leiby, "Social Work and Social History: Some Interpretations," *Social Service Review*, 43, No. 3 (September 1969), 310–18; and Herman D. Stein, "Relevance and the Private Sector in American Social Welfare," *Journal of Jewish Communal Service*, 45, No. 4 (1969), 273–302.

tions in war industries areas. Often, public and private agencies had to meet these increased problems with inadequate personnel, depleted by the call of social workers to service with the armed forces. Finally, war services endangered the maintenance of regular peace-time programs for the aged, the handicapped, the sick, and children.

To solve these problems, a nationwide effort to coordinate all available resources was attempted under the guidance of the Office of Community War Services, which was organized under the Federal Security Agency. The office was guided by an Interdepartmental Advisory Council, with representatives of all federal agencies engaged in health and welfare work. In the defense industrial areas, medical and dental facilities, sanitation, water supply, hospitals, clinics, schools, and housing often were lacking, so that a tremendous effort to provide them was imperative. A serious problem was the lack of recreational facilities for service men on furlough and for war workers in cities in which the population had suddenly increased to many times its former size.[83] The American Red Cross provided medical and casework services in military camps and assisted the families of the servicemen through its Home Service Division. Private social agencies together with public welfare departments cooperated with the defense councils.

The Japanese Evacuation

One event during World War II deserves discussion from the point of view of social welfare: the evacuation of the population of Japanese descent from the states on the West Coast. The Japanese are one of the small minorities (about 127,000 persons) in the United States. Almost 120,000 of them lived in California, Oregon, and Washington. Immediately after Pearl Harbor a wave of suspicion, hatred, and fear against persons of Japanese ancestry engulfed the Pacific Coast. Military leaders were afraid of sabotage and the danger of support of an enemy attack. Racial prejudice was combined with dislike of economic competition. Truck farmers, merchants, laundrymen, restaurant, fruit- and vegetable-market owners, and fishermen urged the removal of Japanese from the West Coast. Others argued that an evacuation would be necessary to protect the Japanese-Americans against harm from mob violence. After the president authorized the evacuation of military zones, Japanese-Americans were asked to move voluntarily from the Pacific Coast inland. Of 100,000 in California 10,000 followed this suggestion, hastily sold their business, land, and property, and tried to settle in the neighboring states. But they encountered difficulties. Utah, Nevada,

---

[83] Federal Security Agency, *Health, Welfare, and Related Aspects of Community War Services* (October 1942); Helen R. Wright, *Social Service in Wartime* (Chicago: University of Chicago Press, 1944); Reginald Robinson, *Serving the Small Community* (New York: Association Press, 1959).

Wyoming, and Arizona prevented them from entering their territory because they considered them "dangerous." On March 2, 1942 General De Witt ordered their removal from West Coast areas. President Roosevelt created the War Relocation Authority on March 18, 1942 as a civilian agency to carry out the evacuation. Social workers and other citizens were concerned about the constitutionality of this measure, since 75,000 of the group were American citizens.[84] However, they assisted in the relocation process at the registration centers. They did their best to advise the Japanese about the disposal of their property, the storage of furniture and equipment, and the safekeeping of valuables, but many Japanese were so upset that they sold everything at great loss and patiently accepted being placed behind barbed wire in ten relocation centers, which were established by the evacuees themselves, in desert regions under command of the army engineers. The War Relocation Authority sought to make life in these centers as bearable as possible. Crowded army barracks (without sufficient privacy for families with many children), lack of constructive work, limited and inadequate wages, and shortage of health and sanitary facilities and teachers for the schools in the camps were serious handicaps. Anxiety about the future and the hostility of the press—and sometimes of the guards and surrounding population—created problems and led, in a few instances, to riots. Japanese who were considered "disloyal" were segregated in Tule Lake, California, while, in the other relocation camps, an intensive outplacement program was carried out.

With the help of local committees, on which members of the American Friends Service Committee, the YWCA, the YMCA, and the Federal Council of Churches of Christ were particularly active, 41,000 persons left the centers and worked in communities all over the country. Life in the relocation centers was trying, especially for adolescents who lost the traditional Oriental respect for their helpless and often embittered parents. Juvenile delinquency, family discord, and political strife were rampant. The removal of families to outside communities solved many difficulties which social workers in the centers tried to alleviate. When Japanese-Americans were permitted to volunteer for army service, the spectacular record of their combat units, particularly in Italy, helped to restore their self-respect and caused a change in public opinion. The War Relocation Authority encouraged the return of the evacuees to their old communities or to other places of their choice as soon as it was permitted by presidential order in 1945.

84 Daisuke Kitagawa, *Isei and Nisei: The Internment Years* (New York: Macmillan, 1967); Bill Hosokawa, *Nisei: The Quiet Americans* (New York: Morrow, 1969); Audrie Girdner and Anne Loftis, *The Great Betrayal: The Evacuation of the Japanese Americans During World War II* (New York: Macmillan, 1969); Robert L. Heilbroner, "Benign Neglect in the U.S.," *Trans-Action,* 7, No. 12 (October 1970), 15–31.

Many older evacuees had suffered under the internment and had lost their initiative so that they first preferred to stay in the camps, a typical damage of "institutionalization." But with the aid of placement officers of the War Relocation Authority and local committees, the difficulties of finding housing, jobs, and acceptance in the communities were finally solved.[85]

SELECTED BIBLIOGRAPHY

Abbott, Edith, *Public Assistance. American Principles and Policies,* Vol. 1. Chicago: University of Chicago Press, 1940.

————, *Some American Pioneers in Social Welfare: Select Documents with Editorial Notes.* Chicago: University of Chicago Press, 1937.

Abbott, Grace, *The Child and the State: Select Documents with Introductory Notes,* 2 vols. Chicago: University of Chicago Press, 1938.

Addams, Jane, *Forty Years at Hull House.* New York: Macmillan, 1935.

————, *Twenty Years at Hull House: with Autobiographical Notes.* New York: Macmillan, 1910.

————, et al., *Philanthropy and Social Progress.* New York: Crowell, 1893.

Best, Harry, *Blindness and the Blind in the United States.* New York: Macmillan, 1934.

————, *Deafness and the Deaf in the United States.* New York: Macmillan, 1943.

————, *Public Provisions for the Mentally Retarded in the United States.* New York: Crowell, 1965.

Blumer, Herbert, "Collective Behavior," in A. M. Lee, ed., *New Outline of the Principles of Sociology.* New York: Barnes & Noble, 1966, pp. 167–222.

Breckinridge, Sophonisba P., *Public Welfare Administration in the United States,* 3rd impression. Chicago: University of Chicago Press, 1935.

Bremner, Robert H., *From the Depths: The Discovery of Poverty in the United States.* New York: New York University Press, 1956.

————, et al., *Children and Youth in America: A Documentary History.* Cambridge, Mass.: Harvard University Press, 1970.

Brown, Josephine C., *Public Relief, 1929–1939.* New York: Holt, Rinehart and Winston, 1940.

Bruno, Frank J., *Trends in Social Work: As Reflected in the Proceedings of the National Conference on Social Work, 1874–1956.* New York: Columbia University Press, 1957.

Cahn, Frances, and Valeska Bary, *Welfare Activities of Federal, State, and Local Governments in California, 1850–1935.* Berkeley: University of California Press, 1936.

[85] U.S. Department of the Interior, War Relocation Authority, *WRA: A Story of Human Conservation* (Washington, D.C.: Government Printing Office, 1947); Dorothy S. Thomas and Richard S. Nishomoto, *The Spoilage* (Berkeley: University of California Press, 1946; Alexander H. Leighton, *The Governing of Men* (Princeton, N.J.: Princeton University Press, 1945; Dorothy Swaine Thomas, *The Salvage: Japanese American Evacuation and Resettlement* (Berkeley: University of California Press, 1952); Carey McWilliams, *Prejudice: Japanese Americans* (Boston: Little, Brown, 1944); Ronald O. Haak, "Co-opting the Oppressors: The Case of the Japanese Americans," *Trans-Action,* 7, No. 12 (October 1970), 23–31; Ford H. Kuramoto, "What Do Asians Want?" *Journal of Education for Social Work,* 7, No. 3 (Fall 1971), 7–18.

CHAMBERS, CLARKE A., *Seedtime of Reform. American Social Service and Social Action, 1918–1933*. Minneapolis: University of Minnesota Press, 1963.

COHEN, NATHAN E., ed., *Social Work in the American Tradition*. New York: Holt, Rinehart and Winston, 1958.

COLL, BLANCHE D., *Perspectives in Public Welfare*. Washington, D.C.: Department of Health, Education and Welfare, 1969.

DEUTSCH, ALBERT, *The Mentally Ill in America: A History of Their Care and Treatment from Colonial Times*. New York: Columbia University Press, 1946.

DEVINE, EDWARD J., *When Social Work Was Young*. New York: Macmillan, 1939.

DURBIN, ELIZABETH F., *Welfare Income and Employment*. New York: Praeger, 1969.

FRENCH, RICHARD SLAYTON, *From Homer to Helen Keller: A Social and Educational Study of the Blind*. New York: American Foundation for the Blind, 1932.

GIRDNER, AUDRIE, and ANNE LOFTIS, *The Great Betrayal: The Evacuation of the Japanese Americans During World War II*. New York: Macmillan, 1969.

GREER, THOMAS H., *American Social Reform Movements: Their Pattern Since 1865*. Englewood Cliffs, N.J.: Prentice-Hall, 1949.

HILLMAN, ARTHUR, *Making Democracy Work*. New York: National Federation of Settlements, 1968.

JOHNSON, ARLIEN, *Public Policy and Private Charities*. Chicago: University of Chicago Press, 1931.

KILLIAN, LEWIS, *The Impossible Revolution?: Black Power and the American Dream*. New York: Random House, 1968.

KLEIN, PHILIP, *From Philanthropy to Social Welfare*. San Francisco: Jossey-Bass, 1968.

KOHS, S. C., *The Roots of Social Work*. New York: Association Press, 1966.

LEE, PORTER, *Social Work as Cause and Function*. New York: Columbia University Press, 1937.

LEIBY, JAMES, *Charity and Corrections in New Jersey: A History of State Welfare Administration*. New Brunswick, N.J.: Rutgers University Press, 1968.

LEWIS, ORLANDO, *The Development of American Prisons and Prison Customs, 1776–1845*. New York: Prison Association, 1922.

LIGHT, IVAN H., *Ethnic Enterprise in America: Business and Welfare Among Chinese, Japanese, and Blacks*. Berkeley: University of California Press, 1972.

LUBOVE, ROY, *The Progressive and the Slums: Tenement Reform in New York City, 1890–1917*. Pittsburgh: University of Pittsburgh Press, 1962.

———, *The Struggle for Social Security: 1900–1935*. Cambridge, Mass.: Harvard University Press, 1968.

MARTS, ARNAUD C., *The Generosity of America: Its Source, Its Achievements*. Englewood Cliffs, N.J.: Prentice-Hall, 1966.

NUGENT, WALTER T. K., *Money and American Society, 1865–1880*. New York: Free Press, 1968.

PUMPHREY, RALPH E., and MURIEL W. PUMPHREY, eds., *The Heritage of American Social Work*. New York: Columbia University Press, 1964.

QUEEN, STUART ALFRED, *Social Work in the Light of History*. Philadelphia: J. B. Lippincott, 1922.

RATNER, LORMAN, *The Pre-Civil War Reform: The Variety of Principles and Programs*. Englewood Cliffs, N.J.: Prentice-Hall, 1967.

REYNOLDS, BERTHA C., *An Unchartered Journey: Fifty Years of Growth in Social Work*. New York: Citadel, 1963.

RICH, MARGARET E., *A Belief in People: A History of Family Social Work*. New York: Family Service Association of America, 1956.

ROMANYSHYN, JOHN M., *Social Welfare: Charity to Justice.* New York: Random House, 1971.

SCHAFFER, ALBERT, et al., *Understanding Social Problems.* Columbus, Ohio: Merrill, 1970.

SCHNEIDER, DAVID M., *History of Public Welfare in New York, 1609–1866.* Chicago: University of Chicago Press, 1938.

SCHNEIDER, DAVID M., and ALBERT DEUTSCH, *The History of Public Welfare in New York State, 1867–1940.* Chicago: University of Chicago Press, 1941.

SIMKHOVITCH, MARY K., *Neighborhood: My Story of Greenwich House.* New York: Norton, 1938.

SPEIZMAN, MILTON D., *Urban America in the Twentieth Century.* New York: Columbia University Press, 1968.

STEINER, GILBERT Y., *The State of Welfare.* Washington, D.C.: Brookings Institution, 1971.

U.S. National Resources Planning Board, *Security, Work and Relief Policies.* Washington, D.C.: Government Printing Office, 1942.

WEAVER, WARREN, *U.S. Philanthropic Foundations.* New York: Harper & Row, 1968.

WILENSKY, HAROLD L., and CHARLES N. LEBEAUX, *Industrial Society and Social Welfare.* New York: Free Press, 1965.

WOLFE, CORINNE H., et al., *Current Issues in Social Work—Seen in Historical Perspective.* New York: Council on Social Work Education, 1962.

WORCESTER, DAISY LEE W., *Grim the Battles.* New York: Exposition Press, 1954.

WRIGHT, HELEN R., et al., *Social Service in Wartime.* Chicago: University of Chicago Press, 1944.

4

social
casework

DEVELOPMENT OF THE CASEWORK PROCESS

During the last quarter of the nineteenth century the workers of the Charity Organization Societies were influenced in their ideas and practice by the recognition of widespread economic and spiritual distress among the masses of low-paid manual laborers, the sick, and the unemployed in the large industrial cities. They realized the lack of helpful, constructive relief from the poor-law authorities and their apathy toward the suffering of the destitute. They also became aware of the waste of energy and funds resulting from the lack of cooperation and information, and of the confusion and duplication of effort among private charitable agencies. The Charity Organization Societies accepted Thomas Chalmers's theory that public poor relief was not effective, and that the individual client needed "rehabilitation" so that he could support himself and his family. They sought to achieve this goal by making personal visits to the poor, by giving advice, admonitions, and financial aid. In each case, the rehabilitation of the poor person was to be carried on after a careful investigation of his conditions and discussions with the applicant and the people in his surroundings. This was the beginning of casework.[1]

In their method of finding a social solution for the personal and economic problems of a client, the Charity Organization Societies spent money for vocational training, tools and equipment, rent for setting up a workshop or a small business, food, clothes, and rent of a room or apartment for the family. These measures were, however, merely incidental to the real purpose of rehabilitating the client. The volunteers and agents of the relief societies considered themselves representatives of the community; they visited the applicant and collected facts on his conditions, family relations, experiences, and abilities. The findings were submitted to a committee, representing the local charities, that decided which action should be taken with the aim of restoring the client to self-support. In this task the "friendly visitor" continued the personal contact with the client, gave him advice and directions to become independent. The client was expected to follow the suggested plan. The necessary funds for rehabilitation, however, were solicited from well-to-do citizens by employed agents of the Charity Organization Society. The personal contact of the volunteer was thus separated from the measures of financial assistance because the societies thought that mixing the two would impair the moral and educational influence and the personal relationship between the friendly visitor and the client.

CHANGING CASEWORK PHILOSOPHY

The approach of the "friendly visitors" was based on the assumption that the client was in his precarious condition because of some fault in his behavior. This moral foundation of the early casework approach became questionable when the "friendly visitors" began to realize that the cause of distress was frequently not a character defect, but the social conditions

---

[1] Gordon Hamilton, *Theory and Practice of Social Case Work* (New York: Columbia University Press, 1947), pp. 17–33; Scott Briar, "Social Casework and Group Work: Historical Foundations," *Encyclopedia 1971*, pp. 1237–45; Robert W. Roberts and Robert H. Nee, eds., *Theories of Social Casework* (Chicago: University of Chicago Press, 1970).

under which the client lived, such as illness of the client or of his family, numerous children, unsanitary, overcrowded housing, low wages, debts, undernourishment, inadequate education, unemployment, and lack of training. This recognition of the influence of environment on the individual was supported, at the turn of the century, by the scientific findings of the "school of environmental determinism" in anthropology, biology, sociology, and economics. Novelists, sociologists, and political scientists exposed the social evils of industrial society and emphasized the need for fundamental social reforms in working conditions and wages, the establishment of schools, housing, hospitals and clinics, the prevention of communicable diseases, and the abolition of night work for women and children.

The effect of these experiences was that the Charity Organization Societies became concerned with advocating social legislation that would prevent destitution, disease, and social disorganization. But, though measures of social reform were improving the living conditions of the poverty-stricken and the low-income group, many families were still in dire want and distress. They needed understanding helpers to listen to them and to advise them so that they might make the right use of such community services as clinics, hospitals, employment bureaus, legal aid, training facilities, and adult education. Under these circumstances, social agencies continued to carry on casework in recognition of the fact that social reform did not solve all individual problems. Social workers also became aware that their interest should not be limited to the individual applicant, especially the breadwinner of the family, but that each member of the family deserved their attention and should be considered in relation to his environment.

The experiences of social workers revealed a serious conflict of values. Industrial society was inclined to embrace a theory of "Social Darwinism," that its unfit members should be eliminated as a natural process, and that interference with such elimination was harmful to a healthy society.[2] However, religious thought and humanitarian philosophy respect the divine nature of man and demand that every human being be assisted, whatever his failures. These two value systems contradict each other. Social workers accepted the "Humanitarian Ethos" as their concept of the responsibility of society for the welfare of individuals in the community. The general public, however, is often still ambivalent about following one or the other

[2] R. H. Tawney, *Religion and the Rise of Capitalism* (Baltimore: Penguin Books, 1947), p. 222; Stowe Persons, ed., *Social Darwinism: Selected Essays of William G. Sumner* (Englewood Cliffs, N.J.: Prentice-Hall, 1963); Richard Hofstadter, *Social Darwinism in American Thought* (Boston: Beacon, 1955), p. 57; and Eugene Mead and Fanchon Mead, *Man Among Men* (Englewood Cliffs, N.J.: Prentice-Hall, 1965), p. 118.

of the two conflicting concepts and is uncertain whether to accept rugged individualism or humanitarian philosophy.[3]

In 1911 Porter R. Lee, director of the New York School of Social Work, stated that social casework is "the method of effecting the understanding of the needs, resources, and reactions of individuals."[4] But there remained at this time a paternalistic, domineering attitude in the relation of the social worker toward the client who came to ask for advice and help. Although theory proclaimed "casework must work with and not for the individual," in practice the caseworker considered himself the best judge of what was the right solution for the client, because of his experience in social questions. Another factor in social casework practice before World War I strengthened the dominant role of the social worker. Social agencies took advantage of the growing number of persons who received training either in special courses or in the newly established schools of social work and employed them instead of untrained volunteers. This meant that the paid social worker assumed most functions in the agency: the initial interview with the applicant, social investigation of his home and his environment, the social diagnosis of the facts found in this investigation, and the development of a plan for treatment or rehabilitation of the applicant and his family. In 1917 Mary E. Richmond, director of the Charity Organization Division of the Russell Sage Foundation, first described this method.[5] Social agencies no longer submitted the findings of social investigations to a local committee, so that the social caseworker became the decisive element in the process of aiding the client.

However, social agencies found that their aim of rehabilitating children and adults could not be achieved by counseling alone. Frequently substantial financial assistance was needed to maintain families during the

[3] Witmer, *Social Work: An Analysis of a Social Institution* (New York: Farrar, 1942), pp. 55, 167–69, 172; Barrows Dunham, *Man Against Myth* (Boston: Little, Brown, 1947), pp. 59–60, 64–65; Elliot Studt, "Social Work Theory and Implications for the Practice of Methods," *Social Work Education Reporter*, 16, No. 2 (June 1968), 22–42.

[4] Porter R. Lee, "Social Function of Case Work," *National Proceedings of Conference of Charities and Corrections* (1911), 260–66; and Elizabeth L. Salomon, "Humanistic Values and Social Casework," *Social Casework*, 48, No. 1 (January 1967), 26–32.

[5] Mary E. Richmond, *Social Diagnosis* (New York: Russell Sage Foundation, 1917). See also Gordon Hamilton, *Theory and Practice of Social Casework* (New York: Columbia University Press, 1947), pp. 11–12, 19; Helen H. Perlman, *Social Casework: A Problem-solving Process* (Chicago: University of Chicago Press, 1957), pp. 84–96; Henry S. Maas, "Social Casework," in Walter A. Friedlander, *Concepts and Methods of Social Work* (Englewood Cliffs, N.J.: Prentice-Hall, 1958), pp. 18–23; Isabel L. Stamm, "Ego Psychology in the Emerging Theoretical Base of Casework," in Alfred J. Kahn, *Issues in American Social Work* (New York: Columbia University Press, 1959), pp. 80–109; and Helen H. Perlman, *Perspectives in Casework* (Philadelphia: Temple University Press, 1971).

period of readjustment, retraining, and rehabilitation, in some instances for long periods. Family welfare and child protective agencies still aimed at supporting people who were not in need of institutionalized care using funds collected from private donors and contributors. By this practice they prevented the public from being aware of the necessity of improving the facilities of public relief authorities, of providing adequate budgets, and competent administration of public relief.

SOCIAL DIAGNOSIS AND THERAPY

Mary Richmond and the early practitioners of social casework required a thorough investigation of the facts and data of the life of the individual who was in need of help. Through social diagnosis, they attempted to analyze these findings and to determine the underlying causes of the client's social and personal difficulties. After this critical examination, followed the interpretation of the specific conditions for the behavior and reactions of the client, based on his individual personality.[6] The therapy was planned on the preceding investigation and the social diagnosis; it was frequently directed toward external improvements in the environment, living conditions, and type and location of work, which were considered of primary importance in the initial period of casework practice.

Methods and practice of social casework were deeply influenced by the recognition of the scientific development of psychology and psychiatry in this country. There were important contributions from the social sciences, such as the studies of child growth by G. Stanley Hall, the investigations of sex problems by Havelock Ellis, and the invention of intelligence tests by Binet and Simon in France and their introduction in the United States by H. H. Goddard. Another decisive influence was the foundation of the mental hygiene movement by Clifford Beers, after the publication of his experiences as a mental patient in his book, *A Mind that Found Itself*, in 1908. These ideas shifted the fundamental interest of social work from economic and sociological emphasis toward psychological and emotional problems of the client. Important factors in this development were the discoveries of Sigmund Freud, psychoanalysis and dynamic psychology, and the work of Freud's followers, Otto Rank, C. G. Jung, Alfred Adler, and others, who founded their own schools.

Before this period only a few social workers had been employed in mental hospitals, especially in children's wards; they helped the psychiatrists

[6] Muriel W. Pumphrey, "Mary Richmond—The Practitioner," *Social Casework*, 42, No. 8 (October 1961), 375–85; Roberts and Nee, eds., *Theories of Social Casework;* William J. Reid and Ann W. Shyne, *Brief and Extended Casework* (New York: Columbia University Press, 1969).

in securing information about the case history and the family conditions of the patient and took care of the patient after his discharge. Some general hospitals felt the need to employ social caseworkers to assist the physician in his diagnosis and treatment by collecting the data on the patient's earlier illnesses and on his social and economic conditions. These social workers were aware of the necessity to make use of the resources of the patient's family as well as of the facilities of the community, of social agencies, employers, and friends, to preserve and strengthen the results of medical treatment.

During World War I the interest of social workers took a further turn from environmental factors to the psychological aspects of human behavior for which psychiatry, psychology, and biology had laid the groundwork. The immediate reason for this intensified psychological concern of social workers was the establishment of "home service divisions" through the American Red Cross, where social workers assisted families whose husbands were serving with the armed forces. These families were different from former clients of the Charity Organization Societies and of the poor relief agencies; most of them had never before been in contact with social agencies. The families were typical American people, a cross section of the entire country. Because the Red Cross is maintained by voluntary contributions of the population, its job was to serve these families, and the old "lady bountiful" attitude was out of place for servicemen's families.[7] The same was true for Red Cross workers serving in hospitals and field stations with the fighting armies in Europe. The large number of neuropsychiatric patients suffering from "shell-shock" created a heavy demand for psychiatric social workers who were trained, for the first time, at Smith College in 1918. Because of the war shortage of psychiatrists, psychiatric social workers were for the first time given substantial responsibility in the treatment of psychoneurotic patients and worked in close contact with the psychiatrists in the armed forces. In this work, it was emphasized that human behavior is not arbitrarily chosen or accidental, but is the result of a lifelong development as well as of family and surroundings on the organism and the emotions of the individual.[8]

Some people have serious difficulties in resolving the conflicts between

7 Virginia Robinson, *A Changing Psychology in Social Work* (Chapel Hill: University of North Carolina Press, 1930),p. 53. See also Stamm, "Ego Psychology in the Emerging Theoretical Base of Casework," in Kahn, *Issues in American Social Work,* pp. 80–109; and Watts, "Casework above the Poverty Line," *Social Service Review,* 38, No. 3 (September 1964), 303–15.

8 Bertha C. Reynolds, *An Unchartered Journey: Fifty Years of Growth in Social Work* (New York: Citadel, 1963), pp. 57–62; Helen H. Perlman, *Persona, Social Role and Personality* (Chicago: University of Chicago Press, 1968); Robert Sunley, "New Dimensions in Reaching-Out Casework," *Social Work,* 13, No. 4 (April 1968), 64–74; Harry Specht, "Casework Practice and Social Policy Formulation," *Social Work,* 13, No. 1 (January 1968), 42–52; Edwin J. Thomas, "Sociobehavioral Techniques and Principles," *Social Work,* 13, No. 1 (January 1968), 12–26.

their desires and the demands of society. Frequently, the patient is not conscious of the motivations for his behavior and attempts to conceal by apparent rationalizations the true motives for his actions. The findings of Sigmund Freud about the unconscious have shown that emotions govern our behavior more than reason. Freud emphasized that early childhood experiences frequently determine the personality development of the adult. This gave new insights to social workers who tried to incorporate psychiatric theories into their concepts.

With a better psychological understanding of human behavior and a more realistic evaluation of economic problems, social casework changed its approach to the client. The full respect of the caseworker for the personal dignity of the client as a human being represents the process of "democratization" of casework. The caseworker accepts the client as he is; he does not attempt to mold him into something else. The change in approach led, in the beginning, from an active influence of the caseworker on the client to an attitude of pronounced "passivity." For some time, caseworkers barely spoke to the client, merely listened to his explanations and tried to accept his statements as well as the motivations which he revealed. The silence of the caseworker forced the client to speak, but often did not give him sufficient help in making decisions. Progress in casework technique was made when the caseworker began to see that effective help for the client was achieved only by using the full understanding of his ideas and feelings as the core of diagnosis and therapy. This enabled the client to work out his emotional problems in a way he himself chose. He had the "right of self-determination" in how much to accept the advice of the caseworker and to use the aid of the social agency or of other community resources.[9]

Since the late 1930s casework has attempted to avoid the extremes of domination or of passivity in relation to the client, and to achieve an equilibrium between these opposite approaches. Caseworkers have learned that social, economic, psychological, and cultural factors influence each individual, and that the concern of casework is not only the client as an individual, but also his relation to his family and community. As the capacity for self-help varies among human beings, the caseworker has to assume the responsibility for helping the client find satisfactory solutions for his individual problems. The caseworker refrains from moral judgments of the client's behavior, but does not approve of attitudes which are harmful

9 Bertha C. Reynolds, "Between Client and Community," *Smith College Studies in Social Work*, 5 (1934), 98–99; Grace Marcus, *Some Aspects of Relief in Family Case Work* (New York: Columbia University Press, 1947), p. 70; Anita J. Faatz, *The Nature of Choice in Casework Process* (Chapel Hill: University of North Carolina Press, 1953); Maas, "Social Casework," in Friedlander, *Concept and Methods of Social Work*, pp. 47–61, 65–79; and Johanna T. Schmidt, "The Use of Purpose in Casework Practice," *Social Work*, 14, No. 1 (January 1969), 77–84.

to the client himself or to others. In addition, there is a trend toward working again with the entire family as a unit. Certain limitations are set by social and cultural standards, sometimes unwritten laws, which may not be violated in our society.[10] The reactions of the community toward ethnic and religious minority groups, toward blacks, Mexicans, Orientals, Indians, or toward recent immigrants require understanding and special consideration by the caseworker.

Some individuals and families are not willing to come to a social agency to ask for help on their own initiative. Such "resistive families" are found particularly in cases of family discord, child neglect, criminal and asocial behavior, juvenile delinquency, and among minority groups. They deny their need for guidance, assistance, and treatment. In such a case the social worker or probation officer must take the initiative, call in the home of the family, and try to understand psychologically the reactions of the clients in order to modify patiently their hostile, defiant attitude. In dealing with a delinquent juvenile gang, a "street corner worker" may first have to join them to be accepted and to gain their confidence before he is able to influence their behavior. We call this approach "supportive" or "aggressive casework," or "out-reaching" social work.[11]

INFLUENCE OF PSYCHOLOGICAL THEORIES

In social casework we deal with human feelings and behavior. For this reason, professional training of social workers includes the study of motivations, the dynamics of human behavior, and the application of psychology in working with people.

The *diagnostic casework theory* derives its philosophy and methods from the theory of personality created by Sigmund Freud and his followers

---

[10] James R. Dumpson, "Public Welfare and the Newcomer in the Community," *Public Welfare*, 19, No. 4 (October 1961), 139–44, 166–67; Bruno Bettelheim and Morris Janowitz, *Social Change and Prejudice* (New York: Free Press, 1964); Robin M. Williams, *Strangers Next Door* (Englewood Cliffs, N.J.: Prentice-Hall, 1964); Milton L. Barron, ed., *American Minorities* (New York: Alfred A. Knopf, 1957); Andrew Billingsley and Amy Billingsley, "Negro Family Life in America," *Social Service Review*, 39, No. 3 (September 1965), 310–19.

[11] Sylvan S. Furman, ed., *Reaching the Unreached* (New York: New York City Youth Board, 1952); Selma Arnold, "Confidential Communication and the Social Worker," *Social Work*, 15, No. 1 (January 1970), 61–67; Fritz Redl, *Controls from Within* (New York: Free Press, 1952); Kermit T. Wiltse, "The 'Hopeless' Family," *Social Welfare Forum* (1958), 135–53; George Brager, "Improving Services for Street-Corner Youth," *Social Work Practice* (1962), 27–40; Ernest A. Herre, "Aggressive Casework in a Protective Service Unit," *Social Casework*, 46, No. 6 (June 1965), 358–62; Ludwig L. Geismar, *Preventive Intervention in Social Work* (Methuen, N.J.: Scarecrow Press, 1969); Dorothy L. Lynn, "Crisis Intervention," *Child Welfare*, 49, No. 3 (March 1970), 152–55.

and applies the principles of "dynamic psychiatry" in the social casework approach.[12] Diagnostic casework accepts personality organization as a composite of differentiated and interacting elements which also are influenced by people's environment, by the social and economic conditions in which they live. Conscious as well as unconscious influences are regarded as determining our human values, behavior, and self-control. Social workers need to comprehend the effects of emotional experiences on human behavior, especially the emotions in early childhood, the feelings of anxiety, frustration, guilt, and tensions caused by the conflict between the "id" (the primitive drives for gratification of all needs) and the "ego" (the socialized force of the individual that becomes aware of its part in human society and of the values of religion, ethics, and civilization).[13]

The relationship to parents, siblings, and other persons in the environment plays an important role in the life experiences of the individual. In Freudian psychology the ego holds the key position in the psychic structure. It performs the most important functions of maintaining a balance between the inner drives and the "superego." The superego is the ideal that a person forms of a human being, usually absorbed from childhood experience with parents, particularly the father. It consists of a synthesis of the rules of desirable conduct, of prohibitions and inhibitions impressed on the child by his parents and his environment. The development of the superego creates the human conscience. The ego reconciles the psychic, emotional needs of the individual with the demands of reality and society. The ego is influenced by inner emotions and external factors, and it functions in self-preservation, perception, reality testing, organization, planning, and judgment. An understanding of the human personality structure, of intrapsychic conflicts and their influence on behavior, is required to achieve change and improvement in attitude. Deviations from normal psychic functions may be recognized, classified, and changed by therapy. The type and intensity of therapeutic action necessary depends on the nature and the extent of the psychosocial disturbance of the individual client. Therapy attempts to remove the disturbance between the individual's emotional needs and the facts of his physical and social environment, and helps the client change and increase his ego capacity. Diagnostic casework encourages

[12] Cora Kasius, ed., *A Comparison of Diagnostic and Functional Casework Concepts* (New York: Family Service Association of America, 1950), pp. 7–13; Hamilton, *Theory and Practice of Social Casework,* pp. 258–62; Stamm, "Ego Psychology in the Emerging Theoretical Base of Casework," in Kahn, *Issues in American Social Work,* pp. 80–109; Helen H. Perlman, 'Social Casework," *Encyclopedia of Social Work 1965,* pp. 708–14; Norman A. Polansky, *Ego Psychology and Communication* (New York: Atherton, 1971).

[13] Heinz Hartmann, "Comments on the Psychoanalytic Theory of the Ego," *Essays on Ego Psychology* (New York: International Universities Press, 1964); Erik H. Erikson, *Insight and Responsibility* (New York: Norton, 1964).

the client to discuss his difficulties and develops a planned treatment directed toward helping the client resolve his inner conflicts, mobilize his ego strength, and lessen environmental pressures by social planning. The diagnostic caseworker assumes the responsibility for evaluating the client's problems and for establishing supportive measures which help him adjust according to his individual needs.[14]

Functional casework was taught primarily at the School of Social Work of the University of Pennsylvania and was based on the theory of "will therapy," developed by Otto Rank. This theory centers around the assumption of an organizing force, the will, in the human personality. It concludes that the interaction of inner instinctual drives of the individual and environmental influences is directed by the individual's autonomous yearning for his "self." This self is the result of transcendental forces composed of inner and environmental experiences by means of the will. Personality growth is achieved by relationships with others, primarily between mother and child, through "projection" of one's needs on the other person. Because such projection cannot lead to complete union in reality, limitations are either accepted or frustration results because of refusal to recognize reality. The client is encouraged to overcome his disturbances and anxieties by his will to solve his psychic problem. The functional caseworker attempts to help the client release his innate capacity. Because psychic disturbances are caused by a destructive use of the relationships of the client, functional casework seeks to replace them by new relationships conducive to constructive use of his "self" and those of other people. In this process, the client directs himself toward his change of attitude, whereas the functional caseworker helps him release his energies toward self-responsibility and self-acceptance. Functional casework calls its function the "helping process" and does not use the diagnostic term "treatment." It is convinced that the client's use of his "self" toward his goals, and with his free choice, are his right, but also his responsibility. The functional approach does not refer to general norms, as does the diagnostic school. The "helping process," according to the functional approach, is limited by the agency setting. The needs of the client can be met only within the framework of agency function, which is considered the keynote. The "client must find his own satisfying solution and ultimate adjustment" among the services which the social agency offers.

Diagnostic casework attempts to help the client adjust to normal

[14] Howard J. Parad and Roger R. Miller, *Ego-Oriented Casework: Problems and Perspectives* (New York: Family Service Association of America, 1963); Berta Fantl, "Integrating Psychological, Social and Cultural Factors in Assertive Casework," in Paul E. Weinberger, *Perspectives on Social Welfare: An Introductory Anthology* (Toronto: Macmillan, 1969), pp. 315–25; Richard A. Pasewark and Dale A. Albers, "Crisis Intervention: Theory in Search of a Program," *Social Work*, 17, No. 2 (March 1972), 70–77.

behavior. It measures success in terms of how far the client approaches normal behavior. This approach aims at more effective treatment through the use of increasing scientific knowledge of the forces affecting human behavior and social adjustment; it seeks objective criteria for measuring and predicting casework results.

The functional theory operates on the assumption that the client himself must determine his goals and choices within the framework of agency services. Its measure of progress is how far the client achieves this self-direction.

Social workers have been concerned about whether social casework might use Carl R. Rogers's *client-centered therapy* as the psychological basis for a particular functional approach. Professor Rogers characterizes his method as "self-directed therapy," which permits the client to gain full confidence in the therapist or counselor and complete awareness of his own personality, so that the client himself can overcome his anxieties and feel able to cope with his problems.[15]

Some social workers use an eclectic theory, applying elements of various schools of psychology as the basis of their approach to the client. The discussion about the specific values of the various schools of psychology in their application for social work has not been closed. An analysis of their essential elements for the practice of social work permits hope that in the future some synthesis between the two psychological methods may be worked out. Such a synthesis might develop new effective skills of social work in helping the client.

CASEWORK PROCEDURE

The modern casework agency offers well-defined services to the client. The caseworker explains these services and discusses with the client in what way he wants to use the agency's facilities and how they may help him solve his problems. No aid is imposed on the client; he decides whether he wants to accept the agency's help. The caseworker explains to the client his own abilities of solving his problems, and what the agency may con-

15 For more information on this specific type of psychotherapy, see Carl R. Rogers, *Counseling and Psychotherapy, Newer Concepts in Practice* (1942), and *Client-Centered Therapy, Its Current Practice, Implications, and Theory* (Boston: Houghton Mifflin, 1951); on psychological theories, see Ruth L. Monroe, *Schools of Psychoanalytic Thought* (New York: Dryden, 1955); Herbert H. Aptekar, *The Dynamics of Casework and Counseling* (Boston: Houghton Mifflin 1955); Lilian Ripple, *Motivation, Capacity, and Opportunity: Studies in Casework Theory and Practice* (Chicago: University of Chicago Press, 1964); Ruth E. Smalley, *Theory for Social Work Practice* (New York: Columbia University Press, 1967); Margaret Schubert, *Interviewing in Social Work Practice* (New York: Council on Social Work Education, 1971).

tribute. Thus, the client gains an understanding of the economic and emotional elements which cause his problems. Casework attempts to awaken the client's strength for self-help and to restore his ability for self-support, thereby maintaining his self-respect and human dignity.

Present-day social casework is facing a number of serious problems. Casework skills are required in all social agencies which work with families and children, with delinquents and adult offenders, and with aged persons. However, many workers, particularly in public welfare agencies and probation and parole services, have no adequate professional training or competence for it. Many social workers are ill-equipped to help destitute black clients and need special training for this service. Some social agencies that want to employ caseworkers with full graduate training and supervised field work experience find it difficult to hire them, because working conditions, salaries, supervision, or the local situation are not desirable. The education of graduate social work students is impeded by the lack of good field work agencies with qualified supervisors and technical facilities and the lack of study stipends.[16]

Another problem confronting social casework is the lack of skilled and experienced caseworkers in some social agencies. Such agencies have heavy turnover and loss of trained workers who wish to take up family life, or who transfer to agencies which are more attractive. There is, furthermore, a need for research studies which attempt to evaluate the successes and failures of casework, to determine the situations in which casework is helpful and where it does not operate with effect. Many caseworkers are inclined to look at each client as a unique phenomenon, failing to recognize the types of human needs and reactions from which a general professional experience can be drawn.[17]

[16] Helen H. Perlman, "Social Casework," *Social Work Year Book* (1960), 535–40; Frances H. Scherz, "Appraisal of Treatment Objectives in Casework Practice," *Social Work Practice* (1962), 158–73; Henry Freeman, et al., "Classification System That Prescribes Treatment," *Social Casework,* 46, No. 7 (July 1965), 423–29; Scott Briar, "The Casework Predicament," *Social Work,* 13, No. 1 (January 1968), 5–11, Max Bruck, "Behavior Modification Theory and Practice," *Social Work,* 13, No. 2 (April 1968), 43–55.

[17] Henry S. Maas, "Group Influences on Client–Worker Interaction," *Social Work,* 9, No. 2 (April 1964), 70–79; David Landy, "Problems of Clients Seeking Help in Our Culture," *Social Welfare Forum* (1960), 127–45; Whitney M. Young, "Reason and Responsibility in the Elimination of Bigotry and Poverty," *Social Welfare Forum* (1968), 141–55; D. D. Bowles, "Making Casework Relevant to Black People," *Child Welfare,* 48, No. 8 (August 1969), 468–75; Gerd Schroeter, "Protection of Confidentiality in the Courts," *Social Problems,* 16, No. 3 (Winter 1969), 376–85.

For examples of research studies in evaluation of casework efficiency, see J. McV. Hunt, et al., *Testing Results in Social Casework; A Field-Test of the Movement Scale* (New York: Family Service Association of America, 1950); Lilian Ripple, "Factors Associated with Continuance in Casework Service," *Social Work,* 3, No. 1 (January 1958), and *Motivation, Capacity, and Opportunity;* Ann W. Shyne, "An Experimental Study of Casework Methods," *Social Casework,* 46, No. 9 (November

Technical methods of recording casework need simplification, clerical operations need streamlining, and the procedure of conferences and consulations needs concentration and more concise action.

Casework services still need to be interpreted to the public, in fact more than health or recreation services, to gain in the community fuller understanding of their value and increased moral and material support.

Recently, caseworkers' functions have been broadened to include not only therapeutic work, but also the roles of "broker," "advocate," and developer of behavior modification. As "broker," the social worker offers the client a single point of entry, either a neighborhood street office or a mobile van, to the many available social services. Here the client, particularly in a slum neighborhood, can be referred to the special service he needs. In view of the wide range of social problems, at least one professional trained worker is necessary to give clients real help.[18] As "advocate," the worker helps the client connect with the relevant part of the social service system. He sees that the client receives help; this may require formal legal intervention in conflict with the social agency, or even representing the client before a court or appeal board. These functions of the caseworker require more knowledge of regulations and legal procedure and a more aggressive attitude than is traditional.[19] "Intervention theory" offers systematic background for such social action on behalf of the client.

The following are trends in present casework practice: (1) caseworkers gain a sharpened concept of the function of social diagnosis and treatment in relation to the facilities of the social agency; (2) caseworkers develop increasing skill in relating their understanding of the client's tensions, fears, and frustration to his social environment and economic conditions; (3) the caseworker takes the initiative in "supportive," "out-reaching," or "aggressive" casework which is necessary with certain types of clients, and works with individuals, families, groups, and communities, as well as in institutions; (4) social agencies, both private and public, are showing a growing awareness of the need for trained, skilled caseworkers in an adequate proportion to the number of clients who need their services, and demonstrating an understanding for the importance of giving early individual and

---

1965), 535–41; Elizabeth G. Meier, "Interaction Between the Person and His Operational Situation," ibid., 542–49; Jane Hanford, "Maximum Use of Casework Service," *Selected Papers in Casework* (1951), 8–10; and Harriet M. Bartlett, "The Generic-Specific Concept in Social Work Education and Practice," in Kahn, *Issues in American Social Work,* pp. 159–90. For case illustrations of social casework practice, see Maas, "Social Casework," in Friedlander, *Concepts and Methods of Social Work,* pp. 16–115.

18 Scott Briar and Henry Miller, *Problems and Issues in Social Casework* (New York: Columbia University Press, 1971), pp. 244 ff, 237 ff.

19 David Wineman and Adrienne James, "The Advocacy Challenge to Schools of Social Work," *Social Work,* 14, No. 2 (April 1969) 22–32; Briar and Miller, *Problems and Issues in Social Casework,* pp. 239–43.

family counseling concerning problems of adjustment; (5) in this period of many social changes, casework is willing to apply its skills to new problems and to work in a team relationship with other professional groups whenever this is essential to help the clients, as well as to train and supervise nonprofessional auxiliary assistants, recruited from the client group; (6) casework is increasingly working with the entire family (instead of with the individual client), with groups, and in community action.

SELECTED BIBLIOGRAPHY

APTEKAR, HERBERT, *The Dynamics of Casework and Counseling*. Boston: Houghton Mifflin, 1955.

BENEDEK, THERESE, *Insight and Personality Adjustment*. New York: Ronald, 1946.

BENNIS, WARREN, G. et al., *The Planning for Change*. New York: Holt, Rinehart and Winston, 1966.

BLUMER, HERBERT, *Symbolic Interactionism: Perspective and Meaning*. Englewood Cliffs, N.J.: Prentice-Hall, 1969.

BRADLEY, KIRK A., *Existentialism and Casework*. New York: Exposition Press, 1969.

BRIAR, SCOTT, and HENRY MILLER, *Problems and Issues in Social Casework*. New York: Columbia University Press, 1971.

FELDMAN, ALBERT G., and FRANCES L. FELDMAN, *The Social Worker in the Community*. New York: Atherton, 1971.

FOREEN, ROBERT, and ROYSTON BAILEY, *Authority in Social Casework*. Oxford: Pergamon, 1968.

FRAZIER, E. FRANKLIN, *The Negro in the United States*, rev. ed. New York: Macmillan, 1957.

GARRET, ANNETTE, *Interviewing: Its Principles and Methods*. New York: Family Welfare Association of America, 1942.

GORDON, HENRIETTA, *Casework Services for Children: Principles and Practice*. Boston: Houghton Mifflin, 1956.

HAMILTON, GORDON, *Theory and Practice of Social Casework*, 2nd ed. New York: Columbia University Press, 1951.

HOLLIS, FLORENCE, *Casework: A Psycho-social Therapy*. New York: Random House, 1964.

———, "Social Casework: The Psychosocial Approach," *Encyclopedia 1971*, pp. 1217–26.

KARDINER, ABRAHAM, *The Individual and His Society*. New York: Columbia University Press, 1939.

KASIUS, CORA, *Principles and Techniques in Social Casework*. New York: Family Service Association of America, 1950.

KENT, BESSIE, *Social Work Supervision in Practice*. Toronto: Pergamon, 1969.

LEVENSTEIN, SIDNEY, *Private Practice in Social Casework: A Profession's Changing Pattern*. New York: Columbia University Press, 1964.

LOWRY, FERN, *Readings in Social Casework*. New York: Columbia University Press, 1939.

MAYER, JOHN E., and NOEL TIMMS, *The Client Speaks: Working Class Impressions of Casework*. New York: Atherton, 1970.

MENDELSON, WALLACE, *Discrimination*. Englewood Cliffs, N.J.: Prentice-Hall, 1962.

NICHOLS, ELIZABETH, *In-Service Casework Training.* New York: Columbia University Press, 1965.

PARAD, HOWARD J., ed., *Psychology and Dynamic Casework.* New York: Family Service Association of America, 1958.

PERLMAN, HELEN H., *Helping: Charlotte Towle on Social Work and Social Casework.* Chicago: University of Chicago Press, 1969.

———, *Perspectives on Social Casework.* Philadelphia: Temple University Press, 1971.

———, *Social Casework, A Problem-solving Process.* Chicago: University of Chicago Press, 1957.

———, "Social Casework: The Problem Solving Approach," *Encyclopedia 1971,* pp. 1206–17.

REGENSBURG, JEANETTE, and SELMA FRAIBERG, *Direct Casework with Children.* New York: Family Service Association of America, 1957.

RICHMOND, MARY E., *Social Diagnosis.* New York: Russell Sage Foundation, 1917.

ROBINSON, VIRGINIA, *A Changing Psychology in Social Work.* Chapel Hill: University of North Carolina Press, 1930.

ROGERS, CARL R., *Counseling and Psychotherapy.* Boston: Houghton Mifflin, 1942.

SCHUBERT, MARGARET, *Interviewing in Social Work Practice: An Introduction.* New York: Council on Social Work Education, 1971.

SMALLEY, RUTH E., "Social Casework: The Functional Approach," *Encyclopedia 1971,* pp. 1195–1206.

———, *Theory for Social Work Practice.* New York: Columbia University Press, 1967.

TAFT, JESSIE, *Counseling and Protective Service as Family Casework: Functional Approach.* Philadelphia: University of Pennsylvania Press, 1946.

TAYLOR, ROBERT K., "Identification and Ego-directed Casework," *Social Work,* 5, No. 1 (January 1960).

TURNER, FRANCIS, *Differential Diagnosis and Treatment in Social Work.* New York: Free Press, 1968.

TURNER, JOHN B., "Racial and Other Minority Groups," *Encyclopedia 1971,* pp. 1068–77.

WESTIN, ALAN F., *Privacy and Freedom.* New York: Athenaeum, 1970.

WHEELER, STANTON, *On Record Files and Dossiers in American Life.* New York: Russell Sage Foundation, 1969.

WILLIAMS, ROBIN M., JR., *Strangers Next Door. Ethnic Relations in American Communities.* Englewood Cliffs, N.J.: Prentice-Hall, 1964.

WITMER, HELEN LELAND, *Social Work: An Analysis of a Social Institution.* New York: Farrar & Rinehart, 1942.

YOUNG, WHITNEY M., "Intergroup Relations and Social Work Practice," *Social Welfare Forum* (1960), 146–53.

———, "Racial Discrimination," in Nathan E. Cohen, ed., *Social Work in the American Tradition.* New York: Holt, Rinehart and Winston, 1958, pp. 340–61.

5

---

social
work
with
groups

Social group work is centered around a "group." It was born partly in the recreational activities of the YWCAs and YMCAs around 1850, and partly in the social reform movement of the settlement houses toward the end of the nineteenth century. It emphasizes the education, development, and cultural growth of the members of the group. It is frequently carried on in voluntary activities during leisure time, under the guidance of a group worker. Although work with groups has concerned agencies identified with the social welfare movement for many years, the first recognition of such work as a social work process occurred in the second decade of this century.[1] The social group work process emphasizes the possibilities for the development and social adjustment of the individual through voluntary group action, and the use of an association with others in a group as a means of furthering socially desirable objectives. This process is determined by the objectives of the agency, the dynamic forces and adjustive efforts within the group itself, and the group worker's skill of observation and interpretation of adjustive and formative efforts within the group and his selection and application of an effective group work technique toward constructive results.[2]

BASIC CONCEPTS OF SOCIAL WORK WITH GROUPS

Social casework is a helping relationship between an individual (the caseworker) and another individual (the client). Social group work, however, is characterized by being carried out in a group setting, and the helping process deals with individuals in their relationship as members of a group.

Gisela Konopka defines the activities of the social group worker as follows: "The group worker enables various types of groups to function in such a way that both group interaction and program activity contribute to the growth of the individual and the achievement of desirable social goals."[3]

Human beings do not grow up isolated from others. Children are born into a family; later they join with other children in informal groups.

[1] See Gertrude Wilson and Gladys Ryland, *Social Group Work Practice. The Creative Use of the Social Process* (Boston: Houghton Mifflin, 1949), pp. 7–16; Gisela Konopka, *Social Group Work: A Helping Process*, 2nd ed. (Englewood Cliffs, N.J.: Prentice-Hall, Inc., 1972), pp. 3–7; William Schwartz and Sergio Salba, *The Practice of Group Work* (New York: Columbia University Press, 1971); and John A. Clausen, *Socializational Society* (Boston: Little, Brown, 1968).

[2] Juanita Luck Cogan, "Social Group Work," *Social Work Year Book* (1960), 540–49; Gisela Konopka, *Social Group Work*, p. 20; Suzanne Schulze, *Group Work in the Institution* (New York: Whiteside, 1954); and William Schwartz, "Group Work and the Social Scene," in Alfred J. Kahn, ed., *Issues in American Social Work* (New York: Columbia University Press, 1959), pp. 110–37.

[3] The ideas and functions of group work are described in more detail in Gisela Konopka, "The Method of Social Group Work," in Walter A. Friedlander, ed., *Concepts and Methods of Social Work* (Englewood Cliffs, N.J.: Prentice-Hall, 1958), pp. 118 (definition), 116–200, and in Konopka, *Social Group Work: A Helping Process*, pp. 23–35; see also Jack Rothman, ed., *Promoting Social Justice in the Multigroup Society: A Casebook for Group Relations Practitioners*, (New York: Council on Social Work Education, 1971).

Adolescents and adults usually join a church, lodge, or other social group, following the natural desire for companionship, belonging, and recognition. In most instances, social casework also is concerned not exclusively with the individual client, but with his family and environment, because they play an important role in causing or alleviating his personal problems. The caseworker functions as a member of a group, just as everyone else in our society.

The social group worker, however, is primarily concerned with the relationship among the members of the group and between the members and himself. The group worker functions mainly through his participation in the interaction between the individuals in the group, but he is not a regular member, identifying himself with the others, absorbed by the activities of the group as such. The worker's functions are guided by his professional understanding of group life and by the individual member's need for his help or for withholding his assistance. This knowledge permits the group worker to give professional service to the group as a whole and to each individual member of the group. To be able to assume this responsibility, the group worker needs to be aware of his professional self. He has to control his personal impulses, values, and preferences, and to concentrate on making it possible for the members of the group to obtain the achievements and personal as well as cultural satisfactions which the group and its activities offer.

Methods of working with groups may be classified into five categories:

1. The *dictatorial or authoritarian method:* The leader orders, the members obey.
2. The *personification method:* The members imitate the group worker and attempt to be like him, but they do not explore and find their own abilities.
3. The *preceptive method:* The worker gives instructions, the group members carry them out, learn skills; but they are not detecting their own resources and capacities
4. The *manipulative method:* The group worker goes with the group through a phase of planning and decision-making. In fact, the group is only accepting a prearranged program of the leader, and is deceived into believing that the group itself came to the decision.
5. The *enabling method:* The group worker helps the members to participate with full responsibility in the life of the group, in its planning and program, in developing their own ideas, skills, and personal attitudes, and to make their own decisions regarding the purposes and actions of the group.[4]

In a democratic society, only the last of these methods is considered

[4] Wilson and Ryland, *Social Group Work Practice,* pp. 60–61; Harleigh Trecker, *Group Work Foundations and Frontiers* (New York: Association Press, 1955); and Konopka, *Social Group Work,* pp. 141–55.

a desirable way of achieving the aims of positive, constructive group life. It helps the individual members enjoy the satisfaction derived from being accepted as a part of the whole, to express themselves, and to participate in the collective action of the group.[5]

DEVELOPMENT AND CHARACTERISTICS OF SOCIAL GROUP WORK

The orientation in the early settlement houses and in other group work agencies was first of a religious and missionary nature, with the purpose of encouraging church participation and Sunday schools and of protecting their members from the moral dangers of city life. But the young people who joined the groups were often more attracted by activities from which they hoped to gain material advantage, education, or pleasure. Similar motives frequently induced children and adolescents in poor quarters to join group work agencies. When, at the beginning of the twentieth century, Boy Scouts and other groups for boys and girls were founded which no longer centered in underprivileged neighborhoods but appealed to middle- and upper-class children as well, the nature of group work organizations and their methods changed.[6] A different use of the group work process was made when mental hospitals and child guidance clinics began to introduce recreational programs as a method of therapy for mentally ill, mentally retarded, and nervous patients. In other group activities the emphasis changed from the mere participation in physical education, sports, crafts, and discussions, to the effect group activities had on the individual member's personal growth and on the collective life of the group. To learn to share experiences with others, to give and take, to clarify differences of opinion and judgment without hostility and frustration, to yield in good spirit to decisions of the majority is even more important for the development of personality than to learn special skills. The process changed from routine direction of activities to conscientious consideration of the desires and needs of the individuals in the group and of those factors which would make the group as a whole the educational and cultural experience the members hoped for, from which

[5] Alan F. Klein, *Society—Democracy—and the Group* (New York: Woman's Press, 1953); Helen U. Phillips, *Essentials of Group Work Skill* (New York: Association Press, 1957); and William Schwartz, "Group Work and the Social Scene," in Kahn, *Issues in American Social Work*, pp. 110–37.

[6] Konopka, *Social Group Work*, pp. 1–34; James F. Short and Fred L. Strodtbeck, *Group Process and Gang Delinquency* (Chicago: University of Chicago Press, 1965); Art Rosenblum, *Aquarian Age or Court War* (Philadelphia: Aquarian Research Foundation, 1970).

they could gain a feeling of belonging together and of mutual solidarity. New methods of group work will have to be applied in communes because of the failure of so many of them.

The group work process relies on scientific, critical elements to measure the interaction among group members, the results of guidance and mutual stimulation from within the group, and the forces which determine the action of gangs and related groups which oppose direction toward socially accepted goals and outside leadership.

The group work process attempts to achieve the following objectives: to provide experiences which integrate the essential needs of the individuals who form the group; to encourage wholesome mental and social attitudes on the part of each participant toward his place in the group and in society; to achieve skill in some leisure-time pursuit; and to provide experience in acceptable social behavior, and in collective, positive activities rather than useless or destructive ones.

PRACTICE OF SOCIAL GROUP WORK

The practice of social group work is determined by the nature and the objectives of the social agency which provides the service, and by the needs which the group and its individual members want to satisfy in their group experience. The group worker is engaged in four different levels of activities:

1. "Basic" social group work, the practice with "primary groups," such as children, adolescents' and adults' clubs, sport and recreation groups, and study and discussion societies
2. Supervision of other group workers, professionals and volunteers
3. Administration of social group work agencies or other organizations through which group work is offered
4. Community organization, planning, and coordination of group work activities[7]

In this chapter we shall discuss mainly the first type of group work—with primary social groups. Group workers most commonly work with this

[7] Wilson and Ryland, *Social Group Work Practice*, pp. 27, 69–78; Nathan E. Cohen, "Implications of the Present Scene for Social Group Work Practice," *Social Welfare Forum* (1955), 48–60; Hans S. Falck, "Social Group Work and Planned Change," *Social Work Practice* (1964), 209–20; Emanuel Tropp, "Social Group Work: The Developmental Approach," *Encyclopedia 1971*, pp. 1246–52.

group; supervision, administration, and community organization in the realm of group work are assigned to a smaller number of experienced and professionally trained people.[8]

Group work organizations in the field of recreation may be classified into four categories according to their activities:

1. Agencies with programs primarily providing recreation and informal education, such as public recreation and adult education in schools, extension divisions of colleges and universities, YWCA, YMCA, boys' and girls' clubs, senior citizens' clubs, and similar private organizations.

2. Agencies conducting recreational and educational programs combined with religious, ideological, and social purposes, such as churches, young people's and women's groups, clubs interested in civic information, adult and workers' education societies.

3. Agencies primarily concerned with other objectives which conduct recreational and educational programs as a support of their main functions, such as settlement houses and community centers (whose main purpose is the establishment of constructive, cooperative neighborhood relations, and the improvement of living and health standards), public housing projects, clubs of labor unions, of factories, and of such youth groups as the 4-H Clubs, which fundamentally want to function as "character-building," vocational, or occupational organizations.

4. Agencies which provide therapy to patients in need of physical, mental, and emotional adjustment (hospitals, rehabilitation centers, mental and child guidance clinics); they use group work as one of the means for achieving their therapeutic objective.[9]

Social group work usually is thought of in connection with leisure time and recreational activities. It is of particular importance, however, in the setting of an institution, such as a children's home, an orphanage, an industrial school, or an old-age home. Daily life in institutions requires an understanding of human behavior, and the capacity to establish personal ties with members of "living groups" as well as of "interest groups" or clubs which

[8] Harleigh B. Trecker, "Community Planning for Group Work," in Charles Hendry, ed., *A Decade of Group Work* (New York: Association Press, 1948), pp. 124–32; Margaret E. Hartford, "Use of Social Group Work in Helping Members Accept Differences," *Social Work Practice* (1964), 221–35; Helen Northern, *Social Work with Groups* (New York: Columbia University Press, 1969).

[9] Grace L. Coyle, *Group Work with American Youth* (New York: Harper & Row, 1948), pp. 6–18; Gisela Konopka, "Group Work and Therapy," in Hendry, *A Decade of Group Work,* p. 41; Arthur Hillman, et al., *Neighborhood Centers Today* (New York: National Federation of Settlements, 1960); Elinor C. Guggenheimer, *Planning for Parks and Recreation Needs in Urban Areas* (New York: Twayne, 1969); and H. Douglas Sessoms, "Recreation in Environmental Planning," *Encyclopedia 1971,* pp. 1077–83.

may form themselves in the institution.[10] Houseparents, teachers, instructors, and administrators assist children or adults to adjust to the demands of group living, and at the same time to develop or to preserve their own personality and cultural satisfaction. The trained social group worker is able to assist, in an institutional setting, in developing the constructive aspects of group living, encouraging the group members to present their ideas, ingenuity, skills, and abilities. He is aware of the dangers of "boss-rule," or dictatorship, and of uncooperative leaders who subdue other members and make them lose their individuality or exclude those whom they do not like. Disturbed and overaggressive members of an institution, frequently found in correctional settings, have special problems complicated by the increased difficulties in the institutional setting in planning and carrying out leisure-time activities, recreational and educational programs, and in bringing to the staff an understanding of group dynamics and group therapy. The group worker takes the initiative in developing recreation for patients and for the staff whenever the institution is not close enough to other sources for providing for leisure time and cultural activities.

The main objective in the social group work process is to stimulate the initiative, the group consciousness, and self-direction in the group. The group worker does not assume the initiative himself, but makes the group members the active, creative forces. The group's program is the framework within which the group experience occurs. The interaction between the group members, learning to be a member of a society, understanding of different opinions and values, and accepting majority decisions as a good sport, are important factors with creative values for personality growth, especially in the development of young persons. The social group worker needs a knowledge of individual and group behavior and of social conditions as well as the ability to work efficiently with groups of people. His leadership requires skill to awake in the members of the group their creative abilities and to develop constructive, socially acceptable activities. His function is to help each individual in the group gain satisfaction and enjoyment through the group relations and activities, and to assist the group as a social unit to find its own objective.[11] Group members have the satisfac-

---

10 For a stimulating discussion of such functions in children's homes, see Netta Berman, "The Group Worker in a Children's Institution," in Susanne Schulze, ed., *Creative Group Living in a Children's Institution* (New York: Association Press, 1951), pp. 117–25; and Louise A. Frey and Ralph L. Colotny, "Illusions and Realities in Current Social Work with Groups," *Social Work*, 9, No. 2 (April 1964), 80–89.

11 Grace L. Coyle, "Social Group Work," *Social Work Year Book* (1954), 480–86; Audrey Trecker and Harleigh B. Trecker, *How to Work With Groups* (New York: Woman's Press, 1952); Robert D. Vinter, et al., *Educational Developments in Social Group Work* (New York: Council on Social Work Education, 1962); Irving Brodsky, "The New Role of the Community Center," *Social Welfare Forum* (1964), 200–216; Harry Lawrence and Martin Sundel, "Behavior Modification in Adult Groups," *Social Work*, 17, No. 2 (March 1972), 34–43.

tion of being with others of their age, of developing social attitudes and skills, and of finding creative outlets for their cultural, artistic, or social abilities which might never have been discovered without group stimulation.

The following sample of group work in practice illustrates this social work process.

Kids in Trouble: Roberto[1][2]

Roberto, a boy of slight build and dark complexion, looks older than his fifteen years. He has gone in gangs with older boys for several years, and consequently, when he was twelve, he appeared before the juvenile court, charged with stealing. Since, he has had a probation officer and has been taken in twice by the police, but not on charges serious enough to bring him before the court again. The probation officer reports that Roberto's home is small and physically inadequate, but that family relations are pleasant enough.

When Roberto was in the seventh grade, his gang started going to a community center in the neighborhood. They had a weekly recreation program of sports, swimming, and dancing, but even here most of the boys were older than Roberto. Much destruction of the building took place, and the solution for the Center, a year later, was to divide the group and form a smaller club for boys and girls who were Roberto's age, many of whom also had juvenile court records.

From the beginning Roberto was loyal in attendance, but very moody, showing enormous distrust of the club leader, who was a woman. For several months he would not talk with the leader, but took great delight in mocking the way she spoke. He seemed to hope that she would be angry about this, but when she only laughed with him, he dropped this mockery. During this sullen, quiet period with Roberto, the leader always invited him to join in activities, but never insisted that he do so.

His favorite activity was to listen to bop records, and occasionally he danced, usually alone. While the other club members planned parties, played ping-pong and basketball, had crafts and dramatic groups, he sat, saying nothing, by the record player. Only once, however, did he outwardly cause trouble, this being on a day when his phonograph records were not available. He got a gang of boys together and they wandered around restlessly, eventually throwing a table down the stairs. When the club leader pointed out that club groups must pay for damage to the building, Roberto admitted that he was responsible and would pay himself, rather than have the whole group pay.

In planning their club program the group asked to have dancing lessons. With this activity, the club leader saw a change in Roberto's attitude. He received a great deal of recognition from the club leader, the members, and the dancing teacher, because he was the best dancer and learned new steps very quickly. When complimen-

[1][2] The authors are indebted to Miss Getrude Wilson, Professor Emeritus of Social Welfare, University of California, Berkeley, for this case illustration. For other perceptive examples of group work practice, see Konopka, *Social Group Work: A Helping Process,* pp. 171–237. See also Sheldon Seller and Joy Taylor, "The Malevolent and Transformation: Implications for Group Work Practice," *Social Work,* 10, No. 3 (July 1965), 82–91; and Hans S. Falk, "Helping Caseworkers Use the Special Group Work Method," *Public Welfare,* 22, No. 2 (April 1964), 125–29.

ted about this, he dropped his tough outward appearance and was more like a shy, modest kid.

Recently, Roberto was elected an officer of the club, and he took his responsibility very seriously. He personally tried to see that all the members' behavior was good at the last dance, and everyone reported that it was the best party the club had had.

GROUP WORK IN OTHER SETTINGS

Cooperation Between Casework and Group Work Agencies

By now it is accepted that close cooperation between caseworkers and group workers helps the people whom social work serves. But for long this concept was not accepted by social workers. Caseworkers often turn to group work agencies, such as the Y's, girls' or boys' clubs, and the 4-H Clubs, for help in behalf of individual children in need of recreation, of companionship, or of developing art and music skills. Experience in group living assists the child or youngster who has difficulties in his family or school, who is lonely or frustrated, or who suffers from excessive sibling rivalry to find new friends, to feel accepted, to develop his ability to get along with others, and to gain initiative and self-reliance.[13]

The caseworker who must refer a child or adolescent to a group work agency considers the child's personality, environment, and age in deciding which type of group will be most helpful for him. An "interest group" attracts the child because of the specific activities carried out in the group. In the "club group" the referred child may find other children of his age who, with the help of the worker, are willing to accept him into their society. A successful referral requires that the group worker has a keen understanding of the personality and emotional needs of the child, knowledge of symptomatic behavior, and the skill to deal sympathetically with the individual child as well as with the group as a whole. Such referrals are made by children's and family welfare agencies, public welfare departments, hospitals, child guidance clinics, and churches. In making a referral, the caseworker finds out which available group, in its composition and

13 Gordon Hamilton, *Theory and Practice of Social Case Work* (New York: Columbia University Press, 1951), pp. 235–36, 242–44; Harleigh B. Trecker, *Group Work—Principles and Practice* (New York: Woman's Press, 1948), pp. 101–2; Mary E. Burns and Paul H. Glaser, "Similarities and Differences in Casework and Group Work Practice," *Social Service Review*, 37, No. 4 (December 1963), 416–28; Scott Briar, "Social Casework and Social Group Work: Historical and Social Science Foundations," *Encyclopedia 1971*, pp. 1237–45; Ronald A. Feldman, "Group Service Programs in Public Welfare," *Public Welfare*, 27, No. 3 (July 1969), 266–71; K. L. Hagberg, "Combining Social Casework and Group Work Methods in a Children's Hospital." *Children* 16, No. 5 (May 1969), 192–97.

leadership, will best serve the needs of the child, and where he promises to be an asset to the other members. Under such circumstances, group experience may help the child make a successful adjustment.

However, the group worker might find a member of the group who needs a personal, intensified relationship and individual assistance which the group worker cannot give, perhaps because there is not enough time to devote to him without neglecting the rest of the group. In such instances the group worker will, with the consent of the child or adolescent and of the parents, refer him to a casework agency for individual treatment. The child remains in the group as long as he is able to enjoy his participation. A cooperative relationship between the group worker and the caseworker may help the child who desires help from both workers and proves capable of using it.

In other cases of referral, the social worker of the agency to which the child is referred assumes the immediate relationship with the child in such a way that the child can attach himself fully to the new worker without conflict from the referral worker. The referral worker, in these cases, restricts himself to following the development of the child through occasional conferences with the new worker.

Group Work with Adults and Aged Persons

Work with groups of young adults, the middle-aged, and elderly persons has gained importance. There is increasing recognition that skilled group work process would make this work more valuable and effective for the members of the group.[14]

During recent decades the proportion of the older generation, over sixty-five years of age, to the total population has steadily increased because of progress in medical science, geriatrics, and improved living standards. However, America has developed its cultural and recreational institutions with strong emphasis on the needs and habits of children and youth and, until recently, has given little attention to the leisure-time needs of older

[14] Leland P. Bradford, "Adult Education as Group Work," L. K. Hall, "Group Work in Religious Education," Eleanor G. Coit and Orlie Pell, "Group Work in the Workers' Education Setting," in Hendry, *A Decade of Group Work*, pp. 52–76; Malcolm S. Knowles, ed., *Handbook of Adult Education in the U.S.* (Chicago: Adult Education Association, 1960); Clark Tibbitts and Wilma Donahue, eds., *Aging in Today's Society* (Englewood Cliffs, N.J.: Prentice-Hall, 1960); Louis Lowy, "The Group in Social Work with the Aged," *Social Work*, 7, No. 4 (October 1962), 43–50; Mark Forman, "Conflict, Controversy, and Confrontation in Group Work with Older Adults," *Social Work*, 12, No. 1 (January 1967), 80–85; Robert D. Vinter, "The Essential Components in Social Group Work Practice," in Weinberger, ed., *Perspectives on Social Welfare*, pp. 298–314.

persons. The growing importance of the older citizens' group requires more consideration, not only in measures of social and economic security, but also in cultural activities and recreation.

With the introduction of old-age insurance and of old-age retirement provisions in civil service and in industrial health and welfare plans, an increasing number of persons aged sixty-five years and older will be unable to obtain jobs in industry. Their life threatens to become dull and lonely without work, so that satisfactory recreational facilities become more and more important for them. The first awareness of this change of emphasis was shown when the William Hodson Center in New York City and settlements in Chicago, primarily the Olivet Institute, in 1940 organized the first "Golden Age Clubs" for elderly people. At present recreational facilities for older citizens exist in many cities.

The organization of leisure time for the aged may be planned by a group of citizens in cooperation with a settlement house, a family welfare agency, a church, or a community center which can provide the meeting place and facilities for group activities. The names of older people living in the selected neighborhood are collected. Visits to the aged, a personal letter of invitation, or announcements in the local press might start the work. As in other recreational activities, programs would be arranged according to the interests and preference of the members of the group after it was organized. They could include games; arts and crafts; music, movies, or television; a discussion of topics of actual cultural or political importance; or just an opportunity for getting together socially and talking with people of like situation. Simple refreshments are important, because some old people rarely have an opportunity to enjoy meals in the company of others. Members of the clubs are limited to those sixty years of age or older, many of them widows or widowers, or couples without children or relatives in the community. There should be no discrimination according to sex, faith, race, or financial status; but experience in senior citizens' groups indicates that Negroes and Latin Americans often are hesitant to join "white clubs" and need special encouragement.

Group activities in homes for the aged have also become an important factor in modern institutional care. They are necessary for the well-being of older people, whose active participation in the program is essential. But, in a home for the aged, the question of health sets limitations to recreational activities, discussions, and dramatic performances.[15]

[15] Herbert Shore, "Group Work Program Development in Homes for the Aged," *Social Service Review*, 26, No. 2 (June 1952), 181–94; Jerome Kaplan, *A Social Program for Older People* (Minneapolis: University of Minnesota Press, 1953); Gordon J. Aldridge, "Old Age as a Social Problem," *Journal of Public Law*, 2, No. 2 (Fall 1954), 333–39; Leo W. Simmons, *Toward Better Understanding of the Aging* (New York: Council on Social Work Education, 1959); Jerome Kaplan and Gordon J. Aldridge, *Social Welfare of the Aging* (New York: Columbia University Press, 1962); Robert W. Kleemeier, ed., *Aging and Leisure* (New York: Oxford Univer-

GROUP THERAPY

The term *group therapy* is frequently used, but often not clearly defined. A great variety of activities, including group discussions with psychiatrists or psychiatric social workers, encounter groups, group meetings in mental hygiene clinics or psychopathic hospitals, and acting in psychodrama, are called group therapy. Careful selection of a suitable group of companions by the group worker is an essential condition for success and for predicting the probable influence of the members of the group on one another.

The primary objective of such groups is to function as a medium for carrying out therapy for their members. Such groups have been composed of individuals who were unable to participate in normal group activities with others of the same age, who could not relate to people and were either too shy and withdrawn, or so hostile and aggressive, that they could not function in a normal group.

Group therapy has unique value. It is not just a simpler, quicker process than individual treatment. It is based on the curative or socializing effect of a group, and on the development of friendly contacts in a secure atmosphere of help provided by the group leader in a controlled environment. In this interaction of the patients with each other, each one feels more secure as he discovers that other members of the group have similar, or even worse, problems, and that his own difficulties are not caused by a unique failure or inadequacy.[16] This recognition permits the patient to identify himself with other members of the group, lessens his anxiety, and develops his readiness to try to help the others, at the same time adjusting himself to the group. This experience encourages the patient by giving him a feeling of solidarity and of getting along with other people. The entire process is made possible through the relationship between the group therapist and the members of the group.[17] In general, group therapy develops

---

sity Press, 1961); Clark Tibbitts, ed., *Societal Aspects of Aging* (Chicago: University of Chicago Press, 1960); Arthur Williams, *Recreation for the Aging* (New York: Association Press, 1953); James K. Whittacker, "Models of Group Development: Implications for Social Group Work Practice," *Social Service Review*, 44, No. 3 (September 1970), 308–22.

[16] A different type of therapy is applied in encounter groups. See Arthur Burton, *Encounter: The Theory and Practice of Encounter Groups* (San Francisco: Jossey-Bass, 1969).

[17] Robert Plank, "An Analysis of a Group Therapy Experiment," *Human Organization*, 10, Nos. 3 and 4 (Fall and Winter, 1951), 5–21, 26–36; William Schwartz, "Small Group Science and Group Work Practice," *Social Work*, 8, No. 4 (October 1963), 39–46; and Martin Loeb, "The Backdrop for Social Research: Theory-Making and Model-Building," in Leonard S. Kogan, ed., *Social Science Theory and Social Work Research* (New York: National Association of Social Workers, 1960).

a feeling of unity among the group members. Therapists, as a rule, are careful to avoid that patients express their feelings of suppressed hostility, aggression, and related drives too forcefully, because it would distort the therapeutic climate of the group; it has to be left to individual treatment. Changes in environment are disturbing to adults and to children with whom group therapy has been practiced. Samuel R. Slavson, one of the outstanding pioneers in the field of child guidance and group therapy, characterizes his method as "activity group therapy," in which the therapeutic effect is produced by the active participation of disturbed or neurotic children or adults in a group which permits them to act out or talk about their anxieties, fears, or aggressive feelings. The patient, who represses his spontaneity because he is afraid of being rebuked or of losing prestige, may be encouraged to talk about his problems when he sees others in the group freely expressing themselves. To achieve such results, the group should be composed of a small number of patients of the same sex and age.[18] The group therapy setting must be informal; it must permit a confidential relation between the therapist and the members of the group.

In such therapeutic groups, even children of preschool age play out their anxieties, tensions, and fantasies. They use for their expression various toys and materials, such as animals, dolls, figures of families, wood blocks, plastics, water colors, and finger paints. The social worker or psychiatrist gives them interpretations of their actions and plays. More intensive psychotherapy is used for disturbed children of elementary school age; different materials are offered to permit them to express their feelings in their play group.

The success of group therapy with children and adults depends on a competent group therapist who needs, at least, to meet the qualifications for individual therapy. Since World War II, psychiatric patients have been treated by group therapy in military and veterans' hospitals and in clinics. In 1943 the American Group Therapy Association was founded. It provides its members—psychiatrists, psychiatric social workers, group therapists, and clinical psychologists—information on research and new experiences, conferences, and exchange of ideas.

---

[18] Samuel R. Slavson, *An Introduction to Group Therapy* (New York: Commonwealth Fund, 1943), pp. 1–2; Grace L. Coyle, "Group Work in Psychiatric Settings," *Social Work*, 4, No. 1 (January 1959); Konopka, "Group Work and Therapy," in Hendry, *A Decade of Group Work*, pp. 264–76; Joseph D. Jacobs, "Social Action as Therapy in a Mental Hospital," *Social Work*, 9, No. 1 (January 1964), 54–61; Beryce W. MacLennan and Naomi Felsenfeld, *Group Counseling and Psychotherapy with Adolescents* (New York: Columbia University Press, 1968); E. J. Anthony, "Reflections on Twenty-Five Years of Group Psychotherapy," *International Journal of Group Psychotherapy*, 18, No. 3 (1968), 277–300.

TRENDS IN THE PRACTICE OF SOCIAL WORK WITH GROUPS

Among new elements in the development of social group work, we may emphasize the following trends:

1. The democratic principle of self-determination is recognized as the genuine American method of social group work. The older form of authoritarian leadership is in the process of being discharged. Democracy implies respect for the personal dignity of each group member. It precludes enforcing the leader's ideas as long as these ideas are not accepted by the majority of the group.

The staff of the group work agency needs to have faith in people's ability to learn and to decide for themselves what they want to do. This idea requires that the group workers work *with* the group, not *for* the group. The group worker is engaged in professional work with groups and with individuals, in recreation and leisure activities, in family services, in public welfare, in health and mental health services, in various institutions, and in correctional work.

2. Certain group work methods are being applied to the expanding program of mass recreation, frequently under the guidance of public recreation departments, schools, and colleges. However, there is a need for the setup of smaller groups to offer individualized services for people who desire personal attention and help.

3. Recreational agencies now accept the need for employment of trained, professional social workers who are able to give competent supervision to volunteer leaders and to work with such groups which need skill, understanding, and experience. The development of the administration and community relations of group work agencies also requires professional skills.

4. It is now recognized that under professional leadership, individual members in groups receive more attention, based on the group worker's understanding of psychiatric concepts of human needs. A new teamwork is developed in which group workers join together with caseworkers, psychiatrists, psychologists, and sociologists to help solve personality problems of group members.

5. Professional leadership has already stimulated a broad literature in the field of social work with groups and the development of scientific research in which social psychology, sociology, and sociometry contribute to a critical evaluation of the validity of group work methods.

6. The tasks and objectives of leisure-time and recreational agencies are being clarified. An adjustment of the program of recreational agencies is under way to meet the actual, essential needs of the community, especially those of lower income and minority groups.

7. In many communities a sincere concern about desirable interracial and intergroup relations is now established. It is leading to mutual understanding and respect among different ethnic and religious groups. Organizations are being encouraged in which membership is open to everyone regardless of creed, race, color, sex, and economic status.

8. The forces of intergroup relations are finding recognition in new provinces: in groups of the aged; in churches, factories, labor unions, cooperatives; and in reformatories, prisons, and institutions for mentally retarded patients. Group dynamics is beginning to play an important role in improving relations between management and workers in industry.[19]

9. Social agencies, professional associations, and schools of social work encourage professional education and attempt to develop the most suitable curriculum for training in group work, as well as criteria for the selection of students. The trend in social work education is to train "generic workers," able to use casework, group work, and community organization work.

10. Professional social workers are assuming the responsibility for improving their competence and skill, for assisting the schools of social work in their teaching methods, and for raising the quality of group work practice. They are attempting to achieve a commonly accepted classification of jobs and the establishment of salaries commensurate with their responsibilities.

11. Public authorities, such as municipal welfare departments, boards of education, and recreation commissions, are assuming financial responsibilities and sponsoring group work services, particularly for teen-agers and the aged.

SELECTED BIBLIOGRAPHY

BLUMENTHAL, LOUIS H., *Administration of Group Work*. New York: Administration Press, 1948.

BURTON, ARTHUR, ed., *Encounter: Theory and Practice of Encounter Groups*. San Francisco: Jossey-Bass, 1969.

COYLE, GRACE L., *Group Experience and Democratic Values*. New York: Woman's Press, 1947.

FELIX, ROBERT H., et al., *Mental Health and Social Welfare*. New York: Columbia University Press, 1961.

HENDRY, CHARLES E., ed., *A Decade of Group Work*. New York: Association Press, 1948.

[19] Paul M. Limbert, "Major Trends and Developments in Professional Aspects of Group Work," in *A Decade of Group Work*, pp. 141 ff., 148–49; Herman D. Stein and Richard A. Cloward, *Social Perspectives in Behavior* (New York: Free Press 1959); Marjorie Murphy, *The Social Group Work Method in Social Work Education* (New York: Council on Social Work Education, 1959); M. K. McCullough and Peter J. Eli, *Social Work with Groups* (New York: Humanities Press, 1969).

Johnstone, Alexander, *Adventures in Social Work*. Fort Wayne, Ind., 1923.

Kaiser, Clara, "Characteristics of Social Work," *Social Welfare Forum* (1957), 158–69.

Klein, Alan F., "Individual Change Through Group Experience," *Social Welfare Forum* (1959), 136–55.

————, *Social Work Through Group Process*. Albany, N.Y.: University Press, 1970.

Konopka, Gisela, *Group Work in the Institution*. New York: Whiteside, 1954.

————, "The Method of Social Group Work," in Walter A. Friedlander, ed., *Concepts and Methods of Social Work*, Chap. 3. Englewood Cliffs, N.J.: Prentice-Hall, 1958.

————, *Social Group Work: A Helping Process*, 2nd ed. Englewood Cliffs, N.J.: Prentice-Hall, 1972.

————, *Therapeutic Group Work with Children*. Minneapolis: University of Minnesota Press, 1949.

Maier, Henry, *Group Work as Part of Residential Treatment*. New York: National Association of Social Workers, 1966.

Merrill, Francis E., *Society and Culture*, 4th ed. Englewood Cliffs, N.J.: Prentice-Hall, 1969.

Miller, Walter B., *Essentials of Group Work Skill*. New York: Association Press, 1957.

Mills, Theodore M., *The Sociology of Small Groups*. Englewood Cliffs, N.J.: Prentice-Hall, 1967.

Murray, Clyde E., Marse G. Bowens, and Russell Hogrefe, eds., *Group Work in Community Life*. New York: Association Press, 1959.

Phillips, Helen U., ed., *Achievement of Responsible Behavior Through Group Work Process*. Philadelphia: University of Pennsylvania Press, 1950.

Roberts, Ron E., *The New Communes: Coming Together in America*. Englewood Cliffs, N.J.: Prentice-Hall, 1971.

Schulze, Susanne, *Creative Group Living in a Children's Institution*. New York: Association Press, 1952.

Schwartz, William, and Serapio R. Zalba, *The Practice of Group Work*. New York: Columbia University Press, 1971.

Sherif, Muzafer, ed., *Intergroup Relations and Leadership*. New York: John Wiley, 1962.

Sullivan, Dorothea F., ed., *Readings in Group Work*. New York: Association Press, 1952.

Thomas, Edwin J., ed., *Behavioral Science for Social Workers*. New York: Free Press, 1967, pp. 425–32.

Trecker, Harleigh B., *Group Work Foundations and Frontiers*. New York: Whiteside, 1955.

————, *Social Group Work: Principles and Practice*, 3rd ed. New York: Whiteside, 1972.

Wilson, Gertrude, *Group Work and Case Work*. New York: Family Service Association of America, 1941.

Wilson, Gertrude, and Gladys Ryland, *Social Group Work Practice*. Boston: Houghton Mifflin, 1949.

6

community
organization

PRINCIPLES

Community organization is the social work process of intervention aimed at bringing about desired changes in human relations and social institutions.[1] Other professions besides social work also try to improve conditions

[1] Arnold Gurin, "Social Planning and Community Organization," *Encyclopedia of Social Work 1971*, p. 1325. Numerous attempts have been made to define community organization; see for example, Wayne McMillen, *Community Organization for Social Welfare* (Chicago: University of Chicago Press, 1949), pp. 2–22; Ernest B. Harper and Arthur Dunham, *Community Organization in Action* (New York: Association Press, 1959), pp. 23–27; and Ralph M. Kramer and Harry Specht, eds., *Readings in Community Organization Practice* (Englewood Cliffs, N.J.: Prentice-Hall, 1969).

in local communities, involving themselves in education, housing, public health, transportation, water supply, and sewage; but our discussion will be restricted to the processes related to social welfare programs and social work concerns.

The concepts of community organization have been derived from various sources, including John Dewey's ideas on liberal education, Kurt Lewin's principles of group dynamics, and sociological theory of community structure. Several disciplines have contributed to community organization theory.[2] Thus many terms have been used to characterize methods of community organization, such as *social welfare planning, social intergroup process, social welfare organization,* and *social engineering.* The National Association of Social Workers has called the process *community planning and development* since 1963. In the field of social welfare the main objectives of community organization are (1) to determine the most important social needs and their priorities, (2) to arrange for careful planning to meet these needs, (3) to coordinate and efficiently mobilize community forces to achieve these goals, and (4) to arrange for active participation of the population, including the recipients of welfare services, in formulating and pursuing the objectives of community organization and development.

In all social service programs in a democratic society, the active social support and the participation of the entire citizenship is essential. This is particularly necessary in community organization, which embodies outspoken concern with the need to improve social conditions and to effect social change. The social worker in the field of community organization, either as professional or as volunteer, must become well acquainted with the social needs in the community and the vital desire of its population for improvement of services and change of conditions. His task is the mobilization of those forces which enable the public and private social service organizations to coordinate their activities, to develop the necessary measures for economic and social improvements and establishment or development of physical and health services and institutions. In such services, social workers combine with city planners in the work of urban renewal and housing development, with public health experts in support for medical institutions and the establishment of community health services (see also Chapters 15 and 16), and with many other professions and citizens' groups in the field of social action. Community welfare work tends to be integrated

---

2 Clarence King, *Organizing for Community Action* (New York: Harper & Row, 1948), p. 22; Arthur Hillman, *Community Organization and Planning* (New York: Macmillan, 1950), pp. 13–14; Genevieve Carter, "Social Community Organization: Methods and Processes," in Walter A. Friedlander, ed., *Concepts and Methods of Social Work* (Englewood Cliffs, N.J.: Prentice-Hall, 1958), pp. 210–13; Murray Ross, "Conceptual Problems in Community Organization," *Social Service Review*, 30, No. 2 (June 1956), 174–84; and Pranal Chatterjee and Raymond Koloski, "The Concept of Community and Community Organization," *Social Work*, 15, No. 3 (July 1970), 82–92.

with the activities of numerous other professional and citizens' efforts, contributing its experience and knowledge of social conditions and human needs.[3]

HISTORY OF COMMUNITY ORGANIZATION

As we saw in Chapter 3, community organization in social welfare was one of the most effective operations of the Charity Organization movement and its councils of social agencies. Their attempts to coordinate the services of various private and public agencies led to improvements in relief for the poor and in raising funds for charitable purposes, as well as to the development of professional social work in the United States.[4]

The financing of voluntary social agencies of sectarian and philanthropic nature was long a major concern of the Charity Organization Societies and their agencies. The increasing number of religious and sectarian organizations led to continuous solicitation of well-to-do citizens for donations and contributions. Bankers, businessmen, lawyers, physicians, and others were approached daily by agencies, hospitals, and dispensaries competing for the favor of donations. Donors could not comprehend that such a variety of services were really necessary, since many of the activities of the organizations seemed to have the same objective. Many donors became annoyed and refused to contribute. In addition, it became known that a number of unscrupulous entrepreneurs pretended to ask donations for charitable purposes while actually betraying the trust of the donors or at least vastly exaggerating the value of the services they represented. For these reasons, community organization services created a separate organization for fund raising on the initiative of Mayor Newton D. Baker in Cleveland, under the title "Federation for Charity and Philanthropy" as a "community chest," later to be renamed "United Fund," which spread to most larger cities and counties of the United States. The United Fund tries to collect the necessary financial resources for voluntary welfare agencies, but also seeks to distribute contributions fairly to the participating agencies, always considering the changing social needs of the population, especially of dis-

---

[3] Arnold Gurin, "Social Planning and Community Organization," p. 1326; Duane W. Beck, "Changing Concepts of Social Work Treatment and Prevention of Problems on a Community Level," in John S. Morgan, et al., *Changing Services for Changing Clients* (New York: National Association of Social Workers, 1969), pp. 37–54; and Whitney Young, Jr., "Social Welfare's Responsibility in Urban Affairs," *Social Welfare Forum* (1967), 15–29.

[4] Frank Bruno, *Trends in Social Work* (New York: Columbia University Press, 1948), p. 194; McMillen, *Community Organization for Social Welfare*, pp. 416–17; Charles F. Grosser, "Community Organization and the Grass Roots," in Paul Weinberger, *Perspectives of Social Welfare* (Toronto: Macmillan, 1969), pp. 347–55.

advantaged minority groups. While for a long time private collections for voluntary welfare agencies seemed the only method of financing, now public welfare organizations have been supplementing private collections for voluntary agencies. Public agencies have assumed the basic responsibility for the provision of economic and social needs of the population since the enactment of the Social Security Act of 1935; private agencies and voluntary organizations now function mainly to supplement public services, particularly in the area of health services and research. However, private agencies still assume a substantial part of the total cost of social services in the United States. Ida Merriam estimates their contribution in recent years at 25 percent of the total expenditure for social welfare services.[5]

STRUCTURE OF COMMUNITY ORGANIZATION

Of the agencies which implement the function of community organization in social welfare, we shall discuss only those which operate on the local level; they are essential for social workers.[6]

Community organization functions in a city or county are carried out by (1) a council on social planning, (2) Community Chest or United Fund, (3) sometimes a coordinating council, (4) neighborhood councils, and (5) public and private social agencies. A social service exchange formerly operated in many cities, but this service has largely ceased.

1. *A Community Welfare Council* or *Council of Social Agencies,* recently called *Council of Social Planning,* exists in almost every city with a population of 100,000 or more, for the purpose of communitywide planning and coordination of the local health, welfare, and recreational services. The organization of the councils is not uniform, but the following features are characteristic of most of them. They are composed of representatives of all social agencies of welfare, health, and recreation which maintain standards acceptable to the council. Often some individuals, such as the mayor of the city and outstanding persons in the fields of philanthropy, health, welfare, and culture are members. The social agencies represented usually include public agencies, such as the department of public welfare, the public health department, the recreation and park commission, the board of education, and the juvenile court. Because public agencies are maintained by taxes, they participate in the work of the Community Wel-

---

[5] Ida C. Merriam, "Financing Social Welfare: Expenditures," *Encyclopedia of Social Work 1971,* pp. 416–24; Charles F. McNeill, "Financing Social Welfare: Voluntary Organizations," ibid., pp. 443–50.

[6] Organizations also exist at the state, federal, and international levels. See Charles I. Schottland, "Federal Planning for Health and Welfare," *Social Welfare Forum* (1963), 97–120.

fare Council without an interest in receiving financial support from money-raising campaigns. Some private agencies also may be members of the council without sharing in general collections for health and welfare purposes. Each social agency participating in the council is usually represented by two members, one the president or another member of the board of directors, and the other a professional social worker, in most instances the executive of the agency. In large cities or counties the council establishes a number of divisions, such as family welfare, child care and adoption, recreation, health and medical care services, and care for the aged, with committees to direct each division. Sometimes the council conducts a separate "Social Planning Bureau," a statistical and research bureau, and a public information bureau.

Councils of Social Agencies were the first form of community organization agencies. Their goal was to coordinate the existing programs of social welfare agencies, limited to voluntary agencies of charitable nature, and to assure a cooperative operation to mitigate or solve the social problems of the community. In contrast to the British charity organization societies (see pp. 33–35), representatives of public welfare agencies were only occasionally involved. Public relief was not considered the objective of the councils. Their main activities were directed toward the elimination of duplication of services, and for this purpose the councils established regular case conferences, social service exchanges, and common employment services. Fundamentally the councils wanted to maintain and strengthen the existing private social agencies. Their executive committees and boards of directors were composed of members of the board of the welfare agencies which had joined to form the council and of their executives. There was very little if any planning for the development of new welfare services, and even the elimination of overlapping and duplicated services was difficult because the agencies involved feared that their boards and employees would lose their jobs.

The second form of councils was the *Community Welfare Council.* It was distinguished from the Council of Social Agencies in that its board and executive committee no longer consisted only of the board and staff members of the constituent welfare agencies, but included outside members of the community, usually influential representatives of banking, industry, and the professions, sometimes of labor organizations but not representatives of the client groups. Still, the major function of the Community Welfare Council remained the coordination of the activities of the member agencies, to avoid duplication of service and waste of funds and to redistribute the services if a change occurred in the organization of some agencies and social institutions such as orphanages, hospitals, clinics, youth centers.

Community Welfare Councils were unable to change the power structure of the community and depended rather on this elite, particularly for their fund raising activities in community chests and campaigns. For this reason it was difficult for them to gain sufficient flexibility to develop broad welfare planning and the creation of new necessary services. This led to the third type of councils, the *Citizen Association for Health and Welfare Planning* or *Council of Social Planning,* which is no longer mainly composed of board and staff members of the voluntary welfare agencies, but of citizens outside these agencies, frequently also officials of public health agencies and city or county welfare departments, and of representatives of labor unions and more and more of some client groups. These associations face some difficulties since members of the local power groups and of local government prefer activities which are not controversial; they are hesitant to suggest changes in which their relatives, friends, customers, and clients have different preferences and opinions, such as race relations, desegregation of housing projects and other issues which do not have the full consensus of the community.[7] An example of the organization of a council is presented in Figure 1. The functions of a Community Welfare Council are frequently classified into the following activities:[8]

(a) *Coordination.* The meetings of the council with its lay board and staff members present to the public and private social agencies and to the citizens a picture of the health and welfare work performed in the community. Usually, the council distributes a bulletin and other pertinent information among its members. In these ways, members have an opportunity to share experiences, to develop mutual understanding, and to work together. Meetings and conferences permit them to identify common problems, to explore unmet needs of the population, and to eliminate duplication of effort. Thus, the council operates as a clearinghouse, permitting better service for the community.

(b) *Fact-finding.* Often, social and health conditions in the community must be investigated to determine the causes and the complexity of problems, the resources available for health and welfare services, and the cost and distribution of such services. Social research and surveys are necessary to acquire reliable knowledge of conditions that need change. Sometimes it is advisable to request outside experts or consultants to conduct such a survey because they are not biased in regard to the conservation of the existing social services and are able to compare conditions with those in other cities or regions. Committees in charge of evaluation of social surveys should be composed both of laymen and of professional

7 Edmund M. Burke, "The Road to Planning," *Social Service Review,* 39, No. 3 (September 1965), 261–70.

8 Campbell G. Murphy, "Community Organization for Social Welfare," *Social Work Year Book* (1960), 186–91; Howard F. Gustafson, "Community Welfare Councils," ibid., 191–98; Arthur Hillman, *Sociology and Social Work* (Washington, D.C.: Public Affairs Press, 1956), pp. 43–45; Wayne McMillen, "Urban and Regional Welfare Planning," *Encyclopedia of Social Work 1965,* pp. 801–7.

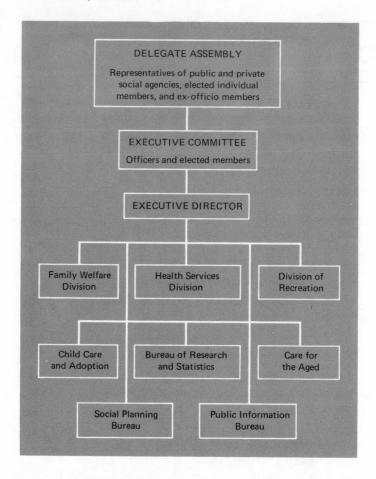

Figure 1.   Organizational Structure of a Council of Social Planning

workers. They should convey the findings and recommendations of the survey, not only to the members of the council, but also to the general public.

(c) *Joint action*. The advantage of a Community Council on Social Planning is that it combines a large number of organizations and mobilizes, through its board and lay members, important forces in the community. As a result, it is able to conduct careful joint planning on the basis of research and examination of the prevailing conditions, and to enlist the support of many groups in carrying out the measures recommended by its fact-finding committee.

(d) *Improving the quality of service*. The observation and evaluation of the quality of services rendered by the social agencies of the community is an important function of the council. The council attempts to improve inadequate services by consulting with board members and by providing intensive staff training courses.

(e) *Common services.* Certain welfare activities are of value to the entire community. Activities such as the compilation of a central index, usually called a "social service exchange," or the maintenance of a central volunteer bureau are the proper responsibilities of a Council on Social Planning. Other services include a central information bureau, or a research and statistical bureau or institute. Further possibilities might include a joint intake bureau for casework, child care, guidance services, a volunteer bureau, or a joint homemaker service.

(f) *Developing public understanding.* One of the essential objectives of the Community Council on Social Planning is to bring the value of the work of social agencies to the attention of the people and to enlist their understanding, concern, and active participation in these services.[9] Social surveys have shown that a large percentage of the citizens have a very vague notion of what social agencies do and why they are necessary. To bring the facts to the people and to impart to them clear, objective, basic information about health and social conditions and the role of social and health agencies is a real challenge for the community welfare council. Such councils may be effective in developing community leaders—lay persons who have a clear understanding of the need for health and welfare services and who are able to convey their knowledge to the people.

2. *The Community Chest* was formed because private social agencies depend on voluntary contributions to finance their services and their personnel. A cooperative method of raising the necessary funds for these activities is required to avoid dissatisfaction and hostility among the people who are called on for contributions to private social agencies and to secure fair support for all essential welfare organizations.[10] As a rule, the Community Chest or the United Fund is governed by a board of directors which represents not only social agencies that are members of the Chest, but also citizens constituting a broad cross-section of the population of the area. In large cities these representatives form a delegate association of the Com-

[9] See Genevieve Carter. "Characteristics of Community Organization Practice in Social Work," in Walter Friedlander, et al., *Concepts and Methods of Social Work* (Englewood Cliffs, N.J.: Prentice-Hall, 1958), 201–9; Lucy P. Carner, "The Youth and Government Project," *National Conference of Social Work, Selected Papers in Group Work and Community Organization* (1952), 12–16; Herman Levin, "Voluntary Organizations in Social Welfare," *Encyclopedia 1971*, pp. 1519–25.

[10] Lyman S. Ford, "Federated Financing," *Encyclopedia of Social Work 1965*, 327–32; Edith Varon, "Communication: Chest, Community, and Agency," *Social Work*, 9, No. 2 (April 1964), 51–57; Robert Morris, ed., *Centrally Planned Change: Prospects and Concepts* (New York: National Association of Social Workers, 1964); and C. F. McNeil, "Financing Social Welfare: Voluntary Organizations," *Encyclopedia 1971*, pp. 443–50.

munity Chest and elect a board of directors, which supervises the operations of the Chest and sets up its policies. The management of the Chest is directed through an executive committee and its officers (president, secretary, and treasurer), as well as through the executive director who usually is appointed by the board of directors. There are laymen and representatives of other social agencies on both the board of directors and the executive committee of the Chest. Frequently they represent the public welfare department, the board of education, the health department, and the recreation commission. They advise the Chest concerning the population's need for voluntary health, recreation, and welfare services, and support the endeavor to raise funds for private agencies. The most important work of the Chest is entrusted to the budget committee and to the campaign committee. The budget committee is composed of some members of the executive committee, other lay persons, and representatives of the Council on Social Planning. Prior to the annual campaign, usually in September, all participating social agencies submit a detailed budget for the subsequent year and request a certain share in the funds to be raised by the drive. The budget committee carefully studies the requests, compares them with former budgets, and discusses each agency's request with its representatives. The budget committee then estimates the total amount of money that may be raised by the campaign and revises, in view of this estimate, the plan for the allocation of funds to individual agencies. The adjusted budget is submitted to the executive committee or to the board of directors for approval.

The campaign committee is in charge of the preparation of the annual drive. It invites church, civic, and youth organizations to enlist volunteers for a house-to-house canvass. It appoints special subcommittees and captains for individual contributions and special drives among industries, apartment houses, service clubs, banks, professional associations, and organized labor groups. The committee supervises the campaign, which usually lasts no longer than one month or six weeks. An illustration of the pattern of Chest organization is shown in Figure 2.

To carry on a successful campaign, the Community Chest has to interpret to the population the necessity, as well as the extent and quality, of recreational, health, and welfare services offered in the community. That a close working relationship with the Council on Social Planning is necessary in this respect is obvious, considering that both agencies have similar objectives. The Chest's interpretation of the need for health and welfare services is a cooperative effort with the public information task of the council and is usually carried out after joint planning. From the financial point of view, the Community Chest promotes the most efficient, coordinated, and well-integrated services. The Chest avoids duplications of work, conducts research regarding the social and health needs, and encourages careful planning and evaluation of projects and welfare operations.

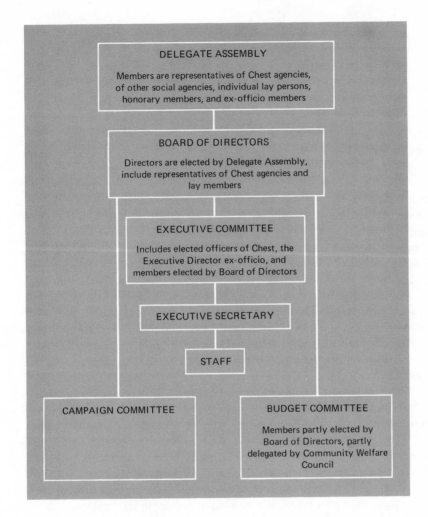

Figure 2. Organizational Structure of a United Fund

Because the Community Chest assumes the responsibility for the financial support of private social agencies, for the fund-raising campaign, and for a fair distribution of the collected contributions, the Council on Social Planning is free to concentrate its attention on social surveys and research, coordination of health, welfare, and recreation services, and program planning.

The principle of joint fund-raising for welfare purposes, as represented by the Community Chest, is basically sound, but Chests and United Funds have not been able to raise the necessary money because of the disunity and competition of the voluntary welfare agencies. The larger health agencies refuse to participate. During recent years, the amount of contributions for health and welfare services collected from federated campaigns was about one-fifth of the total, but the large national health agencies and often the Red Cross raised 80 percent of their funds outside the federated campaign. Public taxes and social insurance benefits are used substantially for payment of social and health services, and it is expected that the rising level of middle-class family income and social insurance benefits enable more people to pay fees for social and health services, insofar as such expenses are not covered by the health insurance for aged people.

A number of important health and welfare agencies, especially the National Tuberculosis Association, the National Foundation, the American Heart Association, the National Society for Crippled Children and Adults, and the American Cancer Society, do not join in the local drive of the Community Chests and insist on carrying on their own campaigns. Citizens have been dissatisfied by near-monthly independent appeals of these health organizations made in addition to the annual campaigns of the Community Chest.[11]

In general, Community Chests welcome special donations and bequests made independently of the regular annual campaign. In some metropolitan cities a separate Community Fund has been organized to receive and administer such donations and bequests for charitable purposes and health and welfare services. There is planned cooperation between the Fund and the local Chest.[12]

In some cities the Community Welfare Council and the Community Chest are combined in a single organization. In other instances, where a separate council and Chest operate, the necessary teamwork is secured by the employment of one executive and staff for both the council and the Community Chest. Both organizations share offices and other facilities and have common research and public relations committees.

(3) *The Coordinating Council* is a citizens' group created for coordinating the social forces of a municipal district to deal with specific social problems (primarily juvenile delinquency). Coordinating Councils have been

---

[11] F. Emerson Andrews, "Fund Raising," in Ernest B. Harper and Arthur Dunham, eds., *Community Organization in Action* (New York: Association Press, 1959), pp. 266–74; Harold J. Seymour, "The Successful Fund-Raising Campaign," ibid., pp. 275–79; Ida C. Merriam, "Financing Social Welfare Services," *Encyclopedia of Social Work 1965*, pp. 344–45; Gordon Manser, ibid., pp. 825–29; C. F. McNeil, "Financing Social Welfare: Voluntary Organizations"; Beatrice Dinerman, "Community Chests: The Ignorant Philanthropists," *The Nation*, 219, No. 12 (March 20, 1970), 269–72.

[12] Essential national coordinating functions are performed by the National Social Welfare Assembly, the National Health Council, and the National Budget and Consultation Committee. Private foundation grants are valuable in the field of youth services, services for the aging, delinquency prevention, and community planning.

discontinued in most cities in recent years or are organized as subcomittees of the Council on Social Planning.

(4) *The Neighborhood Council* is a citizens' committee organized to improve social conditions of particular importance to a certain neighborhood. Some of the neighborhood councils have grown from planning committees in settlement houses; others have been encouraged by a Council of Social Agencies, a Parent-Teacher Association, or other civic or religious societies. During the last years, similar Neighborhood Councils were established in slum regions to serve as agencies for the "Anti-poverty Program," developing community action programs (see Chapter 10.) Social workers usually participate in the work of Neighborhood Councils as individuals or as representatives of their social agencies, but they are a minority; laymen form the majority of the council. The Neighborhood Council is not concerned with the wide range of social welfare and health questions, as is the Community Welfare Council.[13]

The Neighborhood Council frequently attempts to improve local facilities for recreation, parks and playgrounds, or summer camp facilities for school children. It may be concerned with the establishment of a community center, the improvement of sanitary or housing conditions within the area, the founding of a consumers' cooperative to restrict high living costs, or the setting up of garbage collection policies. The new neighborhood councils in the "Antipoverty Program" are mainly the representation of the poor themselves to develop community action and special services for the unemployed and needy families.[14] The local character of the Neighborhood Council encourages intensified interest in its members. In some cities, such as Pittsburgh, Pennsylvania, all Neighborhood Councils have founded a federation, and use the professional staff of the federation for their programs and activities.

[13] A. Hillman, *Community Organization and Planning* (New York: Macmillan, 1950), pp. 218–27; August Vollmer, "Crime Can Be Checked," *Community Organization*, 7 (March–April 1939), 3–4; Robert Morris and Robert H. Binstock, *Feasible Planning for Social Change* (New York: Columbia University Press, 1966); Melvin B. Mogulow, "Neighborhood Service Centers," *Encyclopedia 1971*, pp. 857–65; Roland L. Warren, "Neighborhoods in Urban Areas," ibid., pp. 872–82; and Willis D. Hawley and Frederick M. Wirt, *The Search for Community Power* (Englewood Cliffs, N.J.: Prentice-Hall, 1968).

[14] A very militant action program for social change is recommended by Saul D. Alinsky, *Reveille for Radicals* (Chicago: University of Chicago Press, 1945), and *Citizen Participation and Community Organization in Planning and Urban Renewal* (Chicago: National Association of Housing and Redevelopment Officials, 1962); other aspects are discussed by Daniel P. Moynihan, "Urban Conditions: General," *The Annals*, 371 (May 1967), 165–75; Edward J. Donnell and Marilyn M. Sullivan, "Service Delivery and Social Action Through the Neighborhood Center," *Welfare in Review*, 7, No. 4 (November 1969), 1–18; and Edward J. Donnell and Otto M. Reid, "The Multiservice Neighborhood Center," *Welfare in Review*, 9, No. 3 (June 1971), 1–8.

During the last decade neighborhood centers have gained increasing importance as social agencies. Numerous centers are located in urban districts with large minority populations, especially black neighborhoods, but only a few serve American Indians and Orientals. These centers provide direct client services, social action, information, and client advocacy.

Among the activities of community organization in social welfare, the planning process is assuming vital importance. Social planning is carried out on the local as well as on the state and federal levels above all by public agencies, by municipal, county, and state departments of social services, state bureaus of the budget, voluntary councils on social planning, and on the federal level by the Federal Office of Management and Budget.[15]

(5) *The Social Service Exchange* was a federation of welfare and health agencies which maintained a central, confidential register, and a cooperative clearing service which listed all persons known to health and welfare agencies. Sometimes the title "Social Service Index" or "Confidential Exchange" was used. The purpose of the Social Service Exchange was clearance so that each social agency knew whether persons applying for aid or service received similar or other care by another organization, and so that fraud, duplication of efforts, and waste were avoided.[16]

(6) *Community organization by individual social agencies* is usually executed by high-standard agencies, such as family welfare agencies, child protective or child care agencies, adoption societies, and health services. This secondary function of these agencies may involve the development of recreational facilities in cooperation with lay groups and public authorities, establishment of a mental hygiene clinic or other joint treatment facilities, or the raising of funds for such special goals as the construction of a clinic or hospital. Individual agencies are active in community organization where no council on social planning has been established.

We have discussed so far the structure of local community organization. On the state level only a few State Councils of Social Work coordinate the services of public and private welfare and health agencies. But in a variety of advisory committees and commissions and State Conferences of Social Work, representatives of public and private social agencies work together with lay persons to encourage better use of resources. Certain organi-

15 Robert Perlman and Arnold Gurin, *Community Organization and Social Planning* (New York: John Wiley, 1971); Martin Rein and Robert Morris, "Goals, Structure and Strategies for Community Change," in *Social Work Practice* (New York: Columbia University Press, 1962), p. 135; Roland R. Warren, *Perspectives on the American Community* (Chicago: Rand McNally, 1966). For more detail see Chapter 8.

16 Morton I. Teicher, "Let's Abolish the Social Service Exchange," *Social Work Journal*, 33, No. 1 (January 1952), 28–31; Stephen L. Angell and Frank T. Greving, "A New Look at the Social Service Exchange," *Social Work Journal*, 36, No. 1 (January 1955); and Kenneth I. Williams, "Social Service Exchanges," *Encyclopedia 1971*, pp. 1434–37.

zations have been set up on a regional basis, comprising several states, such as the Regional Conferences of the Child Welfare League of America and the Southern Regional Council, which attempts to improve civic, economic, and racial conditions of the black population in the southern states.

National organizations in the field of social welfare under public and private auspices are also interested in the process of developing adequate standards, and enlisting public support. Their large number makes integration and coordination on the national level difficult. The National Assembly for Social Policy and Development, Inc. represents voluntary health and welfare agencies as their central national organization. The Assembly encourages cooperation of public and private social welfare programs, attempts planning of field services with states and local communities on the national level, and assigns larger roles to its individual members. Community organization is carried on by the National Association of Social Workers,[17] by various national religious and humanitarian organizations, and by such agencies as the American Public Welfare Association, the Child Welfare League of America, the Family Service Association of America, and the United Community Funds and Councils of America. The United States Department of Health, Education and Welfare helps improve standards of service by studies, research, publications, and conferences.

On the international level the functions of most organizations are concerned with welfare and health services in foreign countries and devoted to achieving international cooperation and integration of methods, skills, and resources. United Nations Relief and Rehabilitation Agency during and after World War II, the United Nations, Department of Social Affairs, the Economic and Social Council (ECOSOC), the World Health Organization, and UNESCO are examples of agencies active in international community organization.

SOCIAL ACTION

In the field of community organization, social action has assumed an essential role, particularly during the past decade. Social action is individual or group activity aimed at achieving a change in social policy and at improving social services. Kenneth Pray defines it as "the systematic con-

17 Leonard W. Mayo and Robert M. Webb, "National Organizations in Social Welfare," *Social Work Year Book* (1960), 408–16; Robert E. Bondy, "National Voluntary Organizations," *Encyclopedia of Social Work 1965*, pp. 527–30; Bernard J. Coughlin, *Church and State in Social Welfare* (New York: Columbia University Press, 1964). See also Arnold Gurin, "Factors that Influence Decisions in Community Planning," *Journal of Jewish Communal Service*, 38, No. 1 (Fall 1956), 41–51; Robert Morris, "New Concepts in Community Organization," *Social Welfare Forum* (1961), 128–45; and Daniel Thursz, "The Arsenal of Social Action Strategies: Options for Social Workers," *Social Work*, 16, No. 1 (January 1971), 27–34.

scientious effort directly to influence the basic social conditions and policies out of which arise the problems of social adjustment and maladjustment to which our services as social workers are addressed."[18]

In their casework and group work functions, social workers help individuals and groups. But they also become aware of social phenomena which cause general health and welfare problems. As a result, they recognize the need for social change. Their knowledge qualifies them to participate in social action in cooperation with civic leaders and organizations, churches, city planners, public health officers, and labor groups. Their special competence is based on their value orientation and sense of social responsibility, their commitment to social progress, their awareness of social problems and conditions and the possibilities of their solution, their training in objective observation, analysis and planning, and their skill in organizing people for social progress.[19] For these reasons, social action is an essential part of professional social work and is the responsibility of every social worker.

There are theoretical questions whether social action should be classified as a separate process of social work, but there is no doubt that social workers need to feel responsible for their participation in social action. Essential elements of social action are that group action is necessary, though the initiative may be taken by one or a few individuals; the movement must be concerted; the movement should attempt to achieve social changes in the interest of the people; and the action should be taken in accordance with law.[20]

[18] Kenneth Pray, "Social Work and Social Action," *National Conference of Social Work, Proceedings 1945*, p. 346; see also Daniel Thursz, "Social Action," *Encyclopedia of Social Work 1971*, pp. 1189–95; Eveline M. Burns, "Social Action and the Professional Social Worker," *The Compass* (May 1947), 37–40; Wilbur J. Cohen, "What Every Social Worker Should Know About Political Action," *Social Work*, 11, No. 3 (July 1966), 3–11; Sidney H. Aronson and Clarence C. Sherwood, "Problems in Social Action Research," *Social Work*, 12, No. 4 (October 1967), 89–96; and Joel Fort, "Bureaucracy as a Social Problem," *Journal of Public Social Services*, 1, No. 1 (March 1970), 13–15.

[19] Elizabeth Wickenden, "Social Action," *Social Work Year Book* (1960), 529–35, and "Social Action," *Encyclopedia of Social Work 1965*, pp. 697–703; George A. Brager, "Advocacy and Political Behavior," *Social Work*, 13, No. 2 (April 1968), 5–15; Irwin Epstein, "Social Workers and Social Action," *Social Work*, 13, No. 2 (April 1968), 101–8.

[20] Rudolph T. Danstedt, "Political Action vs. Individualized Treatment in Social Welfare Work," and Clarke A. Chambers, "A Political Perspective on Political Action vs. Individualized Treatment," in *Current Issues in Social Work in Historical Perspective* (New York: Council on Social Work Education, 1962), pp. 45–64; Martin Rein, "Organization for Social Change," *Social Work*, 9, No. 2 (April 1964), 32–41; Thomas D. Sherrard and Richard Murray, "The Church and Neighborhood Community Organization," *Social Work*, 10, No. 3 (July 1965), 3–14; Charles F. Grosser, "Community Development Program Serving the Poor," *Social Work*, 10, No. 3 (July 1965), 15–21; Bernard J. Frieden and Robert Morris, *Urban Planning and*

Social action involves influencing public opinion through information or educational publicity. Promoting social legislation by pressure on legislators is another form of social action. A typical form of social action is the "legislative council," an organization formed by representatives of various civic and church groups, labor unions, and social workers. These councils serve as a clearinghouse for all groups concerned with social legislation, and they organize citizens and organizations for the support of essential measures of social legislation. The public, as well as social workers, often fear social action because they are afraid that "radicals" or "communists" might be pulling the wires. In fact, however, such social reform movements frequently have been begun by rather conservative groups.

The aims of social action include social advance in the practice or interpretation of social work and improvement of conditions of child and woman labor, housing, and slum clearance. It attempts, through social change, to prevent social maladjustment, illness, and social disorganization. At the same time, it is concerned for the well-being, the self-respect, and the dignity of the individual, as are casework and group work.

Social workers have long considered participation in social action to be one of their professional duties because they have intimate knowledge of those social conditions which require reform. Many social workers have been pioneers in social action in the period of social reform and during the Depression (1930 to 1935). Social workers as a profession have been accused of not exercising the influence in social policy and social reform which could be expected from them on the basis of their experiences, because they are exclusively interested in individualized treatment.[21] Social workers who are actively engaged in social action, on the other hand, have been criticized for confusing their civic and professional obligations. Nevertheless, social workers and their professional organizations have taken an energetic interest in the civil rights movement, in school desegregation, and in dynamic support for minority groups in recent years.

Criticisms suggest that a careful rethinking of the social worker's role in social action and social reform, based on his experiences and his professional philosophy and responsibility, is necessary.

Social Policy (New York: Basic Books, 1968); Daniel Thursz, "The Arsenal of Social Action Strategies," *Social Work,* 16, No. 1 (January 1971), 27–34; Rein, *Social Policy: Issues of Choice and Change* (New York: Random House, 1970).

21 Joseph E. Paul, "Social Action for a Different Decade," *Social Service Review,* 45, No. 1 (March 1971), 30–36; Milton Rokeach, *Beliefs, Attitudes, and Values* (San Francisco: Jossey-Bass, 1968); Alan Wade, "Social Work and Political Action," *Social Work,* 9, No. 4 (October 1964), 100–107.

SELECTED BIBLIOGRAPHY

ADRIAN, CHARLES, *Social Science and Community Action.* East Lansing: Michigan State University Press, 1960.

ANDREWS, F. EMERSON, *Corporation Giving.* New York: Russell Sage Foundation, 1952.

————, *Philanthropic Giving.* New York: Russell Sage Foundation, 1950.

BAKER, HELEN CODY, and MARY SWAIN ROUTZAHN, *How to Interpret Social Welfare.* New York: Russell Sage Foundation, 1947.

BUELL, BRADLEY, et al., *Community Planning for Human Services.* New York: Columbia University Press, 1952.

CAMPBELL, ALAN K., *The States and the Urban Crisis* (Englewood Cliffs, N.J.: Prentice-Hall, 1970.

CARTER, GENEVIEVE W., "Social Work Community Organization Methods and Processes," in Walter A. Friedlander, ed., *Concepts and Methods of Social Work.* Englewood Cliffs, N.J.: Prentice-Hall, 1958, pp. 201–82.

CARY, LEE J., ed., *Community Development as a Process.* Columbia: University of Missouri Press, 1970.

CLINARD, MARSHALL B., *Slums and Community Development.* New York: Free Press, 1970.

COHEN, NATHAN E., "Reversing the Process of Social Disorganization," in Alfred J. Kahn, ed., *Issues in American Social Work.* New York: Columbia University Press, 1959, pp. 138–58.

COUGHLIN, BERNARD, "Community Planning: A Challenge to Social Work," *Social Work,* 6, No. 4 (October 1961), 37–42.

DIMOCK, MARSHALL, *The Executive in Action.* New York: Harper, 1945.

DUNHAM, ARTHUR, *The New Community Organization.* New York: Crowell, 1970.

GREEN, HELEN D., *Social Work Practice in Community Organization.* New York: Whiteside, 1954.

GUSTAFSON, HOWARD F., "Emerging Concepts in Community Planning," *Social Welfare Forum* (1960), 154–65.

HARPER, ERNEST B., and ARTHUR DUNHAM, *Community Organization in Action.* New York: Association Press, 1959.

HEATH, MONNA, and ARTHUR DUNHAM, *Trends in Community Organization.* Chicago: University of Chicago Press, 1963.

HILLMAN, ARTHUR, *Community Organization and Planning.* New York: Macmillan, 1950.

————, *Neighborhood Centers Today: Action Programs for a Rapidly Changing World.* New York: National Federation of Settlements, 1960.

JOHNS, RAY E., *The Cooperative Process Among National Social Agencies.* New York: Association Press, 1946.

KING, CLARENCE, *Organizing for Community Action.* New York: Harper, 1948.

KRAMER, RALPH M., "Community Organization and Administration: Integration or Separate but Equal?" *Education for Social Work,* 2, No. 2 (Fall 1966), 48–56.

KRAMER, RALPH M., and HARRY SPECHT, *Reading in Community Organization Practice.* Englewood Cliffs, N.J.: Prentice-Hall, 1969.

LEVIN, HERMAN, "The Essential Voluntary Agency," *Social Work,* 11, No. 1 (January 1966), 98–106.

LIPPITT, RONALD, et al., *The Dynamics of Planned Change.* New York: Harcourt, 1958.

McMILLEN, WAYNE, *Community Organization for Social Welfare,* 6th impression. Chicago: University of Chicago Press, 1954.

———, "Urban and Regional Welfare Planning," *Encyclopedia of Social Work 1965,* pp. 801–7.

NORDHAUS, WILLIAM D., *Invention, Growth and Welfare: A Theoretical Treatment of Technological Change.* Cambridge, Mass.: M.I.T. Press, 1969.

NORTH, CECIL C., *The Community and Social Welfare: A Study in Community Organization.* New York: McGraw-Hill, 1931.

PIFER, ALAN, *The Nongovernmental Organization at Bay.* New York: Carnegie Corp., 1966.

POLSBY, NELSON W., *Community Power and Political Theory.* New Haven, Conn.: Yale University Press, 1963.

ROSS, MURRAY G., *Community Organization Theory and Principles.* New York: Harper, 1955.

SCHOTTLAND, CHARLES I., *Community Organization 1958.* New York: Columbia University Press, 1958.

SHERRARD, THOMAS D., "Planned Community Change," *Social Welfare Forum* (1964), 100–118.

SORENSEN, ROY, *The Art of Board Membership.* New York: Association Press, 1950.

STANTON, ESTHER, *Client Come Last: Volunteers and Welfare Organizations.* Beverly Hills, Calif.: Sage Publications, 1970.

TRETTEN, RUDIE W., *Cities in Crisis.* Englewood Cliffs, N.J.: Prentice-Hall, 1970.

WARREN, ROLAND L., *Politics and the Ghettos.* New York: Atherton Press, 1968.

———, *Studying Your Community.* New York: Russell Sage Foundation, 1955.

WEISSMAN, HAROLD H., *Community Councils and Community Control.* Pittsburgh: University of Pittsburgh Press, 1970.

ZALD, MAYER N., "Organizations as Politics: An Analysis of Community Organization Agencies," *Social Work,* 9, No. 4 (October 1966), 56–65.

Social Action

ALTMEYER, ARTHUR J., "The Dynamics of Social Work," *Social Welfare Forum* (1955), 98–111.

BENNIS, KENNETH D., et al., *The Planning of Change.* New York: Holt, Rinehart and Winston, 1961.

BETTELHEIM, BRUNO, and MORRIS JANOWITZ, *Social Change and Prejudice.* New York: Free Press, 1964.

COSER, LEWIS, *Continuities in the Study of Social Conflict.* New York: Free Press, 1969.

———, *The Function of Social Conflict.* New York: Free Press, 1965.

DE SCHWEINITZ, KARL, "Social Values and Social Action—The Intellectual Base," in Ernest Witte, ed., *Education for Social Work.* New York: Council on Social Work Education, 1956, pp. 55–68.

GREER, THOMAS H., *American Social Reform Movements: Their Pattern Since 1865.* Englewood Cliffs, N.J.: Prentice-Hall, 1949.

LEYS, WAYNE P. R., *Ethics for Policy Decisions.* Englewood Cliffs, N.J.: Prentice-Hall, 1952.

LURIE, HARRY L., "Social Action: A Motive Force in Democracy," *National Conference of Social Work, Proceedings 1941,* 631–41.

MacRAY, R. H., "Social Work and Social Action," *Social Service Review,* 40, No. 1 (March 1966), 1–7.

OHLIN, LLOYD E., "The Development of Social Action Theories," in Ernest Witte, ed., *Education for Social Work, 1958.* New York: Council on Social Work Education, 1958, pp. 77–87.

PERRUCCI, ROBERT, and MARC PILISUK, *The Triple Revolution Emerging—Social Problems in Depth.* Boston: Little, Brown, 1971.

PRAY, KENNETH L. M., "Social Work and Social Action," *National Conference of Social Work, Proceedings* 1941, 348–59.

REIN, MARTIN, *Social Policy: Issues of Choice and Change.* New York: Random House, 1970.

RIOLIN, ALICE M., *Systematic Thinking for Social Action.* Washington, Brookings Institution, 1970.

SCHOTTLAND, CHARLES I., "Social Work Issues in the Political Arena," *Social Welfare Forum* (1953), 18–33.

SOLENDER, SANFORD, "Social Action," *Social Work Year Book* (1957), 517–25.

———, *Citizen Boards at Work: New Challenge to Effective Action.* New York: Association Press, 1970.

WICKENDEN, ELIZABETH, *How to Influence Public Policy—A Short Manual on Social Action.* New York: American Association of Social Workers, 1954.

———, "Social Action," *Encyclopedia of Social Work 1965,* pp. 697–703.

———, "Social Action," *Social Work Year Book* (1960), 529–35.

YOUNG, WHITNEY M., JR., "Services for Racial and Minority Groups," *Encyclopedia of Social Work 1965,* 683–88.

YOUNGDAHL, BENJAMIN, "The Role of Social Agencies in Social Action," *Social Work Journal,* 33, No. 3 (July 1952), 146–48.

7

ancillary social welfare processes

SOCIAL WELFARE ADMINISTRATION

The administration of public and private social agencies is designed to achieve the full effect of the services for which they have been established. In this chapter we shall discuss the principles that rule the administration of social welfare organizations. Administration of social agencies translates the provisions of social legislation and the aims of private philanthropy and religious charities into the dynamics and delivery of services and benefits for humanity. Management of social agencies is oriented to aid people in the most efficient way possible; it has been briefly described as the "art of human relations."[1]

The skills of administration are not limited to social welfare settings. They are derived from public administration and from the techniques of business management. But the special objective of social services—to help human beings—is an element which distinguishes the management of social agencies from that of commercial and industrial enterprises and from other activities that do not directly deal with human beings.

Social work administration involves making judgments and using professional knowledge and skill which differ from those required in business administration, or even in the management of schools, hospitals, and churches.[2]

Administration of public social agencies is complicated by the specific roles legally assigned to the three levels of government: federal, state, and local. The administration is determined by laws and statutes, its budget by decisions of the legislative body that allocates the annual appropriations and indirectly influences the appointment of personnel. Our constitutional principle of the separation of powers has not always been observed in the administration of public welfare, because courts have assumed administrative functions such as the disbursement of mothers' pensions, orphans' allowances, and workmen's compensation. The trend, however, is toward an assignment of executive functions to administrative bodies.

Policies in public welfare administration are primarily established at the state level by state departments of public welfare. State offices of administration and state budget bureaus play a significant role in welfare administration and influence public welfare practice. The policies of federal agencies (such as veterans' services, old-age and survivors' insurance) are determined by the federal government. Public welfare administration, like other government operations, requires clear objectives and policies and an efficient organizational structure with precise staff organization, sound methods of selection, recruitment, and promotion of personnel, decent working conditions, and fiscal accounting and control as guarantees for responsible management.

---

[1] Karl de Schweinitz, *People and Process in Social Security* (Washington, D.C.: American Council on Education, 1948), p. 20. Other definitions are "facilitating activities necessary and incidental to the giving of direct service by a social agency" (Arthur Dunham); "the process of transforming social policy into social service" (John C. Kidneigh); and "the process of defining and attaining the objectives of an organization through a system of coordinated and co-operative effort" (Herman D. Stein); see also Arthur H. Kruse, "Administration of Social Agencies," *Social Work Year Book* (1960), 79–85; Rosemary C. Sarri, "Administration in Social Welfare," *Encyclopedia 1971*, pp. 40–44.

[2] Herman D. Stein, "Administration," *Encyclopedia of Social Work 1965*, pp. 58–62; James D. Thompson, "Elements in Administration," *Social Welfare Forum* (1962), 181–201; and Harry A. Schatz, *Social Work Administration* (New York: Council on Social Work Education, 1970).

There are, nevertheless, important differences from other types of government functions. Social service administration requires thorough experience with the philosophy and methods of social welfare, knowledge of social legislation and social work practice. Above all, public welfare administration demands a sincere appreciation of and devotion to the specific objectives of social welfare and its inherent social philosophy. This identification with the aims and function of social welfare should be required not only of the executive of a social agency and his assistants, but of the entire staff.

Functions of Welfare Administration

The main administrative functions of a private or public social agency may be divided into nine activities: (1) fact-finding; (2) analysis of social conditions and of services to meet human needs; (3) decision on the best way of reaching this objective; (4) planning and allocating resources; (5) setting up organizational structure and work assignments; (6) staffing the agency; (7) supervising and controlling personnel and finances; (8) recording and accounting; and (9) supplying financial resources.[3] The first four functions may be characterized as "enterprise determination," the other five as "enterprise execution."[4]

1. Fact-finding depends on the social agency's program and objectives which, in turn, are determined by whether the agency is a public institution or a private organization. Fact-finding requires research of the social or health conditions which make the planned services of the agency necessary. In case of a public agency, the results of the research findings are submitted to the legislative body which decides about the action to be taken (for instance, the establishment of a child guidance clinic by the county board of supervisors). A private social agency might be set up when the results of the preceding research are presented to a council on social planning or to a group of interested citizens (for instance, proving the need for the foundation of an adoption agency for children of minority groups).

2. An analysis of the social problems which the agency serves permits it to estimate

---

[3] Walter Friedlander, *Concepts and Methods of Social Work* (Englewood Cliffs, N.J.: Prentice-Hall, 1958), pp. 288–92; Herman D. Stein, "Board, Executive, and Staff," *Social Welfare Forum* (1962), 215–30; and David Fanshel, "Administrative Issues in the Organization of Research Activities," *Social Casework*, 14, No. 10 (December 1963), 563–68.

[4] William Brownrigg, *The Human Enterprise Process and Its Administration* (University: University of Alabama Press, 1954); Peter Drucker, *The Practice of Management* (New York: Harper, 1954); Herbert Simon, *Administrative Behavior* (New York: Macmillan, 1957); Harleigh B. Trecker, *New Understandings of Administration* (New York: Association Press, 1961); James D. Thompson, *Organization in Action* (New York: McGraw-Hill, 1967); Harold Wilensky, *Organizational Intelligence* (New York: Basic Books, 1967); Harry Schatz, *Social Work Administration* (New York: Council on Social Work Education, 1970).

the type and number of services that will be needed, and to evaluate the trends for the future, based on statistical data of previous experiences.

3. After the agency diagnoses present social needs, it must decide which alternative course of action to follow, considering its resources, both personal and financial, as well as deciding how it can make the most constructive use of personnel and equipment.

4. Planning and allocating resources is carried out, on the basis of the preceding choice of alternatives, while considering how the objectives of the social agency may best be realized. The immediate and long-range goals of the agency are clarified and policies developed which direct the work of the agency to meet the changing needs of its clients.

5. Setting up the organizational structure of the agency leads to a distribution of duties to the members of the staff with a clear definition of responsibilities concerning their work, delegation of authority, and supervision; a description of staff and line services, and the establishment of standardized operations. It includes the delegation of everyone's authority, so that each member of the staff knows exactly what his assignment and responsibilities are.[5]

6. Personnel administration determines policies on recruitment and employment in the agency, on tenure, promotions, salaries, vacations, and working conditions. A fair evaluation of the performance of the staff is necessary to ensure efficient service and good morale. Rules for retirement and dismissal, inservice training, and grievance procedures are part of personnel administration.

7. Control of the agency's operation secures the proper function of the organization and the attainment of its objectives. It requires coordination of the staff's activities, supervision, and regular communication, consultation services, staff conferences, and financial control measures.

8. Recording and accounting for all essential activities and material expenses of the agency are necessary to provide a reliable analysis of its budgetary operations which have to be reported to its governing body and to the membership or legislative authority under which the social agency works. It allows for an evaluation of the efficiency of the operations and suggests possible improvements. It may be used for recommendations for modifications of the social policy of the agency.

9. The mobilization of the financial resources of the agency depends on its nature and structure. In public agencies, the administration of the budget requires negotiations for the allocation of funds with the federal, state, or local government; in private welfare organizations, money from special campaigns or the Community Chest is relied on for funds. Budget controls guarantee that the money received is spent economically and in accordance with the policies and rules of the agency. Budgeting also describes the allocation of the funds available to the branches and divisions of the agency so that each of them can operate most effectively.[6]

[5] Robert Morris and Martin Rein, "Goals, Structures and Strategies for Community Change," *Social Work Practice* (New York: Columbia University Press, 1962), pp. 139–45; and Ralph M. Kramer, "Ideology, Status and Power in Board–Executive Relationships," *Social Work* 10, No. 4 (October 1965), 107–14.

[6] James D. Thompson, "Common and Uncommon Elements in Administration," *Social Welfare Forum* (1962), 181–201; Alfred J. Kahn, *Theory and Practice of Social Planning* (New York: Russell Sage Foundation, 1969); Jack C. Bloedorn, "Application of the Systems Analysis Approach to Social Welfare Problems and Organizations," *Public Welfare*, 28, No. 3 (July 1970), 280–84.

Organizational Structure

The structure of public social agencies is part of the federal, state, or local government setup. The organization, as a rule, is determined by law or statute as well as by the size of the population and the territory served by the social agency. The legislative body influences the organization, personnel, and content of services by appropriating or withholding funds for the operation of the agency. In private social agencies, either the members or a board of directors exercise the power of ultimate control.

Usually, the governing board of a public or private welfare agency is a commission, such as the board of a state public welfare department, a county welfare commission, or the board of directors of a voluntary welfare agency. Sometimes a single administrator replaces the governing board. He may be supported by an advisory board. In private agencies, the board of directors is usually composed of lay persons. The board and its committees decide on policies, support the mobilization of the necessary resources, and assist in public relations.

The *executive* is the chief administrative officer of the agency. Usually, he is appointed by the board or by another authority, such as the governor of the state, the county board of supervisors, or the city council. He is responsible for the management of the agency and for carrying into effect the program and the policies of the agency that are adopted by the board or by statute. The executive represents the authority of the governing board, but as the chief of the staff, he also maintains the interrelation between the board and the personnel of the agency. The executive is responsible for presenting to the board all essential information so that it can decide on realistic policies.

As the head of the staff, the executive carries the following responsibilities: In personnel management, he must recruit, promote, and dismiss staff members, following the general personnel policy established by the governing body of the agency. Authority of the executive concerning personnel matters should be exercised in cooperation with the staff. The executive remains the final authority in cases where differences arise, and in the judgment of discipline and competence. He is responsible for carrying out clearly the outlined personnel policies and for the procedure to be followed in handling grievances. The executive decides on staff coordination, assignments, and staff development. He is responsible for delegating authority to the members of the staff in connection with assigning duties, leaving sufficient freedom for all of them to exercise their initiative and ingenuity. The executive interprets board policies, community realities, and professional knowledge to the staff and enables its members to participate in advance studies, institutes, and community activities. Communication between the executive and the staff is essential. The members of the staff should have the opportunity to present their experiences, observations, and recommendations in personal contact and at staff meetings to supervisors and to the executive, or, on special occasions, to the board of directors.[7]

The executive is responsible for the establishment of subdivisions of the social agency, such as departments and district or branch offices, and for coordination and cooperation among divisions. It is also his duty to distribute the agency's functions into line, staff (executive and policy functions), and auxiliary services.

The *staff* (personnel) varies according to the nature and size of the agency. In larger agencies, the staff consists of one or more assistant directors, supervisors, social workers, clerical and maintenance workers, and sometimes other professional personnel, such as physicians, nurses, accountants, lawyers, teachers, psychologists, and home economists. In some social agencies, volunteers are engaged in various activities.

Another element of the agency's organization is the management of offices, buildings, or institutions and the procurement, storage, and issuance of supplies. This is particularly important when residential facilities, such as a children's home, a settlement house, a senior citizens' residence, or a correctional institution have to be maintained. Here the proper management of recreational buildings and community centers is essential. Location and equipment of the agency should meet the needs of the people who use its services.

Personnel Administration

Competent, reliable, conscientious personnel is the most important factor in social agency administration, as it is in other professional services, medicine, nursing, law, and teaching.[8] Only a well-trained staff of adequate size can perform social services required for the welfare of the people. In this sense adequate staff means economy, because too few or untrained workers cannot perform qualified social work necessary to achieve the social

[7] Harleigh B. Trecker, *Group Process in Administration* (New York: Woman's Press, 1950); Marshall E. Dimock, *Public Administration,* 3rd ed. (New York: Holt, Rinehart and Winston, 1964); S. Blumenthal, *Management Information Systems* (Englewood Cliffs, N.J.: Prentice-Hall, 1969).

[8] R. Clyde White, *Administration of Public Welfare* (New York: American Book, 1950), p. 327; Virginia S. Ferguson, "Personnel Policies and Practices," *Encyclopedia of Social Work 1965,* pp. 541–46; Mary R. Baker, "Personnel in Social Work," *Encyclopedia of Social Work 1965,* pp. 532–40; Arnulf M. Pins, *Who Chooses Social Work?* (New York: Council on Social Work Education, 1963); Rosemary C. Sarri and Maeda J. Galinsky, "A Conceptual Framework for Group Development," in Robert D. Vinter, ed., *Readings in Group Work Practice* (Ann Arbor: University of Michigan Press, 1967), pp. 72–94; and Joseph H. Kahle, "Structuring and Administering a Modern Voluntary Agency," *Social Work,* 14, No. 4 (October 1969), 21–28.

agency's objectives. Personnel policy of the social agency demands three basic elements: (1) clearly formulated, written standards of employment for specific positions, based on competence; (2) provisions for fair-dealing on grievances; and (3) delegation of final authority to the executive in dealing with matters of competence and discipline.

Appointment of personnel. For a long time, in public and private social agencies, personnel were employed without legal requirements and without specific qualifications. Frequently, appointments were based on private connections with influential people, family relations, favoritism, or political affiliations. In 1829 President Jackson established political patronage, the so-called "spoils system," under the title of "administrative reform" as a practice of rotation-in-office. This type of unregulated appointment was used in federal, state, and local government for over fifty years. Only after the assassination of President Garfield by a rejected applicant for public office, in 1881, did the *Pendleton Act of 1883* change the spoils system. It created the United States Civil Service Commission, composed of three members appointed by the president. Not more than two members of the commission may belong to the same party. The selection of federal employees was to be made on the basis of open competitive examinations. The Pendleton Act established the fundament of *civil service* for the federal government. Many states and municipalities also enacted civil service systems, but some of them neglected to provide the necessary funds for proper administration.[9]

The main responsibilities of the Civil Service Administration are classification of positions, establishment of qualifications and of rates of compensation, recruitment of applicants, and preparation and evaluation of examinations. The job classification determines the requirements (age, education, and experience) that must be fulfilled to take the examination. Qualifications are higher for jobs requiring independent work and supervisory responsibility. In social welfare, it is important that supervisors and persons in responsible positions complete graduate studies at a recognized school of social work.

Merit systems. Merit systems in personnel practice are designed to promote efficiency through a systematic selection of the best available staff, removing the incompetent and promoting the outstanding. The Amendment of the Social Security Act of 1939 required the introduction of an approved merit system for personnel as a condition for receiving federal

9 Ernest F. Witte, "Realities in Staffing Social Welfare Programs," *Social Welfare Forum* (1963), 178–94; Evan Clague, "Social Welfare Personnel," *Social Welfare Forum* (1961), 211–21; Oscar G. Stahl, *Public Personnel Administration* (New York: Harper & Row, 1962); Marshall E. Dimock and Gladys Ogden, *Public Administration* (New York: Holt, Rinehart and Winston, 1969); Daniel Prosser, "Personnel Practices in Social Work," *Encyclopedia 1971,* pp. 893–96.

grants-in-aid, and all states complied with this request. The federal standards require the states to adopt open, competitive examinations as a basis for employment to give qualified persons a fair and equal opportunity for an appointment, and to administer a job classification and equitable pay plan. Under the Hatch Act and many state laws, public employees are barred during their service from participating in political activities. Discrimination because of religious, racial, and political affiliations is prohibited. Promotions are based on length of service and capacity. Where no Civil Service Commissions operate, state merit councils are organized to administer the system.

Under many state merit systems, the state department of public welfare is authorized to determine the qualifications of candidates to be appointed in its administration and in county and city welfare agencies. Frequently a *joint state merit system* is organized, which selects employees for public assistance, child welfare services, public health services, and unemployment insurance administration..

State merit systems should encourage education and training of applicants and enable public welfare agencies to adopt good standards of work, salary, and promotions.[10] Above all, merit systems should develop a professional attitude and a spirit of devoted service in welfare administration, which is of decisive importance for the public.

Specified examinations are given for certain civil service positions and promotions, to secure the recruitment of qualified candidates. Some state and local positions, however, are open only to candidates who have lived a certain period (usually one year) in the state or county, and some even limit positions to persons born in the county or city. Obviously, such requirements are inconsistent with the goal of civil service selection.[11]

Civil service examinations take into consideration education and occupational experience. They consist of written and oral tests which are graded and scored. For positions that require professional skills, graduate education should be a minimum qualification. In practice, there has been a tendency to consider experience as a substitute for graduate education in social work. Since 1969, persons with a Bachelor's degree in social work have been permitted to join the National Association of Social Workers

[10] Marietta Stevenson, *Public Welfare Administration* (New York: Macmillan, 1938), pp. 326–32; National Resources Planning Board, *Security, Work, and Relief Policies* (Washington, D.C.: Government Printing Office, 1942), p. 539; Louise N. Mumm, "The Personnel of Social Welfare," *Social Work Year Book* (1960), 416–26.

[11] Harold Silver, "Personnel Standards and Practices," *Social Work Year Book* (1960), 426–32; Herman D. Stein, "Administrative Implications of Bureaucratic Theory," *Social Work,* 6, No. 3 (July 1961), 14–21; Prosser, "Personnel Practices in Social Work."

and are employed in public welfare departments, mainly as "eligibility workers."[12]

For leading positions, "unassembled examinations," which set high requirements for experience in responsible assignments and permit the Civil Service Commission an individual treatment of the candidates, are often preferred.

All candidates who pass civil service examinations are "certified" for a given position and arranged in the *Eligible List* in order of their grades. For each position a special eligible list is set up which, according to law, may expire within a certain period, usually two years. Veterans and incumbents may have preferential rights, and disabled veterans in some instances are placed on the top of the eligible lists, if they pass, with the assistance of their priority treatment. The appointing officer sometimes has to select the person at the top of the list. More frequently, however, he may select one of the first three on the list. Usually, appointments are made for a probationary period, during which time the candidate may be dismissed. In the case of dismissal, the candidate may ask the Civil Service Commission to restore him to the eligible list, but he may not be recertified to the same agency from which he was discharged.

If a new civil service system is introduced, temporary employees will be appointed and examinations will be given after a certain period. Sometimes, incumbents are "blanketed in," and are not required to take the regular examination; this method, as well as preference for incumbents, defeats the principle of appointment according to ability.

Salaries and tenure. Under civil service and merit systems, compensations are set up in proportion to the requirements for the positions. The positions are classified, as a rule, as clerical, professional, and administrative. In each class, the compensation scale aims to attract competent personnel. In many agencies the clerical salaries of certain employees are higher than those of some professional workers, but some professional salaries may exceed those of administrative positions. There are wide variations in salary range in different positions, regions, and types of practice.[13]

One of the characteristics of the spoils system was uncertainty about length of service. Under the merit system, however, an employee may be

[12] Arnulf Pins, "Changes in Social Work Education," *Social Work,* 16, No. 2 (April 1971), 5–15; Herman Stein, "Social Work Manpower and Training," *Social Work Education Reporter,* 20, No. 1 (January 1972), 23–24.

[13] William B. Tollen, *Study of Staff Losses in Child Welfare and Family Service Agencies* (Washington, D.C.: U.S. Children's Bureau, 1960); U.S. Bureau of Labor Statistics, *Salaries and Working Conditions of Social Welfare Manpower in 1960* (New York: National Social Welfare Assembly, 1961); Mary R. Baker, "Personnel in Social Work," *Encyclopedia of Social Work 1965,* pp. 536–37; *National Association of Social Workers News* (December 1971), 17–26.

dismissed only "for cause." He is entitled to defend himself against charges and to be heard before an impartial referee, a commission, or a board. Tenure requires that an employee be entitled to appeal to an impartial body when he is dismissed, regardless of the cause. The hearing must permit presentation of evidence, careful consideration, and decision by the appeal body with some formal procedure, although no court routine is necessary. However, tenure should not result in the retention of uninterested, mediocre, inefficient employees. This practice has caused severe criticism of bureaucracy. When reductions in staff because of budget cuts or legislative changes make separations necessary, seniority alone should not be the decisive factor; rather, the agency should retain the employees who are most efficient and best qualified for the job.

Promotion. To encourage young people to enter public welfare service there must be opportunity for advancement. Promotions should not be based exclusively on seniority, but also on the service record. This record should evaluate, from an accurate analysis, the specific qualities of the employee's performance. Promotions may also require special examinations. The agency should have an opportunity to hire exceptionally good persons from outside. If there is no competition from outsiders, a close bureaucracy is in danger of becoming self-sufficient, uncritical, indifferent to public opinion, and apathetic in its service to clients. Public welfare personnel should not be recruited solely for the lowest positions and should not be promoted exclusively through the ranks.

Staff development. Inservice training orients a new employee to the organization, the technical setup, the routine work, and the rules and procedures of the agency. It aims at refreshing the skill and knowledge of the staff with regard to methods of work, new developments, changes in legislation and policy, and new professional points of view. However, it is no substitute for professional education for social welfare.

Inservice training is carried on at regular staff meetings, either for the entire staff or certain groups of workers or by special courses or at institutes. Institutes should require serious study and permit staff preparation and follow-up conferences. Study courses usually continue over a longer period and should encourage active and critical participation of the staff members.

Staff development intends to improve the capacity and effective work of public welfare personnel. It uses inservice training and supervision as its principal means, but also educational leaves to attend graduate schools, institutes, and conferences. It seeks to secure continued professional growth of all staff members and to strengthen their skill and interest in performing the best possible service for the public. Staff development leads to an improvement of the quality of work performed in the social agency. The trend in solving the urgent manpower problem in social work is (1) to increase the recruitment and the scholarship programs for graduate education; (2) to strengthen undergraduate education for employment in addition to preparation for graduate studies; (3) to explore the employment of persons according to different levels of skill and responsibilities, and (4) to find ways of using less highly trained auxiliary personnel, particularly among recipients of social services.[14]

Private social agencies do not have to use civil service or merit systems. They establish their employment practices, which are approved by their governing boards. Personnel standards of most private agencies are higher than public service standards. Frequently, standards of recruitment and personnel practice are developed under the auspices of national organizations in which the individual agencies hold membership, such as the Family Service Association of America and the Child Welfare League of America.

Budget and Finance

The financial resources of public welfare agencies are mainly derived from taxes, those of private social agencies from allocations of the local Community Chest, from membership contributions, and from individual donations and bequests.

To determine the necessary resources of a social agency, a budget is prepared. This is an estimate of the expenditure required to carry on the services of the agency. The budget contains a detailed analysis of the services of the agency, of expenditures for aid to clients and for personnel who render services, and of expenditures for office management, buildings, repair, replacement, or expansion when the services of the agency make such expenses necessary.

In a public welfare agency, the budget serves three functions: (1) it is a financial plan of operations for the next fiscal year (sometimes for two years); (2) it serves as a means of obtaining the necessary funds from the legislature (state assembly, county board of supervisors, or the like); and (3) it renders the basis for control of financial transactions.

In preparing the budget, the agency presents the data for the expenditures of the current year and frequently of preceding years, organized according to the major items of the budget to show the statistical trends.[15]

14 Baker, "Personnel in Social Work," pp. 538–40; Bertram M. Beck, "Wanted Now: Social Work Associates," *Social Welfare Forum* (1963), 195–205; Louis Levitt, "Case Aides and Administrative Realities," *Public Welfare*, 28, No. 1 (January 1970), 98–100.

15 Wayne McMillen, "Financing of Social Welfare Services," *Social Work Year Book* (1957), 260–67; Ida C. Merriam, "Financing Social Welfare Expenditures," *Encyclopedia of Social Work 1971*, pp. 416–26. In regard to the tax deduction of charitable contributions, see Gerhard Colm and Theodore Geiger, *The Economy of*

Public welfare is paid for mainly within the general budget of government agencies by three classes of taxes: property taxes, excise taxes, and income taxes.

Property taxes have long been the main financial resource of local government, towns, cities, and counties. Property taxes are levied primarily on real estate, buildings, land, and personal property such as stocks, bonds, and mortgages (liens). Regular household goods and clothes are usually exempt. Property taxes are often classified according to levels of assessed value. For local welfare expenditures property taxes are the primary financial resources, especially where the full burden of general assistance is carried by counties or cities.

Excise taxes are domestic taxes on consumption, mainly sales taxes, which are paid directly by the consumer. They include taxes on liquor, tobacco, cigarettes, cosmetics, and theatre and sports tickets. In several states a general sales tax provides part of the revenue for the welfare expenditures of the state.

Income taxes are levied primarily on net income of individuals and corporations. They are graduated so that individuals and corporations in higher income brackets pay a higher tax. Because of certain deductions and exemptions, the lowest income group frequently is not taxed. Income taxes provide funds for federal and state governments and finance federal and state welfare expenditures.

In addition to these three main classes there are other taxes and fees, on deeds and mortgages, that do not play a major role as resources for welfare budgets.[16]

A social worker in a public welfare agency should be well acquainted with the tax structure and the means of raising the resources for the administration of the welfare services in his community and state. He must have an understanding of the reactions of the population toward taxes to be able to discuss intelligently the social and economic factors involved and to interpret the social effects of the agency's services.

Trends in Social Welfare Administration

Social workers and students are showing an increasing interest in welfare administration. This interest is based on recognition that welfare admin-

---

the American People (Washington, D.C.: National Planning Association, 1961), pp. 112–13; Frank G. Dickinson, ed., *Philanthropy and Public Policy* (New York: National Bureau of Economic Research, 1962); and U.S. Senate, Committee on Finance, *Treasury Report on Private Foundations* (Washington, D.C.: Government Printing Office, 1965).

16 For a more detailed analysis of taxation and public welfare revenues, see White, *Administration of Public Welfare*, pp. 393–414; Ida C. Merriam, "Financing Social Welfare Services," *Social Work Year Book* (1960), 269–72; and Aaron Wildavsky, *The Politics of the Budgetary Process* (Boston: Little, Brown, 1964).

istration is a vital element in the quality of services rendered by social agencies and that effective leadership in social agencies under public and private auspices requires full understanding of, and experience in, social work. Social agency administration is beginning to be identified with social work, except by political appointments aimed at cutting down services.

Schools of social work are assuming responsibility for teaching social welfare administration and integrating the knowledge of this topic with skills in community organization, casework, and group work. Knowledge of social welfare administration embodies the understanding of (a) relationship principles applying to individuals and groups, (b) the totality of the process of social agency administration, (c) the program characteristics of social agencies, and (d) advanced skills required for executive and subexecutive positions.[17]

Theoretical formulations and practical principles of social welfare administration need further clarification and scientific analysis. The interest of social workers goes beyond the questions of external organization and structure of agencies to an exploration of the dynamics of effective social welfare administration.

The responsibility for the administration of public welfare functions in our country rests primarily with the states, counties, and cities. The federal government has assisted state and local governments in providing the funds for adequate welfare services, in equalizing the financial base for public welfare so that the poorer states carry on satisfactory programs, and in developing national standards and goals; but recently this policy has been cancelled.

Personnel in social welfare are being selected, promoted, and retained increasingly on a basis of merit in both public and private agencies. Workers in social welfare administration are qualified by professional education and social work skills, by their human convictions, and by a sense of responsibility toward the clients and toward those who finance welfare services.

In personnel administration, progress is evident, sometimes in collective bargaining agreements with unions in social work or as part of civil service and merit rating systems. The increasing number of retirement annuity provisions in public welfare agencies and the inclusion of social workers in federal old-age and survivors' insurance are signs of this trend. The National Health and Welfare Retirement Association also has developed private retirement plans for the security of social workers.

17 John C. Kidneigh, "Social Work Administration: An Area of Social Work Practice?" *Social Work Journal,* 31, No. 2 (April 1950), 57–61, 79; Eveline M. Burns, "The Role of Government in Social Welfare," *Social Work Journal,* 35, No. 3 (July 1954), 95–102, 124–25; Sue Spencer, *The Administration Method in Social Work Education* (New York: Council on Social Work Education, 1959), pp. 33–52; Michael S. March and Edward Newman, "Financing Social Welfare: Government," *Encyclopedia 1971,* pp. 426–33; Nicos P. Mouzalis, *Organization and Bureaucracy: An Analysis of Modern Theories* (Chicago: Aldine Press, 1968).

Social workers are becoming increasingly aware that public welfare owes to the people and to its representatives a full account of the purposes, policies, and methods of operation, and a breakdown of the expenditures. However, such information must protect the privacy of individuals who receive public welfare services.

The development of higher standards of social agency administration is being furthered by national, state, and local agencies of both public and private character, and by constructive teamwork with members of other professional disciplines.

Public welfare has assumed the responsibility for promoting research. Social research is designed also to improve the quality and the effect of social welfare administration, and to help to alleviate or prevent conditions which result in the need for social services.[18]

SOCIAL WELFARE RESEARCH

Research in social work is the critical inquiry into and the scientific testing of the validity of social work organization, function, and methods in order to verify, generalize, and extend social work knowledge, skill, concepts, and theory.

With the growth of social welfare services organized by both government and private societies, with increasing numbers of persons benefiting from these services, and because of the greater number of workers employed in these agencies, questions are being raised about the efficiency and cost of the methods of social welfare. Professional social workers showed serious interest in the development of social work research, but there is still, among rank-and-file workers, some hesitation because of the time consumed for research investigation and because of doubts over whether it would produce tangible results.

Philip Klein has suggested five types of social research studies: (1) to establish, identify, and measure the need for social service; (2) to measure the services offered; (3) to test, gauge, and evaluate results of social work operation; (4) to test the efficacy of specific social work techniques; and (5) to develop a methodology of social work research.[19]

[18] "Essentials of Public Welfare," A Statement of Principles Prepared by the Welfare Policy Committee of the American Public Welfare Association, *Public Welfare*, 2, No. 1 (January 1953), 5–6; Corinne H. Wolfe, *Competent Staff, A Responsibility of Public Welfare Administration* (Chicago: American Public Welfare Association, 1959); and Peter Woll, *American Bureaucracy* (New York: W. W. Norton, 1963).

[19] Mary E. Macdonald, "Research in Social Work," *Social Work Year Book* (1960), 507–17; Roland L. Warren, *Social Research Consultation: An Experiment in Health and Welfare Planning* (New York: Russell Sage Foundation, 1963); Henry S.

Professional organizations of social work, schools of social work, and public and private welfare organizations have recently shown the desire to provide reliable data to carry on the necessary research studies and to overcome the reluctance of agencies and individuals to support research. There is an increasing number of research workers in federal agencies, state departments of social welfare, many national and regional private organizations, universities, and advanced public and voluntary agencies. In addition, the federal government and private foundations have made money available for research in social work.

Social surveys are conducted to explore the social needs of the population, how adequately these needs are met, and, if they are not being met, what changes are necessary to do so. The first major comprehensive social research project in the United States was the Pittsburgh Survey directed by Paul U. Kellogg in 1909 and financed by the Russell Sage Foundation, which was followed up later by Philip Klein and his associates.[20] Other investigations of health, housing, nutrition, and other social problems of various selected groups of the people, such as migratory workers and children and women in agriculture and certain other industries, were conducted by federal organizations, the Social Security Administration, the Children's Bureau, and the U.S. Department of Labor, and by councils of social agencies and community chests.

Evaluative research in social work is the application of systematic procedures for the purpose of developing, modifying, or expanding knowledge that can be verified by independent investigators.

Social welfare research adopts its concepts from the related social sciences, particularly sociology and psychology, but it also needs to develop special tools. Among social science concepts, for instance, human need, cultural values, social stratification, social class, the satisfaction of human needs by social institutions, social process, and social role are important points to

Maas, *Five Fields of Social Service: Reviews of Research* (New York: National Association of Social Workers, 1966) ; Eleanor B. Sheldon and Wilbert E. Moore, eds., *Indicators of Social Change* (New York: Russell Sage Foundation, 1968) ; Howard E. Freeman and Clarence S. Sherwood, *Social Research and Social Policy* (Englewood Cliffs, N.J.: Prentice-Hall, 1970), pp. 17–30, 39–54.

20 Paul U. Kellogg, ed., *The Pittsburgh Survey* (New York: Russell Sage Foundation, 1909–1914) ; Philip Klein, et al., *A Social Study of Pittsburgh: Community Problems and Social Services of Allegheny County* (New York: Columbia University Press, 1938) ; Arthur J. Vidich, et al., *Reflections on Community Studies* (New York: John Wiley, 1964) ; Clarke A. Chambers, *Paul U. Kellogg and the Survey: Voices for Social Welfare and Social Justice* (Minneapolis: University of Minnesota Press, 1971) ; Walter Buckley, *Sociology and Modern Systems Theory* (Englewood Cliffs, N.J.: Prentice-Hall, 1967) ; Tony Tripod, et al., *The Assessment of Social Research: Guidelines for the Use of Research in Social Work* (Itasca, Ill.: Peacock, 1969) ; Henry S. Maas, *Research in the Social Services: A Five Year Review* (New York: National Association of Social Workers, 1971).

be considered. Other concepts of personality theory, such as individual stress, situational change, personality adjustment, social problems caused by unmet needs, and milieu therapy, are equally valuable for social welfare research, but all of these concepts require further clarification and refinement.[21]

Some of the research studies on the objectives of social welfare have covered the history, structure, and organization of welfare programs. Because the number of social agencies is increasing, people involved with legislation, fund raising, budgeting, and public information desire statistical research to obtain uniform, comparable data on social welfare agencies.

Studies attempt to test and to evaluate the results of the operation of public and private social agencies and to use records of these agencies or interviews to measure the accomplishments against social needs in the community. United Community Funds and Councils publish annually a list of local research projects that during recent years amounted to about 200 studies. The field of international comparative research has been stimulated by the International Conference of Social Work, now called the International Council on Social Welfare, and by the World Congress of Mental Health. Research studies by social workers and students in foreign countries are encouraged by fellowships under the United Nations exchange program and in the United States through the Fulbright Act of 1946.

Social work skills in casework, group work, and community organization are the subjects recently considered for research. Statistical methods to measure the efficacy of the casework process were first applied by the Institute of Welfare Research of the Community Service Society of New York under John McVicker Hunt and his associates. As criteria for "movement in casework," changes in efficiency of the client, in disabling habits, in attitude or understanding, and in the environment are used. There is, among social workers, some question whether it might be possible to find criteria that could not only be rated but also really measured. Studies in related fields, in social group work, sociology, and community organization methods are also being conducted in greater numbers.

The study of *research methodology* in social work has found attention in professional associations and in the literature of social welfare. During the last few years, social welfare research has included social theory, diagnostic and therapy typologies, theory of measurement and sampling, interpretative

[21] Henry S. Maas and Martin Wolins, "Concepts and Methods of Social Work Research," in Cora Kasius, ed., *New Directions in Social Work* (New York: Harper & Row, 1954), pp. 215ff.; Ann W. Shyne, ed., *Use of Judgments as Data in Social Work Research* (New York: National Association of Social Workers, 1959); "Social Work Research," *Encyclopedia of Social Work 1965*, pp. 763–73; David Fanshel, *Research in Social Welfare Administration: Its Contributions and Problems* (New York: National Association of Social Workers, 1962); Eleanor B. Sheldon and Wilbert E. Moore, *Indicators of Social Change* (New York: Russell Sage Foundation, 1968); Davis P. Forcese and Stephen Richter, *Stages of Research: Contemporary Perspectives* (Englewood Cliffs, N.J.: Prentice-Hall, 1970).

theory, social work practice theory, operational research, exploration of new areas for social work practice, identification of relationships among clients, social groups, communities, and social workers, and the creation of continuity in empirical research.[22]

In the area of research methodology, community welfare studies have been carried out mainly with four orientations: (1) as general social surveys with the goal of orienting the public, using random samples of the population, to determine essential unmet social needs; (2) studies for the investigation and appraisal of the demand of the community for new health and social services; (3) social breakdown studies for the exploration of poverty, dependency, disease, delinquency, and crime, and the possibilities of preventing and correcting these social evils; and (4) studies with a standard-setting orientation for the establishment of effective patterns of social adjustment and accurate evaluation of the effect of social services. Henry Maas and Martin Wolins, however, have shown that these methods are still deficient in their methodology and need further careful refinement and conceptualization to improve the reliability and accuracy of the findings and conclusions of social welfare research. For this reason, a new theoretical framework and an empirical evaluation of social welfare research will have to be developed.[23] An important recent means of evaluating the effectiveness of social work programs is the system of social indicators: analytical studies of both quantitative and qualitative data, not merely pulling statistics together, and examination of the results of social measures. These indicators should allow anticipation of future social change.

Social welfare research procedure does not follow definite or rigid rules of execution. Typical research, however, might follow this sequence:

1. Selection of the research subject, as suggested by experience and data from social work practice established in the past by working with individuals, groups, or communities to define and formulate the social problem. The project aims to clarify the problem through application of social theory, or to systematize its various aspects.

---

[22] Ernest Greenwood, "Social Science and Social Work: A Theory of Their Relationship," *Social Service Review*, 29, No. 1 (March 1955), 20–33; Walter Friedlander, ed., *Concepts and Methods of Social Work* (Englewood Cliffs, N.J.: Prentice-Hall, 1958), pp. 292–94; Ann W. Shyne, "Evaluation of Results in Social Work," *Social Work*, 8, No. 4 (October 1963), 26–33; Harry Kitano, "The Concept of 'Precipitant' in Evaluative Research," *Social Work*, 8, No. 4 (October 1963), 34–38; Henry S. Mass, "Social Work Knowledge and Social Responsibility," *Journal of Education in Social Work*, 4, No. 1 (Spring 1968), 37–48.

[23] Maas and Wolins, "Concepts and Methods of Social Work Research," pp. 222–25, 233; Norman A. Polansky, *Social Work Research* (Chicago: University of Chicago Press, 1960); Howard E. Freeman, "The Strategy of Social Policy Research," *Social Welfare Forum* (1963), 143–60; Worth Bateman, "Assessing Program Effectiveness," *Welfare in Review*, 6, No. 1 (February 1968), 1–10; Herman D. Stein, "Assessing Social Agency Effectiveness," *Welfare in Review*, 6, No. 2 (April 1968), 13–18; William Gorman, "Planning, Programming, Budgeting System," *Public Interest*, No. 8 (1967), 408.

2. Formulation of hypotheses to clarify the problems selected for the research.
3. Construction of a research design suited to test the validity of the hypotheses by empirical verification, or by rejection.
4. Fact-finding through observations, interviews, and inquiries to obtain the data and facts required by the research design.
5. Analysis of the collected facts and data to determine whether they logically support or refute the hypotheses of the project.
6. Interpretation and evaluation of the findings and their conclusions; whether they present a convincing answer to the problem or whether they may serve as the basis for further research.[24]

A characteristic trend in recent social work research is the cooperation of social workers with social scientists, thus integrating sociological concepts, organizational analysis, and communication theory.

SELECTED BIBLIOGRAPHY

A. Social Welfare Administration

ATWATER, PIERCE, *Problems of Administration in Social Work*. Minneapolis: University of Minnesota Press, 1940.

BECK, BERTRAM M., "Shaping America's Social Welfare Policy," in Alfred J. Kahn, ed., *Issues in American Social Work*. New York: Columbia University Press, 1959, pp. 191–218.

COHEN, WILBUR J., and FEDELE F. FAURI, *The Objectives of Public Welfare Administration*. Chicago: American Public Welfare Association, 1958.

DE SCHWEINITZ, KARL, *People and Process in Social Security*. Washington, D.C.: American Council on Education, 1948.

DIMOCK, MARSHALL E., and GLADYS O. DIMOCK, *Public Administration*. New York: Rinehart, 1953.

ECKER-RACS, L. L., *The Politics and Economics of State-Local Finance*. Englewood Cliffs, N.J.: Prentice-Hall, 1970.

HANCHETT, HELEN W., et al., *Some Dynamics of Social Agency Administration*. New York: Family Service Association of America, 1946.

HILLMAN, ARTHUR, *Neighborhood Centers Today*. New York: National Federation of Settlements, 1960.

24 Margaret Blenkner, et al., *The Function and Practice of Research in Social Work* (New York: Social Work Research Group, 1955), p. 6; Walter Friedlander, ed., *Concepts and Methods of Social Work* (Englewood Cliffs, N.J.: Prentice-Hall, 1958), pp. 294–95; Dorothy F. Beck, "Potential Approaches to Research in the Family Service Field," *Social Casework*, 11, No. 7 (July 1959); Leonard S. Kogan, "The Utilization of Social Work Research," *Social Casework*, 44, No. 10 (December 1963), 569–74; Bernard Olshansky, "Evaluative Research in Social Planning," *Social Service Review*, 37, No. 4 (December 1963), 429–40; Saul H. Hymans, *Probability Theory* (Englewood Cliffs, N.J.: Prentice-Hall, 1967), pp. 175–213; Aaron Rosenblatt, "The Practitioner's Use and Evaluation of Research," *Social Work*, 13, No. 1 (January 1968), 53–59; John E. Mayer, "Sociology's Relevance for Casework Research," *Social Work*, 14, No. 1 (January 1969), 95–105.

HUNTER, FLOYD, *Community Power Structure—A Study of Decision Makers.* Chapel Hill: University of North Carolina Press, 1953.

KIDNEIGH, JOHN C., "The Quest for Competence in Welfare Administration," *Social Service Review,* 24, No. 2 (June 1950), 172–80.

————, "Social Work Administration, An Area of Social Work Practice," *Social Work Journal,* 31, No. 2 (April 1950), 57–61, 79.

LEPAWSKY, ALBERT, *The Art and Science of Organization and Management.* New York: Alfred A. Knopf, 1949.

McLEAN, F. H., and RALPH ORMSBY, *Organizing a Family Agency.* New York: Family Welfare Association of America, 1944.

MOORE, WILBERT E., *Social Change.* Englewood Cliffs, N.J.: Prentice-Hall, 1963.

MORSTEIN-MARX, FRITZ, ed., *Elements of Public Administration.* Englewood Cliffs, N.J.: Prentice-Hall, 1946.

NOVOGROD, R. JOSEPH, MARSHALL E. DIMOCK, and GLADYS O. DIMOCK, *Casework in Public Administration.* New York: Holt, Rinehart and Winston, 1969.

ROSS, MURRAY F., and CHARLES E. HENDRY, *New Understandings of Leadership.* New York: Association Press, 1957.

SHARKANSKY, IRA, *Public Administration: Policy Making in Government Agencies.* Chicago: Markham, 1969.

SHARTLE, CAROL L., *Executive Performance and Leadership.* Englewood Cliffs, N.J.: Prentice-Hall, 1956.

SIMON, HERBERT A., *Administrative Behavior.* New York: Macmillan, 1957.

STEIN, HERMAN D., "Administration," *Encyclopedia of Social Work 1965,* pp. 58–63.

STEVENSON, MARIETTA, et al., *Public Welfare Administration.* New York: Macmillan, 1938.

TRECKER, HARLEIGH B., *Social Work Administration: Principles and Practices.* New York: Association Press, 1971.

VASEY, WAYNE, *Government and Social Welfare,* Part 3. New York: Holt, Rinehart and Winston, 1958.

WHYTE, WILLIAM F., *Organizational Behavior: Theory and Application.* Homewood, Ill.: Irwin, 1969.

B. Social Welfare Research

AGNEW, NEIL McK., and S. W. PIKE, *The Science Game.* Englewood Cliffs, N.J.: Prentice-Hall, 1969.

ALBERTS, DAVID S., *A Plan for Measuring the Performance of Social Programs: Application of Operations Research Methodology.* New York: Praeger, 1970.

BLALOCK, HUBERT M., *Theory Construction.* Englewood Cliffs, N.J.: Prentice-Hall, 1970.

BLENKNER, MARGARET, et al., *The Function and Practice of Research in Social Work.* New York: Social Work Research Group, 1955.

BRUYN, SEVERYN T., *The Human Perspective in Sociology: The Methodology of Participant Observation.* Englewood Cliffs, N.J.: Prentice-Hall, 1966.

CARO, FRANCIS G., ed., *Readings in Evaluation Research.* New York: Basic Books, 1971.

CHAPIN, F. STUART, *Social Science Research: Its Expanding Horizons.* Minneapolis: University of Minnesota Press, 1953.

DAVIS, JAMES A., *Elementary Survey Analysis.* Englewood Cliffs, N.J.: Prentice-Hall, 1971.

FANSHELL, DAVID, ed., *Research in Social Welfare Administration.* New York: National Association of Social Workers, 1962.

FREEMAN, HOWARD E., and CLARENCE C. SHERWOOD, *Social Research and Social Policy*. Englewood Cliffs, N.J.: Prentice-Hall, 1970.

FRENCH, DAVID G., *An Approach to Measuring Results in Social Work*. New York: Columbia University Press, 1952.

GALTUNG, JOHN, *Theory and Methods of Social Research*. New York: Columbia University Press, 1967.

GORDON, WILLIAM E., "Social Work Research in the Future," in Charles I. Schottland, ed., *Community Organizations 1958*. New York: Columbia University Press, 1958, pp. 104–24.

GREENWOOD, ERNEST, "Social Science and Social Work: A Theory of Their Relationships," *Social Service Review*, 29, No. 1 (March 1955), 20–33.

————, "Social Work Research: A Decade of Reappraisal," *Social Service Review*, 31, No. 3 (September 1957), 311–20.

HERZOG, ELIZABETH, "An Approach to Family Agency Research," *Social Welfare Forum* (1952), 152–60.

————, *Some Guide Lines for Evaluative Research*. Washington, D.C.: U. S. Children's Bureau, 1959.

HYMAN, HERBERT H., et al., *Applications of Methods of Evaluation*. Berkeley: University of California Press, 1962.

KLEIN, PHILIP, and IDA E. MERRIAM, *The Contribution of Research to Social Work*. New York: American Association of Social Workers, 1948.

LUNDBERG, GEORGE A., *Social Research: A Study in Methods Gathering Data*. New York: Longmans, 1951.

MACDONALD, MARY E., "Research in Social Work," *Social Work Year Book* (1960), 507–17.

MAAS, HENRY S., and MARTIN WOLINS, "Concepts and Methods of Social Work Research," in Cora Kasius, ed., *New Directions in Social Work*. New York: Harper, 1954, 215–37.

MAYER, ROBERT R., *Social Planning and Social Change*. Englewood Cliffs, N.J.: Prentice-Hall, 1972.

MORGAN, JOHN S., "Research in Social Work: A Frame of Reference," *Social Work Journal*, 30, No. 4 (October 1949), 148–54.

POLANSKY, NORMAN A., *Social Work Research*. Chicago: University of Chicago Press, 1960.

STEIN, HERMAN D., "Organization Theory and Implications for Administrative Research," in Leonard Kogan, ed., *Social Science Theory and Social Work Research*. New York: National Association of Social Workers, 1960.

SUCHMAN, EDWARD, *Evaluative Research*. New York: Russell Sage Foundation, 1967.

TYLER, RALPH W., "Implications of Research in the Behavioral Sciences," *Social Welfare Forum* (1960), 113–26.

WILKINS, LESLIE T., *Social Deviance: Social Policy, Action, and Research*. Englewood Cliffs, N.J.: Prentice-Hall, 1965.

YOUNG, PAULINE V., *Scientific Social Surveys and Research: An Introduction to the Background, Content, Methods, and Analysis of Social Studies*, 4th ed. Englewood Cliffs, N.J.: Prentice-Hall, 1956.

social welfare programs and practice

8

the organization of social welfare services: an overview

A description of the vast array of social welfare services requires a two-dimensional approach. One dimension is a description of the basic fields of practice in social welfare where social workers contribute to the solution or mitigation of social problems such as poverty, poor housing, and ill health.[1] These fields of practice, described in the ten chapters which follow, are assembled into four main subsystems, each an essential component of basic societal needs. The second dimension is an accounting of the hierarchy

[1] Harriett M. Bartlett, "Social Work Fields of Practice," *Encyclopedia of Social Work 1971*, pp. 1477–81.

of social agencies, both public and private, established at each political and geographic level to meet these needs. Within these agencies social workers use the complete range of methods described in Chapters 4, 5, 6, and 7 in varying combinations to solve the problems presented by the clients, be they individuals, a group, or a community.

The overall organization of social welfare services often appears confusing and illogical. Health care services, for example, are found in many of the fields of practice and at all government levels. Only through an appreciation of the historical development of social services can any logic of the existing structure can be found.

FIELDS OF PRACTICE

For our purposes, a *field of practice* is a cluster of agency settings in which a basic human need is met through professional services. The fields constitute subsystems of the overall welfare system. We conceptualize four major areas of human need for which social welfare has significant responsibility; each of the subsystems has the objective of meeting one type of need. The subsystems are (1) economic security and employment opportunity service; (2) social environment and housing service; (3) health promotion and health care service; and (4) personal and social development service.

Within the framework of these subsystems most social welfare services can be grouped together. However, the subsystems are not all-inclusive compartments; rather, as one would expect, there is considerable overlapping among them.

Closely related to the four subsystems of services is a fifth one, educational services. In this country, education has not usually been conceptualized as a field of social welfare activity, except for the specialty of school social work. We will not discuss education in this book, except to a limited extent; however, we expect that the weak links which now exist between education and social welfare will become stronger in the near future, because many goals are commonly held and new ways of working together are being developed.

Economic Security and Employment Opportunity

The field of economic security and employment opportunity is covered in Chapters 9 and 10, which illustrate current mechanisms and problems in meeting the basic need for food, shelter, and employment as a prerequisite not just for survival, but, as is increasingly advocated, for a gratifying existence. In those chapters we shall explore the public welfare system and social insurance. Significant segments of our population still live in poverty or near-poverty. The War on Poverty during the 1960s failed to provide solutions for victims of racism, industrialization and automation, and rapid urbanization. If the national goal of an adequate income and employment for all who are able to work is more than just words, new mechanisms must be adopted to redistribute income more equitably. Less affluent societies than ours are now trying out such mechanisms. New legislation to provide a minimum guaranteed income is now being considered at a national level, but the concept has not yet been accepted. Even if it were, whether the level of support will be adequate for the poor to escape from poverty remains to be seen.

Social Environment and Housing

Through the centuries the basic need for shelter has come to be a need for more than just a roof over one's head. We usually recognize a minimum standard of comfort, safety, and privacy as the right of every person. The neighborhood, an important part of the environment, should also be attractive and safe. The goal of the Housing Act of 1949 was "a decent home and suitable living environment for every American family."[2]

Public housing, urban renewal, housing finance programs, and Model Cities are part of the services which seek to construct, improve, and maintain the housing and social environment. They are discussed in Chapter 11. Housing is regarded as a secondary setting for social work practice, because the overall responsibility for the development and maintenance of the system is in the hands of planners and administrators from outside the profession of social work. Housing is closely related to transportation, public safety, and environmental protection, all of which are important to the general welfare of the community.

Health Promotion and Health Care

Absence from illness is not an adequate definition of health. An individual is healthy when he can use his full potential, both physical and psychological. The presence of optimal energy, capacity to tolerate stress, full use of genetic inheritance, and environmental mastery are characteristics of positive health. Good health care, both preventive and curative, is a well-articulated goal of our society which is written in legislation. The extent to which this goal is now being met is covered in Chapters 14, 15, and 16.

[2] Julian Hess, "Housing: Federal and State Programs," *Encyclopedia of Social Work 1971*, p. 607.

Chapter 14 provides a description of the preventive approach to physical and mental health. Chapters 15 and 16 illustrate the fragmentation and conflicting approaches of different parts of the subsystem. A hodge-podge of medical and mental health services has proliferated over time, with new components added as patchwork to correct inadequacies. The result is often not only poor medical and mental health care, but unjustifiably costly services and the exclusion of many people from any services at all. A thorough overhaul of the system is essential if comprehensive services are to be provided to meet the needs of all individuals. The health system needs to have greater accountability and a more effective mechanism for self-correction. Health services have also been a secondary setting for social work, which subordinates itself to medical leadership.

Personal and Social Development

In addition to health, housing, income, and employment problems, many individuals also have difficulties of a psychological, intrafamilial, acculturational, or legal nature. This is a cluster of services which help the individual and/or family reach the optimal level of adjustment within the context of the social situation. For example, social work settings deal with problems of dependent and neglected children, families in marital conflict, the aged, and special groups outside the mainstream of society, such as veterans, servicemen, and legal offenders. The internal links among most of these settings are weak, usually arranged on an ad hoc case-by-case basis. Some of the services are sought voluntarily; others are imposed on the client because of society expectation that he conform or adjust to the social code.

Chapter 12 describes one component of this field of practice, family social services; Chapter 13 covers services for children and youth; Chapter 17, services for special needs; and Chapter 18 discusses the settings dealing with crime and delinquency. The bulk of the settings serving families and children are usually thought of as primary settings, because of their sponsorship by social work agencies, whereas those dealing with legal offenders and other clients having special needs are thought of as secondary settings for social work.

CHANGING DIRECTIONS IN SOCIAL WELFARE

The historical overview of social welfare given in Chapters 1, 2, and 3 and in this chapter presents the field as a dynamic one, changing with the economic, political, and social climate. However, in an examination of any particular point in time, it may be difficult to perceive the dynamic nature of social welfare. Even from close range, though, the reader needs to appreciate the extent of the current momentum in the field. Within community and government there is an increasing readiness to reevaluate the causes of social problems. In the past many social welfare services were organized on the premise that the inadequacies of the individual client or his family had brought him to his current condition. After decades of experience with welfare, economic opportunity programs, and health and education programs, we have come to understand that a significant part of social problems is caused by the failure of society. Society has been unable or reluctant to meet the basic needs of those most severely affected by changing social conditions, and when organized services have been available, they have been either inadequately conceived or given in the wrong manner or at the wrong place and time.

We need to seek ways of changing the basic service-giving systems to accommodate better the needs of those they have heretofore neglected, slighted, or bypassed. With a more enlightened understanding of social causality each agency, large or small, public or private, is compelled to reappraise the basis of its service-giving system.

In each of the four fields of practice a number of major trends have strongly affected the current direction of social welfare. Fully developed, these trends will move the welfare system toward becoming more a *public utility* than a device for those who have fallen between the cracks of society. The chapters which follow illustrate where and when these trends are being implemented.

Social agencies are moving away from limiting their activities to ameliorative and rehabilitative programs. They now recognize prevention as a solution to social problems, although admittedly, far too little is known about prevention. Through experimentation and research we expect that rapid progress can be made, as it has been in the field of health. *Prevention* is the mobilization of all physical, social, cultural, and psychological resources for the optimal development of the person. The current fragmentation of social services has often meant that only one resource was used while others were neglected, a situation which has been especially hard on members of oppressed racial or sexual groups. Some agencies have begun to look inward to search out subtle racism, sexism, or ethnic bias.

Social welfare agencies have also tended to reflect traditional social attitudes toward "deviants," whether they be alcoholics, drug addicts, homosexuals, "hippies," or one-parent families. These attitudes are usually seen in admission and treatment policies. But there is change within agencies toward people with different life styles.

Social welfare agencies now recognize the need for greater citizen participation in policy development. This positive step democratizes the field by having individuals take more responsibility for the decisions which affect their lives. Closely related is the trend among social workers to take the role of advocates for their clients (see Chapter 4).

The trend toward decentralization of services—bringing services closer to the client—often means relocating services that were formerly in the center of the community into the districts where the clients live and work. The neighborhood service center is one example of a decentralized office, with multiple services under one roof. It may include a district welfare department, an employment service, a medical and mental health clinic, and a community action program. This type of center aims at comprehensive services where clients with multiple problems can be helped with multiple approaches.

THE STRUCTURE OF THE WELFARE SYSTEM

It is useful to describe public and private social agencies separately. The responsibility of public agencies has usually been limited to serving the needy, the poor, or those with special problems of public concern. In the past these agencies lacked the flexibility of the private agencies to be responsive to a variety of client needs and to be innovative in solving social problems; this is less true today. The administrative structure of agencies established under public auspices differs from that of voluntary or private agencies. Public agencies are based on law or statute, administered within the framework of local, state, or federal government, and financed by taxation. Private agencies are established by individuals or philanthropic, religious, fraternal, or humanitarian groups; their management is the responsibility of a board of directors; and they are supported mainly by contributions, donations, endowments, trust funds, and often participation in the distributions of the Community Chest. Over the past decade, however, private agencies have been able to qualify for the use of public funds related to the goals of public agencies. This more flexible funding arrangement has opened up a wider range of choices for the organization of welfare services.

PUBLIC SOCIAL AGENCIES

Our historical survey has shown that government has gradually assumed the basic responsibility for the maintenance of the social welfare of the people.[3] In the United States this responsibility had long been assumed by voluntary charitable organizations. But the Depression of the 1930s showed that government could no longer avoid its fundamental obligation

---

[3] Rex A. Skidmore and Milton G. Thackary, *Introduction to Social Work* (New York: Appleton, 1964), pp. 55–242. See also Ellen Winston, "Public Welfare," *Encyclopedia of Social Work 1965,* pp. 625–33; Robert D. Vinter, "The Social Structure of Service," in Alfred J. Kahn, ed., *Issues in American Social Work* (New York: Columbia University Press, 1959), pp. 242–69; Charles I. Schottland, "Federal Planning for Health and Welfare," *Social Welfare Forum* (1963), 97–120.

to protect the social welfare of the citizens. This change occurred on all three levels of government—local, state, and federal.

The strength of public welfare agencies lies in their structure. They are established by law; they must provide designated services for all needy people (who are eligible according to legal conditions) without discrimination against race, faith, or color.

Because public welfare agencies are government institutions, their programs and services need to be understood and appreciated by the public. Public welfare agencies need the approval and support of the citizens, because they depend on legislation to appropriate the funds for their services and their administration.[4]

Local Public Welfare Agencies

The largest number of public social agencies operate on a county, city, and township basis. Their structure differs according to state and local statutes. Frequently, a county or city welfare department is directed by a board of commissioners or board of supervisors. In rural counties, the elected officials sometimes administer public welfare services themselves, or they appoint a director or commissioner to be responsible for the administration. In other instances, a city or county welfare department may be managed by a board or a commission of lay citizens appointed by county or state officials; one or several members of the county board of commissioners or supervisors may be members and one of them chairman of the welfare board. This board appoints an executive and controls the operation of the public agency. Although the functions of the public welfare agencies differ widely, there is a trend to consolidate the various activities in one local welfare agency and to coordinate the different assistance and child welfare programs, sometimes including public health functions. Other local public agencies which deal with programs of influence to social welfare are the public health department, the board of education, the juvenile court, the park and recreation commission, the police department, the city planning commission, and the housing authority.

State Departments of Public Welfare

Among the states, there are substantial differences in the organizational setup and the basic policy of their public welfare agency. The large major-

[4] Wayne McMillen, *Community Organization for Social Welfare* (Chicago: University of Chicago Press, 1949), pp. 75–76; Wayne Vasey, *Government and Social Welfare* (New York: Holt, Rinehart and Winston, 1958), pp. 24–33; Robert Morris, "New Concepts in Community Organization," *Social Welfare Forum* (1961), 128–45; Simon Slavin, "Community Action and Institutional Change," *Social Welfare Forum* (1965), 147–61; Melvin A. Glaser, "Public Relations," *Encyclopedia of Social Work 1965*, pp. 618–25.

ity of states have concentrated most, or all, of their public welfare programs in a single agency (department of public welfare, of social welfare, of social security, and recently of human relations).

As a rule, the state department of public welfare is administered by a board whose members are appointed by the governor, and by a "director" or "commissioner," also appointed by the governor. The majority of states leave the immediate administration of general assistance (indigent aid), of the categorical public assistance programs, and of child welfare and health services to counties, cities, townships, and towns. Some states, however, have assumed the entire responsibility for the direct administration of these programs through local state offices. All state departments of public welfare are responsible for the administration of categorical public assistance and child welfare services for which they receive federal grants-in-aid. In several states the administration or the supervision of other state institutions, such as mental hospitals, training schools, schools for the blind and deaf, or correctional programs, probation, and parole services, also falls under their jurisdiction. The question of whether it is desirable to combine all public welfare services under one single department depends on the size and the population of the state and the number of its institutions. We favor such a coordination, but some students of public administration believe that in a large state such a department may be unwieldy. Delegation of authority to qualified division heads and the setup of area offices would secure effective administration.

Some states have Departments of Institutions which house public health services, mental institutions, and corrections under one administrative unit, whereas in other states these are separate departments. The "super-agency concept," exemplified by the federal Department of Health, Education and Welfare, is now used by some states: under one agency chief there are several departments related to the broad field of social welfare. This type of amalgam has the advantage of greater collaboration between departments, avoiding some duplication of effort. Administratively, it is difficult to break down old patterns of organization, so that even a unitary state agency can experience many problems in achieving programs better suited to the state's needs.

Federal Social Welfare Agencies

The main federal agency in the field of public welfare is the Department of Health, Education and Welfare. The Secretary of the Department has full Cabinet rank. An Undersecretary and two Assistant Secretaries of Health, Education and Welfare share with the Secretary the responsibility for the entire area of work, but another Special Assistant Secretary is in charge of health and medical affairs. As in the former Federal Security

Agency, a Commissioner of Social Security, a Surgeon General, and a Commissioner of Education are the head executive officers of the three operating branches of the new Department. All these leading officials of the Department are appointed by the president with the confirmation of the Senate.[5]

Among the social welfare programs, only Old-Age and Survivors' Insurance is directly administered by the Department of Health, Education and Welfare. In other instances, the federal government only approves state plans, establishes rules and standards (based on federal legislation), supervises the operation of the programs in the states, and shares the expenses of the operation by grants-in-aid according to statutory provisions. The Office of Economic Opportunity under the president's Executive Office operated several important programs (Head Start, Community Action, Job Corps), but since 1969 it has served as planning and coordinating agency.

There are, however, important phases of social services administered or supervised by other federal agencies. The Veterans Administration, an independent organization under the president, administers veterans' services directly, throughout the country (see Chapter 17). The Department of Labor is in charge of the United States Employment Service and of the Bureau of Employment Security, which cooperate with the states in the administration of employment services and unemployment compensation (see Chapter 9) and in the protection of child labor (see Chapters 10 and 13). The Civil Service Commission, the Small Business Administration, and the Equal Employment Opportunity Commission administer special programs.

The Bureau of Indian Affairs, United States Department of the Interior, provides educational and medical services as well as land rehabilitation aid, hospitals, schools, and clinics for Indians on the reservations. Immigration and naturalization services for newcomers to the United States are administered by the United States Department of Justice. The Women's Bureau of the United States Department of Labor conducts research and disseminates information on working conditions.

PRIVATE SOCIAL AGENCIES

Private or voluntary social agencies have beeen the pioneers in creating modern social services. In contrast to public social welfare departments, which serve all parts of the states, including the rural regions, private social agencies operate mainly in urban areas. Often they also serve the territory which immediately surrounds the cities, but they are rare in remote rural communities. The efficiency and the standards of private social agencies

[5] Ellen Winston, "The New Welfare Administration," *Public Welfare,* 21, No. 2 (April 1963), 1–2, 39.

have been enhanced by the formation of national organizations of either sectarian or functional character, such as the National Lutheran Council, the National Council of the Protestant Episcopal Church, the Presbyterian Church, the National Conference of Catholic Charities, the National Catholic Welfare Conference, the National Conference of Jewish Communal Service, the Child Welfare League of America, the Family Service Association of America, the National Committee for Mental Hygiene, the National Travelers Aid Association, the National Board of the YWCA, the National Council of YMCA, and the Salvation Army. These national organizations, which are themselves members of the National Social Welfare Assembly as a coordinating body, assist their member agencies in planning, organizing, and budgeting; in the development of professional standards of work and personnel; and in research and participation in the total program of health and welfare services in their community. They share the experiences of other local and regional organizations with their member agencies through conferences, institutes, workshops, consultation, and field services.[6]

The foundation of private social agencies and the continuation of their activities is based on the recognition of the need for this service in the local community. Originally, philanthropists, a group of interested citizens, or a church society became aware of the need for some type of social service, such as a family welfare agency, a children's protective society, or an organization to aid unmarried mothers or crippled children. Currently, the social and health needs of the various groups of the population are considered by the Social Planning Council or Community Welfare Council. There is a careful investigation into what resources exist in the community and what institutions or facilities are missing before the establishment of a new social agency is encouraged and supported. Still, individuals or groups of citizens concerned with social and health conditions in the community may take the initiative, if they are able to secure the necessary moral and financial support, for a new enterprise in health and welfare work, such as a mental hygiene association, a vocational guidance clinic, or a self-help agency such as Alcoholics Anonymous or Synanon for drug addicts, or a suicide prevention center.

Nonsectarian Private Agencies

According to the variety of social and health needs, voluntary organizations have been organized to meet particular problems of family disorganization,

---

[6] Robert E. Bondy, "National Voluntary Organizations," *Encyclopedia of Social Work 1965,* pp. 526–30; Gordon Manser, "Voluntary Organization for Social Welfare," *Encyclopedia of Social Work 1965,* pp. 823–29; Arnold Gurin, "Voluntarism," *Encyclopedia of Social Work 1971,* pp. 1326–27.

juvenile delinquency and truancy, child and adult recreational needs, and diseases such as tuberculosis and poliomyelitis. They have also aided in caring for orphans and neglected children, crippled children, unwed mothers, and the aged and handicapped. As a rule, the interest of one or a few persons is the motivating factor for the establishment of such an organization. After funds have been donated or collected, a constitution and bylaws are usually set up which determine the goal and the place of operation of the agency. It may be incorporated according to statutory provisions of the state where it is organized. In general, the approval of the project is asked from the Council of Social Planning, and the Community Chest if their support is expected.

The responsibility for the management of the agency is entrusted to a board of directors. It is usually composed of persons who had taken the initiative for the foundation of the organization or who had helped in gaining the financial support for it. Typical members of the board of directors are bankers, well-to-do businessmen, physicians, lawyers, a representative of the local welfare and health department, a member of the board of education, and one or two representatives of organized labor and consumers groups. The board also should represent, in a nonsectarian agency, the major religious groups in the community. In most social agencies women form a substantial proportion of the board. It is important to include some women who represent influential women's organizations, such as the League of Women Voters, the Federation of University Women, the Junior League, and businesswomen's clubs. Similarly, the board might have prominent members of men's service clubs and fraternal societies, such as the Masons, Rotary, Shriners, Kiwanis, Elks, American Legion, and Chamber of Commerce. The representation of these different groups in the community is essential to demonstrate to the public and the authorities the broad interest in the goals of the agency and to testify to its integrity and responsibility in carrying out its purpose. Agencies which receive part of their support from the annual drive of the Community Chest are under some obligation to have representatives of different economic levels on their board of directors that formulates the policies of the agency and controls its work and expenditures. Increasingly, it is also expected that racial minorities and potential consumers of the agency be represented on the board.

The board of directors appoints committees which take charge of different administrative functions, because the board usually limits its tasks to the establishment of the general policy of the organization, the appointment of the executive, and the control of the total agency operation. The *executive committee* supervises the current activities and represents the board of directors when the board is not in session. A *nominating committee* prepares suggestions for the election of new board members; sometimes it also proposes suitable persons for appointments as executive, assistant-director, legal counsel, medical consultant, or similar responsible positions in the agency in cooperation with the executive secretary or director.

The *financial or budget committee* controls the expenditures of the agency, prepares the budget for the approval of the executive committee and the board of directors, and often develops plans for raising additional funds or enlisting bequests and donations for the agency. If the agency owns real estate property, such as a school, a hospital, or an administrative building, a *committee of buildings and maintenance* assists the executive in its management. Frequently, there are other *standing committees* on which members of the board, representatives of the professional staff, and lay persons of the community serve. They include a *committee on personnel practice,* which determines the salaries of the staff, recruitment, promotion and vacation policy, regulations, and working conditions. By cooperating with newspapers, radio, television, and civic and religious societies in the community, a *public relations committee* informs the public about the activities of the agency. Because most private social agencies depend financially on the current contributions to the Community Chest, continuous information should be given to the public about the necessity and the value of the agency's activities to convince the citizens that its services are needed and worthy of their contributions. Some agencies that provide services to children, families, unmarried mothers, and handicapped or aged people have a *case committee* with which the professional staff discusses experiences in particular significant cases to keep the board aware of the specific problems which the agency faces, of the methods and changing aspects of the professional work, and of the needs for innovations in policy or practice.

The immediate services of a social agency to individuals or to groups are under the control of the executive-director, appointed by the board of directors, and are carried out by the professional and clerical staff. The social work staff may need special assistance by other professional persons, such as a physician, psychiatrist, lawyer, dietitian or home economist, nurse, psychologist, accountant, and engineer. In casework and recreation agencies of large size, territorial districts are set up under the direction of an assistant executive, and most of them employ one or more supervisors who have the responsibility of working with several caseworkers or group workers and helping them carry out their assignments. This practice of working under a supervisor, rather than as an independent professional practitioner such as a doctor, teacher, or lawyer, has its basis in several facts. The core of social work is the the relation of the worker with human beings, which is based on subjective understanding, individual values, and moral judgments. The professional training in schools of social work provides the beginning worker with the basic professional knowledge and skills, but the introduction of a supervisor in the practical process of operation of the specific agency is still considered desirable. Even more indispensable is the skilled supervision of workers without professional social work education and of paraprofessional indigenous workers hired under the so-called "apprenticeship method" of on-the-job training.[7]

In contrast to public agencies, which according to statutory provision have to accept every client who meets the legal requirements for eligibility, voluntary agencies are not under obligation to serve every applicant. Social workers in private agencies have become convinced that their work will be most effective if the persons who come to the agency fully understand the conditions under which the agency can serve them, what the nature and limitations of the services are, and if the applicant himself decides whether he wishes to use these facilities. Where there is conflict between members of a family, as in cases of marital discord, or neglect of or cruelty to children, social agencies attempt to find measures of protection which are acceptable to the other side; only as a last resort is a court order asked for.

The possibility of the private social agency's limiting its services to special groups, such as to persons suffering from handicaps, particular diseases, or the psychological effects of racial discrimination, enables the organization to offer intensive methods of aid and to interpret the importance of its program to the public. It also has the opportunity of pioneering in new areas, or of serving areas that are controversial and politically unfeasible for government agencies.

Sectarian Social Agencies

In the colonial period of the United States, religious charities played a minor role in social welfare because the settlers brought over from England the tradition of public parish poor relief. The parish, however, was often almost identical with its church. Thus, it was not felt necessary to organize separate church charity activities. Not until the nineteenth century were denominational charities founded by the different religious congregations, primarily to care for orphans and deserted children, but also to provide recreational and educational activities for young people.[8] In addition to wel-

[7] Charlotte Towle, *Common Human Needs* (Chicago: University of Chicago Press, 1945), pp. 95–112; Harold L. Wilensky and Charles N. Lebeaux, *Industrial Society and Social Welfare* (New York: Russell Sage Foundation, 1958), pp. 231–47; S. C. Kohs, *The Roots of Social Work* (New York: Association Press, 1966), pp. 100–176; Arthur Pearls, "New Careers," *Encyclopedia of Social Work 1971*, p. 927.

[8] Sanford Solender, "Social Issues and Religiously Sponsored Social Welfare Agencies," *Social Welfare Forum* (1965), 238–54; Charlotte Towle, "The Role of Supervision in the Union of Cause and Function," *Social Service Review*, 36, No. 4 (December 1962), 396–406, and "The Place of Help in Supervision," *Social Service Review*, 37, No. 4 (December 1963), 403–15; Frances Schmidt and Harold N. Weiner, eds., *Public Relations in Health and Welfare* (New York: Columbia University Press, 1966).

fare aims, these charities pursued those of culture, religion, and education. Religious social agencies are usually supported as though they are nonsectarian voluntary welfare services through Community Chests. However, they also receive contributions, donations, and funds from their membership, from churches, and from special campaigns since they often extend their charity work beyond the boundaries of the local community within the territory of a larger ecclesiastical unit, such as a bishopric, a diocese, or a synod.[9]

One type of sectarian social agency limits its services to the members of the founding denominational group as a part of an extension of its religious training and education. Another type offers welfare service to the entire community without considering this a part of the religious education program. However, the activities of the agency are still sectarian and its officers are "ministers" of the church. A third type is the interdenominational agency serving more than one denomination and transcending the narrow concepts of sectarianism.

As part of the continuing change in the welfare field, sectarian agencies are now modifying the way in which they address social need. The various denominations have always differed in the degree to which they were either sectarian or secular in their interest, occupying different positions on a continuum between those two extremes. Now, however, there is a trend toward greater secularization of all denominational groups. For example, they are showing leadership in reaching out to minority communities, and they are supporting grass-roots groups which want to hasten institutional change related to social welfare. (A concomitant of this movement is the trend for sectarian agencies to employ professional social workers in leadership roles.)

Few data are available on the extent to which sectarian agencies contribute to the total social welfare effort. One piece of information, however, comes from the field of child welfare, in which sectarian agencies do play a significant part. In 1966, of all the institutions caring for dependent and neglected children in the United States, 40 percent were operated under sectarian auspices, 28 percent under nonsectarian auspices, and the remaining 32 percent under public sponsorship.[10]

Protestant social work. As the dominant religious group in this country, Protestant churches have never been concerned about discrimination against their members by public institutions. Numerous humanitarian and

---

[9] Alice D. Taggart, "The Caseworker as Parish Assistant," *Social Casework,* 43, No. 2 (February 1962), 75–79.

[10] William J. Reid, "Sectarian Agencies," *Encyclopedia of Social Work 1971,* p. 1157.

philanthropic charities have been created and maintained by Protestants and their congregations. In addition to such services for the entire community, the individual Protestant denominations have established such religious charities as orphanages, hospitals, homes for the aged and handicapped, settlement houses, reform schools for boys and girls, agencies for the aid of prisoners and their families, and homes for destitute, runaway children. Some of these services were founded as expressions of religious concern for the fate of the underprivileged and needy and were not closely attached to a particular Protestant denomination; but often some contact with one or several church groups was maintained. The social consciousness of the Protestant church was represented by such personalities as Washington Gladden, Josiah Strong, Lyman Abbott, Vida D. Scudder, George Davis Herron, John Graham Brooks, Walter Rauschenbusch, Francis Peabody, Charles R. Henderson, Bishop Scarlett, Bishop Francis McConnell, and Harry Emerson Fosdick.[11]

Lutheran, Episcopal, Baptist, and Methodist churches have organized home missions or city missions in New York and other large cities which led to the establishment of "houses of refuge" and temporary shelters for children and adolescents as well as industrial workshops, settlement houses, summer camps, immigrant services, and various health facilities. The Salvation Army and the Methodist Church have been prominent in the development of "goodwill industries" for the employment and training of the handicapped who are able to earn their living in these "sheltered workshops."[12]

In Protestant social agencies emphasis is laid on the postulate that religious life be nurtured, that religious ethics be integrated into the basic principles of social work by pastoral services, and that the members of the Protestant churches, as volunteers, have a good deal to contribute to the community. Protestant social agencies are operating either under one of the denominations—a local church or a regional, diocesan, or synodical authority—or under a national mission board of the church.

The Young Men's Christian Association (YMCA) and the Young Women's Christian Association (YWCA) are not church organizations in

11 Wade C. Barclay, *The Church and a Christian Society* (New York: Abingdon Press, 1939), p. 56; Dores R. Sharpe, *Walter Rauschenbusch* (New York: Macmillan, 1942), p. 12; F. Ernest Johnson and William J. Villaume, "Protestant Social Services," *Social Work Year Book* (1960), 441–51; Sheldon L. Rahn and Henry J. Whiting, "Protestant Social Services," *Encyclopedia of Social Work 1965,* pp. 587–95.

12 Johnson and Villaume, "Protestant Social Services," pp. 444–45; Charles G. Chakerian, ed., *The Churches and Social Welfare* (Hartford, Conn.: Seminary Foundation, 1955); Rahn and Whiting, "Protestant Social Services," William J. Reid, "Sectarian Agencies," *Encyclopedia of Social Work 1971,* pp. 1154–63.

a sectarian sense, but were founded on religious principles, and most of their members are active in Protestant churches; they are not controlled by any Protestant denomination. Some YWCA and YMCA centers have accepted young people of various creeds to their membership and have thus assumed intersectarian character. But there is controversy in the YWCA and YMCA over the amount of Christianity that is necessary and desirable in their work.[13]

The Salvation Army has been active in the United States since 1880. Its main interest is the religious needs of people. Its family and child welfare services are less important than its work with groups of people who are not reached by other churches or social agencies. Such work includes providing shelters for alcoholics and the homeless and derelict, and maternity homes and placement services for unmarried mothers. Other activities of the Salvation Army include employment service for the handicapped, prison work, and the establishment of social settlements, boys' clubs, and children's institutions.

The American Friends Service Committee, founded in 1917, and the Unitarian Service Committee, established in 1939, have been active in international peace work, social services for foreign relief and rehabilitation, interracial cooperation and also in domestic services for the mentally ill, young and adult prisoners, and community work camps.

For the victims of Nazi persecution, the American Christian Committee for Refugees was organized by the Federal Council of Churches in 1934, and in 1947 the Church World Service developed an extensive program of aid to displaced persons and refugees under its Committee on Displaced Persons. The Church World Service also carries on foreign relief and religious education abroad.

Catholic social work. The social services under the auspices of the Roman Catholic Church are inspired by the religious concepts of the Catholic faith, particularly the virtue of charity. Their main objective is the salvation of the human soul. Catholic social work primarily serves communicants of the Catholic Church, but other clients are not rigorously excluded from the aid of Catholic agencies if their funds and facilities permit caring for such persons without offense to religion or any disadvantage to Catholic applicants. Catholic social workers consider the supernatural element of "charity" as an expression of divine grace, as love of man for the love of

---

[13] Paul Limbert, *Christian Emphasis in YMCA Program* (New York: Association Press, 1951), p. 32; Shelby M. Harrison, *Religion and Social Work—Perspectives and Common Denominators* (New York: National Council of Churches, 1950); Harvey Seifert, *The Church in Community Action* (New York: Abingdon-Cokesbury, 1952); Margaret E. Kuhn, *Houses and People* (New York: National Council of Churches, 1957); Bernard M. Schiffman, "Youth Services," *Encyclopedia of Social Work 1965,* pp. 843–50; Jessie Bernard, et al., "Teen-age Culture," *The Annals,* 338 (November 1961), 1–143.

God; their religious philosophy is primarily based on the teaching of Thomas Aquinas in the thirteenth century.

The structure of Catholic social work follows that of the church organization. The main unit of its services is the diocese. In most of the 112 dioceses of the United States, a director of charities, appointed by the bishop ordinary, coordinates all Catholic welfare activities. As a rule, he is a priest with training in social work. In metropolitan districts the heads of the various departments of the Diocesan Bureau of Social Services or The Associated Catholic Charities are also priests who have received training in social work. The diocesan charities are responsible for the establishment, planning, and financing of all Catholic charitable activities and for cooperation with other voluntary and public social agencies in the area. They are interested in the maintenance of high standards of services and in professional training of young workers in schools of social work In general, the program of the diocesan charities emphasizes child care in foster homes and children's institutions; family casework; cultural, educational, and recreational activities for children and young people; work with juvenile delinquents and endangered youth; and care of the aged and chronically ill.[14] The national agency representing Catholic social work is the National Conference of Catholic Charities, founded in 1910. Its main task is the coordination of all organizations active in Catholic charitable programs and their cooperation with other private and public social agencies.

Volunteer organizations play an essential role in Catholic charitable work in the dioceses. Prominent among them are the Society of St. Vincent de Paul, the Ladies of Charity, the Sisters of the Good Shepherd, and the Knights of Columbus. Volunteer work is mainly devoted to the sick and poor in the parish; to the inmates of hospitals, mental institutions, and prisons; to child care and employment services; and to the maintenance of rest homes and residence clubs for young people and the aged, and shelters for transients and homeless.

Jewish social work. From ancient times, Jewish laws and traditions have made aid to the poor a fundamental religious obligation for the individual and the community. The Bible and Scriptures emphasized the duty of caring for widows, orphans, the blind, and the lame, and of feeding the hungry and sheltering the homeless. The consciousness of the need of soli-

---

[14] Bernard J. Coughlin, *Church and State in Social Welfare* (New York: Columbia University Press, 1965); Mary J. McCormick, *Thomistic Philosophy in Social Casework* (New York: Columbia University Press, 1948); Daniel McColgan, *A Century of Charity* (Milwaukee: Bruce, 1951); Raymond J. Gallagher, "Catholic Social Services," *Encyclopedia of Social Work 1965*, pp. 130–37; Donald P. Gavin, *The National Conference of Catholic Charities 1910–1960* (Milwaukee: Bruce, 1962); Peter C. McCabe and Francis J. Turner, *Catholic Social Work* (Ottawa: Catholic Charities Council, 1965); Kenneth Westhues, "The Roman-Catholic Church and the Field of Social Welfare," *Social Work*, 16, No. 3 (July 1971), 60–65.

darity grew during the Middle Ages when Jews suffered from cruel per-
secutions, mass murder, and expulsions. In the Jewish religion, charity is
called "justice" and has always been an essential part of Jewish ethics.

Jewish social work is religious in origin, but its agencies are secular;
it is not administered by synagogues and congregations. It is mainly financed
by the local religious community. United Jewish Charities were founded in
New York, Chicago, Cincinnati, Cleveland, and a few other large cities
where the bulk of the Jewish population lived. Homes for the aged, community centers, and group work agencies followed later. In 1895 Boston and
Cincinnati organized the first "federations," which were later accepted by
most larger Jewish communities and which became characteristic of the
form of community organization of Jewish social welfare. Their function
was to conduct a unified financial campaign for all Jewish institutions and
agencies. They provided central budgeting for all social agencies according
to their need, and coordinated social work concerning family welfare and
children's services, health and tuberculosis work, hospitals, clinics, group
work, and educational and recreational activities.

The Jewish Welfare Funds raise contributions by a unified central
drive and provide budgeting for domestic and foreign relief needs. They
appeal for contributions to maintain the various Jewish welfare and health
services, particularly for Israel and foreign aid programs, and for such local
services as religious education, vocational training, and special employment
services which cannot obtain Community Chest support. In larger communities the Jewish Community Council coordinates religious, cultural, fraternal,
and social service activities, including relations with other organizations.

Until the Depression of the 1930s, Jewish family societies assumed
major responsibility for Jewish people in need, particularly for immigrants
who were not eligible for public assistance. Since the change of public welfare policies under the influence of the Social Security Act, Jewish family
and child welfare services continue to aid Jews for whom government aid
is not available or whose special religious needs require particular help.[15]

The largest national organization of Jewish social work is the Council
of Jewish Federations and Welfare Funds, with headquarters in New York
and eight regional offices. It coordinates Jewish community resources in
cooperation with local agencies. The National Conference of Jewish Com-

---

[15] George W. Rabinoff, "Jewish Social Work," *Social Work Year Book* (1945),
pp. 203–14; William Avrunin, "Jewish Social Services," *Social Work Year Book*
(1960), pp. 338–44; Philip Bernstein, "Jewish Social Services," *Encyclopedia of Social
Work 1965,* pp. 418–28; "Current Developments in Jewish Communal Service,"
Jewish Journal of Communal Service, 39, No. 1 (Fall 1962), 20–28; Kohs, "Jewish
Social Work," in *The Roots of Social Work,* pp. 119–37; S. P. Goldberg, "Jewish
Communal Services," in *American Jewish Yearbook 1969* (Philadelphia: Jewish Publi-
cation Society), pp. 119–71; Harry L. Lourie, *The Jewish Federation Movement*
(Philadelphia: Jewish Publication Society, 1961).

munal Services serves as a forum for the discussion of problems and experiences and publishes a periodical, *The Journal of Jewish Communal Service.* The Jewish Occupational Council is the clearinghouse for vocational guidance and placement services and formulates programs regarding Jewish economic problems.

Most national and larger local Jewish agencies employ a professionally trained staff, educated in schools of social work.

SOCIAL SERVICES IN RURAL AREAS

The rural population of the United States includes persons living on farms, in villages and towns with less than 2,500 inhabitants, and in the open country; it still comprises about one-third of the total population. However, only 13 percent live beyond commuting distance from a metropolitan area.[16] Although the average income of farmers substantially increased during World War II and the postwar years, there was a decline beginning in 1949. The problems of insufficient income from submarginal land, of difficulties in marketing farm products, and of long-term unemployment, low wages, and insecurity among the migratory farm workers created special needs in certain sections of the rural population. These problems differ in the various agricultural areas of our country, but are most urgent in those states where economic and health conditions are less favorable than in New England, the Middle West, and the far West.[17]

Under these circumstances, a strong national leadership has developed to improve social conditions in rural communities and to develop social services which have long been taken for granted in urban settings. The Office of Child Development in the Department of Health, Education and Welfare is the oldest federal agency particularly concerned, in its maternal and child health services, with rural welfare and health. The Bureau of Indian Affairs in the United States Department of the Interior is another agency which has long been concerned with rural welfare and health on the Indian reservations. In the United States Department of Agriculture, the most important programs for rural communities are administered through

16 Robert L. Barre, "Changing American Environment," *Encyclopedia of Social Work 1971,* p. 277.

17 Grace Browning, "Rural Social Programs," *Social Work Year Book* (1949), 446; Charles P. Loomis and J. Allan Beegle, *Rural Sociology* (Englewood Cliffs, N.J.: Prentice-Hall, 1957), pp. 388–95; Clyde W. Linville, Jr., "Rural Social Programs," *Social Work Year Book* (1957), 500–505; Savilla M. Simons, "Mobility and Social Planning," *Community,* 38, No. 8 (January–February 1963), 10–12, and "Migrants, Transients, and Nonresidents," *Encyclopedia of Social Work 1965,* pp. 512–18; Leon H. Ginsberg, "Rural Social Work," *Encyclopedia of Social Work 1971,* pp. 1138–44.

the Extension Service in the form of free consultation and demonstrations of scientific methods in farming and home economics. A broad adult education program, 4-H Clubs for teen-age boys and girls, and clubs for older rural youth develop agricultural and home economics skills and an appreciation for rural life, as well as an understanding of child care and health preservation. The Extension Service is supported by the Bureau of Home Nutrition and Home Economics, the Bureau of Agricultural Economics, and the Farmers Home Administration, which provides loans, a farm housing plan, and a limited medical care program. The Office of Rural Programs in the Office of Economic Opportunity and the National Institute of Mental Health have been effective in developing rural health and welfare services.

Aid to rural communities in recreation, adult education, and rural health protection is stimulated by the American Country Life Association, the Farm Foundation, the National Education Association, and several farm organizations, such as the National Grange of the Order of Patrons of Husbandry, the American Farm Bureau Federation, and the Farmers' Union.

Before the Depression of the 1930s, needy persons in rural communities depended on uncertain neighborly help or meager local poor relief. The inadequacy of this relief became evident when, in the Depression years, mass unemployment made it difficult to sell agricultural products, and droughts and floods increased the suffering of the rural population in many states. The Federal Emergency Relief Administration and the Farm Security Administration provided financial aid and special measures of assistance in rural communities. In this period, the rural county public welfare departments developed, for the first time, a program of financial assistance. With the support of federal and state funds under the Social Security Act, rural welfare departments gave economic aid to the needy aged and the needy blind, to dependent children, and to disabled persons, as in urban counties. Family and child welfare services were also made possible through federal grants-in-aid.

Professionally trained child welfare workers, supervisors, and consultants are now employed in rural regions for maternal and child care services, for crippled children, and for casework and group work with difficult, endangered, and delinquent children. In the rural communities where these services are not yet available, there are few qualified, trained social workers. Often the county welfare department is the only social agency in such a region. A number of state departments of public welfare supplement the forces of the local county welfare agency by sending field supervisors, consultants, and itinerant clinics to provide medical and psychiatric examinations, guidance, and services to the aging.

Among voluntary social agencies, the local chapter of the American National Red Cross is best known to rural communities. A limited number of other private agencies, including religious organizations, the Salvation Army, the National Tuberculosis Association, the National Travelers Aid, the National Foundation (March of Dimes) and some child-placing and adoption agencies, have field services which serve rural regions.[18]

Social services in the rural community are influenced by its cultural pattern, particular customs, and traditions. The comparative simplicity of the rural village influences attitudes toward assistance expenditures and restricts allowances for education and recreation. Rural relief applicants frequently are accustomed to living on a low economic scale, are shy or apathetic about presenting their requests, and are seemingly grateful to accept meager relief. The relationship between the client and the visiting social worker is more intimate than in the city—more informal and less professional. This is particularly true if the social worker is employed in his home county. If the social worker is not familiar with the rural county, he must first become thoroughly acquainted with its form of government and its health, recreational, and community facilities.

The rural white population in the Northeast and Middle West often is rigid in its moral values and attitudes toward illegitimacy, desertion, birth control, divorce, and sometimes toward drinking and gambling. Social work with the unmarried mother, a nonsupporting husband or father, or an alcoholic is made more difficult in a rural setting because of these rigid attitudes and the closeness of relationships. The high value placed on thrift and frugality encourages the rural population sometimes to refuse aid to families who do not fully conform to the moral standards of the community. The social worker has more difficulty in obtaining information and keeping it confidential because of the curiosity of the neighborhood.

Still unmet are the needs of the migratory and seasonal agricultural workers, many of whom come from black, Spanish-American, Chicano, Filipino, Indian, and Puerto Rican ethnic groups. Because of their migratory work patterns and temporary employment, they have been excluded from many of the social welfare benefits available to the more stationary population. During the 1960s the federal government initiated a series of new legislative acts and amendments of existing laws to bring health care, environmental protective services, education, and minimum-wage laws to this neglected and often exploited group. The dependent children of migratory workers are an especially high-risk group requiring special attention to prevent them from being entrapped in perpetual poverty.

[18] G. Browning, *Rural Public Welfare* (Chicago: University of Chicago Press, 1941), pp. 95–98; Arthur Hillman, *Community Organization and Planning* (New York: Macmillan, 1950), pp. 38–55.

Medical care, hospitals, and public health services in rural counties are poor compared with those in urban regions. There is an incomplete team of public health workers in many of the rural counties, and some counties do not employ even a public health nurse. Most public health nursing in rural sections is carried on through maternal and child health centers. With the aid of federal funds granted under the *Hospital Survey and Construction Act of 1946* (Hill-Burton Act), new hospitals in rural areas have been built, but preventive mental health services are still almost nonexistent in many rural counties. Medical care in isolated areas is very expensive, so that the inhabitants call a doctor only in severe cases, preventing early and quick cure. There is hope that older persons will be better cared for under the *Medicare Program of 1966*. Dental care and lack of proper diets are sometimes special problems encountered by the social worker in a rural community.

Recreational activities and sports in rural regions are conducted under the auspices of high schools, church groups, the 4-H Clubs, the Extension Service of the federal Department of Agriculture, and often also through the YWCA, YMCA, Boy Scouts, and Girl Scouts.

While schools, clinics, and hospitals are improving in most Indian reservations, it still remains urgent that Indians as well as blacks find equal protection under the law against "white backlash," criminal abuse, and even murder by hunting parties, a protection which unfortunately has been denied to them in several instances. Vital interests of several Indian tribes in fishing and hunting rights must be vigorously protected, and treaties of the federal and some state governments must be respected, even if some commercial and industrial interests attempt to nullify such obligations.

SELECTED BIBLIOGRAPHY

Avrunin, William, "Jewish Social Services," *Social Work Year Book* (1960), 338–44.

Bachmann, Ernst, *The Emerging Perspective*. New York: National Council of Churches, 1956.

Bogen, Boris, *Jewish Philanthropy*. Montclair, N.J.: Patterson-Smith, 1969.

Bowers, Swithun, *The Nature and Definition of Social Case Work*. New York: Family Service Association of America, 1949.

Boylan, Marguerite T., *The Catholic Church and Social Welfare*. New York: Greenwich Book Publishers, 1961.

Brauer, Gerald C., "Church and State in Social Welfare," *Social Service Review*, 39, No. 3 (September 1965), 271–82.

Coughlin, Bernard J., *Church and State in Social Welfare*. New York: Columbia University Press, 1965.

Crystal, David, *The Displaced Person and the Social Agency*. New York: United HIAS Service, 1958.

GALLAGHER, RAYMOND J., "Catholic Social Services," *Encyclopedia of Social Work 1965*, pp. 130–37.

GOLDBERG, SAMUEL P., *Jewish Communal Services: Programs and Finances*. New York: Council of Jewish Federations and Welfare Funds, 1969.

JOHNSON, F. ERNEST, and WILLIAM J. VILLAUME, "Protestant Social Services," *Social Work Year Book* (1960), 441–51.

JORNS, AUGUSTE, *The Quakers As Pioneers in Social Work*. New York: Macmillan, 1931.

KOHS, S. C., *The Roots of Social Work*. New York: Association Press, 1966.

LINVILLE, CLYDE W., "Rural Social Programs," *Social Work Year Book* (1957), 500–505.

MENCHER, SAMUEL, "The Future for Voluntarism in American Social Welfare," in Alfred J. Kahn, ed., *Issues in American Social Work*. New York: Columbia University Press, 1959, pp. 219–41.

NIEBUHR, REINHOLD, *The Contribution of Religion to Social Work*. New York: Columbia University Press, 1932.

PURDIE, ARNOLD, *Episcopal Social Welfare Today*. New York: National Council, Protestant Episcopal Church, 1950.

RAHN, SHELDON L., and HENRY J. WHITING, "Protestant Social Services," *Encyclopedia of Social Work 1965*, pp. 587–94.

STIDLEY, LEONARD A., *Sectarian Welfare Federation Among Protestants*. New York: Association Press, 1947.

THOMAS, J. L., *The American Catholic Family*. Englewood Cliffs, N.J.: Prentice-Hall, 1956.

VINTER, ROBERT D., "The Social Structure of Service," in Alfred J. Kahn, ed., *Issues in American Social Work*. New York: Columbia University Press, 1959, pp. 242–69.

WEBB, MURIEL S., *The Social Ministry of the Local Church*. New York: National Council of Churches, 1956.

9

---

social
security
and
income
maintenance

PUBLIC ASSISTANCE

Principles of Income Security

In modern industrial society, the majority of the population depend for their livelihood on their current wages as laborers, workers, and employees, or on their income as self-employed persons. Whenever the breadwinner is unable to work, when he cannot obtain work, or when his death leaves the family in need, outside help is necessary to provide economic protection. The validity of this axiom has recently been supported by the rapid technical development of machines, replacing manual labor and increasingly also white collar workers by automation and cybernetics. Thus the vast number of unemployed in our "affluent society" has called public attention to the lasting problem of the poor (see Chapter 14).

There are two main systems of achieving economic security: (1) a program of *public assistance* (or social assistance), which is financed by taxation, and (2) a program of *social insurance,* financed by contributions of the beneficiary and of his employer.[1] Public assistance may be provided by payments based on the economic and social needs of the applicant, which are determined by a means test, or they may be granted as a "flat-rate allowance" legally fixed with regard to recognized average needs of families of a specific size. Assistance usually is rendered in money so that the recipient is able to purchase the necessities of life, or in kind, such as food, clothing, fuel, and medical supplies. Public assistance may be offered either by accepting the destitute into an institution or by granting aid to the applicant in his home. Because public assistance is granted only to individuals who are in economic need, this fact must be established through some kind of a means test. Modern programs of public assistance characterize the receipt of the payment as a "right" of the applicant, provided that certain legal requirements are fulfilled. The amount of assistance is usually limited by statute and adjusted to the recipient's social and economic conditions, according to his income, resources, and property. The administration of public assistance determines the extent of need, and the amount of assistance often cannot be predicted in advance.

In contrast, social insurance benefits are fully predictable. They are based on legal provisions which provide statutory benefits either on a flat-rate system or in relation to earned wages, income, length of work or loss of working capacity in cases of industrial injuries. Insurance benefits are not dependent on the financial status or the economic need of the insured person. They are provided to the insured who has a legal claim to receive these benefits without arbitrary interference of government authorities. Insurance benefits are financed by contributions from employers, self-employed persons, and workers. In other countries the government often shares contributions for social insurance with the insured and their employers.

Between these two main methods of providing economic security, there is a third approach to income security: a *pension system* based on statute.

[1] Charles I. Schottland, *The Social Security Program in the United States* (New York: Appleton, 1963), pp. 1–6, 9–20; Eveline M. Burns, *Social Security and Public Policy* (New York: McGraw-Hill, 1956), pp. 1–15. See also Milton Friedman, *Capitalism and Freedom* (Chicago: University of Chicago Press, 1962), p. 192; Robert Theobald, *Free Men and Free Markets* (New York: Clarkson Potter, 1965), pp. 89–102; William Haber and Merrill G. Murray, *Unemployment Insurance and the American Economy* (Homewood, Ill.: Irwin, 1966); and Neil W. Chamberlain, ed., *Contemporary Economic Issues* (Homewood, Ill.: Irwin, 1969), pp. 49–107.

In the United States, veterans' pensions to disabled veterans and to survivors of veterans, retirement annuities, and allowances to dependents of military personnel are examples of such pensions which are granted as a matter of legal right to the claimant. Foreign countries have other programs of this nature such as family allowances, and pensions to persons over sixty-five or seventy years of age, or to certain qualified handicapped groups.

To provide economic protection, we use in the United States a dual system, consisting of public assistance on the basis of individual need, and of social insurance programs in which benefits are paid to the insured persons as their legal claim in predetermined, specific contingencies of life (old age, death of breadwinner, unemployment, industrial accident). These two main programs of economic security are supplemented by a system of health and welfare services which provides social services, protective and preventive measures such as child welfare services, recreation, medical and psychiatric care, occupational guidance, and vocational rehabilitation, which are of vital importance for the welfare of the population. Other programs suggested for a more radical income distribution—a "negative income tax" and a "social dividend" (a universal payment to all citizens)—made possible by cybernation, among other developments, seem not to have a realistic chance to be accepted by our present society.

Public programs, such as public employment services and correctional treatment of juvenile and adult offenders, may be classified as public welfare measures in a broader sense only. These public activities are often strengthened and augmented by the work of private social agencies, which contribute to the economic security of the population. This work is carried on under the auspices of religious or nonsectarian philanthropic organizations or of industries and labor unions.

The system of public welfare in the United States has its principal legal foundation in the Social Security Act of 1935 and its subsequent amendments. It provides federal funds for the development and the improvement of standards in specific programs of public assistance and health and welfare services. However, the Social Security Act does not establish a comprehensive federal system; rather, it sets up programs for federal aid in selected and specified types of assistance and welfare services.[2]

Characteristics of Public Assistance

The cost of public assistance is shared by the federal government, the states, counties, and cities. This circumstance has contributed to the fact that the importance of public welfare has been recognized by an increasing propor-

[2] U.S. Bureau of Family Services, "Serving People in Need: Public Assistance Under the Social Security Act," 1964; Advisory Council on Social Security, "The Status of the Social Security Program and Recommendations for Its Improvement,"

tion of the population. The public is, at the same time, more critical of the expenditure of huge sums of money, which necessitates higher taxes, and has become conscious of the marked differences in the amount of benefits received under the various programs in states and counties, and in the standards and methods of their administration. In general, it is now accepted that government, on its various levels, must assume the responsibility of caring for the people who have no means of support. But there is, so far, no unanimity of social philosophy as to how this responsibility should be met, what seems an adequate aid to persons in need, and which government agencies should administer the public welfare services.[3] Under the provisions of the *Social Security Amendment of 1972* (Public Law 92-603), assistance to the needy aged, blind, and disabled is to be financed out of general revenues and administered by the Social Security Administration.

An application of a person in need of material assistance is, as a rule, made at the local department of public welfare. A blind or disabled person may send a relative or friend to submit the request for assistance to the agency. If the application is made in person, the social worker explains how the application form is to be filled out and what information is needed. The applicant may have to include documents for proof of age, data regarding his income and property, or medical certificates about blindness or disability. If the applicant has not come to the welfare office but has written or phoned, a social worker visits the home and gives the necessary explanation. The social worker also checks the facts presented in the application and attempts to make certain that the applicant is eligible for the assistance he is asking for. If further investigations are necessary (for example, about relatives who may support the applicant, or about income and property), these are made within a reasonable time and a notice is sent to the applicant telling him whether he has been accepted for public assistance and how much he will receive monthly. The amount of aid is based on the applicant's individual needs and resources and is often limited by rules of state or local authorities. In the determination of need, all resources of the

---

Social Security Bulletin, 28, No. 3 (March 1965), 3–41; Alfred J. Kahn, "Public Social Services: Policy and Delivery Strategies," *Public Welfare,* 30, No. 1 (Winter 1972), 15–24; Hagith R. Shlonsky, "Welfare Programs and the Social Systems," *Social Service Review,* 45, No. 4 (December 1971), 414–25.

[3] Schottland, *The Social Security Program in the United States,* pp. 93–115; Burns, *Social Security and Public Policy,* pp. 19–26, and "Social Security in Evolution," *Social Service Review,* 39, No. 2 (June 1965), 129–40. See also Michael Harrington, *The Other America* (New York: Macmillan, 1962); Gerhard Colm, "The Economic Base and Limits of Social Welfare," *Monthly Labor Review,* 86, No. 6 (June 1963), 695–700; Leonore A. Epstein, "Unmet Need in a Land of Abundance," *Social Security Bulletin,* 26, No. 5 (May 1963), 3–11; James R. Dumpson, "Hunger and Human Welfare," *Social Welfare Forum* (1961), 87–99; and Frances Fox Piven and Richard A. Cloward, *Regulating the Poor* (New York: Pantheon, 1971).

applicant are considered, especially all insurance benefits under old-age, survivors, and disability insurance; unemployment compensation; workmen's compensation; and the Railroad Retirement Act. Other income considered is interest from real or personal property, rents, veterans' and servicemen's benefits, support from relatives, payments from private life insurance and pension plans, and union welfare funds. If the applicant is eligible, he receives a check at regular intervals, usually once a month. If assistance is denied, the applicant is informed about his right to ask for a hearing or to appeal to another authority, insofar as the categorical types of public assistance are concerned.

Decisions of the public welfare department must be given in writing so that misunderstandings may be avoided, and so that the applicant is able to make an appeal within the period legally stipulated.

In all forms of public assistance, the applicant is required to report promptly to the public welfare department any change in income, economic conditions, address, or other important facts which are essential for granting assistance. The social worker often may help the applicant in other matters regarding his living conditions, health problems, personal questions, and plans for change of his dependent situation.

Categorical Assistance

The goal of public assistance is to provide minimum economic aid to persons who have no other means of supporting themselves. Public assistance is granted only to such people as these, in contrast to social insurance benefits, which are not dependent on economic need.[4] Before the enactment of the Social Security Act in 1935 less than half the states had special relief systems which provided more adequate care than general poor relief for the aged, for blind persons, or for children. Under the Social Security Act the federal government shares in the expenses of four major types of *categorical assistance:* old-age assistance, aid to the blind, aid to dependent children, and aid to the permanently and totally disabled.[5] For the residual part of public assistance, which is called *general assistance* (or indigent aid), no federal standards exist, and no federal money is provided, so that this field remains the sole responsibility of state or local governments. We shall discuss, first, the categorical forms of public assistance, and then the field of general assistance.

[4] Public welfare agencies provide, in addition to financial aid, other essential services, such as casework and medical care; see Kahn, "Public Social Services," 16–18.

[5] The last category was created by the *Amendment of 1950;* for an important evaluation of the entire social security program, see the "Report of the Advisory Council on Social Security," *Social Security Bulletin,* 28, No. 3 (March 1965), 3–41.

Whether public assistance should bear a major burden in providing income security to persons who need such protection is controversial. Whereas before the enactment of social insurance legislation into the Social Security Act, public relief was the only means of public aid to people in distress, it is now but one, and no longer the largest program, within the framework of social security. The number of persons protected by the categorical forms of public assistance is now greater than that of recipients of general assistance.[6]

The federal government until 1973 shared the cost of categorical assistance, but it did not administer these programs.[7]

Under the provisions of the 1972 Amendment to the Social Security Act, the "adult assistance categories"—Old Age Assistance (OAA), Aid to the Blind (AB), and Aid to the Permanently and Totally Disabled (APTD) —were transferred effective January 1, 1974 to the Social Security Administration in the Federal Department of Health, Education and Welfare. Thus, these programs are for the first time in the United States nationally financed and administered by the federal government; until the transfer they had been financed partly by the states and partly by the federal government, and administered by the states.[8] The fourth categorical program, Aid to Families with Dependent Children (AFDC), was not transferred from the Social and Rehabilitation Service in the Department of Health, Education and Welfare by the 1972 Amendment; it will still be administered by state and local authorities. AFDC remains the most controversial public assistance program, both because of its large size and because large proportions of its clients are minority group families, particularly blacks and Chicanos.

Categorical assistance is rendered in the form of money to needy persons or as payment for medical or remedial treatment. Categorical assistance usually does not issue vouchers or supply food, clothes, or fuel in kind to needy persons, as was frequently the case in the past. It may pay the medical expenses for an individual or for all recipients of public assistance through local or statewide prepayment medical care plans. Categorical assistance plans favor and encourage applicants to live in their homes. Fed-

---

[6] *Social Security Bulletin*, 36, No. 2 (February 1973), 52, Table M-25; Burns, *Social Security and Public Policy*, pp. 269–80.

[7] Schottland, *The Social Security Program in the United States*, pp. 41–52; Jerome Cohen, "Social Work and the Culture of Poverty," *Social Work*, No. 1 (January 1964), 3–11; Leonard J. Duhl, "Are We Mentally Prepared for the Elimination of Poverty?" *Social Welfare Forum* (1961), 100–113; Dumpson, "Hunger and Human Welfare," *Social Welfare Forum* (1961), 87–99; and Charles B. Rangel, "The Political Process," *Social Welfare Forum* (1971), 84–89.

[8] Judith D. Moore, "New Law from the 92nd Congress," *Human Needs*, 1, No. 6 (December 1972), 8; Robert M. Ball, "Social Security Amendments of 1972: Summary and Legislative History," *Social Security Bulletin*, 36, No. 3 (March 1973), 3–25.

eral payments are also made to share the expenses of medical and remedial care of needy persons in public medical institutions (hospitals and sanatoriums); psychotic or tubercular patients are included.

Under the *Medical Assistance Program,* enacted by the Amendment of the Social Security Act of 1965, the states must provide inpatient and outpatient hospital services, laboratory and x-ray services, skilled nursing home services for adults, and physicians' services in the doctor's office, the patient's home, or in a hospital nursing home. Additional services may be provided by the states. No cost-sharing or deductible requirements may be imposed by the states for assistance recipients or medically needy patients. For elderly needy patients who are receiving hospitalization under the *Hospital Insurance Program of 1966,* the states must supply assistance payments to meet deductible or cost-sharing payments.

One of the controversial questions in connection with family health and the functions of social agencies is the dissemination of birth-control information in family planning. While well-to-do families sought medical advice and care in such questions, the needy in general have been deprived of proper medical help and have resorted frequently to illegal abortions with severe physical damages as a result.[9] Under the Aid to Dependent Children Program, federal grants differ for the first child and the mother, or other caretaker, and for subsequent children in the family.

The Social Security Act does not define the concept of "need" as a prerequisite for the receipt of public assistance. Each state, therefore, determines what resources and property an individual or a family may have and still be eligible for public assistance. Statutes and regulations of the states on home ownership, savings, cash, and insurance policies, to exclude an applicant from eligibility, vary greatly. Many states, counties, and cities impose liens on the real estate of applicants to secure the refund of general assistance payments after the death of the recipient or when he becomes financially able to repay. To avoid hardship, some regulations require the refund to be made only after the death of the recipient's spouse.

The establishment of these policies means that an applicant for public assistance first must use up his reserves, income, and property (except a limited amount) before he is granted public assistance. This is often hard for an honest applicant, who has saved for a "rainy day," to understand.

Most state laws require not only that the applicant must exhaust his resources before he may receive assistance, but also that his close relatives must support him. Assistance can be given only when the applicant does not receive such support. This "relatives' responsibility" is limited to the

9 "The Right to Birth Control Information in Family Planning," *Social Service Review,* 39, No. 1 (March 1965), 96–101; G. Gurin and P. Gurin "Expectancy Theory in the Study of Poverty," *Journal of Social Issues,* 38, No. 2 (1970), 83–104.

spouse, parents toward their minor children, and adult children toward their parents, but the state laws show differences in their approach. In some states, the requirement of the support of family members is limited according to sliding scales, which are classified according to income and number of dependents of the responsible relative.

The effect of family responsibility is disputed. Some statutes base these provisions on the assumption that by requiring the support of close relatives the family ties are strengthened. In fact, however, the demand for support often is a serious strain on the budget of relatives with modest income, and may lead to a hostile attitude toward those in need that may cause a break-up of friendly relations and serious emotional suffering. In some states, the contribution which relatives owe to the applicant for assistance is deducted from the assistance payment, even if it is not given. This policy violates the sense of the Social Security Act and leads to hardship for the poor, and most states deduct the relative's support only if it is in fact rendered.

The amount of public assistance given to the individual person or to the family is, as a rule, determined on the basis of a budget consisting of the cost figures for food, shelter, fuel, utilities, and clothing. Most states have standard budgets which include several of these items, but leave consideration of rent, nursing, and medical cost to the county or city. The income of the recipient is deducted. Special expenses for medical care, appliances, and medicines may be considered. The financial situation of a number of states sometimes makes it difficult to fulfill the full budgetary needs, so that payments are cut.[10]

Although mobility of labor has been a characteristic of American life, and migrations enable agricultural and industrial development, communities and states have refused to support "strangers" in need of financial help. State residence requirements for welfare benefits have been declared unconstitutional by a decision of the Supreme Court in 1969, but the "intent to remain in the community" is still required. Nonresidents may be refused aid and may be returned to their former place of residence. The hardships which migrants and their families suffer under these conditions has led to a more liberal policy in some states, which now permit residents to receive public assistance payments outside the state; some reciprocal agreements between states permit mutual assistance to their residents. The establishment of a new general assistance category with federal grants-in-aid which would give special consideration to aid for nonresidents might be the best possible solution to this problem.

The development of the public assistance categories from the enactment of the Social Security Act of 1935 until 1970 is shown in Figure 3.

---

[10] See Ida C. Merriam, "Financing Social Welfare Services," *Social Work Encyclopedia 1965*, pp. 342–48; Robert H. Mugge, "Public Assistance Population," *Encyclopedia 1971*, pp. 1028–41.

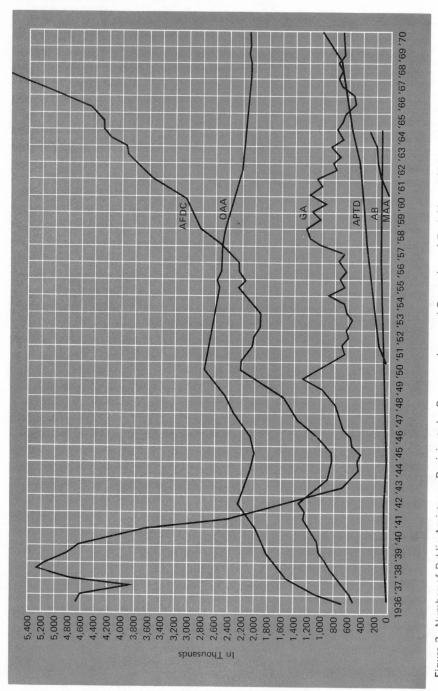

Figure 3. Number of Public Assistance Recipients by Program, June and December of Each Year, 1936 to 1970[11]

[11] *Welfare in Review*, 3, No. 8 (August 1965), 35, and 9, No. 3 (June 1971), 35. For recent development, see Figure 4.

Until the time of the Act, general assistance was the common form of public relief, and under the impact of the Depression, during 1936 and 1937 especially, it still served the largest numbers. In 1941 the new category of old-age assistance reached the same level as general assistance and, since then, has been increasing in importance. After World War II, the number of old-age assistance recipients has steadily grown, while the number of recipients of general assistance has declined with several variations since 1950.

That financial payments under the Aid to Families with Dependent Children became increasingly important is made evident in Figure 3. The number of dependent children has steadily increased. Supplementary aid to mothers and caretakers, which began in 1950, has made this program more effective. Compared to these large programs, the number of persons supported under the aid to the blind, and aid to the permanently and totally disabled, is small, but the social significance of aid to these persons should not be underrated.[12]

Medical Care in Public Assistance

The provision of medical care for public assistance recipients who are ill has long been recognized as a basic need. A 1950 amendment to the Social Security Act permitted the Social Security Administration to participate in the payment of the costs of medical treatment that public assistance recipients required by sharing the costs paid to those who provide the medical care. It limited the amount of the monthly payments to individual recipients. The Amendment of 1956 established a new basis on which the federal government shared in state expenditures for medical care on behalf of public assistance recipients. For the first time, the federal government's payments for this purpose were rendered in addition to the other federal grants-in-aid to public assistance recipients. The purpose of this change was to help the states intensify, extend, and broaden their medical care programs for the recipients of public assistance.[13] It enabled the states to pay directly to doctors, hospitals, medical societies, and insurance agencies that

---

[12] See Peter O. Steiner and Robert Dorfman, *The Economic Status of the Aged* (Berkeley: University of California Press, 1957); and James R. Dumpson, "Our Welfare System—Radical Surgery Needed," *Public Welfare*, 23, No. 4 (October 1965), 226–34.

[13] Edward S. Rogers, "Medical Care," *Encyclopedia of Social Work 1965*, pp. 476–86; Margaret Greenfield, *Medical Care for Welfare Recipients—Basic Problems* (Berkeley: University of California Press, 1957), pp. 1–39; Burns, *Social Security and Public Policy*, Chap. 8; Dorothy P. Rice, "Financing Social Welfare: Health Care," *Encyclopedia 1971*, pp. 433–38; *Social Policy for Health Care* (New York: New York Academy of Medicine, 1969); Nora Piore, "Health as a Social Problem," *Encyclopedia 1971*, pp. 490–503.

provided medical care. The federal government shared, on a 55–45 basis, payment for each recipient of old-age assistance, blind aid, and disabled aid. The former limit for the federal share of fifteen dollars per month was removed by the Amendment of 1965, and the *Public Assistance Health Care Title XIX* requires that the states provide health care, at least such as that of medical assistance for the aged (MAA). The states may average their medical expenses for public assistance recipients and receive one-half from federal funds for these expenditures, within specified limits.

Federal financial participation in medical care expenditures was based on the total amount expended in each month and was unrelated to the maximum payment made to an individual recipient.

State public assistance agencies may maintain a pooled fund to make prepayment arrangements to meet the cost of medical services for public assistance recipients. Fixed payments may be made into the pooled fund each month, in behalf of each public assistance recipient, which are recognized as assistance expenditure for medical care. Premium payments into a pooled fund are still recognized as assistance payments, and will be shared by the federal government, subject to limitation. Pooled fund coverage, or other payment of medical care, may be provided, also, to the "medically needy" who receive no other money payments than that for medical care.

Medical care includes diagnosis or therapy performed by a physician, surgeon, or dentist, nursing services in the home or elsewhere, drugs, medical supplies, appliances, and laboratory fees, which are provided or prescribed by persons authorized by state law to give such services. Of particular importance is medical care for the aged, because the highest rates of chronic disease and disability occur in this group.

The Social Security Amendment of 1965 established a new *Title XIX* of the Act. It replaced the sporadic medical aid to aged persons under the Kerr-Mills laws in several states and the earlier provisions of medical care to recipients of old-age, aid to the blind, to the disabled, and to families with dependent children. The medical assistance program requires that the states provide inpatient and outpatient hospital services, the usual auxiliary services, and physicians' services to receive federal participation for these medical payments.

The states administer this program; eligibility is determined by the state public assistance agency. No deductible amount or cost-sharing may be imposed for hospitalization, and other charges must be related to the income and resources of the recipient.

To encourage the states in developing the medical assistance program, the Social Security Amendment of 1965 assured each state which did not reduce its expenditure for medical assistance an increase of 5 percent of federal participation, and increased the federal grants for compensation and training of professional medical personnel to 75 percent from the former 50 percent.

Despite improvements in health care, the promise of medical service for all who need it has not been fulfilled, and new problems, such as drug addiction among ghetto youth, now threaten.

Old-Age Assistance

The old-age assistance program is an important source of income to retired or unemployable people over sixty-five years of age. It is in effect in all states and the District of Columbia. But the proportion of the aged population assisted by this categorical program varies widely among the states. Frequently, old-age assistance payments supplement insurance benefits that do not adequately meet the economic needs of the aged.[14]

The average payment of old-age assistance varied substantially among the states. Beginning in 1974, the aged, blind, and disabled have received equal assistance payments from the federal government.[15]

Federal grants-in-aid have not been able to raise the level of assistance in low-income states to a really adequate standard. In the majority of states, however, the payments are securing a modest subsistence on a "health and decency level." Many states have monthly maximum payments with limited supplements in case of special needs. In some states, persons are not eligible if they are found begging, have failed to support their minor children, or have committed a felony within the past ten years, but it is these persons who have more difficulties in finding a job, so they are prone to commit new crimes.

Old-age assistance makes it possible, in general, for aged men and women to go on living in their homes, either alone or with their families, and to receive regular monthly cash allowances for their maintenance. If they are unable to manage their households, they may live in boarding homes or in private homes for the aged.[16] During recent years, a good many county almshouses were converted into hospitals for the chronically ill, and patients over sixty-five may therefore receive old-age assistance in these medical institutions.

Special needs, considered in the public assistance payment, frequently arise because of infirmities, special diets required by a physician,

[14] Leonore A. Epstein, "Money Income of Aged Persons," *Social Security Bulletin,* 22, No. 6 (June 1959), 3–11, and "Early Retirement and Work-Life Experience," *Social Security Bulletin,* 29, No. 3 (March 1966), 3–10; *Social Security Bulletin,* 35, No. 1 (January 1972), 50, Table M-15; 58, Table M-24, and 48, Table M-13.

[15] *Welfare in Review,* 4, No. 2 (February 1966), 24, Table 3; *Social Security Bulletin,* 36, No. 2 (February 1973), 59, Table M-27.

[16] James, J. Lally, *The Over 50 Health Manual: A Guide to a Vigorous and Longer Life for People Over 50* (Englewood Cliffs, N.J.: Prentice-Hall, Inc., 1961).

the necessity to eat in restaurants, moving and storage expenses caused by eviction, and housekeeping and laundry service for persons unable to do this themselves.

Aid to the Blind

The second categorical assistance program which the federal government administers beginning in 1974 is aid to the needy blind. A practical definition of "needy blind" was presented in an Oregon statute: "an individual whose vision is so defective as to prevent the performance of ordinary activities for which eyesight is essential." The procedure of application is the same as in old-age assistance. An applicant for aid to the blind is examined by a medical eye specialist (ophthalmologist) or an optometrist.

California, Missouri, Nevada, and Pennsylvania set up special state-financed programs to encourage blind persons to become self-supporting. An example was the California program of Aid to Partially Self-Supporting Blind Residents, which encouraged blind persons to achieve self-support by establishing themselves in business, farming, regular trade, employment in industry or commerce, or the operation of a vending stand. This was done by permitting them to keep $1,000 plus one-half of the exceeding gainful income a year without considering this income in the determination for their monthly assistance payment.

Additional services provided by many states for the blind were free medical examination and treatment, special education of children in schools for the blind, or classes for visually handicapped children, conducted usually under the auspices of the state department of education. Rehabilitation services rendered occupational counseling, vocational guidance, and training for employment or special trades, such as for piano tuning, broom making, handicrafts, or professional work. They were administered by a State Bureau of Vocational Rehabilitation, which served the blind as well as other handicapped people.

Federal grants-in-aid for rehabilitation work are allocated by the Department of Health, Education and Welfare, Office of Vocational Rehabilitation. The federal government provides, as a part of the rehabilitation effort, grants for medical treatment, surgery, hospital care, artificial appliances, adult training centers, placement services, and assistance in providing occupational equipment. Federal grants-in-aid for the needy blind may be used for medical care to remove cataracts by surgery or to conserve vision in cases of glaucoma. Earlier and more effective medical treatment, including eye surgery, is unfortunately still a goal far from being generally achieved for persons with limited means who might be saved from blindness.

Private organizations play an important role in supplementing the services for the blind offered under public auspices. Some of them strengthen educational and rehabilitation work for the blind.[17] Since 1921 the American Foundation for the Blind in New York has served as coordinating agency for all nationwide interests of the blind. In all states, local private groups of the blind and organizations interested in helping the blind are making valuable contributions in the field of social and recreational life of the blind. They help the blind find employment and organize cultural and recreational activities, and pioneer in new adventures for the blind. They promote a better public understanding of the needs of the blind and of the importance of more adequate services and legislation for them.

Aid to the Permanently and Totally Disabled

The Amendment to the Social Security Act of 1950 added a public assistance category for permanently, totally disabled persons in economic need. Until this time, many of them had been meagerly supported by counties and cities under general relief provisions without help from state or federal funds. This category includes adults over eighteen years who have serious physical or mental handicaps. The Social Security Act does not give a definition of "permanently and totally disabled" but allowed the states to define the terms and the conditions of need which entitle one to apply for this categorical aid. The program provides either money payments to adult, invalid persons under sixty-five who are not eligible for old-age assistance, or medical and remedial care for them. This categorical aid was in operation in all states except Arizona, Indiana, Iowa, and Nevada, until it was transferred to the federal government in 1973.

The group of persons under this category consists mainly of people who suffer from physical or mental impairment, which, in medical judgment, offers no indication of a substantial improvement, and which prevents the invalid person from being gainfully employed or from normal homemaking; included are heart diseases, arthritis, and paralysis. The program, however, is not limited to completely helpless people. Economic assistance to these disabled persons resembles the aid to needy blind people. Standards of assistance and special requirements in the states vary. In general, the administration was carried out by the state and local agencies, such as the department of social welfare, which also were in charge of the other categorical assistance programs.[18] It is hoped that medical care and

---

[17] Jacobus Ten Broek and Floyd W. Martin, "The Disabled and the Law of Welfare," *California Law Review*, 54, No. 2 (May 1966), 809–40; Robert A. Scott, "The Selection of Clients by Social Welfare Agencies: The Case of the Blind," *Social Problems*, 14, No. 3 (Winter 1967), 248–57.

[18] Robert Morris, "Chronic Illness and Disability," *Encyclopedia of Social Work 1965*, pp. 145–55; *Social Security Bulletin*, (February 1972), 57, Table M-24; Madeleine Shipsey, "Disability and Physical Handicap," *Encyclopedia 1971*, pp. 228–35.

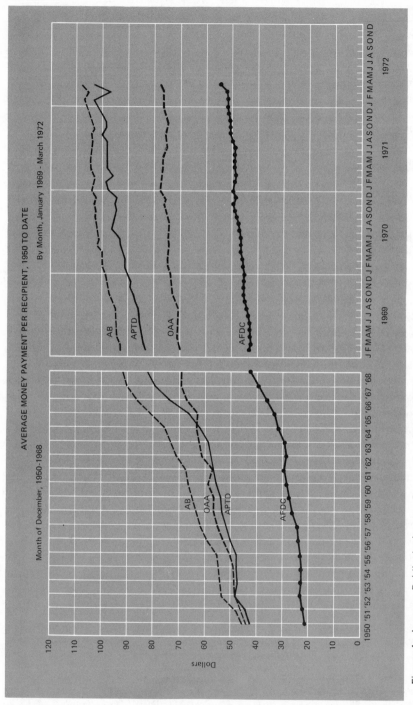

Figure 4. Average Public Assistance Payments, 1950 to 1970

rehabilitation for these invalids will be intensified by more adequate financial support. The categorical assistance may be used for cash payments, remedial care, hospitalization, and medical treatment. Physicians and hospitals may be paid directly in behalf of the patient.

Categorical assistance is given on the basis of the medical findings and the applicant's social and emotional ability to carry out his responsibilities as a wage-earner or homemaker. A permanent physiological or mental impairment may exist from birth or may be caused by illness or accident. It must be a permanent condition, likely to last for life or not to improve or disappear spontaneously. This legal limitation is regrettable, as it prevents rehabilitation. The possibility of improvement or recovery by remedial or therapeutic treatment and vocational rehabilitation, however, does not prohibit the assistance payment. The major causes of permanent disability are cancer, chronic asthma, cystic fibrosis, diabetes, chronic renal disease, blood dyscrasias, and leukemia.

Among the physically handicapped persons in the United States in need of rehabilitation are many permanently and totally disabled.[19] New York supports the largest number of the needy disabled. The expansion of the federal old-age and survivors insurance system to include disabled insured workers fifty to sixty-five years of age also helps a group of the disabled by social insurance benefits. But, because of the limited scope of the Disability Insurance Plan, public assistance to the permanently, totally disabled still remains a major source of support to the severely handicapped (see Figure 4).

Aid to Families with Dependent Children

Destitute children have always constituted a large proportion of the poor. The first White House Conference, in 1909, advocated that children should remain in their homes whenever possible and not be removed for economic reasons. Their mothers should receive "mothers' allowances" so that they would not be forced to give their children away while they worked as domestics or in factories. From this concept grew a program of Aid to Families with Dependent Children as a categorical form of public assistance under the Social Security Act. Its definition of a dependent child is "a needy child under eighteen years of age, who has been deprived of parental support or care by reason of the death, continued absence from the home, or physical or mental incapacity of a parent, and who is living with his father, mother, grandmother, grandfather, brother, sister, stepmother, stepfather, stepbrother, stepsister, uncle, aunt, first cousin, nephew, or niece in

---

[19] Jacobus Ten Broek, "The Right to Live in the World: The Disabled in the Law of Torts," *California Law Review,* 54, No. 2 (May 1966), 841–919.

a place of residence maintained by one or more of such relatives at his own and their own home." This does not include all needy children, such as orphans, who have no close relatives and, therefore, cannot live with them, or children who must be placed in children's institutions.[20] The payment is made to the mother or to the relative who takes care of the child. Upon application, aid must be given with reasonable promptness. The time which elapses between application and payment of aid differs among the states.

The states determine, in their laws and regulations, the requirements for eligibility to receive AFDC (Aid to Families with Dependent Children) and how much shall be paid. Frequently, the need of the child is caused by the desertion of the father; many statutes require a certain period of absence. Usually, aid is given on a standard budget basis which considers the elementary needs of the child and of the mother or the caretaker with regard to local conditions. Only a small number of children receiving aid under the AFDC program are full orphans. Needy children are also supported by the Old-Age, Survivors, and Disability Insurance system, the Veterans Administration, and under Workmen's Compensation Insurance laws of the states, but AFDC maintains more needy children than all other programs together.[21] Very few needy children receive further aid under general assistance because the low standards in most states set limitations which prevent support in addition to insurance benefits or allowances to orphaned children of veterans. An important increase of the program was the inclusion of children of unemployed parents in 1968.

Whenever aid to dependent children is given to a child who has been abandoned by a parent, the state agency has to report the case promptly to the law enforcement authority—usually the district attorney. The purpose of this so-called *"NOLEO"-Amendment of 1950* (notice to law enforcement officials) is to facilitate legal action against the deserting father, to force him to assume his financial responsibility for the support of his child. Nearly all states enacted reciprocal legislation to enforce the support of dependents; but many difficulties still exist in legal procedure against parents in other parts of the country. Mothers sometimes are afraid that court action may prevent their husbands from returning to the family, making them hostile and desiring divorce rather than reconciliation. However, the

[20] See Ernest F. Witte, "Children in the Public Assistance Family," *Child Welfare,* 38, No. 1 (January 1959); Jules H. Berman, "Public Assistance (AFDC)," *Encyclopedia 1971,* pp. 1017–18. A large proportion of dependent children are members of minority groups; for their special conditions, see Chapter 17.

[21] See F. Ivan Nye and Lois W. Hoffman, *The Employed Mother in America* (Chicago: Rand McNally, 1963); M. Elaine Burgess and Daniel O. Price, *An American Dependency Challenge* (Chicago: American Public Welfare Association, 1963); Kermit T. Wiltse: "ADC: Basic Family and Child Welfare Program," *Social Welfare Forum* (1960), 218–31; and Robert Mugge, "Public Assistance Population," *Encyclopedia 1971,* pp. 1033–37.

public resents deserting fathers relinquishing their moral and legal responsibility for the support of their children, and insists that they should be discouraged from unburdening their own obligations on public welfare agencies.

Violent accusations are made, again and again, in newspapers and journals that the public is exploited through the abuse of AFDC, by shiftless, irresponsible people unwilling to work, particularly women who live with various men and have numerous illegitimate children. But even these critics usually admit that cases of abuse are only exceptions, and that the maintenance of family life for the children in economic need, which is made possible by AFDC, protects the vast majority against the dangers of maladjustment, delinquency, and crime.

The federal government shares the expenses for aid to dependent children, and pays one-half of the administrative cost of the program. The federal government's share has been established in accordance with the principle of equalization in favor of the poorer states, on the basis of the state's per capita income during the last three years compared with the national income. The states either meet the entire residual cost for AFDC or divide it among the state and local units of government (counties, cities, and townships).

Since some children in economic need cannot live with relatives and have to be placed in foster families, or in orphanages or other children's institutions, the states support these children either in the same way as "dependent children" or under their general assistance plans. The 1972 amendment makes federal support for foster care possible. For example, California administers categorical assistance under the title "needy children" to children who are deprived of parental support. These children in foster families or children's institutions are supported from state and local funds; but less than 7 percent of needy children live outside their families. Each state is required to set up a special unit for the location of deserting parents which must refer to law enforcement officers and must control fraud.

The American Public Welfare Association conducted an interesting study to determine whether the program of aid to dependent children is successful in conserving the human resources of our nation on which its future depends.[22] The results of this research show that it is necessary to expand and improve financial assistance and social services to children and

[22] Maude Von P. Kemp, et al., *Casework Services in ADC* (Chicago: American Public Welfare Association, 1957); Helen B. Foster, "Family-Centered Services Through ADC," *Social Welfare Forum* (1958), 154–65; Eunice Minton, "Voluntary and Public Relationships in Family Service," *Social Work Practice, 1964* (New York: Columbia University Press, 1964), pp. 41–54; Maurine McKeany, *The Absent Father and Public Policy in the Program of Aid to Dependent Children* (Berkeley: University of California Press, 1960).

young people deprived of sufficient support from their parents. One of the most important achievements of AFDC is that it has encouraged keeping families together. Through this program, child neglect, illegitimate births, delinquency, and crime have occurred less frequently than would have been expected in this endangered and stress-ridden group without such aid. The survey found that one-fourth of the families were still in economic need when the assistance under this program had to be terminated because of its legal restrictions about the age of the children, other income, and return of an absent father. But the study also proved that the assistance payments in many parts of the country are still so low that they barely reach minimum subsistence standards.

The Family Assistance Plan of 1969

In August 1969 President Nixon sent a message to Congress severely criticizing the public assistance program and suggesting new legislation under the title "family assistance program." After long debate in both houses of Congress, the final legislation in 1972 eliminated the major features of the president's suggestions, several forms of assistance to families with dependent children with requirements for work. It also transferred the three types of adult categorical public assistance (discussed in the preceding pages) under federal auspices to the Social Security Administration (which had been administered until 1974 by the Rehabilitation and Social Service Division of HEW), and changed the provisions of Medicare to include the disabled and increase the costs of Medicaid to patients (see Chapter 15). The Revenue Sharing Act of 1972 (PL 92-512) limited the amount of federal matching funds for social services under state governments to $2.5 billion, beginning with fiscal year 1973, with the exception of expenses for the Work Incentive program, and with the condition that no more than 10 percent of the federal grants may be spent for former or potential assistance recipients. Exceptions are permitted for child care, family planning, mentally retarded children, treatment of alcoholics and drug addicts, and foster care.[23]

General Assistance

General assistance is public relief to needy persons who are not eligible for any of the four categorical public assistance programs. The rigid limitations of our public assistance categories explain why numerous persons are not encompassed by this categorical approach; private charity or general

---

[23] Edith G. Levi, "Mr. Nixon's 'Speenhamland'," *Social Work,* 15, No. 1 (January 1970), 7–11; John M. Romanyshyn, *Social Welfare: Charity to Justice* (New York: Random House, 1971), pp. 261–67.

assistance, as a rule, is their only recourse. The requirements for public assistance, such as legal settlement, no relatives to assume support, and exhaustion of all resources and savings apply to general assistance even more rigidly than to the categories of public assistance.[24] One reason for this practice is that general assistance is financed, more than any other economic relief program, by the cities, townships, or counties, which have limited tax funds and must use them for schools, sanitation, police, fire protection, roads, and special local needs. In some states the cost of general assistance is shared between the state and the community or county, with the state frequently paying one-half or more of the expenses. In only ten states is the entire financial burden of general assistance met by the state without a contribution from the communities and counties. Many states prohibit the payment of general assistance when there is an employable person in the family without regard to the fact that he or she may be unable to find work. Since the federal government does not share the cost of general assistance, the poorer states and communities are inclined to spend as little as possible for general assistance.

The uneven treatment of persons in need under general assistance in the various states is characterized by the following facts: In August 1972, 549,000 families received general assistance with an average monthly payment of $73.75. The average payment varied widely from state to state.[25]

"Work-relief" may sometimes be required as a condition for the receipt of general assistance, although it is seldom applied even when state and local statutes authorize this method of determining the willingness of an applicant to work. The assignment of "relief clients" to useless types of work, such as leaf-raking and wood-piling, is rare today.[26]

In some states the administration of general assistance is integrated into the public assistance program at the local level; in other states it is still administered separately. Whenever the state pays the entire cost or shares the expenses for general assistance, the state welfare agency sets the standards of the program, supervises the administration, or carries it out itself. Where no financial aid for general assistance is given to community or county, the local authority determines the methods and form of general assistance, sometimes still granting relief in kind, by vouchers or tickets, which is no longer permitted in categorical assistance. Frequently, persons

[24] Schottland, *The Social Security Program in the United States,* pp. 117–20; Alvin R. Schorr, "Alternatives in Income Maintenance," *Social Work,* 11, No. 3 (July 1966), 22–29; Marc Pilisuk and Phyllis Pilisuk, eds., *How the White Poor Live* (Chicago: Aldine Press, 1971).

[25] Jane de Melto, "The Crisis of the Tenth of the Month," *Public Welfare,* 21, No. 4 (October 1963), 179–225; *Social Security Bulletin,* 36, No. 1 (January 1973), 43, Tables M-25, M-26.

[26] Walter C. Bentrup, "The Profession and the Means Test," *Social Work,* 9, No. 2 (April 1964), 10–17.

who seem employable are denied relief to force them to work regardless of whether a job is, in fact, available, thus forcing them to go begging or to steal. Furthermore, the county or township will not give general assistance until the person has spent his last penny.

General assistance has been called a "patchwork" because each state handles it differently. Principles, standards, administration, and financing vary even within the counties and cities of the same state. Frequently, the treatment of needy persons depends on the local community in which they fall sick or find themselves unemployed. Professional associations in social work have advocated that the federal government share the expenses for general assistance as a special category or combine all public assistance categories into one which would be supported by grants-in-aid or fully paid from the federal government. But Congress and the conscience of the people have not, as yet, been ready to translate this proposal into reality. There is still too much suspicion that an unemployed, able-bodied person asks for relief because of willful idleness, whereas he could find a job and support himself and his family. The public is afraid that public assistance might be made too easy and too generous, and the anxiety of the taxpayers that their burden might be still heavier is understandable in a time of high taxes. Despite these facts, however, the need for integration of all types of public assistance into one unified program, administered by the same agency and staffed with trained social workers, remains an essential goal.

Training and Research

Training of public welfare personnel. Congress authorized, in 1956, federal appropriations to the states to help them increase the number of trained personnel for public welfare programs. A federal share of 80 percent of the total expenses for a period of five years, with an initial appropriation of $5,000,000, was scheduled. The funds were to be used for grants to public or private institutions of higher learning for the education of public welfare personnel and for fellowships, traineeships, study courses, and seminars.[27]

Research and demonstration projects. To learn more about the causes of dependency in our present society, and to find the most effective means of preventing and eliminating dependency, the Amendment of 1956 introduced, under Title XI of the Social Security Act, a new program of cooperative research and demonstration projects. It authorized federal grants to the states, jointly financed cooperative arrangements with the states and with public and nonprofit organizations for sharing the expenses of research

[27] Virginia L. Tannar, "Training for the Expanding Service Programs in Public Welfare," *Social Casework,* 46, No. 10 (December 1965), 599–606; Gertrude Leyendecker, "A Comprehensive Staff Development Program," *Social Casework,* 46, No. 10 (December 1965), 607–14.

and demonstration projects. The projects were to be related to the prevention or reduction of dependency, to the coordination of planning between private and public welfare agencies, or to the improvement of the administration and the effectiveness of programs under the Social Security Act and related measures.

Unfortunately, the Amendment of 1956, calling for federal grants to the states for training of public welfare personnel and for research and demonstration projects, was not followed by actual appropriations of Congress. The Senate Appropriations Committee in June 1959 disallowed the requested funds with the argument that states have made little use of federal funds for educational purposes. However, in 1960 and 1962 appropriations for training grants were made which enabled several states to conduct such programs.

Casework in Public Assistance

Before the Great Depression of 1929, most townships and counties limited their poor relief to meager financial assistance in kind or money, while private charities in urban communities helped a large proportion of the needy and tried to rehabilitate them through casework services based on an understanding of the cause of their poverty. At that time, most poor-law authorities employed untrained personnel, although supervisors were partly professional workers. The changes made under the New Deal transferred the main responsibility for the care of persons in need to the public welfare agencies where many professional social workers from private charities were employed. They applied their belief that the cause of destitution needed to be explored in each individual case to cure it and to prevent its recurrence. Since the enactment of the Social Security Act of 1935 and the creation of public assistance categories (the aged, the blind, dependent children, and later the disabled), the objective of public welfare is undergoing progressive change.[28] Assistance is no longer a "handout," but is rendered to persons in need as a "right." The applicant must be considered in his social, economic, and personal condition, his feelings about relief, and his fear of humiliation.[29] Social work in public assistance agencies, with large case loads and

[28] Tannar, "Training for the Expanding Service Programs"; Alfred H. Katz, "Application of Self-Help Concepts in Current Social Welfare," *Social Work,* 10, No. 3 (July 1965), 68–74; Alfred J. Kahn, "Social Services in Relation to Income Security," *Social Service Review,* 39, No. 4 (December 1965), 381–89.

[29] For an interpretation of the need of casework skills in public welfare, see Charlotte Towle, *Common Human Needs* (Chicago: University of Chicago Press, 1945); Kermit T. Wiltse, *Public Assistance Personnel: Educational Requirements and Training Facilities* (Berkeley: University of California Press, 1959); and Joshua Perman, "Role of Transference in Casework With Public Assistance Families," *Social Work,* 8, No. 4 (October 1963), 47–54.

pressure of work, requires different approaches from those applied in private family and children's agencies. The Amendment of the Social Security Act of 1956 broadened the purpose of public assistance beyond giving financial aid to provide personal services to the recipients, to help them toward independent living. Casework with aged people is directed toward self-care, and in work with the blind and disabled toward self-care and self-support after rehabilitation or training. Casework in the aid to families with dependent children program aims to keep the children in their homes and to maintain and strengthen family life, whereby cooperation with other public and private social and health agencies shall be secured. The purpose of public assistance, therefore, is to assure adequate economic help, keeping in mind the self-respect, the dignity, and the legal rights of recipients. Furthermore, to achieve its purpose, public assistance must be provided with consideration of the goal of financial and personal independence, so that the recipients will be able to live in the community in the same way as other individuals.

The caseworker in a public welfare agency has to be sincerely convinced that an individual in economic need has a rightful claim on society for public assistance. By explaining clearly legal requirements and the policy of the agency, the worker will be able to help the client present the necessary data and facts for establishing "eligibility" for public assistance. This has to be done in a way which expresses the confidence of the worker in the client and his respect for the client, rather than with a hostile attitude which tries to prevent the client from getting aid. The worker has to understand how vitally important money is for everyone in financial stress in our society. In general, clients come to social agencies in times of want and anxiety, and they often are emotionally disturbed. They naturally are more sensitive to their treatment than the average citizen, and they react differently to the kind of approach used by the caseworker. Unfortunately, many untrained workers in public welfare agencies resent the appeal of "welfare rights organizations" or other social workers to live up to these principles. Recently "social services" have been separated from "eligibility work"; the services have been reduced in many public welfare agencies. Professional evaluation of whether this is progress in service to the client is divided.[30]

Casework in public welfare requires professional skills. The caseworker must have skill in personal interviewing; skill in establishing a positive, constructive relationship with the client; training in perception and observation of human beings and in interpreting documents; ability to distinguish between pertinent facts that are essential for the application and

---

[30] Jules H. Berman, "Public Assistance," *Encyclopedia 1971*, pp. 1025–27; Scott Briar, "Money, Politics and Social Services," *Social Work*, 17, No. 6 (November 1972), 2.

personal information not needed for the decision on assistance or service in which the client is interested; skill in recognizing distress and emotional imbalance which requires help from such other sources like a mental hygiene clinic; skill in administration, communication, recording, and reporting; ability to comply with the prescribed policy and procedure of the agency; awareness of the client's social, health, and personal needs and ability to encourage him to use other community resources; ability to plan and organize his work load efficiently; and ability to accept and use supervision with intelligence in the interest of the client.

In rural areas there usually are no private social agencies available for casework services, so that the county welfare department is the only source of help for the client.[31] The caseworker in the urban public agency needs to have accurate knowledge of the services and policies of other agencies in the community, to refer clients who will receive more effective aid to another social agency. The caseworker in public assistance must be careful not to use the client's economic helplessness to force on him an undesired change in attitude or way of life, even if the worker is convinced that such change is in the interest of the client or his family. If the caseworker acts on request of an authoritative agency, such as a court, a parole board, or a youth authority, the source of any specific request should be clearly explained to the client.

The following case may illustrate casework in public assistance.

Case of the Buford Family[32]

The Buford family is a lower-class Negro family, composed of the widowed mother, forty-eight years of age, and eight children, five of whom live in the home. The latter are Cleo (eighteen, in tenth grade in school), John (sixteen, in eleventh grade), Calvin (thirteen, in eighth grade), Marcia (eleven, in third grade), and Alma (eight, in second grade). Two grandchildren also live in the home: Perry (two, son of Mildred), and Dolores (three months, daughter of Cleo). The three children who live outside the home are Mildred (mother of Perry, who is living with and supported by her husband Earl Wilson), Clarissa Loams (married and working part-time as a domestic), and Lindon (separated from his wife and paying alimony to her).

The family live in a rapidly changing rural area bordering on a medium-sized Southern city. There are other Negro families in the neighborhood, but they are surrounded by housing developments with homes in the $25,000 bracket and by large

---

31 See James D. Cowhig, et al., "Rural Youth: Their Problems and Prospects," *American Child*, 46, No. 1 (January 1962), 1–20; Leon H. Ginsberg, "Rural Social Work," *Encyclopedia 1971*, pp. 1138–44.

32 The authors are indebted for this case history to Mrs. Virginia L. Tannar, staff development specialist, Welfare Administration, U.S. Department of Health, Education and Welfare. See also her *Selected Social Work Concepts for Public Welfare Workers* (Washington, D.C.: Bureau of Family Services, Welfare Administration, 1965), pp. 113–16.

farms and estates. The Bufords built their four-room home in 1947 on land they had inherited, intending to build a larger house when they had more resources. The house is a tarpaper shack with shingles. The stovepipe sticks out of the wall, the roof is quite deteriorated, the floors slant precariously. The interior of the home is cluttered, although the floor is swept clean. The furnishings are sparse and there are pieces of rugs on the floors. The family members have little privacy. Four of the children sleep in two very small rooms. The mother, Cleo, and the two grandchildren sleep in the living room. There are electric lights. Wood is used in the space heater and also for cooking and for heating water. The water supply comes from the spring near the house. An outside toilet about fifty feet from the house completes the housing facilities.

The Bufords were first known to the public welfare agencies in January 1948, when Mrs. Buford applied for payment of hospital care for Cleo, then four years old. The child, badly burned when her dress caught fire from a stove, had been hospitalized for several weeks. When the social worker made the home visit, Mrs. Buford was not there, as she was employed as a day worker, but Mr. Buford was present. After a study of eligibility, the agency approved payment of the hospital bill; however, it never was submitted, so the Department of Public Welfare did not expend any funds. The agency received good references for Mr. Buford, a farm laborer.

Four years later in 1952, the mother reapplied for help to pay for the hospitalization of John, then six, for an avulsion wound of the hand; two of his fingers were torn almost off. The doctor at the hospital was alarmed by the child's condition. Payment of the hospital bill was authorized. At that time, Mr. Buford was earning $50 a week as a laborer and the daughter Clarissa was earning $6 for three days of work a week as a domestic.

In early 1954, Mrs. Buford was ill with high blood pressure. She came to the agency to apply for aid, but never followed through in obtaining the necessary data to establish the family's eligibility.

From January 1, 1954 to January 4, 1955, although no assistance was being given, the Public Welfare Department received letters of complaint from neighbors about the children, who were alone because both parents were working. The children were said to be disagreeable and abusive to people. They stripped peach trees of their fruit and were irregular in school attendance. The agency worked with the family on a protective service basis.

Mrs. Buford came to the agency at its request to discuss the complaints. She was hostile and defensive, but after several discussions she gave up her job and stayed at home. She seemed to take responsibility for the family's affairs. After quitting her job she was less hostile to the agency. No assistance was granted to the family at this time. In March 1955, she asked for food because Mr. Buford was again unemployed; however, the family did not follow through with its application for financial aid. In the period between 1948 and 1955 the family had applied to the agency for assistance with problems of unemployment and medical care. The Department of Public Welfare did not pay out funds, but it gave protective services when the children's behavior aroused community reactions.

In June 1955, the school principal telephoned the agency to report the sudden illness and death of Mr. Buford the previous week. Mrs. Buford was quite upset and the children appealed to a neighbor to get their mother to a hospital. There she was treated for high blood pressure and back pains in the emergency ward and sent home the next morning. When the social worker visited the home a few days later, the mother was still very much upset. She went over her husband's death in some detail and with much feeling. He had had a blood clot which caused paralysis of his legs and he had died in a matter of hours. Several weeks later, Mrs. Buford seemed to be more reconciled to the suddenness of his death, feeling that it was better that he did not suffer long. The agency supervisor who saw the children at this time thought that Mildred was alert and intelligent. Lindon, the oldest son, was working in a grocery store and also doing odd jobs. Clarissa was living away from home. The Aid to Families with Dependent Children grant was paid from July to December 1955, when Old-Age and Survivors Insurance Benefits were received. The case was then closed.

On August 15, 1960, almost five years later, Mrs. Buford reapplied for Aid to Families with Dependent Children. Her brother had been helping her with food and clothing and other items but he could not continue doing so. The Old-Age Survivors and Disability Insurance benefits for the three eldest children had terminated as they were out of the home and were no longer eligible. Mrs. Buford was herself employed only one day a week. The current social security benefits were not sufficient to meet the family's financial needs.

When the worker visited the home, she found Mildred there with her small son, born out of wedlock three months before. The girl asked for help also, but she did not wish to name the putative father, who was employed full-time in construction work.

Shortly after her mother's reapplication, Mildred married Earl Wilson, leaving her baby, Perry, with her mother who has continued to care for him. Mildred has given some sporadic support for her child. The family was found eligible for a supplemental Aid to Families with Dependent Children grant in November 1960.

No home visits were made until a new worker visited the family for a reinvestigation of eligibility on May 12, 1961. At this time Cleo was seven months pregnant and out of school. The father of her unborn child was Clyde Wilson, the brother of Mildred's husband. He was giving support to Cleo and he has continued to do so. In September 1961, Cleo returned to school, remaining at home the one day a week when her mother worked, in order to care for her own baby and her sister Mildred's child.

The worker described Mrs. Buford as a large, tall woman weighing 195 pounds, who was very outspoken and who had been hostile to various agency workers. During home visits, she shows herself to be fond of the two illegitimate grandchildren. The two daughters, Mildred and Cleo, apparently do not talk to their mother about their problems and difficulties. Cleo did not tell her mother she was pregnant until she was in her seventh month. Now that the girl is having some marital problems, her mother's attitude is: "She should have known what she was getting into."

Mrs. Buford's brother has helped the family by sending Marcia and Alma to a church camp for two weeks in the summer. He visits the home and is very fond of the children. They attend school regularly and since 1954 neither the school nor the neighbors have made complaints about the children. John has been doing odd jobs such as garden work.

Mrs. Buford's employer speaks well of her and has expressed concern about the living conditions of the family. She asked the welfare department to do something to improve the home. She also believes Mrs. Buford works when she should not, even when she is employed for only one day a week. Her employer has hired John to do garden work in the summer.

Mrs. Buford is currently attending a clinic and having a series of tests. She wants to improve her physical condition in order to become more independent.

In concluding our discussion of public assistance, we might look at the two conflicting philosophies about the best method of aiding people in financial need which we have observed in the development of public relief and in the new concept of public assistance. The traditional policy was the "punitive approach." In England and during the two first centuries of American history, under the impact of Puritan theory and the principles of the British Poor Law, this practice made the receipt of poor relief as intolerable as possible. It was hoped that these conditions would induce people in need to avoid asking for support. The humiliations connected with poor relief—the swearing of the pauper oath, and the posting of pauper lists on the marketplace, in church, and at the city hall—were devised to deter most indigent people from applying for poor relief. One expected they would seek other sources for relief, such as asking relatives and neighbors for help, accepting underpaid work and substandard labor conditions, or even begging, to sustain themselves. Some inclination to revive this punitive method has shown itself in legislation in twenty-three states to deter people in economic need from asking for assistance by opening the assistance rolls for public inspection, and in the attacks against welfare recipients, particularly mothers with several children, as chiselers and lazy people. The experience in those states has not led to any larger reduction in public assistance cases than in other states which continue to keep the names of recipients of public assistance confidential. This is evidence that the number of chiselers and swindlers of public assistance is small, and that the vast majority of recipients are in such urgent need of economic help that at the cost of their self-respect and pride they must apply for assistance, even if their name is exposed to public humiliation. There are some exceptions, such as an old, respectable man who committed suicide a few days after it had been announced that the names of all assistance recipients would be made public. Not only social workers are convinced that this punitive approach is placing an unwarranted humiliation on human beings who are mostly in need without personal fault, and that it will not really reduce the expense of public assistance.

Other reflections of this punitive approach can be seen in the measures taken by some states in denying aid to dependent children of a mother whose husband has deserted her and the children, before she has exhausted all legal efforts to force support from the father. Because these measures disregard hope for the return of the father to the family, a reconciliation of the parents may be discouraged in enforcing them. Certainly, desertion should not be encouraged, in the interest of the family, the mother, and the children; but careful, conscientious counseling of the mother is needed to advise her about the proper efforts she should make to induce her husband to support the children. The same efforts have often been made with unmarried mothers who did not want to destroy the chance of a marriage by hostile enforcement of support from the father of the illegitimate child.

In regard to the treatment of unmarried mothers, some have suggested another punitive measure, demanding the denial of economic aid to children to discourage the mother from promiscuous behavior. Advocates of this method seem to believe that women become pregnant and bear illegitimate children in hope of getting a small assistance (an average of $52.15 per month in 1972) from AFDC which states pay.[33] Social workers have found little evidence of this claim. In fact, vital statistics prove that only 3 to 4 percent of births in the United States occur out of wedlock, and about one-half of these babies are born to teen-age girls who seldom, in their adolescent status, speculate about such a doubtful financial basis for their lives. Most of those women who have several illegitimate children are retarded, feeble-minded, or disturbed persons with serious mental problems. It also should not be overlooked that in depriving the mother of an illegitimate child of public aid, the child is hurt most.

Another punitive treatment of parents is the attitude of some social agencies to refuse aid because housing is not considered adequate. Child welfare workers insist that children should not be endangered by living in vermin-infested, unsanitary places whenever the parents can get better, healthier quarters. But the size of the payments made by AFDC, in many states, is still so low that it would be difficult for widows or unmarried mothers to avoid living in substandard housing conditions. Judges and social workers, aware of the findings of child psychology, do not want to take the responsibility for separating children from their mother as long as she loves the children and does not endanger them. However, the denial of public aid leads to hunger, sickness, and suffering of the children, and to delinquent behavior which is destructive to them and a burden to society.

Thus, the punitive approach with its restrictive, harsh treatment does not produce substantial savings of assistance funds and creates human suffering, bitterness, delinquency, and humiliation as well. In contrast to this attitude stands the philosophy of *rehabilitation,* or *constructive aid.* Practice of this approach has been given less attention in newspapers, radio, and public discussions than the rare incidence of chiseling, abuse of public aid, and the demands for harsh treatment. Particularly important have been measures of rehabilitation for persons with physical handicaps who have been helped by vocational training, placement, and equipment to become financially self-supporting. Rehabilitation services enable these families not only to be removed from public assistance rolls, but also to gain the satisfaction of becoming respected members of their community. Often, some hundred dollars spent on rehabilitation save, in the long run, thousands on relief, and transform the former relief clients into self-supporting citizens. The same approach has been encouraged by Congress in the establishment of the categorical assistance program for disabled adults. As a result, more

33 *Welfare in Review,* 4, No. 10 (October 1966), 32, Table 7; see also Louise C. Youngman, "Social Group Work in the AFDC Program," *Public Welfare,* 23, No. 1 (January 1965), 25–61; *Social Security Bulletin,* 36, No. 1 (January 1973), Table M-27.

adequate and effective medical and orthopedic treatment, vocational guidance, occupational training, psychological counseling, and social casework help may be applied to help them care for themselves and their families again.[34]

In this rehabilitative approach, preventive services play an important role. They protect vulnerable groups so that they do not become destitute, desperate, or hostile toward society. Such a concept includes the establishment of reasonable standards of public aid. This permits the underprivileged to live on a level of decency so that they are not threatened by hunger and cold, contagious diseases, and emotional upset; and may rear their children to become responsible citizens.

Future trends in public assistance depend on two major factors: the social and economic conditions of our country, and the amount of economic security granted the population under the expanded system of social insurance. In times of depression and unemployment, both general and categorical assistance will have to assume greater responsibility for those persons and families who find insufficient protection, or none at all, from unemployment insurance benefits. Many people are still not covered by insurance schemes—casual workers, migratory labor, and other unprotected groups. Thus, a substantial responsibility remains with the public assistance program to protect people against destitution and to help them to become self-supporting again, as much as their health and capacities permit. Efforts to transfer welfare recipients to employment—the work training and work incentive programs—have had only limited success. They cannot help the old, the disabled, children, and mothers of small children to be part of the labor force (see Chapter 10).

The American Public Welfare Association has stated that a unified and comprehensive program of public assistance and medical care for all needy persons including the underemployed should be established. An adequate standard must be maintained for all assistance and broad-based community-wide programs of social services must be developed. Financial assistance should include the present general assistance recipients, all categorical forms of assistance, and foster care for children. Medical assistance should include all medically needy persons. Unnecessary paperwork should be eliminated.[35]

[34] Joyce H. Revels, "Clients and Pressures Unlimited," *Public Welfare,* 23, No. 1 (January 1965), 18–24; Jeanne Giovannoni, "Ethnic Variation in the Care and Protection of Children of Single Parents," in *Illegitimacy: Changing Services for Changing Times* (New York: National Council on Illegitimacy, 1970); Erving Goffman, *Stigma* (Englewood Cliffs, N.J.: Prentice-Hall, 1963); Elizabeth L. Navarre, "Illegitimacy," *Encyclopedia 1971,* pp. 646–53.

[35] American Public Welfare Association, Statement submitted to the Advisory Council on Public Welfare, 12 August 1965. See also Davis McEntire and Joanne Haworth, "The Two Functions of Public Welfare: Income Maintenance and Social Services," *Social Work,* 12, No. 1 (January 1967), 22-31; and Gilbert Y. Steiner, *The State of Welfare* (Washington, D.C.: Brookings Institution, 1971), pp. 34–35.

SOCIAL INSURANCE

Social security in our American form of democratic government is based on three types of services: (1) a program of *social insurance,* which aims primarily to establish a minimum standard of health and decency by providing insurance against the loss of earning capacity; (2) a program of *public assistance* to aid persons in individual economic need; and (3) a program of *welfare and health services* devised to prevent ill health and maladjustment and to meet individual and social needs.[36]

The historical background of social insurance begins in the functions of the medieval craft and merchant guilds, in the twelfth century. Each organized, among its members, mutual aid societies which provided benefits in cases of severe sickness and invalidity, burial expenses, and pensions to widows and orphans after the member's death, in return for regular contributions to the fund. What the required contributions lacked in accuracy of actuarial precision was compensated for by the warm and sympathetic spirit in the benevolent administration of the funds by fellow members in small, closely knit societies.

At the time of the Industrial Revolution, a more comprehensive system of governmental social insurance was first established in Germany under Chancellor Bismarck. The program included sickness and maternity insurance (1883), workmen's compensation (1884), and old-age and invalidity insurance (1889). In England workmen's compensation was enacted in 1897, and unemployment and health insurance was established by the *National Insurance Act of 1911.*

The Nature of Social Insurance

Modern programs of social insurance were established to protect insured workers against the many contingencies of life in an industrial society: unemployment, old-age dependency, industrial accidents, sickness, disability, and death of the breadwinner. Social insurance protection is based on statutory provisions which determine precisely which persons are eligible and the conditions under which benefits are to be paid. As in the practice of commercial insurance, the risk of loss of income or of incurring catastrophic expenses is spread by social insurance over large groups of people and over long periods of time. The few persons who suffer these losses, in a given year, could not meet this risk from their own means or providence.

---

[36] Ida C. Merriam, "The Relation of Social Security and Social Welfare Services," *Social Security Bulletin,* 25, No. 2 (February 1962), 7–14; Virginia L. Tannar, "The Public Welfare Worker in Family Crisis," *Social Welfare Forum* (1962), 202–14.

Social insurance benefits are financed either entirely or in part by contributions of the insured persons, by their employers in their behalf, or by both. Thus, the beneficiaries have a legal as well as an economic and moral claim to the benefits when the contingency occurs. Eligibility and benefits are predictable. Social insurance benefits are a legal right of the insured person without regard to his personal economic need or financial situation; no means test may be required to qualify the insured for benefits. Up to the age of seventy-two, annual earnings of $1,500 are disregarded for any month in which the recipient earns up to $125. After seventy-two all earnings are disregarded. The claim for social insurance is based on the former occupation of the insured person, whether independent or employed, and not on individual financial indigence.[37] The insured, or his survivors, may use the benefits as they please. This implies that the claimants of social insurance benefits are less subject to the discretion of the agencies which administer the social insurance plan than are applicants for public assistance. As a social institution, social insurance provides income security on the basis of presumptive need, not of demonstrated want, and its benefits are determined by the principle of average, common necessities of life rather than individual poverty. In cases of special, increased personal needs, social insurance benefits may have to be supplemented by public assistance payments.

Another difference between social insurance and public assistance is the method of financing. In the United States, social insurance is financed exclusively by the insured persons and their employers, whereas public assistance is financed by taxes. In many foreign systems, taxes supplement these social insurance contributions. Social insurance uses an actuarial base for determining contributions and benefits, but the operational principles of private, commercial insurance and nonprofit social insurance in this respect are not the same. Social insurance benefits in the United States, and in other countries which do not apply a flat-rate system, are related to the previous work and earnings of the insured. In public assistance, this element is without importance; merely the individual want of the applicant is considered.

Social insurance has been preferred to public assistance because social insurance recipients maintain a feeling of self-earned rights, independence, and self-reliance; they have built up social insurance funds by their work; no connection with charity or poor relief exists; and the receipt of social insurance benefits does not impair their social status, the respect of their neighbors, or any citizen's rights. From the standpoint of administration, social insurance provides income security by means of simple procedure.

---

[37] See Robert J. Myers, "Earnings Test under Old-Age, Survivors and Disability Insurance: Basis, Background, and Experience," *Social Security Bulletin,* 27, No. 5 (May 1964), 3–12; and Wilbur J. Cohen, "Social Insurance," *Encyclopedia 1971,* pp. 1277–88.

Individual social-economic investigation is not required, because the benefits are not dependent on personal want of the insured. Social insurance reduces the number of people who are in poverty and have to depend on public assistance payments. In general, the principle of social insurance, as a sound system of necessary basic economic protection against the dangers inherent in an industrial society, is recognized in most countries of the world.

In the United States, the ideals of private enterprise and individual initiative, as well as the fear of government interference and of the financial burden of higher taxes, long delayed the introduction of social insurance.[38] The first social insurance legislation in the United States, which started on a state basis in 1910, was workmen's compensation for the protection of workers, and their families, who were injured or killed by industrial accidents. The Social Security Act of 1935 established old-age insurance as a federal social insurance program and unemployment compensation as a federal-state program. Special social insurance systems have been created for railroad workers and employees, including unemployment, disability, maternity, and retirement insurance benefits. The Social Security Amendments of 1965 established as Title XVIII of the Act a compulsory insurance program for hospital care for persons sixty-five or older and a voluntary supplementary program of insurance for medical and certain related health services.[39]

The basic principle of social security itself has been fully accepted by both political parties in our country with the enactment of the Social Security Act and its amendments.

We shall discuss, first, the three existing types of social insurance in our country: old-age, survivors, and disability insurance; unemployment compensation (both based on the provisions of the Social Security Act); and workmen's compensation established by state legislation. We shall then take up the question of health insurance and family allowances.

Old-Age, Survivors, and Disability Insurance

The Old-Age and Survivors Insurance Program, created by the Social Security Act of 1935, is the only federal program, and the most comprehensive social insurance system in the United States. More than 90 percent of our

[38] See Eveline M. Burns, "Social Security in Evolution," *Social Service Review,* 39, No. 2 (June 1965), 129–40; and Cohen, "Social Insurance," pp. 1277–79; see also Chapter 15.

[39] For a detailed analysis, see Wilbur J. Cohen and Robert M. Ball, "Social Security Amendments of 1965," *Social Security Bulletin,* 28, No. 9 (September 1965), 3–21; and Robert J. Myers and Francisco Bayo, "Hospital Insurance, Supplementary Medical Insurance and Old-Age, Survivors and Disability Insurance," *Social Security Bulletin,* 28, No. 10 (October 1965), 17–28.

working population are covered, and over 28,000,000 people annually receive monthly benefits under its provisions. The purpose of the system is to protect workers and self-employed persons and their families from the economic hazards of old age, disability, and death. The law provides for compulsory contributions from workers, their employers, and self-employed people throughout the period of their gainful employment, and for benefits related to prior earnings to the retired, their families, and the dependent survivors after the death of the breadwinner. The original Social Security Act of 1935 protected only the workers, but the Amendments of 1939 and 1950 changed the emphasis to a family basis. The groups covered were increased and benefits were made more adequate by the Amendments of 1950, 1952, 1954, 1956, 1958, 1965, 1971, and 1972 to compensate the family of the insured for a portion of the loss in income sustained after retirement or through the disability or death of the breadwinner.

Coverage

Insured under old-age, survivors, and disability insurance are workers in "covered employment," in industry, commerce, agriculture, domestic employment, federal employment not covered by special retirement systems, and self-employed persons, including farm operators with yearly earnings of $400 or more. For employees and self-employed persons, earnings are considered up to $7,800 a year. A further increase is planned both for the earnings base and for benefits.

The insurance coverage now includes, as a rule, most farm and domestic workers and self-employed people, such as artisans, craftsmen, artists, store owners, businessmen, fishermen, persons employed in American firms abroad, insurance and traveling salesmen, homeworkers, and farmers.

Excluded from coverage are (1) railroad employees who receive benefits under a special plan; (2) independent farmers with net cash incomes of less than $400 a year; (3) other self-employed persons with annual incomes of less than $400; (4) specified agricultural workers, such as those employed in crude gum processing, and farm hands who are not regularly employed; (5) domestic workers who are not regularly employed; (6) policemen and firemen covered by local or state retirement systems; (7) federal civilian employees covered by staff retirement plans, and (8) employees of subversive organizations.[40]

Agricultural workers are covered only in regular employment, when they earn at least $150 a year for their labor or work twenty days for cash

---

[40] Since 1966 physicians and medical interns have been insured as self-employed persons.

for one employer. If the farm worker changes employers frequently, he thereby loses his status as being regularly employed. The employer has to report cash wages, to withhold the worker's tax, and to pay the entire tax. Board, lodging, meals, and pay in kind are disregarded, however. Crew leaders are treated as self-employed people.[41]

Domestic servants are covered if they are paid cash wages of $50 or more by a single employer during one calendar quarter. Thus, a cleaning woman who works for a number of employers is protected only if she receives from one employer at least $50 in a calendar quarter. For those domestic servants who are covered, the law permits that the husband of the employing couple add the domestic servant in his home to the social security report for commercial employees in his business. Otherwise, the housewife reports the income of the domestic worker on a simple form to the Director of Internal Revenue. Casual domestic work is not included.

Voluntary insurance. (1) Ordained ministers of all creeds and members of religious orders employed by nonprofit organizations are insured unless they request to be excluded. Ministers have self-employed status and pay contributions of one and one-half times the rate of an employee.

(2) State, county, and city employees (other than policemen and firemen) may be insured under old-age and survivors' insurance through voluntary agreements between the state and the federal government, if a majority of the employees vote in a referendum and a majority of the voting members favor coverage under social insurance. No referendum is required by public servants already covered by a retirement plan.

(3) Other employees of nonprofit organizations, such as schools, hospitals, churches, social agencies, foundations for scientific, literary, educational or charitable purposes, who earn at least $50 a calendar quarter, may be insured under the following conditions: the employing organization voluntarily elects to insure its employees, to pay its portion of the contribution, to deduct the employees' share of the tax, and to pay the entire contribution; and at least two-thirds of the employees vote in favor of coverage. Only those members of the present staff who voted in favor of the insurance at an election are insured, but new workers engaged by the nonprofit organization are covered on a compulsory basis after the coverage of the employees has been certified.

Social workers are covered if the agency is willing to pay the taxes and two-thirds of the staff members desire to be insured. They are not covered by old-age insurance if a two-thirds majority is not obtained or if they belong to a minority that voted against coverage. Social workers are insured if they join the staff of an agency which has already secured cover-

---

[41] Edward I. Reinselt and John C. Ellickson, "Farmers and Social Security," *Social Security Bulletin*, 29, No. 3 (March 1966), 11–14; Robert M. Ball, "Social Insurance: Financing," *Encyclopedia 1971*, pp. 1289–90.

age for its employees. If they work for a public welfare agency which does not want to insure its staff, they are not covered. But they are insured if the public welfare agency is willing to insure its staff and secure a state agreement to this end.[42] Workers engaged in private social work practice are covered as self-employed persons if earning over $400 a year.

Eligibility

Workers are insured after they have worked a certain length of time, between one and one-half and ten years, and received more than a minimum income. Employed and self-employed workers are classified according to the length of their work into two groups—the fully insured and the currently insured. A worker is fully insured who, upon retirement at sixty-five years of age or later, or at the time of his death or total disablement, had worked either one-half of the calendar quarters since December 31, 1950 or since he reached the age of twenty-one, whichever is later, but had at least six quarters of coverage, earning a minimum of $50 in each quarter. Self-employed persons, under the same conditions, must have had a minimum income of $400 a year to be counted for fully insured status. If the worker has been covered for forty quarters, whether self-employed or otherwise, he is fully insured for life. A person who has been covered for at least six quarters of the thirteen preceding his death or total disability is considered currently insured. This provision secures for the widow and children of a deceased worker the receipt of survivors benefits even if the worker was not fully insured. It also permits the totally disabled breadwinner to retain his insurance status. Older and disabled workers under sixty have no retirement income except some private industrial pension plans. Recent programs for retraining and employment have little effect for them. Since old-age insurance benefits are reduced at retirement at sixty-two, there is no strong incentive to retire at this age.[43]

Eligible for insurance payments after retirement age (sixty-two for men and women) are: (1) the insured person, (2) his wife if she is herself sixty-two years of age, or (3) his wife if she is younger but has in her care a child, under eighteen years, of the insured husband. If the insured person is a woman, she is entitled to her own primary insurance benefit, and her husband may claim benefits if he is over sixty-five, lives with his wife, and is at least half-supported by her, provided he is either not himself entitled

[42] Eveline M. Burns, "Welfare Reform and Income Security Policies," *Social Welfare Forum* (1970), 46–60.

[43] See Margaret Gordon, "Income Security Programs and the Propensity to Retire," in Richard A. Williams, et al., *Processes of Aging* (Englewood Cliffs, N.J.: Prentice-Hall, 1963), pp. 436–58; and Juanita M. Kreps, "Employment Policy and Income Maintenance for the Aged," in John C. McKinney, et al., *Aging and Social Policy* (New York: Appleton, 1966).

to a primary benefit or is entitled only to one that is less than one-half of his wife's benefit.

After the death of the insured worker, the following survivors may be entitled to insurance benefits: (1) his widow, aged sixty-two; (2) his widow, who is younger but taking care of his child; (3) a divorced wife caring for his child not yet eighteen; (4) unmarried children under eighteen years of age; (5) a dependent widower of sixty-five years of age; and (6) dependent parents (father sixty-five, mother sixty-two). A widow may choose to claim her widow's benefit at the age of sixty at a reduced rate.

The beneficiary may earn, in covered employment or as a self-employed person, $2,100 a year (with future automatic adjustments) and still receive his full benefit. Beneficiaries over seventy-two years of age receive their full benefit even if they have higher earnings. A person seventy-two years of age or older is entitled to receive a social security benefit of $35 a month, a couple $52.50 even if not covered by the provisions of old-age and survivors insurance. They must have lived for five years in the United States, but they need not be American citizens. Claims should be filed three months before the seventy-second birthday of the claimant.[44] A worker between sixty-five and seventy-five who did not receive benefits after 1970 is entitled to a "delayed retirement credit" of 1 percent for each year. A "special minimum primary benefit" of $8.50 multiplied by the worker's years of coverage in excess of ten years, up to thirty years, is provided, with a monthly maximum of $170 for an individual and $255 for a couple.

The same principles apply for self-employed persons who render substantial services in the operation of their own business or trade. A wife or widow under sixty-two loses the right to receive benefit if she is divorced or remarried, or no longer caring for a child under eighteen, but not when the widow was sixty or the widower sixty-two at the time of remarriage. Their benefit is 50 percent of the deceased spouse's primary insurance amount. A child under eighteen loses his benefit rights by marriage.

Disability insurance. In 1954 Congress enacted provisions to freeze the benefit rights of workers who were totally disabled for long periods during their working life. This is similar to a "waiver of premium" in commercial life insurance policies, to prevent the loss of retirement rights of the stricken person. In 1956 cash benefits for severely disabled insured workers between the ages of fifty and sixty-five were provided, financed through a tax increase on employees, employers, and the self-employed. To qualify for disability insurance benefits or for the disability freeze, if the insured worker is under fifty years of age, he must be so severely physically or mentally impaired that he cannot engage in any substantial gainful ac-

---

44 "Social Security Amendments of 1972," *Social Security Bulletin,* 36, No. 1 (January 1973), 1–2; see also "Amendment and Legislative History," *Social Security Bulletin,* 36, No. 3 (March 1973), 3–25.

tivity. Furthermore, he must have been working five of the ten years before the disability occurred and one and one-half years in the three years preceding his disability. The disability must have lasted at least five months, must be expected to continue indefinitely, and must be certified by medical evidence. The determination of disability is usually made by the state vocational rehabilitation agency, which considers age, education, work experience, and vocational prospects. Causes of disability are mainly circulatory and nervous diseases; cancer; mental, psychosomatic, and personality disorders; injuries; tuberculosis; and other infective diseases. Disability insurance for a blind person requires that he is fully insured (if he has as many quarters of coverage as the number of years after age twenty-one or 1950). He does not need to have worked recently. The amount of disability benefits is the same as in old-age insurance and depends on the average earnings of the insured person. Disability benefits are paid in addition to workmen's compensation or other federal disability benefits. In 1958 Congress provided benefits to the dependents of the disabled worker of the same amount as in old-age insurance, and services to their families were added in 1968.

Children whose disability began before they reached age twenty-two are entitled to receive child's benefits as long as either parent receives old-age insurance payments and after the death of the parents as long as they remain disabled. Dependents' applications must be filed within three months after the insured worker's death.

The vocational rehabilitation bureau provides vocational and medical services to disabled adults and children to prepare them for suitable work and to find employment for them. Disability insurance benefits may be withheld from individuals who refuse to accept rehabilitation services without any special reason.[45]

Benefits

The benefits to the insured person, his family, and his survivors are defined as percentages of the monthly "primary insurance amount" to which the insured person is entitled under the law. This amount may be found by two different methods. It may be determined by averaging the wages earned since January 1, 1937 until retirement or death, or by counting only the wages earned since January 1, 1951. The latter method, as a rule, is more advantageous because wages after 1950 were higher than those in the earlier years. All other income, earned in covered employment, is added

[45] Charles I. Schottland, "Social Security Amendments of 1958, A Summary and Legislative History," *Social Security Bulletin,* 21, No. 10 (October 1958), 3–12; Bertram J. Black, "Vocational Rehabilitation," *Encyclopedia of Social Work 1965,* pp. 816–23; E. B. Whitten, "Vocational Rehabilitation," *Encyclopedia 1971,* pp. 236–45.

and divided by the total number of months since 1950, or the attainment of the age of twenty-two. Tips to employees are covered as wages. To raise the average of wages or income, the four years of lowest earnings may be eliminated from the computation. If the insured has twenty quarters of coverage, a "drop-out" of the five lowest income years is permitted. Thus the average income becomes higher, and retired workers receive higher benefits.[46] In fall 1972 the average benefit to a retired worker was $161.45 monthly, to a disabled worker $178.75, to aged widows and widowers $137.25, and to children of deceased insured persons $109.94.[47]

Financing Old-Age and Survivors Insurance

The insurance plan is paid for by a contribution of the employee's wages and the self-employed person's earnings up to $7,800 a year. The employer and the employee each pay 5 percent of the wage; the worker's part is deducted from his wage and sent together with the employer's share to the Bureau of Internal Revenue. Self-employed persons pay 7 percent of their annual earnings up to $7,800.

The taxes are deposited in the Federal Old-Age and Survivors Insurance Trust Fund and the Federal Disability Insurance Trust Fund, whose managing trustee is the Secretary of the Treasury.

Administration

The Old-Age, Survivors, and Disability Insurance Program is administered by the regional offices of the Bureau of Old-Age and Survivors Insurance of the Social Security Administration, Department of Health, Education and Welfare. The central offices of the Bureau, in Washington, D.C. and Baltimore, maintain wage records of all insured persons, issue rules and regulations, and carry on research. The Field Operations Division of the Bureau is part of the Department, with six area offices, several hundred field offices, and over 2,000 field stations.

Procedure

Everyone who is employed or self-employed in work covered by the Social Security Act receives a social security card. This card shows an account number under which the record of the worker's earnings is kept. No one

[46] See Leonore A. Epstein, "Early Retirement and Work Life Experience," *Social Security Bulletin,* 29, No. 3 (March 1966), 3–10; Cohen, "Social Insurance," pp. 1278–79.

[47] *Social Security Bulletin,* 36, No. 1 (January 1973), 1.

should have more than one such card. It permits the insured person to check on his earnings and his insurance rights. The card should be shown to each employer at the beginning of a job.

Before benefits can be paid, the person entitled to them must file an application with the nearest social security field office, the address of which may be obtained from the post office. If the claim is denied or the applicant is dissatisfied with the benefit award, he may ask for reconsideration, or a hearing before a referee. If the applicant is still dissatisfied, he may request a review by the Appeals Council of the Social Security Administration. The decision of the Appeals Council may be contested by an action in the U.S. District Court.[48]

Industrial and Private Pension Plans

Because the benefits provided under the social insurance program of the Social Security Act are modest, individuals, industries, and labor unions have established supplementary pension plans, partly to attract workers to industries when manpower was scarce, as during World War II. Pension and welfare plans have been widely developed as part of collective bargaining contracts since World War II and now cover more than 28,000,000 people. Such plans often provide retirement pensions, disability benefits, early retirement pensions, and survivors benefits. Some also permit "vested interest provisions" for workers who change their jobs or are dismissed before retirement. Many such private plans provide disability benefits supplementing federal provisions. Under most plans, benefits depend on a minimum period of service in the same industrial establishment; this is particularly true of vested interest payments, which usually require ten to fifteen years of service and attainment of forty years of age.[49]

Medicare for the Aged

Hospitalization is more frequently needed for older people than for other age groups. The benefits under old-age and survivors insurance are not high enough to allow the recipients to pay substantial hospital costs, and they badly need financial protection when they have to go to a hospital. Beginning in 1951 the administration and several bills in Congress, such as the

[48] Alfred J. Kahn, "Special Services in Relation to Income Security," *Social Service Review,* 39, No. 4 (December 1965), 381–89.

[49] Clark Kerr, *Social and Economic Implications of Private Pension Plans* (Berkeley: University of California Press, 1949); Harold W. Davey, *Contemporary Collective Bargaining* (Englewood Cliffs, N.J.: Prentice-Hall, 1959); Cohen, "Social Insurance," pp. 1280–81.

Forand Bill of 1958, recommended the introduction of hospitalization insurance.

The *Medicare* program established by the Social Security Amendment of 1965 is a health insurance plan for men and women over sixty-five; it consists of a *compulsory hospital insurance program* and a *supplementary voluntary medical insurance program*. The monthly premium paid by the insured has been $6.30 since 1973, and the federal government pays the same amount. The *compulsory hospital insurance program* covers up to ninety days' hospitalization for one "spell" of illness; however, the patient must pay a total of $40 for the first sixty days of hospitalization and $10 a day for the next thirty days. Ninety days is the limit of the coverage. If outpatient diagnostic services are needed, the program pays 80 percent of the cost once the patient has paid the first $20. After a hospital stay of three days, the program assumes the cost of treatment in an "extended care facility," such as a convalescent home or nursing home up to one hundred days; the first twenty days in such a facility are paid in full by the insurance plan; for the remaining days the patient must pay $5 daily. Home health services are covered for up to one hundred visits after the patient's discharge from a hospital or from a convalescent or nursing home. Each "spell" of illness starts with date of hospitalization and ends sixty days from discharge from the hospital or nursing home. The Social Security Amendment of 1972 extended Medicare to disabled persons.

The *voluntary medical insurance program* pays 80 percent of "reasonable charges" for physicians' services in a hospital, clinic, doctor's office, or patient's home, up to one hundred home health visits by a nurse or homemaker, x-ray, radium and other therapy, diagnostic tests, and related equipment. The patient must pay the first $50 for such service and 20 percent of the remainder. This program is financed by a monthly premium of $3 by the beneficiary and the same amount paid by the federal government out of general revenues. In the Social Security Administration of the United States Department of Health, Education and Welfare a newly-established Bureau of Health Insurance administers the two programs, while the United States Public Health Service remains responsible for professional standards in the operation of the plans. A Health Insurance Benefits Advisory Council was appointed by the Secretary of Health, Education and Welfare. A National Medical Review Committee also was appointed, the majority of which are physicians.[50]

[50] Robert M. Ball, "Health Insurance for People Aged 65 and Over," *Social Security Bulletin,* 29, No. 2 (February 1966), 3–13; Myers and Bayo, "Hospital Insurance, Supplementary Medical Insurance and Old-Age, Survivors and Disability Insurance," *Social Security Bulletin,* 28, No. 10 (October 1965), 17–28; Robert J. Myers, *Medicare* (Bryn Mawr, Pa.: McCahan Foundation, 1970).

The development of old-age and survivors insurance and the new Medicare hospital insurance have brought us a long way toward the goal of this program: to provide protection against destitution and want for people working for a living when their income is cut off by major catastrophes in their lives. (For more details on Medicare and Medicaid, see Chapter 15.) But certain aspects of this goal for all citizens have not been considered yet. The most critical deficiency is the lack of a social insurance program for meeting medical and maternity care costs, particularly the expenses for hospitalization for people under 65.[51]

UNEMPLOYMENT INSURANCE

Concept and Organization

Unemployment has been called the scourge of modern industrial society. Enforced idleness of millions of citizens has caused widespread deprivation. Charles Schottland classifies five types of unemployment: (1) mass unemployment (such as in the Great Depression of the 1930s); (2) individual unemployment, caused by personal reasons; (3) "frictional" unemployment due to disasters, floods, fire, or war; (4) seasonal unemployment, caused by industrial or agricultural conditions; and (5) technological unemployment, caused by changes in production or consumption and by automation and mechanization.[52] The idea of unemployment insurance is to secure an income to replace wages interrupted by loss of employment. Insurance payment is secured for a defined period only, and in instances where loss of employment has occurred through no fault of the worker. At the same time, unemployment insurance attempts to reduce the period of unemployment and the payment of benefits by the procurement of jobs through public employment services.

When the Social Security Act established unemployment insurance in 1935, the United States had just passed through an economic depression with high unemployment and severe suffering. Different from the federal program of old-age and survivors insurance, "unemployment insurance" or "unemployment compensation" was established as a federal-state system. The federal law induced all states to adopt unemployment compensation laws by the so-called "tax offset device." This means that the Social Security Act levied everywhere a tax of 3 percent on the pay-

[51] Herman M. Somers and Anne R. Somers, *Doctors, Patients and Health Insurance* (Washington, D.C.: Brookings Institution, 1961).

[52] Schottland, *The Social Security Program in the United States*, p. 77; William Haber, Wilbur J. Cohen, and Merrill G. Murray, *Unemployment Insurance in the American Economy* (Homewood, Ill.: Irwin, 1966).

roll of all persons who employed eight or more people, for more than twenty weeks a year, and paid them up to $3,000 a year. (Certain types of employment were excluded.) The Amendment of the Social Insurance Act of 1954 extended the coverage to firms hiring four or more workers. Whenever a state employment insurance law has been approved, 90 percent of the federal unemployment tax is credited to the state unemployment insurance fund, and becomes available for unemployment benefits in that state. Under these circumstances, all states enacted unemployment compensation laws because, without a law, employers would have had to pay the federal tax, without possibility of a tax reduction, and the unemployed in their state would not have benefited. All benefits must be paid through public employment offices; taxes must be deposited into the Unemployment Trust Fund, which is administered by the Secretary of the Treasury; the funds must be used only for unemployment compensation; benefits must not be denied for refusal to accept work made available by a strike, lockout, or labor dispute, or because substandard wages are paid; and no one must be forced to join a company union or to join or to resign from a labor union.[53]

Legislation and Administration

All states and the District of Columbia passed unemployment compensation laws that meet the federal requirements; all provide that unemployed workers be registered by the public employment service, which tries to help them find suitable jobs. Each state administers its unemployment compensation law, but the entire cost of administration is paid by the federal government out of the 10 percent of the payroll tax that is reserved for this purpose and not credited to the state fund. It amounts to 0.3 percent of the payroll, while the remaining 2.7 percent is credited to the state. The states have to guarantee correct administration. They must provide, in case of grievance, a fair hearing before an impartial tribunal, and employment of personnel on a merit basis.

Since July 1954 the excess of the federal unemployment insurance tax over expenses has been used for a $200 million reserve, available for interest-free loans to states with depleted reserve accounts. The remainder of the excess is returned to the states for unemployment compensation benefits and administration of the program.

[53] Joseph M. Becker, *In Aid of the Unemployed* (Baltimore: Johns Hopkins Press, 1965); Helen B. Shaffer, "Unemployment Benefits in Prosperity," *Editorial Research Reports*, 1 (March 1965); Paul A. Brinker, *Economic Insecurity and Social Security* (New York: Appleton, 1968), Donald W. Tiffany, James R. Cowan, and Phyllis M. Tiffany, *The Unemployed: A Social-Psychological Portrait* (Englewood Cliffs, N.J.: Prentice-Hall, 1970), pp. 23–37.

The federal administration is the responsibility of the Bureau of Employment Security in the United States Department of Labor. In the states either a special department or commission, or an agency in charge of administration of other labor laws, is responsible for the administration of unemployment insurance. There are questions whether the arrangement is fortunate in that the federal government pays the entire administrative expenses but has little control over the laws which are administered.

Covered Employment

In general, all labor except agricultural, domestic, and homemaking, and service with religious, charitable, scientific, and educational organizations, falls under state laws. Several states, however, have covered one or the other of these groups, and twenty-four state laws protect employees in firms with fewer than four workers; seventeen states even include employment where only one worker is involved. The Amendment of 1954 added about two and one-half million federal government employees to the groups covered by unemployment compensation laws.

About 20 percent of wage and salary workers are not covered, especially state and local government employees, social workers, employees of charitable and nonprofit institutions, domestic, and agricultural workers.

The payroll tax is, in most states, paid by employers only, but Alabama requires contributions from employees, and Rhode Island, California, New Jersey, and New York require such contributions for special temporary disability insurance benefits.

Contributions and benefits are related to wages, with limits on minimum and maximum benefits. The large majority of states determine the duration of unemployment compensation according to past earnings or employment. Weekly maximum benefits and the minimum period for which benefits may be paid differ among the states, from sixteen to twenty-six weeks in one year, based on the statutes and special provisions. These provisions have resulted in a condition in which substantially less than about 50 percent of the average wage received before the loss of the job is paid to the beneficiaries, most often only one-third. This has raised criticism from organized labor that the protection offered by unemployment compensation is not sufficient; this opinion is now generally accepted.

Benefits

Compensation is paid to workers who are able to work and are available for work. Before an unemployed worker may file a claim for unemployment compensation, he has to be registered with the public employment service. Usually, the claim for compensation may be based on loss of the job, for example, the closing down of a factory or dismissal of workers due to lack of orders, or partial loss of work. After filing his claim, the worker has to wait, usually for one week, during which time he does not receive unemployment compensation ("waiting period").

According to unemployment compensation laws, a worker who loses his job is entitled to receive compensation, provided he has earned a certain amount of wages or worked a certain number of weeks, or both, during a so-called "base period"—usually one year preceding his loss of the job with a one-calendar-quarter interval. These requirements aim to limit unemployment compensation to fairly regularly employed workers, but they discriminate against low-paid and migratory workers who may not earn enough during the base period to qualify for benefits.

In some states, the minimum benefit is as low as $3 to $25 per week, while the maximum varies between $36 and $114 a week. Many state laws also determine a maximum amount which, during a given year, may be paid to an unemployed worker. As unemployment compensation is limited to a short period, it does not provide continuous economic security to workers who exhaust the unemployment benefits without finding a new job. For this reason, an extension of benefits by 50 percent was allowed by a legal amendment in 1958, which provided in case of chronic high unemployment an average additional payment of up to $29 for eight weeks. This payment is financed by federal loans to the states. It benefits workers who had exhausted unemployment compensation or who had not been covered before under unemployment insurance.[54]

An unemployed worker may be disqualified for unemployment insurance benefit if he lost his job in a labor dispute, if he was discharged for misconduct on the job, if he left his work voluntarily without good cause, if he refused suitable work without valid reason. Many states disqualify a worker who has not been "actively seeking work" beyond registering with the employment service. In the majority of states, disqualification postpones unemployment compensation for a certain number of weeks, but in others it reduces benefits or even cancels them entirely.

Dependents. In eleven programs, unemployment insurance benefits are supplemented by additional allowances for dependents, ranging from $1 to $17 weekly per dependent, with maximum weekly benefit for the insured and dependents ranging between $36 and $114.

Interstate benefit payment plan. For workers who move from one state to another, reciprocal agreements among forty-five states make it possible that wages earned in several states may be combined to establish eligibility for unemployment compensation.

---

[54] Arnold R. Weber, "The Rich and the Poor," *Social Service Review*, 37, No. 3 (September 1963), 256–58, discusses also the impact of the Manpower Development and Training Act of 1962.

Experience Rating

The payroll tax of 3.2 percent for unemployment compensation may be reduced for employers who were able to maintain regular employment, so that few workers in these firms claimed compensation. The reduction is determined by means of an "experience rating" or "merit rating" according to which the employer's tax can be reduced by the state from the 2.7 percent of the payroll (up to $4,200 a year) to a smaller percentage or even to nothing. The amount paid depends on the ratio of benefits paid to his former workers during a "base period" of one year preceding the year of taxation. The federal proportion of the contribution of 0.32 percent of the payroll is not involved in this reduction.

Students of economics have objected to this method of experience rating on the ground that it defeats the principle of collective responsibility. Stabilization of employment is not an achievement of the individual employer, but depends on the type of industry and production methods. As a result, experience rating favors large firms over small ones. It also drives employers to attempt to defy claims of discharged workers, and it increases administrative cost of unemployment insurance.[55] But the advantages of reduced taxes have induced all states to adopt "experience rating." The specific forms of "merit rating" have led to inequities among the states. They might require an increase of the contribution rates at times of higher unemployment and economic depression when business will be less able to pay higher taxes. Provisions are made that federal advances may be paid when a state unemployment insurance fund approaches insolvency. This provision has not been relied upon as yet. About 2,000,000 workers are covered for supplementary unemployment insurance benefits under collective bargaining contracts.

Disability Insurance Benefits

In six jurisdictions (California, New Jersey, New York, Rhode Island, Puerto Rico, and Hawaii) *Temporary Disability Insurance Laws,* combined with unemployment compensation, provide insurance benefits, also, for a specified period for wage loss due to unemployment caused by illness or

---

[55] E. Burns, *The American Social Security System* (Boston: Houghton Mifflin, 1951), pp. 162–69, and for details about the various types of "experience rating," pp. 156–59; Charles A. Myers, "Experience Rating in Unemployment Compensation," in W. Haber and W. Cohen, eds., *Readings in Social Security* (Englewood Cliffs, N.J.: Prentice-Hall, 1948), pp. 199–200. The question of fraud is discussed in Joseph M. Becker, *The Problem of Abuse in Unemployment Benefits* (New York: Columbia University Press, 1953); Alfred M. Skolnik, "Temporary Disability Insurance Laws in the United States," *Social Security Bulletin,* 15, No. 10 (October 1953), 11–22; and Margaret S. Gordon, "Failures of Unemployment Insurance," *The Nation,* 200, No. 23 (7 June 1965), 610–13.

disability (other than industrial accidents). Disability insurance benefits are paid according to the same scale as that provided under unemployment compensation and to the same workers. Temporary disability insurance is administered by the unemployment insurance agency in three states (for example, by the Employment Stabilization Commission in California). In New York it is administered by the Workmen's Compensation Board. Benefits are the same cash payment as unemployment compensation, but in California, an additional hospitalization benefit for a maximum of $10 a day, for twelve days in one year, is also paid by the Disability Insurance Division. The contributions for disability insurance in California and Rhode Island are made exclusively by 1 percent of the payroll tax paid by the workers (not by the employers!). It is deducted from their wages; in New Jersey and New York both employer and worker contribute. Except in Rhode Island, employers may be insured under an approved "private plan."

RAILROAD WORKERS INSURANCE[56]

Two separate federal social insurance programs protect railroad workers with a unique, comprehensive system. These programs provide benefits for retired workers and their survivors, and for unemployed and disabled railroad men.

The Railroad Retirement System

This system has its legal foundation in the *Railroad Retirement Act of 1937* and its amendments (particularly the *Crosser Act of 1946*). It covers over 8,000,000 employees of railroad companies and related associations and provides the following types of benefits: (1) pensions to retired railroad employees; (2) age annuities to retired workers at sixty-five, or at sixty years of age after thirty years of service; (3) permanent disability annuities; (4) survivors insurance annuities to widows, orphans, and aged dependent parents; (5) lump-sum death insurance benefits for burial expenses; and (6) residual payments guaranteeing the full return of the worker's tax payments plus an allowance in lieu of interest.

The retirement and disability benefits include a monthly compensation computed on the basis of the worker's wage, within certain limits, and survivors insurance annuities related to the last monthly remuneration of the worker. The program is financed by equal contributions from employers

---

[56] See Schottland, "Economic Security Programs for Railroad Workers," *The Social Security Program in the United States,* pp. 131–40; and Robert M. Ball, "Railroad Retirement Program," *Encyclopedia 1971,* pp. 1290–91.

and workers of 9.55 percent of the payroll up to $7,800 a year. The contributions are placed into a Railroad Retirement Trust Account.[57]

The Railroad Unemployment and Temporary Disability System

This system is based on the *Railroad Unemployment Insurance Act of 1938* with several amendments. It covers railroad employees who received at least $150 in wages in the base year preceding the fiscal year in which unemployment or disability occurred. There is a waiting period of seven days for unemployment and disability benefits, both of which are divided into nine classes depending on the amount of annual earnings. All the costs for this system are met by the employers. Their annual contribution rate is determined by their balance in the Railroad Unemployment Insurance Account.

Administration of Railroad Insurance

Both railroad insurance programs just described are administered by the Railroad Retirement Board. It is composed of three members appointed by the president, with consent of the Senate, for five years with overlapping terms. One member is appointed upon recommendation of the railroad carriers, the second upon that of the railroad employees; the chairman is neutral, being recommended by the railroad carriers and the union. The staff is employed under civil service. Nine regional offices and ninety-five branch and district offices receive the claims for the various benefits, determine eligibility, and pay the benefits.

WORKMEN'S COMPENSATION

Workmen's compensation was the first system of social insurance enacted in England and the United States. With the development of modern industry, the provisions of the common law on work injuries proved wholly inadequate. They were based on old master–servant relations in farming and simple trades when injuries were rare, and they limited the injured worker's claim for damage to cases in which the employer had neglected to provide reasonable protection for the safety of the worker. Worse than that, the employer was able to refuse damage recovery on the basis of three "common law defenses": (1) that the worker had assumed the risk of acci-

[57] Maurice C. Hart, "Railroad Retirement Act as Amended in 1965," *Social Security Bulletin*, 29, No. 2 (February 1966), 26–45; Robert M. Myers, *Social Insurance and Allied Government Programs* (Homewood, Ill.: Irwin, 1965).

dents at work, and (2) also the risk of injuries caused by fellow-workers; and (3) that he must prove that he was not negligent when the injury occurred. The worker, or his survivors, had to sue before civil courts, had to pay court and attorney fees, and usually had to wait years until a decision was reached. Thus, many never went to court as they had no means, or accepted whatever poor settlement was offered them. These legal provisions made an injured worker or his widow and orphans helpless victims. The condition was so appalling that many states introduced employers' liability laws, which prohibited the use of the common law defenses, particularly for the mining industry, the railroads, and the merchant marine, where accidents were most frequent. But these laws still offered no adequate protection to injured workers.

The movement for the enactment of legislation to eliminate this social injustice, to clarify the question of fault, and to prevent demoralization was started by social reformers, economists, and the American Association for Labor Legislation. In 1908 the first workmen's compensation law for federal employees was passed, and in 1911 a large number of states enacted this legislation, with the others following soon after. Now, all states have workmen's compensation laws.

Principles and Coverage

Workmen's compensation is based on the principle that the risk of work injuries is an element of industry and that the cost of such injuries is to be considered a part of the cost of production. It should not be blamed on either employer or injured worker. The aim of this program is to assure prompt medical aid, rehabilitation, and cash benefit to the injured worker and his dependents, regardless of who is at fault. But there are still many differences among the state laws.[58] Only about 78 percent of all workers are covered; certain groups of workers are excluded because they are not employed in "hazardous occupations," or because they work in agriculture, domestic service, or casual jobs. About one-half of the states have elective systems of workmen's compensation where the employer is permitted to refuse insurance for his workers if he prefers the risk of being sued for damage by an injured worker or his survivors. Thirty-one states cover all occupational diseases as well as industrial accidents; the other states, only some of these diseases. Eight states do not cover the damage caused by occupational diseases, such as lead poisoning and silicosis, but other systems treat occupational diseases like industrial accidents.

[58] Herman M. Somers and Anne R. Somers, *Workmen's Compensation: Prevention, Insurance and Rehabilitation of Occupational Disability* (New York: John Wiley, 1954), pp. 15–37; Schottland, *The Social Security Program in the United States,* pp. 123–29; Ball, "Railroad Retirement Program," p. 1291.

Because workmen's compensation was the first social insurance in the United States, this legislation was enacted under a great variety of patterns in the different states. No specific type of workmen's compensation has found adoption as the most effective system. In some states the "compulsory," and in others the "elective," method of covering workers and employment is used. Considering organization, there are many states where private insurance companies compete with a public compensation fund. In a minority of states, exclusive private insurance or exclusive public insurance is in operation. "Self-insurance" gives the employer the right not to insure his employees, provided he is able to deposit securities, giving proof of his financial ability to carry his risk. In the majority of the states, the employer can choose whether he wants to: (1) insure with a private insurance company, (2) insure with a state workmen's compensation fund, or (3) apply for self-insurance permission. Four federal laws protect federal employees, longshoremen and harbor workers employees in Washington, D.C., and coal miners.

Usually, injuries that have occurred because of the injured worker's willful misconduct, gross negligence, intoxication, or intentional self-infliction are not granted compensation.

Compensation Benefits

Workmen's compensation laws provide two types of benefits—medical treatment and cash indemnities—as compensation for loss of earning. Cash benefits provide for temporary disability, for total or partial permanent disability, and for the survivors in case of death of the injured worker.

Medical benefits. In the majority of states, full medical care, including first aid, medical and surgical treatment, hospitalization, medicines, and medical and surgical appliances, is provided free to the injured worker. This medical aid, however, is limited in nineteen states either to a certain time or to a maximum amount of expenses. Thirty-one states, however, impose no limit, either on the period of medical treatment or on the amount of medical expenses.[59]

As a rule, the employer or the insurance carrier arranges for medical care and hospitalization, but in some instances the injured worker can choose the physician and hospital. The quality of medical service, nursing care, and rehabilitation service differs widely among the states. Where medical treatment is limited to a certain period or to a definite expense maximum, extensions may sometimes be granted.

Indemnity payments. After a waiting period, usually of seven days,

[59] Earl F. Cheit, *Medical Care under Workmen's Compensation,* Bulletin 244 (Washington, D.C.: Bureau of Labor Standards, 1962); Brinker, *Economic Insecurity and Social Security.*

the injured worker who had to leave his work because of the accident or the occupational disease is entitled to an indemnity payment. The amount of this indemnity is, as a rule, different for temporary disabilities and permanent impairments.

Temporary disability. This is compensated for by a payment based on a percentage of the last wage, which may vary from 50 to 80 percent—frequently it is 66⅔ percent. The worker who receives compensation based on a percentage of his regular wage usually has difficulty meeting high living costs. In a few states, the rate of compensation is higher for married workers, and increased according to the number of dependent children.

There is usually, also, a maximum period for which temporary disability indemnity is paid (frequently five years) or a maximum sum, which amounts to the same limitation.

Permanent disability. In all states compensation is provided for permanent disabilities caused by industrial accidents, and different rates are scheduled for permanent total or partial disability.

Permanent partial disabilities. These are classified either as specific injuries, such as loss of an eye, a hand, or a foot, or as of general nature, such as disability caused by injury to the head or back. For such partial disability compensation is limited in the majority of states to a stated number of weeks, but in several states the weekly payments are fixed sums. In California compensation is rated upon degrees of total disability as classified in a Rating Schedule in relation to nature of injury, occupation, and age of injured worker.

The periods of compensation for specific injuries vary from state to state, which certainly is not logical; they are sometimes paid in addition to the indemnities during temporary disability.

Permanent total disability. If the injured worker is totally disabled by the injury, often defined as having lost 70 percent or more of his working capacity, he receives an indemnity as a smaller proportion of his last wage with weekly and total maximum amounts. The periods range from 250 to 1,000 weeks, and the maximum money amounts from $5,000 to $15,000.

The federal compensation systems and the laws of eighteen states provide for lifelong benefits in case of permanent total disability, but often with reduced rates and dependent on the severity of the disability. In some states, different rates are paid with regard to dependents.

Subsequent injuries. The majority of compensation laws contain provisions to secure benefits for workers who have been injured before, or lost a member of the body, but who suffer another injury which may involve total permanent disability. Without legal provisions, handicapped persons might be refused employment because an employer or the insurance carrier would not take the risk of another injury occurring. To counter this, "second-injury" or "subsequent injuries" funds have been established which, as a rule, secure full compensation for the actual disability to the injured worker without placing undue burden on the new employer.

Death benefits. If the injured worker dies, the economic security of his spouse and children often depends on the death awards under workmen's compensation. In general, they are based on the average weekly wages of the deceased breadwinner, but some states grant a flat pension. Only seven systems provide that death benefits be paid to the widow for life or until remarriage. In the majority of compensation plans, death benefits, again, are limited to payments for a specific period—ranging from 260 to 600 weeks, or up to a maximum amount ranging from $3,500 to $15,000. Weekly minimum and maximum payments usually are similar to those of permanent disability benefits. About two-thirds is cash indemnity to replace wage loss, about one-third payment for hospital care and medical treatment. These laws do not provide adequate economic security for survivors of an injured worker because of the limitations set on the number of weeks and the maximum sums which may be paid. In addition to survivors benefits, many systems pay funeral expenses.

Not all state laws require that reports be made of all industrial accidents and occupational diseases. Therefore no reliable statistics are available. It is estimated that approximately 17,000 workers die from industrial injuries annually throughout the country, that about 100,000 workers suffer permanent total or partial disablement, and that about 2,000,000 persons are temporarily disabled by accidents and occupational diseases at work.[60] But workmen's compensation has encouraged the prevention of accidents through safety measures and has improved the conditions of the victims of occupational accidents and diseases, as well as the social condition of their families.

Administration of Workmen's Compensation

The main objective of the system is to guarantee a simple, fair, convenient, and inexpensive method of settling the claims of injured workers and their dependents. For this reason, in most states, an administrative commission (for example, the Industrial Accident Commission) or board administers the program. Five states, however, still rely on court administration.

State Compensation Insurance Funds are, as a rule, administered by a board of directors, which is independent and separated from the industrial accident commission. State funds are a nonprofit, self-supporting organization. Although the organization does not operate as a private organization

---

[60] Alfred M. Skolnik and Julius W. Hobson, "Workmen's Compensation Payments and Costs in 1964," *Social Security Bulletin*, 29, No. 1 (January 1966), 42–43; Wilbur J. Cohen, "Workmen's Compensation," *Encyclopedia 1971*, pp. 1279–80.

(though in some states commercial insurance companies do carry work-men's compensation insurance), it must comply with the rates and classifi-cations ordered for all insurance companies under state laws. The prevention of industrial accidents and occupational diseases, by improving safety de-vices and instructing workers, is an important function of workmen's com-pensation, but not yet equally achieved in the various systems. Workmen's compensation is financed by the employers because industrial accidents are recognized as part of the cost of production. Oregon requires a one-cent-a-day contribution from the workers. A few other states, as well, require contributions toward medical care.

The federal programs of workmen's compensation for federal civil employees and for longshoremen are administered by the Bureau of Em-ployees' Compensation, United States Department of Labor. The Bureau has twelve branch offices spread about the country.

PERSONNEL IN SOCIAL INSURANCE ADMINISTRATION

The competence of personnel in social insurance administration is, in many respects, related to the skill required in other fields of social welfare administration.[61] Personnel must have a good general education to under-stand laws, rules, and regulations and to explain them clearly and with sympathetic attitude to the public. They must maintain an objective ap-proach as the representatives of a public agency, impartial and polite con-sideration for the applicants, and an awareness of the personality of the person for whom the social insurance program has been established. Beyond these general requirements, and the skills connected with technical problems of legal and financial nature, accounting, and computation, the question has been frequently raised whether specific professional social work skills are required in the administration of social insurance. Under present con-ditions, it is certain that the administration of the various social insurance systems does not require trained professional social workers for most of its functions.

The people who come to social insurance offices to file their claims often incidentally express personal, emotional, or health problems. In the present setup of social insurance administrations no one is prepared to cope

[61] For a discussion of the question of personnel in social insurance administra-tion, see Karl de Schweinitz, *People and Process in Social Security* (Washington, D.C.: American Council of Education, 1948), pp. 62–93; Neota Larsen, "OASI and the Social Services," *Social Work*, 1, No. 3 (July 1956), 12–17; and Donald W. Tiffany, et al., *The Unemployed* (The Counseling Profession), (Englewood Cliffs, N.J.: Prentice-Hall, 1970), pp. 120–32.

with those needs which are not met by the cash benefits and medical care offered under the social insurance program. When claimants reveal psychological problems indicating health or emotional disturbance, anxieties, and fear, personnel not trained professionally to handle these problems cannot recognize their needs and refer them to social agencies equipped to help. To meet these problems of great importance, various foreign social insurance programs employ social workers as consultants who are fully acquainted with the social agencies of the community and their special facilities and services. These workers would be available for insurance benefit recipients who need to be counseled regarding the facilities of other health and welfare services, family and children's agencies, child guidance and mental hygiene clinics, and recreational facilities. In interviews and discussions, they could bring the resources of the community to the attention of the recipients of insurance benefits, who would benefit accordingly.

In other countries, particularly France, Belgium, and England, a much closer integration of social insurance and family allowance benefits with the general system of welfare services has been highly beneficial and is accepted by the population.[62] The establishment of social work consultants in the field offices of the Social Security Administration and the state unemployment compensation and workmen's compensation programs would be valuable progress in the interest of the public.

GAPS IN OUR INSURANCE PROGRAM

Health Insurance

The most flagrant gap in our system of social insurance is the lack of a general system of health insurance. Insurance against the hazard of ill health, by the provision of medical care and cash allowances during the time of illness, was the earliest type of compulsory, public social insurance in many other countries. In fact, the United States is the only great nation which has no general public health insurance program today. Under auspices of the federal government, medical care is given to members of the armed forces, veterans, Indians, and seamen. Under state systems of workmen's compensation, medical care and cash indemnity are provided for workers injured in industrial accidents and occupational diseases. In six jurisdictions, unemployment insurance in the form of disability benefits, but no medical care, is given to insured workers who are unable to work due to illness over a short time. The Medicare program and the voluntary med-

[62] Walter A. Friedlander, "Coordination of Family Welfare Services in France," *Social Service Review*, 27, No. 1 (March 1953), 62–66, and *Individualism and Social Welfare in France* (New York: Free Press, 1962), pp. 167–71, 198–212; Cohen, "Social Insurance," pp. 1285–88.

ical insurance for the elderly are meeting some of the urgent needs of the aged population. Persons who receive various forms of public assistance also, as a rule, receive a certain amount of medical care. Federal grants-in-aid are made for the payment of doctors and hospitals. This program provides medical care for the recipients of public categorical assistance, but it does not protect the other population.

The idea of a compulsory health insurance program has been vigorously opposed in our country. The main objections to such a program are presented by representatives of the medical profession, by some of the commercial insurance companies, by the Christian Science churches, and by drug manufacturing companies. Medical societies fear that compulsory health insurance would lead to a lowering of standards of medical care which would result from overloading doctors, clinics, and hospitals. They claim it would subject the medical profession to bureaucratic control and red tape, and would decrease their income. Some commercial insurance companies are afraid that their accident, hospitalization, and medical care policies would be cancelled and their profits lowered. Drug manufacturing firms which sell patent medicines feel that their products would no longer be bought by health insurance administrators and patients under a health insurance program which would standardize medicines and drugs. The Christian Science churches do not want health insurance because their members believe in cure through prayer, not through medical service. In public discussion, health insurance is often confused with socialized medicine, a system under which doctors and nurses are government employees, and patients have no free choice in selecting doctor, pharmacist, clinic, or hospital. None of these characteristics applies, however, to the concept of health insurance as it operates in other democratic countries.[63]

The need of a large proportion of our population to protect themselves against the heavy cost of serious illnesses, which every year make about 4,000,000 people ill for longer than six months, is obvious. Many families attempt to solve this need by selecting a "medical care prepayment plan"— a voluntary health insurance program. Such plans are established either by nonprofit organizations, such as the Blue Cross and the Blue Shield, which are closely connected with the state medical societies; by some private foundations, labor councils, unions, fraternal societies, and business concerns; or by commercial insurance companies. Approximately 70 percent of the population has some form of hospital insurance, the majority under commercial plans and about 45 percent under Blue Cross plans.

---

[63] J. E. Follman, *Medical Care and Health Insurance. A Study in Social Progress* (Homewood, Ill.: Irwin, 1963); Frank J. Angell, *Health Insurance* (New York: Ronald, 1963); Louis S. Reed, "Private Health Insurance in the United States: An Overview," *Social Security Bulletin*, 28, No. 12 (December 1965), 3–48; Cohen, "Social Insurance," pp. 1279, 1287–88.

The benefits under these plans vary considerably. Most of them offer only hospitalization, only medical care in the doctor's office, or a cash allowance for the patient to compensate for the loss of earnings—frequently only a part payment toward the various expenses. Membership is often limited to persons of low income or to people within specific age limits, and some plans exclude persons who are suffering from various diseases. An analysis of the effect of voluntary insurance plans demonstrated that in 1951, under such arrangements for insured persons, 36.3 percent of hospital costs and 17 percent of costs of hospital, physician, and loss of income were provided; and for 17 percent, medical expenses alone were covered.[64] Only a small proportion of our population has comprehensive insurance in case of sickness, including medical care at home, in the doctor's office, in the hospital, and the necessary operations, medicines, and medical appliances. The premiums for comprehensive health insurance coverage are frequently too high for persons in low-income groups, so that patients most in need of this protection are not able to become members of voluntary plans.

In the discussion of comprehensive compulsory health insurance legislation, the question has come up whether a general public health service, such as that in Great Britain, New Zealand, Australia and Chile, may be preferable to a health insurance plan. It should be seriously considered by Congress.[65]

Maternity Insurance

In many nations, maternity insurance provides for insured women workers and for wives of insured men, medical and maternity ward care, midwife aid, nursing, and medicines at the time of childbirth. Cash allowances of one-half the actual or average wage are paid for periods from about four weeks before, to six weeks after, confinement. This insurance is considerable help to mothers and infants. No public insurance of this type is available in the United States, except to railroad workers.

[64] "Voluntary Insurance Against Sickness: 1948–1951 Estimates," *Social Security Bulletin,* 15, No. 12 (December 1952), 3–7; George W. Cooley, "The Potentials of Voluntary Health Insurance," *Building America's Health,* 4 (1952), pp. 76–82; Edward S. Rogers, "Medical Care," *Social Work Year Book* (1960), 370–74; Joseph Krislov, "Employee Benefit Plans," *Social Security Bulletin,* 28, No. 4 (April 1964), 4–21; Fred J. Cook, *The Plot Against the Patient* (Englewood Cliffs, N.J.: Prentice-Hall, 1967); see also Marjorie Smith Mueller, "Private Health Insurance in 1971," *Social Security Bulletin,* 36, No. 2 (February 1973), 3–22.

[65] Eveline M. Burns, "Further Needs in the Social Insurances," *The American Social Security System* (Boston: Houghton Mifflin, 1949), p. 188; I. S. Falk, "The Need, Potential and Implications of Compulsory Health Insurance," *Building America's Health,* 4 (1952), pp. 66–75; Michael M. Davis, "Needs and Problems of Medical Care," in Cora Kasius, ed., *New Directions in Social Work* (New York: Harper, 1954), pp. 110–30.

Family Allowances

Family allowances were first introduced in France and Belgium, on a voluntary basis, by employers for families with several children. Their goal was to alleviate the financial burden, especially of the mother, of rearing more than one young child and to secure a living standard of health and decency which could not be obtained from the normal wage alone. The individual and health needs of the worker and his family are not considered in the determination of wages and salary. A young bachelor may get along on his wage without difficulty, but his married fellow worker with five young children at home will have difficulty making ends meet with the same wage. Organized labor originally was opposed to family allowances; but later it favored legislation which made the family allowances compulsory, so that their payment is no longer dependent on the discretion of the employer. At present, a large number of countries including Canada and England, the Scandinavian countries, Austria, and Germany have enacted family allowance legislation. There seems, however, no indication that federal or state legislatures in our country are inclined to pass a compulsory family allowance law.[66]

Even the sharpest critics of a humane program of social services admit that public social security policy (including assistance and social security benefits) should provide benefits enough that clients would not be half-starved, half-housed, and half-clothed. The policy should accept a simple formula for benefits, and simple, easily understood procedures with adequate payments to preserve the clients' dignity. Such policy should integrate the present veterans program into the general social security system, eliminate food stamps, and provide special cash benefits for housing not available in public low-rent projects. It should provide enough that the client can at least live within a framework of honorable dependency.[67]

In view of the increase in cybernation, the replacement of human labor by machines, and the growing power of large corporations, the present system of income security cannot secure adequate income maintenance for a substantial number of the poor, the unemployed, and members of racial and religious minorities. Basic changes in our economic system are needed to create a program of income security for all members of society.[68]

66 Herbert Callaghan, "Family Allowances," in William Haber and Wilbur Cohen, eds., *Readings in Social Security* (Englewood Cliffs, N.J.: Prentice-Hall, 1948), pp. 532–37; James C. Wadakin, *Family Allowances* (Miami: University of Miami Press, 1958), and *Children, Poverty, and Family Allowances* (New York: Basic Books, 1969); Scott Briar, "Why Children's Allowances," *Social Work,* 14, No. 1 (January 1969), 5–12.

67 Gilbert Y. Steiner, *The State of Welfare* (Washington, D.C.: Brookings Institution, 1971), pp. 314–38.

68 Robert Perrucci and Marc Pilisuk, *The Triple Revolution: Emerging Social Problems in Depth* (Boston: Little, Brown, 1971), pp. 3–8, 102–14, 157–94, 272–81, 466–75.

SELECTED BIBLIOGRAPHY

A. Public Welfare Policy and Public Assistance

ABBOTT, EDITH, *Public Assistance*. Chicago: University of Chicago Press, 1941.

ABBOTT, GRACE, *The Child and the State*, 2 vols. Chicago: University of Chicago Press, 1938.

————, *From Relief to Social Security*. Chicago: University of Chicago Press, 1941.

DUMPSON, JAMES R., "Our Welfare System—Radical Surgery Needed," *Public Welfare*, 23, No. 4 (October 1965), 226–34.

GOODMAN, LEONARD H., ed., *Economic Progress and Social Welfare*. New York: Columbia University Press, 1966.

GORDON, MARGARET S., *The Economics of Welfare Policies*. New York: Columbia University Press, 1963.

GREENFIELD, MARGARET, *Medical Care for Welfare Recipients—Basic Problems*. Berkeley: University of California Press, 1957.

KAHN, ALFRED J., "Social Services in Relation to Income Security," *Social Service Review*, 39, No. 4 (December 1965), 381–89.

LARSEN, NEOTA, "Protective Services for Older Adults," *Public Welfare*, 22, No. 4 (October 1964), 247–76.

McKEANY, MAURINE, *The Absent Father and Public Policy in the Program of Aid to Dependent Children*. Berkeley: University of California Press, 1960.

MARCUS, GRACE F., *The Nature of Service in Public Assistance Administration*, Public Assistance Report No. 10. Washington, D.C.: Federal Security Agency, 1946.

PERRUCCI, ROBERT, and MARC PILISUK, *The Triple Revolution Emerging: Social Problems in Depth*. Boston: Little, Brown, 1971.

PILISUK, MARC, and PHYLLIS PILISUK, *Poor Americans: How the White Poor Live*. Chicago: Aldine Press, 1971.

SCHOTTLAND, CHARLES I., *The Social Security Program in the United States*. New York: Appleton, 1963.

TANNAR, VIRGINIA L., *Selected Social Work Concepts for Public Welfare Workers*. Washington, D.C.: Bureau of Family Services, 1965.

WICKENDEN, ELIZABETH, *The Needs of Older People and Public Welfare Services to Meet Them*. Chicago: American Public Welfare Association, 1953.

WILTSE, KERMIT T., *Public Assistance Personnel: Educational Requirements and Training Facilities*. Berkeley: University of California Press, 1959.

WINSTON, ELLEN, "Future Social Work Practices and Services," *Public Welfare*, 25, No. 1 (January 1967), 15–20.

————, "Public Welfare—Today and Tomorrow," *Public Welfare*, 22, No. 1 (January 1964), 22–25.

WITTE, ERNEST F., "Who Speaks Now for the Child on Public Assistance?" *Child Welfare* (March 1954).

B. Social Insurance

ALTMEYER, ARTHUR J., *The Formative Years of Social Security*. Madison: University of Wisconsin Press, 1966.

ANGELL, FRANK J., *Health Insurance*. New York: Ronald Press, 1963.

BECKER, JOSEPH M., *In Aid of the Unemployed*. Baltimore: Johns Hopkins University Press, 1965.

BURNS, EVELINE M., *Social Security and Public Policy*. New York: McGraw-Hill, 1956.

———, "Social Security in Evolution," *Social Service Review*, 39, No. 2 (June 1965), 125–40.

DAVIS, MICHAEL M., and DEWEY ANDERSON, *Medical Care for the Individual and the Issue of Compulsory Health Insurance*. Washington, D.C.: Brookings Institution, 1948.

DODD, WALTER F., *Administration of Workmen's Compensation*. New York: Commonwealth Fund, 1937.

EPSTEIN, ABRAHAM, *Insecurity: A Challenge to America*, rev. ed. New York: Random House, 1938.

EWING, OSCAR R., *The Nation's Health*. Washington, D.C.: Federal Security Agency, 1948.

FAULKNER, EDWIN J., *Health Insurance*. New York: McGraw-Hill, 1960.

GORDON, MARGARET S., *The Economics of Welfare Policies*. New York: Columbia University Press, 1963.

HABER, WILLIAM, and WILBUR J. COHEN, eds., *Social Security: Programs, Problems, and Policies*. Homewood, Ill.: Irwin, 1960.

HUNTINGTON, EMILY H., *Cost of Medical Care*. Berkeley: University of California Press, 1951.

KLARMAN, HERBERT E., *Economics of Health*. New York: Columbia University Press, 1965.

McGILL, DAN M., *Fulfilling Pension Expectations*. Homewood, Ill.: Irwin, 1961.

MATHIASEN, GENEVA, *Flexible Retirement*. New York: Putnam, 1957.

MEANS, JAMES H., *Doctors, People, and Government*. Boston: Atlantic, 1953.

MOORE, ELON H., *The Nature of Retirement*. New York: Macmillan, 1959.

MYERS, ROBERT J., *Social Insurance and Allied Government Programs*. Homewood, Ill.: Irwin, 1965.

PICKRELL, JESSE F., *Group Health Insurance*. Homewood, Ill.: Irwin, 1961.

President's Committee on the Health Needs of the Nation, *Building America's Health*, 5 vols. Washington, D.C.: Government Printing Office, 1952.

SCHOTTLAND, CHARLES I., *The Social Security Program in the United States*. New York: Appleton, 1963.

SINAI, NATHAN, *Disability Compensation*. Ann Arbor: University of Michigan Press, 1949.

SOMERS, HERMAN M., and ANNE R. SOMERS, *Workmen's Compensation: Prevention, Insurance and Rehabilitation*. New York: John Wiley, 1954.

———, *Doctors, Patients, and Health Insurance*. Washington, D.C.: Brookings Institution, 1962.

STEINER, GILBERT Y., *The State of Welfare*. Washington, D.C.: Brookings Institution, 1971.

TILLMAN, J. F., *Medical Care and Health Insurance*. Homewood, Ill.: Irwin, 1962.

TITMUSS, RICHARD M., "The Role of Redistribution in Social Policy," *Social Security Bulletin*, 28, No. 6 (June 1965), 14–20.

10

---

antipoverty
programs

DEFINITION OF POVERTY

For the majority of the world's people poverty is a fact of daily life. It has existed in all countries and at all times, and still is a problem of great concern in the United States. Any discussion of poverty and of programs which set about to eliminate it must recognize that poverty is a relative concept and that it varies in different historical and geographical contexts. In social surveys made in the late nineteenth and early twentieth centuries, such as those by Charles Booth (1889) and Seebohn Rowntree (1902), English philanthropists, a bare subsistence income level defined the poverty line. At this level the individual could still purchase the minimum amount of food necessary to keep himself alive; below it he would eventually perish. Since those early studies, the level of purchasing power used to define poverty has been raised considerably, both in Britain and in the United States. As a society becomes more affluent, the poverty line is revised upward.

In the United States the Social Security Administration standard is most frequently used as an official index of poverty. It is based on the Department of Agriculture's estimate of the cost of a temporary, low-budget, nutritious diet for an average household. The food budget is multiplied by three to determine the total budget for subsistence, including rent and other essentials. The rationale for this formula is that the poor spend on the average about one-third of their budget on food. In 1959 the poverty level for a family of four was set at an annual income of $2,973, and in 1969 at $3,743, with the cost of living accounting for most of the increase.[1]

While the Social Security Administration is used in establishing census data on the extent of poverty in the United States, it is highly inadequate for describing the amount of poverty from group to group. For example, it does not take into consideration the differences in consumption needs due to geographic location or life stage, nor does it recognize the grim fact that many millions of Americans live only slightly above the poverty line, but do not have enough income to buy the goods and services deemed necessary by the majority of those who enjoy a high standard of living.

CONCEPTS OF POVERTY

Various ways of conceptualizing poverty have been proposed, dependent not just on size of income, but on a variety of other criteria including the resources available in the community, the attitudes or culture of the group in question, and the "risk characteristics" of individuals. Whole communities have been labeled "pockets of poverty," denoting their limited opportunity of employment, education, and other necessities of life. In such neighborhoods it is not just low income that impoverishes, but also high costs (such as higher food prices in ghetto supermarkets, exorbitant interest rates on loans, and so on) and lack of access to public services that middle-class families take for granted.

Oscar Lewis, the noted cultural anthropologist, and others have proposed the concept of the "culture of poverty." They hold that many of the poor have beliefs, values, and life styles which are not just an adjustment

[1] Robert Harris and Alair Townsend, "Poverty," *Encyclopedia of Social Work 1971*, p. 896.

to low income, but a mind set and way of life which make their poverty self-perpetuating. According to this theory, the poor are mired in despair and resignation, their way of life characterized by fatalism, violence, immediate gratification of desires, and an unstable family structure. Their hopelessness and lassitude prevent them from expending the energy to climb out of poverty. As Charles Valentine points out, however, the concept of "culture" used in this context is a corruption of the anthropological concept of culture, which conceives a more total way of life of a group. Valentine objects that Lewis and other members of the "culture of poverty" school, have let their middle-class biases color their view of the poor. While they use what passes for value-free scientific language, they state conclusions and judgments about the "disintegration" of the Mexican and black family structure and other aspects of the life of the poor which are not totally valid, failing to recognize other important cultural attributes and ways of life. With a similarly judgmental point of view, Daniel Moynihan imposed a middle-class interpretation on census statistics, with the result that he blamed poverty on the poor themselves, failing to recognize the extent to which external factors like racism and unavailability of work perpetuate poverty.[2] We realize now that poor black, Spanish-American, and American Indian subcultures possess amazing coping skills which have helped them to survive in the face of overwhelming adversity.

Alan Little's categorization of the major kinds of poverty includes a type which he calls *inherited poverty*, which fits Lewis's theory; Little also defines *crisis poverty*, *life-cycle poverty*, and *low-earning poverty*.[3] Crisis poverty develops after a major event in a person's life, such as illness and/or unemployment, which cuts off his or her usual source of income. Life-cycle poverty occurs because of the unique demands of a specific stage in life. For a woman of child-bearing age, the strain of supporting too many children, particularly without a husband and/or employment, may drive the family into poverty; for the aged, inability to work and inadequacy of social security benefits may be the cause of poverty. Low-earning poverty is simply the result of temporary or marginal employment and insufficient money to meet family needs.

Inherited poverty is built on Lewis's notion of a self-perpetuating subculture of the poor which provides inadequate knowledge and skills and self-defeating attitudes which keep the poor from succeeding in society. The socialization experience and group attitudes engender a sense of apathy, failure, and dependency. While the children of poor families may desire to change their situation, they often lack both the inner and outer resources to

[2] See Charles Valentine, *Culture and Poverty* (Chicago: University of Chicago Press, 1968), for an excellent critique of the "culture of poverty" thesis.

[3] Alan Little, "Poverty Types," *Encyclopedia of Social Work 1971*, pp. 929–48.

break out of their cultural shackles.[4] It was mainly inherited poverty that was to be attacked by the War on Poverty initiated in the 1960s. Other government mechanisms such as social security, unemployment insurance, and welfare sought to cure or prevent the other types of poverty (crisis, life-cycle, and low-earning poverty).

The various definitions of poverty offered by specialists in this area have been merely classification systems used as vehicles for developing public policy and programs. They all fail to describe the quality of life of the poor.

THE REDISCOVERY OF POVERTY

When the United States recovered from the severe deprivations of the Great Depression of the 1930s and the economic and industrial activities of the nation were intensified by the Second World War, the masses of the middle- and upper-class citizens assumed that widespread poverty no longer existed in America. Social workers, especially those employed in public welfare agencies, never shared this rather naïve belief, but the majority of well-to-do citizens did not ask their opinion.

In 1958 John Kenneth Galbraith of Harvard University published his famous book, *The Affluent Society*.[5] Galbraith explained that severe deprivation no longer was a massive affliction in America, but that poverty caused by low income was still the fate of a minority, including some farm families, particularly migratory workers, and the population of depressed areas such as Appalachia, Piedmont, and the Ozark Plateau, some mining regions, and the Mississippi hill country. Galbraith called this "insular poverty." In addition to naming regional causes, he found that other persons were living in poverty because of poor health, crippling diseases, lack of education and training, alcoholism, drug addiction, excessive procreation, or failure to obtain work because of racial or ethnic discrimination. Their poverty Galbraith called "case poverty," but he did not indicate that their number in the United States was large. In fact, few people paid much attention to Galbraith's assertion that there still was a problem of poverty in the midst of such prosperity; rather, most persons felt a kind of satisfaction in belonging to the "affluent society."

Several years later Michael Harrington, editor of *New America* and *Dissent* and a former social worker, published *The Other America: Poverty*

[4] See Oscar Lewis, *The Children of Sanchez* (New York: Random House, 1961).

[5] John K. Galbraith, *The Affluent Society* (Boston: Houghton Mifflin, 1958), pp. 322–25.

in the United States,[6] but Harrington's book was read in the main by sociologists and social workers. At first ignored, it clearly reported the prevalence of mass poverty in the richest country of the world. Several sociological and economic investigations confirmed the findings of Galbraith and Harrington. Only a year later an article by Dwight MacDonald in *The New Yorker*[7] created a tremendous outcry among politicians, sociologists, and economists about the poverty problem, as well as stimulating discussions in both houses of Congress and in many state assemblies, and numerous presentations in the press, radio, and television. After the publication of MacDonald's article, a flood of books and articles appeared dealing with poverty in the United States, at the same time as the civil rights movement and outbreaks of Negro unrest were finding wide publicity.

The decade preceding the War on Poverty was one of unprecedented economic growth in America. Millions of families for the first time had surplus income to spend on luxuries—the spoils of the affluent society. However, the growth in the gross national product did little to change the lives of millions of others who were not part of the labor force. While the actual incidence of poverty was declining, some people were left out of economic growth and out of the various welfare provisions of the Social Security Act and other health, education, and welfare programs. While programs such as workmen's compensation, unemployment insurance, health insurance, social security, and various pensions and educational plans had indeed made a major contribution to the welfare of the nation, the limit of their capacity to chip away at the block of hardcore poverty had been reached. There remained large clusters of the population who were not benefiting from economic prosperity and who were ineligible for these programs.

WHO ARE THE POOR?

In 1963 the Social Security Administration estimated that of the 187,000,000 people in the United States, 34.6 million, or nearly 1 in 5, were below the poverty line. Many of these people received income under public assistance and social insurance, but the grants and benefits were not enough to keep them from poverty. Overrepresented in this poorest segment of the population, relative to their proportion in the whole population, were families with female heads, the aged, nonwhites, and those in rural areas. Nonwhites represented 1 of every 4 in this group, almost three times their proportion in the population as a whole. In addition to the many families

[6] Michael Harrington, *The Other America: Poverty in the United States* (New York: Macmillan, 1962).

[7] Dwight MacDonald, "Our Invisible Poor," *The New Yorker*, 38 (19 January 1963); Paul Jacobs, "America's Schizophrenic View of the Poor," *The Nation*, 201, No. 8 (20 September 1965), 191–97.

on welfare, among these "poorest of the poor" was also a sizable number of families in which the father or mother was employed, but his or her income was too low and work too irregular to keep poverty from the door. Many of these were migratory and seasonal workers. The disabled constituted another category of the poor.[8]

Michael Harrington and others observed that much of the poverty in America was invisible, that unlike so many other countries, the poor in America could not readily be seen. It is true that when people are housebound because of age or disability, or when they have just enough to clothe and feed themselves, they are not so obvious and do not play on the guilt or pity of society. This was also the period during which the myth of the affluent society reached its peak. But in the early 1960s the existence of the poor began to be dramatized through census data, the press, political campaign promises, and later the emergence of the poor as their own spokesmen. As a result, the face of poverty has become less conveniently hidden from the selective vision of the American public.

FORERUNNERS OF THE WAR ON POVERTY

Conceptual foundations for the War on Poverty were laid during the decade preceding the Kennedy Administration. Two principal demonstration programs, the Ford Foundation Grey Areas Projects and Mobilization for Youth, were developed to experiment with new methods of alleviating social disorganization in congested urban centers.

The Ford Foundation sponsored demonstration projects in four cities, Boston, New Haven, Oakland, and Philadelphia, with the goal of producing institutional change in the various municipal departments concerned with the health, education, and welfare of the slum population. Independent city agencies were established as "umbrella organizations" to effect better coordination and collaboration among the city's education, health, recreation, probation, police, and welfare services.[9]

Mobilization for Youth (MFY), started in 1961, a creative and complex demonstration-research project, was organized to focus on the causes of juvenile delinquency in the ghetto area.[10] The black and Puerto Rican youth on New York's Lower East Side were in danger of becoming juvenile delinquents. The theoretical basis of MFY was the notion that opportunities needed to be provided for youth so that they could embark on careers other than delinquent ones. The approach to the problem of delinquency

[8] Little, "Poverty Types," pp. 938–39.

[9] Daniel P. Moynihan, *Maximum Feasible Misunderstanding: Community Action in the War on Poverty* (New York: Free Press, 1969).

[10] Ibid., p. 55.

was multifaceted, requiring the mobilization of the whole community, not the youth alone. A coordinated group of imaginative projects was created dealing with education, employment, specialized service to individuals and families, and community involvement. The project staff sought to involve the community fully in developing its own ideas about how to solve the problems at hand; such involvement would offset the fact that many of the initial projects were based on ideas originating from the middle-class values and beliefs of professional social workers.

The President's Committee on Juvenile Delinquency, established in 1961, took seriously the notion of a multifaceted approach to social problems generated by the Ford Foundation Grey Areas Projects and the MFY. Leaders in these two seminal programs were influential in shaping the Administration's policy toward the growing employment crisis in the country, especially toward the work-related problems of the young black urban population. The committee assessed the current organization of human services and found that only a few of the voluntary agencies were actually serving the people in poor communities and that the services were fragmented and uncoordinated. Each professional group seemed to be working in its own small orbit with no larger view of the problems and without recognizing the need to link up with the activities of other professionals. Rarely was local political leadership involved in decision-making about serving the poor, nor was the client community involved to any degree in helping shape the direction of services organized on their behalf. Many in high government offices realized that a bold new direction would be required if poverty was to be tackled effectively as a high-priority problem.[11]

The Bureau of the Budget and the Council of Economic Advisers recognized that a new, incisive attack was necessary to change the life circumstances of those bypassed by affluence. President Kennedy strongly encouraged the development of a legislative package to combat poverty. About a month before his assassination in 1963, the Council of Economic Advisers prepared a document called "Program for a Concerted Assault on Poverty." A few months later President Johnson, in his 1964 State of the Union Message, declared "war on poverty." By the end of March 1964 the Economic Opportunity Act was assembled and submitted to Congress; by August it had been passed and signed into law. The Office of Economic Opportunity (OEO) was set up in the Executive Office, where its director, Sargent Shriver, could have easy and close access to the president.[12]

[11] Ibid. See Chapters 3 and 4 for an account of the period when the ideas for the war against poverty were being formulated. Moynihan, a professor on leave from Harvard, was President Kennedy's Assistant in Urban Affairs and Executive Secretary for the National Council of Urban Affairs. He continued on in the Johnson Administration as Assistant Secretary of Labor for Policy Planning and Research. His influence on the War on Poverty Program was significant.

[12] Ibid.

THE STRATEGY

The Economic Opportunity Act was regarded not as an expansion of existing programs to combat poverty, but as the beginning of an all-out campaign to eliminate poverty entirely. Unlike so many previous federal and state welfare programs which were developed to alleviate the effects of poverty, the new law was created to attack its basic causes. Initially, the staff who planned the antipoverty program, as well as the staff throughout the country who were to implement its various aspects, were unfortunately antagonistic to the concept of "welfare." There was also antagonism toward many professional social workers; they were seen as "paternalists" who robbed the poor of their respect and ability to help themselves. The new law sought to provide opportunities for the poor to lift themselves out of the depths of despair, and to help them take advantage of the opportunities already open to them, thus strongly emphasizing the notion of self-help. It underestimated, however, the role of racism in excluding minorities from good education, good housing, and high-paying jobs. Racism was more deeply embedded than the other causes of poverty which the program planned to attack, such as adult illiteracy, unemployment, poor health, overpopulation, and slum housing.

In the planning stage of the War on Poverty, it was recognized that the poor were not taking advantage of the numerous federal and state programs already available to them. A large variety of programs—grants-in-aid, loans, demonstration projects, and educational and technical assistance—were underused by poor people who tended to lack an organization capable of tapping the federal resources. A major goal of the Antipoverty Act was therefore to coordinate, at all levels of government, all the federal agencies with services and resources related to poverty, and to enable the poor to become their beneficiaries. This was no easy task.

The total budget of such existing federal programs ($11.9 billion in 1964) was the base on which specific antipoverty legislation was to be built. The first allocation was $1.5 billion, with much higher appropriations expected in the following years. The program sought primarily to help the young, through education and training opportunities, and thereby to eliminate poverty from the coming generation. The central feature was to be the fullest possible involvement of the poor in planning, developing, and carrying out the war against poverty. There were believed to be untold opportunities that the poor could not take advantage of because they lacked skills, education, and good work habits. By replacing these deficits with marketable attributes, the OEO expected to enable the poor to get jobs, or to get better jobs, and thus to end their poverty. A series of programs showing great promise were spawned from the 1964 Economic Opportunity Act (EOA) and its subsequent amendments. In the education and training field these programs were the Job Corps, the Neighborhood Youth Corps, Adult Basic Education, and Work Experience and Training. In the field of finance they were the Rural Areas Loans and Loans to Small Business. The program receiving the largest annual appropriation was the Community Action Program (CAP) for neighborhood service centers, which was originally responsible for the Head Start Program as well as for Legal Services and Family Planning. The EOA also gave birth to the Volunteers in Service to America (VISTA) and a special small-scale program to assist migrant labor families.

ADMINISTRATION OF THE WAR ON POVERTY

Under the Economic Opportunity Act, the principal responsibility of the Office of Economic Opportunity was to coordinate the newly developing antipoverty programs with preexisting programs in the various federal departments and agencies. OEO itself would assume responsibility for operating some of the new antipoverty programs, and would delegate the administration of others to existing federal agencies within the Departments of Labor and of Health, Education and Welfare; it would then monitor the results. Furthermore, OEO would use its powerful position in the White House to induce these departments to redirect major segments of their ongoing programs to fight the war against poverty. The logic of this coordinating structure was derived from the Ford Foundation Project.[13]

However, the OEO director, Sargent Shriver, insisted on assuming direct operational responsibility for many of the new programs: the Community Action Program, the Job Corps, VISTA, Head Start (a component of CAP), Legal Services, and Neighborhood Health Services. Rightly or wrongly, he believed that the program would fare better if it were directed by a new organization. Thus he became both administrator and coordinator, in theory; in practice he could not effectively do both. It is a principle of administration that coordination should remain separate from operational responsibility for the tasks being coordinated. The coordinating agency needs to be neutral; instead, OEO was directing its own programs while trying to coordinate its activities with those of rival agencies. It appeared that the energy OEO expended in running its programs was taken away from the job of coordination. In the end, OEO was never fully effective in pulling together in a constructive package the cluster of agencies which had the capacity and the responsibility to significantly lower the rate of poverty.[14] The Model Cities program, which included a coordinating

---

[13] Ibid.

[14] James Sundquist, "Coordinating the War on Poverty," *American Annals of Political and Social Science* (September 1969), 41–49.

mechanism at both the federal and the local levels, mandating the co-operation of all relevant federal programs, was a later and hopefully more successfully coordinated effort at fighting urban poverty. (See Chapter 11).

Pressures were eventually put on OEO by the administration and the related federal departments to delegate a number of its program responsibilities. In 1969 the Job Corps and Head Start were transferred to the Departments of Labor and of Health, Education and Welfare, respectively. The president's advisers felt that these departments would be in a more favorable position to administer and coordinate the programs more effectively with their other ongoing programs.

Proponents of OEO and the War on Poverty were uneasy about the possibility of major changes in the program with the inauguration of President Nixon. The anticipated extensive truncation did not at first materialize, and the Economic Opportunity Act was extended for two years; however, OEO was reorganized in 1969 with the objective of minimizing its operating functions and transferring successful programs to other federal departments. Its major responsibility evolved into experimentation and planning with greater emphasis on evaluative research of the experimental and demonstration program.[15]

Ten regional offices of OEO were set up across the nation, paralleling the Department of Labor's Neighborhood Youth Corps offices, to provide technical assistance to local programs in planning and program development, ensuring the enforcement of program policy established by the central office. The regional offices seek to provide "quality control" over local programs.[16]

From the outset, state government was relegated only a minor role in the development of local antipoverty programs. The federal objective was to intervene directly at the local level, cooperating with the community to fight urban problems—"creative federalism." But the governors were uneasy about being bypassed, although their support and technical assistance were requested, and they pushed for a larger degree of control of program resources and activities. As a result the governors were finally given the power to veto any programs which they believed to be poorly planned or administered. This amounted only to token power, however, as the director of OEO reserved the right to override their veto. The veto power, in fact, has served as a check on local programs in danger of going out of control, but it acts mostly as a sop to "states' rights." Governors gained a good deal of political mileage by using their veto power to show opposition to some OEO programs.[17]

15 "Overview," Office of Economic Opportunity Pamphlet No. 1105-2 (Washington, D.C.: U.S. Government Printing Office, 1971), p. 12.

16 Ibid.

17 Sar Levitan, *The Great Societies Poor Law* (Baltimore: Johns Hopkins Press, 1969), pp. 58–62.

THE COMMUNITY ACTION PROGRAM (CAP)

Of all the programs established under the OEO none has been more controversial than the Community Action Program. This program was designed to attack directly the forces which perpetuate poverty. It had perhaps the greatest potential of all the innovations developed under the Act. Planners believed that the Community Action Program, like the Ford Foundation Projects and the MFY, could garner all available local resources to mount a coordinated attack on the local conditions that keep people poor. According to the Act and its subsequent amendments, a community action program has four specific qualities:

1. It mobilizes and uses public and private resources of a community in a comprehensive attack on poverty.
2. It provides services, assistance, and other activities of sufficient variety, scope, and magnitude to give promise of progress toward elimination of poverty or a cause or causes of poverty through developing employment opportunities, improving human performance, motivation, and productivity, or bettering the conditions under which people live, learn, and work.
3. It is directed toward strengthening community capabilities for planning and coordination of federal, state, and other assistance related to the elimination of poverty.
4. It is developed, conducted, and administered with the *maximum feasible participation* of residents of the areas and members of the groups served.[18]

The programs were to be commenced by Community Action Agencies (CAA's) to be organized in target area communities. Most of these agencies were established as corporations independent from local government; however, they were usually organized through the combined efforts of local government and voluntary agencies, including those in local civil rights and social action groups. Social workers, mostly in local welfare planning councils, took active roles throughout the country in organizing for the development of CAP programs. There were rarely two individuals who interpreted the meaning of community action exactly alike. Both the process and the end product of the action to be taken were described differently by those who had planned and taken responsibility for its implementation.

The most troublesome directive of the Act was the one which required "maximum feasible participation" of the residents. This provision, which crept into the Act without much notice from Congress, was a virtual time bomb, exploding in a series of controversies throughout the states as the various programs began to roll. The concept of citizen participation, modeled on community development activities applied to underdeveloped areas in the United States and abroad, when applied to the political climate and

[18] Moynihan, *Maximum Feasible Misunderstanding*, p. 88.

civil rights movement of the mid-1960s, created an explosive mixture and was interpreted by some as a call to revolution. At issue was who should control the governing boards of the CAA; the poor felt that they themselves should. When asked what was maximum feasible participation of the poor, the OEO was at first noncommittal, indicating only that it opposed domination of the CAA's by one faction. In some cities there was open conflict between city hall and militant neighborhood workers who sought control of local action programs. Politicians saw the poor as a bloc of voters whom they could control by holding the purse strings of the poverty programs and by dispensing patronage. If city hall did not maintain control over the poor, someone else might turn them into a strong force against those in power. Well-organized demonstrations and picket lines, some allegedly leading to riots, were sparked by the issue of who should control the CAA.[19] The proportion of representation of the poor on the boards became so much the point of focus that insufficient attention was paid to the quality of participation on the boards. What was needed was more effective leadership from the poor themselves, not from individuals who belonged to a minority race or who had experienced poverty at one time, but who had long since risen in the ranks and been coopted into the power structure.

As a result of the leadership struggles, Congress enacted two amendments which weakened the chances that community action would succeed as a method of confrontation and community change. The 1966 amendment specified that members would be chosen for the CAA boards by local democratic elections (rather than by appointment or other means). The 1967 amendment made it clear that "maximum feasible participation" meant that the poor should represent at least one-third of the CAA board, the remainder of its members being local government officials and other community leaders. The legislation also tightened administrative control of community action programs, requiring all agencies to become instrumentalities of state or local government, although the government could designate a nonprofit organization to establish and operate a program.[20]

Initially, tremendous energy had been released by the promise of an end to poverty. The amendments eliminated much of the conflict over control of the CAA's, but at the same time they dampened the early enthusiasm over the potential impact of community action. For a few years many ghetto dwellers had high hopes of seeing institutional change take place, opening up equal opportunities. When these did not materialize, their disappointment and despair mounted. The demand of the poor

19 See Lillian Rubin, "Maximum Feasible Participation: The Origins, Implications, and Present Status," in Louis Ferman, ed., *Annals of the American Academy of Political Science*, 385, 14–29; Moynihan, *Maximum Feasible Misunderstanding;* and *New York Times,* July 19, 1967. See also Ralph Kramer, *Participation of the Poor: Comparative Community Case Studies in the War on Poverty* (Englewood Cliffs, N.J.: Prentice-Hall, 1969).

20 Rubin, "Maximum Feasible Participation."

for participation, before the lid was put on the Community Action Program, indicated that their despair was not complete, that when there seemed to be a real chance for change, the poor were willing to act to end their powerlessness.

THE OPERATIONS OF A COMMUNITY ACTION AGENCY

Although the CAA's have not been fully controlled by the poor, they are organized through local initiative, by local residents, with a heavy involvement of those who will benefit from their services. In 1971 there were over 900 Community Action Agencies throughout the country in both urban and rural areas.[21] Local initiative has meant that each CAA has special characteristics and unique focus. It has been the responsibility of each CAA to study the extent and causes of poverty in its community and to develop a plan to combat these causes, involving the poor as much as possible in the ensuing activities. Under the 1971 guidelines each agency is charged with the mission of providing the direct services which are appropriate to local poverty needs and of refining the "goals of Community Action by influencing other institutions and by enhancing its own capacity to respond creatively to new poverty situations and traditional methods of dealing with them."[22] The agency is expected to:

1. Develop new information and strategies concerning poverty and encourage joint local planning efforts to implement them through coordination and negotiation with other agencies.
2. Evaluate its own and other antipoverty efforts locally, with an eye to eliminating wasteful and duplicate efforts and strengthening new and promising antipoverty strategies and programs.
3. Mobilize all possible resources within the community, both public and private, to help redress local poverty problems.
4. Effect the necessary changes in existing local institutions, such as welfare and employment agencies, to make them more responsive to the needs of the poor.
5. Launch communitywide education efforts to alter community attitudes and institutional practices affecting the poor.
6. Promote career development activities including increased job opportunities ... and provide increased training and education to upgrade the skills of poor subprofessionals and increase the work incentives of the already employed poor.[23]

[21] Office of Economic Opportunity Pamphlet No. 6000-2 (Washington, D.C.: Office of Operations, 1971), p. 2.

[22] Ibid., p. 7.

[23] Ibid., pp. 7–10.

To carry out the service component of the antipoverty mission, the CAA's have established nearly 3,000 neighborhood service centers in the various poor communities designated as "target areas"; many communities have multiple target areas. Ideally the neighborhood service center houses a variety of employees, such as employment placement officers, legal services officers, youth counselors, general counselors, and neighborhood outreach aides. It may also contain a child care center, a health center, and perhaps even a recreation hall. These services have been established under one roof, to provide staff trained to focus on the multiple causes of poverty. Not all of the programs located in a center are funded or operated with OEO funds; rather, the CAA staff seeks to bring into the neighborhood as many community services as it can to work on the problems of the poor in their area.

The annual national budget for the Community Action Program has been too small (about $300 million) to accomplish many of its goals. Recognizing this fact, the OEO has spurred the local CAA's to act as forceful catalytic agents in opening up the opportunity structure in government and in the private sector for the poor. One of the most impressive activities on the local level has been grass-roots organizing to help the poor have a voice in local politics as it affects their social well-being. According to a widely-distributed OEO pamphlet, "...the concept behind community action is to concentrate financial and philosophic efforts in such a way as to have the maximum impact on the problem, and the maximum leverage to attract additional resources from other institutions in the public and private realms." The pamphlet continues, "Clearly the CAA's are vehicles for local reform, catalysts that show how things can be done differently, more equitably and effectively on behalf of the poor."[24] The CAA's have become a major voice for the poor throughout the country, in many cases lobbying at city hall or the state capital for or against measures which affect the well-being of their community.

To date, however, the CAA has reached no more than a small number of the hardcore poor, even in the target areas. Too little money has been spent to accomplish the program's ambitious goals. Some claim it has done little more than to take the cream off the top of the low-income population, helping those who are perhaps least in need of help. Others charge that the local programs still do not affect the real basis of poverty, that the services they give are still only rehabilitative in nature.[25]

Though both these arguments appear to have validity, still, with all the obstacles, the CAA's have made some important contributions to the

[24] Ibid., p. 6.

[25] See Stanford Kravitz and Ferne Kolodner, "Community Action: Where Has It Been? Where Will It Go?" *Annals of the American Academy of Political Science,* 385 (September 1969), 36–40.

system of bringing services to the poor. They have fostered the growth of interdisciplinary neighborhood service centers throughout the country. Unlike traditional agencies, these centers are decentralized and neighborhood-based, putting services where they can best be used. The CAA's have also demonstrated the benefits of employing the poor as paraprofessionals in jobs such as teacher aides, urban planning aides, and so on, where their knowledge of their community can help social workers and other professionals carry out their work. In these jobs the poor, in turn, can learn professional skills and advance toward a professional career. At the same time, however, they tend to be caught in a web, torn between loyalty to their new profession and loyalty to their community. Thus they are in danger of losing their value as an insistent voice for change as they become more cautious of jeopardizing their professional careers. The danger of cooptation is constant.[26]

HEAD START

Head Start has been one of the most popular programs initiated by OEO. (In 1969 it was transferred to the administration of the Department of Health, Education and Welfare's Office of Child Development.) Initially, the Economic Opportunity Act did not specify education for the very young, and plans to develop the program were not formulated until the spring of 1965.[27] At first it was to be a small experimental summer program to gain knowledge and experience in how best to prepare disadvantaged children for the public schools. For the summer of 1965 the OEO planned to commit only enough money to fund programs for about 100,000 young children. Once the program was announced, however, the OEO was flooded with inquiries and applications. Caught up in the overwhelming national enthusiasm over the development of Head Start, and realizing its political popularity, the OEO hurriedly released enough of its available unearmarked money to allow about half a million children to participate. Few large-scale federal programs have been developed and funded so quickly.[28]

The concept behind Head Start is closely linked with the total theme of the antipoverty program—opportunity. Children who begin their lives in impoverished environments are already at a disadvantage by the time they enter first grade, and they continue to fall farther behind. They often lack the intellectual stimulation, the vocabulary, and the range of cultural ex-

26 Gertrude Goldberg, "Non-Professionals in Human Service," in Charles Grosser, William E. Henry, and James G. Kelley, eds., Non-Professionals in the Human Services (San Francisco: Jossey-Bass, 1969), pp. 12–39.
27 Levitan, The Great Societies Poor Law, p. 135.
28 Ibid., p. 144.

periences which are enjoyed by the more affluent. The Head Start program was developed to compensate for these early deficiencies. Unlike middle-class nursery schools and many kindergartens, which deemphasize academic activities, Head Start stresses basic educational preparedness, seeking to prepare the child at age three, four, or five for grammar school. The average project runs five hours a day.

As in the other local antipoverty programs, maximum involvement of the poor community is encouraged. Parents are expected to participate in both the planning and the ongoing policy development of local Head Start programs.

The young children are given medical and psychological examinations and a range of specialized services such as nursing, social services, and nutrition, as their needs become known by the teachers, teacher aides, and volunteer parents. The program tries to provide both diagnosis and treatment of medical and psychological problems whenever possible. Poor children are usually in greater need of medical care; in Los Angeles, for example, it was found that more than 60 percent of the Head Start children needed medical, psychological, or dental care. These programs can take on the characteristics of child development centers, with the staff and volunteers attending to the developmental needs of the children. Professional social workers interested in early childhood education and development have found Head Start programs a vital place to influence the development of positive child–parent relationships and child growth opportunities.

After its first summer, the Head Start program was extended to year-round operation, with both a summer and a nine-month program. Over the years the number of children in Head Start programs has continued to grow, with more full-time programs being established. Of the monies allocated for community action programs, about two-fifths has been earmarked for Head Start. Even so, the program has been able to serve only a small proportion of the eligible children. To be run properly, Head Start requires a much higher teacher–student ratio than regular public schools. The character of deprivation is such that it cannot be easily erased; a large investment is required to make even small progress. Sar Levitan estimates that to reach all the eligible children, the annual budget for Head Start would have to be $6.5 billion, more than the total OEO budget during its first four years.[29]

The initial assumption of Head Start, that preschool intervention through an educational and cultural enrichment program would prepare young children to function on a par with their nonpoor classmates, has unfortunately not been borne out by evaluative research. The programs have not, it appears, significantly enhanced the intellectual and academic

[29] Ibid., p. 140.

performance of the children they have served. In a major study in 1968, Westinghouse Learning Institute compared Head Start children with control groups. The findings showed that while Head Start children made initial gains over the control group, by the time they reached the third grade the gains had been wiped out. Furthermore, the Head Start children fell far below the national norm on scores measuring cognitive development.[30] The question remains whether the program has failed to reach these children, whether better-planned programs could have more beneficial results; or whether Head Start is really too late—perhaps the children must be reached while they are still in their mothers' arms, that is, their mothers should be educated for more effective child rearing.

The director of Head Start, Edward Zeigler, remarked that the Westinghouse study was looking only at the children's I.Q. and that it failed to consider the multiple purposes of Head Start, which also aims at improving the children's health and self-esteem and at involving the parents in improving their children's lives.[31] The controversy over the effects of Head Start has not been without its benefits; the organization now plans a more thorough evaluation of the total impact of services on the child. It is also engaging in research which will evaluate the effectiveness of various models and techniques of early childhood education.

Another federal program allied with Head Start is Follow Through, administered in a similar way. It was begun in 1967 to grant funds to primary schools to enhance language and intellectual skills and provide medical and dental care to Head Start children once they entered first grade. It was designed to "be operated by local educational agencies with a view to changing their approach to primary grade education of disadvantaged children." The program has never reached the scope of Head Start, however; eighty programs served only 12,000 children during the year 1968–69.[32]

LEGAL SERVICES PROGRAM

Legal services for the low-income population have long been available. Legal Aid Societies were organized to assist people with legal problems who could not afford private attorneys (see Chapter 13). Too few of these agencies were available, however, and many were staffed only by part-time legal

---

[30] For a good discussion of the effectiveness of Head Start, see Norma Radin, "Preschool Programs in Child Welfare," *Encyclopedia of Social Work 1971*, pp. 131–37.

[31] Ibid., p. 134.

[32] Levitan, *The Great Societies Poor Law*, p. 163.

volunteers. They could serve only a small number of cases and were usually situated in locations inconvenient for the poor. Furthermore, poor people generally distrusted lawyers and the courts and avoided using them.

OEO, recognizing the legal needs of the poor, was successful in having Congress pass in 1965 an amendment to the Economic Opportunity Act establishing the Legal Services Program. The formal objectives of the program are to provide "traditional legal assistance in establishing or asserting clearly defined rights; legal analysis and representation directed toward reform where the law is vague, uncertain, or destructively complex; legal representation where the law appears to be contrary to the interests of the slum community; and legal representation in contexts that appear to be nonlegal."[33]

The local Legal Services Program is administered through the Office of Legal Services of the OEO. The CAA has the option of operating a Legal Services Program itself or delegating the responsibility to an existing community Legal Aid Society program. As do other antipoverty programs, each local Legal Services Program has a large degree of autonomy in developing its services. It is under the administration of a board of directors composed of lawyers, interested laymen, and representatives of the poor. The board sets priorities for the program and standards to be followed, within broad guidelines established at the national level.

Legal Services, like other OEO programs, is usually located in the neighborhood of the poor, often within the Neighborhood Service Center. A few have been set up in buses so that they can be even more available to clients. In 1970 there were 850 neighborhood law offices in America, located in the 265 communities with CAA programs. The legal services were staffed by 2,000 attorneys, who were paid a regular salary and who provided free legal aid to the poor. The number of clients helped by these attorneys each year was approximately 1,000,000. Because the lawyers sympathized with the problems of the poor and were easily available, many of the poor overcame their resistance to attorneys and sought help more freely on a large variety of legal problems. The majority of legal problems brought to Legal Service lawyers are in the areas of family relations and consumer law.

Starting in the lower courts, several cases handled through the Legal Services Program have resulted in important decisions affecting the legal rights of groups of poor people. In one such major decision the United States Supreme Court declared unconstitutional state laws which required otherwise eligible clients to wait for a year to establish residency before they could receive welfare grants.[34]

33 Ibid., p. 129.
34 "Legal Services," OEO Pamphlet No. 6140-5 (Washington, D.C.: Government Printing Office, 1971).

VOCATIONAL PROGRAM

Originally, the Office of Economic Opportunity decided to operate one major youth education-employment program, the Job Corps, itself, and to delegate responsibility for another, the Neighborhood Youth Corps, to the Department of Labor. In addition, the Department of Labor has had responsibility for administering other programs such as the Concentrated Employment Program, to improve economic opportunity for young people.

The Job Corps, although patterned after the Civilian Conservation Corps (CCC) established as a sort of antipoverty program during the Depression of the 1930s, was directed at a much more intractable problem. The CCC tried to provide education and employment for a cross section of the nation's population hit by the Great Depression; the Job Corps was given the mission of preparing for employment sixteen- to twenty-one-year-old school dropouts who were largely from hardcore poor families.

The Job Corps program consisted of both educational and vocational skill components, with medical care and counseling services also available. By 1969, eighty-two rural residential centers housing up to 250 youths each, and twenty-four urban centers, some with a capacity of 3,000 trainees, were set up. The urban centers were operated mostly by private corporations such as IBM, Philco, and Litton Industries, and the rural centers under the auspices of the Departments of Interior and Agriculture. At its peak in mid-1967, the Job Corps had the capacity to serve 43,000 young men and women. The program was unpopular with youth, however, and each year after 1967 it dwindled in size. By mid-1969, fifty-nine centers had closed and only 20,000 youth were enrolled in the programs.[35] In 1972 the Job Corps was discontinued.

The Job Corps had many critics. Congress was especially concerned at the per capita expense of the program, which in the first year was as much as $15,000 per year, per trainee.[36] It was also charged that the Corps did not really help a large number of individuals to enter the labor market, and those that did enter did so at the bottom, still lacking the skills they need to move them into higher positions with greater responsibilities. When major lay-offs occurred, as during the 1970–72 recession, the ex–Job Corps trainees were the first to be let go. Their response, naturally, was extreme anger and frustration.

Another criticism was that the private industries which ran Job Corps training programs made substantial risk-free profits from the enterprise. Job training programs also reimbursed companies for training employees

[35] Levitan, *The Great Societies Poor Law*, pp. 305–6.

[36] Joseph Kershaw, *Government Against Poverty* (Washington, D.C.: The Brookings Institute, 1970).

whom they would have had to train anyhow; this amounted to a subsidy of business.[37]

The Neighborhood Youth Corps, somewhat smaller than the Job Corps, also is a work-training program for youth between sixteen and twenty-one. Monies are made available to nonprofit organizations like recreation programs, park departments, and public schools to establish on-the-job training for school dropouts or those still in school, allowing up to thirty hours per week of employment. Wages on these jobs have been extremely low, ranging between $1.25 and $1.60 per hour.[38] Nevertheless, this program has been much more popular, attracting 600,000 young adults for the year 1970.[39] About 1,500 projects have already been funded for the NYC, with the summer program attracting the most participation. While this OEO-sponsored program has been more favorably received, the character of employment and on-the-job training obtained by many of the youths has been rather menial and has not prepared them for high-paying jobs later on.

The Concentrated Employment Program, started in 1967, is another manpower program which combines the resources of OEO and the Department of Labor. It concentrates on employment problems in sections of the country hardest hit by unemployment. The local employment service joins with the Community Action Program to provide a broad range of services for putting men and women to work, such as counseling, training, and job placement.

SPECIAL EMPHASIS PROGRAMS

Although the primary emphasis of the antipoverty program was initially on youth, the OEO has singled out four other groups for special attention: older persons, Indians, migrants, and rural families. The Office of Special Programs was started in 1970 to coordinate resources available for solving the economic problems of these groups. In 1971 the OEO estimated that of every hundred people sixty-five or older, thirty are poor, and of every hundred Indians living on reservations, eighty are poor. For rural dwellers the figure is twenty-three; for migrant laborers, ninety. For the United States as a whole, the OEO estimated that thirteen of every hundred are poor, using the standard measure of poverty.[40]

37 David Wellman, "The Wrong Way to Find Jobs for Negroes," *Transaction,* 5, No. 5 (April 1960), 8–18.

38 Kershaw, *Government Against Poverty,* pp. 30–31.

39 "Overview," OEO Pamphlet No. 1105-2.

40 "Special Programs," OEO Pamphlet No. 6100-1 (Washington, D.C.: Government Printing Office, 1971).

As a coordinating body, the Office of Economic Opportunity does not administer programs, but helps set policy and improve the functioning of the various other offices and local programs designed to help these special categories of people. In cooperation with the Office of Program Development and the Office of Planning, Research and Evaluation, new experimental and demonstration projects are started in various areas of the country to test out more effective approaches to deal with hardcore poverty. In the area of Indian problems, for instance, the OEO is supporting the first Indian community college, a Navajo college planned, controlled, and operated by Indians; it serves more than 650 students. Another demonstration project is training eighty Indians to become attorneys. The OEO also supports twenty health projects concentrating on the prevention, treatment, and rehabilitation of alcoholism among Indians.[41]

Briefly, other programs sponsored by OEO include the Neighborhood Health Centers Program, Family Planning, Work Experience Program (replaced in 1967 by the Work Incentive Program), Rural Area Loans, and Loans to Small Business. These programs have broadened the array of mechanisms to combat poverty; however, none of them has been funded sufficiently to meet its objectives.

CONCLUSION

Is the OEO winning the War on Poverty? According to the *Encyclopedia of Social Work,* during the 1960s the number of poor persons decreased sharply, from 40,000,000 in 1960 to 24,000,000 in 1969. The decline was largely caused not by government programs, however, but by a period of sustained economic expansion. The rewards went mainly to those poor families headed by nonaged working men who could join the labor force. Among these families there was a 40 percent decrease in the number of poor, while there was only a 6 percent decrease among aged families, and only a 0.5 percent decrease among families headed by women (a special target group of the antipoverty program). Furthermore, the rate of decline in the number of poor families is now slowing down, and if the 1970–72 recession continues, the number of poor may again begin to rise.[42] Thus, the overall impact of the War on Poverty has been disappointing. Though some worthwhile experience in social programs has been gained, the OEO has not materially reduced poverty in the United States.

Using 1967 figures, Sar Levitan estimated that it would take between twenty and twenty-five billion dollars annually, in addition to funds already

41 Ibid.
42 Harris and Townsend, "Poverty," p. 898.

committed to federal programs, to raise the poor above the poverty level
and to provide them with enough incentive to remain in the labor force
if possible.[43] This figure compares modestly to the over $100 billion the
Southeast Asian War has drained from society in direct costs alone. However, at no time was there any indication that either the president or Congress was prepared to commit a sum of that size to antipoverty programs.
The amount allotted in 1965 for the first six months of the program $800
million; in 1966, $1.5 billion, in 1967, $1.6 billion, in 1968, $1.8 billion, in
1969, $1.9 billion, and in 1970, $2 billion.

Accounting for inflation, the size of the annual program increase over
the last few years dwindles to almost nothing. The Vietnam War siphoned
off money from social programs and made it impossible for a poorly funded
antipoverty program to integrate the poor into the working class through
programs to change the opportunity structure. The policy of escalating the
war did temporarily decrease unemployment by building war industries,
thus raising the income of millions of families who would otherwise have
fallen below the poverty line. But even before the deescalation of the war
began at the end of 1971, these families and many others began to be
recipients of social security, public assistance, and food stamps.

Although it was bold in its initial conception, even with a much higher
level of funding the antipoverty program would still have been limited in its
ability to eliminate poverty. A major step toward that goal would be a
guaranteed income and a reordering of our national priorities to place at
a considerably higher level the objective of removing the barriers which
keep many disadvantaged groups from sharing more completely in the
wealth of the land.

SELECTED BIBLIOGRAPHY

Baldwin, James, *Notes of a Native Son.* New York: Dial Press, 1963.

Boulding, Kenneth E., "Reflections on Poverty," *Social Welfare Forum* (1961),
45–58.

Bredemeyer, Harry C., "New Strategies for the War on Poverty," *Trans-action,* 2
(November–December 1964), 3–8.

Brown, Claude. *Manchild in the Promised Land.* New York: Macmillan, 1965.

Clark, K. B., *Dark Ghetto: Dilemmas of Social Power.* New York: Harper & Row,
1965.

Cloward, R. A., and R. M. Elman, "Poverty, Injustice and the Welfare State,"
Nation, 202 (28 February 1966), 230–35, (7 March 1966), 264–68.

Cohen, Jerome, "Social Work and the Culture of Poverty," *Social Work,* 9, No. 1
(January 1964)), 3–11.

Coles, Robert, *Children of Crisis: A Study of Courage and Fear.* Boston: Little,
Brown, 1967.

[43] Levitan, *The Great Societies Poor Law,* p. 316.

————, "It's the Same, But It's Different," *Daedalus*, 44, No. 4 (Fall 1965), 1107–32.

COLLINS, LEROY, and WHITNEY M. YOUNG, "Civil Rights—Unfinished Business," *Social Welfare Forum* (1965), 35–54.

COMER, J. P., "The Social Power of the Negro," *Scientific American*, 216, No. 4 (1967), 21–27.

COSER, LEWIS A., "The Sociology of Poverty," *Social Problems*, 13, No. 2 (1965), 140–48.

DEUTSCH, MARTIN, et al., *The Disadvantaged Child: Studies of the Social Environment and the Learning Process*. New York: Basic Books, 1967.

ELMAN, RICHARD M., *The Poorhouse State: The American Way of Life on Public Assistance*. New York: Dell, 1966.

ERIKSON, E. H., "The Concept of Identity in Race Relations: Notes and Queries," *Daedalus*, 95, No. 1 (1966), 145–71.

FEIN, R., "Economic and Social Profile of the Negro American," *Daedalus*, 94 (1965), 815–46.

FISHMAN, LEO, ed., *Poverty Amid Affluence*. New Haven, Conn.: Yale University Press, 1966.

FRAZIER, E. FRANKLIN, *The Negro Family in the United States*. Chicago: University of Chicago Press, 1939. Rev. ed. by Nathan Glazer, 1966.

GINZBERG, ELI, et al., *The Middle-Class Negro in the White Man's World*. New York: Columbia University Press, 1967.

GLADWIN, THOMAS, "The Anthropologist's View of Poverty," *Social Welfare Forum* (1961), 73–86.

GLAZER, NATHAN, *Beyond the Melting Pot: The Negroes, Puerto Ricans, Jews, Italians and Irish of New York City*. Cambridge, Mass.: MIT Press and Harvard University Press, 1963.

GRIER, GEORGE, and EUNICE GRIER, *Equality and Beyond: Housing Segregation and the Goals of a Great Society*. Chicago: Quadrangle, 1966.

HANDLIN, OSCAR, *The New Comers: Negroes and Puerto Ricans in a Changing Metropolis*. New York: Doubleday, 1962.

HARE, NATHAN, "Recent Trends in the Occupational Mobility of Negroes 1930–1960: An Intra-cohort Analysis," *Social Forces*, 44 (December 1965), 66–73.

HELLER, CELIA S., *Mexican-American Youth: Forgotten Youth at the Crossroads*. New York: Random House, 1966.

HERZOG, E., "Is There a 'Breakdown' of the Negro Family?" *Social Work*, 11, No. 1 (1966), 3–10.

LEVITAN, SAR A., *Programs in Aid of the Poor for the 1970's*. Baltimore: Johns Hopkins Press, 1969.

LEWIS, OSCAR, *La Vida: A Puerto Rican Family in the Culture of Poverty—San Juan and New York*. New York: Random House, 1965.

LOURIE, NORMAN V., "Poverty," in Nathan E. Cohen, ed., *Social Work and Social Problems*. New York: National Association of Social Workers, 1964, pp. 1–40.

MCWILLIAMS, CAREY, *North from Mexico: The Spanish-Speaking People of the United States*. New York: Greenwood Press, 1968.

MERRIAM, IDA C., "Welfare and Its Measurements," in Eleanor B. Sheldon and Wilbert E. Moore, eds., *Indicators of Social Change*. New York: Russell Sage Foundation, 1968.

MYRDAL, GUNNAR, *American Dilemma*. New York: McGraw-Hill, 1964.

ORSHANSKY, M., "Counting the Poor: Another Look at the Poverty Profile," *Social Security Bulletin*, 28 (January 1965), 3–29.

PARKER, SEYMOUR, and ROBERT J. KLEINER, *Mental Illness in the Urban Negro Community*. New York: Free Press, 1967.

PILISUK, MARC, and PHYLLIS PILISUK, eds., *Poor Americans: How the White Poor Live.* New York: Transaction Books, 1971.

RAINWATER, LEE, and KAROL K. WIENSTEIN, *And the Poor Get Children.* Chicago: Quadrangle, 1960.

"Rights of Man," *Ebony,* 21 (October 1966), 142–43.

SCHORR, ALVIN L., *Poor Kids—A Report on Children in Poverty.* New York: Basic Books, 1966.

SEXTON, PATRICIA CAYO, *Spanish Harlem: An Anatomy of Poverty.* New York: Harper & Row, 1965.

SHRIVER, SARGENT, "Poverty in the United States, What Next?" *Social Welfare Forum* (1965), 55–65.

TITMUSS, R., "Poverty vs. Inequality: Diagnosis," *Nation,* 200 (February 1965), 130–33.

UNITED NATIONS: *Economic and Social Consequences of Racial Discriminatory Practices.* New York: United Nations, 1963.

11

---

housing
and
the   *H. deb. Hachlen, Ph.D.*
social
environment

Satisfactory housing and a supportive physical and social environment are essential to sustain *human* life. In concerning itself with housing and the environment, social welfare encroaches somewhat on other professional territory, such as city planning and architecture. However, where environment is inadequate for human beings, it is legitimate for social welfare to be concerned and to encourage an organized professional effort aimed at developing environments that promote human growth. For over a century, the field of social welfare has included in its scope the quality of housing (see page 84). More recently, it has also been concerned with the physical and social environment of the community as a whole, as it affects the well-being of the people.

Obviously, safety and sufficient shelter from the elements are basic requirements for survival. However, it has not always been recognized that physical and psychological growth, the expression of human potential, and reproduction can occur successfully only when elements in the social environment are adequately ordered. Furthermore, when the social environment is impoverished, disorganized, or conflict-ridden, as is often the case in slums, a certain proportion of the population will show gross signs of maladaptation, and their growth potential will be thwarted.[1]

A growing body of literature in the biological and social sciences shows the impact on man of the environment which he has shaped. One study shows that when people are inundated with noise of a high decibel level, undesirable physical and psychological effects occur. Another study deals with the psychological impact of forced relocation from one housing area to another.[2] While we still lack a definitive understanding of how and why man reacts as he does to an impoverished, disintegrating, or disruptive environment, enough information is available to show that the quality of housing and the broader environment directly influence the quality of life. Social science research has also brought the tragic realization that public housing programs designed to improve living conditions of those trapped in poor environments have often had the opposite effect. For example, government efforts to eliminate slums frequently have the unforeseen consequence of breaking up the culture and way of life of a stable subpopulation, fostering among residents a feeling of alienation and despair.[3]

From their study of the animal world including the human species, environmentalists conclude that environmental influences are most profound when they are brought to bear during the prenatal or postnatal period, or in early childhood. When these influences are negative, they often have permanent and irreversible effects.[4] Man is one of the most adaptable anthropoids, able to survive under extreme physical hardship, including extreme climatic conditions, inadequate food supply, and disruptive living conditions. Nevertheless, as noxious elements accumulate in the environment, certain aspects of his adaptation have negative effects over the long run, not only on present but also on future generations of the human species. For example, man can initially adapt to overcrowded living conditions, but as time passes he responds adaptively but negatively to the loss of privacy and lack of social satisfaction that results. The consequence may be

[1] Rene Dubos, "Environmental Determinants of Human Life," in David C. Class, ed., *Environmental Influences,* Proceedings of a Conference under the Auspices of The Russell Sage Foundation and Rockefeller University (New York: Rockefeller Foundation University Press and Russell Sage Foundation, 1968), pp. 138–54.

[2] Marc Fried, "Grieving for a Lost Home," in L. Duhl, ed., *The Urban Condition* (New York: Basic Books, 1963), pp. 151–57.

[3] Ibid.

[4] Dubos, "Environmental Determinants of Human Life," p. 138.

social isolation and anomie, as seen in densely populated residential areas. The ill effects of exploiting man's adaptive capacity endangers subsequent generations. The likelihood of unanticipated negative consequences is of major concern to social welfare institutions, and must be faced by the caseworker, group worker, community organizer, and planner alike.

Environments can favor growth as well as threaten it, as we know from common knowledge and from scientific evidence. It has long been recognized that a milieu with rich resources, warmth and consistency in human relationships, and sufficient stimulation favors physical and emotional growth, just as deprived, conflict-ridden, and disruptive situations tend to stunt or warp growth for many. However, only recently have we had the scientific evidence to demonstrate that environments which segregate and isolate individuals, restrict functions, limit stimulation, and maintain low self-expectations are likely to have devastating effects. This was the prime reason for the 1954 Supreme Court decision to end school segregation.[5] Unhealthy environments occur both in deprived areas of the community and in various institutions such as hospitals, prisons, and the armed forces.[6]

Increasingly, the field of social welfare is acknowledging the importance of the social and physical environment as it affects man. The task is to translate common knowledge and scientific proof into policies and programs which will improve living conditions, life circumstances, and growth opportunities for all groups. Man's genetic inheritance provides great potential for the development of innate intelligence and creativity, which make life satisfying and joyful. Rarely does this potential come to fruition. The major key to its development is an environment which optimally meets his needs and provides a variety of choices and opportunities. As social workers become more aware of the nature of man's adaptive potential and the effects of varying environmental influences on him, they can be increasingly effective in building new social welfare policies and programs favorable to the human condition.

ENVIRONMENT, HOUSING, AND WELL-BEING

Ethology is the objective study of the behavior of various species of animal, including man over the life cycle; it allows accurate comparisons between species. Ethology posits two facets of the relationship between the animal and its environment which may have special significance for man.

[5] United States Supreme Court, *Brown* v. *Board of Education, Topeka, Kansas* (74 U.S. 689, 1954).

[6] Robert Apte, *Halfway House* (London: Messrs. Bell, 1968).

Territoriality and *personal space* are useful in explaining animal behavior (and perhaps human behavior) with respect to the physical environment. In drawing conclusions about human behavior from studies of the behavior of lower animals, however, we must recognize that we are extrapolating beyond known data.

The concept of territoriality refers to the importance to the individual of the geographic area as a source of security; the animal feels safe in familiar territory, and uneasy or fearful outside. In the animal kingdom, territory has an especially important function in relationship to the locale where mating and the rearing of offspring take place. This concept seems to be operative for humans. For example, in slum areas of the city it is common to find that many young people have not ventured beyond the territorial limits of their neighborhood, probably as much because of a general need for security of the familiar as from lack of opportunity. Inter-group conflict over territory is a key issue in gang warfare occurring in overcrowded slum areas of cities.

Personal space is the physical space between the individual and other objects and individuals around him. Personal space, in contrast to territory, is a fluid concept; it travels with the individual wherever he goes. A lack of or invasion of privacy is an infringement of the individual's personal space, and possibly an attack on his feeling of integrity. In his experimental study of hospitalized schizophrenics, David Hebbs showed that limiting the personal space of patients produces hallucinations and other thought disorders.[7] These simplistic concepts can help us understand many of our reactions to the organization of the environment around us.

Another environmental concept comes from anthropological research. Cultural anthropologists have pointed out that there are many cultural differences in the reactions of groups of people to their environment, because of the different perceptual worlds in which they live. For example, Edward Hall says:

> Consider for a moment the difference between a Greek who garners information from the way people use their eyes and look at him, and the Navajo Indian whose eyes must never meet those of another person. Or consider the disparity between a German who must screen both sight and sound in order to have privacy, and the Italian who is involved with people visually or auditorially almost twenty-four hours a day. Compare the sensory world of the New England American, who must stay out of other people's olfactory range and who avoids breathing on anyone, and the Arab who has great difficulty interacting with others in any

[7] David B. Hebbs, *The Organization of Behavior* (New York: John Wiley, 1949). See also Robert Sommer and Robert Dewar, "The Physical Environment of the Ward," in George Rosen, ed., *The Hospital in Modern Society* (New York: The Free Press, 1960).

situation in which he is not warmly wrapped in the olfactory cloud of his companion. All the senses are involved in the perception space; there is auditory, tactile, kinesthetic, and even thermal space . . . . The kind of private and public spaces that should be created for people in towns and cities depends upon their position on the involvement scale.[8]

For most individuals reared in Western cultures, the privacy afforded by the enclosure of four walls is essential for existence; without such privacy a sense of security, dignity, and self-esteem would vanish. Yet there are subcultures such as in some of the largest cities of India where whole generations of families have managed to be born, reared, to live, and to die on the open sidewalks and still maintain a sense of dignity and integrity. To understand the meaning of environment, therefore, we must go far beyond the details of housing construction, to the culture that dictates the values, mores, and expectations of a group of people. For example, we learn from Marc Fried's study of the West End in Boston that the old run-down neighborhood, for all its shabby slum conditions, was far more attractive to many of the residents than the new homes provided by the city. Residents held in high regard their close-knit relationships, influenced by the closed-in physical characteristics of the neighborhood.[9] The ghetto, with its enforced or semi-enforced togetherness and cultural homogeneity, has positive as well as negative connotations for many people.

Most research on the effects of housing has been limited to public housing. This makes it difficult to generalize about private housing or about smaller types of housing units. D. Wilmer and associates reviewed forty studies made in the United States and Europe which investigated the relationship between the quality of housing and social pathology or health.[10] While the methodology of these studies suffered from the lack of control groups with which to compare the populations living in public housing, the majority of the studies (twenty-six out of forty) found a clear correlation between poor housing (for example, dilapidated and overcrowded) and poor health and social adjustment. Because of the lack of adequate statistical controls, however, it was not possible to determine whether the poor health and adjustment were due to the bad housing or vice versa. Because the studies were limited to the poor in densely populated urban areas where many subjects also suffered from unemployment, discrimination, and a limited choice of life possibilities, the cause-and-effect relationship between poor housing and various indices of social disorganization was impossible to

[8] Dubos, "Environmental Determinants of Human Life," p. 138.

[9] Fried, "Grieving for a Lost Home."

[10] D. Wilmer, R. P. Walkley, T. Pinkerton, and M. Tayback, "The Housing Environment and Family Life," in *A Longitudinal Study of the Effects of Housing on Morbidity and Mental Health* (Baltimore: Johns Hopkins Press, 1962).

determine. Furthermore, the flats studied were in dilapidated buildings in run-down neighborhoods. The effects of the inferior living conditions could not be isolated from the influences of the unsightly and insecure surroundings.

Wilmer and associates, in an attempt to "find effects on behavior of man's physical environment" and to "test the belief and conviction among social planners and officials in public agencies that improvement in housing leads to an improvement in health and the amelioration of social ills" investigated 300 ex-slum families living in a new public housing project.[11] Over a three-year period they compared this group of families with a comparable group of 300 families who continued to live in slum housing. Statistical measures of physical and mental health and school achievement were taken for both groups. Although the experimental families moved into new surroundings which were markedly superior to the slum dwellings, by the end of five months they showed higher rates of communicable disease than those who remained in the slums. After the initial period, however, there was a sharp diminution of illness among children and persons under thirty-five. For both boys and girls there was about a 20 percent drop in the number of illness episodes; accident rates were about one-third lower. Among those over thirty-five, however, there was little difference in the incidence of illness between experimental and control groups. Generalizing the results of this study, Wilmer found that the following illnesses could be attributed to bad housing: tuberculosis, pneumonia, acute respiratory infections, infectious diseases such as measles, chickenpox and whooping cough, infectious and noninfectious skin diseases, and digestive diseases such as typhoid, dysentery, and diarrhea. All these illnesses can be prevented.

Architects are becoming increasingly interested in designing buildings which include internal space in a manner which will evoke the type of behavior for which the setting was planned. Most of their knowledge of this topic, however, has unfortunately come only through trial and error. Socially-oriented architects are interested in the symbolic language and meaning communicated by spatial design and organization, seeing this as the vital content on which to base their designs. For instance, a room can give many clues to its use. A square room with chairs arranged in a circle in the center encourages different thoughts and behavior than a rectangular room with chairs lined along the opposing walls.

Housing can have many architecturally created characteristics such as privacy, intimacy, accessibility, adaptability, and comfort, which evoke a variety of human responses. It can encourage people to come together as groups, or to isolate themselves. According to Clifford Moller, spatial design, can affect the well-being of people in the following manner:

11 Ibid., p. 11.

1. There is a continuous reaction on the part of each individual to the enclosed spaces in which he finds himself, to such phenomena as size, scale, proportion, openness, closure, light, color. It has been discovered, for example, that ambiguous spaces (spaces in which size, shape, extent, and the purpose for which the space is to be used are not properly defined) arouse feelings of insecurity.
2. Architectural space conditions interpersonal and family relationships through the possibilities it allows for privacy, contact, quiet, circulation, etc.
3. Architectural space conditions extrafamilial contacts—whom the family meets, how they relate to the community.
4. Architectural space is one of the determinants of a person's status.[12]

A new field of study, ecological psychology, has emerged in recent years. Roger Barker has studied the effects of location on human behavior.[13] Rooms of similar size, but in different locations—for example in a home, a bar, a school, and a church—each evoke different responses, obviously related to the cultural meaning of each location. Vary the site of the room or the number of people in it and behavior will also change.

Crowding, an easy factor to measure, has frequently been studied. It has been described as a major factor with negative influences when it reaches certain limits. More than one person per room is the usual standard for overcrowding in the United States. Crowding can negatively influence the social and psychological well-being of the family in many ways. A child raised in overcrowded surroundings, for example, often lacks a sense of individuality and self-sufficiency. Continuous close contact with others often causes irritability and flashes of violence, and the most negative aspects of the parents' personalities emerge. For the child this is a poor adult example with which to identify, and the child often becomes disillusioned with the adult world. In a crowded home many important tasks and activities such as studying, cooking, sleeping, and sex are accomplished only with deep frustration, interruptions, and dissatisfaction. When privacy is not assured, the child comes to see sex as a purely physical expression rather than an aspect of caring human relationship. Too often overcrowded quarters allows too little sleep, resulting in constant fatigue.[14] Because physical space is limited, time is employed to separate activities. According to Molly Harrington, in overcrowded situations "management of time becomes supremely important; there can be little margin between meticulous order and chaos."[15]

[12] Clifford B. Moller, *Architectural Environment and Our Mental Health* (New York: Horizon Press, 1968), pp. 15–18.

[13] Roger G. Barker, *Ecological Psychology* (Stanford, Calif.: Stanford University Press, 1968).

[14] James S. Plant, "Some Psychiatric Aspects of Crowded Living Conditions," *American Journal of Psychology*, 9, No. 5, (March 1938), 849–68.

[15] Molly Harrington, "Resettlement and Self-Image," *Human Relations*, 18 (May 1968), 115.

Too little space for inside activities frequently drives the child into the streets and the father into the tavern, perhaps away from important activities at home like making repairs, studying, or child rearing. While the consequences are not always negative, they have the cumulative effect of breaking down the fragile ties which unite the family. All these potential effects of overcrowding multiply and are experienced by slum dwellers as another aspect of their deprivation. For the slum dweller to improve his economic and social situation, the daily handicaps must be overcome.

High-rise apartments are another potentially hazardous component of housing, especially for children. Because there is little space and it is difficult for mothers to allow their children outside their visual control, childhood independence is hampered; such children often have difficulty on entering school in separating from their mothers. However, once the child reaches adolescence he is likely to flee from the confinement of what is now considered an isolated, often conflict-ridden cell. At this point, control by parents becomes tenuous. Also, in the large multistory apartments families often lose the sense of neighborhood and do not become acquainted with their neighbors. Physical closeness causes people to guard their social and psychological distance to protect their privacy, independence, and individuality.

Wilmer compared those who moved into new public housing with those still in slums to determine the psychological effects of the move.[16] In the group that moved he found a reduction of anxiety and conflict in the home, and a higher degree of positive interaction with their neighbors. The new residents felt an increased pride in their neighborhood and were more active in the upkeep of their homes. As a result of the move they felt a sense of improvement in their situation in life. Comparing the school performance of the children in both groups, Wilmer found little difference in test scores; in the two-year follow-up study, however, he found that the children living in the improved housing "were considerably more likely to be promoted at a normal pace, control children being held back more often for one or more semesters."[17]

Not all families or groups of families respond favorably to changed living conditions, even when the new ones are physically more desirable. Their reaction depends on cultural affiliations, the social values of the group, the meaning of the neighborhood, and the conditions under which they move. For the aged and the physically handicapped, the degree of isolation from family and peers and the accessibility of services and communications are often even more meaningful than the living space and the condition of the housing and neighborhood (see page 346).

[16] Wilmer, "The Housing Environment and Family Life," pp. 201–12.
[17] Ibid., p. 252.

Our discussion of the factors of health and social and psychological well-being in relationship to housing and the environment has been fragmentary but sufficient to indicate the complexity of the subject. It is extremely difficult to determine whether bad housing per se is a cause or an effect of poverty, poor health, and various other indices of social pathology. Perhaps it is truest to say that poor housing is just another crooked spoke in the wheel of despair, along with disease, mental illness, crime, unemployment, family breakdown, alienation, and ignorance. *At the hub of this wheel are racism and poverty.* Improving any one of these aspects of social disorganization will affect the others; however, to eliminate all of them, one must attack the source: racism and poverty. Housing, for example, is a product which can be bought, sold, and leased on the open market. Adequate incomes for families to rent or purchase satisfactory accommodations will do more to improve the housing market than any other type of intervention. However, even if the benefits of "the great society" are shared more equitably, we still have much to learn about using the environment so that it can work for man and not against him.

URBAN GROWTH

The entrance of the federal government into massive programs for housing and the urban environment came with the realization that there was a growing housing crisis in the cities. The rate of movement from rural areas to cities had been increasing constantly, as had the number of city dwellers. The percentage of city and metropolitan dwellers in the total population was 25 percent in 1880, 50 percent in 1915, 70 percent by 1967, and a projected 85 percent by the year 2000. The percentage of isolated rural families has declined until at the present time only 13 percent of the nation is out of commuting distance from the center of a metropolitan area.

Until 1920 the largest shift of population and the greatest rate of growth were in the central city; later the rate of growth there declined, but the suburbs began to grow at a rapid rate, and continued to grow. Since midcentury, however, the central city area has not shown appreciable growth, and in some cities it has declined. In Manhattan, for instance, the density per square mile dropped from 101,000 to 69,000 between 1910 and 1968.

The characteristics of the population have also shifted markedly as cities have grown. Once the central city was composed mainly of middle- to lower-income white families, many of them foreign-born; over the past three decades the composition has shifted to larger percentages of blacks, Puerto Ricans, Mexicans, and single male Caucasians. In the largest cities especially, blacks are increasingly replacing the whites who retreat from the open conflict and stress of the central city. The percentage of whites living in the central cities of the largest metropolitan areas was 34 percent in 1950, 30 percent in 1960, and 27 percent in 1966. Conversely, blacks represented 43 percent in 1950, 51 percent in 1960, and 56 percent in 1966 of the central city population of these metropolitan areas.[18]

This influx does not mean, however, that the central city has become a black community in the sense of the positive aspects of a "community"; the population is always shifting, with new waves of migrants coming from the rural South. Social problems are rife. The outflow of white residents was accompanied by the outflow of industry and small business. There are too few jobs nearby to support the new residents of the central city, especially those with few skills, as well as too few profitable businesses and industries to contribute to the city's tax base. A 1967 census of the hundred largest metropolitan areas in the country found that the number of families in the central city poverty area was three times as great as in the cities as a whole. While many white families still live in the central city, surveys show that the percentage of them living in dilapidated housing is much smaller than for black families.[19] The slum area of the central city, caught in a downward spiral of poverty, rapidly changing population, despair, and dilapidated housing, is in drastic need of all-out efforts for positive redevelopment and renewal.

HISTORY OF HOUSING LEGISLATION IN THE UNITED STATES

With the rapid development of the United States in the nineteenth century, the building of houses for quick profits in the cities, often of shoddy materials, left endless rows of dismal buildings which are now unsightly slums and black ghettos. These houses were often located just beyond the main business district. As the occupants became more affluent, they moved to the outer areas of the city and later to the suburbs, leaving their old homes to successive waves of immigrants or migrants coming into the cities. The character of the construction was often such that rooms lacked any exposure to fresh air or light, and sanitary facilities were either absent or inadequate, exposing the residents to dangers of illness or accident. Many of the nineteenth century and early twentieth century apartments and flats, built originally for one family, have now been subdivided and frequently house many where before there were few.

[18] Robert L. Barre, "Changing American Environment," *Encyclopedia of Social Work 1971*, p. 282.

[19] M. Scott, "Housing and Urban Planning," *Encyclopedia of Social Work 1965*, p. 391.

The first housing legislation passed in the United States was on a municipal level: in 1867 New York City enacted a *Tenement House Law*. Maintaining public health was the main purpose of the law, and to this end it established city codes to ensure adequate light, space, and water supply. This sanitary provision was intended more to prevent epidemics than to protect the well-being of the tenants. The New York law became a model for the rest of the country, and many cities and states passed similar legislation. A perpetual problem with the legislation, however (except in renewal areas) has been that it has primarily affected new construction, and inadequate houses built before restrictive legislation have often been left unaltered, unaffected by beneficial codes.

Before the 1930s the federal government paid little attention to the problem of housing other than to provide a small number of housing units (16,000) for workers in World War I industries, and to encourage the establishment of local standards for housing through the Federal Bureau of Standards.

During the Depression of the 1930s, federal housing legislation started with the *Home Loan Act of 1932*. Under the New Deal, the *National Housing Act of 1934* guaranteed mortgages, the Public Works Administration built low-cost housing projects, and the *U.S. Housing Act of 1937* provided federal grants to local housing authorities which were expanded under later amendments. During World War II, additional war housing projects were financed under the *Lanham Act*, which created residential facilities for 8,000,000 persons. After the war, in 1947, the Housing and Home Finance Agency replaced the National Housing Agency. It consisted of five divisions: (1) the Federal Housing Administration for sound home financing through loan insurance programs; (2) the Public Housing Administration for the administration of federally aided low-rent public housing projects; (3) the Federal National Mortgage Association for home mortgages procured through secondary market facilities; (4) the Community Facilities Administration for loans to educational institutions and hospitals for housing of students, faculty, interns, and student nurses, and for public works of local or state governments; and (5) the Urban Renewal Administration for slum clearance, urban renewal planning and financing, and the rehabilitation of blighted areas.

M. Scott, discussing the role of the federal government in housing, states sardonically, "...almost all housing programs in this country have been regarded as instruments for accelerating or retarding activities in the economically sensitive construction industry." He continues, "The effort to meet human need for decent housing has thus been subordinated to economic considerations, national defense policies, and at times purely political goals of the administration."[20]

[20] Ibid., p. 282.

HOUSING AND URBAN DEVELOPMENT AFTER WORLD WAR II

The lack of wartime construction and the "baby boom" following World War II made the housing shortage especially acute. A congressional committee reported in 1948 that only an annual construction of 1,500,000 nonfarm houses for the next ten years would meet the existing need (15,000,-000 houses by 1958). The following year the *Federal Housing Act of 1949* committed $1.5 billion of government funds for the improvement of housing, mainly in residential areas. The theme was "a decent home and a suitable living environment for every American family." It authorized over a six-year period the annual construction of 135,000 public housing units.[21]

It was a forward step for Congress to initiate legislation for eliminating housing shortages and improving the environment of the cities. Few were aware, however, of the economic, social, and political complexities of this move. Local commercial and political maneuvering to obtain federal funds made it possible for the national authorities to dictate criteria or standards required for funding and to decide which communities were to be helped. This apparently benign method of control caused increasing local and state resentment of federal influence. The results of the first half-decade of the Act were not as anticipated. Blighted buildings were torn down and replaced with apartments which housed mostly middle- and upper-class tenants, while the displaced residents were pushed further into the slums, their condition becoming more overcrowded. By 1960, 85,000 families had been displaced into interim dwellings in 200 cities.[22] Rents in the newly constructed buildings were too high to attract more than a few of the former residents. Strong resentment grew among those who had been displaced by the more expensive apartments.

The legal mechanism by which the government could commandeer land from private owners to further the goal of urban renewal was established in the first postwar decade. The Constitution states, "...nor shall private property be taken for public use, without just compensation." The Constitution made it clear that "for public use" is not the same as "for public purpose"; but this constitutional provision, the *law of eminent domain*, was undermined by the 1949 housing law which allowed "...that the acquisition and the assembly of real property and the leasing or sale thereof for redevelopment pursuant to a project area redevelopment plan...is hereby declared to be a public use." Thus a significant amount of the land already taken under the federal urban redevelopment schemes could be used

---

21 Julian Hess, "Federal and State Housing Programs," *Encyclopedia of Social Work 1971*, p. 607.

22 Peter Marris, "A Report on Urban Renewal in the United States," in Duhl, ed., *The Urban Condition*, pp. 113–34.

by private owners for private use. This decision, of course, caused considerable unrest in the slum area. In 1954, in the case of *Berman* v. *Parker,* the United States Supreme Court sidestepped the issue of whether the law of eminent domain was to be ignored in urban planning, and merely upheld the constitutionality of this federal urban redevelopment legislation, which adversely affects the poor.[23]

In the same year, during the Eisenhower Administration, the housing law was amended and the concept of *urban renewal* was promulgated, a broader concept than redevelopment, concerned as much with slum area renewal as with housing. A new concept of planning was introduced, involving not just building new homes but also building or upgrading neighborhoods. The implications of this new operation for social work as a profession became increasingly apparent.

Urban renewal consists of three levels of activities: (1) prevention of blight where there is satisfactory housing; (2) redevelopment of slums; and (3) rehabilitation of areas with partial blight (urban renewal).

The new law tried to assure that some of the imbalances causing social inequities among slum dwellers did not reoccur. To qualify for loans, a city had to develop what was called a *workable program* of community improvement, requiring that a master city plan be developed along with modern building codes. Also the local housing authority had to have adequate personnel to ensure enforcement of codes, a method of analyzing the extent of blight in neighborhoods, and financial resources to pay the local share, and it had to provide satisfactory housing for all families who were to be replaced by renewal. A final requirement was that there be citizen participation in the renewal activities. This last requirement was a harbinger of the *participation of the poor* which later became a basic theme of the Community Action Programs of the War on Poverty. The proviso was designed to ensure more consideration on the part of the planners of the immediate needs of those directly affected by the renewal operation.

In 1956 the planning concept of urban renewal was further broadened to include the "general neighborhood" in renewal plans, not just a specific project. The law allowed the plans to be executed over a period of ten years. Piecemeal approaches to urban blight were therefore discouraged. Progress was slow, and where urban renewal occurred, the construction did little to improve either the plight of most residents or the overall condition of the slum. Those relocated either were removed to other accommodations with little improvement in environmental circumstances, or the move itself was accomplished with insufficient consideration

---

[23] Martin Anderson, "The Sophistry that Made Urban Renewal Possible," *Law and Contemporary Problems* (Winter 1965), 198–211.

for the needs of the family and the integrity of the individual. Relocation was especially difficult for one-parent families, the aged, and the handicapped. Insufficient resources were available to help them cope with the stresses of relocation. The West End study showed that many of the inhabitants who were forced to relocate suffered a marked depression, often lasting as long as a year after the move.[24] Both the relocation experience itself and the disruption of a stable way of life were responsible. Housing or rehousing per se will not make or break a family, although it may be the final blow in a series of untoward situations. A holistic approach, attacking racism, poor schooling, and unemployment, is needed to break the cycle of poverty, of which poor housing is merely a symptom.

The process of "unslumming" the slum is complicated. The best approach is not to tear buildings down and cause slum people to flee, only to be replaced by a new group of unresourceful deprived residents, regardless of the quality of new housing. Breaking the cycle of inadequacy and deprivation requires that the slum community itself become as responsible as possible for *changing its destiny.* Jane Jacobs, a significant contributor to the conceptual thinking about slum improvement, suggests that slum dwellers be helped to become residents of a stable community, achieving all the networks of relationships, communications, and resources of stable communities elsewhere. Outside assistance is needed to help these residents improve their morale, social functioning, and physical surroundings.

> Neither slum shifting nor slum immuring breaks that key link in the perpetuation of slums—the tendency (or necessity) for too many people to leave too fast. Both these devices merely aggravate and intensify the processes of perpetual movement backward. Only unslumming overcomes American city slums, or ever has overcome them . . . . Conventional planning approaches to slums and slum dwellers are thoroughly paternalistic. The trouble with paternalists is that they want to make impossibly profound changes, and they choose impossibly superficial means for doing so. To overcome slums we must regard slum dwellers as people capable of understanding and acting upon their own self-interest, which they certainly are. We need to discern, respect and build upon the forces for regeneration that exist in slums themselves, and that demonstrably work in real cities. This is far from trying to patronize people into a better life, and it is far from what is done today.[25]

HOUSING PROGRESS

By the end of the 1950s there were some signs of improvement in the nation's housing situation, but much remained to be done. The 1960 census

[24] Fried, "Grieving for a Lost Home," 151–57.

[25] Jane Jacobs, *The Death and Life of Great American Cities,* New York: Random House, Inc., 1961), p. 270.

revealed that the number of people living in overcrowded housing decreased approximately 9 percent during the decade, and those living in substandard housing decreased by 40 percent. During this period, 4.3 million homes were upgraded. However, approximately 1,000,000 people moved from standard to substandard housing. At the time of the 1960 census, 16 percent of all American families, or 8,500,000 families, were still living in conditions considered substandard. Six million, or 12 percent, were living in over-crowded quarters. Three-quarters of these families were below the poverty line of $4,000 annual income. Nearly half had to pay on the average about 35 percent of their income in rent.

How did nonwhite families fare during this period? Since much of the effort was focused on slum housing, did they partake of the improve-ments? Between 1950 and 1960 the percentage of white families living in substandard housing dropped from 32 percent to 13 percent. During this same period nonwhite families made gains, too, dropping from 72 percent in inferior housing to 44 percent. This still left a substantial margin of dif-ference, 31 percent, between the number of white and nonwhite families living in poor housing.[26] Federal housing policies have done little to narrow the gap between whites and nonwhites. The problem of racism, of course, has been the significant factor in this continued inequity. Discrimination and de facto segregation have made it impossible for nonwhites as a group to have their choice of housing, restricting them to the slum areas. At the same time, urban renewal has enabled whites, poorly housed in the central city, to escape into the outer areas of the city and into the suburbs.

RELOCATION AND ITS EFFECTS

When the federal government first entered the field of housing, re-location was seen as a goal in itself. Little consideration was given to the human aspects of the removal of a family from one place to another. As experience was garnered, official and unofficial policy studies made, and neighborhood reactions listened to, it was recognized that the act of re-locating people, aside from the exchange of dwellings, was a significant event requiring special consideration. The storms of protest pointed out the negative components of relocation. Officials, including social workers, could see an important opportunity to help compensate families for the inequities of the present system. Not only were the displaced families not receiving the benefit of the new housing; renewal agencies were of little assistance to them in finding even an equivalent replacement for their old homes. Often the new rents were even more than what they had given up. In

[26] Michael A. Stegman, "Low Income Housing," *Encyclopedia of Social Work 1971,* pp. 617–18.

addition, a substantial number of those directly affected had special problems because of age or physical condition, and were eligible for welfare services which were not being received. Any sensitivity shown to the needs of these groups before the 1960s was due more to responsible local leadership than to national policies.

The Housing Act amendments of 1961, 1964, and 1966 went a long way toward correcting the weaknesses of the former legislation, giving the population undergoing relocation special consideration to compensate them for the hardships encountered. These amendments called for special assistance programs to be set up in relocation areas to determine the needs of families, and to provide services to meet those needs. A house-to-house diagnostic survey was required to determine for each individual family where and how assistance could be given. The new laws also sought to establish greater uniformity of administration from one area to another, including uniform financial compensation for families being displaced. By 1966 the operations of local renewal activities, previously diversely administrated, had been brought under the administration of one central agency in an attempt to avoid the inconsistencies and lack of coordination characteristic of the earlier decentralized administrative structure. The amendments sought to establish a comprehensive set of services that would deal with the vicissitudes of the economic, social and psychological problems associated with relocations.[27] However, as with other local programs, there is great variation in the style and quality of local administration.

The range of activities required to relieve the psychological, social, economic, and physical burden of the move is broad. When a neighborhood is first designated for renewal, early contact must be established with the residents as a group to prepare them for the events which will take place. This should be done early enough so that a positive working relationship can be established between the renewal agency and the neighborhood. Misapprehensions, rumors, and distortions must be dealt with so that people do not panic. The establishment of communication centers, both at the construction sites and centrally, affords greater chance for the flow of valid information and greater opportunity for the involvement of the community in the planning. Communications must be set up with community health and welfare agencies in the area to determine where gaps in the needed services will exist and to establish a system of interagency coordination.

Contact with those who are likely to be relocated may be effected early in the operation by different teams. The teams should provide information about the events to take place, determine individual family need by a diagnostic survey, and begin counseling or referral to other community agencies if necessary. Many renewal agencies maintain a cadre of profes-

27 Demetrius S. Iatridis, "Urban Planning and Development," *Encyclopedia of Social Work 1971*, p. 314.

sional social workers and aides to provide casework. A series of activities are taken on as concomitants of the actual move, for example, house hunting, house selection, and direct assistance during the move. The San Francisco Urban Renewal Agency provides a home economist to assist in redecorating for those families who will be going to temporary accommodations. The agency also provides direct financial compensation for the actual cost of the transition.

In addition, many civil rights issues arise as a result of the process of relocation. When procedures are not followed according to the law, as is often the case, relocation for a community can be, if not permanently, at least temporarily held up by the courts. San Francisco, attempting to deal with each case fairly and according to the law, has established a system of review and appeals, thus preventing the renewal process from violating the rights of the potential victim. Other renewal agencies have attempted to affect the social well-being of the individual or family, following relocation, through the formation of neighborhood social groups to help families adjust to their new environment. Unfortunately, few renewal agencies have the quality or quantity of personnel and services to take the sting out of their major activity, tearing down slums and building replacements. Too often, relocation as a result of renewal is a painful process which falls far short of the ideals set down by government policy.

By the middle of the 1960s the War on Poverty was in full swing, concentrating much of its effort on urban problems, especially those related to the central city. In 1965 a new federal department, Housing and Urban Development (HUD), was formed to increase government efforts to solve the environmental problems of the cities. HUD runs the following federal programs:

1. Federal Housing Administration (FHA)
2. Federal National Mortgage Administration (Fanny Mae)
3. Government National Mortgage Administration (Ginny Mae)
4. Home Loan Bank Board
5. Federal Savings and Loan Association
6. Operation Breakthrough
7. Urban Renewal Program
8. Model Cities

MODEL CITIES PROGRAM

The Model Cities Program was established by the *Demonstration Cities and Development Act of 1966*. Embodied in the Act is a more advanced concept of urban renewal which promulgates the "unslumming" or rehabilitation of entire neighborhoods. The viewpoints of such people as Herbert Gans, Marc Fried, and Jane Jacobs in regard to the prevention of neighborhood disruption and the promotion of neighborhood growth through comprehensive, multifaceted planning, including citizen involvement, were incorporated in the legislation. The Act had a demonstration concept, expecting several cities to create comprehensive plans which would integrate the social with the physical aspects of community renewal, and in doing so, attack the multicausal problems in the blighted slum areas.

The program had the following four goals:

1. To renew entire slum neighborhoods by combined use of physical and social development programs
2. To increase substantially the supply of standard housing of low and moderate cost
3. To make marked progress in reducing social and educational disadvantages, ill health, underemployment, and enforced illness
4. To contribute toward a well-balanced city

A major intent of the Act was to have the Model Cities projects make full use of the manifold grant programs available through the Department of Health, Education and Welfare, to carry out the plans. Coordination of the application and funding of these grants would occur at both federal and local levels.[28] It is too soon to predict, let alone evaluate, the eventual outcome of this major legislation. Because of the Vietnam War, the funds available were not sufficient to carry out the program. Those programs which have been initiated have not been in operation long enough to reach their goals, and hence are difficult to evaluate.

The New York City Experience

The New York City program gives some useful information about the planning process for model cities, and provides important clues to the issues and dilemmas which arise in connection with the program. In New York City two superagencies, the Housing and Development Authority and the Human Resources Agency, contain the main citywide programs affecting housing, such as renewal, social services, welfare services, community development, antipoverty activities, and manpower training. Representatives from these two agencies, the mayor's office, the City Planning Commission, the Housing Authority, the Council Against Poverty, and the Bureau of the Budget con-

---

28 Edward M. Kaitz and Herbert Harvey Hyman, *Urban Planning for Social Welfare: A Model Cities Approach* (New York: Praeger, 1970), pp. 3–40.

vened in 1967 to form the Model Cities Committee to guide the development of the new City Demonstration Agency.

Numerous innovative proposals for neighborhood improvement under the Model Cities proviso were presented to the planners of the City Demonstration Agency for approval. These included the development of neighborhood manpower centers, minibusing to places of work, rental information offices, cooperative housing for the poor, multiservice centers, mobile medical care units for the homebound, vocational education schemes and community colleges, manpower training with built-in career ladder concepts, recreation programs of various types, centers for early childhood education, a variety of employment schemes, housing assistance to newcomers, schemes to improve landlord–tenant relations, and family planning clinics. The various programs were rated by the Model Cities Committee according to criteria set down by the Model Cities legislation (see page 320). Those rated highest were neighborhood manpower centers, minibusing to work, housing offices, community corporations, and cooperative housing for the poor. Analysis of employment problems within the target neighborhoods revealed that the lack of jobs, the lack of needed skills, and the paucity of available light industry were the major factors in perpetuating the poverty cycle. Employment through economic development therefore was chosen as the tool to help the New York City Model Cities residents become part of the mainstream of the community.

It was found in New York that planning for economic development, even on a project-by-project basis, involves complex coordination between the private sector of the economy, the many public agencies concerned, and the community groups to be affected. Also required is the development or pooling of community-oriented services to assure that the poor take advantage of new employment programs and other activities necessary to break the cycle of dependency. Ten percent of the cost of these services comes directly from Model Cities funds, the remainder from other local, state, federal, and private funds.

As the New York City program demonstrated, some key dilemmas in model cities programs must be resolved before they will achieve their objectives. The concept of Model Cities rests on the spirit of cooperation among a series of actors who have heretofore often played adversaries. For example, the city government and private business interests each are expected to give up some of their control over local resources. This ideal is difficult to achieve, though hopefully not impossible. While the goals of Model Cities are to establish more comprehensive long-range planning to solve the problems of the central city, and to incorporate local residents in the planning, the crisis in the city is such that residents want action, not promises for the future. However, the Model Cities requirement to employ residents, many of whom have few skills, to change the face of their community, often conflicts with the requirement of efficiency in construction. Furthermore, unions have a major stake in the financial rewards to be gained from Model Cities building projects and therefore resist hiring low-skilled residents. Finally, there is the problem of choosing priorities; each interest group sees its resource or service as the central one for change, be it private capital, education, social services, or housing. Program priorities become subject to controversy and impede progress.[29]

CRISES IN THE CENTRAL CITY

The events of the summer of 1967 demonstrated clearly that much of the nearly two decades of government programs to improve the quality of life in the central city, specifically in black ghettos, had been of little value, and had even been detrimental in some situations. Racial violence broke out in Newark, then in Detroit, and then spread to other communities throughout the nation. During the first nine months of 1967, 164 disorders were recorded in 128 cities, with varying degrees of violence and destruction. Of these, 39 were serious, involving fires, looting, and sniping, lasting at least one day or more, and requiring state police and/or federal forces for control. During this period, 25 cities had two or three episodes of violence. A study of 67 cities which experienced violence accounted for 83 deaths and almost 2,000 injuries. Fire caused great damage in Cincinnati and in Detroit, where damage was estimated at $45 million. The violence, unplanned and unanticipated (at least by the white community), came about after months of mounting tensions. The typical rioter was described as a teenager or young adult, a lifelong resident of his city. He had dropped out of school and had either inadequate employment or none at all. He identified strongly with his race, being distrustful of whites, police, and middle-class blacks.

The Kerner Commission, which investigated the riots, found twelve major grievances, the strongest of which concerned police practice, unemployment and underemployment, and inadequate housing.[30] The Commission found that white racism, at the heart of the violence, was responsible for the "explosive mixture" which set off the disorders. Its report claimed that pervasive discrimination and segregation, black migration into the central city and white exodus out of it, and the establishment of black ghettos with substandard housing were the most salient features underlying the widespread disorder. At another level were the frustrated hopes of

29 Ibid., pp. 64–99, 169–83.

30 *Report of the National Advisory Commission on Civil Disorders* (New York: Bantam Books, 1968), pp. 7–8.

minorities, the legitimization of violence as a form of protest, and the feeling of powerlessness.

In concluding its findings and making recommendations, the Commission stated: "No American white or black can escape the consequences of the continuing social and economic decay of our major cities. Only a commitment to national action on an unprecedented scale can shape a future compatible with the historic ideals of American society." The manifold recommendations, some of sweeping generality and others very specific, touched on education, employment, the welfare system, interracial communications, and housing. The recommendations on housing followed a thorough and scathing criticism of the inadequacies and ineffectiveness of federal housing policies to date. The housing recommendations of the Kerner Commission included the following: provision of 600,000 low- and moderate-income housing in 1969 and 6,000,000 units over the next five years; a below-market interest rate program; an expanded urban renewal program; enactment of a comprehensive national enforceable open-occupancy law; more low- and moderate-income housing outside ghetto areas; and an expanded supply of housing suitable for low-income families.[31]

GOVERNMENT PROGRAMS SINCE 1968

The Kerner Report recommendations in regard to housing were carried out only to a minor extent. Congressional action in 1968 did authorize programs for rent supplements, but the size of the appropriation was too meager to make any substantial improvement.

Under the Nixon Administration, urban renewal and Model Cities programs received still smaller appropriations. Vietnam War expenditures cut into the monies available to fight the war on poverty in the cities. Emphasis was placed on building units housing one or two families, with incentives to encourage private business to create supply. The "Turnkey One" program is an example. Small homes are built by private parties according to government specifications; on completion they are purchased with government funds by the local housing authority, which rents them at low cost to those who would otherwise qualify for public housing. Low-interest and low-rent supplement programs were made possible and practical under the 1968 Housing and Urban Redevelopment Act. Section 235 of the Act enables families with low incomes, usually between $4,000 and $8,500, to purchase homes or cooperative housing, paying as little as 1 percent interest. The subsidy is reduced incrementally as the family income increases, taking into consideration their need to pay for insurance and taxes. After income ex-

[31] Ibid., p. 475.

ceeds a certain point, there is no more subsidy. Section 236 of the Act has a similar proviso, except that the government subsidizes the difference between the basic cost and the allowance of a fair profit to the landlord for the housing unit so that it is possible for him to rent the dwelling at low cost.[32]

Subsidized rent programs have received favorable press coverage. They are one alternative to building unsightly blocks of public housing, and they make it feasible for low-income families to live in areas outside the slum district. That their rents or house payments are subsidized is generally unknown to the neighbors; therefore they avoid the stigma of living in public housing. Rent supplement programs are administered through the Federal Housing Administration (FHA), which by law limits the amount of the supplement to 70 percent of the market value of the rental. Nonprofit corporations wishing to sponsor low-rent housing can also receive support from the FHA. These groups, usually started by churches, fraternal organizations, cooperatives, or unions, can qualify for interest-free loans and can obtain technical assistance in planning their projects. Eventually, as the organization develops other sources of financing for the group home, they must repay the initial loan into a revolving fund.

THE NEW TOWN MOVEMENT

A number of totally new communities have been built in England, starting before World War II and gaining momentum during the postwar years. Their purpose has been to provide more ideal communities and to overcome many of the noxious elements which make life in the central city overbearing. A site selected for a new town is usually away from urban centers. After comprehensive planning, a totally new community is built to accomplish several interlocking goals. The goals include checking unplanned growth of cities by draining off their population, providing new environments which have been thoughtfully developed, avoiding many of the errors which have been compounded in existing communities, and establishing a "model community" in which life will be healthier and happier. The establishment in the area of a new industry to employ the residents is usually part of the plan, as is the provision for all necessary utilities and services.

In 1968 housing legislation in the United States made a significant advance in the *New Communities Act*, which makes it possible for private developers to obtain financing and overcome previous legal barriers to planning new communities. To date, HUD has made commitments to assist

[32] Hess, "Federal and State Housing Programs," p. 608.

with the development of five new town projects.[33] Reston, Virginia and Columbia, Maryland are two new towns which are already partly settled.

Experience in England has shown that it takes over ten years from the initial planning stages until the settlement of the new towns. Opinions of those who have studied the new towns in England have been equivocal; some compare life there unfavorably with life in the residents' original communities, while others find that they are the best solution to overcoming the stresses and strains of the city. The move to a new town can at least initially be a stressful event for a family, especially if it separates them from old kinship ties and a rewarding or supportive cultural environment.[34] Now that the enabling legislation is available, we await the development of new towns in America to evaluate their contribution to human welfare.

COMMUNITY PARTICIPATION IN HOUSING AND URBAN DEVELOPMENT

Under the 1954 Housing Act, cities were required to demonstrate community participation in their planning to qualify for urban renewal. Since that time there have been numerous amendments to the housing laws, as well as new laws which have reendorsed the requirement of community participation. Community representatives must be included on planning and operating committees of local programs funded by HUD, such as Public Housing, FHA, Workable Programs for Community Improvement, Urban Renewal, and Model Cities. The concept of citizen participation is based on the expectation that programs are better, more acceptable, and more successful when the people who are their beneficiaries have some influence in the policies which govern their development and direction.

In reality, the idea of citizen participation can mean anything from residents occasionally being consulted, to regularly giving advice, to sharing in policy development, to actually controlling the program. Key issues in citizen participation are: Who are the citizens? Whom do they represent? What proportion of the committee members should be from the target community and what proportion professionals, government, or influential community leaders? The most acceptable definition of a citizen in this case might be anyone who is either poor or the recipient of federal services, most likely a minority group member. Those in control of local government become uneasy when the majority of members of a citizens' committee are actually representatives of the poor, rather than from the power structure. Community leaders are less shaken by the thought of a majority vote of the poor against

---

[33] Iatridis, "Urban Planning and Development," p. 315.

[34] Lord Tayor and Sidney Chave, *Mental Health and Environment* (Boston: Little, Brown, 1964).

the "establishment" when the committee functions only in an advisory capacity. However, when the citizens' committee has been established either to share responsibility with the municipal government or to have full responsibility for decision-making, the potential for conflict becomes great. The city fathers' concern is that the "citizens" will either get out of control or make the wrong decisions, counter to the wishes of the community as a whole.

Each of the federal housing programs seems to have a different concept of citizen participation and what is expected from the citizens' group. The federal government merely gives guidelines, and what happens locally varies considerably. In some communities programs have been effectively halted because citizen groups believe the redevelopment plans will affect them negatively. In other communities the citizens participating on committees have contributed substantially to moving along plans for housing and urban development. At the heart of the concept of local citizen involvement is the democratic value that people in our society should have a major voice in matters that affect their lives.

The current policy on citizen participation in the Model Cities Program reveals the government's reaction to the fear that citizens' groups might take control of the planning. Initial legislation on Model Cities stipulated that a community is eligible for the program only if its plan includes widespread citizen participation. Standards were set up to ensure that the neighborhood would have clear and direct access to the decision-making processes. A year later, however, after a change in the Model Cities administration in Washington, a new ruling evolved which clearly limited the powers of the citizens' board. The ruling stipulated that any community participation structure should "not impede the city's ability to take responsibility for developing the plan" for Model Cities, thus shifting control to local governments.[35] Apparently the Nixon Administration became concerned with the dangers of a Model Cities program dominated by a neighborhood power bloc, as it had been concerned about the Community Action Programs under the OEO, and chose to nip any such developments in the bud.

TENANT UNION MOVEMENT

Perhaps more immediately significant in terms of citizen input in affecting the housing situation for poor people is the tenant union movement. In 1963 a tenant union was organized in Harlem to deal with the housing situation there. By 1969 over 700 tenant unions existed in the

---

[35] Melvin B. Mogulof, *Citizen Participation: A Review and Commentary on Federal Policies and Practices* (Washington, D.C.: The Urban Institute, 1970), p. 71.

United States; they affiliated with the National Tenants Organization, formed in that year. The concept of collective bargaining for tenants to achieve lower rents and a more equitable tenant–landlord contract has proven very effective. The tactics of the local unions are familiar, ranging from confrontation and rent strikes to the formation of pressure groups to improve or ensure implementation of local housing laws and codes. Over sixty cities throughout the country have experienced rent strikes. However, tenant unions have found confrontation with private property owners less effective than dealing with the public housing establishment, which under federal law encourages the organization of tenant groups to participate in local housing policy. At the state and national levels the National Tenant Union (NTU) represents the local unions. It has been successful in negotiating with HUD the establishment of a new model lease and a uniform grievance procedure which HUD recommends to the local housing projects under its jurisdiction. The procedure uses a variety of political methods to seek change in housing. Although it is new, it has obviously important potential impact. For instance, with support from the NTU Congress passed the *Brooke Amendment* prohibiting local housing authorities from charging more than one-quarter of the tenant's income as rent. The NTU supports the grass-roots development of strong local unions, regarding its role principally as supporting local efforts through national leadership. Perhaps one of the greatest challenges the NTU faces is developing a methodology to influence private landlords to improve the quality of poor housing and the milieu in which the housing is located, while charging equitable rents. This goal may require social action at the local level and further legislative support to bring more resources to bear on this type of housing.[36]

GROUPS REQUIRING SPECIAL HOUSING

The Aged

With the breakdown in American society of the extended family, the local group, and the nuclear family, and the resultant physical dislocation of its members, it has become necessary to plan for the housing needs of each age group. In earlier periods people were born, lived a full life, and died in the same house, almost always in the presence of a large family and neighbors. Today space needs grow and decline as the family grows and declines. By the time most individuals or married couples reach their fifties or sixties,

[36] Peter Marcus, "The Rise of Tenant Organizations," *The Nation*, 213, No. 2 (19 July 1971), 47.

their requirement for space changes. As older people become infirm and less able to do chores and move about, they need to live in an environment which suits their new life style. Some, of course, move into boarding houses and institutions, often because that is all that is available, but many wish to continue living independently.

There is increasing interest in housing especially designed for the elderly. In such homes the elderly can continue to live meaningful lives and to develop as useful members of the community. The designers and planners of special houses or retirement communities need to provide for services such as medical care, housekeeping, nursing, meals and shopping, and leisure-time activities.

The *Federal Housing Acts of 1956, 1959, and 1961* all carried provisions for special housing for the aged, financed on a similar basis as the other types of housing provided for in the law. Additionally, in 1965 Congress authorized a special rent supplement program to subsidize rents above 25 percent of their income for elderly persons who were eiglible for the program.

Although research has made advances, we still know too little about suitable housing for the elderly. Questions such as the following need to be answered: What would their choices of housing be? What effect does special housing have on their participation in the community? Are they happier when surrounded mainly by their peers? At what age should they be encouraged to change dwellings? Experience gained in the large variety of housing developments springing up around the nation, such as retirement villages, residence clubs, retirement hotels, and multiple dwelling units in high-rise buildings will eventually tell us which housing patterns are best. However, if the answers come too late we may be saddled with numerous buildings ill-suited to the people in them.

Housing for the Physically Handicapped

After World War II the Veterans Administration gave special attention to the housing needs of veterans with gross physical handicaps. In an attempt to give independent living status to handicapped returning veterans, many of whom were amputees, paraplegics, or quadraplegics, the VA helped finance specially designed houses with wide doorways, ramps instead of steps, and specially adapted kitchens, allowing residents to maneuver as independently as possible in a wheelchair.

The 1964 Housing Act broadened housing benefits for the elderly to include the physically handicapped. It featured a low-income housing program for them as a demonstration of what could be done to foster inpendent living. The program allowed, through subsidies, $1,100 or more per room for equipment and construction, plus an annual operating subsidy of

$120.[37] These units could be built either as single or multiple dwellings for handicapped individuals, or as a special unit in a multidwelling building mostly for nonhandicapped people. There are certain advantages in having handicapped people living in the same building; it cuts down their physical isolation and enables them to share cooperatively in services which would be too costly to provide individually. However, as in the case of the elderly, isolation from people in the mainstream of life can foster the feeling that society has abandoned them.

SOCIAL WORK ROLES IN HOUSING AND URBAN CHANGE

The total range of social work methods—casework, group work, community organization, and administration—are applicable to the field of housing and urban social change. While the profession of social work has long been identified with the need to improve housing and the urban environment, too few social workers have either chosen or been employed to work in this field, regardless of the need and manifold opportunities.

As far back as the last quarter of the nineteenth century, in England Octavia Hill and other social reformers took leadership in organizing special housing for poor multiproblem families (see pages 33, 36). In the early part of this century social workers in settlement houses were concerned about the abysmal living conditions of immigrants and sought to have housing codes adopted by local authorities and landlords.

After World War I, however, the major social work emphasis was on providing casework services for families caught in impoverished living conditions. This trend has persisted, notwithstanding some development of social work interest in social policy and planning around housing needs. It is becoming increasingly clear to the profession that other types of social work intervention may have even more important consequences for those trapped in the decaying, unsanitary, overcrowded slums of our great cities. Of highest priority are those professional interventions that could bring about significant changes in the quality of the environment itself, and to weaken those forces which block positive community change. Therefore, the social work professional's major focus should increasingly be on environmental change, using community development techniques to involve residents in obtaining a secure, satisfying, and resourceful milieu. This does not, of course, obviate the necessity for continued provision of rehabilitative services to those who are affected by the social change process.

[37] Geneva Mathiasen, "Housing for Special Groups," *Encyclopedia of Social Work 1971,* pp. 639–40.

Social workers may find employment in three major areas in the broad field of housing: (1) in public housing departments, (2) in urban renewal and relocation departments, and (3) in other public and private agencies concerned with social planning. Most public housing departments in the larger cities employ a small number of social workers to help residents with their social, economic, and emotional problems. Public housing families often have multiple problems connected with low income. Moreover, many public housing residents are isolated, often aged, with few resources available to them. The concentration of problem families in a small area provides a unique situation for creative intervention services, where the special needs of subgroups of residents can be attended to. Unfortunately, however, there are usually too few social workers available to organize and provide these services themselves; rather, most workers are used as interagency liaison workers and coordinators of services. They must rely on social services available to the community at large, refering residents to the community agencies after diagnosis of their problem. For example, if a female resident needs day care for her child so that she can work, or if a male resident needs employment counseling, they must be referred to the existing community agencies. Too frequently these agencies have either long waiting lists or restrictive intake policies which make referral difficult or even impossible.

Public housing projects often have tenant organizations formed for mutual assistance among the residents. These organizations carry out activities ranging from child care and sewing classes to grievance committees. The tenant groups also come together to develop and seek enforcement of mutually agreeable rules and procedures for cooperative living in public housing. The Department of Housing and Urban Development has encouraged the formation of tenants' organizations, looking favorably on the advisory role that they often play vis-á-vis the local housing authority. Social workers are often instrumental in helping to organize the tenant groups and have been available to them as advocates and consultants.

Social workers are also employed to develop and implement the services established under the 1966 Amendment of the Housing Act, providing aid to uprooted families being resettled. Some cities have fared better than others in developing comprehensive social services for residents undergoing relocation. The usual pattern is for a local department of urban renewal to hire a small number of trained social workers plus a larger number of untrained welfare workers. As in the case of public housing, the expectation is that residents can be referred to local public and private agencies for the necessary services. The requirement of a comprehensive diagnostic survey, with the necessity of identifying the gap between the residents' need and the availability of social services, informs agency administrators about the extent of the unmet need. Ideally, there are enough trained staff to provide and/

or develop the additional services required to humanize the relocation process. In the San Francisco Urban Renewal Agency, for instance, a large number of professional workers with an added staff of nontrained workers practices casework, group work, and community organization interventions to ensure a smooth transition in the moving process. The Golden Gate Project, serving principally the skid-row area, has been set up to engage every resident in threat of being uprooted in an evaluation of his immediate and long-term needs. Social rehabilitation is the keynote. The renewal project will demolish the numerous run-down hotels housing single men, many elderly, and alcoholics. This will disrupt long-established ways of life. Social work knowledge of social planning, administration, and individualized services are all being employed to make this relocation project a success. The activities of this project cannot, however, be carried out without the cooperation and coordination of the manifold other community agencies such as health and welfare departments, police, and the Salvation Army, which serve this highly handicapped population. A large interagency committee has therefore been established to coordinate services. The planning must be sufficiently farsighted and comprehensive so that the men will not be forced out only to move into the adjacent nonrenewal areas, recreating there the same life of anomie and exploitative social environment from which they are being moved. This has happened in other cities. Only through the thorough integration of social planning and physical planning can this consequence be avoided.[38]

In other agencies such as community councils, city social planning departments, Model Cities agencies, and private consulting firms, social workers may play a significant role in affecting the quality of housing and the urban environment. Social workers trained in community organization and social planning are employed to work at the grass-roots level as enablers and advocates for the poor and minority groups to bring about positive neighborhood change. At the community level they are hired as social planners to employ technology in helping planning committees determine the direction of the change. Social planning as a social work method calls for skills in data-gathering and analysis, the projection of trends, estimating community need, and the analysis of various policy choices. Once the choices and goals are determined, for example, in the location and nature of services for a renewal project, the next task is program planning and, finally, implementation of the plan. Social workers may also be employed, following the establishment of the services, to evaluate the quality of services in meeting initial project goals. These findings can provide feedback to those responsible for the administration of services, enabling them to make improvements, alterations, and additions where necessary. Knowledge and

[38] For example, see David Preston, "Social Work in Public Housing," *Encyclopedia of Social Work 1971,* pp. 622–27.

skills obtained by social workers in developing and implementing various demonstration projects in juvenile delinquency, such as Mobilization for Youth, and in antipoverty agencies, are applicable, often invaluable, to working in the field of housing, urban renewal, and Model Cities programs.

SELECTED BIBLIOGRAPHY

ALDRICH, C. D., and E. MEDKOFF, "Relocation of Aged and Disabled: A Mortality Study," *Journal of the American Geriatric Society*, 11, No. 3 (March 1963), 185–94.

BROLIN, B. C., and JOHN ZEISEL, "Mass Housing: Social Research and Design," *Architectural Forum*, 29, No. 1 (July–August 1968), 66–71.

CITRINE, LOUISE, and CATHERINE B. MOORE, "Social Workers Take Over Relocation," *Journal of Housing*, 14, No. 8 (1957), 329–33.

Department of Housing and Urban Development, *Content Analysis of First Round Model Cities Applications*. Washington, D.C.: Government Printing Office, 1968.

DEWITT, MARGARET L., "Relocation Case Work Yields Positive Results for Seriously Deprived Families," *Journal of Housing*, 20, No. 6 (1963), 323–25.

DUBOS, RENÉ, *Man Adapting*. New Haven, Conn.: Yale University Press, 1965.

FARR, LEE E., "Medical Consequences of Environmental Noises," *Journal of the American Medical Association*, 202 (16 October 1967), 171–74.

FRIEDEN, BERNARD J., "Toward Equality of Urban Opportunity," *Journal of the American Institute of Planners*, 31, No. 4 (November 1965), 320–30.

GANS, HERBERT, "Human Implications of Current Redevelopment and Relocation Planning," *Journal of the American Institute of Planners*, 25, 1 (February 1959), 15–25.

GRIER, GEORGE, and EUNICE GRIER, *Equality and Beyond: Housing Segregation and the Goals of the Great Society*. Chicago: Quadrangle, 1966.

Guide to Federal Low- and Moderate-Income Housing and Community Development Programs. Washington, D.C.: National Urban Coalition, 1970.

HARTMAN, CHESTER, "The Housing of Relocated Families," *Journal of the American Institute of Planners*, 30, No. 4 (November 1964), 266–86.

HOLE, VERE, "Social Effects of Planned Rehousing," *Town Planning Review*, 30, No. 2 (July 1959), 161–73.

MARGOLIS, RICHARD, and DIANE MARGOLIS, *How the Federal Government Builds Ghettos*. New York: National Committee Against Discrimination in Housing, 1967.

National Commission on Urban Problems, *Building the American City*. Washington, D.C.: Government Printing office, 1969.

Patterns of Living and Housing of Middle-Aged and Older People, Proceedings of Research Conference on Patterns of Living and Housing of Middle-Aged and Older People. Washington, D.C.: Health, Education and Welfare, Public Health Services Publication No. 1496, 1965.

President's Committee on Urban Housing, *A Decent Home*. Washington, D.C.: Government Printing Office, 1969.

ROSENBERG, GERHARD, "High Population Densities in Relation to Social Behavior," *Ekistics*, 25 (June 1968), 425–27.

SCHORR, ALVIN L., "National Community and Housing Policy," *Social Service Review*, 39, No. 4 (December 1965), 433–43.

————, *Slums and Social Insecurity*. Washington, D.C.: Health, Education and Welfare, 1963.

SOMMER, ROBERT, *Personal Space*. Englewood Cliffs, N.J.: Prentice-Hall, 1969.

U.S. Bureau of the Census, "Social and Economic Conditions of Negroes in the United States," *Current Population Reports*, Series P-23, No. 24 (October 1967).

U.S. House of Representatives, *Housing and Urban Development Act of 1969*. Washington, D.C.: Government Printing Office, 1969.

12

family
social
services

The family is the basic unit of society. In the family individuals receive most of their personal satisfactions, and perhaps most important, the personality of the child is formed. Within the family sexual relations are regularized; children are given nurture and education; and food, clothing, and the dwelling place for its members are provided. In illness the family renders care. It is the center of warm affection for its members (as long as normal, healthy conditions prevail). Regardless of the social changes of modern industrial society, family life has values for most individuals that cannot be found elsewhere. This is true despite the "generation gap," a mistrust between many parents and children, which may be exaggerated in the literature. It is desirable, in terms of these values, to the individual members of

the family as well as to society, that family life be protected and strengthened.[1] Family service of social agencies has the purpose of preserving
healthy family life; the aim of family casework is to help the individuals in
the family develop their capacities to lead personally satisfying and socially
useful lives.

Social anthropology has described the influence of tradition, habits,
customs, and the pattern of social organization on the behavior of human
beings. Sociology recognizes these factors as essential determinants in human
values, ambitions, and reactions. Knowledge of the decisive role of culture
in the formation of the human personality is essential in family casework,
because the individual may be understood at times in terms of his environment. The role of the family in society, however, is not static. In our pre-
dominantly industrial, urban society, many features of the earlier rural
family have changed. Margaret Mead went so far as to characterize the
new pattern of the American family as follows:

> The typical American couple is composed of two people with no common
> childhood associations or traditions, living apart from the relatives of either,
> without responsibilities for their family shared as in other countries and in earlier
> American society with other relatives and neighbors. Divorce has increased to its
> present rate for a variety of reasons related to the complexities of modern society,
> and is self-increasing in that prospective partners approach marriage with the
> tacit—often explicit—understanding that divorce is an acceptable way of
> "resolving" marital difficulties.[2]

Whether we consider the changes in the pattern of family life either a
"progress" or a "decline," compared with the quiet satisfaction of earlier
rural family life, these changes undoubtedly have created many serious
problems which afflict the members of the families concerned. Margaret
Mead explains: "To the extent that we continue to act as if the family were
what it used to be, we compromise our capacity to understand its limitations, and also we delay the development of the community services, the
education, and the counseling we need."[3] The community services Mead
mentions are primarily family welfare services.

---

[1] Andrew G. Truxal and Francis E. Merrill, *Marriage and the Family in American Culture* (Englewood Cliffs, N.J.: Prentice-Hall, 1953), pp. 29–51, 349–74; John
Biesanz and Mavis Biesanz, *Modern Society* (Englewood Cliffs, N.J.: Prentice-Hall,
1956), pp. 203–47; William J. Goode, *The Family* (Englewood Cliffs, N.J.: Prentice-
Hall, 1964), pp. 1–18.

[2] Margaret Mead, "What Is Happening to the American Family?" *Journal of
Social Casework* (November 1947), 322–23; quoted by permission of the Family
Service Association of America. See also Truxal and Merrill, *Marriage and the Family
in American Culture*, pp. 583–603; Philip Fellin, "Reappraisal of Changes in American Family Patterns," *Social Casework*, 45, No. 5 (May 1964), 263–67.

[3] Mead, "What is Happening to the American Family," 327; See also Talcott
Parsons, "The Kinship System of the Contemporary United States," in Herman D.
Stein and Richard A. Cloward, eds., *Social Perspectives on Behavior* (New York:

The present "conjugal family" or "family of procreation" consists of the two marriage partners and their children. There is less connection with the parental families of both partners, their "families of orientation," and with other relatives, which frequently causes an isolation of the conjugal family.

The difficulties which arise in the life of the family vary greatly. There may be lack of harmony between husband and wife, emotional instability of either, economic problems caused by failure of good home management, or small income, or unemployment, sickness, accidents, health problems, lack of support, or desertion of the breadwinner. We find problems in the relations of parents or adults with children, sometimes leading to neglect or cruelty, housing problems, financial need for the mother to obtain work and to place the children, or delinquency or other maladjustment of the children. Personal and family difficulties are usually caused by a combination of various elements, frequently involving several members of the family and based on social, economic, emotional, and physical factors. Therefore, an improvement in unsatisfactory family situations may be obtained by helping the members of the family to see the reasons for their difficulties. Changes in the environment or in the economic conditions in which the family lives may help improve relationships between its members.

Other social problems are caused by the "new morality" in Western nations: young couples living together without marriage or in communes, often with their children, without the advantage of an "extended family." Further research is needed to assess the social results of new forms of communal living.

In former times, family casework depended mainly on the overt behavior of the people for both social diagnosis and cure. If a husband neglected his wife and children because he was devoted to drink, the social worker advised him to stop drinking and threatened him with legal measures or jail. Now family casework attempts to explore the motives for his drinking and to find ways to convince him, by insight into his personality, of the necessity for his changing his habits and of going to a clinic for therapy.

Some characteristics of the present form of American family life may be called "democratic"; husband and wife have a larger amount of equality than did former generations and are aware of their equality. In the choice of a mate, greater freedom is granted the young couple than in other cul-

Free Press, 1958), pp. 7–19; Florence R. Kluckhohn, "Variations in the Basic Values of Family Systems," *Social Casework,* 39, No. 2 (February–March 1958), 63–72; Elizabeth Herzog, "Unmarried Mothers," *Children,* 14, No. 3 (June 1967), 105–10; Andrew Billingsley and Jeanne Giovannoni," One-Parent Family," *Encyclopedia 1971,* pp. 362–73; Ron E. Roberts, *The New Communes: Coming Together in America* (Englewood Cliffs, N.J.: Prentice-Hall, 1971).

tures. After marriage, the young couple seeks to obtain independence from the families of each partner and rejects interference from parents and relatives. The "conjugal" or "nuclear family," however, lacks the moral, economic, and social status support which the "extended" or "joint family" offers. This is typical for Asian, African, and most European countries. In principle, decisions on their way of life in the United States are reached between the couple, sometimes with participation of adolescent children. The changes in the family pattern of the past to new forms of family living sometimes lead to conflicts for those who cannot accept new customs, and require aid for adjustment. The influence of the women's liberation movement is strongly felt in our society. Progress in psychology and psychiatry, as well as in natural sciences, enables the caseworker to recognize difficulties in family life which formerly were not detected. The ability to diagnose the nature of each member of the family often helps to find a solution for them if they have problems.

FAMILY SERVICE AGENCIES

Both public and private social agencies frequently offer family services. In public welfare agencies, family casework, as a rule, is offered in connection with the granting of public assistance, particularly in the program of aid to dependent children.[4] Recently, however, many welfare departments have separated financial aid and social services. Financial help for the maintenance of a family in need is an accepted function of the public welfare department, provided that the family meets the legal eligibility requirements for assistance. Private family welfare agencies, therefore, frequently refer applicants who ask mainly for financial support to the public welfare agency. Private family service agencies are primarily concerned with personal problems and the emotional maladjustment of members of the family. Their casework attempts to help solve such problems, by counseling in health, educational, and adjustment questions, and to overcome disturbances to normal, healthy family living. Counseling may include giving advice on family budget and home management and on vocational opportunities by

---

[4] Clark W. Blackburn, "Family Social Work," *Encyclopedia of Social Work 1965*, pp. 309–19; Howard J. Parad, "Preventive Casework," *Social Welfare Forum* (1961), 178–93. See also Sanford N. Sherman, "The Sociopsychological Character of Family Group Treatment," and Frances L. Beatman, "The Training of Workers for Family Group Treatment," *Social Casework*, 45, No. 4 (April 1964), 195–208; Scott Briar, "The Family as an Organization," *Social Service Review*, 38, No. 3 (September 1964), 247–55; Atlee L. Stroup, "Family Formation," *Encyclopedia 1971*, pp. 352–62; Salo Rosenbaum and Ian Alger, eds., *The Marriage Relationship* (New York: Basic Books, 1968).

referring the client to employment services and occupational guidance centers. Often, family casework includes premarital counseling when the social worker is consulted by the young couple or the parents. It is concerned with marital disturbances—helping the couple to gain better mutual understanding and satisfaction—and with the adjustment of difficulties which have arisen between parents and children.[5]

Most family welfare agencies are situated in urban areas, but surrounding rural communities are often included in their activities. Little family welfare service is available in most rural areas, which are remote from cities, except for social work rendered by the county welfare department to persons receiving financial assistance, and occasionally by Red Cross chapters.

Many private family service agencies are nonsectarian and help families regardless of their creed and ethnic background. Family service agencies of high standards are organized in the Family Service Association of America. The Association accepts only such agencies that guarantee the clients a well-developed program of services, employ a qualified professional staff and maintain an adequate agency structure and a sound financial policy.[6] In 1971 the Family Service Association had over 300 agency members; most of them are private social agencies, but a number of public welfare departments which provide family services and meet the requirements of the Association have also been accepted as members.[7]

The staff of the family service agency depends on the size and resources of the community. It usually consists of an executive director, one or more supervisors, and a group of caseworkers competently trained for family work. In private agencies a board of directors must be active and responsible; a public agency needs an advisory board on family work to be accepted as a member of the Family Service Association. The executive is in charge of the organization, administration, and liaison work with the board and other agencies, but in a small community he may also serve as casework supervisor or even carry a case load himself. Funds for the private family service agency are provided from the annual campaign of the Community Chest, from contributions of members, interest on endowments, and other donations. Persons may come to the family service agency

5 For a discussion of the main characteristics of Catholic social agencies, see Kenneth Westhues, "The Roman Catholic Church and the Field of Social Welfare," *Social Work,* 16, No. 3 (July 1971), 60–65.

6 The Association formerly was named "Family Welfare Association of America," and its noted monthly journal, *The Family,* now is called *Social Casework.*

7 L. L. Geismar and Michael A. La Sorte, *Understanding the Multi-Problem Family* (New York: Association Press, 1964); Marvin B. Sussman, "Family" *Encyclopedia 1971,* pp. 329–40; Reuben Hill, *Family Developments over three Generations* (Cambridge, Mass.: Harvard University Press, 1970).

on their own initiative, informed by the radio or the press, on advice of friends, a minister, or neighbors. They may also come on referral by other social agencies, public or private.

The first interview usually takes place at the office of the agency. The applicant explains why he came to the agency, which difficulties have induced him to ask for help or advice, and what he expects from the agency. The caseworker listens to the applicant's story and helps him by friendly encouragement and sympathy to present his explanation. The caseworker will frequently discover that the reasons which the applicant presents are not the real core of his troubles, and that he, in fact, wants help concerning problems other than those he discusses first—such as legal advice, employment, and vocational training. The caseworker will clearly explain to the client what services the agency is able to offer, and under what conditions. He will leave the client free to decide whether or not he wishes to use these services, but he may well help him make a decision which lies in his interest and in that of his family. After the interview the caseworker records the client's description of his problems and their causes in a "case history." If the client decides to make use of agency services, the caseworker attempts to help the client solve his problems by applying his capacities, as well as by relying on facilities in the community. The length of contact, the frequency of interviews, and the intensity of the helping relationship of the caseworker vary according to the circumstances.[8]

Although private family service agencies are asked for help mainly in personal and emotional problems, request for financial assistance also is frequently made. Sometimes financial aid is given to clients where it is necessary to implement other services given by the agency (casework, counseling, legal advice), and where financial assistance is an integral part of the family casework process. Such support may be necessary for clients who feel they cannot apply for public relief, who are not eligible for it, or who need it while their case is being investigated by the public welfare department. Financial help is given in emergencies for the maintenance of the household before public assistance can be obtained, and for recreational or educational purposes for which public funds might not be available. Among the clients who need material help, particularly, are nonresidents, families who have not gained settlement rights and therefore are not eligible for public assistance. In this category might be new immigrants who cannot apply for material assistance to public welfare agencies unless their economic need has been caused by events which could not be anticipated at the time of their immigration to the United States.

---

[8] For a discussion of the serious problem of "family polarization," including youth in communes, see Kenneth Borell, "The Generation Gap—Age or Issue," *Social Work*, 16, No. 3 (July 1971), 91–96.

The following case illustrates the approach of family welfare casework.

Case of the Webb Family

Mr. and Mrs. W, a couple in their forties with three children, were referred by their minister because they had reached an impasse in their management of money. There was no real financial need. Just prior to the referral, Mrs. W had suddenly bought a new washing machine. This had upset Mr. W and he had threatened to leave home. The minister indicated that Mr. W was extremely thrifty, was a good workman, and had held his job for years. To the community, the church, and friends they appeared to be a substantial family.

Mr. and Mrs. W were interviewed separately. Mr W stressed the need to save as much as possible for the family's future; he wanted his family to have more security than he had had as a child. Mr. W's preoccupation with money, his stubbornness, and his orderliness were all traits suggestive of a rigid personality pattern. Mrs. W was more anxious than her husband. She had been having various aches and pains which she attributed to her approaching menopause. She expressed a desire for outside activities and for a more attractive home.

Psychiatric consultation confirmed the caseworker's impression that Mr. W's capacity for change was limited. His defenses seemed effective and his activities, such as hoarding money, fishing, and hunting, were socially acceptable. Mrs. W, also controlling, used money as a tool to express aggression against her husband. Each capitalized on the other's vulnerability and used similar defenses of projection, denial, and rationalization.

Casework treatment was directed toward fortifying Mr. and Mrs. W's defenses and toward helping Mrs. W relate to her husband in a less aggressive way.

Because of Mr. W's absorption with his own needs, he did not realize that he was not providing some of the things that were important to his wife and to the management of the home. The caseworker pointed out that he could continue to manage the finances, but that he could also afford to spend more for certain items for the home; that this would enable his family to manage better and his children to get more enjoyment, and would be an investment for himself and his family.

Mrs. W was helped to realize that her earlier acceptance of her husband's ways of doing things made it difficult for him to accept her change of attitude and behavior.

The caseworker's acceptance of Mrs. W helped her to discuss the day-by-day events in order to see why she was now acting differently. She could bring out her need for more money than she was getting and was helped to realize that it was important for her to let her husband know what she wanted so that he could have a part in planning expenditures for things that were needed. Both Mr. and Mrs. W were able to make some modifications in their behavior. Through this treatment, the marital balance was restored and the marital relationship improved.

The caseworker, in this type of treatment, attempts to help the marital partners clarify factors in the current situation and their reactions to them, with the aim of helping them achieve greater ability to meet social responsibilities. The aims of this method are to support existing strengths and to produce modification of adaptive patterns, but not to help the client achieve basic personality change.[9]

9 This case illustration is quoted from Eleanor A. Moore, "Casework Skills in Marriage Counseling," *Social Casework,* 34, No. 6 (June 1953), 255–58, by permission of the Family Service Association of America; see also John A. Rose, "A Reevaluation of the Concept of Separation for Child Welfare," *Child Welfare,* 41, No. 10 (December 1962), 444–58.

FEE CHARGING IN FAMILY SERVICE AGENCIES

Family welfare agencies generally provide their service to the clients without charge. It has been known for some time, however, that some clients want to pay for casework service and counseling. They feel that they can afford to pay for such professional service in the same way as they pay their doctor or lawyer, and they express their preference to pay for casework, rather than to have to ask for free service. Family service agencies which offer such paid service use a graduated scale so that the client pays a fee according to his financial ability. The agencies have made it possible, thereby, for a type of client to use casework who otherwise would never have been willing to seek counsel from any charity agency. This type of client includes bankers, merchants, factory workers, engineers, teachers, white-collar employees, artists, and craftsmen.

There are about 530 fee-charging family service agencies in the country, most of them in large cities. Casework with paying clients includes all aspects of social problems, personal, emotional, and family difficulties, employment questions, placement of children in summer camps or in schools and of adults in rest homes, sanatoriums, old-age homes, and mental institutions. Most family service agencies are satisfied with their clients' reactions about fee charging and consider this form of service a real contribution to the needs of the public.[10] However, the interest in fee charging has recently declined because of the strong emphasis on counseling the poor.

PRINCIPLES OF FAMILY SERVICE

The goal of family casework in social agencies is to help the individual client and the members of his family achieve harmonious relationships in their family life. Recent years have seen a growing emphasis on education as a process for strengthening the relationships of the members of the family, their mutual affection and cooperation. Some of these activities have been called "family life education"[11] and have been carried on by social workers in family service agencies. However, these agencies share the effort for

[10] Alice D. Taggart, et al., *Fee Charging in a Family Agency* (New York: Family Welfare Association of America, 1944); Ruth Fitzdale, "The Rising Demand for Private Casework Services," *Social Welfare Forum* (1961), 194–204; Nathaniel Goodman, "Fee Charging," *Encyclopedia 1971*, pp. 413–15.

[11] Helen L. Witmer, *Social Work: An Analysis of a Social Institution* (New York: Farrar & Rinehart, 1942), pp. 246–47; Frances L. Feldman, *The Family in a Money World* (New York: Family Service Association of America, 1957); Dorothy F. Beck, *Patterns in Use of Family Service* (New York: Family Service Association of America, 1962); Clark W. Blackburn, "Family Social Work," *Encyclopedia of Social Work 1965*, pp. 309–18.

family protection with programs of adult education, parent-teacher associations, discussion groups of young married couples, and church and mothers' clubs. The Family Service Association defines family service as a "process by which people are helped, through group discussion, to broaden their understanding of family relationships." The specific role of the caseworker here is to devote full interest to the individual who is in anxiety or trouble, and to be aware of the resources of the community which may help in this process.

In our urban-industrial civilization, the family has assumed a highly individualistic pattern which often has not been conducive to the happiness of all its members. Marriage counseling is, in most family service agencies, one of the essential activities of the caseworker's assignment. It regularly includes premarital guidance, wherein the caseworker helps the two marriage partners to decide whether their plan promises happiness to both of them in their social, sexual, and cultural relationship, especially with regard to economic and occupational conditions, employment of the wife, relationship to parents and relatives of both partners, and health and behavior problems.[12] In both premarital and marital counseling regarding conflicts of husband and wife, the caseworker may advise them to consult clinics and physicians, whenever medical and psychiatric problems seem to be important for their decisions. She or he suggests the use of a mental hygiene clinic or a psychiatrist if sexual maladjustment and behavior patterns make it advisable to explore the chances of successful therapy. Family casework attempts to settle conflicts between parents and children in which the rights of children to choose play, companionship, and activities are not recognized in accordance with their age. In some instances, the family service agency shares the responsibility of premarital, marital, and child counseling with other community facilities engaged in this work. In 1965 a special project named "ENABLE" was established to provide family counseling services in poverty neighborhoods; it is funded by the Office of Economic Opportunity and uses caseworkers and nonprofessional "community organizers" who have had some training.

12 Judson T. and Mary G. Landis, *Personal Adjustment, Marriage, and Family Living* (Englewood Cliffs, N.J.: Prentice-Hall, 1956); Otto Pollak, "The Broken Family," in Nathan E. Cohen, ed., *Social Work and Social Problems* (New York: National Association of Social Workers, 1964), pp. 332–39; Frances L. Beatman, et al., "Current Issues in Family Treatment," *Social Casework*, 47, No. 2 (February 1966), 75–81; Alvin Schorr, "Income Maintenance and the Birth Rate," *Social Security Bulletin*, 28, No. 12 (December 1965), 22–30; Lawrence Q. Crawley, et al., *Reproduction, Sex, and Preparation for Marriage* (Englewood Cliffs, N.J.: Prentice-Hall, 1964); Katherine B. Oettinger, "This Most Profound Challenge," *Children*, 12, No. 6 (November–December 1965), 211–14; John Rock, *The Time Has Come* (New York: Knopf, 1963); Earl J. Beatt, "Family Services," *Encyclopedia 1971*, pp. 396–97; Abbott L. Ferris, *Indicators of Change in the American Family* (New York: Russell Sage Foundation, 1969).

The main element in family casework is counseling all members of the family to prevent individual and family disorganization, mutual hostility, unhappiness, and breakdown. If differences of opinion, apathy, or anxieties develop, the family caseworker tries to help the members of the family understand one another better and to create among them the desire of mutual assistance to overcome these threats to their successful family life. This service is given to people who are willing to use it constructively, whether or not they are in economic need.

Modern family service is convinced that most clients will make real use of a plan of rehabilitation only when they share in the planning, and when their desire for self-support and responsibility for their life is fully considered. To carry on such a plan, the social caseworker frequently helps to straighten out differences and tensions within the family, and to change the environmental or health situation by arranging financial assistance, finding housing at reasonable cost and a satisfactory job, and securing necessary medical or psychiatric treatment through the use of community facilities, hospitals, and clinics.

This type of social casework includes so-called "supportive work"—encouragement and supervision rendered to parents to secure constructive relations with the children or other members of the family. Family casework requires that the social worker possess a full understanding of the client's personality, motivations, behavior, and his situation within the family. On this basis the caseworker assists the client in developing plans to meet his difficulties. The caseworker's task is to inform the client which institutions are available that may be helpful in the solution of his problems, and to explain the nature and conditions of these services. If the client desires to use some of these facilities, the caseworker arranges for the necessary contact and referral. But the client himself makes the final decision; he exercises his right of self-determination.[13]

In his or her relationship with the client and his family, the caseworker encourages all members of the family to use their thoughts and resources, thus preserving and strengthening their energy and independence. The caseworker helps the client overcome his anxieties and confusions, which are a barrier to finding a way out of his difficulties. In enabling the client to

[13] Lola Selby, "Supportive Treatment: The Development of a Concept and a Helping Method," *Social Service Review*, 30, No. 4 (December 1956), 400–414; Carol H. Meyer, "Individualizing the Multi-problem Family," *Social Casework*, 44, No. 5 (May 1963), 267–72; David Hallowitz, "Individual Treatment of the Child in the Context of Family Therapy," *Social Casework*, 47, No. 2 (February 1966), 82–86; Scott Briar, "The Family as an Organization," *Social Service Review*, 38, No. 3 (September 1964), 247–55; Wilma Donahue, *Living in the Multigeneration Family* (Ann Arbor: University of Michigan Press, 1969); Louis Kriesberg, *Mothers in Poverty: A Study of Fatherless Families* (Chicago: Aldine Press, 1970); Paul Bohannan, ed., *Divorce and After: An Analysis of the Emotional and Social Problems of Divorce* (Garden City, N.Y.: Doubleday, 1970).

make his own decision in his affairs, the caseworker strengthens his self-reliance and self-respect, explaining to the client what the facilities and limitations of the family service organization are, so that he knows what to expect from the agency according to its policies and resources, and what his role must be.

The characteristic problems which families face today are based on economic, environmental, health, and psychological conditions. Economic suffering is often caused by illness in the family, which also causes great anxiety and personal difficulties. It is especially unfortunate that the achievements of medical science are not always readily available to patients of modest means or low income. Unemployment, change of jobs, and low wages also impair a normal, happy family life.

Family discord is sometimes caused by hasty marriages of young couples who are driven together by a short-lived passion and who use marriage as a device to create a semblance of love and security. Counseling alone may not produce sincere affection, patience, and the tolerance necessary for successful adjustment to married life, but it may well be a medium for gaining mutual understanding as a background to strive for such an adjustment.

In the preceding chapters we discussed the fact that basic financial needs of families without income or resources are increasingly met by public assistance and social insurance payments. The role of the private family service agency under sectarian or humanitarian auspices has primarily helped in emotional and personal troubles. However, families in financial distress frequently suffer from dissatisfaction, frictions, and hostilities, and need help with these problems as well. For this reason, private family service agencies sometimes give temporary financial aid or supplement public assistance payments to enable the client to reestablish normal family life.

SPECIAL SERVICES IN THE FAMILY WELFARE FIELD

We shall now discuss a few activities of family service agencies which deal with the problems of clients who have particular needs.

Services to the Aged

The number of aged people, in relation to the entire population, is steadily increasing in all countries. This condition has called attention to their specific needs. In 1850 only 2.6 percent of the population was sixty-five years of age or older; in 1950, 7.7 percent, and in 1958, 8.6 percent had reached this age. The average life expectancy has advanced from forty years in 1850, to forty-nine years in 1900, to sixty years in 1930, to sixty-three years in 1940, to seventy years in 1959, and to eighty-two years in 1972. Improved living conditions and sanitation, easier work and shorter hours due to machinery, and advances in medical science, nutrition, and health education have contributed to the longer life span. But society has not yet succeeded in sufficiently filling the lengthened life of older persons with useful activities and cultural satisfaction.

Our methods of public assistance, social insurance, industrial pension plans, and private insurance provisions have emphasized securing economic protection for older people who cannot work any longer. But social workers have become aware that "senior citizens," living in enforced retirement, often suffer not only from chronic diseases and frailties of their age, but also from the unhappiness caused by their feeling of uselessness, loneliness, or despair. In addition, family welfare and social group work agencies are in full agreement that communities must pool all their resources to offer older persons more than the bare necessities of life—food, clothing, shelter, and medical care. Senior citizens need understanding, sympathy, companionship, and acceptance in the community to continue a way of life that gives them some amount of satisfaction.[14] When an old person loses the ability to take care of himself, and his family is not able to care for and nurse him, a protective environment has to be found for him. The services of the community must be mobilized to help the aged meet their personal, economic, medical, and social needs, and to offer cultural, educational, recreational, and vocational projects for the lonely and unemployed.

In the past, a "home for the aged" was considered the traditional place where an older person could find shelter when he could not live in his home or with his family. At present, social agencies consider institutions only one of several possibilities to care for old people. For the chronically sick, hospitals, special institutions, homes for the aged, and family foster care with the support of medical and nursing services are beginning to be used.

Family welfare agencies have noted that older people express the desire to be counseled by caseworkers with special experience, sympathy, and skill in working with the aged and their families. If housekeepers are

---

[14] Family Service Association of America, *Casework with the Aging* (New York, 1961); Ethel Shanas, et al., *The Multi-Generation Family* (Trenton: New Jersey Division of Aging, 1964); Charles T. O'Reilly, "Caseworker Attitudes and Service to Older Clients," *Public Welfare*, 21, No. 2 (April 1963), 29–42; Esther Twente, "Aging, Strength, and Creativity," *Social Work*, 10, No. 3 (July 1965), 105–10; Neota Larsen, "Protective Services for Older Adults," *Public Welfare*, 22, No. 4 (October 1964), 249–60; Robert Kestenbaum, *New Thoughts on Old Age* (New York: Springer, 1964); Gladys Worthington, "Older Persons as Community Service Volunteers," *Social Work*, 8, No. 4 (October 1963), 71–75; Elaine M. Brody, "Aging," *Encyclopedia 1971*, pp. 51–74.

provided for older people, the family welfare agency prepares them for a longer period of service than is customary with other age groups, and for taking care of the shopping, cleaning, and cooking, as well as giving some personal aid.

Family welfare agencies develop placement services to board older people with private families, and supervise boarding homes for older people who either pay the monthly board themselves or receive aid from relatives, public assistance, or the family agency. They assist older people in finding convalescent and nursing homes, sometimes supplementing private resources or old-age assistance payments to secure adequate medical and nursing care.

Clubs and community centers for the aged have been established recently to give older citizens the feeling that they are not unwanted, and to offer them opportunities to apply their experience and creative abilities, or to learn new skills, to gain the satisfaction of accomplishment.[15] Recreational activities of the aged are not limited to clubs and centers, but are included in modern homes for the aged and in hospitals and homes for the chronically ill.

Homemaker Services

In families, problems arise if the mother is absent or sick and no adult member of the family nor any relatives and friends are available to care for the children, the working father, or sick or aged members of the family. Family service and child care agencies have found that in such instances the temporary breakup of the family may be avoided by providing the family with a "housekeeper" or "homemaker."[16] Homemakers are carefully selected and trained in advance by social agencies which provide this type of service. When a family asks for homemaker service, the agency decides whether that family may receive this aid under the rules of the agency. The social worker explains the relationship and duties of the homemaker in the family and makes arrangements for the family's contribution to the salary of the

15 Wilma Donahue, ed., *Education for Later Maturity* (New York: Whiteside, 1955); Jerome Kaplan, *A Social Program for Older People* (Minneapolis: University of Minnesota Press, 1953); E. Grant Youmans, "Some Environmental Factors in the Health of Older Persons," *Geriatrics* (July 1962), 442–50; Worthington, "Older Persons as Community Service Volunteers," 71–75; Barbara Carter, "Organizing the Old Folks," *Reporter* (12 March 1964), 31–32; Louis L. Bennett, "Protective Services for the Aged," *Social Service Review*, 39, No. 3 (September 1965), 283–93; Caroline S. Ford, "Ego-Adaptive Mechanisms of Older Persons," *Social Casework*, 46, No. 1 (January 1965), 16–21. Special housing needs of the aged are discussed in Chapter 11.

16 John T. McDowell, "A Community Approach to the Home: Homemaker Service," *The Annals*, 355 (September 1964), 62–68; Johnnie U. Williams, "The Caseworker–Homemaker Team," *Public Welfare*, 23 (October 1965), 275–95; Evelyn Hart, *Homemaker Services for Families and Individuals* (New York: Public Affairs, 1965); Roberta Hunt, "Homemaker Services," *Encyclopedia 1971*, pp. 583–86.

homemaker. If circumstances allow, an interview between the mother and the homemaker is arranged so that the mother may explain her wishes for the care of the family and the special duties which home management entails. This contact usually eliminates the mother's anxiety and feeling of jealousy.

In general, the homemaker is sent to a home only for limited periods of time. She tries to continue the regular routine of home management, diets, and child care. The children have the advantage of remaining with their father in their home with little change in their accustomed life. If the family has no means for paying the homemaker, the social agency's budget often provides funds for assuming this expense. As a rule, the agency guarantees the payment of the salary to the homemaker and collects from the family according to its ability to pay. In 1971 over 1,800 family and child care agencies offered homemaker service, among them 1,050 public welfare agencies. Most homemakers are employed on a full-time basis. The social agencies assume training and supervision of the homemakers, frequently by their own supervisors and caseworkers.[17] To bolster the short supply of homemakers, the training and employment of "homemaker's assistants" have been suggested, a proposal which promises success.

Services to Travelers and Migrants

Travelers and migrants (or immigrants) often encounter serious difficulties en route. They become stranded without means, are without funds for food or shelter, or need medical care. They face these difficulties in a strange environment where they do not know anyone and do not know what means of help may be available. Family welfare agencies, therefore, have been giving aid to transients for many years, but since they are often limited by policy to serve the resident population, specialized services are necessary.

These services are rendered primarily by the Travelers Aid Association. Through its branches, usually located in railroad stations, bus terminals, and piers, this agency is prepared to assist travelers and transients in need on a "short-contact" basis. The problems the agency handles vary from giving information on trains, buses, planes, and hotel accommodations to locating families and friends, and providing information on vocational and employment opportunities, as well as financial aid and medical or hospital assistance.

Runaway children and adolescents, without realistic plans, are among the groups which frequently become charges of the Travelers Aid Societies. Wayward children may be cared for by a children's agency until return to

[17] Adelaide A. Werner, "Homemaker Service," *Encyclopedia of Social Work 1965*, 381–86; Worthington, "Older Persons as Community Service Volunteers," 71–75; Hunt, "Homemaker Services," p. 585.

their home is arranged. Then they might be put on a train or bus and agreements made with other social agencies en route to help in the safe return of the child, unless his problems require that a social worker or an attendant accompany him all the way home. Other help might be necessary for aged or invalid, crippled, blind, or mentally disturbed people who have tried to travel alone but are found in need of direction.

The need for aid to travelers is particularly great in periods of war, defense, or economic distress when many people are on the move. As in peacetime, the Societies assist not only travelers who are just on their way, but also migrants looking for a new home and refugees and displaced persons who have not received help in settlement and adjustment by other social agencies. Since 1917 the National Travelers Aid Association has coordinated local Travelers Aid Societies, established in 103 places, with enough representatives in other communities to allow about 2,900 cities to use their services.[18] The casework in each Travelers Aid Society requires a thorough knowledge of all community resources within the city where the agency is located, special contact with facilities in other cities, and the ability to refer the client to places where his needs really will be met.

Travelers Aid Societies, public welfare departments, and private family service agencies are engaged in helping migratory agricultural workers. Agricultural production, particularly at harvest time, relies partly on seasonal labor. Most workers cannot make a living in one place because of crop specialization and changes in the sharecropper system. They are often unskilled, earn their principal income from temporary employment, and move several times a year. Their total number is estimated at 1,300,000, of whom about 473,000 are foreign workers, mainly Mexicans. Housing outside labor camps is frequently inadequate and improvement of sanitary conditions necessary. Communicable diseases are widespread, and migratory workers are often denied public health service and economic assistance. Their children work to supplement the low wages of the parents, and communities sometimes do not enforce school attendance laws for migratory children to avoid overcrowding of classrooms and higher costs. Local recreation services do not encourage migratory children to participate, so that their mothers have to take them into the fields.

Rural migratory workers have long been without protection of minimum wages and unionization. Only in 1962 did the *Migrant Health Act* provide for some modest health services. About half of the migrants work less than twenty-five days a year, so that over 6,000,000 of them live in dire poverty. The Economic Opportunity Program has rendered some remedial education, youth projects, day care facilities, and housing services.

---

[18] Savilla M. Simons, "Migration and Resettlement Services," *Encyclopedia 1971*, pp. 836–44; Dale Wright, *They Harvest Despair: The Migrant Farm Worker* (Boston: Beacon Press, 1965); Myrtle R. Reul, "Communicating with the Migrant," *Child Welfare*, 49, No. 3 (March 1970), 137–45.

SELECTED BIBLIOGRAPHY

ACKERMAN, NATHAN W., *Treating the Troubled Family*. New York: Basic Books, 1966.

BILLINGSLEY, ANDREW, *Black Families in White America*. Englewood Cliffs, N.J.: Prentice-Hall, 1968.

BIRREN, JAMES E., *The Psychology of Aging*. Englewood Cliffs, N.J.: Prentice-Hall, 1964.

CARTER, HUGH, and PAUL C. GLICK, *Marriage and Divorce: A Social and Economic Study*. Cambridge, Mass.: Harvard University Press, 1970.

CELLA, CHARLES P., and RODNEY P. LANE, eds., *Basic Issues in Coordinating Family and Child Welfare Programs*. Philadelphia: University of Pennsylvania Press, 1964.

COSER, ROSE, and GERARD ROKOF, "Women in the Occupational World," *Social Problems*, 18, No. 4 (Spring 1971), 535–53.

DIZARD, JAN, *Social Change in the Family*. Chicago: University of Chicago Press, 1968.

EDWARD, JOHN N., ed., *The Family and Change*. New York: Alfred A. Knopf, 1969.

FELDMAN, FRANCES L., and FRANCES SCHERZ, *Family Social Welfare*. New York: Atherton Press, 1967.

GLASSER, PAUL H., and LOIS N. GLASSER, *Families in Crisis*. New York: Harper & Row, 1970.

GOMBERG, M. ROBERT, and FRANCES T. LEVINSON, *Diagnosis and Process in Family Counseling*. New York: Family Service Association of America, 1951.

GOODE, WILLIAM J., *The Family*. Englewood Cliffs, N.J.: Prentice-Hall, 1964.

HARRIS, C. C., *The Family: An Introduction*. New York: Praeger, 1969.

HAUSER, PHILIP M., *The Population Dilemma*, 2nd ed. Englewood Cliffs, N.J.: Prentice-Hall, 1969.

HEBERLE, RUDOLF, *Social Movements*. New York: Appleton, 1957.

HEER, DAVID M., *Society and Population*. Englewood Cliffs, N.J.: Prentice-Hall, 1968.

HERZOG, ELIZABETH, "Unmarried Mothers," *Child Welfare*, 41, No. 8 (October 1962), 339–50.

HESS, ROBERT D., and GERALD HANDEL, *Family Worlds: A Psychosocial Approach to Family Life*. Chicago: University of Chicago Press, 1959.

HOFFMAN, ADELINE, ed., *The Daily Needs and Interests of Older People*. Springfield, Ill.: Charles C Thomas, 1970.

HOLLIS, FLORENCE, *Women in Marital Conflict: A Casework Study*. New York: Family Service Association of America, 1949.

KAPLAN, JEROME, *A Social Program for Older People*. Minneapolis: University of Minnesota Press, 1953.

KASIUS, CORA, ed., *A Comparison of Diagnostic and Functional Casework Concepts*. New York: Family Service Association of America, 1950.

KISER, CLYDE V., *Research in Family Planning*. Princeton, N.J.: Princeton University Press, 1962.

KIMMEL, DOROTHY D., *Homemaker Service for Older People*. Chicago: American Public Welfare Association, 1955.

LANDIS, JUDSON T., and MARY G. LANDIS, *Building a Successful Marriage*, 6th ed. Englewood Cliffs, N.J.: Prentice-Hall, Inc., 1973.

LANGSLEY, D. G., et al., "Family Crisis Therapy," *Family Process*, 7, No. 2 (February 1968), 145–58.

LOOMIS, CHARLES P., and ALLAN BEEGLE, *Rural Social Systems*. Englewood Cliffs, N.J.: Prentice-Hall, 1950.

MARTINSON, FLOYD M., *Family in Society*. New York: Dodd, Mead, 1970.

MOORE, WILBERT E., *Social Change*. Englewood Cliffs, N.J.: Prentice-Hall, 1963.

PLANT, JAMES S., *Personality and the Cultural Pattern*. New York: Commonwealth Fund, 1937.

POHEK, MARGUERITE V., *Teachers' Source Book on Aging*. New York: Council on Social Work Education, 1964.

POLLAK, GERTRUDE, "Sexual Dynamics of Parents Without Partners," *Social Work*, 15, No. 2 (April 1970), 79–85.

RAINWATER, LEE, *Family Design: Marital Sexuality, Family Size and Contraception*. Chicago: Aldine Press, 1967.

REISS, IRA L., *The Family System in America*. New York: Holt, Rinehart and Winston, 1971.

RICH, MARGARET, *A Belief in People*. New York: Family Service Association, 1956.

ROBERTS, RON E., *The New Communes: Coming Together in America*. Englewood Cliffs, N.J.: Prentice-Hall, 1971.

ROGERS, CARL R., *Counseling and Psychotherapy Newer Concepts in Practice*. Boston: Houghton Mifflin, 1942.

SATYR, VIRGINIA, *Conjoint Family Therapy*. Palo Alto, Calif.: Science and Behavior Press, 1967.

SCHULZ, DAVID A., *The Changing Family: Its Function and Future*. Englewood Cliffs, N.J.: Prentice-Hall, 1972.

SHANAS, ETHEL, and GORDON F. STREIB, *Social Structure and the Family: Generational Relations*. Englewood Cliffs, N.J.: Prentice-Hall, 1965.

SIMONS, SAVILLA M., "Services to Uprooted and Unsettled Families," *Social Welfare Forum* (1962), 169–80.

SMELSER, NEIL J., *The Sociology of Economic Life*. Englewood Cliffs, N.J.: Prentice-Hall, 1963.

STEIN, HERMAN D., *Careers for Men in Family Social Work*. New York: Family Service Association of America, 1946.

STRAUSS, MURRAY A., *Family Analysis*. Chicago: Rand McNally, 1969.

TAFT, JESSIE, ed., *Family Casework and Counseling*. Philadelphia: University of Pennsylvania Press, 1948.

TIBBITTS, CLARK, and WILMA DONAHUE, *Social and Psychological Aspects of Aging*. New York: Columbia University Press, 1962.

TRUXAL, ANDREW G., and FRANCIS E. MERRILL, *Marriage and the Family in American Culture*. Englewood Cliffs, N.J.: Prentice-Hall, 1953.

VINCENT, CLARK E., *Unmarried Mothers*. New York: Free Press, 1961.

WHITMAN, HOWARD, *A Brighter Later Life*. Englewood Cliffs, N.J.: Prentice-Hall, 1961.

YOUNG, LEONTINE, *Out of Wedlock*. New York: McGraw-Hill, 1954.

13

services
to
children
and
youth

CHILDREN'S NEEDS FOR SPECIAL SERVICES

Care for orphans and abandoned children is one of the oldest forms of charity. It was originally carried out by the church. Recognition that children need a different type of care from adults is only a recent development, and the modern term "child welfare" has assumed a broader meaning. It is not only concerned with care for destitute, neglected, deserted, sick, handicapped, or maladjusted and delinquent children. "Child welfare" also incorporates the social, economic, and health activities of public and private welfare agencies which secure and protect the well-being of all children in their physical, intellectual, and emotional development.[1]

Scientific progress in anthropology, biology, medicine, psychology, and social research during the past hundred years has changed the attitude of society toward the child. He is no longer treated as an adult person of smaller stature, but as a human being with a different rhythm of life, and with different laws of biological and mental growth. The child follows drives, social forces, and motivations which are basically different from those governing adult behavior. To the child the world is identical with his personality; fantasy and reality are not yet separated. Only in the period of adolescence do reality and fantasy begin to part.

As we have seen, during the colonial period in the United States dependent children were indentured for many years as cheap labor. Young children were boarded out to foster families or were later placed in the almshouses. The high death rate and low life expectancy of the period left numerous children alone and destitute. The Colonies were ill prepared for their care. Relatives, neighbors, church members, and a few national groups or religious societies took care of some dependent children. But usually, the overseer of the poor chose indiscriminately to place them out—which was cheapest for the community.

During the nineteenth century more and more children were brought into the almshouses. They lived in dark, overcrowded, filthy rooms, without adequate food and clothing, herded together with adults suffering from various physical and mental diseases. The typical conditions in these almshouses were revealed in an investigation in New York in 1857.[2] The committee described the poorhouses as the most disgraceful memorials of public charity, "where the misfortune of poverty is visited with greater deprivations of comfortable food, lodging, clothing, warmth, and ventilation than constitute the usual penalty of crime." Children should never have been permitted to enter the poorhouses. Young children were forced to pass their most impressionable years in the midst of such "vicious associations as will stamp them for a life of future infamy and crime." The

1 David Fanshel, "Child Welfare," *Encyclopedia 1971,* pp. 99–103; Alfred Kadushin, *Child Welfare Services* (New York: Macmillan, 1967); Robert H. Bremner, *Children and Youth in America* (Cambridge, Mass.: Harvard University Press, 1970–71), 2 vols.

2 Sophonisba P. Breckinridge, *Public Welfare Administration in the United States* (Chicago: University of Chicago Press, 1935), pp. 149–58; Grace Abbott, *The Child and the State,* Vol. 2 (Chicago: University of Chicago Press, 1938), pp. 3–9, 51–54; Ralph E. Pumphrey and Muriel W. Pumphrey, eds., *The Heritage of American Social Work* (New York: Columbia University Press, 1964), pp. 49–51; Nathan E. Cohen, ed., *Social Work in the American Tradition* (New York: Holt, Rinehart and Winston, 1958), pp. 22–26, 71–75; Clarke A. Chambers, *Seedtime of Reform* (Minneapolis: University of Minnesota Press, 1963), pp. 27–58.

committee recommended that children be removed from the poorhouses and placed in orphanages or asylums in which they would be educated according to the needs of their age. The idea of saving destitute children from the dangers of the "mixed almshouse" was the first, but not the only, cause for the rapid growth of orphan asylums during the nineteenth and early twentieth centuries. There was also the need to find a place for other children whose health and morale were endangered by conditions in their families, who were neglected, and who were roaming the streets in large cities. A special problem existed for Negro children, for whom no care at all could be found. Religious societies wanted children to be placed in orphanages where they would be brought up in the faith of their parents.[3]

Before the nineteenth century only a few orphanages had been established in this country. The first was built by the French Ursuline Sisters in New Orleans in 1729, to place homeless orphans whose parents had been killed by Indian massacres, and the first public children's asylum was the Charleston Orphan House, founded in 1790 in South Carolina. In the large cities, private orphanages and children's branches of public almshouses, or asylums, took care of an increasing number of dependent and neglected children. In smaller communities and rural counties the segregation of children from adults took a long time, and children remained exposed to the undesirable influence of adult rogues and vagabonds who, as inmates, still were used to care for the children in almshouses and even some public orphan asylums. The Congress of State Boards of Charities in 1875 challenged the state legislatures to remove all children from county poorhouses, city almshouses, jails, and from all associations with adult paupers and criminals, and to place them in families, asylums, reformatories, or other children's institutions.

Child placement in families in the form of indenture, which had been customary in the colonial period, led in most instances to neglect of the child's needs for affection and education and to his being overworked and exploited as cheap domestic labor. In fact, the almshouse at first seemed to promise better treatment and education when it was proposed as a method of relief in the 1820s. The disadvantages of bringing up children in almshouses, asylums, and orphanages, however, were recognized fairly early. Children reared in institutions became dull, without vigor and initiative.

Around 1850 runaway, wayward children became a problem in some metropolitan areas. The New York police complained that over 10,000 vagrant children were running loose in the streets, begging and stealing. On the initiative of Charles Loring Brace, the New York Children's Aid Society

[3] Henry W. Thurston, *The Dependent Child* (New York: Columbia University Press, 1930), pp. 40, 90; Maurice O. Hunt, "Child Welfare," *Social Work Year Book* (1960), 141–57; Ralph Pumphrey, "Social Welfare History," *Encyclopedia 1971*, pp. 1448–50.

was founded in 1853 to locate rural foster homes for neglected children.[4] The main activity of the newly founded Society became the organization of a "mass deportation" of underprivileged or homeless children to farmers and mechanics in rural communities of the midwestern states. Many children found homes in the rural families where they were placed, but others did not adjust to the unfamiliar country life and agricultural work. The majority of the farmers who asked for children were poor and wanted cheap labor, without being too deeply interested in rehabilitating them.

In Baltimore, Boston, Brooklyn, and Philadelphia, Children's Aid Societies followed the New York example. In Chicago Martin Van Buren Van Arsdale founded in 1883 the American Educational Society, the first statewide child placing agency for Illinois, which later expanded its services as the National Children's Home Society with charters in other states. Several states began to place children in foster homes under the auspices of state boards of charities, later departments of social welfare. They tried to select foster homes in which the children would not be treated only as an economic asset. Their inspectors provided a certain amount of supervision by visiting the families from time to time. Since the Children's Aid Societies, however, did not pay board to the foster parents, they felt they could not require higher standards of care which were desirable for the children. Placement in rural regions in other states, frequently far from the former residence of the child, usually led to a permanent breakup of the child's ties with his family and made it difficult for the family to maintain contact or to take back the child.

A profound influence on the life of children during the industrial-urban development of the United States was exercised through the change of the goals of education under the leadership of John Dewey. His educational philosophy centered around the growth and development of the child.[5]

Foster care was a forward step compared with the shortcomings of orphanages and other children's homes which existed in that period. Children's asylums did not meet any individual needs of the children. They were mostly mass institutions with huge dormitories. The children lacked personal attention and understanding, received treatment in groups rather than as individuals, and missed the feeling of belonging and the love of parents and

---

[4] Emma Brace, *The Life and Letters of Charles Loring Brace* (New York: Scribner, 1894); Edith Abbott, *Some American Pioneers in Social Welfare* (Select Documents) (Chicago: University of Chicago Press, 1937). For recent developments in foster care, see Henry S. Maas and Richard E. Engler, *Children in Need of Parents* (New York: Columbia University Press, 1959); and Helen Stone, *Reflections on Foster Care* (New York: Child Welfare League, 1969).

[5] See Thomas N. Bonner, et al., *The Contemporary World* (Englewood Cliffs, N.J.: Prentice-Hall, 1965), pp. 315–17; and Henry W. Maier, *Three Theories of Child Development* (New York: Harper & Row, 1965), pp. 221–38.

family. Only toward the end of the nineteenth century did some children's institutions recognize these deficiencies and introduce the "cottage plan." Large dormitories were replaced by small family-like groups living in separate buildings with a housemother and a housefather who were to function as a substitute for a real family. Even with such improvements, care of children in institutions deprived them of growing up in the normal setting of the community, playing with the neighbors, going to school, and returning to "their home." This is why the introduction of carefully selected and supervised foster homes seemed a better solution to the problem.

The latest idea in the development of methods for child protection is that, whenever possible, the child should be left in his family. We have already noted that until the end of the nineteenth century many children were taken from their parents because of their poverty, and because it was thought that a pauper family could not properly bring up a child. The findings of modern psychology and psychoanalysis, as well as the observations of the juvenile courts and social agencies dealing with difficult and maladjusted children, proved, however, that it would be advisable to enable children to remain at home with their mothers and siblings. Economic aid granted to the mother would allow her to rear her children instead of forcing her to give the children away and work in a factory, on a farm, or as a domestic worker. The first White House Conference on the Care of Dependent Children, in 1909, emphasized the need of financial help to mothers to preserve the family.[6] However, if this was not a desirable solution for the child, placement in a foster home or in a children's institution was necessary, sometimes in permanent foster care or in an adoptive family.

Originally, private agencies carried a major share of responsibility for maintaining the family in cases of death of the father, divorce, or desertion, but more and more public funds were made available for this purpose. The function of aid to dependent children with the support of federal and state funds is, at present, the main factor in overcoming the problems of financial maintenance of needy children in their families in the United States. This support enables these families to provide a minimum of shelter, food, clothing, medical care, education, and recreation for their children. Our public social welfare services thus contribute to the maintenance of family life for the entire population. Other institutions and measures, such as public health services, schools, minimum wages and hours, agricultural subsidies, low-rent housing, social insurance benefits, and other recreation facilities, also play an important role to this effect.

6 Maas and Engler, *Children in Need of Parents,* pp. 378–97; Martin Wolins, *Selecting Foster Parents* (New York: Columbia University Press, 1963), pp. 1–6, 108–30; Beatrice L. Garrett, "Meeting the Crisis in Foster Family Care," *Children,* 13, No. 1 (January–February 1966), 2–8; Catherine Pratt, "Foster Parents as Agency Employees," *Children,* 13, No. 1 (January–February 1966) 14–15; Seth Low, "Foster Care of Children—Major National Trends and Prospects," *Welfare in Review,* 4, No. 9 (October 1966), 12–21.

Dangerous as economic deficiencies are for the development of the child in his family, they are not the only problems which require child welfare activities. Children are often endangered not only by poverty, insufficient income, and sickness in the family, but also by neglect or rejection, lack of understanding or love, or because the parents are unable to educate them. For these reasons, casework for children is a vital necessity, and private family and child care agencies as well as the child welfare divisions of city and county welfare departments have developed casework for children as an integral part of their programs.

Child welfare services are rendered by providing (1) economic and personal aid to children living in their homes, (2) substitute families or an adoptive home for children who have no home or cannot remain with their families, and (3) institutional care in children's homes and orphanages when children, for particular reasons, cannot be left in their homes or in foster families. Casework for the child in his home considers the individual needs of the child for well-being and health. It uses such facilities of the community as day nurseries, recreation, organized children's and youth activities, and clinics. In general, casework with the parents or the foster parents is indispensable in the interest of the child. Still more vital is individual service to children who cannot remain in their families and for whom, therefore, substitute care has to be provided, either in a foster home or in a children's institution.[7]

WELFARE AND HEALTH SERVICES FOR CHILDREN

Public child welfare services in the states are supported by Federal grants-in-aid, when approved by the United States Children's Bureau, since 1969 a division of the Office of Child Development in the Department of Health, Education and Welfare. They include maternal and child health, crippled children services, and "child welfare services for the protection of homeless, dependent, neglected and endangered children in urban and rural areas."[8] An Advisory Council on Child Welfare Services reports findings and recommendations to the Secretary of HEW and Congress. Private social

[7] For an analysis of the shortcomings of present child protective services, see Alfred Kadushin, "Child Welfare: Adoption and Foster Care," *Encyclopedia 1971,* pp. 110–11.

[8] *Child welfare services* is a technical term used in the Social Security Act to designate preventive and protective activities as distinguished from material aid under public assistance. See Alfred J. Kahn, "Planning for the Welfare of Children," *Social Welfare Forum* (1966), 165–87, and *Planning Community Services for Children in Trouble* (New York: Columbia University Press, 1963); Kermit T. Wiltse, "Aid to Families with Dependent Children," *The Annals,* 355 (September 1964), 75–81; Julia Ann Bishop, "Helping Neglectful Parents," *The Annals,* 355 (September 1964), 82–89; and David Gottlieb and Ann L. Heinsohn, *America's Other Youth: Growing Up Poor* (Englewood Cliffs, N.J.: Prentice-Hall, 1971).

agencies continue to supplement public child welfare services. Federal grants are in direct proportion to the total child population and in inverse proportion to state per-capita income. State and local funds must match federal grants.

The treatment of minority group children—blacks, Puerto Ricans, Mexican-Americans, American Indians, Appalachian poor whites—is still very inadequate. Child welfare workers need to be trained to understand the specific culture and values of these groups in order to respect their differences and to meet their needs, which differ from those of white middle-class Americans.

Maternal and Child-Health Services

Services to promote the health of mothers and young children are supported by annual federal grants.[9] The states share the expenses and administer the program through the state health agency. Rating personnel on a merit basis and efficient administration are required; reports must be made, and the funds must be used for improvement of local services. Cooperation with medical, nursing, and private welfare organizations is required, and demonstration services in deprived areas and for groups in particular need have to be arranged. The federal allotment is composed of a uniform rate to all states—a sum based on the ratio of live births in the state to the total in the United States, and on the individual need of the state for financial assistance to carry out its maternal and child-health program. The services include well-baby clinics for regular medical examinations of young children and advice to their mothers; prenatal clinics; home delivery nursing; infant and child health conferences; school, dental, and mental health services; advisory and consultation services; and training programs for pediatricians, dentists, nurses, nutritionists, and social workers. The necessity for further improvement of specialized medical care for young children and school children in rural areas is generally recognized. In the prevention of infant mortality, the United States is in eleventh place, behind Holland, Sweden, Ireland, and Switzerland, among others. During recent years even in urban areas of the United States infant mortality was 25.3 per thousand live births (compared with 15.3 for Sweden and Holland); for blacks, it was 35 to 40, due to slum conditions, lack of prenatal care, poverty, and premature birth.

During World War II the federal government provided free "emergency maternity and infant care" to wives of servicemen of the lower ranks, including medical care for infants during their first year. The costs of this program were met entirely by federal funds, and its remarkable success

---

[9] *Social Security Bulletin*, 28, No. 9 (September 1965), 21. The amendments of 1967 stressed care for crippled children, education of retarded children, and dental care.

showed the value of comprehensive medical care. From 1939 to 1948, the mortality rate of infants under one month decreased by 24 percent, that of children under one year by 48 percent, from one to four years by 50 percent, and maternal mortality by 71 percent.[10]

Services for Crippled Children

Services for crippled children are administered at the federal level by the United States Public Health Service. The Social Security Act defines these services as locating crippled children and providing medical, surgical, corrective, and other services and care, and facilities for diagnosis, hospitalization, and aftercare. They include provision of aids and prosthetic appliances, physiotherapy, medical social services, and maintenance of a state crippled children's registry. The federal grant of $15,000,000 annually is allocated by a uniform grant of $60,000 to each state, and a portion of $4,320,000 on the basis of the state's particular need for this program in relation to the number of crippled children; this amount must be matched by state, local, or private funds. These grants were increased to $45,000,000 in 1966, and there were further increases of $5,000,000 each year to 1969. The remaining $7,500,000 are allotted according to each state's need and in proportion to urban and rural child population without the requirement of matching funds. The state relies on local public and private social agencies, public health nurses, physicians, midwives, hospitals, and nursery and kindergarten teachers, as well as elementary school teachers, to locate crippled children. Federal grants of $5,000,000 in 1966, $10,000,000 in 1967, and $17,500,000 beginning in 1968 are provided for aid in training professional personnel for the care of crippled and retarded children. They amounted in 1969 to over $140,000,000. In 1962 the President's Panel on Mental Retardation requested inclusion of these children in state programs for crippled children.[11] In all states, diagnosis and treatment cover children with severe crippling conditions, such as clubfoot, harelip, and cleft palate. Other diseases, such as rheumatic fever, heart diseases, cerebral palsy, eye and speech defects, ear diseases, epilepsy, and dental defects requiring orthodontia, are covered in some state programs (at present frequently only on a demonstration basis). Usually, the program is administered by state and local health departments. In urban areas of most states, special classes for the instruction of crippled, deaf, and blind children are organized.

Private crippled children's agencies, established and supported by such fraternal orders as the Shriners, the Elks, and the Rotary Clubs and also

[10] Children's Bureau, *Changes in Infant, Childhood, and Maternal Mortality Over the Decade 1939–1948,* Statistical Series, No. 6 (1950); Betty M. Flint, *The Security of Infants* (Chicago: University of Chicago Press, 1959); Virginia Insley, "Maternal and Child Health," *Encyclopedia 1971,* pp. 552–60.

[11] *Social Security Bulletin,* 28, No. 9 (September 1965), 21.

by religious and nonsectarian societies, have been the pioneers in this field. They built the first orthopedic hospitals and clinics and encouraged state legislation for crippled children preceding the Social Security Act of 1935. Despite the more generous federal and state appropriations granted recently for crippled children, supplementation by private social agencies is still urgently needed, since most states do not yet provide adequate diagnostic services or the expensive treatment for many crippling diseases.[12]

Child Welfare Services

When the Social Security Act of 1935 was passed, nearly 7,500,000 boys and girls were "on relief," 300,000 children were dependent or neglected, and about 200,000 children annually came before the juvenile courts. Help and protection for these children was left mainly to private social agencies and to the inadequate powers of local communities. With the support of federal grants-in-aid, public services for the protection of the unfortunate homeless, orphaned, abandoned, dependent, or neglected children and for children in danger of delinquency, have been greatly strengthened. The *Amendment of the Social Security Act of 1958* no longer limited federal grants to rural and special emergency areas. Every state now has a child welfare division in its public welfare department, and local child welfare departments are more efficiently operated. These public services include casework with parents and relatives for the improvement of unsatisfactory family and personal relationships of the child, and help in economic and social difficulties. Children with physical, mental, and emotional handicaps receive aid. Special attention is given to children born out of wedlock, and foster families or institutional care are provided for children who need to live away from their homes. Public child welfare authorities are responsible for the supervision of foster homes and children's institutions. These child welfare services also provide assistance to courts which handle children's cases, to schools, to child guidance and mental hygiene clinics, and to other health agencies concerned with individual children.[13] Frequently, they co-

---

[12] Dean W. Roberts, et al., "The Physically Handicapped," *Social Work Year Book* (1960), 432–40; U.S. Children's Bureau, *Services for Crippled Children* (1952); William M. Cruickshank, *Psychology of Exceptional Children and Youth* (Englewood Cliffs, N.J.: Prentice-Hall, 1955); Dorothy Zietz, *Child Welfare—Principles and Methods* (New York: John Wiley, 1969), pp. 205–40; James Robertson, ed., *Hospitals and Children: A Parent's Eye View* (New York: International University Press, 1963); Emma N. Plank, *Working with Children in Hospitals* (Cleveland: Western Reserve University Press, 1962).

[13] Fred Delli Quadri, "Child Welfare," *Social Work Year Book* (1957), 146–57; Wayne Vasey, *Government and Social Welfare* (New York: Holt, Rinehart and Winston, 1958), pp. 186–202; Shirley Braverman, "The Informal Peer Group as an Adjunct to Treatment of the Adolescent," *Social Casework*, 47, No. 3 (March 1966), 152–57; Henry S. Maas, *Five Fields of Social Service* (New York: National Association of Social Workers, 1966).

operate with group work agencies for the protection of children. The child caseworker also is concerned with the promotion of an understanding of the needs of children in the community, and with the encouragement and development of such public or private facilities as day care centers, nursery schools, group work agencies, community centers, and recreation places for children and adolescents.

Each state receives from the federal government a flat amount of $60,000 and shares in the balance of the appropriation according to the proportion of its population under eighteen years to the total population in the United States under that age.[14] The federal grants may be used for returning a runaway child under the age of eighteen to his home community when his parents or relatives, a social agency or institution cannot meet the expense. The principal advantage of these child welfare services is that they employ trained child welfare workers and consultants to improve the work of local welfare departments, institutions, public and private child and family welfare agencies, clinics, and community centers. The facilities and the experience of voluntary organizations may be used as well. The states may authorize coordinated programs for child care and protection with private social agencies in the field of group work and casework, and cooperate with probation departments of juvenile courts and police juvenile aid bureaus. Child welfare work is devoted to strengthening family life and permitting the child to grow up in his family. Children should not be deprived of the emotional security derived from family life because of economic need. In case of personal or emotional difficulties within the family, the child welfare worker will try to help in an adjustment by counseling the child and parents. He or she will assist in making available other facilities, such as participation in a children's or youth group or in recreational activities, or the use of a mental hygiene or child guidance clinic. Only if a child cannot remain in his family for reasons of health, education, or adjustment will he be placed in a foster home or a children's home.

The functions of child welfare divisions of each state department of public welfare include the development of standards for child care and for adoption procedure, licensing and inspection of children's institutions and foster families, and the promotion of legislation for child protection. In some states, the child welfare division also administers state institutions for delinquent and mentally and physically handicapped children. In other states, a separate state agency, such as the California Youth Authority, is in charge of all institutions, or assumes the responsibility for prevention and treatment of juvenile delinquency.

[14] The Social Security Act of 1935 considered the entire rural population ratio, but the Amendment of 1950 replaced this factor by the ratio of rural children and youth under eighteen years of age; see Margaret Purvine and Andrew Billingsley, "Protective Service as a Social System," *Journal of Public Social Services*, 1, No. 1 (March 1970), 34–45.

PROTECTIVE SERVICES FOR CHILDREN

The need for special protective services for children has been recognized in the United States since the 1870s, when the first societies for the prevention of cruelty to children were established in New York, New Hampshire, California, Massachusetts, and Pennsylvania. Later such societies were founded in all other states, some combined with societies for the prevention of cruelty to animals. Recently the child welfare divisions of public welfare departments have widely assumed the responsibility of protecting children from neglect, abandonment, exploitation, and abuse. While these services first emphasized legal prosecution and punishment of the parents or guardians, their present aim is to prevent recurring neglect and abuse of children by providing help, counsel, and casework services to parents and guardians. Sometimes parent groups for discussion of problems concerning children supplement individual services to the family. Other community resources are used to help the families of such children overcome their problems. But since most people who need such protective services do not apply for them, present facilities are not sufficient to protect all endangered children, particularly those of middle- and upper-class background who are less likely to be referred to a social agency.

That the general public is not aware of the extent of child neglect and abuse explains the lack of adequate resources for measures to protect children against neglect, cruelty, and abuse, especially sexual abuse.[15]

FOSTER FAMILY CARE

There are children who cannot live with their families; children who are orphans without relatives; abandoned children whose parents are unknown; children who have been deserted by their parents; and children whose parents are unable to keep them because of illness or confinement to prison. Some parents also may be a direct threat to their children. For such children, as a rule, placement in a foster home is considered. The social agency which handles foster family placement needs to know the child well enough to find the proper home for him. The caseworker helps the child accept the

[15] Erik Erikson, *Childhood and Society* (New York: W. W. Norton, 1963), p. 267; Andrew Billingsley, *The Social Worker in a Child Protective Agency* (New York: National Association of Social Workers, 1965); Helen R. Jetter, *Children's Problems and Services in Child Welfare Programs* (Washington, D.C.: Department of Health, Education and Welfare, 1963); Robert M. Mulford and Morton I. Cohen, *Neglecting Parents* (Denver: American Humane Association, 1968); David Bakan, *Slaughter of the Innocents* (San Francisco: Jossey-Bass, 1971); L. C. Lane, "Youth, the Counterculture and the Social Worker," *Child Welfare*, 50, No. 1 (October 1971), 573–81.

necessity for placement and share, as much as his age permits, the plans for his foster family. The caseworker also sustains the child in this inescapably anxious period. The child receives medical and psychological examinations, and the child-placing agency considers his social and cultural background; his relation to all members of the family, the neighborhood, and school; his behavior, attitudes, and personal preferences, as well as the wishes of his parents (whenever this is possible). Working together with the parents, the child, and the foster parents to secure a mutually satisfactory solution for all persons concerned, the social agency attempts to find the foster home best suited to the individual child's needs.

In selecting a foster family,[16] the social agency considers whether the family will provide the right home for healthy and normal development of the particular child, but it also gives attention to the financial situation, housing conditions, neighborhood, and housekeeping standards. The educational, spiritual, and religious background of the foster parents deserves serious thought as well. Professional skill in foster placement is needed for fitting together the child's emotional, intellectual, and physical needs with the abilities of foster parents, to achieve the best possible adjustment and satisfaction for both child and foster family.

In the foster family, a harmonious relationship between the parents is necessary, and, if there are children or other relatives, the entire family group should be congenial. They also must have (particularly the foster mother) a sincere interest in children, because a child in a foster home requires, above all, love and understanding to adjust to a new family environment. The main motivation of families applying for a foster child should be their desire to rear such a child as if he were their own. Families who apply merely for financial reasons, or who want to get a child primarily for their emotional satisfaction, without being able to give the child warmth and understanding, should not be accepted. It is often difficult for the child welfare worker to refuse applicants who want badly to be foster parents; sometimes it is necessary to refer such applicants to a family service agency to help them in their own personal problems.[17] As a rule, it is desirable

16 See Martin Wolins, *Selecting Foster Parents: The Ideal and the Reality* (New York: Columbia University Press), 1963, pp. 131–39; Kathryn Close, "An Encounter with Foster Parents," *Children,* 18, No. 4 (August 1971), 138–42; Elizabeth Herzog, "Finding Families for Black Children," *Children,* 18, No. 4 (August 1971), 143–48.

17 Dorothy Hutchinson, *In Quest of Foster Parents: A Point of View on Home-finding* (New York: Columbia University Press, 1943), pp. 13–15; Jean Charnley, *The Art of Child Placement* (Minneapolis: University of Minnesota Press, 1955); Henrietta L. Gordon, *Casework Services for Children* (Boston: Houghton Mifflin, 1956), pp. 34–156; Maas and Engler, *Children in Need of Parents* pp. 1–8, 378–97; Elizabeth G. Meier, "Child Neglect," in Nathan E. Cohen, ed., *Social Work and Social Problems* (New York: National Association of Social Workers, 1964), pp. 153–200; Aaron Rosenthal and John E. Mayer, "Reduction of Uncertainty in Child Placement Decisions," *Social Work,* 15, No. 4 (October 1970), 52–59.

that the foster parents be about the same age as the natural parents of the child. However, practical experience shows that older, well-suited foster parents often establish an excellent relationship with the child if he responds to their affection and understanding. Foster parents need to accept that the child's ultimate security is with his natural family, that he will return to them, and that his ties to his parents or other close relatives are not to be weakened or destroyed.

In general, the child-placing agency assumes the supervision of the foster home after the child has been placed. Of course, the foster family has responsibility for the physical care of the child, and for his education. The child caseworker helps the child and the foster parents adjust to each other and solve the difficulties and disappointments which are rarely missing in any family. The child frequently brings to the foster home his suspicions, anxieties, resistance, or hostility. The caseworker aids the foster parents in their effort to overcome these problems and to give the child the security he longs for. Whenever possible, the caseworker attempts to preserve the child's interest in his natural family, and to keep alive the family's feeling of responsibility for the child, because in the majority of cases, the child finally will return to it. Sometimes, visits of the parents with the foster family, or of the child with the mother or siblings are arranged, but this has to be done with the full cooperation of the foster family. In cases of conflict, the caseworker will consider the welfare and happiness of the child as the decisive factor in such arrangements.

Some child welfare and family service agencies use temporary foster homes to place children in emergencies until they find a more permanent family home in which the child will feel accepted and secure. During this period, the child himself, who in his own family has experienced the neglect and domestic discord that leads to running away, stealing, or other expressions of maladjustment, has time to adapt himself to the idea of living with another understanding family.

Among the various types of foster homes, only one plays a major role in present child care practice: the boarding home. Here, the foster parents receive payment for their service, either by the parents, relatives, guardian of the child, juvenile court, or by the social agency which places the child. Free foster homes, in which the foster parents do not receive any remuneration, are rare today, because such families usually are not willing to submit to the standards, conditions, and supervision of the social agency or to the special needs of the child. There are sectarian agencies which still find free homes in a few instances. Wage homes, or work homes, in which the older child is maintained in exchange for the work he does for the foster family, are infrequently relied on for placing children.

The adoption home provides a different type of care. The child is placed without payment of board and with the understanding that the adoptive parents will accept the child as a permanent member of the family if the placement of the child proves to be mutually satisfactory.

ADOPTION

Adoption is the legal, social, and psychological method of providing a family for children who have lost their natural parents or who cannot be reared by them under sound conditions. Adoption, as a legal proceeding of the courts, establishes the relationship of parent and child between persons who are not related by nature. Through adoption, the child in effect becomes a permanent member of the adopting family. Often children are adopted by relatives or by a stepparent, but the legal and social safeguards of present adoption laws are basically designed to protect children who are not related to the adopting family.[18]

Adoption was part of Roman law and was brought from France and Spain to Louisiana and Texas in the seventeenth century. The first state to introduce adoption legislation under common law was Massachusetts in 1851. At present, every state has an adoption statute, though they vary widely from state to state. One objective of adoption law is *to protect the child* from unnecessary separation from his natural parents; from adoption by unfit parents; and from interference by his natural parents after a successful adoption has been arranged. Another objective is *to protect the natural parents*, particularly the unmarried mother, from unwise decisions made under emotional stress or economic pressure, which they might greatly regret later. Still another is *to protect the adopting parents* from taking a permanent responsibility for children whose health, heredity, or physical and mental capacities might lead to their disappointment, and also to protect them from disturbance of their relationship with the adopted child by threats or blackmail from the natural parents.

More than half of nonrelative adoptions concern illegitimate children. Others involve premarital, extramarital, and unwanted children. Nearly 98 percent of children placed for adoption are under one year of age. In some states a trend exists to limit the adoption placements to licensed social agencies, but it is questionable whether one should attempt to prevent parents

---

[18] Florence G. Brown, "Adoption," *Social Work Year Book* (1960), 85–90; Michael Schapiro, *A Study of Adoption Practice*, 2 vols. (New York: Child Welfare League of America, 1956); Gordon, *Casework Services for Children*, pp. 223–309; Helen Witmer, et al., *Independent Adoptions* (New York: Russell Sage Foundation, 1963); Bernice R. Boehm, "Adoption," *Encyclopedia of Social Work 1965*, pp. 63–68; Irving W. Fellner, "Recruiting Adoptive Applicants," *Social Work*, 13, No. 1 (January 1968), 92–100; Shirley A. Reece and Barbara Levin, "Psychiatric Disturbances in Adopted Children," *Social Work*, 13, No. 1 (January 1968), 101–11; Bernice Madison and Michael Shapiro, "Permanent and Long-Term Foster Family Care," *Child Welfare*, 49, No. 3 (March 1970), 131–36.

from placing their child, particularly with relatives or friends. In adoptions carried out under agency auspices, the natural parents (or the unmarried mother) "relinquish" the child to a licensed social agency which then takes full responsibility for the placement of the child in an adoptive home not known to the natural parents. This decision is made only after careful interviews. Many an unmarried girl comes to the agency during her pregnancy and wants to relinquish her baby immediately. Frequently, she is motivated by fear, shame, or feeling of guilt, and might be very unhappy later about a hasty decision. She is counseled about all the possibilities which exist, such as aid to dependent children, foster care, and other temporary arrangements which might help her keep her child for a time before making her decision over whether to rear him. Adoption should be a free, well-considered plan, not a hasty decision of the mother under emotional and economic pressure.

Typical features of adoption laws are that adult persons may adopt a child only with the consent of the natural parents or of the unmarried mother, that the adoptive parents must be at least ten years older than the child, and that the child has to give his consent to the adoption if he is twelve or fourteen years or older. The consent of the natural parent or parents has to be given before the court (frequently the juvenile court or the probate court), or before the state department of social welfare or a licensed adoption agency. In general, a social investigation by a public or private welfare agency is required so that the court can be fully informed of all essential factors before it makes a decision on the petition. As a rule, the child is placed in the adoption home for a trial period from six months to one year under supervision of a social agency until the final decision of the court on adoption is rendered. During this time, the development of the child in his new environment is observed by the social worker, and the adoptive parents have an opportunity to find out whether they really want to have this child as a member of their family.[19]

Throughout the United States, there is a demand from childless couples for children to adopt, particularly babies. There are, however, not enough children available for adoption to meet this demand. This discrepancy explains the public criticism that adoption agencies are too strict in their postulations, preventing people who wish to adopt a child from getting the desired child, and that a family is denied to homeless children. Social agencies have become conscious of this widespread criticism and are

---

[19] American adoption laws of today do not, in general, limit adoption to a married couple, or a couple that cannot have children. But the practice of social agencies and courts has been to place children for adoption into "full families" to give the child the opportunity for normal development. Georgia alone legally limits adoptions to married couples. See Alfred L. Kasprowicz, "Interpreting Rejection to Adoptive Parents," *Social Work,* 9, No. 1 (January 1964), 98–108; Lillian Ripple, "A Follow-Up Study of Adopted Children," *Social Service Review,* 42, No. 4 (December 1968), 479–99.

trying to find ways to improve their service and to curtail the waiting period preceding adoption. They also are anxious to create better public understanding of the reasons for the time involved in this process.[20] These conditions have encouraged the "black market in babies" in which unscrupulous employees of maternity wards, together with other middlemen, abuse the anxiety of unmarried girls and the sentimental attitude of well-to-do childless couples desirous of receiving a baby. Arrangement is made for adoption placement before, or immediately after, the birth of the child in exchange for the payment of substantial amounts of money (sometimes from both parties), called a "gratitude donation." This "selling of babies" results in handsome profits for the managers of this business, and no questions or investigations delay the placement of such a baby. However, unhappiness for the child and the adopting parents often results.

Similar manipulations, which are not based exclusively on greed, are called the "gray market in babies." They are carried on by people who attempt to please a couple wishing to have a child by persuading fearful unmarried mothers to give up the child immediately after birth. There is no competent method of determining whether this action really will be in the interest of the child and the mother. Trained workers of an adoption agency are the only ones professionally qualified to counsel with the mother, to acquaint her with alternatives to adoption placement, and to proceed with skillful study of the child's parental background and potentialities to suit him to the adopted home. Although child placements by unauthorized persons are prohibited in some states, these "independent adoptions" are still very frequent, and the unmarried mother or the natural parents are usually entitled to place their child in a family of their choice. The danger in these "independent adoptions" is that the mother may not have time or insight to form a clear opinion of whether she really wants to give away her child. She may be unable to assess the qualities of the adoptive family. The child may unnecessarily lose his natural mother. This method also involves the risk for the adopting parents that the child in his mental and physical health, temperament, and personality may not fit into their family. For these reasons, agency adoption offers greater security to the three parties concerned—the child, the natural parents, and the adoptive parents.

[20] Joseph H. Reid, "Principles, Values, and Assumptions Underlying Adoption Practice," *Social Work*, 2, No. 1 (January 1957), 22–29; Evelyn I. Smith, *Readings in Adoptions* (New York: Philosophical Library, 1963); Witmer, *Independent Adoptions;* Sanford N. Katz, "Community Decision-Makers and the Promotion of Values in the Adoption of Children," *Social Service Review*, 38, No. 1 (March 1964), 26–41; John A. Rose, "A Reevaluation of the Concept of Separation for Child Welfare," *Child Welfare*, 41, No. 10 (December 1962), 441–58; Carmolla May, "Unmarried Parents," *Public Welfare*, 21, No. 4 (October 1963), 191–226; Alfred Kadushin, *Adopting Older Children* (New York: Columbia University Press, 1970); Benson Jaffe and David Fanshel, *How They Fared in Adoption* (New York: Columbia University Press, 1970).

If the parents or the unmarried mother are determined to relinquish the child, the social agency makes a thorough study of the child with medical examination, psychological tests, and information about the social and health background of the child's mother and father. Also, their hereditary, racial, and constitutional type is studied. The agency attempts to find an adoptive home in which these factors are similar. Relinquishing the child to the agency also assures the parents that their identity and that of the adoptive parents are concealed from each other so that embarrassment, jealousy, friction, interference, and blackmail are avoided. However, the concept that adoptive children should be matched in physical appearance and personality to those of the adopting parents no longer is generally accepted. Recent research has shown that adoption of foreign children has led to very satisfactory adaptation to American culture and to happy family life.[21]

Some adoption agencies are more often placing newborn babies in their first months of life in adoption homes because they have become convinced that the child's stay in a new permanent home without any change of environment offers the best chances for his emotional development. Agencies investigate and select suitable adoption families from their applicants before a child is available for adoption. More adoptive couples are willing, at present, to take the risk involved in adopting a very young child than in former times. The so-called "intelligence test" of the infant to check the probability of his normal mental growth is, as a rule, no longer considered necessary. Only a medical statement is required by the adoption agency that the baby has not suffered injury or damage in delivery. In these early adoptions, as in others, the mother of the child is counseled by the caseworker of the agency so that she is able to weigh the reasons for or against relinquishment of the child before she decides whether to have him adopted.

The role of the adoption worker is very responsible. He must be well aware of his feelings and attitudes in order to give objective but warmhearted understanding to the needs of the three parties in the adoption process, and to perform a service satisfactory to the community.

In the selection of the adopting parents, the social agency looks for families who are in good physical and mental health and are emotionally and economically able to rear the child. After the child is placed with the selected family, the social agency generally maintains contact with the child and the new parents for one year. This is done to give help in whatever adjustment difficulties might arise, and to observe whether the child satis-

---

[21] Susan T. Pettis, "Cultural Factors in Adoption of Oriental Immigrant Children," *Social Work*, 7, No. 4 (October 1962), 22–25; Harriet Fricke, "Inter-racial Adoption: The Little Revolution," *Social Work*, 10, No. 3 (July 1965), 92–97; Carl Schoenberg, "Adoption: The Created Family," *The Annals*, 355 (September 1964), 69–74; Andrew Billingsley and Jean Giovannoni, "Research Perspectives on Interracial Adoptions," in R. R. Miller, ed., *Race, Research, and Reason: Social Work Perspectives* (New York: National Association of Social Workers, 1969), pp. 57–79.

factorily takes roots in the new family. If the adjustment is satisfactory, the social agency recommends that the court grant the adoption.[22] In general, the courts follow the social agency's suggestion, which is based on its work with natural parents, child, and adopting parents. In many states court hearings are not open to the public, but the older child is usually present to give his consent. The decree of adoption declares that the child is the child and legal heir of the adopting parents and acquires the same rights, privileges, and obligations as a child born to them.

There are two other types of adoption: the stepparent adoption, and adoption of an illegitimate child by his natural father. Under stepparent adoption, the child remains with his mother, whether she was not married before, widowed, or divorced. The petition for adoption is filed with the court by the stepfather, and requires the formal consent of the mother. It is done so that the child has the same legal status and name as other children in the family. In these cases, social investigations are often carried out by the probation officer of the court. A father who wants to adopt his natural child has to undergo different procedures in the various states. For instance, in California he must acknowledge the child as his own before the court, receive him into his family, and treat him like a legitimate child. He needs the formal consent of the natural mother if she is alive, and also of his wife if he is married.

CHILDREN OF UNMARRIED PARENTS

Programs to meet the needs of the unmarried mother and to offer care and protection to her child are among the most important services organized by family and children's agencies. The unmarried mother often moves away from her home community to avoid the embarrassment and disdain which, even today, frequently are connected with this situation. The social agency may have to assist in arrangements for the confinement and for the care of the child. Obviously, the illegitimate child needs just as much affection and feeling of belonging as any other child, and for this reason children's agencies usually attempt to permit the mother to stay with the baby until she decides what she wants done with the child. The child born out of wedlock, fundamentally, should not be treated differently from other children in providing for his needs of protection and care. His moth-

---

[22] If the child does not adjust well, the social agency removes him and makes another arrangement; however, because careful selection is made, such cases are rare. See Clark E. Vincent, *Unmarried Mothers* (New York: Free Press, 1961); Ethel Branham, "One-Parent Adoptions," *Children,* 17, No. 3 (June 1970), 103–7; Jaffe and Fanshel, *How They Fared in Adoption;* Peter J. Kasius, "Exploring Adoption Hangups," *Public Welfare,* 29, No. 2 (Spring 1971), 189–93; Benjamin Schlesinger, *The One-Parent Family* (Toronto: University of Toronto Press, 1969).

er, as well, frequently needs intensive help and counseling by the caseworker to avoid unwise plans for herself and for the child. The unmarried father, also, should be included in the work of the social agency, to help and encourage him to meet his moral and financial responsibilities for the child.[23]

GUARDIANSHIP

Guardianship is the establishment of legal protection for children when the parents are dead, incapacitated, incompetent, or have failed in their duty toward the children.[24] The guardian is a substitute for the parent, but he is not liable for the child's support. The guardianship ends with the child's majority or with his marriage. In case of death of the father, the mother is the *natural guardian* of the children, and the unmarried mother is the *sole guardian* of her child. *Testamentary guardians* are named in the will of the deceased parents, and often are relatives or friends of the family; *public guardians,* as a rule county officials, are provided in ten states for the protection of children; there are *guardians of estate* to manage property rights of the ward, and *guardians ad litem* who are appointed by the court for special purposes, mainly legal proceedings. The legal provisions for guardianship in most states are enacted in the laws on infancy and guardianship, but too much emphasis still is placed on the management of estate and too little on the protection of the child's healthful placement, education, and guidance. In addition to testamentary guardians, guardians are appointed by various courts, such as the probate court, the juvenile court, orphans', or surrogate court. In some states the probation officer of a rural juvenile court is guardian for the wards of the court. The investigation of the fitness of guardians before their appointment, and supervision of the

---

[23] Some states have adopted the *Uniform Illegitimacy Law* drafted by the National Conference of Commissioners on Uniform State Laws in 1922, by which both the mother and the unmarried father are responsible for support, maintenance, and education of the illegitimate child. See Blanche Bernstein and Mignon Sauber, *Deterrents to Early Prenatal and Social Services* (New York: Community Council, 1960) and *Research Perspectives on the Unmarried Mother* (New York: Child Welfare League of America, 1962); Vincent, *Unmarried Mothers;* Helen H. Perlman, "Unmarried Mothers," in Cohen, *Social Work and Social Problems,* pp. 270–320; Hanna M. Adams and Ursula M. Gallagher, "Facts and Observations about Illegitimacy," *Children,* 10, No. 2 (March–April 1963), 43–48; Sanford N. Katz, "Legal Protection for the Unmarried Mother and Her Child," 55–59; Witmer, *Independent Adoptions;* Mildred Arnold, 'New Trends in Adoption Practice," *Social Welfare Forum* (1959), 125–35; Fricke, "Inter-racial Adoption," *Social Work,* 10, No. 3 (July 1965), 92–97; *Illegitimacy: Changing Services for Changing Times* (New York: National Council on Illegitimacy, 1970), pp. 54–69.

[24] Irving Weisman, et al., *Guardianship for Children,* Publication No. 330 (Washington, D.C.: U.S. Children's Bureau, 1949), p. 19; Leontine Young, *Out of Wedlock* (New York: McGraw-Hill, 1954); Ruth L. Butcher and Marion O. Robinson, *The Unmarried Mother* (New York: Public Affairs Committee, 1959).

activities of guardians, are necessary for the protection of children, but these measures unfortunately are seldom carried out.[25]

CHILDREN IN INSTITUTIONS

In the nineteenth century destitute and orphaned children were customarily cared for in orphanages and asylums. The trend since then has been away from institutional care. The main reason is that children's institutions require from the child an adjustment to a large number of other children, educators, and staff members in an atmosphere unlike home. That children become "institutionalized," that they lose their personality in conforming to strict, general regulations, and that they have no opportunity to develop their individuality, their mental, physical and creative abilities, and are apt to become docile and dull have been the main arguments against institutional care. Life in an institution makes a certain routine necessary that often limits warm personal relationships with the personnel and other children in the home and easily inhibits the development of initiative in the child. However, the modern children's institution offers an opportunity for an experience in more constructive group living, regular physical care, a healthy diet, an atmosphere provided by friendly, interested, trained educators concerned with the well-being of the child, and medical (often psychiatric) aid and trained social work service.

Modern children's institutions have tried to overcome the problems presented by mass education and living in large dormitories by the establishment of the "cottage plan." The institution is decentralized into a number of cottages, usually accommodating a group of about twenty girls and boys with a couple of cottage parents. Instead of dormitories, small sleeping rooms for two to four children, and living and dining rooms are used in which the children feel more as if they are "at home."[26]

Which children need institutional care? Infants and preschool-age children who cannot remain with their families are rarely placed in institutions, but into foster families. It also is an accepted principle that institutional care for children should be a temporary placement, and not planned until the child has fully grown up. The following groups usually seem to

[25] Hazeltine Byrd Taylor, *Law of Guardian and Ward* (Chicago: University of Chicago Press, 1935), p. 5; Mary Stanton, "The Administration of Guardianship by a Local Probate Court," *Social Service Review,* 14, No. 4 (December 1945), 495–505; Irving Weisman, "Guardianship: Every Child's Right," *The Annals,* 355 (September 1964), 134–39.

[26] For examples of various types of children's homes and of the life of the children in such institutions, see Howard W. Hopkirk, *Institutions Serving Children* (New York: Russell Sage Foundation, 1944); and Margrit Meyer, "Family Ties and the Institutional Child," *Children,* 16, No. 6 (December 1969), 226–31.

need institutional care: (1) children who, because of severe illness or injury of the parents, have to leave their home and who are so strongly emotionally tied to the parents that they or the parents feel threatened by a placement in another family; (2) children who, because of family disturbances, tensions, or divorce, have become so difficult that they cannot remain in their family, but who also are unable to establish sound emotional relationship with a foster family; (3) children who have been so badly disappointed or so deeply hurt by previous foster placement that they are unfit to become, at this point, an integral part of a new family; (4) children presenting such difficult health or behavior problems that they are not acceptable to foster families, and are in need of professional observation and guidance, as well as medical or psychiatric treatment in a controlled environment; (5) large family groups of siblings who do not want to be separated, but who, otherwise, would have to be split up among several foster families; (6) older children and adolescents who are breaking away from their natural families and would tend to break away from the foster family as well; and (7) adolescents who for various reasons arising from within their families need only short-term care and would profit more from the experience of group living during such a period.[27]

Placement of a child in an institution often seems easier for parents to accept than placement in a foster family because it does not threaten to the same degree their own role as parents. Effective treatment of children in an institution requires that the children receive a friendly, home-like reception in a small group according to the cottage system; that medical and, if necessary, psychiatric examination and service be available; and that the individual needs of the children be met by trained casework service. It is also necessary that educational, recreational, and vocational facilities be of a high standard, and that the work in the institution be fully devoted to the development of the children into useful members of the community.

Recently, the special merits of children's institutions have been recognized for certain types of difficult, disturbed, predelinquent children. Institutions have long been used for the care of feeble-minded, blind, deaf, deaf-mute, epileptic, and crippled children in need of special education, and also for delinquent children who are so dangerous to the community and to themselves that placement in a family does not promise success. There is a new trend toward keeping blind and deaf children in their own or in foster families and toward encouraging them to take part in normal

[27] Helen R. Hagan, "Foster Care of Children," *Social Work Year Book* (1957), 267–74; Elizabeth G. Meier, "Foster Care for Children," *Social Work Year Book* (1960), 277–80; Joseph F. Meisels and Martin B. Loeb, "Unanswered Questions about Foster Care," *Social Service Review*, 30, No. 3 (September 1956), 239–59; Wolins, *Selecting Foster Parents*, pp. 12–27; Howard W. Polsky and Daniel S. Claster, *The Dynamics of Residential Treatment* (Chapel Hill: University of North Carolina Press, 1968), pp. 178–84.

activities as much as possible. Furthermore, special classes for handicapped children in public schools are now limited to subjects in which their health makes it impossible for them to learn together with normal children. These developments were necessary because the number of institutions that offer intensive treatment with psychotherapy and skillful therapeutic group living experience for seriously disturbed children and adolescents is not sufficient.[28]

The number of children placed in public and private institutions is still large. The United States Children's Bureau estimated that in 1969, the number of children living in public institutions was 85,000, and it is assumed that about the same number reside in private children's institutions. The median number of children in homes for neglected and dependent children was 46, and the number in institutions for delinquent children was 110.[29] The establishment of small, well-staffed institutions which give individualized, personal care to each child and provide understanding for young and disturbed children seems most desirable.

A special type of care which lies between that given in an institution and a foster family is that provided in a "group home." The group home accommodates between six and ten children or adolescents in a house or spacious apartment. The housemother or houseparents are in a position to let the children participate in home management in the same manner they would be required to in a large family, and the personal contact between the foster parents and children is the same as it is in a family of substantial size. This type of care might well be used as a transition from institutional placement to a foster family or to the return of the child or adolescent to his own family.[30] A new form of living arrangement of adoles-

28 Susanne Schulze, *Creative Group Living in a Children's Institution* (New York: Association Press, 1951), pp. 158–86; Hansel H. Hollingsworth, "The Child-Caring Institution on the Move," *The Annals,* 355 (September 1964), 42–48; Henry W. Maier, *Three Theories of Child Development* (New York: Harper & Row, 1965), pp. 207–40; "Children in Need of Institutional Care," in Joseph S. Roucek, ed., *The Unusual Child* (New York: Philosophical Library, 1962), pp. 161–76; Fritz Redl, *When We Deal with Children* (New York: Free Press, 1966).

29 I. Richard Pearlman and Jack Wiener, *Children Living in Selected Public Institutions* (Washington, D.C.: Children's Bureau, 1950); Joseph H. Reid and Helen R. Hagan, *Residential Treatment of Emotionally Disturbed Children* (New York: Child Welfare League of America, 1952); Gisela Konopka, *Group Work in the Institution* (New York: Whiteside Press, 1954); Joseph L. Reidy, "An Approach to Family-Centered Treatment in a State Institution," *American Journal of Orthopsychiatry,* 32, No. 1 (January 1962), 133–42; Henry W. Maier, "Residential Treatment of Children," *Encyclopedia of Social Work 1965,* pp. 660–65; John Matushima, "Child Welfare: Institutions," *Encyclopedia 1971,* pp. 120–28.

30 Hagan, "Foster Care of Children," 270; F. Fischer, *The Group Home: An Innovation in Child Placement* (New York: Child Welfare League of America, 1952); Haim G. Ginot, *Between Parent and Child* (New York: Macmillan, 1965); Robert Glasser, *Reality Therapy* (New York: Harper & Row, 1965); Ron E. Roberts, *The New Communes: Coming Together in America* (Englewood Cliffs, N.J.: Prentice-Hall, 1971); Gisela Konopka, "Adolescence in the 1970s," *Child Welfare,* 50, No. 10 (October 1971), 553–59.

cents and young adults, "youth communes," is developing as a self-help institution without official sanction.

DAY NURSERIES AND CHILD CARE CENTERS

Day nurseries provide care for children between two and five years of age during the day while their mothers are at work. These nurseries have become necessary because of the increasing employment of women in industry. At first, only custodial care was offered. More recently, however, day nurseries have assumed broader responsibilities for the health and education of the children. These include social casework with parents and relatives, mothers' study groups, and cooperation with children's and family service agencies whenever the children require additional services or special treatment.

Nursery schools are educational institutions for preschool children which attempt to develop the mental, physical, social, and emotional capacities of the children, and to help them form desirable habits and behavior patterns. These schools are not limited to caring for children, but, like the day nurseries, devote considerable effort to parent education through conferences, study groups, and mothers' participation in the nursery school activities and in discussions with the nursery school staff.

When numerous women went into industrial work during World War II, the establishment of day care centers for school children became imperative. Funds were provided by the *Lanham Act* for their organization and operation during the war, and after the war, state subsidies in several states have made the continuation of day care centers possible. Their number has decreased during recent years because children are now accepted in the centers only if the income of their parents does not exceed certain limits, or if their parents are veterans. It seems desirable that day care centers be made a permanent part of child welfare services. They function as valuable substitutes for family care during the time when the mother is not available at home; improve the health, education, and social attitudes of the children; give them a healthy outlet for their energies in play, games, and leisure time activities; and above all, provide an experience in group living (aside from that gained in school) with other children of the same age. The potentialities of day care centers could be increased if trained social caseworkers were employed as intake workers and to establish the individual contacts with the children and their families which prove constructive in such relationships. Until now, few day care centers have been able to use caseworkers for this service, but some have made arrangements with family welfare or children's agencies for members of their staff to establish liaison work as "outposts" in the centers.

SCHOOL LUNCHES

During the Depression, and later during World War II, school lunches were provided in many schools to safeguard the health of children who were fed no breakfast at home. The program was financed partly by the parents, partly by local communities and private social organizations, and was supported by Lanham Act funds. In 1946 the *National School Lunch Act* appropriated federal funds to be administered by the Department of Agriculture, to encourage the proper nutrition of children and, at the same time, to increase domestic consumption of farm products on a permanent basis. Under supervision of the various state departments of education, which finance an increasing proportion of the program, some schools make the lunch available to children regardless of their race, religion, and ability of their parents to pay.[31] Unfortunately, many schools do not provide free school lunches. Only seventeen states have appropriated funds, and some provide so little that the aim of the law is sabotaged.

SCHOOL SOCIAL WORK

Until the end of the nineteenth century, the concept prevailed that children with reasonable physical care would grow into normal, happy adulthood. But scientific investigation of psychological, sociological, and psychiatric principles regarding personality development has discovered the greater importance of the growing-up process and its lasting effects on the total human personality. The introduction of programs of social work in schools was felt to be necessary, almost at the same time, in Boston; Hartford, Connecticut; and New York City in 1906 and 1907. The programs were established under the title "visiting teachers' work," because the difficulties which children had in schools frequently were caused by faulty relationships within the family or environment, or by the child's personal problems which could not be well handled by the teachers in school.

In Boston, the West End Neighborhood Association, a social settlement, and the Women's Education Association, a parent-teacher group, each engaged a social worker, called a "home and school visitor," to assist the schools in overcoming misunderstanding between the families and the schools. In Hartford the director of the Henry Barnard School Clinic, a psychological clinic, requested the employment of a "visiting teacher" to coordinate the work in school, family, and clinic and to prevent serious

31 Recently school lunches have played an essential role in the preschool programs of Head Start. See N. Deming Hoyt, "The School and American Culture," *Social Work*, 9, No. 2 (April 1964), 90–97; and J. L. Frost and G. L. Hawkes, *The Disadvantaged Child*, 2nd ed. (Boston: Houghton Mifflin; 1970), pp. 197–201.

maladjustment of children. In New York two settlement houses, Hartley House and Greenwich Neighborhood House, each assigned a social worker to assist in the home–school relationships of children and to meet the social problems which seemed to cause trouble for children in schools. Other cities followed these examples, and in 1913 Rochester, New York established the first public municipal system of visiting teachers with the requirement that they have social work training.[32]

The program of school social work was greatly strengthened by funds granted by the Commonwealth Fund in New York, in 1921, to serve in the prevention of juvenile delinquency. The program was designed to develop four different, but coordinated, programs: (1) demonstration projects for visiting teachers in thirty communities; (2) child guidance clinics established with the advice of the National Committee of Mental Hygiene; (3) psychiatric studies of difficult, predelinquent, and delinquent children in connection with schools and juvenile courts; and (4) the training of social workers, visiting teachers, and psychologists for competent work in the field of delinquency prevention.

The Commonwealth Fund insisted that the communities, which received allocations for visiting teacher work, share one-third of the expenses during a demonstration period of five years; after that it helped, for another three years, to train personnel to understand behavior problems. After this experience, many cities, including smaller and rural towns, developed school social work programs. The American Association of Visiting Teachers was organized in 1916 and renamed the National Association of School Social Workers in 1945; since 1955, it has been incorporated into the National Association of Social Workers. Some states require the employment of at least one school social worker in each community; others, such as Michigan and California, use state funds to support the school districts or communities in school social work. Four hundred fifty to five hundred cities are estimated to have full-time school social workers, but many more have part-time service.[33]

[32] Lela B. Costin, "Historical Review of School Social Work," *Social Casework,* 50, No. 8 (October 1969), 439–53; Arlien Johnson, *School Social Work* (New York: National Association of Social Workers, 1962).

[33] Mildred Sikkema, "School Social Services," *Social Work Year Book* (1951), 448; Florence Poole, "School Social Services," *Social Work Year Book* (1954), 467–69; Johnson, *School Social Work,* and "Social Work Practice in Schools," *Encyclopedia of Social Work 1965,* pp. 672–79; Horace W. Lundberg, ed., *School Social Work—A Service to Schools* (Washington, D.C.: U.S. Office of Education, 1964); J. M. Berlin, "Working with Children Who Won't Go to School," *Children,* 12, No. 3 (May–June 1965), 109–12; Wallace M. Cornell, "Differential Approach to School Social Work," *Social Work,* 8, No. 4 (October 1963), 76–80; Mary A. Sarvin and Marianne Pennekamp, *Collaboration in School Guidance* (New York: Brunner-Mazel, 1970); Rosemary C. Sarri and Frank F. Maple, eds., *The School in the Community* (Washington, D.C.: National Association of Social Workers, 1973).

The school social worker helps individual children who have difficulties making a satisfactory school adjustment. These difficulties may be expressed in truancy, failure in school subjects, and timid, fearful, withdrawing, or overaggressive behavior. Other indications may be stealing, taking narcotic drugs, fighting, sullenness, resentfulness, inability to get along with other children or to accept the authority of the teacher, or demand for special attention. The classroom teacher will ask for the help of the school social worker for such children. The social worker usually observes the child in class first, and then discusses his problems with the teacher and principal. He learns more about the child's difficulties from school records, the school nurse, the attendance or truant officer, and, above all, from the child himself. Sometimes a discussion with the child changes his attitude. The school social worker, in most instances, contacts the parents after the interview with the child in order to understand his difficulties and to ask for the parents' help to improve the child's adjustment in school.

The school social worker will also interpret the methods and philosophy of the school to the parents to enlist their active cooperation. In this way, he helps the school establish constructive parent–school relationships. He interprets the school program to parent-teacher associations, civic groups, and the community, and participates in faculty meetings, school committees, and group projects. The school social worker maintains an independent role in the interest of the child, so that the child trusts him and does not identify him fully with the school authority. He works with four parties: the child, the family, the school staff, and the community. He attempts to change attitudes of the child, the parents, teachers, and community groups which are detrimental to the adjustment of the child and to the requirements of the school. The maladjusted child is often a serious handicap to other children in his class.

The social worker's functions vary in different communities. Whether he should also serve as a truant or attendance officer is questionable, but the execution of the compulsory school attendance laws is not limited to police, or legal means. It is also debatable how much a school social worker in cooperation with the teacher and the school counselor may effectively prevent the development of mental disorders. Practical experience has shown that the school social worker is frequently successful in solving behavior problems and disciplinary questions. Sometimes he is able, through the ues of other community resources, group work agencies, and family welfare services, to improve the conditions in the family which caused the child's failure or maladjustment in school, and thus change the child's behavior.

The school social worker should have professional training in social work and understanding of the educational process of the school, possess the ability to work with children and adults, and be able to operate in a team relationship with the school faculty. He needs humor, imagination, flexibility, and a good knowledge of the resources of the community.

CHILD LABOR PROTECTION

Children worked in the fields and the trades since the first settlements in America were established. They were cheap, willing, useful workers in a time when labor was scarce. Children represented a large proportion (more than half) of the labor force in this period. The philosophy of the Puritans and Quakers taught that labor was the right way for children to learn farming or craftwork and to become thrifty and industrious as well. During the seventeenth and eighteenth centuries children were apprenticed to a farmer, craftsman, or merchant and lived in the master's family. When the factory system developed in the nineteenth century, parents no longer apprenticed their children but sent them to factories where they earned higher wages.[34]

The first laws limiting daily working hours of young children to ten hours were enacted in some of the northern industrial states, beginning in Massachusetts and Connecticut. At first, child labor laws passed by the states applied to manufacturing shops and textile mills only. The maximum age of the children covered by these laws differed from twelve to sixteen years. None of these statutes, however, required proof of age from working children, nor did they provide for inspectors to enforce the observation of the laws,[35] so they were not effective. Children continued to be employed for long hours, at night, at dangerous work, and even in occupations in restaurants, music halls, bar rooms, and dance halls which damaged their morale.

The early trade unions complained of the excessive hours children had to work, and began before 1860 to demand universal education for them, but they were fighting for their members' benefit as well as for that of children when they attempted to secure a shorter working day.

When industries expanded and the use of machine power increased, after the War between the States, the number of children working in factories and mines grew larger, and the demand for child labor legislation and means to enforce the statutes became stronger. The main arguments

[34] Grace Abbott, *The Child and the State,* I (Chicago: University of Chicago Press, 1938), pp. 189–91; Clarke A. Chambers, *Seedtime of Reform, 1918–1933* (Minneapolis: University of Minnesota Press, 1963), pp. 28–49; Walter I. Trattner, *Crusade for Children* (Chicago: Quadrangle Books, 1971).

[35] Abbott, *The Child and the State,* I. pp. 260, 405. These laws were widely disregarded, since children, parents, and employers were interested in child labor for profit, and fellow employees were either indifferent or afraid to report violations of the laws.

were the health damage to the child, interference with the child's education, and the depressing effect of children's work on the wages of adult workers. Another reason for the demand to restrict child labor in factories was that children took the places of adults, a complaint which was raised particularly in periods of large-scale unemployment during the last two decades of the nineteenth century.

Following the example set by Massachusetts in 1836, the states enacted compulsory school attendance laws, but progress was slow in the face of stubborn opposition both from parents who did not want to lose the income from the labor of their children and from employers who preferred to use cheap child labor. The industrial states began to introduce factory inspectors to supervise and enforce child labor statutes after social reformers, educators, and social workers showed their concern for the damage which excessive child labor did to the health and education of the children. Among the leaders of the movement for the protection of children were Jane Addams, Florence Kelley (who became the first factory inspector in the state of Illinois),[36] Julia Lathrop, Edith and Grace Abbott, and Sophonisba P. Breckinridge. But public opinion was sharply divided over the question of child labor laws, and the influential groups which had opposed this legislation earlier continued to do so for a long time afterwards. By the end of the nineteenth century, most industrial states had enacted child labor legislation which limited the daily hours of work of children and young persons to nine or ten hours, and prohibited work of children during school hours and at night. This usually applied to children employed in manufacturing, mining, and industry. Employment in particularly dangerous occupations was, as a rule, prohibited for children and adolescents under sixteen years of age, whereas child labor laws, in general, applied to children only up to twelve, thirteen, or fourteen years. Children working in agriculture and as domestic servants were not protected at all.

The provisions of these state laws were not well enforced throughout the country, because the staff of factory inspectors was insufficient, and many judges were not disposed to fine parents or employers for violating the laws. Conditions in most southern states were far worse, for they had almost no child labor legislation at all. In several states children could be legally employed in the cotton mills as young as twelve years of age. The exploitation of these children, their poor health, and lack of school attendance led to the organization of the National Child Labor Committee in 1904, under the leadership of the Reverend Edgar Gardner Murphy and Alexander J. McKelway. The committee urged that the employment of the "poor white children" in the southern states be restricted, as it was in

---

[36] See Josephine Goldmark, *Impatient Crusader: Florence Kelley's Life Story* (Urbana: University of Illinois Press, 1953), pp. 78–92.

the industrial states, to a minimum age of fourteen years. The southern mill owners denounced the campaign for a federal child labor law as "the effort of northern agitators to kill the infant industries of the South" and argued that because of the widespread poverty of the southern states, the children were much better off in the mills than in their homes. The Committee is now called the National Committee on Employment of Youth.

Proposals for a federal child labor law, dating from 1906, either failed to pass both houses of Congress or were declared unconstitutional. A constitutional amendment was introduced in 1924, and was passed by both houses of Congress. However, it failed to gain ratification by the necessary number of states.[37] Since that date no further ratification has taken place, so that the amendment has not become effective.

The application of two federal laws, before they were declared unconstitutional, and the campaigns for the child labor amendment, however, had the effect of clarifying in the minds of the public the necessity for protection of children against excessive and damaging labor. Thus they led indirectly to important improvements in the child labor laws of most states and to raising the standards and methods of their operations.

Other social forces that contributed to a decline in child labor were the growth of union strength, a rise in the level of the national income which made education possible for more children, and then the Depression of 1930–35, which encouraged factory owners to dismiss children in order to employ adults who had lost their jobs.

In 1932 industry again started to employ children because they were cheaper labor than adults. After the *National Industrial Recovery Act of 1933*, which limited the employment of children younger than sixteen, was declared unconstitutional, the number of young children employed rose.[38] The *Fair Labor Standards Act* (so-called "Wage Hours Act") of 1938 prohibited the employment (during school hours) of children under sixteen years of age in industries engaged in interstate commerce and producing

[37] The reader will find the decision of the United States Supreme Court in *Hammer* v. *Dagenhart* of June 3, 1918, which declared the child labor law unconstitutional; for the famous dissenting opinion of Chief Justice Oliver Wendell Holmes, see Abbott, *The Child and the State*, I, pp. 493, 495 ff., 502–6. See also Martin Hamburger, "Protection from Participation as Deprivation of Rights," *New Generation*, 53, No. 3 (Summer 1971), 1–6; Dale B. Kloak, "Laboring Youngsters," *New Generation*, 53, No. 3 (Summer 1971), 7–10.

[38] Other federal laws affecting child labor were the *Walsh-Healy Act of 1936*, establishing a minimum age of sixteen years for boys and eighteen years for girls for employment in production under federal contract, and the *Sugar Act* of 1937, which prohibited federal subsidies to sugar growers employing children under fourteen—or children under sixteen longer than eight hours daily. See Rudolph A. Oswald, "Reinvigorate Child Labor Laws," *New Generation*, 53, No. 3 (Summer 1971), 11–14; Robert Taggart III, "The Case for Less Restrictive Regulations," *New Generation*, 53, No. 3 (Summer 1971), 14–19.

goods for shipment to other states, and (at any time) in mining, manufacturing, and processing industries. Agricultural work outside school hours
is not included in this law.

The Child Labor Branch of the Department of Labor is assigned to
enforce the provisions of the Fair Labor Standards Act. Its small staff of
inspectors, however, can only make sample inspections on special complaint,
so that relatively few industries employing child labor are visited. Inspections reveal that a tendency to disregard the federal child labor provisions
is prevalent. The great majority of the violations concern the employment
of children under sixteen without special permit.

Certain progress in state child labor legislation has led to the enactment, in twenty-three states, of a basic sixteen-year minimum age for work
in factories and to the prohibition of employment of young people during
school hours. Twenty-two states do not permit gainful employment for
children under fourteen years during school hours. But only six states protect agricultural labor and domestic services under these provisions.

Eighteen states have not yet enacted adequate child labor legislation,
and the extension of the sixteen-year minimum age to these states is one of
the urgent tasks for future legislation.[39] Another problem which has not
been solved is the extension of child labor protection to agriculture, domestic services, street trades, and industrial homework. Agriculture still relies
most extensively on the employment of children. In California, New
Jersey, New York, Connecticut, and Hawaii special laws for the control
of child labor in agriculture have been established, but in the other states
much remains to be done. At present, in view of the high rate of unemployment, it seems necessary to create job opportunities for adolescents that will
enable them to develop skills for positions in the labor force, part-time
while in school. The private sector of our economy is unlikely to provide
such jobs; thus public agencies must create them. A flexible strategy of
balancing protection with work opportunities is needed.

The exemption of agricultural work from the child labor provisions of
most states causes children of sharecroppers and low-income farm families
to be kept from school by farm work in rural areas and permits six-year-
old children to work as cotton pickers. The enforcement of school attendance laws often is inadequate. The federal child labor law does not protect
children employed in agricultural work, either during the long summer

---

[39] Since the Fair Labor Standards Act does not cover intrastate industries,
children under sixteen are frequently employed in retail stores, bakeries, garages,
beauty parlors, repair shops, hotels, restaurants, motels, bowling alleys, theaters, on
merry-go-rounds, in offices, and domestic services without federal protection and often
without state protection. Walter I. Trattner, "The Fight Against Child Labor,"
Welfare in Review, 8, No. 5 (October 1970), 17–26; Eli E. Cohen, "Protection vs.
Opportunity," *New Generation,* 53, No. 3 (Summer 1971), 24–28.

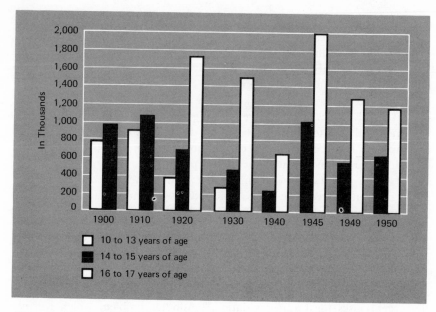

Figure 5.   Employed Children and Minors in the United States, 1900–1950

vacation or after school hours. These children may have to work at an early age, sometimes for long hours under the hot sun and occasionally in backbreaking, monotonous labor. This is true not only for children of migratory farm workers whose miserable conditions frequently arouse public concern, but also for other children of farm families, though their exploitation may be less known.

The selling and distribution of newspapers by small boys, classified as "independent little merchants," is of questionable value as business experience. Twenty-seven states have no regulations of hours and working conditions for newsboys, and only four have adequate protective legislation. Newspapers profit from the "little merchant system" by making the children responsible for uncollectible subscription rates and by escaping the payment of workmen's compensation contributions which would be due if the children were employed. Thus the children are not protected if they are injured on their jobs.

Changing economic conditions and technical progress induce employers to prefer high school graduates when there is no shortage of workers. Children who leave school early have little chance for satisfactory jobs and advancement. Uniform protection of children against damaging child labor, enforcement of compulsory education laws, federal aid to elementary and secondary schools, and scholarships to help students complete their secondary education will assist in educating children to become responsible citizens.

SELECTED BIBLIOGRAPHY

ABBOTT, GRACE, *The Child and the State,* I. Chicago: University of Chicago Press, 1938.

ADDAMS, JANE, *Spirit of Youth and the City Streets.* New York: Macmillan, 1900.

AMOS, WILLIAM E., and JEAN D. GREMBS, *Counseling the Disadvantaged Youth.* Englewood Cliffs, N.J.: Prentice-Hall, 1969.

BAYLOR, E. M., and E. D. MONACHESI, *Rehabilitation of Children: The Theory and Practice of Child Placement.* New York: Harper, 1939.

BEALER, ROBERT C., and FERN K. WILLITS, "Rural Youth," *The Annals,* 338 (November 1961), 63–69.

BEREITER, CARL, and SIEGFRIED ENGELMAN, *Teaching Disadvantaged Children in the Pre-school.* Englewood Cliffs, N.J.: Prentice-Hall, 1966.

BERGER, BENNETT M., *Looking for America: Essays on Youth, Suburbia and Other Obsessions.* Englewood Cliffs, N.J.: Prentice-Hall, 1971.

BERNARD, JESSIE, ed., "Teen-age Culture," *The Annals,* 338 (November 1961), 1–136.

BIRMINGHAM, JOHN, *Our Time Is Now: Notes from the High School Underground.* New York: Praeger, 1970.

BURMEISTER, EVA, *Forty-five in the Family: The History of a Home for Children.* New York: Columbia University Press, 1949.

————, *Tough Times and Tender Moments in Child Care Work.* New York: Columbia University Press, 1967.

BURTON, LINDY, *Vulnerable Children.* New York: Schocken Books, 1968.

BUXBAUM, EDITH, *Troubled Children in a Troubled World.* New York: International Universities Press, 1970.

CAPLAN, GERALD, ed., *Prevention of Mental Disorders in Children.* New York: Basic Books, 1961.

CAPLAN, GERALD, and SERGE LEBOVICE, *Adolescence: Psychosocial Perspectives.* New York: Basic Books, 1969.

COLES, ROBERT, *Erik H. Erikson: The Growth of His Work.* Boston: Little, Brown, 1970.

DENZIN, NORMAN K., et al., "Wednesday's Child: Drugging and Schooling," *Transaction,* 8, No. 9 (August 1971), 28–72.

DU BOIS, V. E. B., "Florence Kelley," *Social Work,* 11, No. 4 (October 1966), 98–100.

ERIKSON, ERIK H., *Childhood and Society.* New York: W. W. Norton, 1950.

FREDERICKSEN, HAZEL, *The Child and His Welfare,* 2nd ed. San Francisco: W. H. Freeman, 1957.

FRIEDLANDER, WALTER, and EARL DEWEY MYERS, *Child Welfare in Germany Before and After Naziism.* Chicago: University of Chicago Press, 1940.

GERSITZ, JAMES, and SYLVIA GLICKMAN, "Solving Deficiencies in Services to Unmarried Parents," *Public Welfare,* 27, No. 3 (July 1969), 261–65.

GINZBERG, ELI, ed., *Values and Ideals of American Youth.* New York: Columbia University Press, 1961.

GOLDMARK, JOSEPHINE, *Impatient Crusader: Florence Kelley's Life Story.* Urbana: University of Illinois Press, 1953.

GORDON, HENRIETTA L., *Casework Services for Children*. Boston: Houghton Mifflin, 1956.

HEALY, WILLIAM, et al., *Reconstructing Behavior in Youth*. New York: Alfred A. Knopf, 1929.

HELFER, RAY E., and C. HENRY KEMPE, *The Battered Child*. Chicago: University of Chicago Press, 1968.

HILL, JOHN P., and JEV SHELTON, *Adolescent Development and Behavior*. Englewood Cliffs, N.J.: Prentice-Hall, 1971.

HUTCHINSON, DOROTHY, *In Quest of Foster Parents*. New York: Columbia University Press, 1940.

KADUSHIN, ALFRED, *Child Welfare Services*. New York: Macmillan, 1967.

KAHN, ALFRED J., ed., *Planning Community Services for Children in Trouble*. New York: Columbia University Press, 1963.

KENISTON, KENNETH, *The Uncommitted: Alienated Youth in American Society*. New York: Harcourt Brace, 1965.

KONOPKA, GISELA, *The Adolescent Girl in Conflict*. Englewood Cliffs, N.J.: Prentice-Hall, 1966.

———, *Therapeutic Group Work with Children*. Minneapolis: University of Minnesota Press, 1949.

LANDRETH, CATHERINE, *The Psychology of Early Childhood*. New York: Alfred A. Knopf, 1958.

LEWIS, OSCAR, *The Children of Sanchez*. New York: Random House, 1961.

LUMPKIN, KATHARINE DuPRE, and DOROTHY DOUGLAS WOLFF, *Child Workers in America*. New York: McBride, 1937.

MAAS, HENRY S., and RICHARD E. ENGLER, Jr., *Children in Need of Parents*. New York: Columbia University Press, 1959.

MacLENNAN, BERYCE W., and NAOMI FELSENFELD, *Group Counseling and Psychotherapy with Adolescents*. New York: Columbia University Press, 1968.

McWILLIAMS, CAREY, *Factories in the Field*. Boston: Little, Brown, 1939.

MAIER, HENRY W., *Three Theories of Child Development*. New York: Harper & Row, 1965.

MALONE, CHARLES, *The Drifters: Children of Disorganized Lower Class Families*. Boston: Little, Brown, 1967.

MANNING, PETER K., and MARCELLO TRUZZI, eds., *Youth and Sociology*. Englewood Cliffs, N.J.: Prentice-Hall, 1972.

MEYER, ELIZABETH G., "Child Neglect," in Nathan E. Cohen ed., *Social Work and Social Problems*. New York: National Association of Social Workers, 1964, pp. 153–200.

MULFORD, ROBERT M., et al., *In the Interest of Children*. Denver: Humane Association, 1968.

MULFOLD, ROBERT M., and HANS HOEL, *Protective-Preventive Services*. Denver: Humane Association, 1970.

PLANK, EMMA N., *Working with Children in Hospitals*. Cleveland: Western Reserve University Press, 1962.

RAINER, JOSEPH D., *Family and Mental Health Problems in a Deaf Population*. New York: Columbia University Press, 1963.

REDL, FRITZ, and DAVID WINEMAN, *The Aggressive Child*. New York: Free Press, 1957.

REID, JOSEPH H., and HELEN R. HAGAN, *Residential Treatment of Emotionally Disturbed Children*. New York: Child Welfare League of America, 1952.

RIESE, HERTHA, *Heal the Hurt Child*. Chicago: University of Chicago Press, 1962.

SARVIS, MARY A., and MARIANNE PENNEKAMP, *Collaboration in School Guidance.* New York: Brunner-Mazel, 1970.

SCHULZE, SUSANNE, *Creative Group Living in Children's Institutions.* New York: Association Press, 1951.

SHAPIRO, MICHAEL, *A Study of Adoption Practice,* 3 vols. New York: Child Welfare League of America, 1956, 1957.

SMITH, WILLIAM CARLSON, *The Stepchild.* Chicago: University of Chicago Press, 1953.

THURSTON, HENRY W., *The Dependent Child.* New York: Columbia University Press, 1930.

VINCENT, CLARK E., *Unmarried Mothers.* New York: Free Press, 1961.

WEISSMAN, IRVING, et al., *Guardianship: A Way of Fulfilling Public Responsibility for Children.* Washington, D.C.: U.S. Children's Bureau, 1949.

WITMER, HELEN LELAND, and RUTH KOTINSKY, *Personality in the Making.* New York: Harper, 1953.

WOLFF, SULA, *Children Under Stress.* Baltimore: Penguin Books, 1969.

WOLINS, MARTIN, "Group Care: Friend or Foe?" *Social Work,* 14, No. 1 (January 1969), 35–53.

————, *Selecting Foster Parents: The Ideal and the Reality.* New York: Columbia University Press, 1963.

YOUNG, LEONTINE, *Out of Wedlock.* New York: McGraw-Hill, 1954.

————, *Wednesday's Children: A Study of Child Neglect and Abuse.* New York: McGraw-Hill, 1964.

ZALBA, SERAPIO R., "The Abused Child," *Social Work,* 11, No. 4 (October 1966), 3–16, and *Social Work,* 12, No. 1 (January 1967), 70–79.

ZEITZ, DOROTHY, *Child Welfare—Principles and Methods.* New York: John Wiley, 1969.

14

public
health
services

The notion of welfare extends beyond survival to a broader concept of well-being and "the good life," an essential element of which is freedom from disease. Public health and medical care, mental health and psychiatric care are intrinsic to social welfare. Within the field of social welfare education we consider two components in the development of an effective health system. The first is a theoretical analysis of the intricate connection between social forces and individual biological processes. Without such an understanding our efforts to combat disease would be clumsy and often misdirected. The second is the practical matter of the effective delivery of preventive health and medical care services, for which social work skills are needed.

The topic of mental health is often dealt with separately from public health, but the two are closely related. The dimensions of mental health are well understood through the public health approach because the latter is a multidisciplinary and preventive focus. It includes educational techniques and concepts from the social and behavioral sciences, in addition to the epidemiological core of public health practice. Consequently in this chapter, to better describe the links, mental health is discussed concurrently with public health. In Chapters 15 and 16 medical and psychiatric care are discussed separately, to facilitate presentation of the information.

Although it has not always been true in the United States, good health is now considered a basic right of every citizen. Our health system is gradually being transformed, albeit unevenly and with much reluctance, to accommodate those who because of age, social class, race, or handicapped condition would not otherwise have access to adequate health services.

One of the key issues confronting the formulation of health and medical care policy in the United States is the question whether "health promotion and protection" should take priority over or for that matter assume equal status with the treatment of illness. This split in health values was already articulated in the ancient world, illustrated by the Greek myth of the goddess Hygeia and the god Aesculapius. Hygeia, whose Greek name means "health," symbolized a "healthy mind in a healthy body," *mens sana in corpore sano,* achieved by leading a "hygienic" life in accordance with the laws of nature. An active cult worshipped this goddess until the fifth century B.C., when the fame of Aesculapius began to achieve dominance. Aesculapius was known as a healer and was famous for both his surgical and medicinal cures. As his popularity spread through the ancient world, Hygeia was gradually derogated to the role of one of his handmaidens. Today, Hygeia is still a handmaiden in our health system. The treatment of illness (medical care) receives the greater attention and share of resources. Hygeia is always appealing but is still given second place to the magic potions of Aesculapius.[1]

The concepts of the *promotion of health* and the *prevention of illness* are operationalized through that part of the health system called public health. The practice of public health has been part of society at least since biblical times. Each historical era has had its concept of disease and a complementary notion of what should be done to eradicate it.[2] While significant progress has been made over the centuries in understanding disease and developing measures to combat it, less progress has been made in understanding its counterpart—health, and how to further it. Health is still a poorly defined idea.

1 Rene Dubos, *The Mirage of Health* (New York: Anchor Books, 1959), pp. 113–43.

2 John J. Hanlon, *Principles of Public Health Administration* (St. Louis: C. V. Mosby, 1969), pp. 14–43.

DEFINITION OF HEALTH

Medicine traditionally defines health as the absence of gross illness. The medical student is concerned with abnormality and pathology. In the absence of any indices of disease, the patient is regarded as healthy. Claude Bernard's concept of "dynamic equilibrium" within the internal body environment and Walter Cannon's concept of "homeostasis of body systems" suggest, however, that health is a complex state, just as is illness.[3] Some implications of this complexity are suggested by the question,"health for what purpose?" Different tasks require different qualities of health. For example, the jobs of college professor and coal miner require different physical and mental capacities, both related to health. The physical requirements for living in an Antarctic outpost differ from those required for a Mediterranean climate. When we consider health as more than a simple absence of illness—that is, a positive state of well-being—the economic and social conditions of the individual and his community are central. An ingrown toenail may be debilitating to a society matron, but chronic dysentery may be considered normal for a migrant agricultural laborer.

The World Health Organization says that "health is a state of complete physical, mental and social well-being and not merely the absence of disease or infirmity."[4] This concept of health, then, is not strictly physiological. It includes factors other than pathology and suggests a latitude in definition from country to country. The very idea of "public health medicine" implies a juncture between the natural and social sciences. While it may employ methods from the natural sciences, its goals are social. The aim of public health as a field is to promote health, prevent disease, and treat illness to maintain or assist individuals in their adjustment to society.

A useful definition of public health is offered by C. Winslow:

Public Health is the Science and Art of (1) preventing disease, (2) prolonging life, and (3) promoting health and efficiency through organized community effort for

(a) the sanitation of the environment,

(b) the control of communicable infections,

(c) the education of the individual in personal hygiene,

(d) the organization of medical and nursing services for the early diagnosis and preventive treatment of disease, and

---

[3] See for example Claude Bernard, *An Introduction to the Study of Experimental Medicine* (New York: Macmillan, 1927); and Walter B. Cannon, *Bodily Changes in Pain, Hunger, Fear and Emotional Excitement* (New York: Appleton, 1929).

[4] Constitution of the World Health Organization.

(e) the development of the social machinery to insure everyone a standard of living adequate for the maintenance of health, so organizing these benefits as to enable every citizen to realize his birthright of health and longevity.[5]

HISTORY OF PUBLIC HEALTH EFFORTS

Although Winslow's definition dates back fifty years, it remains useful today because the explicit concepts of environment and community effort are germane to current public health work. These ideas were not new in Winslow's time; they can be traced to ancient societies.

The concepts of community contagion and preventive dietary practices are found in the Bible. Health and dietary laws were strictly adhered to by the entire community. In contrast to the Hebrews, who applied what can be considered preventive practices for religious and theological reasons, the Greeks practiced personal hygiene for the sake of man himself. Hippocrates, the father of medicine, was the first to point out that the causes of common and frequent epidemics were related to man, his culture, and his physical environment. The word *epidemic* comes from the Greek *epi*, "upon," and *demos*, "people," a disease falling upon a specific group of people at a specific time. Hippocrates also pointed out that epidemics were not sporadic events, attacking people at random. Different segments of the community were affected by different types of disease, some segments being more vulnerable to attack than others. He recognized that factors such as age, climate, economic position, and the geographic location of the homes in the community affected susceptibility to illness. He theorized that illness was caused when the four bodily humors—blood, phlegm, black bile, and yellow bile—were attacked by the four environmental elements—earth, water, fire, and air. While Hippocrates was not able to gain specific insights into causal factors of disease, his linking together of man, his life style, and environmental elements still provides the foundation of public health knowledge and practice.[6]

The Romans initiated the practice of public health as a community system. Their contribution was not so much in the area of enhancing our understanding of the factors causing ill health, as in their skills in public health, engineering, and construction administration. The Romans built a large aqueduct and sewer system, the necessary foundation of any community's public health effort. The division of Rome into administrative districts to supervise the operation of these essential systems also represented significant progress. The Romans also were concerned with other potentially harmful

---

[5] C. Winslow, "The Untilled Field of Public Health," *Modern Medicine*, 2 (March 1950), 183.

[6] Dubos, *The Mirage of Health.*

factors such as foul air, hazardous constructions, decaying foods, littered streets, houses of prostitution, and public bath houses.[7]

As Europe entered the Dark Ages, the achievements in public health practices within the Roman Empire were lost. Only in the monasteries were rules of personal hygiene and environmental health practices strictly observed. The medieval towns which developed at the end of the Dark Ages grew in an unplanned manner. Houses were built close together with walls that circled the towns for protection. Living standards were low, sanitation was poor, and ventilation, light, and nutrition were inadequate. Little wonder that the populace was subject to rampant epidemics. In the Middle Ages Europe suffered wave after wave of major epidemics. According to Hanlon, during the fourteenth century bubonic plague epidemic Europe lost 25,000,000 lives.[8]

Every society attempts to explain and thereby control catastrophies such as plagues. Some cultures attribute them to the wrath of a god; others blame the devil; sometimes astrology is the explanatory source. Early theorists developed the concept of contagion, but could not carry it further except to advocate quarantine as a method of control. This was first practiced in Dubrovnic in 1377. A group known as the Miasmists believed that the spread of disease was caused by the quality of the physical environment. They believed that foul air emitted from the earth spread disease, and that by cleaning the environment they could bring health back to the community.[9]

The great epidemics of Europe and the United States lasted until the end of the nineteenth century. It is interesting that the tide of human destruction was brought to a rapid decline through practice based on the theory of the Miasmists. Although this theory is basically incorrect, the approach espoused by public health leaders in controlling disease was essentially effective. Without knowledge of the specific causes of the major diseases, this approach to disease control significantly reduced death from typhus, malaria, cholera, and typhoid. The world had to await the development of bacteriology for an explanation of their specific causes.

The Industrial Revolution intensified the health problems of the urban population. Towns grew into cities, and the overcrowded housing and poor sanitation only made the larger urban communities increasingly unsalutary. (See Chapter 10 on housing.) For the first time national governments in Europe and America became concerned about the health of their citizens. It became apparent to government that mass illness meant a reduction of economic productivity and contributed to general social instability. The

---

[7] Hanlon, *Principles of Public Health Administration,* 17.

[8] Ibid.

[9] Ibid.

growing industries depended on a healthy working force, and high productivity was the basis of their revenue and strength. Consequently, larger units of government than the cities became involved in the effort to reduce disease.

The Sanitation Movement

During the 1830s, while studying the administration of the Elizabethan Poor Laws for the British Parliament, Edwin Chadwick was struck by the unhealthy living environment of the poor and laboring classes (see Chapter 2, pages 22-25.) At the time a major cholera epidemic broke out. In his travels throughout England Chadwick saw enough poor-quality dwellings and slum conditions to indicate a direct connection between an unsanitary environment and rampant disease. The 1842 document resulting from his study, *Report on the Sanitary Condition of the Labouring Population and on the Means of its Improvement,* became the basis for *The Public Health Act of 1848.* This Act was the first major attempt on a national basis to improve the healthfulness of the human environment. It was enabling legislation which gave broad health powers to local authorities. Following suit, many American states and cities established boards of health. However, the scope of their effectiveness was limited because they were not always able to control the spread of disease in the surrounding geographic areas. Not until 1879 did Congress establish the National Health Board. While this board has since undergone many changes, it was the first major step by the federal government in preventive medicine.[10]

Breakthroughs in scientific knowledge and the development of technology in the nineteenth century led to the discovery of the specific causes of major communicable diseases. Microorganisms could be seen with the new higher-powered microscopes. Inoculation techniques were developed to protect the individual from harmful bacilli. As more was learned about the transmission of disease, it was recognized that it is usually more than the presence of a specific organism which causes the outbreak of an epidemic. More often, mass outbreaks of illness result from a disturbance of the delicate balance between the host, the agent, and the environment.

From the turn of the century to the present, public health history is replete with triumphant breakthroughs in man's ability to control major crippling or killing diseases. Progress has been swift, and today immunization is such an accepted practice in Western culture that it receives little public attention. Only when there is a breakdown in controls and specific disease

[10] Lenor S. Goerke and Ernest L. Stebbins, *Mustard's Introduction to Public Health,* 5th ed. (New York: Macmillan, 1968).

rates rise (as is currently true with venereal disease, cholera, and drug abuse) does the general public become alarmed and aware of the existence of public health.

THE PRACTICE OF PREVENTION IN PUBLIC HEALTH

Over the past half-century, as public health has become more sophisticated about causes of epidemics and the measures necessary to maintain community health, it has taken on a broad interdisciplinary approach. To accomplish its goal, it uses a broad array of technical knowledge. The first specialists in public health were those with medical and biological knowledge such as the sanitarian, public health nurse, virologist, epidemiologist, and occupational and industrial health specialists; now, however, the health team also includes specialists in the social sciences: social worker, anthropologist, health educator, sociologist, and social psychologist.

As a result of public health efforts, there has been in this century a significant change in the leading causes of death. While in the nineteenth century acute infectious diseases were responsible for a majority of deaths, in the United States chronic diseases now claim the majority of lives. In 1900 the ten highest causes of death included four groups of infectious diseases: influenza and pneumonia, diarrhea and enteritis, diphtheria, and meningitis. By 1950 the only acute infectious disease on the list was influenza and pneumonia.[11] As public health technology has progressed in controlling rampant disease, more attention and commensurately more resources have been devoted to the chronic diseases and other health hazards.

Public health has waged an aggressive war against the major illnesses, organizing one campaign after another to eradicate disease. Through research efforts we are beginning to understand, however, that the etiology and treatment of such problems as heart disease, pathology of the digestive system, cancer, and tuberculosis involve social, cultural, and psychological factors. These factors range from cultural patterns affecting whole groups of people to psychological stress phenomena affecting the individual. The conquest of disease and disability on the part of public health now means looking beyond the responsible microorganisms and physical environment to the social environment and emotional life of the population. In this area social work knowledge and skills have found a place in the scheme of public health. Tuberculosis, alcoholism, suicide, accidents, prematurity, and drug abuse are major health problems with important social components; they can also be considered major social problems.

[11] Hugh R. Leavell and E. G. Clark, *Textbook of Preventive Medicine* (New York: McGraw-Hill, 1955), p. 149.

It is instructive to contrast the practice of public health in the United States to that of social welfare. Social welfare activities generally proceed through amelioration, rehabilitation, or remediation. In only a few problem areas such as delinquency and child guidance has social work attempted to apply the concept of prevention. In public health practice, however, prevention is given the highest priority; it is conceptualized as a continuum, with absolute prevention at one end and rehabilitation (the prevention of further disability) at the other. Leavell and Clark divide this continuum into the following five levels.

1. *Health Promotion.* The procedures employed in promoting health are not directed at any particular disease or disorder but serve to further general health and well-being. Health education and motivation are vitally important in this connection. Procedures which promote health include a good standard of nutrition which is adjusted to the various developmental phases of life, taking into account rapid growth and development in infancy and early childhood, the physiologic changes that are associated with adolescence, the extra demands of pregnancy, and the variations in nutritional requirements of the aged as compared with those of the young adult.

2. *Specific Protection.* This is prevention in its strictest sense and comprises measures applicable to a particular disease or group of diseases in order to intercept the causes before they involve man, such causes being related to the agent, the host himself, or the environment.

3. *Early Recognition and Prompt Treatment.* The obvious objectives of early recognition and prompt treatment are (a) to prevent spread to others if the disease is a communicable one; (b) to cure or arrest the disease process; (c) to prevent complications or sequelae; (d) to shorten the period of disability. The foundation of the ideal control program is case finding in the early stage of disease, when treatment is most effective.

4. *Disability Limitation.* Under this head is included prevention or delaying of the consequences of clinically advanced or nonpreventable or noncurable disease.

5. *Rehabilitation.* This is more than stopping a disease process; it is the prevention of complete disability after anatomic and physiologic changes are no longer reversible, and its positive objective is to return the affected individual to a useful place in society.[12]

In strategic allocation of manpower and other resources, more efficiency is achieved and less suffering occurs if prevention is achieved at the first level, then the second, and so forth.

The preceding conceptual scheme is applicable to all diseases, whether physical, social, or psychological in origin. We know too little about some diseases to accomplish anything except at the rehabilitative level. But with others we can work at each level. Of course, this is not a static condition; it changes with advances in knowledge and technology. Barely two decades

[12] Ibid., pp. 50–51.

ago we knew about poliomyelitis only enough to help a victim survive the acute illness crisis and then to rehabilitate him. Now, through the use of Salk vaccine, we are able to provide specific protection from the polio virus. Earlier in this century general paresis (syphilis), often requiring prolonged hospitalization, was a major source of mental disorder. Untreated, it is a progressive disease. Now we know enough about the disease to apply preventive measures at the first four levels, and to do some good even at the fifth level. But in this case, as in many others, the available knowledge is not fully used for the benefit of society. The United States is experiencing a major national venereal disease epidemic. It is at the level of changing attitudes toward health and health care that much prevention can take place.

From the outset public health has differed from social work in its orientation toward service to the community rather than service to the individual. In social work practice the greatest effort is placed on individualizing the client for the purpose of care or treatment, and it is frequently suggested that this is the best way to help the individual change. Public health, however, thinks, plans, and operates on the basis of aggregates. It is population-oriented. In practice this means that the individual is considered part of a group which may be at the risk of becoming ill. This is a principal feature in the planning and delivery of preventive health services. This does not mean that the individual is ignored in public health programs—there are many individualized services, such as those provided by public health nurses. Furthermore, in recent years there has been a growing trend for public health services to employ social workers to better serve individuals and families who need preventive attention. Social workers bring to the practice of public health practical knowledge of the dynamics of individual and family functioning which can enhance the total practice of public health.[13]

The idea of preventive psychiatry germinated in the child guidance movement, which received its major impetus in 1922 when the Commonwealth Fund financed eight experimental clinics. The aim of the movement was to study the sources of delinquency and to find other means of dealing with it than to incarcerate the youthful offender. The movement aimed mainly at providing preventive measures for children identified as potential delinquents. Pressing demand for services, however, gradually transformed the Child Guidance Clinics from their focus on prevention to a focus on treatment after the fact.[14]

As in public health in general, prevention in the field of mental health depends on controlling the community factors which affect the emotional

[13] See *Public Health Concepts in Social Work Education*, proceedings of a seminar at Princeton University, 4–9 March 1962 (New York: Council on Social Work Education, 1962).

[14] Martin Nacman, "Social Workers in Mental Health Services," *Encyclopedia of Social Work 1971*, p. 824.

health of the individual or group.[15] This requires an understanding of the variety of stresses, internal and external, predictable and unpredictable, which affect adaptation. At a time of a life crisis effective preventive measure can often be applied. A life crisis may be caused by the loss of a family member, physical dismemberment, or a role change. Prevention of mental illness is achieved by a successful resolution of the crisis. Personal change to reinstate the former equilibrium is a major goal of the intervention. While crisis is an event affecting the single individual, the public health approach is to locate and help specific subpopulations exposed to crisis situations, for example, individuals undergoing rapid or forced geographic relocation. Effective efforts can be made to prepare such groups to cope with the crises. The approach relies heavily on techniques of mental health education and "anticipatory guidance" as a way of preparing an individual in advance for a major life change.[16]

An important contribution to preventive psychiatry, resulting from a study of families under acute stress, explained how individuals reorganized their emotional and social perspectives to cope with changing life circumstances.[17] The study demonstrated that a variety of prophylaxic measures can be taken either to prevent the negative effects of serious crises on individuals, or to limit the degree of their severity.

Mental health preventive measures have always been the stepchild, Hygeia, of the psychiatric services. Only with the enactment of the *Community Mental Health Centers Act of 1963* did the need for preventive mental health services receive the endorsement of the federal government. Part of the impetus for this step was the agonizing recognition of the extent of mental illness in America, the abominable conditions in most of our mental hospitals, and the great cost of mental illness to the country. From 1955 to 1961 the national Joint Commission on Mental Illness and Health had met to analyze and evaluate the problem of mental illness in America and to develop recommendations for effective legislation to reduce its incidence and consequences. The Joint Commission's final report[18] and the Mental Health Act of 1963 did not go far enough, however, in promoting the deployment of preventive services. This was partly because we still have in-

15 Paul V. Lemkau, *Mental Health in Public Health,* 2nd ed. (New York: McGraw-Hill, 1955), pp. 11–15.

16 See Gerald Caplan, *Principles of Preventive Psychiatry* (New York: Basic Books, 1964). Anticipatory guidance techniques were well demonstrated in the Peace Corps. Trainees were given assistance in anticipating the stresses they would be exposed to, before being placed in overseas assignments.

17 Eric Lindemann and L. Dawes, "The Use of Psychoanalytic Constructs in Preventive Psychiatry," *Psychoanalytic Study of the Child* (New York: International Universities Press, 1952), VII, pp. 429–48.

18 Joint Commission on Mental Illness and Health, *Action for Mental Health* (New York: Basic Books, 1961).

sufficient knowledge on the specific etiology of emotional disorders and insufficient ability to control the known factors to demonstrate with confidence our capacity to "prevent." This has undoubtedly made it harder for the mental health field to demand a larger portion of the tax dollar.

PUBLIC HEALTH METHODS

It is necessary to monitor health in the community in order to promote health. Public health has employed vital statistics as its primary method of measuring the extent of illness and the effectiveness of programs of prevention. Rates of specific illness per hundred-thousand of the population are the standard measure. Two types of rates are used: incidence rates and prevalence rates. The *incidence rate* measures the *amount of new illness* occurring at any specific period; the *prevalence rate* measures the *total amount of illness* extant in a population at any one period.[19] By monitoring changes in incidence and prevalence rates, public health personnel can measure the effectiveness of their programs. Rate increases indicate that something has caused an imbalance in the previous equilibrium in the community's health. Statistics collected on a demographic and geographic basis reveal the subpopulation most affected by the outbreak. The subpopulation may be defined, for example, by age, social class, occupation, eating habits, or ethnic group. Often, identifying such a subpopulation becomes the first step in locating the chain of factors which cause the increase in a particular disease. Intervention may then occur at various levels to interrupt the sequence of events causing the illness and affecting the mortality rates. We know in advance that certain subpopulations have a high risk of incurring specific illnesses. We can therefore plan a prevention program to lessen the risk. For example, an analysis of the incidence rates of premature births in most urban areas will show that the subpopulation which contributes disproportionately to this condition is composed of poor, young black women living in ghetto areas. Major contributing factors are poor nutrition, lack of prenatal medical care, and the generally poor physical environment. The public health approach to prevention in this case is an aggressive health education program which encourages an adequate diet and periodic medical checkups, as well as improved housing. Proper diet and medical care often depend on the presence of a good system of welfare services. Hence, public health programs need to be well coordinated with local social services.

The same kind of procedure is useful in dealing with mental health problems. Suppose that the rate of attempted suicide has risen in the community. Analysis of the statistics shows a cluster of suicide attempts in one

---

[19] E. Gurney Clark, "An Epidemiologic Approach to Preventive Medicine," in Leavell and Clark, eds., *Textbook of Preventive Medicine,* pp. 28–64.

geographic area. Further analysis shows that many victims are wives of naval personnel, living near a naval base, whose husbands are away much of the time. Through the use of crisis theory, public health officials understand that the loss of their husbands, although temporary, has caused a change in their social roles, enhancing their dependency needs and resulting in feelings of isolation and depression. Concomitantly, there is excessive drinking. An effective community prevention program should provide group counseling and individualized casework services for these women. A variety of other activities should be planned in advance by the military or civilian mental health authorities to limit their feelings of dependency and isolation and prepare them for this difficult period in their lives. In both the preceding examples of high-risk populations, one of the major factors in the problem is social. Effective prevention requires intervention on a group basis.[20]

We have insufficient knowledge to explain adequately the etiology of most mental disorders. After decades of research, little insight has been gained into the specific origins of such conditions as schizophrenia and manic-depressive psychosis. In fact, many in the field now consider present diagnostic labels to be meaningless.[21] How, then, can mental health personnel reduce the rate of mental disorder in the way public health workers reduce diesase rates? We do know, at least, that the social and physical environment are closely linked with the incidence and prevalence of mental illness. Numerous studies have shown that social class, cultural attributes, minority group status, and their corollaries, such as housing and living conditions, existing social services, and unacceptable social roles, are associated with the rates of mental disorder. Individual life experiences like severe physical illness, social and physical deprivation, loss of parents, and neglect increase the likelihood of mental disorder. The Midtown Manhattan Study found that a series of these factors or events in various combination render an individual even more vulnerable to emotional illness than a single such factor or episode.[22] Prevention should then consist of minimizing the occurrence of these events, and/or mitigating the circumstances in which they happen. In addition, we need to provide those basic sociocultural experiences which promote human growth. In doing so, we will be contributing to prevention in the best way we now know how. As Bernard Bloom has pointed out, it was during the sanitation movement when the environment was

[20] See Howard Parad, *Crisis Intervention, Selected Readings* (New York: Family Service Association of America, 1965), p. 368. This volume provides excellent coverage of the theoretical practice aspects of crisis intervention.

[21] For a clear explanation of this problem, see Bruce P. Dohrenwend and Barbara Snell Dohrenwend, "The Problem of Validity in Field Studies of Psychological Disorder," *Social Status and Psychological Disorder: A Causal Inquiry* (New York: John Wiley, 1969), Chap. 7.

[22] T. S. Langner and S. T. Michael, *Life Stress and Mental Health* (New York: Free Press, 1963).

cleaned up that the greatest amount of progress was made in stopping the spread of disease.[23] This was before the specific microorganisms which cause illness had been identified. Perhaps mental health personnel, in their broad community activities to improve the psychosocial environment, can be successful in reducing rates of mental disorder, even before we fully understand the complicated biosociopsychological dynamics.

Public health is a field with continually changing priorities. As success is achieved in dealing with one problem, increasing efforts are applied to others which before seemed to be less important. Furthermore, as medical problems are solved, unforeseen social problems often arise. We now have sufficient knowledge of about ten of the twenty major causes of death in the United States to prolong life. However, much more is known about prevention of these illnesses than is being used. If the cult of Hygeia were more ascribed to today, with emphasis on more exercise, better eating habits, the elimination of smoking, and safer automobiles and highways, the death rate from heart diseases, cancer, and accidents would undoubtedly decrease. But death rates from other causes would rise. The result of a highly successful public health campaign to eliminate major chronic illness would be the prolongation of life, but certainly not the elimination of death. The idealist as well as the cynic may come to see this as a mixed blessing. Already the highly developed countries are experiencing a crisis in medical care, welfare, and housing programs because of the longer life span of their populations. While good medical care keeps individuals physically alive, the social, emotional, and economic life of many of the aged is far less desirable than most would choose. The changing structure of the family and the local group has done little to make advanced old age worth living. Many European nations have done more to promote the general welfare of the aged than has America. In Scandinavia, for example, housing, medical care, and social programs for the aged are well organized. This is a social policy area which needs greater attention from our national, state, and local policy makers. In the absence of a humanitarian social policy toward the aged, we will find that the prolongation of life will simply increase the number of disaffected elderly. While they may continue to live medically, many will be socially dead.

THE ORGANIZATION OF PUBLIC HEALTH SERVICES

An understanding of the organization of public health services clarifies the contribution of each level of government in solving public health

[23] Bernard Bloom, "The Medical Model, Miasma Theory and Community Mental Health," *Journal of Community Mental Health,* 1, No. 4, 333.

problems. Public health services are organized on five levels: local (city or county), regional, state, national, and international. The division of responsibility among local, regional, and state health authorities varies considerably from state to state. Unfortunately, the quality of health services also varies considerably throughout the fifty states, depending not only on the economic development of the area, but also on the citizens' attitudes toward health. While it has usually been the responsibility of city government to provide direct public health services, recently there has been a trend to switch to larger units of government such as the county. With greater administrative specialization many problems can be handled better by larger administrative units. Often regional solutions are better than local ones; however, this depends on the characteristics of the area, whether it is urban or rural, sparsely or densely populated. Disease is not limited within geographic boundaries, and administrative units depend on good work relationships with one another, whether they are units of equal authority or subordinate or superior to one another. Only through coordinated efforts and cooperation among governmental units can public health problems be solved or brought under control.

The federal government has assumed broad powers in public health under its Constitutional mandate to "promote the general welfare." The bulk of the federal effort is through direct grants and grants-in-aid to states and lower levels of government to improve the quality of health services. Congress has approved programs to fund research, train health workers, support the delivery of health services, and upgrade the quality of planning and administration of local health services.[24]

Until 1953, when the Department of Health, Education and Welfare was organized, federal health services were dispersed among many departments of the government. The United States Public Health Service, a subsection of the Department of Health, Education and Welfare, brought most of the health agencies under its auspices, thereby reducing overlap and improving coordination of activities. However, the division of responsibilities among the various subsidiary bureaus can still be an administrative nightmare, especially at budget time when each area of health interest vies with the others to maintain if not extend the scope of its operations.

The mission of the United States Public Service is to support both health training and research and to help state governments use new information and techniques to promote health, prevent and control diseases, and develop community health services. The Public Health Service also runs hospitals and medical services for various groups of people who depend on the federal government, such as merchant seamen, the Coast Guard, Indians, and Eskimos. St. Elizabeth's Hospital in Washington, D. C. is one of these

[24] Hanlon, *Principles of Public Health Administration*, pp. 224–35.

responsibilities, operated by the government since the beginning of the nineteenth century; however, it is now being transferred to the District government.

The Public Health Service contains three main divisions: the Consumer Protection and Environment Health Service, the Health Services and Mental Health Administration, and the National Institute of Health. The last two are especially important to social welfare because they support research and training, and promote direct services dealing with those public health problems that have important social components. Under the Health Services and Mental Health Administration are the National Institute of Mental Health, the Regional Medical Programs, and two centers dealing with communicable and chronic diseases, which contain separate research and training programs. Under the National Institutes of Health are a number of institutes and bureaus concerned with research and training in the following areas: health manpower, child health and human development, neurological disease and blindness allergy and infectious disease, cancer and heart diseases, arthritis and metabolic disease, and dental and general medical disease.[25]

The National Institute of Mental Health is itself a complex bureaucratic organization providing a variety of specialized programs. It is concerned with research, training, and support to state and local mental health programs. The Institute was established in 1949 by the *National Mental Health Act of 1946* and has grown steadily since that time. Research into the causes of mental disorder and training of psychiatric personnel (social workers, psychologists, psychiatrists, and psychiatric nurses) received major impetus. One of the important outgrowths of the Institute's work was the establishment of community-oriented mental health services. With the Institute's encouragement, several states such as Massachusetts and California passed legislation in the 1950s enabling the growth of comprehensive mental health services.

It is important to note that while the mandate of the Institute is in part the promotion of mental health and prevention of mental disorder, the struggle over spending on prevention versus spending on treatment continues. After the *Community Mental Health Centers Act of 1963* (see Chapter 16), which provides funds to aid in the development of comprehensive mental health centers, was passed, it was expected that there would be a departure from a total emphasis on treatment of mental illness and a concomitant growth in efforts toward prevention. This, however, has not yet materialized.

Within HEW myriads of other divisions and bureaus provide health or health-related services. For example, the Maternal and Child Health Service in the Health Services and Mental Health Administration is con-

25 Ibid.

cerned with improving maternal and child health and providing services to crippled children.[26] The Medical Services Administration is concerned with the problem of medical care for dependent children, the blind, and the permanently and totally disabled. The Rehabilitation Services Administration, the Administration on Aging, and the Office of Education also have programs which provide special kinds of health or health-related services. Many of these programs promote treatment and rehabilitation as well as prevention.

The Departments of Agriculture, Commerce, Interior, Justice, Treasury, Labor, and Housing and Urban Development also operate many health programs. Some of these might be considered preventive because of the standard-setting aspects of their services. These are established to protect certain high-risk groups such as malnourished school children, mine workers, new immigrants, working mothers, young workers, migratory workers, drug addicts, and Head Start children.

A maze of federal programs exists concerned with the field of health. Although there is a trend toward bringing these programs under one administration to achieve a higher degree of coordination and to prevent duplication, at the same time there is a continuous proliferation of new programs which serve newly identified high-risk groups. We leave to Chapters 15 and 16 the discussion of those federal health programs that provide direct medical care and psychiatric services.

STATE RESPONSIBILITIES

Under the United States Constitution, each state is charged with the task of guarding the health of the population within its borders. The usual pattern is for the state to pass to local government the major responsibility for direct health services. However, the state retains the authority to set standards, to monitor the overall health level in the state, and to enforce statewide regulations. State health departments also take responsibility for statewide health planning and coordination with the federal government.

Most state health departments have bureaus concerned with administration and finance, hospitals, vital statistics, health education, laboratories, preventive medicine, environmental health, maternal and child health, public health nursing, and nutrition. At least half the states' health departments have programs concerned with chronic disease control, crippled children's

[26] See Myron E. Wegman, "Maternal and Child Health," in Leavell and Clark, eds., *Textbook of Preventive Medicine;* and Hanlon, *Principles of Public Health Administration,* Chap. 18, for a discussion of the maternal–child health problem area. There are important implications for social work contributions to this area of public health practice. See also Joanna Gorman, ed., *Social Work in Maternal and Child Health Programs* (Berkeley: University of California Press, 1968).

services, dental health, occupational health, and mental health.[27] There is usually a bureau or division of local health services which provides a structure for health personnel to relate to local health departments to facilitate their work. Several health departments also have public health social work bureaus to facilitate the social work component of the department's task. An effective state health department is one which provides maximum assistance to the local health department in carrying out its goals.

LOCAL HEALTH DEPARTMENTS

The majority of public health services to the community and the individual are rendered through local health departments. Increasingly the standard administrative unit of government for delivering local services is the county rather than the city or township. The recommended minimum size of a population served by a health department is 50,000 people. The American Public Health Association lists the following as necessary activities of a local health department:

1. Recording and analysis of health data such as reports of births, deaths, marriages, divorces, and notifiable diseases, and the maintenance of registers of individuals known to have certain diseases or impairments. This also includes the conduct of special surveys, the collection and interpretation of morbidity data from a variety of sources. In addition they conduct periodic evaluation of community health needs and services.

2. Health Education and Information Services to stimulate the public to recognize health problems that exist, to study the resources available for meeting the problems, and to develop and put into action programs designed to solve them. They also provide individual instruction by public health nurses and other personnel as in the case of families in which communicable disease has occurred, and of mothers attending well-baby conferences. Other activities are the organization of courses such as parents' classes, and the development of a well-rounded program of professional education designed to assist the local health professions to maintain and improve the quality of services.

3. Supervision and regulation of food, water, and milk supplies, control of water and air pollution, prevention of occupational diseases and accidents, control of human and animal sources of infection, regulation of housing, hospitals, nursing homes, and other health facilities.

4. Provision of environmental health services.

5. Administration of personal health services such as immunization against infectious diseases, advisory health maintenance service, as in child health conferences, prenatal clinics, parents' classes, and public health nursing visits, case finding surveys of the general population, chest x-ray surveys for TB and serologic tests for syphilis, provision of diagnostic aids to physicians, and provision of diagnostic

[27] Hanlon, *Principles of Public Health Administration,* pp. 221–24.

and treatment services for specific diseases such as syphilis, tuberculosis, defects in children and expectant mothers, orthopedic, cardiac, and other crippling impairments in children.

6. Operation of health facilities.
7. Coordination of activities and resources in order to provide effective leadership in meeting community health needs. (This is to be done through community organization activities to prevent duplication and overlapping, and to plan for the development of comprehensive health service.)[28]

The following subdivisions at least are common in most health departments: public health nursing, health education, sanitation, maternal and child health, communicable disease control, and laboratories. Many locales also have divisions dealing with mental health and chronic diseases. While many of these functions have implications for social work, of special interest to social workers are the divisions of public health nursing, health education, maternal and child care, and mental health. These services are usually organized under a Board of Health, appointed by the city or county government. The Board of Health usually appoints a physician to be chief of the health department. In the past there has been a dearth of physicians trained in public health concepts and methods who have the administrative experience necessary to take these responsible positions. The smaller urban and rural departments have had to settle for directors who are less qualified or not trained in public health, and consequently many of their programs have suffered from a lack of informed leadership.

Public health nursing and health education as disciplines have much in common with social work, as well as some differences. Traditionally public health nurses have placed great emphasis on the educational component of preventive medicine. Their concern is the basic family unit and its environment. Their services are given not only during times of illness or crisis, but in normal times as well.

Families needing service are found through health-screening clinics and various follow-up clinics. Public health nurses make periodic visits to homes of high-risk groups. They use these contacts to teach families about adequate nutrition and hygiene and to help prepare the members for unanticipated changes in the life cycle, such as the effects on a child of the birth of a sibling. They practice the whole range of prevention services, from health promotion to rehabilitation.

The public health nurse often works with expectant mothers, postpartum mothers, and infants below school age. Through prenatal and postnatal clinics, immunization clinics, and home visits, the district public health nurse comes to know the whole family's health and social needs. She is able to

[28] Ibid., pp. 215–21.

maintain their trust and confidence because she is seen by the family as someone who contributes to their general well-being.[29]

Families in the high-risk group typically served by public health
nurses often have severe social and emotional problems. Social workers col-
laborate with public health nurses who are not trained to deal with these
problems, when special assistance in understanding psychosocial dynamics
and case management techniques is required. The nurse assumes responsibility for the health care and the social worker assists her with social and
emotional aspects of the problems. Some health departments employ social
workers directly as consultants; others use mental health personnel as consultants to the nurses. The consultation service may come from a mental
health division within the health department or from a mental health center
administered under another authority.

Health departments also employ health educators to carry out broad
community education programs. Depending on the department in which
they work, their activities range from education through the use of mass
media to community organization activities for health services. The health
team relies on the health educator as an expert in communicating information about health and illness to the community. He is able to work with
minority groups because he understands their perception of health problems
and health services. Knowing their social and cultural mores, the health
educator advises and collaborates with health personnel in developing preventive programs which are more acceptable to and better used by the client
groups.[30]

Public health personnel from several disciplines make unique contributions to the multifaceted maternal and child health bureau team. The staff
in these bureaus is small, but through surveillance of the health status of
mothers and children, consultation with other units, program planning within the department, and coordination with community health and welfare
services, their contribution to lowering rates of mortality and illness has been
important. Expectant and young mothers, the foetus, and the infant are
vulnerable to disease and other developmental hazards and require health
education and direct services at each successive stage of development. As-
tounding progress has been made during this century in reducing infant and
maternal mortality, prematurity, brain damage, mental retardation, con-
genital malformations, and other effects of an unhealthy pregnancy. Yet,

29 Ibid., pp. 585–600. See also Zella Bryant, "The Public Health Nurse's
Expanding Responsibilities," *Public Health Reports,* 76, No. 10 (October 1961),
857–60.

30 See M. Derryberry, "The Role of Health Education in a Public Health
Program," *Public Health Report,* 62 (November 1947); and B. J. Robert, J. Gross-
man, and W. Griffith, "Public Health Educators' Bookshelf," *Journal of Public
Health,* 53 (January 1961), 3–12.

without the constant vigilance of the staff of these programs and their attention to the mothers and infants, mortality rates would quickly rise.[31]

Although infant and maternal mortality rates in the United States have decreased 75 percent since the turn of the century, there are still wide local and regional differences based on social class, race or ethnicity, and availability of medical care.[32] In areas where inequality of income distribution is related to these factors, the infant mortality is much higher. In spite of the affluence in the United States, infant mortality in this country still far exceeds that in several European countries with lower per capita incomes.

The practice of encouraging family planning is increasing in many local health departments. This once extremely controversial area of public services was the domain of voluntary agencies such as the Planned Parenthood Federation. Knowledge about various birth control methods has multiplied in the last two decades. The effects on the family of an unplanned child and the effects on society of overpopulation have now been more broadly recognized. Consequently, prior anti–birth control attitudes among large segments of society have been significantly modified. Numerous public health departments supported by state and federal policies and programs have expanded their protection of the mother or potential mother by opening clinics and providing contraceptive information and supplies. Knowledge about family planning has, in many areas, crept into the curricula of the secondary schools. It is now considered enlightened public health practice both to curb the "population explosion" and to protect the physical, social, and emotional well-being of the mother and family through family planning.[33]

To date social work experience in regard to family planning has been limited, with only a few individuals taking leadership in this important but neglected area of practice. The social worker's knowledge of family dynamics, human motivation, and psychosocial behavior would seem to have great use in the current movement to consciously control family size with the aim of improving the quality of family life. There is a unique opportunity, as yet not fully explored, for public health and social work professions to join, sharing knowledge and skills, communication networks, and domains, to effectively meet the challenge for a salutary approach to solving the population problem. This approach should be concerned with the immediate well-being of families, allowing a range of options around family growth, and at the same time it should protect our society and future societies from the disaster of overpopulation. With the current upheaval in the welfare system,

---

[31] Hanlon, *Principles of Public Health Administration,* Chap. 18.

[32] Ibid., p. 367.

[33] See "Public Health Programs in Family Planning," supplement to the January issue of *American Journal of Public Health* (October 1964).

and the restructuring of social work education, a large number of social workers should be more interested in assuming responsibility for leadership in the field of family planning.[34]

ORGANIZATION AND ORIENTATION OF MENTAL HEALTH SERVICES UNDER LOCAL PUBLIC HEALTH DEPARTMENTS

Many local health departments hire mental health personnel to enhance their work. Some departments have a bureau of mental health, while others obtain mental health consultants from outside the department. A public health–oriented mental health program is organized not only to provide an array of services to the high-risk populations in the community, but also to enhance the practice of public health workers assisting their clientele with emotional problems.

Public health–oriented mental health workers tend to be population-rather than individual-oriented. This means singling out groups or subgroups of individuals who are especially vulnerable to breakdown because of their life stages, social situations, and cultural mores. Young school dropouts, the unemployed, unmarried mothers, the recently bereaved, the recently retired, immigrant families, and families affected by the birth of a premature or malformed child are all experiencing crises and are especially vulnerable to social maladjustment and potential breakdown. Many people, of course, go through these crises unscathed, and may even be psychologically strengthened by them. However, there are some who are permanently thrown off equilibrium. These are mostly individuals who do not have the inner and outer resources necessary to cope with the extreme stress of their changing life situations.

Mental health personnel in public health settings organize their programs to do preventive work with groups such as these. This means that mental health workers assist other community workers to identify and aid high-risk cases. The community workers may be probation officers, social workers, public health nurses, ministers, teachers, or public housing workers, who carry a large number of cases and are in close touch with the problem when and where it occurs. Once the vulnerable individuals are identified, the mental health worker assists the community worker through consultation and collaboration to serve his client better.[35]

---

[34] See Florence Hazelkorn, ed., "Family Planning, The Role of Social Work," in *Perspectives in Social Work,* II, No. 1 (Garden City, N.Y.: Adelphi University School of Social Work, 1968).

[35] Caplan, *Principles of Preventive Psychiatry.*

VOLUNTARY HEALTH ORGANIZATIONS

Approximately 100,000 voluntary health organizations in the United States are almost totally dependent on nontax dollars for support. Most are financed by voluntary contributions from individuals, but a few are supported by philanthropic foundations such as the Rosenwald, Rockefeller, Milbank Memorial, and Kellogg Foundations. Most of these organizations have local semiautonomous chapters, but they also may have offices on the state, regional, or national level.[36]

The programs of voluntary health organizations do not fall easily into the categories of prevention or treatment. Rather, many such programs provide both of these services. Their mission may fit into one of the following types: concern with one particular disease, such as tuberculosis or muscular dystrophy; concern with an organ of the body, such as the heart or eyes; concern with a special group, such as crippled children, mothers, or the aged; concern with a specific social problem, such as overpopulation or accidents.

Starting with the Anti-Tuberculosis Society of Philadelphia in 1892, voluntary health organizations have proliferated at a fantastic rate. Their financing is increasingly problematic and competition among them for the elusive voluntary contribution is intense. Nevertheless, they have taken the lead in dramatizing the problems of specific groups in the population, working toward understanding the etiology of problems and obtaining the treatment and rehabilitation. The gamut of activities practiced by these agencies includes dramatizing health needs, education, demonstrating specific services, supporting research, supplementing governmental activities, promoting health legislation, and developing support for further contributions to carry on their work. Rarely has one of these national organizations gone out of business, even after its major objectives have been reached; instead, they seek out new objectives and continue with new types of activities.[37]

SELECTED BIBLIOGRAPHY

"Concepts of Mental Health and Consultation—Their Application in Public Health Social Work," Publication No. 2072. Washington, D.C.: U.S. Public Health Service, 1970.

[36] Hanlon, *Principles of Public Health Administration.* See also Sol Levine and Paul E. White, "The Community of Health Organizations," in Howard E. Freeman, Sol Levine, and Leo G. Reeder, eds., *Handbook of Medical Sociology* (Englewood Cliffs, N.J.: Prentice-Hall, 1963), pp. 321–47.

[37] Ibid., p. 337.

"Educational Qualifications of Social Workers in Public Health Programs," *American Journal of Public Health*, 42, No. 2 (February 1962), 317–24.

ELIOT, M. M., "The Children's Bureau: Fifty Years of Public Responsibility for Action in Behalf of Children," *American Journal of Public Health*, 52 (April 1962), 676–91.

FREEMAN, R. and E. HOLMES, *Administration of Public Health Services*. Philadelphia: W. B. Saunders, 1960.

Functions and Qualifications in the Practice of Public Health Nursing. New York: American Nurses Association, Public Health Nurses Section, 1964.

HANLON, J. J., F. B. ROGERS, and G. ROSEN, "A Bookshelf on the History and Philosophy of Public Health," *American Journal of Public Health*, 50 (April 1960), 445–58.

HAZELKORN, FLORENCE, ed., "Mothers-at-Risk," in *Perspectives in Social Work*, I, No. 1. Garden City, N.Y.: Adelphi University School of Social Work, 1966.

JAMES, G., "Poverty as an Obstacle to Health Progress in our Cities," *American Journal of Public Health*, 55 (November 1965), 1757–71.

LESSER, ARTHUR J., "The Federal Government in Child Health Care," *Pediatric Clinics of North America*, 16, No. 4 (November 1969), 891–900.

OJEMANN, R., *Four Basic Aspects of Preventive Psychiatry*. Iowa City: University of Iowa Press, 1957.

Proceedings of Tri-Regional Workshop on Planning and Implementing Social Work Programs in Community Health Services for Mothers and Children. Pittsburgh: University of Pittsburgh, Public Health Social Work Program, 1968.

Protection and Promotion of Mental Health in Schools. Washington, D.C.: U.S. Department of Health, Education and Welfare, Public Health Service, 1965, Monograph 5.

Public Health Concepts in Social Work Education. Washington, D.C.: U.S. Department of Health, Education and Welfare, 1962.

RAPOPORT, LYDIA, "The Concept of Prevention in Social Work," *Social Work*, 5, No. 1 (January 1961), 3–12.

ROBERTS, B. G., J. GROSSMAN, and W. GRIFFITH, "The Public Health Educator's Bookshelf," *American Journal of Public Health*, 53 (April 1963), 531–43.

ROSEN, G., *A History of Public Health*. New York: MD Publishers, 1958.

SCHIFF, SHELDON K., and G. KELLAM SHEPPARD, "A Community-wide Mental Health Program of Prevention and Early Treatment in First Grade," Psychiatric Research Report No. 21. New York: American Psychiatric Association, 1957.

SILVERMAN, PHYLLIS R., "Services to the Widowed: First Steps in a Program of Preventive Intervention," *Community Mental Health Journal*, 3 (1967), 37–44.

SIMMONS, L. W., and H. G. WOLFF, *Social Science in Medicine*. New York: Russell Sage Foundation, 1954.

"The Social Worker and Family Planning," *Proceedings of the Annual Institute for Public Health Social Workers*. Berkeley: University of California, 1970.

medical
care
and
social
work

Acute and chronic illness and premature death due to lack of access to good medical care or failure to take advantage of care have long made medical care a topic of prime concern to the field of social welfare. The threat of loss of income and the accumulation of medical debts because of serious illness affects the majority of the families in the United States. Medical care is as central to the needs of any organized society as food, clothing, and shelter. We have come to realize that success of medical care is based as much on the adequacy of the delivery system as it is on the knowledge and skill of the medical personnel. In this chapter we are concerned not with medical knowledge and treatment methods per se, but with the organizational, economic, and social aspects of medical care and the strains on the present system. Medical care is an important field of practice for social workers, who play significant roles in facilitating the delivery of medical services at the individual, group, and community levels. Because this is a broad topic, with an expanding body of knowledge, this chapter raises only the main points which seem relevant to social welfare.

Medical care encompasses the entire continuum of preventive and curative health services. Chapter 14 covered the public health aspects of this field; Chapter 15 deals mainly with the provision of diagnostic, treatment, and rehabilitative services.

BRIEF HISTORY OF PUBLIC MEDICAL CARE

If the concept of health preservation was associated historically with cleanliness, purity, and sanitation, then the concept of treatment of illness has been associated, at least until recent centuries, with magic, conjury, shamanism, and trial-and-error medical practice. The wondrous cures of Aesculapius and the physicians who followed him were based as much on the suggestibility of the patient as on knowledge of illness and its causes. Though some useful medical information was gained during the practice of three or four millennia of folk medicine, it is fair to say that until the Industrial Revolution the practice of medicine was primitive, and organized medical care did not exist.[1]

The provision of medical care for the poor in colonial America was based on a principle of charity established under the Elizabethan Poor Laws (see Chapters 2 and 3). Private physicians were employed by the local authorities on a fee-for-services basis to treat the poor in their homes. Patients who were infirm or required custodial care or isolation were sent to the pesthouse or almshouse, which was under the auspices of local government.

The forerunner of the modern hospital originated in eighteenth century England through the efforts of private philanthropy and church organizations. At first these hospitals cared mainly for the chronically ill who were impoverished, and little treatment was available. However, with scientific and medical advancements in treatment, the hospitals began to attract patients of all classes. The local public general hospital grew from the poorhouses and county hospitals set up to serve the destitute. These general hospitals served the "medically indigent," those receiving public assistance plus those who qualified for public medical care because of their low income. The concept of medical indigency recognizes a broader responsibility of

---

[1] For example, see Arturo Castiglioni, *A History of Medicine* (New York: Alfred A. Knopf, 1941); G. Rosen, *A History of Public Health* (New York: MD Publications, 1958); and Richard H. Shryock, *The Development of Modern Medicine* (New York: Alfred A. Knopf, 1947).

government for the health of the citizens than under the Elizabethan Poor Laws by extending medical care to those who are otherwise self-supporting, but cannot afford hospital treatment or care.

In the nineteenth century, in addition to public assistance medical care for the indigent at the local level, the federal and state governments met the medical care needs of special population groups: the federal government gave services to merchant seamen, the military, veterans, and prisoners; and the state governments served tuberculosis patients and the mentally ill. The federal government's role in funding medical care services expanded significantly with the passage of the Social Security Act in 1935. The philosophy underlying this Act gave rise first to medical care for handicapped children (the Crippled Children's Service, see Chapter 13), and later to more complete medical care for such groups as the aged, the blind, and the totally disabled. This principle has been expanded to other groups with special needs; it is described later in this chapter.

THE ORGANIZATION OF MEDICAL CARE

For a better understanding of contemporary problems in medical care in the United States and of the need for reform, we should be familiar with the existing medical system and the various methods of medical care payment. This knowledge is important to social workers, as it clarifies their various roles and gives some idea of how they can influence the modification of the system.

The medical care system in the average American community is composed of four basic substructures: medical personnel in solo practice; group medical practice; the hospital, its clinics, and allied services; and the public health subsystem. Each of these substructures has unique features. While each is related to the others, the four are characteristically unintegrated and frequently lack effective coordination and continuity. The method of accountability for quality of practice is sporadic and often singularly lacking.

The notion of private or solo practice is a carryover from the earliest days of medicine. The physician sees the patient in his own office, which is furnished with equipment bought with his capital. Solo practice is part of the free enterprise system, and the physician is in competition with his colleagues. He has built up a following of patients whom he must satisfy to ensure their return visit. The keynote and one of the major strengths of this type of practice is the doctor-patient relationship, regarded as sacrosanct. The doctor in private practice cherishes his autonomy from other professionals and is accountable only to the patient. Supervision of his activities is minimal or nil. Except through consultation referrals and use of various laboratories and hospitals, the solo physician works in relative isolation from his colleagues.

Medical knowledge is now so vast and the array of special techniques and specializations so extensive that it is difficult for even the most competent physician to meet the needs of any individual or family completely. While many physicians still cling to solo practice, medical technology and contemporary health care problems require that they modify the conditions under which they serve the public.

Group medical practice includes various patterns of medical services brought together under a variety of auspices. One type of group practice is organized under the initiative of the physicians themselves to satisfy their professional needs and to improve on the quality of medical care. For example, several physicians can share one waiting room, examining room, and laboratory; one can cover for the other while he is away. Each may have a different specialty, complementing the work of the other. Another type of group practice is organized by a third party to provide medical care for its constituency. The third party may be a union, a business, a factory, or a government agency. Collective membership makes the demand for medical services sufficient for a number of physicians to come together to provide the gamut of medical services to members of the group. Services can be provided either on a fee-for-service basis or in exchange for a predetermined monthly sum. Or the agency purchasing medical care can either contract with a medical group for the services, or actually employ the medical personnel itself. In general, group practice appears to be more efficient than solo practice, improving the organizational, economic, qualitative, and supervisory aspects of health service delivery.

The third subsystem includes the hospital and all of the clinical specialty services organized around it. While the hospital is hierarchical, there is usually cooperation among the staff with the aim of achieving teamwork. Although the hospital has become more skillful in treating disease and injury, it is having more difficulty treating the patient as a whole person. The application of medical technology without special attention to the patient can depersonalize medical care.

In Chapter 14 we described the role of the federal, state, and local government in organizing and providing public health services. These units of government also play a role in providing direct hospital care services to specific groups of people. State and local governments have developed hospitals and sanatariums because of the need to isolate patients with communicable diseases which might threaten the community, and because of the need to serve the totally disabled who require continuous care. Such state institutions include tuberculosis sanatariums, mental hospitals, and hospitals for the chronically ill. In addition, there are, of course, county and city general hospitals for the medically indigent. Often the work of these hospitals is supplemented by outpatient services.

The federal government, too, has aided in organizing and providing a spectrum of hospital care services for specific categories of individuals, such as merchant seamen, disabled veterans, those in military service and their dependents, dependent Indians, lepers, and drug addicts. The total number receiving some form of hospital care under federal government auspices is sizable. Much of the care, however, is fragmented in nature and is often available only for a specific illness, or only at a specific period in the person's life.

Many of the nonprofit providers of medical care are voluntary hospitals. These hospitals, dependent on voluntary gifts, private fees, and government funds, are generally operated by a board of directors who set the goals and determine who will be served, usually patients suffering from acute illnesses of short duration who are treated on an inpatient basis. Because of their voluntary status, such hospitals are relatively independent of outside control over admission policies and fees. However, to qualify for federal reimbursement from programs like Medicare, voluntary hospitals must conform to laws and regulations, including the civil rights laws.

The hospital has become the center of the medical care system. Because of the concentration of highly skilled technicians, specialists, and equipment within its walls, it is the most logical place for physicians to come together to obtain consultation, share experiences, and voluntarily develop a system of peer evaluation. Hospitals can be and often are a place where the standards of practice can be set and raised.

The lack of sufficient beds and the spiraling cost of hospital care, plus the inappropriateness of keeping patients in hospitals during certain phases of illness, have generated new modes of administering medical care while the patient is still nonambulatory. These services, such as nursing and convalescent homes, are all part of the complicated hospital subsystem. Nursing homes and convalescent homes are now being built at a rapid rate. Most of them are established on the profit principle; their development has had a major impetus from the Medicare and Medical Assistance to the Aged programs. The per diem cost of care can be considerably less in a nursing home than in a regular hospital because of the reduced need for specialized personnel and equipment. Frequently, however, convalescent homes suffer from a lack of specialists and of adequately trained nursing personnel skilled in physical and social rehabilitation.

Organized home care programs, another part of the hospital subsystem, can facilitate immensely the continuity of medical care. As yet, they have not grown enough in number to meet the potential demand. Home care is a program of organized hospital services delivered directly to the patient in his home. These services allow a patient to return home more quickly after the acute phase of an illness and still receive all the specialized services he might otherwise have received while hospitalized: services from nurses, the laboratory, physical and occupational therapists, the medical social worker, homemaker aides, and, of course, the doctor. Organized properly, home care can cut down the time spent in the hospital, reduce the cost of medical care, and in many cases facilitate recovery by keeping the patient in his home with his family. Effective organization and coordination of home care service is difficult to achieve, but it is a highly worthwhile objective.[2]

The fourth subsystem, public health, has been discussed in some detail in Chapter 14. Ideally, public health should not be regarded as a separate entity from medical care, because it is significantly interdependent with other aspects of the health service system. Furthermore, many of the health department's activities might be handled more effectively by the family doctor. It is mainly the lack of appreciation or concern on the part of physicians for the preventive aspects of medicine that has spurred the public health field to assume so many responsibilities. Nevertheless, physicians often depend on the public health system's laboratories and nursing service, and public health departments frequently work through private physicians to control the spread of communicable disease.

Our health system in a hodge-podge that has grown out of a variety of historical trends rather than out of conscious planning. Care is often fragmented, and is oriented toward treating episodic illnesses rather than toward maintaining the health of the whole person or family. Over time or simultaneously, one person might receive services from any or all of the four subsystems, but few individuals, rich or poor, can be said to receive really comprehensive continuous services from the care available to them. Some of the current high cost of care, in fact, can be attributed to the inefficiency, overlap of effort, and gaps in the system. Consumer groups are beginning to press for a better-organized comprehensive health system which would give quality care at lower cost. As yet, however, their voice is not strong enough to overcome the opposition of the medical profession and other forces resisting change in the medical care system.

COMPREHENSIVE HEALTH PLANNING

The *Comprehensive Health Planning Act of 1966* (PL 89-749) set about to correct the haphazard manner in which the national health system has developed. Even with the continued expansion of medical care services, there are still major gaps. Furthermore, there are often unnecessary duplications of program efforts in one geographic area. The result of previous federal legislation was mainly segmental planning around hospital construction and health facilities development. The Comprehensive Health Planning Act, however, aims at a more total approach which would encourage state- and area-wide efforts to assure continuous planning for future needs.

[2] Martin Cherkasky, "The Montefiore Hospital Home Care Program," *Medical Care in Transition,* 1 (January 1964), 8–11.

To qualify for the federal planning grants, a state has to establish a statewide planning agency with an advisory board composed of both consumers and health professionals. The state agency must state clearly its goals, the content of its plan, and the methods to be used in planning. The law provides qualified states and "planning areas" with grants for planning plus additional grants to maintain and develop medical care, public health, and mental health programs.

If the effectiveness of the law were measured by the number of states which qualified for grants, it would be considered a resounding triumph, as all but one state and territory have established comprehensive planning programs. In practice, however, all the local, state, public, and private agencies have entered into planning and competition over goals, ideas, and funds has become fierce. It is perhaps too soon to determine if and how the planning agencies will eventually improve the areawide organization and methods of delivery of health service. The direct rewards of better planning may in themselves be insufficient to voluntarily induce a more responsible health subsystem. Rather, we may have to experience an even greater crisis in the health system to evoke cooperation from the public, nonprofit, and private interest groups which compose the medical care industry.

FINANCING MEDICAL CARE

More than $75 billion are spent annually on medical care in the United States. Health is big business in America, employing over 3,000,000 people. The cost of medical care, already exorbitant, is steadily rising. In 1928–29, for example, medical care constituted 3.6 percent of the gross national product. In 1960–61 it constituted 5.4 percent, and by 1971 it had risen to 7.6 percent. From 1927 to 1971 the amount of family income spent annually on medical care rose from $27 to $358, a much higher rate of increase than that of average income over this period. Within one recent year the average cost of medical care per family increased by 15 percent. Furthermore, over the past two decades the total amount spent on medical care multiplied five times; at least half of this was due to rising costs.[3]

The largest growth in costs has been in the cost of hospital care. Although the average length of hospital stays is down, the number of annual admissions has risen considerably. The reasons for the spiraling costs of medical care are manifold. The increasing affluence of our society has increased the demand for health care, in turn leading to an overall increase in life expectancy and a rise in the number of chronic illnesses. Knowledge and technique in medicine have progressed considerably during the last two dec-

3 Dory P. Rice and Barbara S. Cooper, "National Health Expenditure 1929–71," *Social Security Bulletin,* 34, No. 1 (1971), 3–18.

ades, including a greater range of life-saving treatment interventions. The cost in terms of personnel and equipment to employ the new medical developments is extreme. The heavy demand for medical advances has been greater than anticipated; however, hospitals in the same area have duplicated expensive equipment which they use only seldom. In addition, pharmaceutical companies have taken excessive profits from the drugs they manufacture.

POVERTY AND HEALTH

The economics of medical care has always been a problem for the majority of citizens. The average family is ill prepared to shoulder the cost of a major illness of one of its members. Over the past twenty-five years the population has shown great interest in participating in one of the many insurance schemes to better cover the cost of medical care. However, insurance plans have been directed mainly at employed persons and their families; those either marginally employed or unemployed are frequently left without any health coverage.[4]

As we have seen in regard to other social problems, illness is strongly associated with poverty.[5] Many categories of illnesses such as childhood diseases, tuberculosis, and chronic illnesses are found disproportionately more

Table 1   Days of disability per person per year by major form of disability and family income, United States, July 1963–June 1964.

Major Form of Disability	Family Income					
	All Incomes (Includes Unknown Incomes)	Under $2,000	$2,000–$3,999	$4,000–$6,999	$7,000–$9,999	$10,000 or Over
Restricted activity[a]	16.2	22.4	17.7	15.2	14.3	14.1
Bed disability[a]	6.0	8.1	6.6	5.9	5.5	5.6
Lost from work[b]	5.5	8.2	7.1	6.0	4.4	4.2

Source: Monroe Lerner, "Social Differences in Physical Health," in Kosa, Antonovsky, and Zola, eds., *Poverty and Health: A Sociological Analysis,* p. 102.

[a]All figures except those in "All incomes" have been adjusted to the age and sex distribution of the total civilian noninstitutional population of the United States.

[b]Per currently employed person per year. Persons aged seventeen years and over. All figures except those in "All incomes" have been adjusted to the age and sex distribution of the currently employed population of the United States.

[4] See pages 274–76.

[5] For a comprehensive analysis of this topic, see John Kosa, Aaron Antonovsky, and Irving Kenneth Zola, *Poverty and Health: A Sociological Analysis* (Cambridge, Mass.: Harvard University Press, 1969).

often among the poor than in the middle class. The poor are hampered by their inadequate diet and undesirable working and living conditions. They are more frequently disabled, and for longer periods of time, and hence more frequently in need of care (see Table 1). In addition, the poor must spend a larger proportion of their income on medical care; thus they often do not obtain treatment when they most need it. When hospitalized, they spend longer periods in the hospital on the average because of their poorer health. With fewer personal and family resources, they have less money available to speed discharge of the patient to his home. It is often more costly, therefore, to provide the poor with equivalent-quality services. This fact in itself makes it important for the government to take greater leadership in providing more preventive, diagnostic, and clinical services for the poor.

FINANCING MEDICAL CARE FOR THE POOR

Individuals who are considered medically indigent and not entitled to insurance benefits usually receive their care through the county hospital system and public clinics. A means test is almost always required. Some poor can obtain care at charitable hospitals, paying according to their ability. The federal government also finances, in part, the cost of medical care through the vehicle of public assistance (Social Security Act, Amendment of 1965, Title XIX). The government shares the cost according to the per capita income of the state extending medical care under the Aid to the Blind, Aid to Families with Dependent Children, and Aid to the Totally and Permanently Disabled programs and to other needy. These funds are limited, and each state decides whether it will develop a medical care program for welfare recipients. The money is usually paid by the Welfare Department directly to the vendor of medical services. By January 1970 all but two states had established Medicaid programs.[6]

Old age is the period during which the most illness occurs, yet the aged have the least income or earning power to pay for medical care. In the area of medical care for the aged Congress acted by establishing the Medicare program (Title XVIII of the Social Security Act of 1965). For those over sixty-five years of age, this program signified an important factor in making up the difference between what they could purchase in medical care and the actual cost of hospitalization and out-of-hospital treatment (see Chapters 9 and 11).

Presently there are still large numbers of people who have no health plan or highly inadequate means for financing medical care. This group consists mainly of those who live above the poverty line but do not belong to

6 Dorothy P. Rice, "Financing Social Welfare: Health Care," *Encyclopedia of Social Work 1971,* pp. 437–38.

any union or organization which has a plan for health care coverage. In addition, large groups of middle-class families, many of whom are self-employed, have not been able to enroll in a comprehensive health plan or in insurance schemes such as Blue Cross and Blue Shield.

Neighborhood Health Centers

A new subsystem of medical care, Neighborhood Health Centers, was developed during the War on Poverty to supplement existing health care systems. These centers, financed by the Office of Economic Opportunity and the United States Public Health Service, were begun in "high-risk" communities in many sections of the United States. By 1970 these two federal agencies had funded eighty-three programs serving approximately 2,000,000 people.[7]

The Neighborhood Health Centers were set up to give comprehensive outpatient care. They have been organized in a variety of ways: contracting with private practitioners, acting as coordinating agencies, or as comprehensive outpatient clinics. Many centers, like the West Oakland Health Center in Oakland, California, are administered by a lay board. Most employ the principle of community involvement in policy making whenever possible. The centers make a point of using indigenous manpower in the delivery of medical care. Health outreach aides and new careers schemes have been developed to provide job openings for residents of the poverty areas served by the centers. Neighborhood Health Centers need skillful, experienced leadership to operate effectively and fulfill their great potential. Their financial base has not been secure enough to guarantee their continued existence over the long run.

HEALTH MAINTENANCE ORGANIZATIONS

The prepaid medical care plans which have been operating in the United States for a number of years have served as prototypes for a new direction in medical care administration: the Health Maintenance Organization (HMO). Since 1971 the Department of Health, Education and Welfare has been encouraging this development by providing funds to health agencies for the planning of HMO's. A bill was passed which makes available guaranteed low-interest loans for the initiation of local HMO's. Embodied in the idea of the HMO is the concept of a comprehensive prepaid medical program such as the Kaiser Foundation has operated on the West Coast since World War II. HEW has been criticized, however, for not having developed national

---

[7] See Chapter 12 on neighborhood health centers in antipoverty programs. See also Herbert Notkin, "Health Care System: Ambulatory Care," *Encyclopedia 1971,* pp. 528–29.

standards for the new programs, and because the legislation is only a step toward reducing the cost of care, helping the providers rather than improving or rebuilding the whole antiquated delivery system.[8] Unless the HMO's can also address themselves to providing radically new methods for improving the quality and accessibility of medical care, this new direction will have little impact on the nation's health.

Despite all the federal government's efforts to correct deficiencies in the existing medical care system, it has still done little more than to provide care to certain groups of people for whom it was otherwise unavailable .There is still no federal agency responsible for monitoring the nation's health care system, let alone a compulsory national health insurance program providing universal coverage for medical care services, or a comprehensive health service available to all, as in Great Britain.[9]

SOCIAL FACTORS IN ILLNESS BEHAVIOR

Even when quality medical care is freely available, it is used infrequently by certain groups of people and misused by others. This is true of both the preventive and treatment aspects of health service. For example, one nation-wide health study found that only one-third of the sample eligible for health care visited a physician for a medical checkup over a five-year period, and only half took advantage of a free tuberculosis test over a ten-year period.[10] Medical statistics also reveal major intergroup differences on who uses medical care, when they use it, and under what circumstances they are willing to take advantage of it. A sociological and psychological perspective on illness and the use of health services can enhance our understanding of the importance of the social component in medicine and medical care. This perspective will be useful at all levels of medical care delivery, in broad policy formation, in organizing clinical services, and in developing special approaches for families from different backgrounds. In brief, study of the sociological and psychological perspective contributes to the following areas of knowledge:

1. The nonmedical etiological factors leading to illness
   a. Stress reactions and illness
   b. Psychological reactions to illness which exacerbate existing disease
   c. Effects of social environment on physical well-being

8 Call Des and Ann Lawrence, "Health Policy Advisory Center," Health-Pac Bulletin No. 26 (December 1971).

9 See Evelyn Burns, "Health Care System," *Encyclopedia 1972*, pp. 510–23; and Charles P. Loomis and Zona K. Loomis, "Social Systems for Health," *Social Systems* (Princeton, N.J.: Van Nostrand, 1960), pp. 298–334.

10 Irwin M. Rosenstock, "Prevention of Illness and Maintenance of Health," in Kosa, Antonovsky, and Zola, eds., *Poverty and Health*, p. 170.

2. The reaction patterns of the individual and his family to the illness, affecting treatment and outcome
3. The existence of psychological, cultural, and social policy issues which shape both the delivery and use of services

Chapter 14 introduced the concept of stress. Stress can be both physiological and psychological; the two types are so closely interrelated that it is often difficult to differentiate them. Individuals and groups of people under varying degrees of psychological stress have been studied intensively by medical teams and psychologists. Some of the stress studies have observed individuals under laboratory conditions, while others have surveyed groups of people actually undergoing the stress of extreme social change, such as wartime conditions. These studies point out that excessive psychological stress can have a major impact on the health of individuals or groups.[11] In the laboratory actual bodily changes are demonstrated under stress. We do not mean to ignore the importance of biological and physical factors in illness, but merely to point out the definite relationship between external social and psychological stress and human bodily response.

Within the field of medicine, a specialty, psychosomatic medicine, has been developed to better understand the relationship of the body to psychosocial stress, and to develop treatment programs to serve individuals experiencing excessive bodily response to such stress. A growing number of physicians recognize the importance of psychosocial stress and consider it in diagnosis and treatment. This branch of medicine also has been a fertile field for the practice of medical social work. Physicians vary in their estimates of the percentage of patients whose complaints have psychosomatic origins; however, some physicians estimates this at well over 50 percent. In some illnesses undue stress is not the primary cause of the symptoms, but is a salient factor influencing the eruption of the disease or disability. A case in point is tuberculosis. A study in Seattle found that exposure to the tubercle bacillus and the physical and environmental factors conducive to tuberculosis were not the only conditions encouraging its outbreak, but that certain social and psychological factors also increased the likelihood of onset of the disease. Psychological stress contributed by social isolation and disruption of life style enchanced the likelihood of contracting tuberculosis.[12]

[11] See David Mechanic, *Medical Sociology: A Selective View* (New York: Free Press, 1968), pp. 294–322; Hans Selye, *The Stress of Life* (New York: McGraw-Hill, 1956); and L. E. Hinkle and H. G. Wolff, "Health and the Social Environment: Experimental Investigations," in A. Leighton, et al., eds., *Explorations in Social Psychiatry* (New York: Basic Books, 1957), pp. 105–32.

[12] Stanley H. King, "Social Psychological Factors in Illness," in Howard E. Freeman, Sol E. Levine, and Leo G. Reeder, eds. *Handbook of Medical Sociology* (Englewood Cliffs, N.J.: Prentice-Hall, 1963), pp. 99–121.

The psychological effects of aging are still imperfectly understood; however, it has long been recognized that the emotional impact of a chronic illness on the aging person is extremely stressful. The fear and despair which accompany a long-term illness can lower the individual's physiological threshold for coping, having a stream of physical and psychological results.

The social and physical environment in which the individual lives can also contribute to illness. This can happen either through the customs, beliefs, and taboos of the society or through its pressures. Proneness to disease may be affected by type of dwelling, life style, hygienic habits, diet, or types of individual interaction.[13] For example, persons in many agrarian communities live in very close contact with animals. Proximity to animals can cause certain debilitating fly-borne diseases, and yet because of cultural traditions, it is difficult for members of the society to accept other, more healthful living arrangements. Many of these diseases could be avoided were it not for their inadequate knowledge and/or cultural inhibitions.[14]

A rather extensive range of sociocultural responses to the signs and symptoms of illness have been recognized by social workers, sociologists, and psychologists. These response patterns are closely related to the socioeconomic level of the individual experiencing the symptoms. Sensitivity to these patterns of responding to illness is useful both for the health worker trying to understand the individual, and for the program planner responsible for organizing medical care services.

Before we discuss response patterns, it will be useful to introduce the sociological concept of the *sick role,* valuable in describing the actions of the patient during his period of disability. In most societies the individual who is ill is considered to be suffering, and is therefore granted a special role, differing from his usual one, in which certain privileges are allowed. For the person to sustain the role for any period of time, his illness needs to be recognized and accepted by a doctor, or perhaps by a member of his family or by his employer. When the illness is legitimized the individual may consider himself a patient. With the assumption of the sick role he is able to modify his usual social responsibilities to his family and his job, and others modify their expectations of him.

Not only do his obligations to others change, but their obligations to him change as well. Relatives and employers are supposed to relieve him of certain activities and show signs of helpfulness and concern. In exchange for this newly gained social dispensation, the ill individual is expected to do

---

13 See Chapter 11, page 319.

14 See Ozzie Simmons, "Popular and Modern Medicine in Mestizo Communities of Coastal Peru and Chile," and Harold A. Gould, "The Implications of Technological Change for Folk and Scientific Medicine," in Dorrian Apple, ed., *Sociological Studies of Health and Sickness: 1960 Source Book for the Health Professionals* (New York: McGraw-Hill, 1960), pp. 69–99.

everything in his power to cooperate with the physician to return to normal health. This frequently means accepting a passive-dependent state while others do things to him or for him. For the individual to accept this role, he has to perceive the illness or symptoms as serious enough to require a definite, changed role. This concept is relative, however, and applies more to gravely acute and chronic illnesses than to minor or temporary ones.[15]

There can be varying patterns of response of different groups to the same illness. The response is often related either to the cultural meaning of the illness itself (whether it is regarded as important or insignificant, acceptable or shameful, and so on), or to the extent that it is considered a danger to life and independence. Different social classes appraise illnesses differently, and accordingly either act or do not act on the symptoms when they appear. Table 2 shows the responses of three different social classes asked whether selected symptoms would motivate them to see their doctor.

Table 2   Percentage of respondents in each social class recognizing specified symptoms as needing medical attention

Symptom	Class I (N = 51)	Class II (N = 335)	Class III (N = 128)
Loss of appetite	57	55	20
Persistent backache	53	44	19
Continued coughing	77	78	23
Persistent joint and muscle pains	80	47	19
Blood in stool	98	89	60
Blood in urine	100	93	69
Excessive vaginal bleeding	92	83	54
Swelling of ankles	77	76	23
Loss of weight	80	51	21
Bleeding gums	79	51	20
Chronic fatigue	80	53	19
Shortness of breath	77	55	21
Persistent headaches	80	56	22
Fainting spells	80	51	33
Pain in chest	80	51	31
Lump in breast	94	71	44
Lump in abdomen	92	65	34

Source: Earl Lomon Koos, "Illness in Regionville," in Dorrian Apple, ed., *Sociological Studies in Health and Sickness* (New York: McGraw-Hill, 1960).

Both class and cultural differences enter into the recognition of symptoms, the willingness to define oneself as "sick," the willingness to seek treat-

[15] See Talcott Parsons, *The Social System* (New York: Free Press, 1951); and Mechanic, *Medical Sociology*, pp. 79–85.

ment, and the ability to obtain the treatment one seeks. The lower class in general makes less use of medical care services, partly, of course, because the cost is too great or the facilities are far away or hard to get to, but partly because the poor put less faith in doctors are are perhaps treated with less understanding by health personnel.

One study found that symptoms of mental illness are more prevalent in the lower class than in the middle or upper class, with both a greater number of episodes and a longer average duration of each episode. Among the poor, however, appearance and disappearance of symptoms were more related to concrete external events in their lives than among other classes. Perhaps unwanted in-laws moved in, crowding the household, and symptoms appeared; or, after weeks of unemployment, the subject finally got a job, and symptoms disappeared. Among other classes symptoms did not respond so readily to changes in life circumstances.[16]

Amazingly, different cultures and classes have different degrees of tolerance to pain. Among those doing manual labor, certain symptoms may be regarded as expected in the normal routine of things, and they may not seem worth the trouble or expense of seeing a doctor. One study found cultural differences among Jews, Italians, Irish, and "Old Americans" in their recognition of the response to pain. Both Italians and Jews paid a great deal of attention to their pain, talked about it, and worried about it. When their symptoms were relieved, the Italians forgot about being sick, while the Jews continued to worry about whether the illness itself had been cured, and whether they might suffer a relapse. The Old Americans were more matter-of-fact, trusting the doctors and believing in the care; they tried to cause as little trouble as possible and kept quiet about their pain.[17]

Individuals and groups also vary in the degree to which they are willing to play the sick role, disrupting job and family social activities. Medical care is placed somewhere on the hierarchy of values, and symptoms have to be of a certain magnitude before time, energy, and money are spent on them. In some families, particularly poor ones, a person may have a back symptom for years and never seek a doctor, for example, because "my mother had a bad back for years, and it never killed her."

Class differences in consumption of medical care are in part a result of different ability to pay—the poor cannot afford the quantity or quality of medical care they need. In countries such as Great Britain where services are given on the basis of need rather than means, class differences in use of medical care services are smaller than in the United States. Nevertheless,

---

[16] Bruce P. Dohrenwend and Barbara Snell Dohrenwend, *Social Status and Psychological Disorder: A Causal Inquiry* (New York: John Wiley, 1969), pp. 131–50.

[17] Mark Zborowski, "Cultural Components in Responses to Pain," in Apple, ed., *Sociological Studies of Health and Sickness*, pp. 118–33.

there are also noneconomic factors which discourage the poor and the ethnic minorities from getting the care they need: prejudice among health personnel, institutional racism, and inadequate provision of special attention for immigrants whose English is poor. Furthermore, cultural inhibitions frequently make a poor or minority person uncomfortable in a hospital or doctor's office, which may discourage them from seeking care. The recent trend toward greater consumer participation in the organization and management of medical care programs may lessen these problems. Experience has shown that when these programs include minority group individuals on their staff and policy-making boards, the programs have been well used by low-income groups.[18]

Regardless of the many forces affecting response to perceived symptoms, individuals take similar cognitive steps in their appraisal of the situation. When a person first notices symptoms, he determines the possible threat of the problem to his current functioning. The symptoms and their threat arouse anxiety, which leads him to use available medical knowledge and problem-solving skills to deal with his anxiety and discomfort. This may mean seeking one or another form of medical care, including advice from friends, home remedies, a visit to the physician or curandero (native witch doctor in Spanish-American communities in Colorado and New Mexico), or perhaps denial of the symptoms. The factors mentioned previously shape the direction the individual takes to control his symptoms.

The fields of psychology, psychiatry, and social work have made us aware of the large variety of psychological reactions to physical illness and disability. In addition to understanding the stress factors that may have been an important precursor to a serious illness, it is essential to understand the nature of the individual and his family's emotional reactions to his symptoms. For example, it has been found to be helpful for the personnel giving services directly to the patient, be they doctor, nurse, or social worker, to appraise the patient's emotions and motivation for recovery. While emotional reactions vary considerably according to the patient's personal history and innate characteristics, his age or life stage also plays a key role. Infants, children, adults, and the aged react differently to a similar illness or accident. Emotions are also differently affected by the characteristics of the particular illness, whether it is acute or chronic in nature. Different categories of illness and disability evoke different emotional responses. Venereal disease, for instance, may engender feelings of guilt in its victims because of the stigma attached to it. Likewise, tuberculosis evokes fear, anxiety, and shame among those who suffer from it. However, as community attitudes toward various illnesses change, psychological and social responses to them also change.[19]

[18] For further discussion of this concept, see Chapters 10 and 11.
[19] See Joan K. Jackson and Thomas H. Holmes, "Alcoholism and Tuberculo-

Individuals understandably respond to chronic disabilities and terminal illnesses with depression and despair. A variety of psychological defense mechanisms come into play when an individual is confronted with a crippling condition. Mechanisms such as denial of illness, withdrawal from social contacts, and blame of others for the condition are frequently encountered. Similarly, the family's feelings are aroused by the illness; they use various defense mechanisms to deal with the realization of the patient's illness and its meaning to them. On the other hand, it is not uncommon for individuals who have willingly accepted the sick role to enjoy the side benefits of invalidism so much that they are not willing to relinquish the role when their health improves. Too much acceptance of the secondary advantages of illness can impede recovery. Another related phenomenon is the patient's acceptance of a chronic-dependent role. For some patients a long-term illness and strong dependency needs make the chronic dependent position more acceptable, on a continuing basis, than risking the emotional effects of recovery. The fear of being discharged into a world with high expectations can impede the patient's progress.[20]

It is important to distinguish between psychological reactions to the illness itself and the reaction to the treatment environment. Medical procedures such as amputations and removal of certain organs can evoke gross psychological responses, especially when the change has some specifically emotionally-charged meaning to the individual. For example, a hysterectomy may bring on an especially severe depression in a young woman anxious to build a family. Social-psychological research has recognized that the medical institution itself, because of its structure and manner of caring for patients, has an extremely influential role in encouraging the patient to accept a chronic sick role. This is especially true of institutions that deal with long-term medical problems found among the aged, the mentally ill, the chronically disabled, and alcoholics. More progressive treatment programs have devised ways to prevent this type of social breakdown from occurring.[21] However, most hospitals have given insufficient attention to this aspect of sociomedical care. The medical treatment team is increasingly dependent on social workers and other allied health professionals to attend to these factors and to help create a hospital environment that will prevent the occurrence of nonfunctional dependency.

---

sis," in Apple, ed., *Sociological Studies of Health and Sickness,* pp. 175–85; and King, "Social Psychological Factors in Illness."

20 Mechanic, *Medical Sociology.*

21 Russell Barton, *Institutional Neurosis* (Bristol: John Wright & Sons, 1959). See also Ernest M. Gruenberg, S. Brandon, and R. Kasius, "Identifying Cases of Social Breakdown Syndrome, Evaluating the Effectiveness of Mental Health Services," *Milbank Memorial Fund Quarterly,* 44, No. 1 (January 1966), 150–55.

SOCIAL WORK IN MEDICAL SETTINGS

In view of the variety of social and psychological responses to illness and disability and the need to understand and deal with them, it is understandable that within the medical setting a specialty of social work practice has developed. Physicians consider social work an allied medical discipline, and where social workers are employed, they have become an integral part of the medical team. In collaboration with the doctors, nurses, and other therapists, medical social workers take part in the study, diagnostic, and treatment-planning process for the patient, or for groups of patients with similar needs. The primary aim of medical social workers is to help restore the patient's social functioning. They help him resolve the social and emotional problems that keep him from reaching a satisfactory level of adjustment to or recovery from the illness. In addition, they provide all-important links between the world of medicine, the family, and the world of social services. Medical social workers are found in most aspects of hospital services, be they acute, chronic, or rehabilitative.[22]

History of Medical Social Work

The medical social worker has four main precursors. The first was the recognition, in England in the 1880s, that discharged patients of mental hospitals needed aftercare in their homes to avoid recurrence of their illness. "Visitors" went to the patient's home and advised family and friends about the necessary care of the patient after his discharge. A second source of medical social work were the "lady almoners" in English hospitals; they organized on the initiative of Sir Charles S. Loch in London in the 1890s, and served as volunteer receptionists, made social investigations, and decided whether applicants should be admitted as free patients to the hospital, and what charity organization might be asked to assume the patient's support.[23] Visiting nurses were the third precursors of medical social workers. In 1893 Lillian Wald

---

[22] See Beatrice Phillips, "Health Services: Social Workers," *Encyclopedia 1971*, pp. 565–75; Harriett M. Bartlett, *Social Work Practice in the Health Field* (New York: National Association of Social Workers, 1961); and Bess Dana, "Social Work in the University Medical Center," *Johns Hopkins Medical Journal*, 124, No. 5 (May 1969), 277–92.

[23] Ida M. Cannon, *Social Work in Hospitals: A Contribution to Progressive Medicine* (New York: Russell Sage Foundation, 1930), pp. 5–15, and *On the Social Frontier of Medicine* (Cambridge, Mass.: Harvard University Press, 1952), pp. 46–94; Eleanor E. Cockrill, "Medical Social Work," *Social Work Year Book* (1960), 375–82; Elizabeth P. Rice, "Social Work Practices in Medical and Health Services," *Encyclopedia 1965*, pp. 470–76; Ava H. Parks, "Short-term Casework in a Medical Setting," *Social Work*, 8, No. 4 (October 1963), 89–94; Richard H. Klemer, *Counseling in Marital and Sexual Problems* (Baltimore: Williams & Wilkins, 1965).

and Mary Brewster of the Henry Street Settlement House in New York began to visit the homes of sick people in the neighborhood who were too poor to pay for medical and nursing care. They found that many social and personal problems were caused by the illness of the patients. Some hospitals in New York learned from the experiences of the Henry Settlement House that visits in the home might improve greatly the effect of medical treatment; they sent nurses from the hospital staff for aftercare and supervision of discharged patients. The fourth precursor of the medical social worker was medical students trained in social agencies. Dr. Charles P. Emerson of Johns Hopkins University, Baltimore, in 1902 wanted to include the study of social and emotional problems in medical education and requested that his students serve as volunteers with charity agencies to gain an understanding of the influence of social, economic, and living conditions on the illness of patients.

On the basis of these experiences, medical social work was established in 1905, at four different places at almost the same time. Social workers became members of the staff at Massachusetts General Hospital in Boston, at Bellevue Hospital in New York, at Johns Hopkins Hospital in Baltimore, and at the Berkeley Infirmary in Boston.

The medical specialist is no longer able to be acquainted with the living conditions, income, environment, habits, and personality of the patient, as was the old family doctor. Therefore, the medical social worker has had to make the personal contact with patient and family, to investigate social and personal conditions of the patient, and to supply the factual background to the physician to help him in diagnosis and treatment. Dr. Richard C. Cabot of Massachusetts General Hospital was the first to recognize the need for a social worker to help the patient, after his return from the hospital, to observe the orders of the physician, to instruct the family in diets, and to administer medical prescriptions.[24]

The most typical role for the medical social worker is that of a caseworker, either in a hospital or in a clinic. In these settings the worker studies the patient's social situation with the aim of understanding the psychological stresses he is undergoing and the resources available to him during and after treatment. Through interviews with the patient and his family, the worker can gain a perspective on the social and emotional components of the illness and how they may affect treatment and recovery. A detailed knowledge of the effects of the specific illness and its course is essential to the worker in understanding how to develop a meaningful medical-social treatment plan for him and his family. Often several posthospital placement options are open fol-

---

[24] Dr. Cabot's use of medical social work began in an experience with a small boy cured of an acute gastric condition after careful medical treatment. A few days after his release, the boy was returned by his mother in the old, ill condition. When this happened a second and third time, it became evident that observation in the family and instruction to the mother were needed to preserve the health of the child.

lowing the acute phase of illness. Knowledge of these options and a determination of how the patient might respond to each of them is required. The medical caseworker's job is a dynamic one which requires constant expansion of his knowledge. With the development of new techniques for prolonging life through heart transplants, artificial organs, and miracle drugs, the social worker must learn to help in dealing with the resulting new types of medical-social problems. Indeed, in many medical centers medical social workers become highly specialized in understanding the dynamics of specific illness or disease categories.[25] With a broader acceptance of psychosomatic components of illness on the part of the physician, the medical caseworker is in the position of working ever closer with the medical treatment team in understanding and treating the soma, the psyche, and the patient's environment.

Medical social workers can be found in the whole range of settings dealing with the direct delivery of medical service, including clinics, hospitals, rehabilitation services, nursing homes, organized home care programs, and the like. They also work in public welfare departments, where they administer and supervise medical assistance programs, especially those concerned with the aged, the mentally disturbed, the mentally retarded, and the physically disabled. Through their understanding of the dynamics of illness, they are able to interpret to other welfare workers the social and psychological needs of the patient or his family, arising from his illness. In so doing, they help to develop the individualized health planning required for the patient, and to coordinate it with other health and welfare services. Medical social workers frequently teach medical school courses. As medical school faculty, they impart their professional knowledge of the sociopsychological aspect of illness and the social dynamics of medical care.

SELECTED BIBLIOGRAPHY

ANDERSON, ODIN W., *Health Services in a Land of Plenty*. Chicago: University of Chicago Press, 1968.

BRESLOW, LESTER, "The Urgency of Social Action for Health," *American Journal of Public Health*, 60, No. 1 (January 1970), 10–16.

BROWN, ESTHER LUCILE, *Newer Dimensions of Patient Care: Patients as People*. New York: Russell Sage Foundation, 1964.

BURNS, EVELINE M., "Some Major Policy Decisions Facing the United States in the Financing and Organization of Health Care, *New Directions in Public Policy for Health Care* (December 1966), 1072–88.

Comprehensive Health Planning, Selective Readings. New York: Health Insurance Institute, 1969.

[25] For example, see Zelda P. Leader Foster, "How Social Work Can Influence Hospital Management of Fatal Illness," *Social Work*, 10, No. 4 (October 1965), 30–53; and David M. Kaplan and Edward A. Mason, "Maternal Reactions to Premature Birth Viewed as an Acute Emotional Disorder," in Howard Parad ed., *Crisis Intervention* (New York: Family Service Association, 1965), pp. 118–28.

CORNING, PETER A., *The Evolution of Medicare from Idea to Law,* Research Report No. 29. Washington, D.C.: U.S. Department of Health, Education and Welfare, Social Security Administration, 1969.

Delivery of Health Services for the Poor, A Program Analysis. Washington, D.C.: U.S. Department of Health, Education and Welfare, Office of the Assistant Secretary for Planning and Evaluation, 1967.

FALK, LESLIE A., "The Negro American's Health and the Medical Committee for Human Rights," *Medical Care,* 4, No. 3 (July–September 1966), 171–77.

Hospitals and Coordinated Home Care Programs. Chicago: American Hospital Association, 1966.

LERNER, MONROE, "The Level of Physical Health of the Poverty Population," *Medical Care,* 6, No. 5 (September–October 1968), 335–67.

MACNAMARA, MARGARET, "The Family in Stress: Social Work Before and After Renal Homotransplantation," *Social Work,* 14, No. 4. (October 1969), 89–97.

Medical Industrial Complex, Health-PAC Bulletin. New York: Health Policy Advisory Center, 1969.

Medicare and Medicaid: Problems, Issues and Alternatives, Report of the Staff to the Committee on Finance, U.S. Senate. Washington, D.C.: U.S. Government Printing Office, 1970.

"Neighborhood Health Centers," *Medical Care,* 8, No. 2 (March–April 1970).

PHILLIPS, BEATRICE, "Social Service Programs Require Imaginative Staff Deployment," *Hospitals,* 43, No. 18 (16 September 1969), 101–5.

ROSEN, G., *The Hospital: Historical Sociology of a Community Institution.* London: Macmillan, 1963.

SILVER, GEORGE A., "New Types of Personnel and Changing Roles of Health Professionals," *Bulletin of the New York Academy of Medicine,* 42, No. 12 (December 1966), 12–17.

WEINERMAN, E. R., "Research into the Organization of Medical Practice," *Milbank Memorial Fund Quarterly,* 44, No. 4 (October 1966), 104–45.

WEISS, EDWARD, and O. SPURGEON ENGLISH, *Psychosomatic Medicine.* Philadelphia: W. B. Saunders, 1943.

WOLFE, P. H. and GENEVIEVE TEED, "A Study of the Work of a Medical Social Worker in a Group Medical Practice," *Canadian Medical Association Journal,* 96 (27 May 1969), 1407–16.

16

---

mental
health
services
and social
work

We have separated our presentation of mental disorder from the chapter
on medical care, even though we know that this division is somewhat arbitrary, because the two systems of treatment and care have different historical
roots and are, by and large, administered separately. Gross mental disorder
in the form of bizarre and disturbing behavior or severe retardation is
usually defined as "deviant" from "normal" behavior, which in turn is
defined by each culture according to its unique societal context.[1] Some

[1] Daniel Offer and Melvin Sabshin, *Normality: Theoretical and Clinical Concepts in Mental Health* (New York: Basic Books, 1966), p. 253.

societies are more tolerant toward individuals who exhibit unusual behavior; extremely deviant behavior generally evokes strong responses, and often leads to the exclusion of the deviant individual from the community.

The problem faced by any society in defining mental disorder(s) is that abnormal behavior tends to merge with borderline and "normal" behavior so that division between normality and abnormality becomes arbitrary. Also, one specific act or piece of behavior itself is usually not enough to define a person as disordered. Mental health and mental illness cannot be considered dichotomous, but rather as the ends of a continuum. While it is not too difficult to identify and classify those who fall at either end of the continuum, it is riskier to label most people who fall between the extremes. The labeling process is dangerous because it sets the individual apart from the majority and frequently provides the society with a rationale for treating him differently, often punitively.

The range of acceptable human behavior is so broad and changes so from place to place and time to time that the designation "normal" probably has as much to do with mores as with objective knowledge about the psychopathology of an individual. A person may indeed be psychologically disturbed (diseased), but labels such as schizophrenic, paranoiac, and neurotic are socially defined, in large part, and subjectively diagnosed. Psychiatrists, even those trained at the same school, frequently disagree on the diagnosis of a particular patient.[2] Because it is difficult for psychiatrists to understand patients of different social classes and ethnic backgrounds, they tend to diagnose poorer patients more severely.[3] The scientific approach to the diagnosis of mental disorders is still too inaccurate to distinguish clearly between different categories and subcategories of mental disorders. The standard system of psychiatric nomenclature of mental disorders is based on the description of symptoms or clusters of symptoms, and does not explain either the cause of the condition, in many categories, or the course treatment should take.

BRIEF HISTORY OF MENTAL HEALTH CARE

The history of man's treatment of the mentally disordered is fascinating but blood curdling (see Chapter 2 for background on the care of the mentally retarded). It reveals that each society has developed a unique way

---

[2] Lawrence C. Kolb, Viola Bernard, and Bruce P. Dohrenwend, "The Problem of Validity in Field Studies of Psychological Disorder," in Bruce P. Dohrenwend and Barbara Snell Dohrenwend, eds., *Urban Challenges to Psychiatry* (New York: John Wiley, 1969), pp. 429–60.

[3] Joel Fischer, "Negroes and Whites and Rates of Mental Illness," *Psychiatry*, 32, No. 4 (November 1969), 428–46.

of viewing the problem and treating the disturbed people.[4] Treatment has varied according to the meaning society has attached to the particular form of deviant behavior. In some societies deviants are valued highly, even treated as prophets or "divine" beings with unusual powers to do good. In others abnormal behavior is regarded as an evil threat to be suppressed or rooted out. Sometimes deviant individuals have been tortured and put to death. In Western Europe and the United States before the nineteenth century, the mentally disordered were quartered in "mad houses" where they were often chained to the walls.[5] Kept in barren, unsanitary rooms, the "insane" and "idiots" mixed freely. Children and adults were kept together. Harsh treatment and ridicule were heaped upon them, with no regard for their well-being. Local communities hired wardens to care for the mentally disordered in squalid, overcrowded buildings, paying for their care on a per capita basis at a predetermined rate. If the warden could care for them for less, he could pocket the remainder of the payment. By the end of the eighteenth century, with the development of interest in medical science, some of the enlightened hospitals in Western Europe and America began to take a more humane attitude toward the insane. Physicians became scientifically interested in insanity, observing patients more systematically and listening to their illogical mutterings.[6] Various systems of classification began to develop for the physicians' observations. Ironically, these early forerunners of psychiatry had little inkling that much of the behavior they observed in the mad houses resulted from "chronic breakdown syndrome," the side effect of long periods of institutionalization. Simultaneously in both England and France and then in America changes began to occur in the treatment of the insane. In England the impetus came from a book called *Treatise on the Moral Treatment of the Insane.* The author, William Tuke (1732–1822), was a Quaker, and his notions about "moral treatment" were influential in changing attitudes toward the care of the mentally disturbed.[7] The use of the word *moral* has changed since the time of Tuke. Psychiatrists of his time used the word as a synonym of *psychological* and *emotional.* They believed that the insane had experienced a variety of stresses which affected their ability to reason, and that "moral treatment" would provide the proper influences to help them return to normal. Tuke believed that the custodians of the insane should treat their patients with humanity and dignity, and he rejected the brutality which characterized English wardens. He founded the first asylum for the insane at York, in northern England.

4 George Rosen, *Madness in Society, Chapters in the Historical Sociology of Mental Illness* (New York: Harper & Row, 1969).

5 Ibid., pp. 172–95.

6 Franz G. Alexander and Sheldon T. Selesnick, *The History of Psychiatry* (New York: Harper & Row, 1966), pp. 112–13.

7 Ibid., p. 120

Tuke himself lived at the hospital, called the Retreat, and treated the patients as members of his family.[8] His principle of "moral treatment" spread to America, where Benjamin Rush (1745–1813) introduced the idea in his mental hospital in Philadelphia. (See pages 69–71 on the early history of care for the insane in the United States.) During the same period in France, informed by the spirit of scientific rationality and the French Revolution, Philippe Pinel (1745–1825) unshackled the insane from the walls, first at Bicêtre, the *grange aux gueux* (beggars farm), and later at La Salpêtriere, the insane asylum.[9] Pinel's notion, revolutionary in its time, was that the mentally disturbed were not criminals, but were ill, and that humanitarian treatment could make them normal. Some of his contributions were to improve their physical surroundings, to reject violence and chains as a way of subduing unruly patients, and to introduce segregation of violent from nonviolent patients, men from women, and chronic from short-term patients. He also introduced therapeutic occupations for mental patients. Tuke in England, Pinel in France, and Rush in the United States were the first to recognize the crucial importance of the physician–patient relationship as a unique tool in the treatment of emotional disorders.

The concept of "moral treatment" of the insane spread to many places in the United States. In 1817 the first hospital in the United States exclusively dedicated to providing moral treatment was built by the Pennsylvania Quakers. Patterned after the York Retreat, it became the model for other similar hospitals. By 1847 thirty hospitals for moral treatment under philanthropic auspices had been established from New Hampshire to South Carolina.[10] Several state-financed hospitals practicing moral treatment were also constructed during this period. The Worcester State Hospital in Massachusetts kept accurate records of the patients using its facilities and reported what can be considered remarkable success in treating its patients by means of moral therapy. During its first twenty years of operation, of all the patients admitted who had been ill less than one year before admission, 66 percent were discharged "recovered" and 5 percent "improved."[11] Similar results were reported by other hospitals at that time. However, the early golden era of psychiatry was not long-lasting. Tuke's theories, while far in advance of his time, were costly to implement and perhaps unsuited to a young country undergoing population expansion and rapid urbanization. To be effective, hospitals for moral treatment had to be small and have an adequate staff. Local governments responsible for raising taxes for the care

8 Sanbourne J. Bockhoven, "Moral Treatment in American Psychiatry," in O. Hobart Mowrer, ed., *Morality and Mental Health* (Chicago: Rand McNally, 1967), pp. 172–95.

9 Alexander and Selesnick, *The History of Psychiatry*, pp. 112–13.

10 Bockhoven, "Moral Treatment in American Psychiatry," p. 179.

11 Ibid., p. 180.

of the insane, however, chose not to give much support to hospitals for the care of the mentally ill and mentally retarded. The hospitals therefore grew in size and became overcrowded. Frequently psychiatric patients mingled with the poor, the disabled, and criminals. These institutions, still called "poor houses," were overcrowded and understaffed, exploited patients by employing them in hospital industries, and provided inadequate diet and miserable surroundings.

For the most part there was little progress during the nineteenth century in the scientific inquiry into the origin of mental disorders, except for developments in the field of neuroanatomy. Wardens of the poor houses and superintendents of the insane asylums were more concerned about caring for the buildings and managing their adjacent dairies and farms than assuring the well-being of inmates.

Significant reforms in the day-to-day care of mental patients were achieved through the efforts of reformer Dorothea Lynde Dix (1802–1887). Her singular efforts led to the establishment of thirty-two new institutions for the mentally disordered.[12] Dix's work is praised highly, yet in retrospect it is ironic that the current national trend in the field of mental health is aimed at dissolving or transforming these institutions, which have now outgrown their usefulness. Most of the hospitals were located deep in the countryside, where they removed patients from their families and the facilities and activities of the community. With the patients out of sight, the community took little interest in their fate at the hands of an apathetic staff.

Clifford Beers's book, *A Mind that Found Itself* (1908), reached a wide audience and was instrumental in the development of mental health associations.[13] The book was a recollection of Beers's emotional torture and recovery from mental illness, and it sensitized the public to the plight of mentally disordered people and the necessity for treatment. The mental health societies, under Beers's leadership, successfully demonstrated the extent of mental disorders and the need for more, improved services. Under his influence the concept of outpatient treatment as a prevention of hospitalization became widespread.

While efforts were being made to improve the hospital environment for the mentally disordered, some scientists were attempting to understand the origins of mental illness and to develop effective treatment for it. Sigmund Freud, founder of the psychoanalytic school, was the most significant figure in this development; his influence has penetrated every phase of intellectual life, from clinical treatment to political analysis. Freud's theories ranged from historical explanations, as in *Civilization and Its Discontent* and

_____

[12] Ralph L. Pumphrey and Muriel W. Pumphrey, eds., *The Heritage of American Social Work* (New York: Columbia University Press, 1961), pp. 126–32.

[13] Clifford W. Beers, *A Mind that Found Itself* (New York: Longmans, Green, 1908).

Moses and Monotheism, to the most precise and detailed studies of the individual psyche.[14] During the 1920s and '30s the development of social work, the direction of casework techniques, and the rise of psychiatric casework as a field were profoundly shaped by Freud's influence.[15] His theory of neurosis has been an especially strong influence in shaping treatment modalities in small inpatient units and in clinical settings, but it has been used less with psychotic patients in larger hospital settings.

Freud and his followers theorized about the stages of psychosexual development from earliest infancy through adulthood. They held that the earliest years of development influence the future growth of the personality, and that the successful completion of each stage in development, if the conflicts which characterize the stage are properly resolved, leaves the developing person with strength to grow and mature. If in the process of maturation a child misses some basic experience essential to development, or undergoes some emotional trauma which hinders or arrests emotional growth, personality disorders result in the child or adult. Earlier many scientists had believed that personality disorders flowed from genetic or physiological conditions which could not be changed; Freud's psychoanalytic research developed a body of theory and wider range of techniques by which treatment of severe neuroses and emotional problems could be postulated. The trained psychoanalyst or analytically trained psychotherapist could, through an intensive therapeutic relationship with a patient, reveal the sources of early problems, help to bring them into the patient's consciousness, and thereby help him resolve these problems.[16] Analysis, or therapy, requires high motivation on the part of the patient to enter into and continue the therapeutic process. However, in large hospital settings where patients are often brought against their will, the general atmosphere does not lead to such motivation and Freud's theories have not been so useful.

The realization that emotional disorder results from childhood development led to the establishment of psychological services for young people. In the initial decade of the twentieth century juvenile courts began to consider psychological reasons for wayward behavior.[17] The first child guidance clinic was founded in Chicago in 1909 by Dr. William Healy, and in 1927 the Commonwealth Fund provided funds to establish demonstration child

[14] Sigmund Freud, *The Standard Edition of the Complete Psychological Works of Sigmund Freud,* 23 vols., trans. James Strachey (London: The Hogarth Press, 1953–1964).

[15] Gordon Hamilton, *The Theory and Practice of Social Casework* (New York: Columbia University Press, 1941) Carol H. Meyer, *Social Work Practice* (New York: Free Press, 1970), pp. 42–44.

[16] Ernest Jones, *The Life and Work of Sigmund Freud* (New York: Basic Books, 1953–1957), 3 vols.

[17] August Aichhorn, *The Wayward Youth* (London: Image Press, 1951), p. 236.

guidance clinics in different areas of the country.[18] The goal of these clinics was prevention of psychological disorders, but in actuality they came to deal mainly with treatment of already identified behavior disorders. While many of Freud's early followers remained close to him and elaborated his original theories, some, like Carl Jung and Alfred Adler, broke away to form separate schools of psychological thought and treatment.[19] Today there are still orthodox Freudians practicing psychoanalysis, as well as numerous offshoots from his school and from other schools as well.

For the most part advances in the care and treatment of the hospitalized mentally disordered during the first four decades of the twentieth century were undramatic. Only a few specific organic causes of mental illness and mental retardation were uncovered. General paresis, a progressive organic condition ending in insanity, was linked to syphilis; pellagra, a condition generating psychiatric symptoms, was linked to a dietary deficiency, as was phenylkitornuria, a condition resulting in mental retardation. While psychoanalytic explanations and psychoanalysis were beginning to be more widely accepted in America, many psychiatrists and other physicians still stoutly rejected them and continued to hold the belief that genetic endowment, metabolic disorders, and infectious diseases were the basis of mental disorder. Within medical circles there is still the strong belief that most mental disorders are physiological, though psychoanalytic concepts have taken a firm foothold in psychiatry and have spread widely in the other mental health professions.

The notion that mental illness is akin to other physical illnesses gave rise to the expectation that it could be treated medically or even surgically. In the eighteenth century bloodletting was used widely to treat the insane. By the mid-twentieth century other extreme forms of physical treatment of the mentally ill were extensively practiced. Electroconvulsive therapy (ECT) and prefrontal lobotomy, surgical alteration of a section of the brain, were the new nostrums to "remove" the illness from the patient.[20] These physiological approaches were of little lasting therapeutic value, although they made the hospital routine easier for the staff, as patients were more subdued and easier to control.

Until the end of World War II there were few psychiatric outpatient clinics. Most of these services were privately sponsored and used mostly by middle-class patients. In the major cities psychiatrists opened private practices similar to traditional medical practice. Only the wealthy could afford the cost of private treatment, and the majority of people still depended on state mental hospitals for treatment. Those with lesser forms of illness, such as

18 Alexander and Selesnick, *The History of Psychiatry*, p. 377.
19 Ibid., pp. 226–52.
20 Ibid., pp. 271–96.

mild neuroses, did not enter hospitals. They rarely found their way to medical treatment, but often obtained help from social workers employed in family agencies, ministers, friends, even bartenders and beauticians.

Preenlistment screening during World War II rejected about 5.7 percent (856,200) of the inductees because of neuropsychiatric disorders.[21] Among returning servicemen 37 percent (387,000) of those discharged with service-connected medical conditions were diagnosed as mentally ill. This enormous need for psychiatric services galvanized Congress to establish a national health policy for increasing psychiatric services. Veterans Administration Hospital facilities were greatly expanded, as was their recruitment and training of psychiatric personnel. The VA psychiatric training program was the first major step on a national level to increase the number of trained mental health professionals (psychiatric social workers, psychologists, and psychiatrists). This in turn increased the stature of psychodynamic theory as the basis for treating mental disorders.[22]

Another major advance in the development of psychiatric services was the passage of the *National Mental Health Act* in 1946. It established the National Institute of Mental Health, which provided grants-in-aid for states to train personnel, fund research, and encourage the development of local mental health services.[23] The annual budget of the Institute continually increased during the 1960s; the number of outpatient clinics, for example, increased threefold during the first fifteen years of the Institute's existence.

The late 1940s and the 1950s marked the expansion of psychiatric services into the community, but the major facility for the treatment of mental disorders remained the state psychiatric hospital. Most patients were released in less than six months' time, but there was a steady accretion of long-term patients with chronic mental illness, mostly diagnosed as schizophrenia and diseases of the aged. Few hospitals had sufficient funds to provide high-quality psychiatric care. Most institutions still suffered from understaffing, overcrowding, and lack of skilled leadership. Throughout the postwar period dramatic reports of maltreatment and neglect of the mentally ill were published. The movie *Snake Pit,* dramatizing the worst aspects of the insane asylum, was a shocking exposé of the bizarre reality of life in a mental hospital.

Medical personnel in psychiatric hospitals relied heavily on electro-convulsive therapy as a way of handling patients' problems. Ideally, the therapy was supposed to treat the patient's psychotic disorder. Some patients

---

21 James Lowry, "Mental Hygiene," *Social Work Year Book* (1951), 321.

22 Morris S. Schwartz and Charlotte Green Schwartz, *Social Approaches to Mental Patient Care* (New York: Columbia University Press, 1964), p. 32.

23 Ruth I. Knee and Warren C. Lamson, "Mental Health Services," *Encyclopedia of Social Work 1971*, pp. 805–8.

did respond to this radical treatment, but many experienced relapses following a "successful" course of shock treatment. Too often these extreme forms of treatment were used to promote social control of difficult patients, rather than as therapy.[24]

While lobotomies and leucotomies were not so routine as ECT, these surgical procedures were popular in many institutions.[25] Some tormented individuals were helped by such surgery, but the irreversible nature of these operations meant that any chance for the patient to return to self-sufficiency was lost. Predictability of the outcome of the surgery was very low because not enough was known about the brain and the specific origins of mental disorders. The number of lobotomies dwindled, but presently there is a resurgence of interest in this type of procedure as a way of managing individuals with long histories of criminal behavior.

Behavioral scientists' increasing knowledge of the social dynamics of the mental hospital were an impetus to change traditional methods of hospital psychiatry. They brought into clear focus the effects of the hospital social structure, especially the authoritarian hierarchy among the staff, on the patient.[26] They demonstrated how the hospital socialization process did as much to impede the patient's progress as to promote it.[27] Much of the bizarre psychopathology displayed by long-term patients was caused by the institutional process.[28] In some hospitals it was demonstrated, however, that an organized resocialization and reacculturation program could reverse, to some extent, the psychopathic process and shorten the period of hospitalization of mental patients.[29]

In the late 1940s in Great Britain, France, and the United States, a number of social psychiatrists, working with social workers and psychologists, began to experiment with a variety of alternate models of institutional care and treatment for the mentally ill. Some of these services, like the day hospital, were designed to prevent institutionalization, while others, like social therapeutic clubs, halfway houses, rehabilitation workshops, and therapeutic communities, were aimed at shortening hospitaliza-

[24] For a dramatic illustration, see Ken Kesey, *One Flew Over the Cuckoo's Nest* (New York: Viking Press, 1962).

[25] Franz G. Alexander and Sheldon Selesnick, *The History of Psychiatry* (New York: Harper & Row, 1966), pp. 285–97.

[26] A. Stanton and Morris Schwartz, *The Mental Hospital* (New York: Basic Books, 1954); W. Caudill, *The Psychiatric Hospital as a Small Society* (Cambridge, Mass.: Commonwealth Fund, 1958).

[27] Stanton and Schwartz, *The Mental Hospital.*

[28] Russell Barton, *Institutional Neurosis* (Bristol: John Wright & Sons, 1959); Ernest W. Gruenberg, S. Brandon, and R. Kasius, "Identifying Cases of Social Breakdown Syndrome, Evaluating the Effectiveness of Mental Health Services," *Milbank Memorial Fund Quarterly,* 44, No. 1, (January 1966), 150–55.

[29] Schwartz and Schwartz, *Social Approaches to Mental Patient Care.*

tion, minimizing its negative features, and thereby speeding rehabilitation.[30]

The use of psychoactive drugs was another significant development of this period. Both tranquilizers and stimulants were found useful in controlling behavior. The initial hope was that they could cure psychoses, but it was soon realized that they were useful primarily because they made other therapeutic modalities possible—patients could be more accessible to treatment. That the staff could control bizarre and often threatening behavior meant that some of the policies and restrictive procedures of the hospital environment could be liberalized or eliminated. Staff morale quickly improved and the prevalent attitude of despair gave way to hope. Through the use of drugs many long-term patients improved enough to return to the community.

In 1955 Congress passed the *Mental Health Study Act,* which authorized the formation of the Joint Commission on Mental Illness and Health (see Chapter 14). The task of the Joint Commission was to recommend to Congress, after seeking divergent viewpoints, measures for the improvement of care and treatment of mental illness. The congressional mandate of the Commission stated that it "should be ready to recommend a radical reconstruction of the present system, if such is indicated, rather than advocating a patch-up of our present system." The Commission produced ten reports over the next six years, culminating in the report "Action for Mental Health," submitted to Congress in 1961.[31] The report acknowledged the new treatment approaches in psychiatry from the previous decade, and recommended a major change in the system of care of the mentally ill. The Commission recommended that no hospital be larger than 1,000 beds (some hospitals at the time had over 10,000 patients). Its report stated that hospitals should be used for intensive treatment rather than for the care of chronic patients; this meant revamping the existing system for giving care. Perhaps the most important recommendation was that psychiatric care should shift from the state mental hospital to mental health centers in the communities. The Commission made a strong case for treating mentally ill patients in the community, near their homes, thus avoiding the crippling effects of institutionalization. It recommended the establishment of a spectrum of community-based services to provide continuous and comprehensive aid to the mentally disordered and to meet the needs of all social

---

30 Robert Apte, *Halfway Houses: A New Dilemma in Institutional Care* (London: Bell & Sons, 1968); Maxwell Jones, *The Therapeutic Community* (New York: Basic Books, 1953); Milton Greenblatt and Benjamin Simon, "Rehabilitation of the Mentally Ill," Publication No. 58 (Washington, D.C.: American Association for the Advancement of Science, 1959).

31 Joint Commission on Mental Illness and Health, *Action for Mental Health,* Final Report of the Joint Commission on Mental Illness, (New York: Basic Books, 1961).

classes. To that end it recommended that the federal government play a major role in financing the mental health system. The Commission also encouraged a commitment to long-term basic research on the etiology of mental illness, and more flexible use of available manpower to serve the needs of those with emotional problems.

The report was criticized for its obvious bias in favor of improving the system of treatment for those already diagnosed as mentally ill, instead of a more balanced approach including primary prevention as well as secondary and tertiary prevention.[32] The majority of the professionals who wrote the report were psychiatrists with a professional investment in clinical psychiatry. They stated:

> We have assumed that the mental hygiene movement has diverted attention from the core problem of major mental illness. It is our purpose to redirect attention to the possibilities of improving the mental health of the mentally ill. It is not our purpose, however, to dismiss the many measures of public information, mental health education, and child and adult guidance that may enhance an understanding of one's own and others' behavior and so build self-confidence, reduce anxiety, and result in better social adjustment and greater personal satisfaction. But our main concern here, in recommendations for a program attacking mental illness, is with various levels of service beginning with secondary prevention—early treatment of beginning disturbances to ward off more serious illness, if possible—and continuing through intensive and protracted treatment of the acutely and chronically ill.[33]

MENTAL ILLNESS AS A SOCIAL PROBLEM

Mental illness is not just an individual or family problem; it is also a social problem of great magnitude. As we have seen, mental illness has been regarded differently at different times; certainly it has not always been considered a serious social problem. Presently there is increased interest in mental illness as a social problem of major concern. Sociologist Robert Nisbet defines a social problem as "breakdowns or deviations in social behavior, involving a considerable number of people, which are of serious concern to many members of society in which the aberrations occur. At bottom, social problems are problems of moral value;...because the behavior involved... is widely regarded as immoral, illegal, or potentially destructive of some established institution."[34]

The important aspects of mental illness as a social problem which we

[32] Ibid., p. 338.

[33] Ibid., pp. 330–31.

[34] Robert Merton and Robert A. Nisbet, *Contemporary Social Problems* (New York: Harcourt Brace, 1961), p. 11.

shall discuss are (1) the extent and cost to society of mental illness, (2) the legal and moral issues centered around the social control of deviant behavior, and (3) the stigma attached to the mentally ill and their families.

Extent and Cost of Mental Illness

The prevalence of mental disorders has been of considerable interest during the past thirty years, the topic of studies of many kinds. Findings have differed, and evaluation is difficult because there has been no uniform standard of what constitutes mental illness, and what differentiates severe, moderate, and mild disorders. However, there is agreement that mental illness in one form or another touches on nearly every family at some point in life.

Mental health statistical reports show that over 1,000,000 individuals annually are treated in mental hospitals, and over 1,500,000 individuals annually are seen in clinics and private physicians' offices for diagnosis and treatment of mental disorders.[35] Of those hospitalized, 45.6 percent are diagnosed as schizophrenics, 12.2 percent as senile, and 7.6 percent and 6.7 percent respectively as suffering from manic-depressive psychoses and syphilitic psychoses. Another 3 percent of patients suffer from involutional and alcoholic psychoses, while 6 percent suffer from mental retardation. Over half of all hospital beds for all illnesses (medical and psychiatric) are occupied by schizophrenics.[36] Until fifteen years ago schizophrenia was believed to require long periods of hospitalization, and as a result there was continual growth in the number of hospital patients.

Comprehensive community surveys, while their findings vary vastly, indicate that the number of patients actually treated in hospital or community facilities is only a fraction of those who have serious emotional problems, the "tip of the iceberg." The Midtown Manhattan Study, perhaps the most rigorous of the prevalence surveys in the United States, sampled at random 1,660 residents of a population of 110,000 individuals living in downtown Manhattan.[37] They were interviewed in detail to determine the extent of emotional disorder. Each person was given a mental health rating established by psychiatrists involved in the research project. A six-step scale described the level of mental health functioning of the sample, based on the presence and severity of psychiatric symptoms. The scale ranged from no evidence of symptom formation through mild, moderate, and serious symptom formation, to incapacitation.

[35] John J. Hanlon, *Principles of Public Health Administration* (Saint Louis: C. V. Mosby, 1969), pp. 425–26.

[36] Ibid., p. 425.

[37] I. S. Langner and S. T. Michael, *Life Stress and Mental Health* (New York: Free Press, 1963).

Table 1   Scale of mental health functioning from Midtown Manhattan Study

Well (no symptoms)		18%
Mild symptoms		36%
Moderate symptoms		21.8%
Impaired		
Marked symptoms	13.2%	
Severe symptoms	7.5%	
Incapacitated	2.7%	23.4%
Total		99.2%

Startlingly, in Midtown Manhattan over 45 percent of the people were judged to have from moderate to severe symptoms of poor mental health. One might assume that this was a product of the "life stress" in New York City, but a similar survey of the extent of mental illness in Kalamazoo, Michigan found overall prevalence rates only slightly lower than in Manhattan. (The authors of the Kalamazoo study believed that the difference in rates was caused by a difference in the definition of illness between the two studies.) [38]

An important criticism of both studies is that symptoms per se are not indicative of mental disorders. Psychiatric symptoms appear and disappear quickly in many people. It is the *persistence of symptoms* that signifies mental illness.[39] In addition, our definition of mental illness is still very vague. Social attitudes differ over what constitutes deviant behavior of psychiatric concern. Members of different cultures and of different groups in the same culture have different tolerances toward variations in behavior. Mental health professionals usually come from the middle stratum of our society, and their bias shapes the psychiatric labeling process.

Further, the degree of affluence of a society permits it to allow more or fewer segments of its population to play the sick role. Our society permits and perhaps unintentionally encourages a certain proportion of its population to be socially dependent as mental patients. Conversely, in the Soviet Union, the psychiatric system shows no particular interest in treatment of or care for the psychoneurotic individual. The Soviet Union, of course, does have neurotic citizens, but its government has chosen not to burden the economy with providing care for people who are psychoneurotic, and it therefore denies the existence of neuroses. Social, economic, and even political factors strongly affect our ability to clearly understand the real

[38] J. G. Manis, et al., "Estimating the Prevalence of Mental Illness," *American Sociological Review*, 29 (1964), 84–89.

[39] Bruce Dohrenwend and Barbara Snell Dohrenwend, eds., *Social Status and Psychological Disorder: A Causal Inquiry* (New York: John Wiley, 1969).

extent of mental disorders.[40] Nevertheless, it is certain that the number of those who seek help for their emotional problems far exceeds the capacity of existing programs to help them, and the addition of new services in a community has almost always brought an increase in demand for still more services.

The cost of mental disorder can be thought of both in terms of human suffering and crippling and in terms of the actual dollar-and-cents cost. The latter is extremely difficult to measure, the former impossible. No one can fully appraise the effect of a suicide on the survivors, or the effect of a sadistic or psychotic school teacher on his class. It is clear that devastating incidents such as these have far-ranging effects.

Various attempts have been made to measure the cost of mental illness in monetary terms. The items included in and excluded from the calculations can make a great difference in the final results. Rashi Fein completed a study for the Joint Commission Report on Mental Illness in 1958 and concluded that the cost of mental illness was $2.4 billion in the year 1952. She included both the cost of care and the loss in earning power of those institutionalized.[41] R. L. Conley, M. Conwell, and S. G. Arrill developed a more comprehensive approach to determining the cost of mental illness.[42] In their estimate they included the costs of prevention and treatment of all types of mental illness, whether the patient was in or out of the hospital, and the cost of lower productivity among the mentally ill. The sum of all the components in their analysis exceeded $20 billion for the year 1968 (see Table 2).

Legal Aspects of Mental Illness

When society cannot solve a social problem by informal means, sanctions are used to maintain order and control deviant behavior. A common belief is that mental patients are dangerous to the community and to themselves. While there are instances of psychotic "madmen" who do physical harm to others or are self-destructive, there is no evidence that mental patients are proportionally more dangerous or self-destructive than the population at large. More common, however, are disturbed individuals who need psychiatric treatment but do not recognize their need. Still others realize that they are emotionally in trouble, but do not have the capacity to ask for or accept help.

---

40 For evidence of this fact, see ibid., pp. 9–31.

41 Rashi Fein, *Economics of Mental Illness* (New York: Basic Books, 1958).

42 R. L. Conley, M. Conwell, and S. G. Arrill, *Cost of Mental Illness, 1968,* Statistical Note 30 (Washington, D.C.: Biometry Branch Office of Program Planning and Evaluation, National Institute of Mental Health, 1970).

An informal way to bring the mentally ill into custody or care has long existed in America. A request from family or neighbors to the legal authorities to take responsibility for an insane individual was all that was needed to institutionalize a troubled or troublesome person. However, without provisions to protect the civil rights of the individual, occasional abuses occurred. The formal system of handling problems of this nature evolved in the mid-nineteenth century. Most state laws follow the Massachusetts law of 1848, under which individuals can be apprehended against their will only if they are held dangerous to themselves or others. The involuntary detention is expected to help rehabilitate them. Typically, commitment laws provide that a disturbed person may be detained against his will in a psychiatric hospital or jail for two to five days, under a signed allegation from an interested party that the person is dangerous to himself or others or in need of care and/or treatment. A formal court hearing presided over by a judge, is required; the individual is confronted with witnesses, usually family or friends, and with medical testimony that he is behaving in a deviant way and is considered mentally ill. If the judge accepts the testimony and the accused or his legal defender cannot prove otherwise, the accused is adjudged insane, a legal term, and committed to a psychiatric hospital. He remains in the hospital until he is considered no longer in need of care or treatment.

The law varies somewhat from state to state, and legal procedures may vary considerably even within states.[43] The execution of these laws has been noticeably inconsistent, and the criteria for evidence and proof are imprecise.[44] The laws have worked to the disadvantage of the poor, racial minorities, and the foreign-born. Formal hearings often lack sensitivity to the needs and emotional condition of the patient. Some patients respond to the allegation as if they are being charged with a criminal act, not being assisted to obtain help for an emotional problem. Individuals are often brought to care against their will, with the involvement of the police or sheriff, and therefore they do not cooperate or accept help. On the other hand, some disturbed people are denied treatment or asylum in emergencies because they do not fit the legal category of insanity. Not only is the immediate procedure of commitment a traumatic event for a person already suffering under the stress of his illness, but once he is hospitalized, he may also lose many of his legal rights. When someone is declared legally insane, the implication is that he is incompetent to negotiate his affairs. A California study in 1966 found that under some conditions insane persons have been denied as many as sixteen of their constitutional rights, including the right to vote,

---

[43] California Legislature, *The Dilemma of Mental Commitments in California: A Background Document* (1968), p. 204.

[44] Ibid., p. 38.

Table 2 Estimate of amount and distribution of current cost of mental illness, 1968 (in thousands)

Type of Cost		Borne by General Population	Borne by Mental Ill and Families
I. Treatment and prevention	4,130,974	3,419,849	711,125
A. Direct services	3,860,481		
B. Training and fellowships	93,000		
C. Research	109,771		
D. Development of new facilities	63,766		
E. Management	3,956		
II. Cost of reduction in productive activity	16,906,000	4,074,100	12,831,900
III. Publically provided maintenance	1,253,284	1,253,284	
A. Federal			
1. Veterans administration	564,279		
2. Federal Civil service	52,029		
3. Railroad retirement	6,800		
4. Social Security payments	397,403		
5. Aid to Disabled	42,489		
6. Aid to Blind	3,597		
7. Medicaid	26,429		
8. Other medical assistance	1,188		
B. State and local			
1. General assistance	99,101		
2. State and local expenditures	59,969		
Total cost	22,290,258	8,747,233	13,543,025

Adapted from Conley, Conwell, and Willner, *Cost of Mental Illness, 1968,* Statistical Note 30 (Washington, D.C.: Biometry Branch Office of Program Planning and Evaluation, National Institute of Mental Health, 1970), Tables 2, 3.

to hold public office, to possess firearms, to maintain custody of children, and to obtain a marriage license. By comparison, a convicted felon loses only nine civil rights.[45]

There is a growing national awareness that the present system unjustly deprives people of their civil rights, as well as beginning the inpatient treat-

[45] Ibid., pp. 5–56.

ment process on the wrong track by handling the mentally disturbed person insensitively. Discontent with the commitment provisions was heightened by the civil rights movement, causing some states to begin to take action. California, for example, completely rewrote its laws on hospital admission procedures and guardianship of the mentally disordered in 1969.[46] The California certification law seeks to broaden the possibility that mentally disordered individuals will come voluntarily into care.[47] With the expansion of community-based mental health services and outpatient treatment, there is a trend toward more voluntary hospital admissions.

The key issue in devising a humanitarian way of bringing disordered people into treatment is the potential conflict between the needs of the individual and the protection of society. The protection of people and property has been used to arbitrarily deprive the disordered of their civil liberties without due process of law. Notwithstanding the recognition that most mentally disordered individuals pose no threat, notorious cases like those of Lee Harvey Oswald, Richard Speck, and Sirhan Sirhan, linked to mental illness, will continue to make it difficult to modify laws so that persons who behave deviantly will receive equal protection. Without a liberalization and humanization of the laws of commitment, large numbers of disturbed patients will continue to be victims of the very system which should help them.

Stigma

Another important aspect of mental disorder as a social problem is the stigma attached to it. According to Ervin Goffman, a stigma is "an attribute that is deeply discrediting."[48] Mental illness is seen as a blemish on the individual character: the person is not just stigmatized as deviant from normal, but also highly disvalued for his traits. The mentally retarded are not usually so stigmatized, because they have no control over their condition; however, the mentally ill person is thought to have some measure of control over his behavior, and his actions are therefore regarded as reprehensible.

In effect the stigma of mental illness sets the person off from the rest of society, handicapping his ability to have healthy relationships with others and thereby causing secondary deviancy, that is, a set of adaptive devices such as a low valuation of oneself and a feeling of shame. Often a person has problems finding reemployment and in social relations because people know he has been mentally ill, even though he may have recovered fully.

---

[46] *California Mental Health Services Act, 1971; Lanterman-Petris-Short Act of 1969,* (Sacramento: State of California Human Relations Agency, 1971), pp. 16–23.

[47] Ibid., p. 16.

[48] Ervin Goffman, *Stigma* (Englewood Cliffs, N.J.: Prentice-Hall, 1963), p. 3.

Individuals who are chronically mentally ill and show signs of illness are kept at arm's length, ridiculed, and often denied needed opportunities.

The stigma attached to mental illness has decreased since the seventeenth and eighteenth centuries, when it was based on a moralistic view of "will." In recent decades the mental health movement has sought through mass education to equate mental illness with physical illness. There is now less stigma attached to individuals with a history of psychiatric hospitalization, but stigma has not fully disappeared. Individuals with overt signs of mental illness are still treated differently, encounter hostility, and find many doors closed to them. While there is less ridicule than in previous periods, the pity shown them is just another form of stigma. It is the goal of the mental health movement to change public attitudes toward mental disorders.

PROGRAMS FOR TREATMENT AND CARE OF THE MENTALLY ILL

Chapter 14 applied the concept of prevention to the problem of mental illness and discussed the possibilities of primary prevention under health promotion and specific protection. In this section we introduce the concepts of secondary and tertiary prevention, thus covering the three levels in the prevention of mental illness, as described by Gerald Caplan. These concepts are valuable not only as a way of describing and classifying types of activity in the treatment of mental illness, but also because they generate ideas on how to maximize efforts to cut the rise of these disorders.

Secondary prevention is the effort to shorten the duration of mental illness primarily through early detection and treatment, and also through more effective treatment of established cases. Maximizing the chances for early detection of mental illness requires that mental health practice extend to all kinds of institutions where people live and work. The ability to identify high-risk groups and individuals who are on the verge of mental breakdown is crucial, since people usually seek treatment in a hospital or neighborhood center only after the problem is relatively well developed and hence more difficult to treat. The aim of secondary prevention is to enlarge the opportunity for early treatment.

Tertiary prevention carries the concept of rehabilitation from the mental hospital back to the community. The purpose of tertiary prevention is to decrease the extent of disability in the community due to long-established mental disorder. Rehabilitation is helping the individual to adjust to his residual handicap. In contrast, tertiary prevention programs work with psychiatrically handicapped individuals in groups to develop their social potential. Their subjects are largely individuals labeled chronic schizophrenics. Like secondary prevention, tertiary prevention programs are planned to reintegrate the patient as fully as possible into the life of the community. They take advantage of the strengths of the individual and the resources of the community to resocialize him into acceptable social roles.[49]

We can expect that prevention will reduce the rates and cost of mental illness because it allows us to conceptualize the relationship of environment to all stages of mental illness. Therefore, our intervention in the process can be more than a patch-up job on an individual; it can deal with the very factors which affect and exacerbate mental illness.

ORGANIZATION OF PSYCHIATRIC SERVICES

Under the Community Mental Health Centers Act of 1964 numerous state and local programs are organizing or changing to develop programs and construct buildings to meet the letter if not the spirit of the law. The current national organization of mental health services has the characteristics of a patchwork quilt. Traditional psychiatric services have three main components: the inpatient system, the aftercare system, and the community treatment system.

Inpatient System

Psychiatric hospitalization is usually reserved for patients who have severe mental problems with labels such as schizophrenia, manic-depressive psychoses, severe reactive depressions, dangerous sociopathic behavior, or numerous conditions causing organic psychoses. There are four types of hospitals: large state mental hospitals, Veterans Administration Psychiatric Hospitals, small private psychiatric hospitals, and psychiatric sections in general hospitals.

About 85 percent of all psychiatric hospitals beds are in state mental hospitals.[50] This type of institution has provoked the greatest criticism of mental health services. State mental hospitals grew from the earliest institutions set up to provide protection from, and asylum for, the legally insane (see pages 69 to 71). In large state hospitals, hospital superintendents usually have no control over who is admitted; instead, they must accept individuals under court order. Because of government sponsorship, state hospitals are subject to the vagaries of political, economic, and social pressure. Characteristically they are understaffed and their personnel are poorly trained. State hospitals range in size up to 10,000 beds, and because they lack adequate resources, less emphasis is placed on treatment and more on

---

[49] Gerald Caplan, *Principles of Community Mental Health* (New York: Basic Books, 1964), pp. 113–27.

[50] Schwartz and Schwartz, *Social Approaches to Mental Patient Care*, p. 102.

custody. Even today, some hospitals have so many chronic patients that insufficient energy and services are available to treat the acutely ill patients who have good prospects of recovery.

Great effort has been expended in the past fifteen years to upgrade state mental hospitals to provide better quality treatment, rehabilitation, and care. Funds provided by the National Institute of Mental Health and other sources have been used to experiment with new approaches to inpatient treatment.[51] But most state hospitals have failed to overcome longstanding liabilities. This failure has been the major impetus in the development of the concept of comprehensive mental health centers.

Veterans Administration Hospitals, in general, are smaller and better staffed and use more progressive approaches to treatment than state hospitals. After World War II, they provided significant national leadership in hospital psychiatry. Because they had better-trained personnel and were more committed to experimentation and research, they were able to develop and use the newest methods available in both social and somatic therapies. Now, however, VA hospitals no longer provide leadership in hospital psychiatry, perhaps because of their continuous involvement with the aging World War I and II veteran population. The critical psychosocial and psychological problems of veterans of the Vietnam War, including widespread drug abuse, may lead to sorely needed rejuvenation of the VA hospital system.

Private psychiatric hospitals are usually much smaller than state and VA hospitals, and are supported mainly by patient fees and medical insurance. They generally maintain higher staff–patient ratios, and the patient's opportunity for close contact with his family and his private physician is greater. He is not lost in the large group of patients, as is likely in larger, public institutions.

In the 1950s psychiatric units or sections began to appear in general hospitals.[52] These units are often small and can be coordinated with the services of the rest of the hospital. Patients with acute emotional problems are admitted and given short-term psychiatric treatment. Patient turnover rates are very high. These units have demonstrated the value of local treatment programs which can respond quickly to emergency psychiatric needs, diminishing the likelihood that the patient will be separated from his family and community for a prolonged period.

Aftercare System

It is important to distinguish between two general types of population which leave mental hospitals. One group were acutely ill, but responded quickly and positively to their stay. Within a short period of time, they are able to

51 Ibid., pp. 101–10.
52 Ibid., p. 108.

return to their home and work. The others have chronic emotional problems; they were ill long before entering a hospital, or remained in the hospital for a prolonged period of time, or perhaps both. These patients frequently develop secondary symptoms as part of their adjustment to life in the hospital.[53] When members of the second group leave the hospital, they usually require considerable assistance in readjusting to life in the community. They are frequently lonely, isolated individuals with few personal or family resources. A large number are unmarried. Many have lost (or perhaps never acquired) the social and work skills which would enable them to function in the community. The first group of patients, while they may still need psychotherapy or medication, require little or no assistance in reacculturation to life outside the hospital; the second group frequently require considerable help. In many states commitment laws have been used in conjunction with psychiatric aftercare. Many patients are released and returned to the community but still show symptoms of the illness for which they were hospitalized. Since many patients continue to need rehabilitation service, some states have organized programs to follow patients for an extended period after their release from the hospital. They have added to the commitment law a "leave of absence" provision which compels the patient to return to the hospital without court action if he again becomes seriously disturbed. Aftercare programs also include social services provided by a psychiatric social worker or a public health nurse to help the former patient readjust to society.[54]

Initially the concept of aftercare was vague, wrapped in the cloak of "posthospital supervision." However, during the last fifteen years it has been conceptualized as a form of tertiary prevention. Mental health professionals have become more aware of the crippling effects of long-term hospitalization and of the need to develop effective methods of resocializing and acculturating mental patients to the community. Such services include activities such as industrial workshops and therapeutic social clubs.

The states vary greatly in their development of aftercare systems. Some states, such as California and New York, have had well-organized systems for many decades, while others still have no well-organized service.[55] The Veterans Administration has developed a good aftercare system for mentally ill veterans.[56] Throughout the 1950s and 1960s many new modes of rehabilitation were developed and demonstrated, leaving a rich variety of possibilities for a comprehensive aftercare system. These will be discussed later.

[53] Russel Barton, *Institutional Neurosis.*

[54] Joint Commission on Mental Illness and Health, *Action for Mental Health,* pp. 178–89.

[55] Schwartz and Schwartz, *Social Approaches to Mental Patient Care,* Chap. 13.

[56] N. W. Hollier and R. W. Harrison, "A Home-Care Program in the Community," *Mental Hygiene,* 40 (1956), 574–82.

Community Treatment Facilities

Community treatment facilities include clinical services and mental health practitioners working in solo practice. The concept of a clinic for psychiatric patients dates only from the beginning of the century, when it arose with the optimism that mental illnesses could be treated. Most early clinics were associated with teaching hospitals connected with university medical schools. Later there was a gradual development of clinical services sponsored by federal, state, and local government, as well as clinics under private financial auspices. Clinics were often geared to special groups such as children, delinquents, veterans, neurotics, alcoholics, or those who could pay the fee, so that only a limited number in any area had access to the nearby clinic. Even so, these clinical services almost always had long waiting lists of people seeking psychotherapy (up to a year's wait). These services have been available mostly to middle-class people with psychoneuroses or behavior problems. However, because there are positive benefits from the skillful development of the diagnostic psychological study and the employment of the team approach to treatment, the traditional clinic has made a major contribution to present understanding of the dynamics of mental disorders.

Private psychiatric practice has been unavailable to meet the general public's demand for outpatient psychiatric services. Operating on a fee-for-service basis, private psychiatrists have attracted well-to-do patients. Because of the high fees and the necessity of frequent visits, few troubled individuals in the middle and lower classes have been able to visit private psychiatrists. Usually they receive no treatment, short-term clinic treatment, or medication from their general practitioner. If they are seriously ill, they go to a state hospital. In contrast, people who are relatively well-off visit private psychiatrists for psychoanalysis or other mental health professionals schooled in dynamic psychology. Between the extremes of state hospital and private practitioner, there is a range of psychiatric services which vary in intensity and method employed, available according to the patient's ability to pay. The 1960s saw the development of a long list of new outpatient treatment modalities which were variations or adaptations of traditional Freudian approaches, some individually- and some group-oriented, such as transactional analysis, gestalt therapy, family therapy, multiple impact therapy, and Synanon games.

THE COMMUNITY MENTAL HEALTH CENTER

The community mental health center must be described in terms of ideals rather than solid accomplishments, since a decade after the 1963 Mental Health Act only one-fourth of the nation's communities had established centers.[57] In 1971 about 300 were in operation, with an additional 180 in the planning stage. The Act provided for joint federal-local funding to build and staff the centers, yet the amount of money budgeted for new programs has been severely limited. The vast expenditures on the Vietnam War prevented the mental health program from receiving much of the money that had been projected for it.

President Kennedy's message to Congress preceding the enactment of the legislation called for a program to

> bestow the full benefits of our society on those who suffered from mental disabilities;
>
> prevent the occurrence of mental illness ... wherever and whenever possible;
>
> provide for early diagnosis and continuous and comprehensive care, in the community, of those suffering from these disorders;
>
> stimulate improvement in the level of care given the mentally disabled in our state and private institutions and reorient those programs to a community-centered approach;
>
> reduce, over a number of years, and by hundreds of thousands, the persons confined to these institutions;
>
> retain in, and return to, the community the mentally ill, and restore and revitalize their lives through better health programs and strengthened educational and rehabilitation service; and
>
> reinforce the will and capacity of our communities to meet these problems, in order that the communities, in turn, can reinforce the will and capacity of individuals and individual families.[58]

The 1963 legislation proposed a well-rounded, balanced program which would provide leadership in prevention, treatment, and care of the mentally ill, located in the community rather than the hospital. The program would offer a comprehensive range of services, linked together to provide continuity and individual attention. To achieve this ideal, the centers would provide several if not all of the following services: precare (broad diagnostic and evaluation service); acute inpatient service; outpatient service; day-care service, night-care service (partial hospitalization); emergency service, continuously available; rehabilitation; consultation; mental health education; supervised aftercare; and research and training.

The 1963 legislation also called for a new basis for planning and organizing mental health services. In an effort to provide programs of optimum size—large enough to allow specialization yet not too large and

[57] Constance Holden, "Community Mental Health Centers: Growing Movement Seeks Identity," *Science*, 194, No. 4014 (10 December 1971), 1110–13.

[58] John F. Kennedy, "Message from the President of the United States Relative to Mental Illness and Mental Retardation," 5 February 1963 (Washington, D.C.: House of Representatives, Document No. 58).

unwieldy—it suggested that each center should serve a population of 75,000 to 200,000. The boundaries of the community served should be drawn so as to include areas having meaningful political, social, and economic interconnection. This type of planning, called "catchment area planning," can provide a sound basis for establishing preventive and treatment services and for monitoring changes in the incidence and prevalence of mental disorders resulting from the center's total program.[59]

A central feature of the community mental health center is an effective intake (entry) service which efficiently screens candidates for admission to one of the center's services. Admission to the wrong service or denial of admission may mean time lost in treating a person at a time when he can best use the service. A program that meets his specific needs at the point of acute crisis, instead of placing him on a waiting list, may save months of treatment later on. For the patient it may mean the difference between satisfactory resolution of the crisis and chronic depression. If the center offers a choice of full-time, day only, or night only hospitalization, it can come closer to meshing with the patient's specific needs.

Ideally the center's programs are linked so that the patient can progress from one to another during various phases of his illness. Historically, psychiatric patients tended to become permanent fixtures in the institution to which they were sent, whether hospital, clinic, or aftercare service. Each system became sluggish because of the lack of turnover of patients.[60] The mental health center with its range of options minimizes this problem and seeks the reintegration of the individual into the community. Acute patients may need only one or two of the services, because the pattern of quick onset and immediate psychiatric attention avoids the negative consequences of hospitalization. Patients with long-term or chronic illness, however, need a spectrum of services because they depend on a larger variety of social and psychological supports.

The planners of psychiatric care are showing unprecedented creativity in developing services for the chronic patient, from the therapeutic community in the hospital to the creation of community lodges.[61] Combinations of the following services can provide the disabled person's psychological, social, housing, employment, and recreation needs:[62] therapeutic community, hospital rehabilitation ward, hospital member-employee program, foster family care home, day hospital program and night hospital, halfway house, supervised hostel, unsupervised hostel, community lodge, sheltered workshop, therapeutic social club, aftercare supervision, ex-patient self-help group, and community rehabilitation center.

59 Community Mental Health Centers Act of 1963, pp. 88–164.
60 Apte, *Halfway Houses.*
61 Maxwell Jones, *The Therapeutic Community.*
62 Schwartz and Schwartz, *Social Approaches to Mental Patient Care.*

Although there is some overlap in the purposes of and methods employed in these types of services, each has unique features. Together they provide the patient with a transition from living in a total institution to living as an independent member of the community. The main objective of these tertiary prevention programs is to help chronic patients relocate, resocialize, and reacculturate into community life. While living in or attending one of these transitional services, the patient can be exposed to increasing stress as he learns to live more independently. Within the boundaries of these programs, which vary in their protectiveness, it is still possible, given adequate staff, to provide the patient individualized help with his emotional and social problems.[63]

Consultation services are an integral part of the community mental health center. Consultation is not offered directly to the patient population, but to professional and community agencies concerned with the mental problems of their clients. It seeks to enhance their capacity to deal with those who are already ill or in danger of becoming ill.[64] The mental health consultant and the health educator play a vital role in expanding the preventive and treatment efforts of the center into the network of other agencies which deal with mental health–related problems. In addition to improving the skills of other care-givers, these professionals can help educate the community about the environmental and personal factors that cause emotional stress and eventually result in mental disorder.

The Mental Health Center Act does not require that a single organization administer and provide all the possible services. Recognizing that each community has existing services and desires to solve its individual problems, the Act allows for a variety of administrative patterns. As a consequence, many different models of community mental health services exist. To communities with long-established psychiatric inpatient services, the Act has meant financial resources for additional buildings and staff, perhaps with the addition of a day hospital or consultation service. For other communities or catchment areas with no existing facilities, the law has provided the means to build an entire new program. The totally new programs have not been so hamstrung as those already in existence by established procedures, rigidities, and loyalties, and have therefore been somewhat more balanced and comprehensive.

The *mental health consortium* allows well-established specialty services, each under different sponsorship and administration, to establish a center by means of contractual arrangements. The new organization receives federal funds to establish a mental health center, to coordinate the activities of existing programs, and to provide necessary additional services. This type

[63] Apte, *Halfway Houses.*

[64] Lydia Rapoport, "Consultation in Social Work," *Encyclopedia of Social Work 1971,* pp. 156–61.

of center, frequently little more than a paper organization at first, is charged with providing leadership in mental health planning and fostering cooperation and coordination between the existing agencies.

The quality and orientation of a center's program is somewhat related to its sponsorship, be that a medical institution, a public health department, or an independently administered mental health agency.

Community health centers are expected to contribute toward decreasing the number of patients in state hospitals and helping mental patients stay in their own homes. The assumption is that they will remain healthier if they learn to cope with their problems while in their accustomed surroundings. The community care movement has excellent theoretical foundations, but without adequate manpower to carry it out skillfully it may bring us to another crisis in the mental health system. In practice, when disturbed patients remain in or are transfered to their homes or to halfway houses and are not given needed mental health services, they are likely to be as miserable and debilitated as if they were in a large hospital with ample resources.[65] Moreover, if mental patients are only partially aided by outpatient services or local psychiatric hospital facilities and then neglected, their symptoms will burden their families and the community as a whole, which may lack adequate services. In England in 1961 Richard Titmuss cautioned mental health officials not to oversell the idea of community care without being able to deliver the required services.[66] In California a recent proposal to phase out all state mental hospitals with the expectation that patients would be cared for in their communities brought a strong public outcry.

FINANCING MENTAL HEALTH CENTERS

Mental Health centers are financed by federal, state, and local government funds, foundations, patient fees, and health plans. In addition to consultation services and technical assistance available from the NIMH, the Mental Health Center legislation provides two types of basic federal support: for the renovation, construction, or purchase of physical facilities for the mental health center, and for staffing these facilities. Grants to local governments or nonprofit foundations cover one-third to two-thirds of the cost of building and site. Staffing grants are based on a formula which requires local and/or state participation, with a declining amount given over a fifty-one-month period. For the first fifteen months 75 percent of the personnel cost is borne by the federal government, and by the final year

65 Apte, *Halfway Houses.*
66 Richard M. Titmuss, "Community Care—Fact or Fiction?" speech to conference of the National Association for Mental Health, 9 March 1961, London.

the federal share declines to 30 percent.[67] It is uncertain whether sufficient federal government funds will be allocated to continue to promote the growth of mental health centers, or if their development will slow like that of so many other progressive federal programs. President Nixon's controversial budget for 1974 eliminated funds for the construction and staffing of additional mental health centers; however, Congress and mental health lobbyists made a strong drive to restore this important item. Shrinking federal allocations may mean that existing programs may have to concentrate only on serious cases, neglecting prevention, early treatment, and mental health promotion.

MENTAL RETARDATION

This chapter has dealt principally with mental illness. Mental retardation is another major category served by the mental health system. The history of treatment of the mentally retarded in many aspects parallels that of the mentally ill. Both shared the fate of the insane in the madhouses and asylums of earlier centuries. However, early in the twentieth century, as public awareness of the retarded grew, facilities were developed to provide separate care for those with life-long handicaps in intellectual functioning.

Mental retardation is "subaverage general intellectual functioning which originates in the developmental period and is associated with impairment in adaptive behavior."[68] Within that definition are included individuals with capacities ranging from mild retardation and ability to function normally in a semiprotected environment to total disability and need of continuous nursing care. Physical disability is a frequent concomitant of retardation. An estimated 3 percent of the American population—5,400,000 —are retarded; however, 90 percent are only moderately retarded and can assume some responsibility for themselves.

The causes of mental retardation are complex, ranging from heredity, metabolic dysfunction, prenatal illness, prematurity, and birth injury to illness and accidents in early childhood. Mental retardation is also associated with poverty and its psychosocial and sociocultural consequences. While they have lower intelligence, the majority of mentally subnormal children are still complex human beings and social, cultural, and environmental influences can affect their intellectual attainment and adjustment either positively or negatively.

[67] Department of Health, Education and Welfare, *National Institute of Mental Health Support Programs*, Public Health Service Publication No. 1700 (Washington, D.C.: Government Printing Office, 1968).

[68] Rick Heber, "Modification in the Manual on Terminology and Classification in Mental Retardation," *American Journal of Mental Deficiency*, 65, No. 4 (January 1961), 499–500.

The needs of the mentally retarded and their families are manifold, including diagnostic testing, special education, counselling, physical and social rehabilitative services, and special care facilities. Until a few decades ago public services institutionalized the more severely affected and ignored those whose intelligence was at the upper extreme of retardation, because it was felt that little could be done to help them. Today personnel with a more sophisticated understanding of mental retardation place great emphasis on care in the home, with supportive services including vocational workshops and social activity groups, evaluation, and training. In a proper learning environment geared to his needs, the retarded person can develop many useful skills and a greater degree of self-reliance. There are psychological consequences which frequently affect the child and his family adversely. Their seeds are usually sown at the child's birth, in the form of ambivalence, guilt, and overprotection. Counseling services can deal with such feelings so that the child is freer to learn and his parents are more prepared to help him.

Each state has developed its own system of care for the retarded, and quality varies considerably from state to state. These services are often linked organizationally with services for the mentally ill. The past two decades have seen a major expansion of services and facilities for the retarded, largely because of a self-help movement which originated among parents of mentally retarded children. The National Association for Retarded Children, founded in 1950, has a membership of 100,000 people, mostly parents, with over 1,000 local chapters. It has greatly influenced national legislation on behalf of the retarded.

Much federal legislation to improve the resources for the care of the mentally ill has also had specific provisions for the mentally retarded. Thus, the National Mental Health Act of 1948 provided funds for training personnel to serve the retarded; the 1963 Mental Retardation Facilities and Community Mental Health Centers Construction Act provided resources for research and treatment centers, and the 1965 and 1967 amendments of this Act allowed for additional construction and professional personnel to operate these centers. The total HEW allotment for services for the mentally retarded in 1969 was $510 million. This is a good beginning, but it does not meet all the special needs of this population.

MANPOWER FOR THE MENTAL HEALTH SERVICES

There has never been ample manpower to provide the quality of services needed to solve the problem of mental disorders. Most of those who work in the mental health services provide custodial care for hospitalized patients. Considerably fewer give actual treatment, either on an inpatient or an outpatient basis. An infinitesimal number are engaged in research and preventive activities. As mental hospitals decrease in size, we hope that more trained personnel will be used in treatment, prevention, and research.

Accompanying the major changes in the system of treatment and care of the mentally disordered is a change in the nature of training and use of manpower. Traditionally, mental health personnel have been divided into two main groups. One group includes the large number of workers who lack professional education and whose main responsibility is to provide twenty-four-hour care for patients in hospitals for the mentally ill and mentally retarded. These are practical nurses, attendants, psychiatric technicians, and allied nontrained nursing personnel. The group is arranged in a hierarchy of personnel who supervise, administer, and govern the patients' institutional life. While these staff do not have professional degrees, many of them, in addition to on-the-job training, have received college or specialized education related to their work.

The other major group, the "professionals," includes psychiatrists, psychiatric social workers, psychiatric nurses, psychologists, and occupational and recreational therapists. In addition to providing therapeutic service, they usually administer and supervise various aspects of services provided by those without professional degrees. Outpatient services are provided mainly by this group. Traditionally psychiatrists, psychiatric social workers, psychologists, and in some instances psychiatric nurses have composed a clinical team. Each member of the team had a relatively well-defined role, with little overlapping; however, more recently considerable role duplication has occurred.

Volunteers have long been used in mental hospitals and facilities for the retarded, although they have been regarded as auxiliary to the treatment process. Volunteers spend several hours a week entertaining or reading to mental patients or retarded children, doing errands for them, or even taking them on outings. Another kind of volunteer activity is self-help. The first such group was Alcoholics Anonymous. Working inside and outside the institution, seeking to strengthen, support, and assist other alcoholics, AA members have contributed vast energy to fighting a persistent problem. The AA self-help model has proved useful and is now spreading to other groups with mental problems.

As the mental health establishment is slowly changing, the traditional hierarchical structure of authority is also beginning to change. Though administrative authority and power still rest with those who have medical or other advanced degrees, professional roles are now more diffused. There is little agreement on the amount and type of education required for work in the field of mental health. The division of tasks within the psychiatric team is no longer so clearly defined, and the roles of different disciplines are more interchangeable.[69] In many centers for the mentally ill and retarded, personnel are assigned to tasks as much on the basis of demonstrated skills and experience as on the basis of their academic degrees. For example, in many mental health centers psychiatrists do community organization, traditionally a social work responsibility, while social workers are administrators. Obviously, the knowledge and skills needed for community mental health practice are much broader than those provided by traditional psychiatrically-oriented education. The methods and skills are not the province of any single discipline, but draw on psychology, health education, medicine, social work, and other, related disciplines. All the mental health disciplines, both in practice and through their official organizations, are broadening the professional foundation of their roles and functions.

Changes also affect those without professional training. While the performance of therapy was formerly reserved for the professional, it is increasingly recognized that everyone in the mental health system has a potentially therapeutic role. In the early 1950s it was acknowledged that if the hospital community was to help the patient recover, then all the ward staff who had day-to-day contact with the patients must accept therapeutic roles.[70] Consequently, in many hospitals ward staff at several levels have been given more training in individual and group therapeutic methods, and assigned more responsibility for conducting treatment programs. Throughout the United States, financial support received from National Institute of Mental Health has opened educational opportunities for all levels of mental health personnel to increase their competence and responsibility.

Outside the hospital, in clinical and aftercare programs, new roles are opening up to the non-professional. Working-class and minority people with good potential for mental health work are hired through such programs as New Careers. Many mental health centers employing New Careersmen purposely recruit their workers from the same class and ethnic groups as their clientele. Experience has demonstrated that in many cases New Careers workers with training and supervision have a good understanding of patients' problems, communicate well with them, and can be of great help with the social and emotional aspects of their difficulties.[71] In some community mental health centers New Careers workers with prior histories of alcoholism and drug abuse have been recruited to work with clients who

69 Lydia Rapoport and Robert Apte, "Advanced Education for Practice in Community Mental Health," *Social Work Education Reporter* 6, No. 4 (December 1968), 24–28.

70 Maxwell Jones, *The Therapeutic Community.*

71 Frank Riessman, Jerome Cohen, and Arthur Pearl, *Mental Health of the Poor: New Treatment Approaches for Low Income People* (New York: Free Press, 1964).

have similar problems. The combination of having successfully overcome a personal drinking or drug problem and understanding the culture and rationalizations of the alcoholics and addicts, gives the worker special knowledge and skills unavailable to others. One mental health program employed nontrained widows who had successfully mastered the bereavement crisis to find recently widowed women and help them over this serious life crisis.

Other self-help groups have been organized by gamblers, neurotics, drug addicts (Synanon), and ex-mental patients. These groups, some of which are nationwide, are often far better able to satisfy their members' needs for understanding, social support, and specialty services than professionally-run programs. Various government bureaus and mental health centers have supported the self-help movements by providing encouragement, technical assistance, and consultation.

Suicide prevention centers, which have sprung up throughout the United States since the late 1960s, are another type of volunteer organization involved in mental health. Most suicide centers are staffed with nonprofessional volunteers who are given special training in suicidology. These centers offer a telephone crisis intervention and referral service up to twenty-four hours a day for people who are contemplating suicide or having emotional problems.[72]

THE SOCIAL WORKER IN THE MENTAL HEALTH SYSTEM

Social workers have been significant in mental health services since the establishment of the early psychiatric clinics. The character of their participation has, however, changed. Originally the social worker was regarded as an assistant to the psychiatrist, providing him with background information about the mental patient or retarded child. History taking, family contacts, and environmental planning were the main duties of the worker.[73] As more social workers received professional education, and schools of social work added psychiatric information and psychoanalytic theory to their curricula, the social worker began to assume more treatment responsibility. Some institutions limited the roles of social workers; in others they were equal members of the psychiatric team, but under the leadership of the psychiatrist. The psychiatrist treated the patient, whether child or

---

[72] See Anson Haughton, "Suicide Prevention Programs in the U.S.—An Overview," in *Bulletin of Suicidology* (Washington, D.C.: Department of Health, Education and Welfare, National Institute of Mental Health, 1968), pp. 25–29. See also Alfred H. Katz, "Application of Self-Help Concepts in Current Social Welfare," *Social Work*, 10, No. 3 (July 1965), 680–83.

[73] Lois Meredith French, *Psychiatric Social Work* (New York: Commonwealth Fund, 1940), p. 344.

adult, while the social worker assisted with members of the patient's family.

During the 1920s and 30s many of the more progressive clinics allowed social workers to practice psychotherapy. Because medical knowledge is needed to discover any underlying organic causes of mental disorder, their lack of medical training had always been at issue. The clinical setting, supervised by a psychiatrist, provided the conditions necessary to allow the extension of the social worker's role in therapy. Within the social work profession a debate was generated over whether the worker was practicing casework or psychotherapy while working with psychiatric patients. This debate is still going on, however, it is important to note that both are problem-solving methods, borrowing knowledge from many of the same sources and requiring similar training. Both methods can encourage very broad or very limited changes in the patient's adjustment to life.

Until the 1950s social workers mainly practiced individual casework or psychotherapy with patients. Later they extended their techniques to group therapy and then family therapy. In hospitals more attention was paid to the ward environment, and therapeutic community programs were initiated. Social workers led in demonstrating the applicability of these milieu therapeutic techniques. Social workers practicing in mental health have both perpetuated the traditional and been among the vanguard in developing and demonstrating new modes of problem-solving.

Today more schools of social work educate social workers for a much wider range of roles in mental health. The aim is to give them competence in both the individual and the group approach to treating emotional disorders. The graduate student is taught to look at the multiple levels of stress which affect mental health. Besides recognizing intrapsychic, interpersonal, and intrafamilial forces, they are taught to understand how community structure and social forces affect emotional health. In many schools, graduate education also includes the opportunity to develop some understanding of community organization so that the student is able to judge which mental health problems can best be solved at the community level. However, because the job of the mental health worker has grown so broad, a two-year graduate program is insufficient to give the student all the needed skills. To meet the increasing expectations, the social worker must be committed to education beyond the master's degree. Some individuals meet this commitment by individual study and professional development on the job; others attend continuing education workshops and institutes; still others return to the university for advanced education.[74]

With the advent of the community mental health center, work requirements for the social worker have broadened. The traditional skills of casework and group therapy are still his most heavily used methods. However,

[74] Rapoport and Apte, "Advanced Education for Practice in Community Mental Health."

the mission of the center is also to combat the problems of employment, housing, and education which create undesirable stress within the community. Social work roles now include consultation and planning. As consultants they may be available to teachers, physicians, nurses, welfare workers, probation officers, judges, and a host of other agents in the community who need assistance in improving their ability to cope with the mental disorders of clients. As planners they may play important roles in developing transitional services for mental patients and the retarded, or they may work with other agencies to develop mental health–related services. Experienced social workers in the mental health system also assume educational roles. Teaching is usually on a tutorial basis, available to any of the various mental health disciplines. Social workers have also taken an active role in the education of the New Careers employees.

Finally, there is a growing trend for social workers to assume leadership and administrative roles in community mental health centers. About half the states now allow social workers to be center directors.[75] A competent administrator does not need medical education; many of the skills required for administrative jobs can be found among social workers, such as sensitivity and skill in dealing with personnel planning, and social policy issues. Mental health centers, in addition to treating patients, must develop excellent working relationships with a variety of community agencies which depend on the center for services. A capable social worker with the right kind of experience often proves a very able administrator.

SELECTED BIBLIOGRAPHY

Albee, George W., "Energizing Concepts of Mental Illness and Models of Treatment: The Psychological Point of View," *American Journal of Psychiatry*, 125, No. 7 (January 1969), 871–72.

Arnoff, F. N., E. A. Rubenstein, and J. C. Speisman, eds., *Manpower for Mental Health*. Chicago: Aldine, 1969.

Barker, Robert C., and T. L. Briggs, *Differential Use of Social Work Power*. New York: National Association of Social Workers, 1968.

Beers, Clifford W., *A Mind that Found Itself: An Autobiography*. New York: Doubleday, 1935.

Bellak, Leopold, *Handbook of Community Psychiatry and Community Mental Health*. New York: Grave and Stratton, 1964.

Bowlby, John, "Maternal Care and Mental Health," Monograph Series #2. Geneva: World Health Organization, 1951.

Cohen, Felix, and Arthur C. Huntley, "The Psychiatric Day Hospital," *Mental Hospitals*, 16, No. 7 (July 1965), 21–26.

Cumming, Elaine, and John Cumming, *Closed Ranks: An Experiment in Mental Health Education*. Cambridge, Mass.: Harvard University Press, 1957.

[75] Personal communication of the authors with National Institute of Mental Health Staff, Rockville, Md.

————, *Ego and Milieu*. New York: Atherton Press, 1963.

DEUTSCH, ALBERT, *The Mentally Ill in America: A History of their Care and Treatment from Colonial Times*. New York: Columbia University Press, 1946.

DINCIN, JENNY, "Utilization of Professional Staff in Psychiatric Rehabilitation," *Social Work*, 10, No. 1 (1965), 51–57.

ENGLISH, O. SPURGEON, and GERALD H. J. PEARSON, *Emotional Problems of Living: Avoiding the Neurotic Pattern*. New York: W. W. Norton, 1946.

ERIKSON, ERIK H., *Childhood and Society*. New York: W. W. Norton, 1950.

FARNDALE, JAMES, *The Day Hospital Movement in Great Britain*. New York: Pergamon Press, 1961.

GLASSCOTE, RAYMOND M., J. N. SUSSEX, E. CUMMING, and L. H. SMITH, *The Community Mental Health Center: An Interim Appraisal*. Washington, D.C.: Joint Information Service of the American Psychiatric Association and National Association for Mental Health, 1969.

GREENBLATT, MILTON, D. J. LEVINSON, and R. H. WILLIAMS, eds., *The Patient and the Mental Hospital*. New York: Free Press, 1957.

JAHODA, MARIE, *Current Concepts of Positive Mental Health*. New York: Basic Books, 1954.

Joint Commission on Mental Health of Children, *Crisis in Childhood Mental Health: Challenge for the 1970's*. New York: Harper & Row, 1970.

JONES, ERNEST. *The Life and Work of Sigmund Freud*. New York: Basic Books, 1953.

KIRKLAND, MARGARET H., "Institutions for the Retarded: Their Place in the Continuum of Services," *Mental Retardation*, 5, No. 2 (April 1967), 5–8.

KRAFT, ALAN D., SIDNEY M. GLASSMAN, and W. W. JEPSON, *Partial Hospitalization for the Mentally Ill: A Study of the Programs and Problems*. Washington, D.C.: Joint Information Service of the American Psychiatric Association and the National Association of Mental Health, 1969.

LINDEMANN, ERICH, "Symptomatology and Management of Acute Grief," *American Journal of Psychiatry*, 101, No. 2 (September 1944), 141–48.

PADULA, HELEN, R. M. GLASSCOTE, and ELAINE CUMMING, *Approaches to the Care of Long-Term Mental Patients*. Washington, D.C.: Joint Information Service of American Psychiatric Association and National Association for Mental Health, 1968.

ROSE, ARNOLD M., *Mental Health and Mental Disorder*. New York: W. W. Norton, 1955.

SABSHIN, MELVIN, and DANIEL OFFER, *Normality*. New York: Basic Books, 1966.

STRAUSS, ANSELM, et al., *Psychiatric Ideologies and Institutions*. New York: Free Press, 1964.

SUSSMAN, MARVIN B., ed., *Sociology and Rehabilitation*. New York: American Sociological Association, 1965.

SZASZ, THOMAS S., *Myth of Mental Illness*. New York: Harper & Row, 1961.

WILLIAMS, RICHARD H., ed., *The Prevention of Disability in Mental Disorders*. Bethesda, Md.: National Institute of Mental Health, 1962.

ZUSMAN, JACK, "Sociology and Mental Illness," *Archives of General Psychiatry*, 15, No. 12 (December 1966), 630–40.

17

services
for
special
needs

SERVICES TO VETERANS AND THE ARMED FORCES

Legislation for the welfare of veterans was first enacted in colonial times. Numerous laws, which were changed after each major war, provided land grants, homestead privileges, medical care, and various types of pensions and monetary grants to veterans, their survivors, and their dependents.[1] At present, veterans services have two main goals: (1) to compensate the

---

[1] For the history of veterans services in the United States, see Chapter 3, pages 99–100.

veteran and his family as much as possible for the sacrifice he has made for his country and to prevent his suffering economic loss from his military service; and (2) to demonstrate to the veteran and his family the nation's gratitude for his risking his life or health in the service.[2]

The first group of measures includes compensation to disabled veterans and to survivors, medical care, hospitalization, vocational rehabilitation, educational aid, and job reinstatement. The second category comprises mustering-out pay, preference in civil service positions, bonuses, priorities in housing, and loans for purchasing homes, farms, and businesses. Emphasis has been placed by veterans services on rehabilitation—helping the veteran to regain his position in the community.

The social and economic benefits granted to veterans and their families may be divided into five categories: (1) medical care, hospitalization, and social services; (2) compensation and pensions to disabled veterans and to survivors of deceased veterans, life insurance, and social insurance benefits protection; (3) education, training, and vocational rehabilitation; (4) job reinstatement, preference in civil service positions, and employment services; and (5) economic privileges, including mustering-out pay, readjustment allowance, and loan guarantees for the purchase of a house, a farm, or a business. (For the medical and mental health services of the Veterans Administration, see Chapters 14 and 15; for its housing services, see Chapter 11.)

By June 30, 1958 the veteran population in the United States was 22,727,000 and it remained largely unchanged by 1965. About one of every eight citizens was a veteran, and veterans and their families make up 44 percent of our total population.[3] Their number, however, is increasing substantially with the return of veterans from the Vietnam War.

The major part of veterans' benefits is provided by the federal government, because veterans, since the independence of our country, have been the largest group of "federal wards." In September 1972 veterans and their dependents receiving federal benefits numbered 5,629,000. Our main discussion, therefore, will concern the federal program. But most of the states also have established veterans' departments to supplement federal aid. State activities are indicated briefly below.

---

2 Eveline M. Burns, *The American Social Security System* (Boston: Houghton Mifflin, 1949), p. 266; Gustavus A. Weber and Lawrence F. Schmeckebier, *The Veterans Administration* (Washington, D.C.: Brookings Institution, 1934), pp. 4, 5, 320; Omar N. Bradley, "The Veterans' Administration," *National Conference of Social Work, Proceedings* (1946), 353–59; Claribel H. Moncure, "Veterans' Benefits and Services," *Social Work Year Book* (1960), 591–600; Veterans Administration, *Federal Benefits for Veterans and Dependents* (Washington, D.C.: Government Printing Office, 1963); Margaret Neville, "Veterans Benefits and Services," *Encyclopedia of Social Work 1965*, pp. 809–16; Delwin M. Anderson, "Veterans Services," *Encyclopedia of Social Work 1971*, pp. 1513–18.

3 The Administrator of Veterans Affairs, *Annual Report, 1958*, Chap. 17 (Washington, D.C.: Government Printing Office, 1959), pp. 138–39; and *Social Security Bulletin*, 36, No. 1 (January 1973), 39, Table M-3.

Medical Care, Hospitalization, and Social Services for Veterans

In accordance with the current emphasis of veterans services on rehabilitation, the federal program provides free hospitalization and medical and dental care to veterans in need of treatment for service-connected illnesses and disabilities. The honorably discharged veteran may be admitted to a Veterans Administration hospital or another authorized hospital. For nonservice-connected illnesses, the veteran may be admitted to a hospital when beds are available and if he is unable to pay the cost of hospitalization and confirms this under oath. In emergencies, immediate hospitalization is granted. This includes prosthetic and other appliances, chaplaincy, library facilities, recreational activities, rehabilitation, and social services. In 1965 the Veterans Administration operated 168 hospitals, 4 of them for tuberculosis, 38 for neuropsychiatric, and 126 for general and surgical treatment.[4] Psychiatric therapy is integrated into the general program, and aftercare is administered in foster homes, halfway houses, and nursing homes. Vocational training and special rehabilitation centers have been set up for blind, deaf, and hard-of-hearing veterans. Blind veterans also are entitled to seeing-eye dogs and electronic and mechanical equipment; legless veterans to payment up to $1,600 for the purchase of a special automobile. The veterans' pension program is not supposed to be a complete income-support program, but to supplement other sources of income. However, pensioners should not be reduced to indigence.

Veterans and their survivors are in a much more favorable position than recipients of public assistance, or even beneficiaries of social security allowances. Their pensions, which are not based on a war-connected disability, are characterized as a compensation for military service, and are regarded as justified regardless of economic need, unlike public assistance benefits. Veterans' pensions are maintained partly by the lobbying power of the major veterans' organization. Social security allowances have already been paid by the beneficiaries' prior contributions and those of their employers, but veterans' pensions have no similar economic base.

The social worker's function is to help the veteran in his rehabilitation by enabling him to use to his best advantage the various benefits to which he is especially entitled, and other community resources. Casework with the veteran who is ill or disabled deals with personal and family problems, employment, economic questions, and particularly with his attitude and feelings

[4] Burns, *The American Social Security System*, pp. 267–68; Neville, "Veterans' Benefits and Services," 810–13; *Annual Report of Administration of Veterans Affairs, 1958* (Washington, D.C.: Government Printing Office, 1960), pp. 5–7; Administrator of Veterans Services, *Annual Report* (1965), 18, 23; Delwin M. Anderson and Jean M. Dockhorn, "Differential Use of Staff," *NASW Personnel Information*, 8, No. 6 (November 1965), 1, 43; Gilbert Y. Steiner, *The State of Welfare* (Washington, D.C.: Brookings Institution, 1971), pp. 14, 28, 232, 237–79.

regarding his handicap, his relationship with others, and questions of his adjustment. The caseworker helps the patient understand the nature of his illness and treatment, and to face obstacles within himself and in his environment which stand in the way of his rehabilitation. The patient is informed about facilities for occupational and physical therapy, vocational guidance and training, and opportunities to gain a general education. The social worker explains to the patient the doctor's advice and prescriptions regarding medication, proper diet, rest, and life habits and helps him leave the hospital with confidence in his ability to reestablish himself.

In neuropsychiatric hospitals, the psychiatric social worker helps the veteran and his family become familiar with the nature of his nervous disease, the expected length of treatment, and the time of discharge. Particularly important is to make patient and family understand how essential complete treatment is for the cure and future life of the veteran.

To assist the men in the armed forces and their families in personal and social problems, the Army uses medical and psychiatric social workers of its own staff, in cooperation with the Medical Service Corps; the Navy relies on civilian social workers, and the Air Force on the Office of Community Services.[5] The American Red Cross offers family services to the dependents of men in the armed forces and to the personnel of the Navy.

Domiciliary care in thirty-three special institutions is available for veterans who, because of their disability, are so severely incapacitated that they are unable to earn a living or are unwilling to live in the community.[6] Veterans in need of medical and dental treatment for service-connected ailments which do not require hospitalization are cared for in thirty-two outpatient clinics. There they receive medical, psychiatric, and dental treatment and medical supplies and appliances. To make it unnecessary for veterans to travel long distances, and to relieve the crowded hospitals and clinics, Hometown Medical Care Plans have been authorized in most states under which veterans may be treated by private physicians and psychiatrists. The Veterans Administration is authorized to reallocate hospital beds according to shifts in the veteran population around the country.

Social services are available to veterans in domiciliary institutions and outpatient clinics, as well as in hospitals. The American system of veterans' aid is characterized by the large expenditures for veterans when they become old and are in financial need, often forty years and longer after a war.[7]

5 John H. Hurley, "National Defense and Social Welfare," *Social Work Year Book* (1957), 380–81; William S. Rooney, "Military Social Services," *Encyclopedia of Social Work 1965*, pp. 518–20; Joseph J. Bevilacqua and Ralph M. Morgan, "Military Social Work," *Encyclopedia 1971*, pp. 851–55.

6 The Veterans Administration maintains thirty-three homes for domiciliary care for 17,500 veterans, and sixty-seven mental hygiene clinics.

7 Mildred Maroney, "Veterans Benefits," in Lewis Meriam and Karl Schlotterbeck, eds., *The Cost and Financing of Social Security* (Washington D.C.: Brookings Institution, 1950), pp. 96–97; see also Steiner, *The State of Welfare*, pp. 237–79.

Economic Compensation for Disabled Veterans and Their Families

Compensation for service-connected disabilities for veterans who have lost at least 10 percent of their earning capacity is based on degree of wartime disability and period of military service. The monthly compensation ranges from $18 to $190, but additional compensation for severe disabilities, such as blindness and loss of a hand, foot, or eye, permit a monthly compensation of $47 up to a maximum of $440. Veterans with disabilities rated at 50 percent or more receive additional allowances for a wife, children, and dependent parents. After the veteran's death, his survivors are entitled to "dependency and indemnity compensation."

For nonservice-connected disabilities a veteran with a permanent and total disability may receive a pension ranging from $66.15 to $135.45 a month, provided that he is in economic need. Pensions are also paid to the widow and minor children if need is proved. The difference between compensation and pension is that the first is paid for all incapacities and is independent of income and financial status of the veteran, whereas pensions are paid only for total nonservice-connected disability and only to veterans or survivors whose income is lower than a statutory limit.[8] Since 1960 veterans have received higher pensions if they have low incomes or dependents.

Veterans of World War I were protected through life insurance, and veterans of World War II were entitled to purchase the same amounts by National Service Life Insurance policies. There are more than 6,000,000 policies in force; both systems are administered by the Veterans Administration.

Survivors of veterans discharged before July 26, 1951 who passed away within three years after their discharge are entitled to their full social insurance benefits under the Old-Age and Survivors Insurance. Burial expenses for a deceased veteran are reimbursed to relatives or friends.

Education and Vocational Rehabilitation

Under the *Servicemen's Readjustment Act of 1944* (so-called "GI Bill of Rights") and its amendments, a program of general education and training was made available to honorably discharged veterans with ninety days or more of service. The period of subsidized education varies from one to four years. Training may be performed in industry, business, or workshops providing apprentice or on-the-job training. War orphans eighteen to twenty-three years of age receive educational assistance for three years. The *GI*

[8] George F. Rohrlich, "Veterans Pensions in Retrospect and in Prospect," *Social Service Review*, 31, No. 4 (December 1957), 427–41.

Education Act of October 24, 1972 raised the allowance for a single veteran to $220 a month, for a married veteran to $261, for a veteran with one child to $298, and allowed $18 more for each additional child.

Vocational rehabilitation is provided under the *Act Providing Vocational Rehabilitation of Disabled Veterans,* of 1943, to restore the employability of disabled war veterans.[9] The training period for vocational rehabilitation is not limited, but after four years approval of the Veterans Administration is required. Training allowance for disabled veterans is paid in addition to disability compensation and retirement pay. The vocational rehabilitation plan is carefully supervised; courses have to be continued so that the benefits will not be wasted and the training will suit the individual needs of the veteran. In hospitals of the Veterans Administration and the Navy, vocational guidance and counseling are provided so that disabled veterans may prepare their rehabilitation training in advance. Veterans returning from the Vietnam War face particular problems because of the high unemployment and the scarcity of available jobs. This is especially true for minority veterans, such as blacks and Chicanos.

Job Reinstatement and Preference in Civil Service

The *Veterans Readjustment Act* provides the right of the veteran to be reemployed in his former job with special regulations of conflicting interests. In civil service examinations and tests a special priority of 5 points for veterans and 10 points for disabled veterans made the eligibility for, and the appointment of, veterans and their widows to civil service positions easier. These priorities apply to federal civil service, but in most states also to state and local government civil service jobs.

Special job counseling and placement services are available to the veteran. Policies for effective placement of veterans are established through the Veterans Placement Service Board, whose chairman is the veterans' administrator. Veterans' employment representatives serve in all state employment organizations and many local employment services. Particular attention is given to counseling and placement services for physically handicapped veterans who had been prepared by vocational rehabilitation. The *Vocational Education Act of 1963* provides federal funds to state and local governments for vocational training of adolescents in high school and after school, and of unemployed and underemployed adults to meet changing

9 Roger Cumming, "Veterans Services," *Social Work Year Book* (1954), 522–28; Virginia C. Karl, "Veterans Benefits and Services," *Social Work Year Book* (1957), 573–84; Moncure, "Veterans' Benefits and Services," 595–98; Ruth Cooper, "Social Work in Vocational Rehabilitation," *Social Work,* 8, No. 1 (January 1963), 92–98; James M. Fendrich, "The Returning Black Vietnam Era Veteran," *Social Service Review,* 46, No. 1 (March 1972), 60–75.

manpower needs and job opportunities. But the general economic conditions after the Vietnam War leave many returning veterans in difficult conditions.

Economic Privileges

At the time of honorable discharge, the veteran receives mustering-out pay and a special type of federally financed unemployment benefit, called "Readjustment Allowance." Since 1952 unemployment insurance benefits have been paid to veterans under two different programs. (1) The general state unemployment insurance laws provide pay to veterans who have established benefit rights after their return to civilian life or, in twenty states where unemployed veterans receive insurance benefits, on the basis of "frozen wage credits" earned before their military service. (2) *The Veterans Readjustment Assistance Act of 1952,* provides weekly benefits to unemployed veterans with active service after June 27, 1950, including the Korean conflict and the Vietnam War, for twenty-six weeks. A veteran must first claim benefits for which he is eligible under a state unemployment compensation law or the Railroad Unemployment Insurance Act.

Self-employed veterans in trade, business, profession, or other vocations are entitled to readjustment allowance if they had net earnings of less than $100 in the previous month.

Veterans and widows of deceased veterans received help in building a home, establishing a business, or buying a farm in the form of a guarantee of up to 60 percent of the loan from private lending societies or individuals until 1960. For veterans of the Korean Conflict these benefits were available until 1965. Veterans also receive priorities in housing located in public housing projects built with funds of the Lanham Act of 1950, and in securing homesteads on public land. Disabled veterans receive aid in obtaining suitable homes.[10]

Organization of the Veterans Administration

Federal organization. Veterans' benefits are administered by the Veterans Administration. The policy-making body is the central office in Washington, D.C., which is responsible for the supervision of the entire program. The various fields of the administration, covering legal problems, claims, appeals, vocational rehabilitation, education, and life insurance, are assigned to staff units. Social services are a subdivision of the Department of Medicine and Surgery in the central, district, and regional offices. Social services are available to veterans receiving medical treatment and care.

Operating functions are decentralized and delegated to 5 district offices, 57 regional offices, and 532 field stations. They handle disability and

---

[10] June A. Willenz, "The Returning Vietnam Veterans: A Challenge to the Nation's Conscience," *American Veterans Committee Bulletin* (December 1972), 7–9.

death awards, training and education, and other benefits. Readjustment allowances are paid by the state unemployment compensation agencies, which are also reimbursed for their administrative costs incurred by this cooperation.

State veterans programs. Although the federal government assumes the basic responsibility for veterans' services, all states provide additional benefits to veterans. These services supplement the federal benefits or continue them after their expiration. The benefits include information and counseling centers, preference in civil service or public employment, tax and license fee exemptions, and domiciliary care in thirty-three state soldiers' homes. Other state benefits are financial aid to needy veterans, bonuses, pensions, and burial expenses to indigent veterans. Several states supply guarantees for loans to veterans for the purchase of a home, farm, or business, sometimes up to a higher maximum than the federal program allows. In other state programs, land settlement, homesteads, or institutional care for children are available to veterans and their families.

The state veterans' departments or commissions administer or supervise these services for veterans, but in a few instances private veterans' organizations or the various state departments of public welfare are charged with providing benefits.

Community services for veterans. Among social agencies, some are particularly active in services for veterans. Through its local chapters, the American National Red Cross assists veterans in the presentation of claims for their legal benefits. The home service divisions of the chapters offer casework services, and in special instances, financial aid to veterans and their families. Several veterans' organizations, such as the American Legion and the Veterans of Foreign Wars of the United States, also help veterans with filing their claims; in rehabilitation; in securing housing or loans for purchasing homes, farms, and business; in obtaining employment or hospitalization; and in obtaining family and child welfare services.

Beyond the federal and state programs, local community services assist the veteran and his family because the veteran should also receive the consideration and aid given to other citizens. Such services are offered by public and private agencies such as local health and welfare departments, employment services, vocational rehabilitation centers, family and child welfare agencies, and mental hygiene and child guidance clinics.

SOCIAL SERVICES FOR MINORITY GROUPS

Major social problems in the United States, particularly the urban crisis, have racial overtones. Blacks, Chicanos, Puerto-Ricans, American Indians, and Asiatic people experience discrimination in employment, housing, and health care, and many live in poverty. Special social services and social action are necessary to improve their social, economic, and health conditions. Especially in the cities, the financial burden of public welfare and health services has caused resentment among the middle classes and the well-to-do against the racial minorities which suffer from a disproportionate amount of unemployment, underemployment, illness, inadequate housing, lack of equal education, and involvement in delinquency and crime, for which the minority group members are scarcely responsible.

The white majority tend to deny that there is discrimination against racial minorities and to accuse the members of minorities, especially blacks, of being responsible for their poor housing, undesirable jobs, and ill health. Such feelings of hostility have recently been aggravated by black power movements such as the Black Muslims and the Black Panthers and by the strong support among blacks for the welfare rights movement, which insists on equal rights for all and demands an end of discrimination against welfare recipients and minority group members in housing, employment, salaries, and political and economic status.[11]

The so-called "Kerner Report," written by the National Advisory Commission on Civil Disorders (1968), emphasized the seriousness of the problem of racial discrimination: "Our nation is moving toward two societies, one black, one white—separate and unequal." To prevent this development, the Commission recommended the following objectives:

> Opening up opportunities to those who are restricted by racial segregation and discrimination, and eliminating all barriers to their choice of jobs, education and housing.
>
> Removing the frustration of powerlessness among the disadvantaged by providing the means for them to deal with the problems that affect their own lives and by increasing the capacity of our public and private institutions to respond to these problems.
>
> Increasing communication across racial lines to destroy stereotypes, to halt polarization, end distrust and hostility, and create common ground for efforts toward public order and social justice.[12]

Unfortunately most of the Commission's recommendations have not been followed. Some open-housing legislation has been enacted and several

[11] Whitney Young, "Racial Discrimination," in Nathan E. Cohen, ed., *Social Work and Social Problems* (New York: National Association of Social Workers, 1964), p. 340; Hugh Davis and Ted R. Gurr, *Violence in America,* vol. 2 (Washington, D.C.: Government Printing Office, 1969), pp. 317–40; David Boroff, ed., *The State of the Nation* (Englewood Cliffs, N.J.: Prentice-Hall, 1965), pp. 179–80; John M. Romany-shyn, *Social Welfare: Charity to Justice* (New York: Random House, 1971), pp. 128–33.

[12] *Report of the National Advisory Commission on Civil Disorders* (Washington, D.C.: Government Printing Office, 1968), pp. 1, 17, 23; Gary T. Marx, *Racial Conflict: Tension and Change in American Society* (Boston: Little, Brown, 1971).

programs to employ the hard-core unemployed have been carried out. There remain the serious tasks of improving the health and housing conditions in urban ghettos and many rural regions and of achieving real equality in employment by removing discrimination caused by racial prejudice and injustice. The war on poverty has failed to effect these necessary social changes; it has neither brought about the promised "full participation of the poor" nor fulfilled the rising expectation of equal rights and dignity for all minorities.

The problem of racism in social agencies, both public and private, cannot be solved by token action such as appointing one or two minority group members to the board of directors. A whole-hearted change of the power structure of social agencies is needed to ensure democratic leadership and full participation in the organization of the consumers of their services, the poor and the minorities. Only such participation can eradicate suspicion that social agencies help their clients so that the clients will accept the rules and values of the dominant majority and sacrifice their desire for independence. Client representatives should have equal say in determining the policies and practices of the social services; heretofore the white majorities have been the only real power in the agencies.[13]

Blacks are not the only minority group discriminated against in the United States. Chicanos, or Mexican-Americans, are more numerous than blacks in California, New Mexico, and Arizona. Originally Chicanos numbered about 300,000 in the United States; their number has grown to about 8,000,000, and they have maintained their Spanish language, their culture, and their national identity. Most Chicanos live in California and New Mexico, but some, mostly migrant laborers, live on the shores of Lake Superior. Many Chicanos have close relatives in Mexico. So-called "commuters" live in Mexico, but work in the United States. In earlier years Indians, Chinese, Filipinos, and other Asians were used for stoop labor on large industrial farms in the American Southwest and for railroad construction; they were also employed in the garment, electronics, chemical,

13 Andrew Billingsley, *Children of the Storm: Black Children and American Child Welfare* (New York: Harcourt Brace Jovanovich, 1972); Dan W. Dodson, "Institutional Racism in Social Welfare Agencies," *Social Welfare Forum* (1970), 88–98; Louis Knowles and Kenneth Prewitt, *Institutional Racism in America* (Englewood Cliffs, N.J.: Prentice-Hall, 1971); Roger Daniels and Harry H. L. Kitano, *American Racism: Exploration of the Nature of Prejudice* (Englewood Cliffs, N.J.: Prentice-Hall, 1970), pp. 117–30; Richard B. Sherman, ed., *The Negro and the City* (Englewood Cliffs, N.J.: Prentice-Hall, 1970), pp. 171–80; John F. Kain, ed., *Race and Poverty: The Economics of Discrimination* (Englewood Cliffs, N.J.: Prentice-Hall, 1969), pp. 23–31, 38–44. For an example of the difficulties in establishing full participation of minority group members in social agencies, see Ralph M. Kramer, *Participation of the Poor: Comparative Community Case Studies in the War on Poverty* (Englewood Cliffs, N.J.: Prentice-Hall, 1969). This study describes the work of Community Action Programs in five California communities under the Economic Opportunity Act.

steel, and rubber industries and in hotels, restaurants, hospitals, and other service work. Now, however, Chicanos and Puerto Ricans are the main labor source for all these occupations.

Presently the Chicano movement is largely a youth movement for political and economic equality for Latin Americans, for example the Alianza Federal de Pueblos Libres and La Raza. There is also the Farm Workers Union under the leadership of Cesar Chavez. All demand recognition of their full civil rights and equal dignity with Anglo-Americans.[14]

Another minority group which suffers from discrimination and racial prejudice in the United States, although most of them are citizens and "whites," are the Puerto Ricans. In contrast to his status in his homeland, in the United States the Puerto Rican is considered "colored." He is usually forced into an urban ghetto, limited to low-paying jobs, and not accepted as equal by the bourgeois middle class. Unemployment among Puerto Ricans as well as among Chicanos is much higher than among the Anglo population. Imitating the "black revolution," young Puerto Ricans, most of whom live in New York, have taken a militant stand against Anglo racism. However, they face the problem of trying to establish a Puerto Rican culture after having lost most of their national language and habits. The majority of Puerto Ricans speak English and would no longer be considered natives if they returned to Puerto Rico; they have become a "lost generation."

There are about 1,600,000 Puerto Ricans in the United States, of whom 1,100,000 live in New York City. Between 20 and 30 percent of them are unemployed or underemployed, working as unskilled laborers or semi-skilled blue-collar workers with inadequate and only temporary wages. Thus they often require public assistance and medical services; in addition, drug abuse and conflicts with police aggravate conditions among Puerto Rican youth.[15]

Although the concept of the inferiority of minority groups has been discredited by legislation and court decisions, old prejudices are still potent against all of them. American Indian tribes are particularly subject to such prejudice, since they have largely been kept on reservations and have only recently resettled among the general population. Social work with American Indians requires different skills and approaches from social work with other groups, and each tribe should be treated according to its special cultural and religious habits. Most tribes still emphasize the extended family

[14] Bert Corona, "The Chicano People: An Oppressed National Minority," *New Generation,* 53, No. 4 (Fall 1971), 1–6; Leo Grebler, Joan W. Moore, and Ralph Guzman, *The Mexican-American People: The Nation's Second Largest Minority* (New York: Free Press, 1970), pp. 578–97. For a discussion of the special health needs of minority groups, see Chapter 15.

[15] Eduardo Seda Bonilla, "The Identity of the 'Niuyorricians'," and Andres Torres, "Puerto Rican Employment in New York," *New Generation,* 53, No 4 (Fall 1971), 6–17.

and strong cooperation among relatives. New organizations of tribes in some states, regions, and even on the national level insist on preserving the cultural heritage of the Indian people. Their slow integration into the general economy has led to an increase of the Indian population to about 600,000. But further improvement of health and social services, both on reservations and for Indians living among the general population, are necessary to compensate this minority group for the injustice done to them during previous centuries.[16]

Although the *Civil Rights Act of 1964* eliminated legal inequality between the white majority and the various minority groups in America, serious barriers to full equality in economic opportunity and social conditions remain. The minority groups still discriminated against in employment, civil service, housing facilities, and citizens' rights are blacks, Spanish-speaking groups (Chicanos and Puerto Ricans), American Indians, Asian groups (primarily Chinese and Japanese, but also immigrants from other Asian countries), and refugees from Africa. The National Advisory Commission on Civil Disorders, appointed by President Johnson in 1967, stated that only a commitment to national action on an unprecedented scale can shape a future compatible with the historic ideal of American society, and that the major need is to generate a new will, namely to tax ourselves to the extent necessary to meet the vital needs of the nation, to wipe out the severe injustices and inequalities in the life of minority group members, particularly in city ghettos.

Many organizations devote their efforts to this goal. The most influential are the Congress of Racial Equality (CORE), the National Association for the Advancement of Colored People (NAACP), and the National Urban League among blacks, the "Casa de Raza" among Chicanos, the Association for American Indian Affairs among American Indians, and the National Welfare Rights Organization for welfare clients, mostly black mothers receiving public assistance.[17]

PUBLIC EMPLOYMENT SERVICES

One of the social institutions of paramount importance for industry and labor is the public employment service. Local and a few state employment offices were established as early as the nineteenth century. The first

[16] Walter A. Lurie, "Intergroup Relations," *Encyclopedia of Social Work 1971,* pp. 671–72; Evelyn L. Blanchard, "Social Work with American Indians," *Social Work Forum* (1972), 276–80; James R. Dumpson, "Breaking the Barriers to an Open Society," *Social Work Forum* (1972), 3–19.

[17] Lurie, "Intergroup Relations," pp. 668–76; Dumpson, "Breaking the Barriers to an Open Society," 3–19; *Report of the National Advisory Commission on Civil Disorders,* pp. 16–29.

state offices were opened in Ohio in 1890, in New York in 1896, and in Wisconsin in 1901. The particular employment problems of new immigrants which were emphasized by the Immigrants Protective Society under Grace Abbott in Chicago led to the setting up of an information service for immigrants in the United States Bureau of Immigration in 1907, which was changed into an employment office in 1914. The manpower problems of World War I resulted in the establishment of the U.S. Employment Service in the Federal Department of Labor.

Only in the depths of the Depression, after the New Deal government had assumed responsibility, were the public employment services reactivated. The *Wagner-Peyser Act of 1933* developed, again, a national system of public employment services with financial support of federal funds and with special emphasis on placement of war veterans and agricultural labor. Federal grants permitted the states to organize their employment bureaus and to introduce modern methods of placement with the use of aptitude and vocational tests for occupational classification, by employing qualified personnel. In 1939 the United States Employment Service was incorporated as Bureau of Employment Security in the Social Security Administration. After Pearl Harbor, in December 1941, state employment offices were merged with the federal service because of the need of a uniform policy for war needs. After the war, in November 1946, the public employment services were returned to the states. They are operating now as state agencies, usually under the Department of Employment and in close cooperation with the state unemployment insurance administration.[18] The Bureau of Employment Security, including the United States Employment Service, was attached to the United States Department of Labor in 1950.

The function of the employment services is "to bring workers and employers together." They assist in the effective recruitment and placement of labor, helping workers to find suitable and, if possible, stable employment. As well, they help employers find qualified employees. This function is carried out by registration and classification of workers who are seeking jobs upon consideration of their vocational capacity. Employment services obtain from employers information on job openings and their requirements, and they refer job applicants, if necessary, to other employment offices where workers are needed. The employment service is thus the connecting link between the employer in need of labor and the worker in need of a job.

<hr>

[18] Arthur W. Motley, "Employment Services," *Social Work Year Book* (1957), 232–39; William U. Norwood, Jr., "Employment Services," *Social Work Year Book* (1960), 240–45; Paul E. Mott, *The Organization of Society* (Englewood Cliffs, N.J.: Prentice-Hall, 1965), pp. 210–18; Louis Levine, "Placement and Vocational Services," *Encyclopedia of Social Work 1965,* pp. 546–52; William G. Bowen and T. Aldrich Finegan, *The Economics of Labor Force Participation* (Princeton, N.J.: Princeton University Press, 1968); Glen G. Cain, "Labor Force," *Encyclopedia 1971,* pp. 693–709.

Only seldom do employment services attempt to develop special training or retraining courses or to assume a role in channeling the flow of labor to areas with better placement facilities. This has been recently attempted by the Office of Economic Opportunity and its regional and local stations as the Work Incentive program (WIN) with questionable success, and was suggested again by President Nixon's Family Assistance Program.

SOCIAL WORKERS IN INDUSTRY

During World War I industrial social work in the United States developed under the name "industrial counseling" in a number of plants, particularly in war factories. Between the world wars, a few large companies —the Metropolitan Life Insurance Company, the Hawthorne Works of the Western Electric Company in Chicago, and the R. H. Macy department store in New York—employed industrial counselors. Their main function was to help employees with personal and family problems, in questions of health, care of children, marital problems, and financial difficulties. Other companies followed these examples.[19]

With the development of defense production and the ensuing spread of war industries during World War II, many plants, yards, and docks engaged industrial counselors, particularly for women.[20] Organized labor became concerned that industrial counselors in the plants might be biased in their approach to personal and work problems in favor of the employer who had hired them, and might lack understanding of and sympathy for labor unions. In some instances, the counselors or "welfare workers" were even accused of serving as labor spies for management, so that the workers had no confidence in them. Therefore, both CIO and AFL developed, with the cooperation of local welfare councils, a new program of "union counselors" under union sponsorship and control.[21] Social workers on the staff

---

[19] Mary Palevsky, *Counseling Services for Industrial Workers* (New York: Family Welfare Association of America, 1945), p. 4; B. A. Kogan, "Some Labor Union Enterprises in Public Health Economics," *American Journal of Public Health,* 38 (July 1948), 945–46.

[20] There is no specialization in industrial social work in the United States such as has developed in France. See Harold L. Wilensky and Charles W. Lebeaux, *Industrial Society and Social Welfare* (New York: Russell Sage Foundation, 1958), p. 162; Walter A. Friedlander, *Individualism and Social Welfare* (New York: Free Press, 1962), pp. 222–23; Melvin A. Glasser, "Labor and Industrial Health and Welfare Services," *Encyclopedia 1971,* pp. 744–49; and Elma P. Cole, "Unions in Social Work," *Encyclopedia 1971,* pp. 1507–11.

[21] Robert L. Kinney, "Union Counseling Bridges a Gap," *Survey Midmonthly* (April 1945), 106–8; Mary Palevsky, *Counseling Services for Industrial Workers* (New York: Family Welfare Association of America, 1945), pp. 5–8, 35–36; Arthur Hillman, "Labor Joins the Chicago Council," *Community,* 22, No. 3 (November 1946), 48–53.

of the Welfare Council, or Council of Social Agencies, or on one of the affiliated organizations were asked to offer training to selected rank-and-file workers who had the confidence of their fellow workers. The training courses did not attempt to make social workers out of rank-and-file union members. They tried to give the volunteers an understanding of simple interviewing technique and taught that grievances of a fellow worker about his work and his supervisor belonged to the shop steward as representative of the union, and that questions of family disturbances and personal, social, psychological, and health problems should be referred to the proper social and health agencies in the community. The training courses, for this reason, included instruction about the public and private social agencies in the community, their function in the field of family and child welfare, health treatment, and relief, and their policies and limitations.

The union counselors were able to answer simple legal and jurisdictional questions. The active participation of union members in the counseling process was of significance. It represented a new, positive approach to their concern in social welfare. Serious social and personal problems, however, were referred to the social agency best suited to help. The most advisable arrangement was that a union staff member or a social worker who enjoyed the full confidence of labor served on the staff of the Welfare Council or of the Community Chest so that any difficult questions could be referred to him. He then contacted the special social agency able to help the person or family in need of service. In some places, a central referral bureau for all inquiries from union counselors and their "clients" was set up, but in other cities the union counselor (union community service director) referred inquiring workers directly to the competent social agencies. This integration of social services with labor union counseling proved of value to union members to help them overcome family disturbances, to receive neglected medical and dental care, and to replace oppressing debts with reasonable loans. It also helped to avoid unnecessary duplication of available community services by special institutions of labor unions.

Many problems (frequently concerning marital difficulties and health and child adjustment questions) brought to the attention of industrial counselors are the same as those encountered in family casework. The short period of training of union counselors limited their information basically to a survey of community welfare and health organizations and to an understanding of the necessity of referring serious problems to a central, experienced representative, if possible a trained social worker. The difficulty of preparing rank-and-file workers in plants sufficiently, within a short period, for counseling, has led to another approach in which professional workers assume the task of industrial counseling. This has been experienced in the Workers Personal Service Bureau, organized through the Brooklyn Council for Social Planning in cooperation with eighty New York unions. In a number of industries, "in-plant counseling" either by industrial counselors employed by management or by union counselors who advise fellow workers with the consent of management during certain hours on working time, during lunch hours, or after work has been continued.

A few labor unions have established professional social work under their auspices. The National Maritime Union (AFL-CIO), in cooperation with the United Seamen's Service, has organized a Personal Service Department as a casework agency in New York. During World War II, branch units were operating in New Orleans and San Francisco. Casework is available to members of the American Merchant Marine who have family and other personal and health problems, and referrals are made to other social agencies when they may be of help to the seamen.

Trained, experienced social workers are also employed in some of the health and welfare plans administered under union auspices, for example, in the rehabilitation service of the United Mine Workers of America Welfare and Retirement Fund. Some also are employed in centers for aged and unemployed workers and their families founded by the United Automobile Workers of America, and in the Community Service Activities of the AFL-CIO. However, no special industrial social work has developed so far in the United States, in contrast to France, Belgium, Germany, Russia, most Latin American countries, and India.

ORGANIZED LABOR AND SOCIAL WORK

Labor unions in the United States have historically favored protective legislation with regard to child labor and women's work, workmen's compensation, and old-age insurance. However, before the Great Depression, when the pressing need for unemployment insurance as well as for wage and hours legislation was clearly demonstrated, their attitude was one of ambivalence toward this type of social legislation.[22] Since the Depression a positive endorsement of social legislation, including collective bargaining, social security provisions, and extension of social insurance, has become the unanimous attitude of organized labor in our country.

Originally, labor unions manifested substantial suspicion of, and very little sympathy for, public and private social work. Even when industrial workers, during World War I, substantially contributed to Community Chest drives, they were indifferent about the aims and methods of charitable agencies and the programs that the drives supported. The social worker still

22 John A. Fitch, "Samuel Gompers and the Labor Movement," *The Survey* (June 1950), 291–92; Albert Deutsch, "Get Together, Labor and Social Work," *Social Work Today* (April 1942), 13; Walter Friedlander, "Labour Unions and Social Workers," *International Social Work*, 13, No. 4 (Spring 1970), 18–30.

was considered as a person doling out largesse and being a representative o a wealthy, bourgeois class, instead of helping neighbors on a plane of equality Rank-and-file workers criticized their employers for paying low wages bu boasting of their generous contributions to charities. They found that pri vate social agencies sometimes were used to discourage persons in financia need from joining labor unions, and that relief even was abused as a too to break strikes. During World War II this attitude changed. It began witl the organization of war relief drives by both the AFL and the CIO to help the suffering people of those countries which had been attacked by the Axis powers. When these contributions reached an annual amount of abou $50,000,000 in 1942, the National War Fund and the American Red Cross recognized the need of integrating this important source of income into the general welfare campaign. It was evident that several competing drives would result in discontent and conflict among the population, and that only a unified, concerted appeal for war relief as well as domestic health and wel-fare services would be successful. Organized labor decided to join forces and to cooperate in the National War Fund, through special war relief com-mittees of the AFL and the CIO. Representatives of labor groups were employed in Community Chests, and labor began to play a more significant role in social work.

Their role was not limited to aiding the local, state, and national Community Chests and the Red Cross in the united fund-raising appeals in factory, plants, docks, and union meetings. In view of the essential efforts of organized labor in raising the large amounts needed for domestic and foreign war relief activities, it was only natural that labor leaders were no longer satisfied with mere "window dressing" representation of labor on boards of social agencies, Community Chests, and Welfare Councils.[23] Their participation in fund-raising campaigns, social welfare planning, and policy development of individual agencies led to understanding and a sincere interest among labor unions and their membership in social work. Labor representatives were able to interpret to union members the need for, and the value of, health and welfare services for their families and for the whole working class, as well as for the sick, old, infirm, and needy children of the community.

In the postwar era the interest of labor unions in the support of social services through participation in Community Chest campaigns has con-tinued. Closely connected with this active help in raising the necessary funds for voluntary welfare and health agencies is the participation of labor re-

---

[23] Howard Keeler, "Unions in Social Work," *Social Work Year Book* (1951), 518–19; Brent Taylor, "Labor Becomes a Big Giver," *Survey Graphic* (February 1943), 447–48; Hillman, "Labor Joins the Chicago Council," 48 ff; Cole, "Unions in Social Work," pp. 1507–11; Howard Hush, "Collective Bargaining in Voluntary Agencies," *Social Casework,* 50, No. 4 (April 1969), 210–13.

presentatives in community welfare councils, which are concerned with the planning of development, concentration, or expansion of social welfare, health, and defense facilities. Labor feels that these services should not be handled by a few wealthy people alone, but by representatives of the common man as well. The third result of this sharing in participation of union representatives in policy-making boards and committees of social agencies (though it usually is only a modest participation in view of the economic and social importance of labor) is that union members and their families are more aware of, and more willing to use, the services of health and welfare agencies. Union members are independent people, little accustomed to turning to public or private social agencies in time of difficulty. Union counselors have recently been able to dissipate the distrust of union members against social agencies and enable them to use services of the community. The experience of union representatives in social agencies has developed mutual respect between labor and social workers. The participation of organized labor in social work is increasingly accepted as a method for more effective interpretation of social work to the public, and as a fair and constructive relationship. Finally, the cooperation of unions in social work planning will bring into focus unmet needs of the community so that Community Chests and Welfare Planning Councils will realize more easily where essential, actual health and welfare needs require new or expanded services.

The Community Services Committee of the AFL-CIO is actively engaged in supporting the work of community welfare councils in planning and improving standards of social services, both on the federal level and in states and local communities. The fund raising for health and welfare is strengthened by the helpful recommendations of organized labor and their active participation in campaigns and collections all over the country. The director of the Community Services Committee, Leo Perlis, is urging community chests and federated funds to allocate money for professional social work education; he has been honored for his valuable cooperation by the Council on Social Work Education.

SELECTED BIBLIOGRAPHY

A. Services to Veterans and the Armed Forces

ANDERSON, DELWIN M., "Veterans Services," *Encyclopedia of Social Work 1971*, pp. 1513–18.

APAKA, TSUNEKO A., and KATHLEEN B. SANGES, "The Group Approach in a General Hospital (Veterans Administration)," *Social Work*, 7, No. 4 (October 1962), 59–60.

BURNS, EVELINE M., *The American Social Security System*, Chap. 10, Income Securit Measures for Veterans." Boston: Houghton Mifflin, 1949, pp. 265–92.

CUMMING, ROGER, "Veterans' Benefits and Services," *Social Work Year Book* (1954) 521–29.

GRAY, CARL R. Jr., "The Veterans' Administration," *The American Annual* (1952).

KARL, VIRGINIA C., "Veterans Benefits and Services," *Social Work Year Book* (1957) 573–84.

MAGNUSON, PAUL B., "Medical Care for Veterans," *The Annals*, 273 (January 1951)

NEVILLE, MARGARET, "Veterans' Benefits and Services," *Encyclopedia of Social Wor 1965*, pp. 809–16.

ROHRLICH, GEORGE F., "Veterans Pensions in Retrospect and in Prospect," *Socia Service Review*, 31, No. 4 (December 1957), 427–41.

ROSS, ELIZABETH H., "Social Work's Responsibility for Veterans," *National Con ference of Social Work, Proceedings* (1946), 336–41.

STIPE, JACK H., "Social Services in the Veterans Administration," *Journal of Socia Casework*, 29 (February 1948), 43–48.

United States Veterans Administration, *Federal Benefits for Veterans and Dependents* Washington, D.C.: Government Printing Office, 1963.

WEBER, GUSTAVUS A., and LAWRENCE F. SCHMECKEBIER, *The Veterans Administra tion: Its History, Activities, and Organization*, Service Monographs of the U.S. Government, No. 66. Washington, D.C.: Brookings Institution, 1934.

B. Problems of Racism

BECKER, GARY S., *The Economics of Discrimination*. Chicago: University of Chicago Press, 1957.

BERNARD, JESSIE, *Marriage and Family among Negroes*. Englewood Cliffs, N.J.: Prentice-Hall, 1966.

BILLINGSLEY, ANDREW, *Black Families in White America*. Englewood Cliffs, N.J.: Prentice-Hall, 1968.

CAPLOVITZ, DAVID, *The Poor Pay More: Consumer Practices of Low-Income Families*. New York: Free Press, 1963.

CLARK, KENNETH, *Dark Ghetto*. New York: Harper & Row, 1965.

DANIELS, ROGER, and HARRY H. L. KITANO, *American Racism: Exploration of the Nature of Prejudice*. Englewood Cliffs, N.J.: Prentice-Hall, 1970.

DUNCAN, BEVERLY, and PHILIP M. HAUSER, *Housing a Metropolis—Chicago*. New York: Free Press, 1960.

GLAZER, NATHAN, and DANIEL P. MOYNIHAN, *Beyond the Melting Pot*. Cambridge, Mass.: MIT Press, 1963.

GREBLER, LEO, JOAN W. MOORE, and RALPH GUZMAN, *The Mexican-American People: The Nation's Second Largest Minority*. New York: Free Press, 1970.

GRIER, WILLIAM H., and PRICE M. COBBS, *Black Rage*. New York: Basic Books, 1968.

KAIN, JOHN F., *Race and Poverty: The Economics of Discrimination*. Englewood Cliffs, N.J.: Prentice-Hall, 1969.

KITANO, HARRY H. L., *Japanese Americans: The Evolution of a Subculture*. Engle wood Cliffs, N.J.: Prentice-Hall, 1969.

KLUCKHOLM, CLYDE, ed., *Personality in Nature, Society and Culture*. New York: Alfred A. Knopf, 1967.

KNOWLES, LOUIS, and KENNETH PREWITT, *Institutional Racism in America*. Engle wood Cliffs, N.J.: Prentice-Hall, 1971.

LEE, ROSE HUM, *The Chinese in the United States*. Chicago: University of Chicago Press, 1960.

MARX, GARY T., *Racial Conflict: Tension and Change in American Society.* Boston: Little, Brown, 1971.

MYRDAL, GUNNAR, *An American Dilemma: The Negro Problem and Modern Democracy.* New York: Harper & Row, 1962.

NORTHRUP, HERBERT, and RICHARD L. ROWAN, eds., *The Negro and Employment Opportunity.* Ann Arbor, Mich.: Industrial Relations Institute, 1965.

SCHULZ, DAVID A., *Coming Up Black: Patterns of Negro Socialization.* Englewood Cliffs, N.J.: Prentice-Hall, 1969.

SHERMAN, RICHARD B., *The Negro and the City.* Englewood Cliffs, N.J.: Prentice-Hall, 1970.

STEINER, GILBERT Y., *Social Insecurity: The Politics of Welfare.* Chicago: Rand McNally, 1966.

YOUNG, WHITNEY M. Jr., *To Be Equal.* New York: McGraw-Hill, 1964.

C. Industry and Social Welfare

BECKER, HARRY, *Labor's Stake in Employment and Retirement.* Detroit: United Auto Workers, 1949.

————, ed., "Organized Labor and the Problem of Medical Care," *The Annals,* 273 (January 1951), 122–30.

BRYANT, CLIFTON D., *The Social Dimensions of Work.* Englewood Cliffs, N.J.: Prentice-Hall, 1972.

CAIN, GLEN G., *Married Women in the Labor Force.* Chicago: University of Chicago Press, 1966.

CRUIKSHANK, NELSON H., "Labor's Role in the Broad Field of Social Work and Community Responsibility." New York: Community Chests and Councils, 1950.

DAVEY, HAROLD W., *Contemporary Collective Bargaining,* 2nd ed. Englewood Cliffs, N.J.: Prentice-Hall, 1959.

DEUTSCH, ALBERT, "American Labor and Social Work," *Science and Society* (Fall 1944), 289–304.

DIAMOND, DANIEL, and HROCH BEDROSIN, *Industry Hiring Requirements and the Employment of Disadvantaged Groups.* New York: New York University Press, 1970.

GOLDNER, WILLIAM, *Pensions Under Collective Bargaining.* Berkeley: University of California, Institute of Industrial Relations, 1950.

GORDON, M. S., and R. A. GORDON, *Prosperity and Unemployment.* New York: John Wiley, 1966.

HILL, HERBERT, "Business, Labor, and Jobs in the Ghetto," *Issues in Industrial Society,* 1, No. 1 (1969), 3–18.

KATZ, ARTHUR, *Unions in the Profession of Social Work.* New York: Community and Social Agency Employees Union, Local 1707, 1963.

KEELER, HOWARD, "Unions and Social Work," *Social Work Year Book* (1951), 518–22.

KRAMER, KENNETH L., "Labor's Goals for Social Security," *Social Work Journal,* 31, No. 1 (January 1950), 16–19.

KRAMER, LEO, *Labor's Paradox.* New York: John Wiley, 1962.

Labor Participation in Organized Health and Welfare Activities Other than Fund Raising. New York: Community Chests and Councils, 1943.

LEVITAN, SAR A., and GARTH L. MANGUM, *Federal Training and Work Programs in the Sixties.* Ann Arbor: University of Michigan Press, 1969.

484   social welfare programs and practice

MANGUM, GARTH L., "Guaranteeing Employment in the Public Sector." Washington, D.C.: National Association for Community Development, 1968.

MINKOFF, NATHANIEL M., "Trade Union Welfare Plans," *Monthly Labor Review*, 64, No. 2 (February 1947), 201–14.

PALEVSKY, MARY, *Counseling Services for Industrial Workers*. New York: Family Welfare Association of America, 1945.

PECHMAN, JOSEPH A., *Social Security: Perspectives for Reform*. Washington, D.C.: Brookings Institution, 1968.

POHLMANN, KENNETH E., "Rehabilitation of Disabled Miners," *American Journal of Public Health*, 42, No. 7 (July 1952), 791–94.

REHR, HELEN, "Problems for a Profession in a Strike Situation," *Social Work*, 5, No. 3 (July 1960), 22–28.

SHANAS, ETHEL, *Old People in Three Industrial Societies*. New York: Atherton Press, 1968.

SIFF, HILDA, "Labor Unions in Health and Welfare Agencies," *Encyclopedia of Social Work 1965*, pp. 443–47.

UDY, STANLEY H., Jr., *Work in Traditional and Modern Society*. Englewood Cliffs, N.J.: Prentice-Hall, 1970.

VAN KLEECK, MARY, "Social Work on the Industrial Frontier," *The Compass* (November 1944), 3–7.

18

---

social
work
and
correctional
services

CAUSES OF DELINQUENCY AND CRIME

Social services for children, youth, and adults who violate laws are an important part of modern social work. These services developed only after the criminal courts already had a long history. Thus, court authorities have been reluctant to recognize the value of the services of social workers whose techniques and skills had not yet taken definite form. We shall discuss, first, the social services rendered to children and young persons who have difficulties in abiding by the legal rules of community life, and then proceed to social services for the adult offender.

Maladjustment and delinquent behavior of children and youth are among the most serious problems of our society.[1] From the point of view of social work, it seems necessary to help children and adolescents to avoid asocial behavior, whether or not they are brought before a court or pronounced delinquent. Social work helps young people abide by the rules of social conduct required by tradition or statute. These efforts include the development of social attitudes and modes of behavior which are not necessarily embodied in legal provisions.[2] Thus, juvenile protection in social work is concerned with maladjusted children and youth whose delinquency brings them before the law, but also with those who, although not violating laws, prove difficult to educate in the family, or who are endangering others in school and in the streets.

Deviant behavior cannot be treated alike in all children because of the different circumstances under which it occurs. One difficult child may be accepted or even encouraged in his delinquent behavior by his family and neighbors, according to the mores of a certain area or community; another child under the same conditions may be brought to a social agency or referred to a child guidance clinic; and still another may be denounced to the police, arrested, and cited before the juvenile court. The economic status of the parents, customs of the local community, and cultural patterns of the social group to which the child belongs are essential factors in determining what happens to a delinquent child. The White House Conference of 1930 defined delinquency as juvenile misconduct that might be dealt with under the law. But from the point of view of social work, it is desirable to help the child before he gets in trouble and police authorities and juvenile courts are forced to interfere with his life.

No exact statistical data on the extent of juvenile delinquency in our country are available. But it is estimated that about 1,500,000 children under eighteen are arrested for delinquency each year and that about the same

---

[1] For a full discussion of the topic, see Negley K. Teeters and John Otto Reinemann, *The Challenge of Delinquency: Causation, Treatment, and Prevention of Juvenile Delinquency* (Englewood Cliffs, N.J.: Prentice-Hall, 1950), Chap. 1; John R. Ellingston, *Protecting Our Children from Criminal Careers* (Englewood Cliffs, N.J.: Prentice-Hall, 1948), Chaps 1, 2; Don C. Gibbons, *Changing the Lawbreaker* (Englewood Cliffs, N.J.: Prentice-Hall, 1965), pp. 1–20; Frank E. Hartung, *Crime, Law and Society* (Detroit: Wayne State University Press, 1965), pp. 15–36; Max Siporin, "Deviant Behavior Theory in Social Work," *Social Work*, 10, No. 3 (July 1965), 59–67; Don C. Gibbons, *Society, Crime, and Criminal Careers,* 5th ed. (Englewood Cliffs, N.J.: Prentice-Hall, 1973); Edwin M. Schur, *Our Criminal Society* (Englewood Cliffs, N.J.: Prentice-Hall, 1969), pp. 1–9, 12–21, 121–57; James F. Short, Jr., and Marvin E. Wolfgang, eds., "Collective Violence," *The Annals*, 391 (September 1970), 1–176.

[2] Helen L. Witmer. *Social Work: An Analysis of a Social Institution* (New York: Farrar & Rinehart, 1942), p. 383; John Cumming and Elaine Cumming, *Ego and Milieu* (New York: Atherton Press, 1962); Edwin M. Lemert, *Human Deviance, Social Problems and Social Control* (Englewood Cliffs, N.J.: Prentice-Hall, 1967), pp. 3–30.

number are not brought before a juvenile court, although they also are involved in crime.[3]

There are many theories concerning the causes of delinquency. Cesare Lombroso, the noted Italian anthropologist and criminologist, taught that the criminal was born, doomed by certain biological characteristics to lead a life of crime. Today few scientists adhere to this "constitutional school of criminality." Most students of criminology are convinced that crime and delinquency are caused not by any single source, be it heredity, biological structure, or environmental influences, but usually by several factors working together. This is termed the "multiple causation theory." Among the various factors may be included hereditary and biological influences, such as poor health, physical handicaps, abnormalities, glandular disturbances, various degrees of mental deficiency or even psychosis, emotional instability, insecurity, uncontrolled sexual drives, or neurotic behavior. Other factors may be environment; neglect or rejection by parents, siblings, and friends; detrimental influences of a broken home; and criminal attitudes of the family, neighbors, or predatory gangs in a slum area. There may also be poverty in the family, gambling, bad companions, irregular or poor education, lack of healthy recreation, excitement through the radio, television, the newspapers, crime stories, comic books, and movies.

Another theory, the "differential association theory," interprets delinquency as a learned behavior based on deviant patterns, isolated from common, legally accepted behavior, and nurtured by the surrounding "culture."

Research studies, particularly those of Sheldon and Eleanor Glueck and Clifford Shaw, have shown that certain young persons may become delinquent while others remain law-abiding citizens under the same hereditary conditions and in the same environment.[4]

3 Katherine B. Oettinger, "Current Concerns of the Children's Bureau," *Children*, 5, No. 4 (July–August 1958), 123–28; Benjamin Fine, *1,000,000 Delinquents* (New York: World, 1955); Sophia M. Robison, "Juvenile Delinquency," *Encyclopedia of Social Work 1965*, pp. 429–40; Thorsten Sellin and Marvin E. Wolfgang, *The Measurement of Delinquency* (New York: John Wiley, 1964); Milton G. Rektor, "Crime and Delinquency," *Encyclopedia 1971*, pp. 162–72.

4 Sheldon Glueck and Eleanor Glueck, *One Thousand Delinquents* (Cambridge, Mass.: Harvard University Press, 1934); Clifford Shaw, *Brothers in Crime* (Chicago: University of Chicago Press, 1938); Miriam van Waters, *Youth in Conflict* (New York: Republic Printing Co., 1925); Albert K. Cohen, *Delinquent Boys: The Culture of the Gang* (New York: Free Press, 1955); Sophia M. Robison, *Juvenile Delinquency: Its Nature and Control* (New York: Holt, Rinehart and Winston, 1960); William E. Amos and Charles E. Wellford, *Delinquency Prevention: Theory and Practice* (Englewood Cliffs, N.J.: Prentice-Hall, 1967); Leslie Wilkins, *Social Deviance* (Englewood Cliffs, N.J.: Prentice-Hall, 1965), pp. 36–55; Daniel Glaser, "Differential Association and Criminological Prediction," *Social Problems*, 8, No. 1 (Summer 1960), 6–14; Donald R. Cressey, "The Theory of Differential Association," *Social Problems*, 8, No. 1 (Summer 1960), 2–6; Walter B. Miller, "Implications of Urban Lower Class Culture for Social Work," *Social Service Review*, 33, No. 3

Because human behavior is determined in part by customs and culture, much delinquency is based on the conflicting values within and between cultural groups. A frequently mentioned example of such a conflict is the difference between the customs of foreign-born parents and their native-born children. Children are ashamed of the "strange" habits and values of their parents; as a rule, they accept those of their play companions and classmates in school. In fact, our present civilization is not ruled by a single set of cultural and ethical values, but by several conflicting systems. This conflict is more evident in the United States than in other countries due to the mobility of its population, their different ethnic backgrounds, and the lack of a strict class system.[5]

Cultural anthropology explains the divergence in sexual customs and habits; in approval or disapproval of street fighting, gang rule, stealing of money, food, or automobiles; fraud, cheating in measures and weights; gambling and betting; riding freight trains, trucks, and busses; truancy; illicit manufacture of liquor; and the use of drugs, among various minority groups and underprivileged classes of our population. Whenever youngsters act in conformity to the customs of their group, but in violation of the written law or the habit of other groups, the lawbreaker and his family and friends often consider it merely an unfortunate accident to be caught by the police and reprimanded by the court.

More general, and not dependent on the particular customs of minority groups, is the conflict existing between the teaching of religious and moral ethics on the one hand, and on the other, the practical demands of the economic rules of society. Religious teaching and social philosophy ask the individual to love others, and praise mutual aid and cooperation. In conflict with this humanitarian ideal, the principle of ruthless economic competition and individual achievement in terms of success, wealth, property, and high income regardless of its source, as a measurement of efficiency, urge the child to excel others in school and to aim at economic success, even at the expense of others. It is obvious that many children and youngsters find it difficult to establish a balance between these conflicting theories.[6]

(September 1959), 219–36; Bertram M. Beck, "Can Social Work Prevent Social Problems?" *Social Welfare Forum* (1961), 180–93; Stanton Wheeler, ed., *Controlling Delinquents* (New York: John Wiley, 1968); Martin Gold, "Crime and Delinquency: Control and Prevention," *Encyclopedia 1971,* pp. 172–81.

[5] Ellingston, *Protecting Our Children from Criminal Careers,* pp. 13–27; Fritz Redl and David Wineman, *The Aggressive Child* (New York: Free Press (1957); Gibbons, *Changing the Lawbreaker,* pp. 74–96; Inabel B. Lindsay, "The Influence of Cultural Factors," in *Current Issues in Social Work in Historical Perspective* (New York: Council on Social Work Education, 1962), pp. 23–29; William J. Brenner, "Court Decisions and Crime," *Crime and Delinquency,* 15, No. 4 (October 1969), 449–58.

[6] Franz Alexander and William Healy, *The Roots of Crime* (New York: Alfred A. Knopf, 1935); Bernard Lander, *Toward an Understanding of Juvenile Delinquency*

In view of the increasing rates of juvenile delinquency and adult crime, the numerous professional organizations of law enforcement, public and private social and correctional services, and educational agencies assembled in 1964, under the leadership of the Council on Social Work Education, the Council on Crime and Delinquency, the American Sociological Association, and the American Correctional Association, at Arden House of Columbia University, with the support of the Ford Foundation, for a conference on manpower and training for corrections. The Arden House Conference established a Joint Commission on Correctional Manpower and Training which succeeded with the help of several members of Congress in moving Congress to enact the *Correctional Rehabilitation Study Act of 1965.* The Act provided $2,100,000 for a three-year study of the nature of crime and delinquency, the necessary manpower for more effective prevention and control of crime and for rehabilitation of juvenile and adult offenders. Private donations from individuals and foundations for this research and training were encouraged.[7] The Arden House Conference stated that social work had so far neglected to emphasize the need of value changes in correctional rehabilitation and that concepts of self-determination and the nonjudgmental approach needed to be modified in correctional work which tries to establish in the offender respect for others and responsibility for his behavior, as well as to curb his destructive actions.

THE JUVENILE COURT

After the French Penal Code under Napoleon provided for a minimum age at which children could be made responsible for offenses, and for a different treatment of young lawbreakers, the postulate of differentiation

---

(New York: Columbia University Press, 1953); William McCord et al., *Origins of Crime* (New York: Columbia University Press, 1959); Sophia M. Robison, *The Adolescent: His Search for Understanding* (New York: Fordham University Press, 1963); Sanford Bates, "Organized Crime and the Correctional Process," *Crime and Delinquency,* 8, No. 4 (October 1962), 390–98; Serapio R. Zalba, "Battered Children," *Transaction,* 8, No. 10 (August 1971), 58–61.

[7] Charles S. Prigmore, *Manpower and Training for Corrections* (New York: Council on Social Work Education, 1966); Peter P. Lejins, "The Joint Commission on Correctional Manpower and Training," *Crime and Delinquency,* 12, No. 3 (July 1966), 217–20; Elliot Studt, "Social Work Practice in Correctional Services," *Encyclopedia 1965,* pp. 219–25; and "Crime and Delinquency: Institutions," *Encyclopedia 1971,* pp. 186–91.

In 1967, the President's Commission on Law Enforcement and Administration of Justice published *The Challenge of Crime in a Free Society* and a Task Force report, *Organized Crime,* which revealed the necessity of changing methods of crime prevention and of rehabilitating delinquents and adult offenders. A separate task force report, *Juvenile Delinquency and Youth Crime* (1967), discussed the nature of juvenile delinquency, the practice of juvenile courts, prevention, control, and cultural elements in delinquency.

spread to most Western countries. The English Courts of Chancery already had been protecting the interests of children under seven years of age, who were considered incapable of "criminal intent." Children between seven and fourteen could be punished by the courts, provided the prosecutor was able to prove their capacity of entertaining criminal intent. Children over fourteen were punished as adult criminals.

In the United States, the press and charity societies complained that children begging in the streets, or pilfering, needed protection and reformation rather than punishment of the type that adults received. It became evident that harsh punishment, particularly the death sentence, against children was out of proportion to the child's responsibility, and that children placed in jails or prisons with adult criminals were really becoming trained in crime and vice by the older inmates.

In the 1820s New York, Boston, and Philadelphia established "houses of refuge" for wayward or delinquent children and youngsters to separate them from adult criminals.

The first juvenile court was created in Chicago on July 1, 1899. Since 1891 a group of citizens under the leadership of Jane Addams and Judge Harvey B. Hurd had urged the Chicago Bar Association to encourage the state legislature to enact legislation for the protection of children and for their segregation from adult offenders. The law was adopted on April 14, 1899 with the aim of treatment and supervision of dependent, neglected, and delinquent children.[8] The juvenile court judge had to combine legal skill with the knowledge of human behavior to help the child in his adjustment.

The law established the jurisdiction of circuit and county courts over children's cases. It based the entire process of investigation, court hearing, and judicial disposition on the idea of rehabilitation of the juvenile delinquent. The juvenile court is not a criminal court; it does not make charges against the child, who therefore is not in need of a defense lawyer, although this concept has recently been questioned. There is no jury to determine the guilt or innocence of the child. Rather, the court attempts to understand the causes for the behavior of the child or adolescent and orders measures to be taken for his adjustment and rehabilitation.

In the same year in which the Chicago juvenile court was established, 1899, Judge Benjamin B. Lindsay organized a special children's court under the Board of Education in Denver, Colorado, which developed into a juvenile court in 1903. Other states have followed the Illinois example, so that at

---

8 Grace Abbott, *The Child and the State,* vol. 2 (Chicago: University of Chicago Press, 1938), pp. 303–31; Margaret K. Rosenheim, ed., *Justice for the Child: The Juvenile Court in Transition* (New York: Free Press, 1962); Amos and Wellford, *Delinquency Prevention: Theory and Practice,* pp. 208–23; Robert M. Emerson, *Judging Delinquents: Content and Process in Juvenile Court* (Chicago: Aldine Press, 1969).

present all states, as well as the federal government, have juvenile courts. The operation of the juvenile court may be best characterized by its comparison with the adult criminal court. An adult who has committed an offense is, as a rule, arrested and after a hearing before a magistrate either summarily punished by a fine or jail sentence, held for trial in jail, or released under bail or on his pledge to appear in court. After a criminal investigation, the prosecuting attorney submits the evidence to a jury, requesting an indictment of the accused. If the jury finds that the evidence does not justify an indictment, the accused is released. If the indictment is pronounced by the jury, the trial proceeds. The defendant is entitled to have an attorney to represent him. At the arraignment he pleads guilty or not guilty; in the latter case, a trial jury of twelve members brings in, on examination of the facts and cross-examination of the witnesses by the prosecuting officer and the defense lawyer, a verdict of guilty or not guilty.

The procedure of the juvenile court is very different. Its jurisdiction covers, in the majority of states, youth under eighteen years of age. As a rule, neglected and dependent children also are under the jurisdiction of the juvenile court, and in some states are placed under adoption, guardianship, or committed to institutions for handicapped and mentally defective or ill children. The action of the juvenile court usually is initiated by petition; no jury is asked for an indictment. In a famous decision, *Gault* v. *Arizona* (1967), the Supreme Court decided that the child and his parents must be notified of their right to be represented by counsel, and if they cannot afford to hire an attorney, he must be appointed by the court.[9]

If a juvenile offender is arrested after violating the law, he should be placed in a detention home, not in a jail with adults. Despite the knowledge that children and youthful offenders are trained in crime, distrust society, and become more hostile to good citizenship as a result of being kept in jail, prohibition of jail detention varies widely among the states. Often, exceptions are possible for older youth or by order of the juvenile court judge. Frequently the young offender is heard before a referee or a probation officer at once or the next day, and released on his promise of good behavior, or held for the juvenile court session in the detention home. Many juvenile courts place the child under the supervision of a probation officer when the youngster is released before the final court hearing.

THE DETENTION HOME

The detention home, 'or juvenile hall; receives children who may be classified into three main categories: (1) children in need of protection, such as dependent, neglected, and abused children without proper care,

---

[9] *Task Force Report: Juvenile Delinquency and Youth Crime* (Washington, D.C.: Government Printing Office, 1967), pp. 57–76.

lost children in need of emergency shelter, mental defectives awaiting commitment, and habitual truants who are being returned to their parents; (2) children in temporary custody, such as children who are runaways from their natural or foster families and from children's institutions, and children who must serve as witnesses to secure their presence in court; and (3) juveniles expecting trial before the juvenile court, and children awaiting transfer to a training school or another institution after court decision.

In some detention homes, dependent and neglected children are kept separate from delinquent children. Many children remain only a day or a night in the detention home until they return to their families, but for three types of children longer placement in the detention home is frequently necessary: (1) children and youngsters beyond the control of their parents, foster parents, and guardians, who cannot be prevented from committing new delinquencies, such as serious assault, sexual attacks, burglary, armed robbery; (2) children who are in physical or moral danger in their families or are without a home; and (3) children whose attendance or uninfluenced testimony at a court hearing or whose placement in an institution can be assured only by detention.[10]

The detention home is administered by (1) the juvenile court (sometimes the chief probation officer is superintendent of the home), (2) the county authorities (board of supervisors or commissioners), (3) a local public welfare department, (4) the state's department of social welfare, or (5) a private child welfare agency.

Services to the child in the detention home include physical and custodial care, medical and dental treatment, recreation, instruction according to the age of the child and the length of his stay, and religious services. Although a certain security against escape is necessary, the detention home should avoid an atmosphere of fear and repression. More recently, the need of professional casework and clinical services for emotionally disturbed children has been acknowledged, as well as stimulating, cheerful group activities in workshops, play, and recreation so that the children are occupied and socially interested. However, many detention homes are still far from meeting these standards, which require employment of trained personnel, a superintendent, teachers, caseworkers, group workers, and supervisors. The observation in the detention home of the child's health, mental

---

[10] Sherwood Norman, "The Detention Home," *The Annals,* 261 (January 1949), 158–65; Teeters and Reinemann, *The Challenge of Delinquency,* pp. 237–46; Wayne R. La Fave, *Arrest: The Decision to Take a Suspect into Custody* (Boston: Little, Brown, 1965); Paul W. Tappan and Ivan Nicolle, "Juvenile Delinquents and their Treatment," *The Annals,* 339 (January 1962), 157–70; Anthony Platt, *The Child Savers: The Invention of Delinquency* (Chicago: University of Chicago Press, 1969); Seymour L. Halleck, "Criminal Behavior," *The Center Magazine,* 11, No. 2 (March 1969), 86–88; Jeffni G. Murphy, "Preventive Detention and Psychotherapy," *Dissent* (October 1970), 448–60; Milton G. Rector, "Correction in the United States," *Crime and Delinquency,* 13, No. 1 (January 1967), 1–162.

abilities, and behavior renders valuable information for the court, the probation staff, and social agencies which may later help the child.

Because most children are held only a few days or weeks in a detention home, little systematic, academic, or technical education and personality adjustment is possible. The children are of different age groups. Most of them are sent home again or are placed in a foster home or another children's institution before they are well acquainted with the detention home staff.

With an accepting, friendly attitude toward the child the staff some times is able to break through the fearful or hostile defense which most children bring to the detention home after they have been arrested. The establishment of contact between the child and the caseworker, group worker, or counselor may be the beginning of a treatment process. An intensive influence on corrective adjustment of the child can seldom occur during such a short period. But the child is protected against destructive influences, is well cared for physically, and the family and society are protected against the child's delinquent actions for the period of detention. Whenever the child feels that the staff takes a sincere interest in his well-being and is willing to help him, a start in his treatment may be made in the detention home.

JUVENILE COURT PROCEDURE

A major characteristic of juvenile court procedure is the social investigation, conducted by the probation officer attached to the juvenile court. It supplies the data for gaining an understanding of the personality of the young offender, his family, social and economic conditions, and the motive of his offense, to determine the plan for treatment and rehabilitation.

The probation officer needs knowledge of human behavior and personality for his interview with the child and his family. It is not easy to make contact with delinquent children because they frequently carry over toward the police, the probation officer, and the social worker their resentments against their parents or against authority in general. The delinquent child is unable to deal with his problems himself, but also avoids revealing them to adults. He may have been hurt by others and inconsistently treated by his parents or teachers. Then, the child is distrustful and fears being betrayed and punished. To hide this fear, delinquent children give themselves an air of reckless bravery and of callous hardness.

In cases of juvenile delinquents, the probation officer, as a rule, will have to make a home call to see the youngster and his family. He will not wait until the youth comes into his office. He studies the nature and circumstances of the offense, former delinquencies of the child, the family background with an analysis of its personal, educational, and economic conditions, the question of employment, housing, and moral conditions, as well as the health status of the child and the family. In the child's history, his relation to parents, siblings, and neighbors; personality traits; conduct and behavior; the physical and emotional effect of illness; his religious and school experiences; his work records; recreational activities; and his outlook for the future need exploration. The probation officer evaluates these data in relation to the cultural and social conditions in which the youngster is living, and presents his recommendations to the court with the aim of finding measures which will be most helpful to the child. Physical as well as mental examinations of the young offender are desirable to interpret his personality. Mental tests by a psychologist or a psychiatric diagnosis depend on local facilities available to the juvenile court. Different psychological tests may be used to explain the child's intelligence, the areas of his maladjustment, and the possibilities of rehabilitation and adjustment.

Juvenile courts frequently dispose of minor cases of delinquency informally without filing a petition, preparing a court record, or holding a court hearing. The arrangement of such an informal adjustment may be assigned by the judge to a probation officer, the chief probation officer, or a referee, sometimes even to a juvenile bureau or crime prevention division of the local police department.[11] At the court hearing the child meets the judge of the juvenile court, often for the first time. The meeting should be dignified, but free from judicial technicalities which might frighten the child and his parents. The court hearing is centered around the questions of why the child has become delinquent and what measures may be most effective in preventing further delinquencies and in promoting the child's readjustment. The establishment of the facts of the specific delinquency is less relevant.

As a rule, the juvenile court hearing is private; the general public and the press are excluded. The presence of spectators is harmful to the youngster because in an open court hearing either he finds himself the center of attraction and is inclined to act as a hero, therefore appearing tough and nonrepentant, or he risks losing the respect of his fellows and neighbors by showing regret for his behavior. The parents of the child, necessary witnesses, and the probation officer are present; representatives of social agencies and of the school authorities may be admitted. The atmosphere of the court hearing should create confidence in the child and his parents that the judge is willing to help them solve the youth's problems. But this procedure is not followed by all juvenile courts. Recently "teen-age juries" have been suggested for juvenile offenders, but it is doubtful whether they could provide a fair trial or reduce delinquency. A research project in 1965 indicated that the decision

11 Ellingston, *Protecting Our Children from Criminal Careers,* pp. 214–15; Alfred J. Kahn, *A Court for Children* (New York: Columbia University Press, 1953); William A. Lofquist, "The Framework and Experience of Juvenile Probation," *Social Casework,* 48 (January 1967), 17–21; National Council on Crime and Delinquency, "Teen-Age Juries," *Crime and Delinquency,* 12, No. 4 (October 1966), 305–9; Amos and Wellford, *Delinquency Prevention;* John R. Stratton and Robert M. Terry, *Prevention of Delinquency* (New York: Macmillan, 1968).

on juvenile offenses would best remain with the juvenile court, but that an "advisory youth committee" would be desirable which could tutor school dropouts and assist them in finding jobs.

The disposition of the juvenile court may be one of the following:

1. The child may be placed, with a reprimand by the judge, under supervision of his parents in his home.
2. The child may be placed on probation.
3. The child may be taken away from his home and placed in a foster family, either through a social agency or under the auspices of the juvenile court.
4. The judge may order the medical or psychiatric examination of the child and place the child for this purpose in a hospital, a children's institution, or a suitable family.
5. The judge may order the commitment of the child to the custody and guardianship of a public or private social agency or children's institution, frequently a training school or industrial school.
6. The judge may order restitution or reparation for damage caused by the child's delinquency.

The adjudication in juvenile court is not a penal conviction and does not constitute a criminal record. However, many juvenile court laws do not yet provide that the disposition of the juvenile court shall not disqualify the young person for any future civil service appointment.

The decision of a criminal court against an adult offender may be changed only by another sentence of an appellate court, but the disposition of the juvenile court may be modified by the judge according to the needs of the child. The right to appeal the decree of the juvenile court to an appellate court is limited in several state laws to questions of law, errors of fact, or certain decisions, such as commitment to a training school or removal from the custody of the parents.

In a few instances, adolescent courts or boys' courts have been established to separate the trial and treatment of persons between seventeen and twenty-one years of age from that of adult offenders.[12] The development of adolescent courts has been hampered by a hostile attitude of the public toward a mild or "sentimental" treatment of nearly adult offenders.

12 Teeters and Reinemann, *The Challenge of Delinquency*, pp. 328–33, 344–54; Clyde B. Vedder, *The Juvenile Offender* (New York: Doubleday, 1954); Rosenheim, *Justice for the Child;* Wilkins, *Social Deviance*, pp. 157–77; Robert M. Mennel, "Origins of the Juvenile Court," *Crime and Delinquency*, 18 No. 1 (January 1972), 68–78; Michael H. Langley, H. Ray Graves, and Betty Norris, "The Juvenile Court and Individualized Treatment," *Crime and Delinquency*, 18, No. 1 (January 1972), 79–92; Justine W. Polier, "The Invisible Legal Rights of the Poor," *Children*, 12, No. 6 (November–December 1965), 215–20; Renée Berg, "Social Work Practice and the Trend toward a Legalistic Juvenile Court," *Social Casework*, 47, No. 2 (February 1966), 93–97; Orman W. Ketcham, "The Juvenile Court for 1975," *Social Service Review*, 40, No. 3 (September 1966), 283–88; Edwin J. Thomas, "Role Problems of Offenders and Correctional Workers," *Crime and Delinquency*, 12, No. 4 (October 1966), 354–64.

PROBATION

"Probation is a process of treatment, prescribed by the court for persons convicted of offenses against the law, during which the individual on probation lives in the community and regulates his own life under conditions imposed by the court (or other constituted authority) and is subject to supervision by a probation officer."[13]

Characteristic of probation, therefore, is the postponement of either the final judgment or the execution of the sentence combined with certain conditions imposed by the court, under the guidance and supervision of the probation officer. In practice, it is not uncommon that an adult offender is ordered, first, to serve a certain period in jail or prison and then, under suspension of sentence, to live freely in the community on condition of good behavior under supervision. For juvenile delinquents, the probation order of the juvenile court allows the youth to live at liberty in his home or in the custody of a relative, friend, or foster parents, under supervision of the probation officer, instead of being committed to a correctional institution or training school.

The social elements of probation are threefold: (1) probation permits the probationer to live a normal life in the community and to readjust to socially acceptable attitudes without being confined, during this period, to a penal or correctional institution; (2) it is granted, on the basis of a social investigation by the court, assuming that the probationer will be able to live a lawful life and may be expected to do so; and (3) it is a process of adjustment with the supervision of a probation officer.

Probation has its legal basis in the authority of the court under common law to suspend sentence and to allow the convicted offender to remain at liberty upon condition of good behavior.[14] As a practical method, probation was introduced in the United States as early as 1841 by John Augustus, a Boston shoemaker. He provided bail for a poor drunkard who was threatened to be sentenced to the house of correction, and assumed his supervision during a period of "probation." John Augustus, encouraged by the success of his

---

[13] National Commission on Law Observance and Law Enforcement, *Penal Institutions, Probation and Parole,* Report No. 9, Wickersham Report (1931), p. 184; see also Gertrude M. Hengerer, "Organizing Probation Services," *National Probation and Parole Association Yearbook* (1953), 45–49; Charles Shireman, "Crime and Delinquency: Probation and Parole," *Encyclopedia 1971,* pp. 191–96; Howard G. Brown and William R. Downs, "Juvenile Courts and the Gault Decision," *Children,* 15, No. 3 (June 1968), 87–96; and Charles W. Tenney, "The Utopian World of the Juvenile Court," *The Annals,* 383 (May 1969), 101–18.

[14] John Otto Reinemann, "Probation and the Juvenile Delinquent," *The Annals,* 261 (January 1949), 109. See also David Dressler, *Practice and Theory of Probation and Parole* (New York: Columbia University Press, 1959); Robert A. Dentler and Kai T. Ericson, "The Function of Deviance in Groups," *Social Problems* (Fall 1959), 98–107; and Robert D. Vinter, "The Juvenile Court as an Institution," in President's Commission on Law Enforcement, *Juvenile Delinquency and Youth Crime* (Washington, D.C.: Government Printing Office, 1967), pp. 84–90.

first case, continued to bail, supervise, and assist about 2,000 adults and juveniles until his death in 1859. He also advocated the establishment of an asylum for the treatment of alcoholics.

The first probation law for adult offenders was enacted in 1878, in Massachusetts, and since 1959 all the states, the federal government, and the District of Columbia have had probation laws.

Probation provisions vary among the states and even among the individual courts. Probation is not just leniency. It is an educational measure of treating an offender through supervision while he lives in the community. The cost of probation is only a small fraction of that of institutional commitment. Its advantages are as follows: the probationer remains in his home; his social status is not impaired; he is able to support himself and his family and to pay restitution to the victim of the offense; and he may be rehabilitated with the aid of the probation officer, who can use the resources of the community and take advantage of the fact that the probationer's status discourages him from committing new offenses. Research on the effectiveness of prevention and control of juvenile delinquency and on the reduction of recidivism shows that granting probation to all first offenders but those guilty of severe assault and cruel crimes proves more successful than incarceration.[15]

Requisite for an effective probation system is the employment of skilled social workers trained in casework, in the use of community resources, in understanding the behavior of juvenile and adult offenders, and in cooperation with psychiatrists and psychologists. During recent years standards for probation officers have risen, and in some states civil service requirements and merit systems have been set up. Much remains to be done.

Usually, the probation service is attached to the court, and the appointment of the probation officers is made by the judge. But some exceptions have been made. For example, the probation service has been established as an independent agency, in the Los Angeles County Probation Department, the New York City Youth Board, or on a statewide level, as the California Youth Authority, the Youth Conservation Commission in Minnesota, the Youth Service Commission in Wisconsin, the State Department of Correction in New York, and the State Department of Public Assistance (Division of Child Welfare) in West Virginia.

The probation officer begins with a social investigation in the case of a juvenile court hearing. For the criminal court, the investigation, as a rule, is ordered only after a verdict of guilty is rendered against the adult offender, particularly if the judge is considering not sending the offender to a penal institution. The investigation requires that the probation officer understand the motivations, feelings, and attitudes of the offender, and the influences which neighborhood gangs and other elements may have had on his behavior. The probation officer cannot apply his standards of life and morals to the offender;

15 M. A. Lewin, "Crime and Punishment and Social Science," *The Public Interest*, 27 (Spring 1972), 96–103.

his function is to help the person who is in trouble with the law. He will consider the offender's personality, physiological equipment, mental and intellectual capacities, life experiences, cultural background, and setting.

When the probation officer interviews the young person, he gives him a chance to express his difficulties and discuss his social and personal situation. The probation officer explores with him possibilities of making changes in work, environment, or social relations, and joining church or group activities which may be helpful in his adjustment. In presenting data on the young delinquent collected in the family, school, and neighborhood, the probation officer has to distinguish between objective facts and his interpretation of the situation and the young offender's personality.

For juvenile delinquents, as well as for adult offenders, the probation officer recommends probation to the court only if he is convinced that the offender will be able to use it constructively for his adjustment. If he feels that the offender is not ready to adjust himself in the community, he suggests commitment to an institution.

After the court has placed an adult offender or a juvenile delinquent under probation, the probation officer supervises him as a helping service, but under the authority of the court. Whether it is good practice to have the same probation officer carry out the social investigation and the supervision, or whether these two main activities should be separated and assigned to different groups of probation officers, has been the subject of discussion.[16]

In general, girls' supervision and often that of boys under twelve are assigned to women probation officers, and cases of boys over twelve years of age to men. The regional principle, according to which a certain geographical area is assigned to the individual probation officer who supervises the children and young persons in this area, is considered economical and practical.

The probation officer recognizes the positive possibilities of authority and its implications for the probationer. He knows that this authoritative element is a necessary function of the judiciary system and of the probation process. However, he should be free of a feeling of vindictiveness and moral superiority toward the probationer which would prevent him from interpreting the court decision objectively and the meaning of probation to the probationer in an acceptable way. He will explain that the court's requirements, such as making regular reports to the probation officer or the court, planning permanent work, and avoiding drugs and excessive drinking, must be strictly followed. The probation officer will make it clear that the probationer

16 Chester H. Bartoo, "Hidden Factors Behind a Probation Officer's Recommendations," *Crime and Delinquency*, 9, No. 3 (July 1963), 276–81; Henry W. Maier, "Adolescenthood," *Social Casework*, 46, No. 1 (January 1965), 3–9; President's Commission on Law Enforcement, "Parole," pp. 60–71, "Probation," pp. 27–44, in *The Challenge of Crime in a Free Society* (Washington, D.C.: Government Printing Office, 1967); Marvin E. Wolfgang, "Violence USA: Riots and Crime," *Crime and Delinquency*, 14, No. 4 (October 1968), 289–305.

is free to ask for his help, but that the responsibility for complying with these court orders is his own, and that the success of the probation process depends on his attitude and behavior. During this period, the probation officer assists the probationer in his personal, emotional difficulties as well as in environmental problems, housing, employment, schooling, and group and cultural relations. Despite the authoritative element in probation, the probation officer should not direct the life of the probationer, depriving him of the responsibility for his decisions.[17] The recent trend toward therapy in penology pursues the objective of rehabilitation, no longer the goal of retribution. New forms of "community treatment" are being used, although their superiority has not been demonstrated.

The probationer has to be educated to assume responsibility; the probation officer will not always supervise his life. The relationship between probation officer and probationer must be based on understanding, respect, sincerity, and confidence in the sphere of authority that is a part of the court's jurisdiction. Revocation of probation will be recommended by the probation officer if he is convinced that the probationer cannot profit from a continuation of the probation service, and if he violates the rules of probation so flagrantly that institutional treatment seems necessary. However, the probation officer should be well aware that failure of probation might be due to his inability to find the right contact with the probationer or to mobilize other community resources. Such reasons would not justify the revocation of probation.

TRAINING SCHOOLS (CORRECTIONAL INSTITUTIONS)

Children and adolescents who are not granted probation by a juvenile court because their rehabilitation cannot be achieved in their home or in a foster family are committed to a training school, frequently called "industrial school" or "reform school."[18] The first local school of this type in the United

17 Dale Braxton, "Family Casework and Juvenile First Offenders," *Social Casework*, 47, No. 2 (February 1966), 87–92; Robert D. Vinter, "Justice for the Juvenile —Myth or Reality?" in Catherine Feblen, ed., *The Administration of Justice in America* (Newark: University of Delaware Press, 1970), pp. 55–73; Francis A. Allen, *The Borderland of Criminal Justice*, vol. 1 (Chicago: University of Chicago Press, 1964), pp. 26ff; Thomas Young, Charles Shireman, et al., "Findings from Experiments in Treatment in Correctional Institutions," *Social Service Review*, 46, No. 1 (March 1972), 38–59.

18 Though the terminology is not unanimously accepted, we want to speak of "reformatories" only as penal institutions for young offenders sentenced by the criminal court, or for adult offenders sentenced for the first time. Some schools for truant children are called "parental schools." See Gibbons, *Changing the Lawbreaker*, pp. 212–20; Elliot Studt, "Crime and Delinquency: Institutions," *Encyclopedia 1971*, pp. 186–91; and James F. Short and Marvin E. Wolfgang, eds., "Collective Violence," *The Annals*, 341 (September 1970), 1–176.

States was the New York City House of Refuge, founded in 1825 by the Society for Reformation of Juvenile Delinquents, to save neglected and vagrant children from the destructive influence of adult prisons. Other schools followed in Boston, Philadelphia, and New Orleans, but only in 1847 was the first state reform school established in Massachusetts. In 1959 there were 130 state industrial schools, a number of county and municipal schools, and about as many private training schools providing care for dependent, neglected, truant, and delinquent children and youths ranging from six to twenty-one years of age.

Some of these institutions have maintained practices of mass treatment, a repressive attitude, and even corporal punishment. Others offer little more than physical and custodial care; they accept the policy that the school is the place where troublesome and disturbing children may be placed primarily for the safety of the population of their home community, and that such children and adolescents should be controlled in the school by the denial of their liberty, enforcement of some general education and vocational training, and strict regulation of their activities. A third type of training school, however, has developed an integrated program of rehabilitation for these children and youths by providing a positive plan for group living under educational guidance. They offer medical and mental health supervision; spiritual, religious, academic, and vocational training; recreation; and leisure-time activities, permitting as much freedom and choice as possible. This type of school still represents a controlled environment in which the children have to accept limitations on their freedom and have to conform to the rules of group living, but it contributes to a constructive development of the children and prepares them for the return to life with their family or in their home community.

Only the last type of training school will achieve a positive change of personality, readjustment, and rehabilitation in children and adolescents committed to the school. Many schools suffer from their geographical isolation, which makes it difficult to teach the children how to live in a normal community, how to get along with other groups, how to participate in community activities, and how to use services outside the school. The isolation makes it difficult to find competent personnel interested in professional growth and in the adjustment of young persons. Despite these facts, there is often pressure by the population to remove training schools, particularly for older, aggressive boys, from the metropolitan centers to protect themselves from them. In the interest of the readjustment of difficult and disturbed children, the purpose of protection of the community should be considered only of secondary importance, and the construction of new schools in isolated regions should be abandoned. A relevant example of a modern, efficient program for the rehabilitation of delinquent adolescents is the experiment of the New York State Division for Youth.

One of the main obstacles to the successful rehabilitation of difficult and disturbed children is the lack of trained and competent personnel. In many institutions, employees have no proper training for their challenging job—they are former guards in jails or custodians without educational background or skill. Others, however, are well prepared by education, studies, and experience in child development, social work, and psychology to work with children in need of understanding and readjustment. There is in many training schools a trend toward the selection of a really qualified superintendent and staff who, as a team, will be able to help the children overcome the difficulties in personality and behavior which brought them into the training school.

Aftercare (or postinstitutional care, or parole) is an important factor for securing the effect of the institutional treatment of children and adolescents in training schools. As a rule, the children return to homes and neighborhoods which are far from ideal. There is no complete agreement as to who should be responsible for aftercare, what the content and procedure of aftercare should be, and what training is necessary for this service, nor are there, in general, sufficient funds available. Aftercare might be carried on by a parole officer of the training school, or by a statewide central aftercare agency for released children and adolescents, or by a child or family casework agency in the local community. Of utmost importance is the employment of well-trained personnel, which is possible only if adequate salaries, professional inservice training, and possibilities of promotion are secured.[19]

YOUTH CORRECTION AUTHORITIES

After World War I, widespread juvenile delinquency aroused the interest and concern of many legislators, judges, social workers, and sociologists. In lieu of retributive punishment, which had failed, the American Law Institute, composed of outstanding lawyers, criminologists, and judges, suggested a new approach to educating and treating youthful offenders. In 1940 it published a model *Youth Correction Authority Act,* proposing that the state legislatures establish preventive protection and correctional treatment of young offenders. The American Law Institute suggested that a Youth Correction Authority in the state should coordinate all facilities in educa-

---

[19] Rosemary C. Sarri and Robert D. Vinter, "Group Treatment Strategies in Juvenile Correctional Programs," *Crime and Delinquency,* 11, No. 4 (October 1965), 326–40; Gilbert Y. Steiner, "Day-Care Centers: Hype or Hope?" *Trans-action,* 8, No. 10 (August 1971), 50–57; Harry Finkelstein, "Limitations in Residential Treatment," *Crime and Delinquency,* 14, No. 3 (July 1968), 240–44; Gene Post, et al., "Day-Care Programs for Delinquents: A New Treatment Approach," *Crime and Delinquency,* 14, No. 4 (October 1968), 353–59; Milton Luger, "Innovations in the Treatment of Juvenile Offenders," *The Annals,* 381 (January 1969), 60–70.

tional, medical, and rehabilitation work for juvenile delinquents carried on in social agencies, children's institutions, training schools, clinics, and hospitals. Whenever necessary, the Authority itself should establish and operate detention homes, observation clinics, and corrective institutions.

The first state to write the suggestion of the American Law Institute into law was California.[20] The 1941 California Youth Correction Authority Act embodied all essential features of the model act. (In 1943 the name of the organization was changed to "Youth Authority.") Professor August Vollmer of the University of California, president of the California Prison Association, was mainly responsible for this legislative action. The Authority was to offer consultation services to local communities, conduct research on the causes of juvenile delinquency, and develop preventive services and diagnostic and treatment facilities.

One of the Youth Authority's major objectives is to protect society more effectively against the danger of crime by substituting for the old unsuccessful methods of retribution and punishment measures of education, correction, and rehabilitation of young offenders. The other major objective is prevention of delinquency.

The first step in the rehabilitation of young offenders referred to the Youth Authority by the juvenile courts is a clinical diagnosis in a reception center. Studies by a physician, psychiatrist, psychologist, social worker, and teacher secure an understanding of the personality and motives of the adolescent, and of the factors which led to his antisocial action. On the basis of clinical observation, the youngster then is classified according to his age, sex, mental capacities, emotional stability, aptitudes, and personal interests, and the treatment is determined on these factors. The subsequent therapy and adjustment is carried on under a program of reeducation and work assignments formulated to meet the individual needs and capacities of the youth. After adjustment of the young person in a selected institution is achieved, parole supervision is provided with careful preparation of the adolescent's return to his family or to the community. Before the release of the young offender, the Youth Authority contacts his family, his employer, and sometimes other people in the community to ensure his acceptance when he returns. Parole service offers guidance for the young offender in the beginning of his new life in the community.

The second objective, delinquency prevention, is partly pursued by the systematic development of facilities for sports, recreation, and leisure-time activities for children and young persons in the community. The program

[20] For an analysis of the development of the California Youth Authority and its operation, see Ellingston, *Protecting Our Children from Criminal Careers*, pp. 55–345; Teeters and Reinemann, *The Challenge of Delinquency*, pp. 354–68. See also David S. Milne, "Public Youth Agencies," *Crime and Delinquency*, 9, No. 3 (July 1963), 297–305; and Studt, "Crime and Delinquency: Institutions." The California Youth Authority now is an independent State agency.

includes the establishment or improvement of probation departments, police juvenile bureaus, and detention homes (in California called "juvenile halls") to secure better services for children and adolescents who are in trouble. Another aspect of the preventive activities is the creation of community councils for the coordination of the various social services to youth. Youth groups are invited to participate in recreation work in community and youth centers and other constructive cultural group action.

The Youth Authority succeeded in establishing smaller schools and forestry camps for the different age groups, with consideration of their character and behavior problems. Classification considers maturity, behavior, and vocational and personal aptitudes of the children. The necessary isolation of children in correctional schools is alleviated through contacts with the surrounding communities so that the children are prepared for their return to the family. Forestry camps for older boys acquaint the youngster with normal work habits in forestry projects, forest fire and blister rust control, road construction, and lumber mill work. Younger boys are placed in several ranch schools whose program is applied to the abilities of their age, including instruction in farming and animal husbandry.

The number of girls with delinquency records is much smaller. In the schools, the girls are divided according to age groups; special techniques are used for adjusting mentally retarded children. Recreation, art, craft, and hobby programs supplement vocational and social adjustment in class work. Homemaking, garden work, and housekeeping instruction is provided, but gifted girls are encouraged to prepare themselves for higher education.

The Delinquency Prevention Section assists community efforts to prevent and to reduce juvenile delinquency. Preventive work is more effective than punishment, but it has to be done on the local level in the community and neighborhood. The Youth Authority encourages community programs of social agencies, civil groups, youth groups, and individuals for sports and recreation, which divert youth from criminal actions. Consultants are sent to the counties to help coordinate recreational facilities with detention homes and juvenile control.

The Youth Authority Board has the final decision for the release of the youngster, but the Parole Section prepares his return to the community by securing, in advance, a job in business, industry, or agriculture, an apprentice position, or the possibility of entering school. If the family is not able to take the youth back, a foster home may be necessary. After the return of the adolescent, the parole officer is responsible for counsel, advice, and supervision until discharge of the youth from parole. Sometimes a return to one of the institutions of the Youth Authority for further education and training is necessary.

The integrated program of the Youth Authority has resulted in broader public understanding of the modern concept of rehabilitation of maladjusted youth. It has encouraged coordination of correctional facilities in the communities, the counties, and the state, and a working relationship between the Youth Authority, and other judicial, civic, and social institutions.

Similar arrangements have been made in Minnesota which formed the Youth Conservation Commission, and in Wisconsin which established a Youth Service Commission under the Department of Public Welfare. New York has set up a State Division for Youth and in New York City a City Youth Board which has engaged numerous citizens' groups and social agencies in coordinated action for prevention of juvenile delinquency in particularly endangered areas. In Massachusetts, the Youth Service Board deals with offenders of juvenile court age, and Texas formed a State Youth Development Council to conduct research and administer state institutions for delinquent children. It seems that the advantages of a united state authority in the field of juvenile delinquency are becoming recognized. But it might be seriously considered whether such state agencies would not be even more effective if they were coordinated under the Child Welfare Division of the state's department of public welfare. Such an organization could use all the facilities in the field of child welfare and maintain the contact with counties and communities without being limited to the specific field of juvenile delinquency.

DELINQUENCY PREVENTION AND CONTROL

During the past decades, knowledge of delinquency and some of its causes has grown and proved the necessity that people in the community understand that children are not "born to become criminals." We have seen that the causes of delinquency are complex and variable. They may be classified into three groups: individual factors, home factors, and neighborhood factors.[21]

Among the individual factors which lead a child into difficulties are biological conditions, such as glandular disorders, physical handicaps, and biological weakness, conducive to abnormal development or behavior. Mentally retarded children and youth of below-average intelligence, as well as psychopathic, nervous, unpredictable, and irresponsible adolescents, easily fall prey to asocial actions. The mentally ill may endanger themselves and others.

[21] Ellingston, *Protecting Our Children from Criminal Careers,* pp. 337–42; Gisela Konopka, "Co-ordination of Services as a Means of Delinquency Prevention," *The Annals,* 322 (March 1959), 30–37, and *The Adolescent Girl in Conflict* (Englewood Cliffs, N.J.: Prentice-Hall, 1966), pp. 134–40; Malcolm W. Klein, "Juvenile Gangs, Police and Detached Workers: Controversies over Intervention," *Social Service Review,* 39, No. 2 (June 1965), 183–90; Howard J. Parad, *Crisis Intervention* (New York: Family Service Association, 1965); Gisela Konopka, "Our Outcast Youth," *Social Work,* 15, No. 4 (October 1970), 76–86.

A third set of individual factors leading to delinquent behavior includes emotional instabilities caused by inferiority complexes, inner conflicts, temperamental disorders, and sex abnormalities. A fourth cause of delinquency is early childhood habits which create anxieties, truancy, runaway tendencies, and the abuse of alcohol or narcotic drugs.

Destructive influences of home life are a second group of factors leading to crime. The disorganized, divorced, or separated family in which children are mistreated or neglected causes delinquency; illegitimate children growing up without love and proper care are a part of this group. Other factors are families with quarreling, disunited parents who are in disagreement about education and discipline; and living in inadequate housing without sufficient privacy for the members of the family. The lack of leisure time and recreation, and too-heavy work responsibilities make children tired or rebellious and drive them into the streets. Other causes of conflict in the family may be differences of values and customs between the generations, particularly of parents of foreign descent, or the lack of spiritual and religious attachment to a church or an ethical philosophy.

The third group of neighborhood factors is particularly dangerous in blighted areas where the gang leader easily becomes the hero for young children and where street-corner associations are the rule. Examples of drunkenness, vice, and adult crime influence the young. In rural regions, the lack of healthy recreation and of a community center may induce youths to make the "highway night spot" their gathering place with gamblers, prostitutes, and other dubious acquaintances. In such neighborhoods, schools and churches should open their meeting halls and playgrounds for sports, recreational, and cultural activities; youth organizations and citizens' groups should assume the responsibility for carrying on these programs. Harmful commercial amusements appealing to sexual drives of adolescents, unsupervised dance halls where teen-agers and adults mix and where liquor is sold, and certain movies, magazines, and books may push youths into troublesome adventures.

To counteract these dangers which lead youths to crime, whole-hearted teamwork of public and private agencies devoted to the task of crime prevention is necessary. These include schools, churches, parent-teacher associations, youth organizations, group work agencies (such as YMCA, YWCA, YMHA, Boy Scouts, Girl Scouts, and boys' clubs), probation officers of the juvenile court, social workers, and policemen and officers of juvenile bureaus of police departments. All these groups should assist parents and guardians in locating difficult children in danger of maladjustment, and in recognizing early symptoms of unhappiness, conflict, and asocial behavior.

Recent research studies show that a small percentage of multiproblem families are the source of more than 75 percent of all juvenile delinquency. These families are characterized by desertion, alcoholism, divorce, mental illness, drug addiction, and crime. Their children tend to become asocial. Coordinated social services for these problem families, staffed by trained personnel, are necessary to help through counseling, casework, and group work, and can prevent a good deal of deviant behavior. Child guidance and mental hygiene clinics need to have more therapeutic facilities.[22]

The development of youth activities and social group work, as well as the strengthening of recreational facilities, promise desirable change. The cooperation of schools, churches, and social agencies with the juvenile police is essential to help underprivileged and endangered children in slum areas.

The first national attempt to prevent juvenile delinquency was the enactment of the *Juvenile Delinquency and Youth Offenses Act of 1961*. Its objective is the participation of the federal government in developing techniques for the prevention and control of juvenile and youth offenses, and in encouraging the coordination of efforts among government and nongovernment educational, employment, health, welfare, law-enforcement, correctional, and other agencies concerned with such problems. The statute encouraged demonstration projects in the field of delinquency prevention and called attention to the high delinquency rate among school dropouts, unemployed youth, and adolescents in deprived families. The act was to be implemented by the Department of Health, Education and Welfare in consultation with the President's Committee on Juvenile Delinquency. Demonstration projects were selected primarily in urban slums which so far had offered youngsters in this environment little incentive to conforming behavior and few opportunities for decent employment and desirable jobs. The policy of the projects is aimed at community action for changes in the social environment and in occupational chances of its youth, rather than attempting to change the personality of the underprivileged youth.[23] Programs for the prevention and control of delinquency need to study its immediate causes and analyze its various types to develop different therapies. Modern technical preventive programs may be used; the schools and the community should be involved

[22] William C. Kvaraceus and Walter B. Miller, *Delinquent Behavior* (Washington, D.C.: National Education Association, 1959); Alfred J. Kahn, "Planning for the Welfare of Children," *Social Welfare Forum* (1966), 165–87; Lewis Yablonsky, *The Violent Gang* (New York: Macmillan, 1962); Saul Pilnick, "Guided Group Interaction," *Encyclopedia 1971*, pp. 181–86; David Matza and Gresham M. Sykes, "Juvenile Delinquency and Subterranean Values," *American Sociological Review*, 26, No. 5 (October 1961), 712–19; Milne, "Public Youth Agencies," *Crime and Delinquency*, 9, No. 3 (July 1963), 297–305.

[23] See Melvin B. Mogulof, "Design for Community Action," in Amos and Wellford, eds., *Delinquency Prevention: Theory and Practice*, pp. 225–31; Alfred J. Kahn, *Planning Community Services for Children in Trouble* (New York: Columbia University Press, 1963; Milton Burdman, "Realism in Community-Based Correctional Services," *The Annals*, 381 (January 1969), 71–80; Stanton Wheeler, Leonard S. Contrell Jr., and Anne Romasco, *Juvenile Delinquency: Its Prevention and Control* (New York: Russell Sage Foundation, 1966).

in preventive action. Alternatives to probation or incarceration are needed to find new ways of delinquency prevention.

An important part in delinquency control may be taken by newspapers, magazines, radio, television, and motion pictures in reporting on juvenile delinquency in terms of its causes and protection of youth, rather than stressing the sensational aspects, scandals, and a false heroism in delinquent behavior.

Mobilization for Youth, New York

One interesting model of a youth delinquency prevention program is Mobilization for Youth in New York. It was established in 1962, after careful theoretical preparation by the faculty of the New York School of Social Work at Columbia University, with the objective to reduce juvenile delinquency on Manhattan's Lower East Side in New York. The pilot project was based on the experiences of the various settlement houses in the region, particularly Henry Street Settlement House, and the theory that in a slum neighborhood like the Manhattan Lower East Side delinquency is caused by the lack of opportunity for young people to find meaningful jobs with the chance of upward social mobility.[24] It was hoped that the new project might help these unemployed youth to get social status and possibilities similar to young people in normal neighborhoods. The main goal of the project is to change the environment rather than attempt to rehabilitate individual youngsters, and to achieve such change by educational measures, a job-finding program, and a welfare system which encourages young persons instead of punishing and frustrating them.[25]

The project works mainly with young Puerto Ricans and members of other minority groups, many of them members of juvenile gangs, who have been unable to find themselves a way out of unemployment and misery. These are, of course, the youngsters most difficult to work with; for that reason they had previously been left out in planning of delinquency prevention. To reach these people, MFY established several "area storefront helping stations" staffed with public health nurses, social workers, lawyers, vocational counselors, and psychiatric consultants. To supplement the services of these centers, baby-care facilities and a "drop-in day care station" were set up by

---

[24] Richard A. Cloward and Lloyd E. Ohlin, *Delinquency and Opportunity: A Theory of Delinquent Gangs* (New York: Free Press, 1960); see also Helen Hall, *Unfinished Business in Neighborhood and Nation* (New York: Macmillan, 1971), pp. 269–76.

[25] Bertram M. Beck, "A (New) Social Work Model," *Social Service Review*, 2, No. 3 (September 1966), 270–74; Richard A. Cloward and Richard M. Elman, "Advocacy in the Ghetto," *Trans-action*, 4, No. 2 (December 1966), 27–35.

MFY since they were essential to serve the persons coming for help and advice in emergencies. One of the controversial aspects of the work of the organization was that it had to assume the role of defender of the justified complaints and requests of the poverty-stricken people who came for help. This advocacy function brought criticism from the police, the municipal welfare department, and landlords, whose actions and decisions were being questioned. The *New York Daily News* accused MFY of being infested with communists or their fellow-travelers, of fomenting racial unrest and riots, and of being ridden by corruption, but these accusations proved to be wrong and the organization is continuing its efforts of community development within New York. It has organized demonstrations against abuse of tenants by landlords who refused to provide badly needed sanitation facilities and repairs, and picket lines against stores charging exorbitant prices. In the MFY area the active participation of the low-income families has been engaged both in the administration of the war against poverty activities and in a voter registration program.

The final evaluation of the new methods of community development of MFY will be possible only after several more years, but this experiment deserves attention. A number of similar projects of legal protection and social workers' advocacy for poor clients in other states are now accepted policies in community action.

ADULT DELINQUENCY AND SOCIAL WORK

The vast majority of adult offenders sentenced for felonies or minor crimes are kept in prisons or penitentiaries, segregated for years from normal life and left without responsibility for themselves and their families. Only a minority of younger prisoners are assigned to open institutions, such as prison farms and camps where life is less abnormal and the inmates are prepared for the return to law-abiding life, the goal of commitment. Only a small percentage of offenders committed to penal institutions are hardened criminals who have to be kept in prison for the protection of society. Long confinement within prison walls brings the prisoner into a state of mind which makes it rather difficult for him to accept a normal attitude toward life and society, although he is expected to react in this way on his release from prison. In particular, young offenders, maladjusted or misled by gangs and older fellows, are often bedeviled by hard-boiled criminals in prison whenever they are not strictly separated from such elements, as they are in reformatories. Homosexuality is frequent in many penal institutions, a difficult problem for the administration, which is unable to provide outlets for normal drives of young, vigorous men. Much of the nervous tension, unrest, disorder, or violence is caused by sexual frustration and perversion.[26] The difficult problem of the insane criminal is still unsolved. The M'Naghten test is still used in most states.

Penal institutions are classified into prisons, penitentiaries, reformatories, and jails. They are divided into institutions of maximum, medium, and minimum security dependent on the restraint they offer against possible escape. Most city and county jails, prison farms, and forestry camps are of medium or minimum security type. In penal institutions religious services are offered by chaplains of the major faiths. Chaplains frequently participate in the classification process of the inmates and assist in educational activities for the prisoners, library services, and counseling. Crime prevention will not occur because of penal institutions, but only by means of social planning to stop the breeding of potential criminals. Such measures are intended under a Correctional Training and Employment Plan proposed by Senators Jacob Javits, Philip Hart, and Edward Kennedy.

The honor system used in some prisons permits the offender to move up according to his attitude and cooperation, to live in sections which offer better opportunities to learn self-control and to get acquainted with the outside community. The prisoner is usually assigned to work in a shop or on a farm similar to where he will be employed after his discharge. Privileges accorded to him are based on his adjustment to social demands, and as a result he accepts responsibilities for himself and for his neighbors. Open institutions are still rare, but they help to adjust the prisoner to normal life.

The oldest, but most neglected, type of prison in our penal system is the county and city jail, of which there are about 3,900 in the United States. The jail serves as a place of detention for (1) adult offenders after arrest, pending trial or release on bail; (2) witnesses who otherwise may not appear in court or who have asked for protection before the hearing; (3) convicted offenders before they are taken to a prison or penitentiary; and (4) offenders

---

[26] For further study of adult crime and its treatment, see Harry E. Barnes and Negley K. Teeters, *New Horizons in Criminology*, 3rd ed. (Englewood Cliffs, N.J.: Prentice-Hall, 1959); Max Grunhut, *Penal Reform, A Comparative Study* (New York: Appleton, 1948); Kenyon J. Scudder, *Prisoners Are People* (New York: Doubleday, 1952); Gibbons, *Changing the Lawbreaker*, pp. 253–82; Gus Tyler, "The Roots of Organized Crime," *Crime and Delinquency*, 8, No. 4 (October 1962), 325–38, and "Combating Organized Crime," *The Annals*, 347 (May 1963), 1–112; Elmer H. Johnson, "The Present Level of Social Work in Prisons," *Crime and Delinquency*, 9, No. 3 (July 1963), 290–96; Alfred H. Katz, "Lay Group Counseling," *Crime and Delinquency*, 9, No. 3 (July 1963), 282–89; Gresham M. Sykes, *The Society of Captives* (Princeton, N.J.: Princeton University Press, 1958); Joseph W. Eaton, *Stone Walls Do Not a Prison Make* (Springfield, Ill.: Charles C Thomas, 1962); Sheldon Glueck, *Law and Psychiatry: Cold War or Entente Cordiale?* (Baltimore: Johns Hopkins Press, 1962); President's Task Force, *Corrections*, pp. 45–59; Marvin E. Wolfgang, et al., *The Sociology of Crime and Delinquency* (New York: John Wiley, 1962).

sentenced to jail as place of commitment. About 3,000,000 citizens annually spend some time in jail. The basic problems of the jail are threefold: (1) It lacks the means of rehabilitation—it fails to understand and influence the convicted offender and, therefore, to prevent recidivism. Jail confinement does not deter many adult offenders from committing new violations of the law, nor does it change their attitudes or behavior. (2) It lacks adequate health facilities, medical and dental care, mental hygiene, and facilities for the treatment of alcoholism. (3) It costs society the wasteful expense, placed on the public and private social agencies, of supporting the families of those confined to jail.[27]

The emotional situation of a convict is well described in the following statement of one who experienced prison life:

> I was recently released from solitary confinement after being held therein for thirty-seven months. A silent system was imposed upon me, and to even whisper to the man in the next cell resulted in being beaten by guards, sprayed with chemical mace, blackjacked, stomped, and thrown into a strip-cell naked to sleep on a concrete floor without bedding, cover, wash basin, or even a toilet. To let a moan escape your lips resulted in another beating . . . . I now only think of killing those who have beaten me and treated me like a dog.[28]

Under such circumstances, the usual results of a prison or jail experience on the prisoner are not rehabilitation, readjustment, and change of basic attitude toward society, but a retardation in maturity and frequently actual regression. This is brought about because the prisoner experiences the confinement as a replica of his child dependency. Other means than prison and penitentiary confinement have to be sought to solve the social problem of crime. Terrifying demonstrations of the need of change in prison management are the reports of the Arkansas prison system and the recent events at the Attica prison, New York.[29]

[27] Richard A. Cloward, et al., *Theoretical Studies in the Organization of the Prison* (New York: Social Science Research Council, 1960); Donald R. Cressey, *The Prison: Studies in Institutional Organization and Change* (New York: Holt, Rinehart and Winston, 1961); Vincent O'Leary, "Citizen Involvement in Corrections," *The Annals*, 381 (January 1969), 99–108; Norwal Morris and Frank Zimring, "Deterrence and Corrections," *The Annals*, 381 (January 1969), 137–46.

[28] Philip G. Zimbardo, "Pathology of Imprisonment," *Society*, 9, No. 6 (April 1972), 4.

[29] For a stimulating account of the Chino (California) Institution for Men, an open institution for adult offenders that prepares them to return to the community and to decent civilian life, see Scudder, *Prisoners Are People*. See also Robert M. Lindner, *Stone Walls and Men* (New York: Odyssey, 1946), pp. 418–22; Giles Mayfair and Dorrick Singleton, *The Offenders: The Case Against Legal Vengeance* (New York: Simon & Schuster, 1957); Sykes, *The Society of Captives;* Tom Murton, "One Year of Prison Reform," *The Nation*, 210, No. 1 (12 January 1970), 12–17; Robert Martinson, "The Paradox of Prison Reform," *The New Republic*, 166, No. 16, 18 (15 and 29 April 1972), 17–19, 21–23.

The most advanced type of penal institution is the reformatory, primarily intended for the reception of young adult male offenders and offenders sentenced for the first time. It is frequently limited to persons up to twenty-five or thirty years of age. The Elmira (New York) reformatory was the first such institution. At present, there are one or more reformatories in every state. Some of these institutions are built on the cottage plan, permitting individual treatment. Several reformatories, however, are still using the cell-block system and mass treatment; to help prevent the inmates from escaping some have watch towers that house sharpshooting guards. Progressive reformatories develop a conscientious program of clinical diagnosis, classification, and systematic adjustment similar to the process of treatment of juvenile delinquents, and some avoid the title "reformatory" because so many institutions have failed to achieve their goal of rehabilitation.

Most penitentiaries, prisons, and reformatories are equipped with prison industries, including several types of workshops with modern machinery, as well as facilities for agricultural work. Usually the agricultural products and goods manufactured in prison industry are used exclusively in public institutions such as hospitals, schools, and correctional facilities, to avoid competition with free labor and private industries on the open market ("state use system").

A difficult social problem is the treatment of "white-collar crime," committed by respectable-looking citizens who avoid punishment by pleading no contest in court, or draw light sentences that are hardly felt as punishment.[30]

The modern concept of rehabilitation makes it necessary to give up the outdated approach of retaliation against the offender for his attack against society. One of the essential elements in developing the reformatory into an institution of rehabilitation is to supplement the present technical and industrial facilities with programs for personal adjustment, to emphasize therapy rather than punishment. Rehabilitation is, in fact, neither punishment nor retaliation, but social adjustment, education, and preparation of the offender for living a normal citizen's life. To achieve such reeducation, social casework in correctional institutions is indispensable. We recognize that casework services are not available in many penal institutions, but at least the need for casework with prisoners is theoretically accepted. Offenders in prison or jail have, in general, a deep need for personal attention and help.

The nature of the penal institution certainly makes individual work with prisoners rather difficult, and it sets definite limits to personal contact, which is the essential tool of social casework. Despite these limitations, there are possibilities for individual work with the convict, provided that skilled,

[30] Milton G. Rector, "Crime and Delinquency," *Encyclopedia 1971*, pp. 167–69.

competent social workers are available. A number of state prisons and reformatories, and most federal penal institutions, have social service departments with trained personnel, which offer the inmates not only medical care, psychological tests, general education, and vocational training, but also social services. These facilities are important for achieving the goal of rehabilitation of the prisoner. In recent years experiments with work-furloughs for prisoners have had excellent results in several states.

The federal *Prisoner Rehabilitation Act of 1965* authorizes the Attorney General to extend the services of community guidance centers to adult offenders, to allow selected prisoners to work at paid employment in communities near the penal institution, and to grant furloughs to prisoners in case of emergency.

Intelligent wardens and superintendents of penal institutions accept the social worker as a vital part of the team of institutional personnel. There is no doubt that prison walls and bars are not conducive to letting the inmate cooperate in counseling and casework. But the social worker still can function successfully in such an authoritative setting if he is skilled enough to overcome the barriers erected by the prison environment. This applies to work with inmates who express the desire to consult the social worker, or who are referred to him by the medical officer, the psychologist, or by the classification clinic, when intensive casework seems necessary.[31] Recently, organizations of the prisoners themselves have begun to participate in measures of reform and improvement of penal conditions.

In fact, the best time for the social worker to make contact with a prisoner is when he has just entered the prison or jail. The initial shock of the first day or night in the prison and of meeting the other inmates makes the prisoner bewildered, afraid, and often hateful of everyone. The social worker will give him a chance to discuss the hard realities of prison life, his possibilities for his future, and his educational and vocational opportunities, limited as they might seem to the prisoner. The social worker has to determine how much help the inmate needs, and whether he is able to use social casework assistance at this time. Frequently the prisoner may hide his real feelings, and the social worker has to understand that he needs time before he is able to take advantage of casework service. The social worker certainly should not overwhelm him with suggestions and offers of assistance until the prisoner is really asking for his service. Sometimes he will need advice and help with specific problems, such as contact with his family and friends, arrangements of obligations he left behind, changes in the prison, assignment to a specific training unit, or transfer to other living quarters.

---

[31] Elliot Studt, "Worker–Client Authority Relationship in Social Work," *Social Work*, 4, No. 1 (January 1959), 18–28; Gibbons, *Changing the Lawbreaker*, pp. 189–220; Norval Morris, "Prison in Evolution," in T. Grygier, et al., *Criminology in Transition* (London: Tavistock, 1965), pp. 267–92.

The problem of personnel in correctional institutions—not only of social workers, but also of all other personnel—has long been the exceedingly poor working conditions: low salaries, confusion concerning objectives, conflict between punitive and rehabilitative philosophies, inadequate budgets, ill-defined tasks, isolation from the outside world, and ineffective programs for rehabilitation of adult and juvenile offenders.[32] It was hoped that the enactment of the federal *Correctional Rehabilitation Study Act* of 1965 would change these conditions; however, these hopes have not been realized. But there is widespread recognition that serious effort must be made to improve conditions and to introduce in correctional institutions, as well as in community services for offenders, decent treatment for white as well as minority offenders, by appointing qualified personnel.

The main task of the social worker in prison is to help the convict explore his attitude toward his crime, sentence, and confinement. The social worker will try to help him clarify his thinking about his action, change his attitude toward society, and develop new plans for his future life. In this respect, the social worker might give advice about the use of the prison library, vocational training and studies, and adaptation to the rules of the prison.

Finally, the social worker will have a substantial role in preparing the convict for his release and return to the community. To this end, he helps the convict take an honest attitude toward prison regulations and toward the request for work, and also attempts to explain to him that an important element for permitting his release is a new outlook toward society and its laws. Often, it is difficult for the social worker to convince the prisoner that he himself has responsibility for his change and readjustment. It is easier for the convict to conform on the surface with official rules, but to remain unchanged in his mind. The social worker tries to bring the prisoner to the insight that, after release, his chance of success requires a definite change in his behavior, which results only from a positive attitude toward society.

PAROLE

Parole is the release of a prisoner under supervision before the expiration of his sentence, with the provision that he may be returned to the prison if he violates the conditions of his parole. Whereas probation, as we saw, is a judicial decision of the court, parole is an administrative act usually taken either by the parole board or the board of directors of the prison. In the United States, the first parole system was introduced at Elmira Reformatory (New York) in 1877. Since that time, all states have developed programs of parole.

---

[32] Charles S. Prigmore, "Epilogue," *Manpower and Training for Corrections* (New York: Council on Social Work Education, 1966), pp. 246–49.

Parole requires that the prisoner be returned to the prison to finish his sentence if he commits a new crime or a serious technical violation of his parole. Examples are failing to report to the parole officer, changing his job or home, leaving the community without permission of the parole authority, or indicating that he might commit another criminal act.

The decision on parole, which is of such vital importance for the prisoner, should be based on an impartial, careful investigation of his personality and conduct. It should consider reliable information about the prisoner's background, life experiences, family and neighborhood, health, and the situation that will confront him after his release. In preparation for the release, the parole officer tries to determine whether the family of the prisoner and his neighbors will welcome him back and assist him in adjusting to normal life. The officer will enlist cooperation of social agencies or other groups which may help the prisoner in this adjustment, especially in obtaining employment, so that he can support his family, maintain his self-respect, and become part of the community.

The supervision of the released prisoner by the parole officer is a responsible job. The caseload of the parole officer should not be so large that it prohibits conscientious supervision. It requires trained and skilled personnel acquainted with human behavior, social casework, and conditions in correctional institutions, plus the ability to encourage the parolee to assume responsibility for his life in the community. The parole officer also has to interpret the parolee's situation to the community, and he must be familiar with laws and regulations. At present, many parole officers do not meet these requirements, but it is hoped that courts and parole authorities will increasingly require adequate education and professional training for parole officers who carry such a heavy responsibility.[33]

The parole system permits an indeterminate sentence so that the parole authority may set the date and the conditions of parole according to the progress made by each prisoner. Recently, serious doubts have been raised about the effect of the indeterminate sentence because it rewards the offender who pretends to be rehabilitated, and may prevent a real change of attitude toward crime.

The advantages of parole are that the public receives protection through the supervision of the parolee, that it gives the prisoner an incentive for good behavior, and that it sends him into the community with the goal of being

[33] Kenyon J. Scudder, "Prisons Will Not Solve Our Crime Problem," *Federal Probation* (March 1954), 32–39; Gibbons, *Changing the Lawbreaker*, pp. 220–27; Amos and Wellford, eds., *Delinquency Prevention: Theory and Practice*, pp. 187–206; Task Force Report, *Corrections*, pp. 60–71; Stuart Adams, "Some Findings from Correctional Caseload Research," *Federal Probation*, 37, No. 4 (December 1967), 48–57; John Irwin, *The Felon* (Englewood Cliffs, N.J.: Prentice-Hall, 1970), pp. 107–48.

a law-abiding citizen, rather than with the intention of settling a score with society. Parole permits recommendation for release when favorable conditions are found and acts as a bridge between the abnormal environment of the segregated prison and the life under personal responsibility in the community. Parole makes our system of treatment of the offender less expensive than does long detainment in penal institutions and offers an opportunity to correct mistakes or injustices which have been made in judgment.[34]

The particular difficulty of parole is that the parolee, after serving part of his sentence in a prison or penitentiary, returns to the community with a great handicap. Family, neighbors, employer, and coworkers learn that he has "served time." In addition to this shame, the parolee is pressed by the threat of being returned to the prison for violation of parole conditions. Sometimes parolees are returned to prison for minor transgressions, such as forgetting to report to the parole officer, changing a job, drinking, or marrying without special permission. There is some question whether minor violations should not be overlooked by a capable parole officer and the return ordered only if a serious offense is committed. Often parolees are very lonely and looking for companionship. The parole officer assists them in finding connections, but in most instances he has to supervise so many people with different needs that it is hard for him to help the individual efficiently.

About 42,000 persons are released each year on parole from penal institutions in the United States, and the number who have to be returned to the prison varies between 15 and 40 percent of this group.[35]

Prisoners under parole or after final discharge are assisted in many larger communities by private organizations which provide casework and usually material assistance. The oldest of these organizations is the Pennsylvania Prison Society. The social workers of these voluntary agencies help the released prisoner, particularly if the prisoner is a woman, by giving counsel, clothes, and financial assistance and securing employment. Their work frequently includes the reestablishment of constructive relations with the family of the former convict. Private organizations have in this respect the advantage of being less distrusted by the offenders and his family, and being more flexible in their policies of assistance and help.

An important factor in the control of delinquency and crime would be better training of policemen. Since their function is not limited to legal mat-

---

34 Sanford Bates, *Prisons and Beyond* (New York: Macmillan, 1936), pp. 250–51; Bertram M. Beck, "A Reassessment of Casework as a Method," in *Social Work Practice* (New York: Columbia University Press, 1964), pp. 55–73.

35 Frank T. Flynn, "Courts and Social Work," *Social Work Year Book* (1954), 150–54; *National Prisoner Statistics* (July 1959), p. 2; David Dressler, *Practice and Theory of Probation and Parole* (New York: Columbia University Press, 1959); Task Force Report, *Corrections,* pp. 82–92; Shireman, et al., "Findings from Experiments in Treatment in Correctional Institutions."

ters, but includes judgments, civility and human understanding instead of crude behavior might result in more effective crime control.[36]

A recently developed means of assisting in the rehabilitation of released prisoners or juvenile delinquents is the *halfway house,* a residential facility, particularly useful for persons from slum areas or without family relations who thus avoid being forced to return to their old neighborhoods where they are under the influence of former gang or crime companions. They live in the halfway house until they have found suitable employment and personal contacts which help them return to a better life.[37] The parolees work during the day in jobs sometimes found by their parole officer or friends of the halfway house; they return there after work and receive informal treatment by the staff or professional consultants of the parole department. There are, so far, only few such institutions, some of them organized by church groups and the American Friends Service Committee, others by public correctional authorities.

Prison societies, which sometimes assume a neutral name, such as "Service League," assist in gaining the cooperation of the community to give a hand to the returned prisoner and to offer him a chance for normal work and life. They provide information services, conduct research and studies, and participate in suggestions for the improvement of legislation and penal institutions. Especially well known in this reform work is the Osborne Association, which for many years has organized important research and surveys of correctional institutions in the United States; it has stimulated penal legislation of the federal government and the states. The American Prison Association, founded in 1870, also improves by forums, conferences, and professional proposals the standards of our penal institutions. In addition to social workers, probation and parole officers, religious groups and civic organizations also advocate further reform of the treatment of the adult offenders and the introduction of methods of effective rehabilitation in our correctional system.

SELECTED BIBLIOGRAPHY

AICHHORN, AUGUST, *Wayward Youth.* New York: Viking Press, 1952.
AMOS, WILLIAM E., and CHARLES F. WELLFORD, eds., *Delinquency Prevention: Theory and Practice.* Englewood Cliffs, N.J.: Prentice-Hall, 1967.
ARNOLD, WILLIAM R., *Juveniles on Parole.* New York: Random House, 1970.

[36] Egon Bittner, *The Functions of the Police in Modern Society* (Chevy Chase, Md.: National Institute of Mental Health, 1970), pp. 31–35, 65–71, 86, 120.

[37] See Robert F. Kennedy, "Halfway Houses Pay Off," *Crime and Delinquency,* 10, No. 1 (January 1964), 1–7; Apte, *Halfway Houses;* Harold L. Rausch and Charlotte L. Rausch, *The Halfway-House Movement: A Search for Sanity* (New York: Appleton, 1968).

BARNES, HARRY ELMER, and NEGLEY K. TEETERS, *New Horizons in Criminology,* 3rd ed. Englewood Cliffs, N.J.: Prentice-Hall, 1959.

BATES, SANFORD, *Prisons and Beyond.* New York: Macmillan, 1936.

BECKER, HOWARD, *The Other Side: Perspectives on Deviance.* New York: Free Press, 1964.

BERNSTEIN, SAUL, *Youth on the Streets: Work with Alienated Youth Groups.* New York: Association Press, 1964.

BITTNER, EGON, *The Functions of the Police in Modern Society.* Chevy Chase, Md.: National Institute of Mental Health, 1970.

BLOCH, HERBERT, and GILBERT GEIS, *Man, Crime and Society.* New York: Random House, 1962.

BROWN, RICHARD MAXWELL, ed., *American Violence.* Englewood Cliffs, N.J.: Prentice-Hall, 1970.

BURDMAN, MILTON, "The Conflict Between Freedom and Order," *Crime and Delinquency,* 15, No. 3 (July 1969), 371–76.

CARTER, ROBERT M., DANIEL GLASER, and LESLIE T. WILKINS, *Correctional Institutions.* Philadelphia: J. P. Lippincott, 1972.

CARTER, ROBERT M., and LESLIE T. WILKINS, eds., *Probation and Parole: Selected Readings.* New York: John Wiley, 1970.

CAVAN, RUTH S., and JORDAN T. CAVAN, *Delinquency and Crime.* Philadelphia: J. P. Lippincott, 1968.

CICOUREL, AARON V., *The Social Organization of Juvenile Justice.* New York: John Wiley, 1968.

CLINARD, MARSHALL B., *Anomie and Deviant Behavior.* New York: Free Press, 1964.

———, *Sociology of Deviant Behavior.* New York: Holt, Rinehart and Winston, 1963.

CLOWARD, RICHARD A., and LLOYD E. OHLIN, *Delinquency and Opportunity: A Theory of Delinquent Gangs.* New York: Free Press, 1960.

———, et al., *Theoretical Studies in Social Organization of the Prison.* New York: Social Science Research Council, 1960.

COHEN, ALBERT K., *Delinquent Boys: The Culture of the Gang.* New York: Free Press, 1951.

———, *Deviance and Control.* Englewood Cliffs, N.J.: Prentice-Hall, 1966.

CONRAD, JOHN P., *Crime and Its Correction: An International Survey of Attitudes and Practices.* Berkeley: University of California Press, 1965.

CRESSEY, DONALD R., *The Prison.* New York: Holt, Rinehart and Winston, 1961.

———, and DAVID A. WARD, *Delinquency, Crime and Social Process.* New York: Harper & Row, 1969.

DEUTSCH, ALBERT, *Our Rejected Children.* Boston: Little, Brown, 1950.

DRESSLER, DAVID, *Practice and Theory of Probation and Parole,* 2nd ed. New York: Columbia University Press, 1969.

EATON, JOSEPH W., *Stone Walls Do Not a Prison Make.* Springfield, Ill.: Charles C. Thomas, 1962.

ELLINGSTON, JOHN R., *Protecting Our Children from Criminal Careers.* Englewood Cliffs, N.J.: Prentice-Hall, 1948.

ERIKSON, ERIK H., ed., *Youth: Change and Challenge.* New York: Basic Books, 1961.

ERIKSON, KAI T., *Wayward Puritans.* New York: John Wiley, 1966.

GARDINER, JOHN A., *The Politics of Corruption.* New York: Rusell Sage Foundation, 1970.

GIBBONS, DON C., *Changing the Lawbreaker: The Treatment of Delinquents and Criminals.* Englewood Cliffs, N.J.: Prentice-Hall, 1965.

————, *Delinquent Behavior*. Englewood Cliffs, N.J.: Prentice-Hall, 1970.

GLASER, DANIEL, *Crime in the City*. New York: Harper & Row, 1970.

————, *The Effectiveness of a Prison and Parole System*. Indianapolis: Bobbs-Merrill, 1964.

GLUECK, SHELDON, and ELEANOR T. GLUECK, *Family Environment and Delinquency*. Boston: Houghton Mifflin, 1962.

————, *Toward a Typology of Juvenile Offenders*. New York: Grune and Stratton, 1970.

————, *Unraveling Juvenile Delinquency*. New York: Commonwealth Fund, 1950.

HARTUNG, FRANK E., *Crime, Law and Society*. Detroit: Wayne State University Press, 1965.

HERMAN, MELVIN, et al., *Work, Youth, and Unemployment*. New York: Crowell, 1968.

HOLLINGSHEAD, AUGUST B., *Elmstown's Youth*. New York: John Wiley, 1949.

IRWIN, JOHN, *The Felon*. Englewood Cliffs, N.J.: Prentice-Hall, 1970.

JONES, HARRY W., *The Courts, the Public, and the Law Explosion*. Englewood Cliffs, N.J.: Prentice-Hall, 1965.

KASSEBAUM, GENE, DAVID A. WARD, and DANIEL M. WILNER, *Prison Treatment and Parole Survival*. New York: John Wiley, 1971.

KLEIN, MALCOLM W., *Street Gangs and Street Workers*. Englewood Cliffs, N.J.: Prentice-Hall, 1971.

————, and BARBARA G. MYERHOFF, *Juvenile Gangs in Context: Theory, Research, and Action*. Englewood Cliffs, N.J.: Prentice-Hall, 1967.

KONOPKA, GISELA, *The Adolescent Girl in Conflict*. Englewood Cliffs, N.J.: Prentice-Hall, 1966.

KORN, RICHARD R., and LLOYD W. McCORKLE, *Criminology and Penology*. New York: Holt, Rinehart and Winston, 1959.

KVARACEUS, WILLIAM C., and WALTER B. MILLER, *Delinquent Behavior: Culture and the Individual*. Washington, D.C.: National Education Association, 1959.

LARSEN, OTTO N., *Violence and the Mass Media*. New York: Harper & Row, 1968.

LEMERT, EDWIN M., *Human Deviance, Social Problems and Social Control*. Englewood Cliffs, N.J.: Prentice-Hall, 1967.

LINDNER, ROBERT M., *Stone Walls and Men*. New York: Odyssey, 1946.

McDONALD, LYNN, *Social Class and Delinquency*. Hamden, Conn.: Archon, 1969.

McLENNAN, BARBARA N., *Crime in Urban Society*. Cambridge, Mass.: Harvard University Press, 1970.

MATZA, DAVID, *Becoming Delinquent*. Englewood Cliffs, N.J.: Prentice-Hall, 1969.

————, *Delinquency and Drift*. New York: John Wiley, 1964.

MEYER, HENRY J., et al., *Girls at Vocational High*. New York: Russell Sage Foundation, 1965.

MITCHELL, J. PAUL, *Race Riots in Black and White*. Englewood Cliffs, N.J.: Prentice-Hall, 1970.

MOMBOISSE, RAYMOND M., *Riots, Revolts, and Insurrections*. Springfield, Ill.: Charles C Thomas, 1967.

MORRIS, NORVAL, and GORDON HAWKINS, *The Honest Politician's Guide to Crime Control*. Chicago: University of Chicago Press, 1970.

NEUMEYER, MARTIN H., *Juvenile Delinquency in Modern Society*. New York: Van Nostrand, 1955.

OHLIN, LLOYD E., *Sociology and the Field of Corrections*. New York: Russell Sage Foundation, 1956.

OLAVSON, FREDERICK A., *Justice and Social Policy*. Englewood Cliffs, N.J.: Prentice-Hall, 1961.

PACKER, HERBERT L., *The Limits of Criminal Sanction*. Stanford, Calif.: Stanford University Press, 1968.

PIGEON, HELEN D., et al., *Principles and Methods in Dealing with Offenders*. New York: National Probation Association, 1949.

POLIER, JUSTICE W., *Everyone's Children: Nobody's Child*. New York: Charles Scribner's Sons, 1941.

POLLACK, OTTO, *The Criminology of Women*. Philadelphia: University of Pennsylvania Press, 1970.

POLSKY, HOWARD W., *Cottage Six*. New York: Russell Sage Foundation, 1962.

PRIGMORE, CHARLES S., *Manpower and Training for Corrections. Proceedings of Arden House Conference, June 1964*. New York: Council of Social Work Education, 1966.

RECKLESS, WALTER C., *The Crime Problem*. New York: Appleton, 1955.

RECTOR, MILTON G., "Crime and Delinquency," *Encyclopedia of Social Work 1971*, pp. 163–72.

REDL, FRITZ, and DAVID WINEMAN, *Children Who Hate*. New York: Free Press, 1951.

REISS, ALBERT J., Jr., *The Police and the Public*. New Haven, Conn.: Yale University Press, 1971.

ROSE, ARNOLD M., and CAROLINE B. ROSE, eds., *Minority Problems*. New York: Harper & Row, 1965.

SCHRAG, CLARENCE, *Crime and Justice: American Style*. Rockville, Md.: National Institute of Mental Health, 1971.

SCHUR, ERWIN M., *Crimes Without Victims: Deviant Behavior and Public Policy*. Englewood Cliffs, N.J.: Prentice-Hall, 1965.

———, *Our Criminal Society: The Social and Legal Sources of Crime in America*. Englewood Cliffs, N.J.: Prentice-Hall, 1969.

SCHWITZGEBEL, RALPH K., *Development and Legal Regulation of Coercive Behavior: Motivation Techniques with Offenders*. Chevy Chase, Md.: National Institute of Mental Health, 1971.

SCUDDER, KENYON T., *Prisoners Are People*. New York: Doubleday, 1952.

SELLIN, THORSTEN, and MARVIN E. WOLFGANG, *The Measurement of Delinquency*. New York: John Wiley, 1964.

SHERIF, MUZAFER, and CAROLYN W. SHERIF, *Problems of Youth: Transition to Adulthood in a Changing World*. Chicago: Aldine Press, 1965.

SHORT, JAMES F., *Gang Delinquency and Delinquent Subcultures*. New York: Harper & Row, 1968.

———, and FRED STRODTBECK, *Group Process and Gang Delinquency*. Chicago: University of Chicago Press, 1965.

SLAVSON, S. R., *Reclaiming the Delinquent: New Tools for Group Treatment*. New York: Free Press, 1965.

SPERGEL, IRVING, *Racketville, Slumtown, Haulburg: An Exploratory Study of Delinquent Subcultures*. Chicago: University of Chicago Press, 1964.

———, *Street Gang Work: Theory and Practice*. Reading, Mass.: Addison-Wesley, 1966.

STEBBINS, ROBERT A., *Commitment to Deviance: The Nonprofessional Criminal in the Community*. Westport, Conn.: Greenwood Press, 1971.

STREET, DAVID, et al., *Organization for Treatment: A Comparative Study of Institutions for Delinquents*. New York: Free Press, 1966.

STUDT, ELLIOT T., *A Conceptual Approach to Teaching Materials: Illustrations from the Field of Corrections*. New York: Council on Social Work Education, 1965.

SUTHERLAND, EDWIN H., and DONALD CRESSEY, *Principles of Criminology*. Philadelphia: J. P. Lippincott, 1966.

SUTTLES, GERALD D., *The Social Order of the Slum*. Chicago: University of Chicago Press, 1968.

SYKES, GRESHAM M., *Crime and Society*, 2nd ed. New York: Random House, 1967.

————, *The Society of Captives*. Princeton, N.J.: Princeton University Press, 1958.

TEETERS, NEGLEY K., and JOHN O. REINEMANN, *The Challenge of Delinquency*. Englewood Cliffs, N.J.: Prentice-Hall, 1950.

TEN-BROECK, JACOBUS, *The Law of the Poor*. San Francisco: Chandler, 1966.

VAN WATERS, MIRIAM, *Youth in Conflict*. New York: Republic Co., 1927.

VORENBERG, JAMES, et al., *The Challenge of Crime in a Free Society*. Report by the President's Commission on Law Enforcement and Administration of Justice. Washington, D.C.: Government Printing Office, 1967.

WARD, DAVID A., and GENE G. KASSEBAUM, *Women's Prison: Sex and Social Structure*. Chicago: Aldine, 1965.

WEEKS, HERBERT A., *Youthful Offenders at Highfields*. Ann Arbor: University of Michigan Press, 1958.

WERTHMAN, CARY & IRVING PILIAVIN, *Gang Members and Police*. New York: John Wiley, 1967.

WESTON, PAUL B., *Supervision in the Administration of Justice: Police, Corrections, Courts*. Springfield, Ill.: Charles C. Thomas, 1965.

WHYTE, WILLIAM F., *Street Corner Society*. Chicago: University of Chicago Press, 1943.

WILKINS, LESLIE T., *Social Deviance: Social Policy, Action, and Research*. Englewood Cliffs, N.J.: Prentice-Hall, 1965.

WOLFGANG, MARVIN E., ed., *Crime and Culture*. New York: John Wiley, 1968.

19

professional education, practice, and issues in social work

DEVELOPMENT OF THE PROFESSION

The forerunners of social work, individual citizens giving alms to people in need, and charities under auspices of the churches, were known in ancient times. But social work as a profession is young. It grew mainly from the Humanitarian Movement of the nineteenth century, which attempted to improve the desperate conditions of the poor, to achieve social reform by legislation, and to awaken the social conscience of the public. The need for professional education in social work was emphasized in 1893 for the first time, by Anna L. Dawes at the International Congress of Charities, Corrections and Philanthropy, held in Chicago. In the Charity Organization Societies the necessity of preparation for charitable work was recognized, but not until 1898 was the first six-weeks' training course set up by the New York Charity Organization Society. It later was extended to six months and developed into the New York School of Social Work, since 1940 affiliated with Columbia University.[1]

In Chicago the Institute of Social Science opened in 1901 under the leadership of Graham Taylor, Sophonisba P. Breckinridge, and Edith Abbott, then became the School of Civics and Philanthropy, and later the School of Social Service Administration of the University of Chicago. Boston, Philadelphia, and St. Louis established similar schools of social work in 1904 and 1908. The Boston School of Social Workers, under Jeffrey Brackett, was sponsored by Harvard University and Simmons College for Women. Since that time, the recognition of social work as a profession has made remarkable progress. Until academic education was begun, social workers were trained under an apprenticeship system without systematic, scientific knowledge. Their technical skill depended on the executives of the charity agencies where they served as volunteers. During the first decade of this century the necessity of social reform as well as of competent individual service became evident in connection with social problems caused by mass emigration from European countries. The rapidly developing industrialization and urbanization of our country created social problems and human suffering that called for skillful personnel to administer social services. The Great Depression of the 1930s brought unexpected economic distress to large masses of the population and showed that trained social workers were indispensable.

There were in most professions, for example in law, ministry, and medicine, three stages in the development of professional education: (1) an apprenticeship under an experienced practitioner, (2) the establishment of private schools, and (3) the recognition of universities that a professional school should be part of their academic program.

The criteria for any profession have been stated as the following:

1. Special competence, acquired through intellectual training, which develops skills and requires the use of independent, responsible judgment, not merely mechanical skills.
2. Distinct techniques capable of communication through an orderly and specialized educational discipline, with application of knowledge and skills based on academic learning.

[1] Edith Abbott, *Social Welfare and Professional Education*, rev. ed. (Chicago: University of Chicago Press, 1942); Ernest V. Hollis and Alice L. Taylor, *Social Work Education in the United States* (New York: Columbia University Press, 1951), pp. 3–52; Nathan E. Cohen, *Social Work in the American Tradition* (New York: Dryden, 1958), pp. 8–15; John C. Kidneigh, "History of American Social Work," *Encyclopedia of Social Work 1965*, pp. 9–19; Werner W. Boehm, "Education for Social Work," *Encyclopedia of Social Work 1971*, pp. 257–259; Charles S. Levy, "The Value Base of Social Work," *Education for Social Work*, 9, No. 1 (Winter 1973), 34–42.

3. Practitioners who become conscious of common bonds and organize as a professional association for the promotion of high standards and of common interests.

4. The professional association has concern for the development of standards of service for the profession as a whole as expressed by a code of ethics, provision for specialized education, and the use of specialized knowledge and skill to apply them in the public interest.

5. A professional person has a sense of personal responsibility and accountability to others in the same field for the kinds of standards he sets for himself.[2]

Not until the end of World War I did social work begin to be recognized as a profession. There is a marked difference in this respect from other professions, such as law, medicine, teaching, and the ministry. The recent changes in the attitude of the people toward public relief and charities, which we discussed earlier, led to new positive concepts with regard to the persons who performed new types of services. This historical fact explains the delay of the acceptance of social work as a profession in the United States.

There is no longer any doubt that social work satisfies the criteria for a profession. The social worker has to study the scientific principles of human behavior and the structure and organization of social institutions. With these principles before him, he has to develop, under his own responsibility, knowledge and skill in working with people under specific social, economic, and emotional conditions. Social work has organized professional associations which maintain standards of performance and behavior embodied in a code of ethics. Social work recognizes its responsibility for competent service with integrity, for the welfare of human beings whom it serves.

The number of graduate schools of social work in the United States and Canada has increased, by 1971 to 83 accredited by the Council on Social Work Education, and there are now 223 undergraduate departments of social work.

The youth of the social work profession explains why more than half the persons employed in social work positions have not received professional education in social work. A study, *Social Work Education in the United States,* by Ernest V. Hollis and Alice L. Taylor, questions whether it might be necessary to classify the functions in social agencies into those services which require graduate, professional training, and other activities which may be performed by persons who do not have graduate education, but are prepared for simpler, technical work.

2 Benjamin E. Youngdahl, "Social Work as a Profession," *Social Work Year Book* (1949), 497–98; "Social Work at the Crossroads," *Social Work Journal,* 34, No. 3 (July 1953), 111–13; Nathan E. Cohen, "Social Work as a Profession," *Social Work Year Book* (1957), 553–62; John C. Kidneigh, "Social Work as a Profession," *Social Work Year Book* (1960), 563–73; Ernest Greenwood, "The Elements of Professionalization (Social Work)," in Howard M. Vollmer and Donald L. Mills, eds., *Professionalization* (Englewood Cliffs, N.J.: Prentice-Hall, 1966), pp. 9–19; Boehm, "Education for Social Work," pp. 259, 263.

In fact, the proportion of trained social workers is slowly increasing, and there is a growing awareness on the part of social agency boards and public welfare commissions, as well as among the public, that professionally trained social workers are needed for the responsible, competent performance of social services. Thus, social work gradually is being accepted along with the older professions—the ministry, law, teaching, and medicine. In four states, the title "social worker" is officially protected (California, New York, Rhode Island, and Oklahoma). In New York, social workers may refuse to disclose professional information to courts and authorities.

On the other hand, there is a trend toward employing persons without graduate degrees in social work (paraprofessionals) as auxiliary social worker aides. Since 1970 persons holding a baccalaureate degree in social work have been entitled to membership in the National Association of Social Workers.[3]

Philosophies of social work different from those developed in the United States were presented at the Congress of the International Association of Schools of Social Work at The Hague, Netherlands, in August 1972. Their main points are as follows. *Animation* is an ideology of social work, developed in France, based on the experience of students living in groups or communities with the purpose of facilitating access to their cultural heritage in order to control their lives and engage in social action. *Conscientization,* developed in Chile by Paulo Freire, is an action philosophy aiming to make the masses aware of their needs and their responsibilities to effect social change. *Agology* aims to use various sciences as basic elements of social work, so that social work will be a scientific approach to social change. Agology developed in the Netherlands and gained followers in several other European countries. Whether these new philosophies will be helpful in integrating concepts of social work cannot be told at this time.[4]

*

SOCIAL WORK EDUCATION

Undergraduate Education

Preparation for social work requires high school study with the qualifications to enter college. In college, undergraduate study includes a broad course in liberal arts with emphasis on social sciences, sociology, social welfare, history, philosophy, economics, psychology, political science, cultural anthropology, and physical and biological science.

[3] Henry J. Meyer, "Profession of Social Work: Contemporary Characteristics," *Encyclopedia 1971,* pp. 959–71; Charles Grosser, et al., *Nonprofessionals in the Human Services* (San Francisco: Jossey-Bass, 1969); Martin Rein, "Social Work in Search of a Radical Profession," *Social Work,* 15, No. 2 (April 1970), 13–28.

[4] Eileen Younghusband, "Which Way for Social Work?" *Community Development Journal,* 8, No. 1 (January 1973), 2–5.

Because the number of social welfare positions exceeds the present total number of professionally trained people in social work, a substantial group of social agencies employ persons on graduation from college. These positions are mainly junior positions in public welfare departments, in recreation and leisure-time organizations, in probation services of juvenile courts, in institutions for children and adults, in personnel work in commerce and industry, in social security administration, unemployment insurance, and workmen's compensation, and in public employment services.

The undergraduate program acquaints the student with the basic concepts and major findings of the social sciences, psychology, sociology, and economics. It also gives him some understanding of the importance of biology, genetics, history and principles of government, social philosophy, public health, and family problems. The undergraduate student gains a broad background of present society and of man as an individual and as a member of various groups. He then learns to arrive at some integrated perspective of the relations between human behavior and the demands of society. He learns to state his opinion clearly and interpret the facts and his ideas to other people.

On the basis of these studies, the student has several choices: (1) to apply for advanced, graduate, professional training in social work, city planning, law, public administration, or public health; (2) to use his preparation for accepting employment in a position which does not require graduate training; or (3) to consider this undergraduate program as preparation for informed, intelligent citizenship which brings him an understanding of social welfare concepts, the wide range of social problems, and the motivation to help solve them.[5] The last group may include businessmen, housewives, local officials, state legislators, teachers, labor leaders, and citizens in other occupations. There is increasing recognition of the value of undergraduate social work education for entry positions in social work.

A typical, undergraduate social welfare major program includes the following courses: (1) In lower division—general psychology, general economics, elementary statistics and research, introduction to sociology, history,

---

5 Katherine A. Kendall, *Undergraduate Preparation for the Social Services* (New York: Council on Social Work Education, 1954); Herbert Bisno, *The Place of the Undergraduate Curriculum in Social Work Education* (New York: Council on Social Work Education, 1959), and *Social Welfare Content in Undergraduate Education*, New York: Council on Social Work Education, 1962); Ernest F. Witte, "The Purposes of Undergraduate Education for Social Welfare," *Journal of Education for Social Work*, 1, No. 2 (Fall 1965), 53–60; John M. Romanshyn, "Undergraduate Social Welfare Sequence," *Public Welfare* (July 1964), 202–22; Carl G. Pettijohn, "Undergraduate Social Work Education," *Public Welfare* (July 1965), 155–60; Mereb Mossman, et al., *Recent Thoughts on Undergraduate Social Welfare Education* (New York: Council on Social Work Education, 1964); Arnulf M. Pins, "Challenge and Change in Social Work Education," *Social Work Education Reporter*, 17, No. 1 (March 1969), 34A–34D; John B. Turner, "Education for Practice with Minorities," *Social Work*, 17, No. 3 (May 1972), 112–18.

biology, and anthropology. (2) In upper division—concepts, history, and system of social welfare, methods of social work, public assistance, child welfare, social security, social problems and social institutions, social legislation and reform, social philosophy, child and adolescent psychology, mental deficiency, abnormal psychology, social psychology. It also may include introduction to clinical psychology, municipal and state government, public administration, problems of poverty, labor economics, public finance and taxation, and crime prevention and correction. Other courses may deal with problems of juvenile delinquency, race relations and culture, migration, study of group behavior, community recreation, dynamics of culture, medical sociology, child hygiene, and housing and planning.

Some colleges offer facilities for their students to make observations in social agencies to know something of the practice of social welfare, under the name of "field experience." The value of these courses is disputed. Graduate schools of social work find that field work as clinical practice of social work processes is a vital part of graduate education, but is successful only through integration with academic courses in casework, group work, and community organization under responsible supervision. The attempt to provide practical experience of sufficient breadth and intensity in the undergraduate program poses the problem of securing conscientious and reliable field supervision, and of curtailing unduly the time required for a broad liberal education, and a background in the social sciences and humanities. Social agencies, on the other side, use inservice training, as well as seminars, institutes, and extension courses of universities, to supplement theoretical knowledge and skills of staff members who have no professional training.

Professional Education for Social Work

Graduate training for social work requires, as a rule, the successful completion of two academic years of study in an accredited school of social work, leading to the granting of the master's degree. Prerequisite for acceptance to graduate school is the bachelor's degree, preferably in social welfare or the social sciences, and personal qualification for the profession of social work. Most schools accept students older than thirty-five years only if they have demonstrated good capacity for social work. Graduate social work education is characterized by its close integration of academic courses in the school with practical field work in a selected social agency under careful supervision.

The aims of professional education in social work are to develop competence in three major areas: (1) conceptual and perceptual understanding; (2) skills in methods, procedures, and processes; and (3) personal professional qualities.[6]

---

[6] Hollis and Taylor, *Social Work Education in the United States*, pp. 220–25; Charlotte Towle, *The Learner in Education for the Professions, as Seen in Education*

The first category includes understanding of individual and group behavior, the significance of human behavior in relation to social environment,
and the historical perspective of social welfare development and of religious,
economic, political, and social movements. It requires a grounding in the
social sciences, the structure and philosophy of government, the nature of
social change, the causes and effect of cultural factors, and principles of social
security. It also demands knowledge of the principles, objectives, and processes in social casework, group work, community organization, supervision,
intergroup relations, public administration, social policies and planning, and
social research. The curriculum includes the study of public relations, standards of social legislation; the administration of social welfare, community
structure, and resources; the study of human growth; and the significance of
physical, social, and emotional deviations from normal behavior.

The skills of professional social work include the ability to establish and
maintain purposeful and constructive relationships with individuals, groups,
and communities. The most important skill in the helping process is that of
enabling an individual, a group, or a community to identify and clarify problems and needs, and to solve them by their own initiative in a socially desirable way. The social worker learns to use his resources in professional
relationships based on self-understanding, control of personal needs and feelings, and warmth of response. Other skills are those of social administration,
planning, social action; use of scientific methods in research and practice;
skill in teamwork with other professions; ability in communication, staff
development, supervision, and volunteer and student training; and preparation for social work teaching and social statesmanship.

The personal, professional qualities that graduate training aims to
develop include genuine warmth, sensitivity to, and liking for people, and
the capacity to identify with a variety of persons. A professional philosophy
comprises a high degree of social conscience and conscientiousness, emotional,
mental, and physical stability, maturity, self-security, imagination, resourceful-
ness, flexibility, as well as personal integrity, courage, and a sincere conviction
about the values of social work. Professional concepts make the student capable of standing up for the rights of people even against hostile public attitudes.[7]

for Social Work. (Chicago: University of Chicago Press, 1954), pp. 233–46; Ernest
P. Witte, "Education for Social Work," *Social Work Year Book* (1960), 223–40;
Werner W. Boehm, *Objectives for the Social Work Curriculum of the Future* (New
York: Council on Social Work Education, 1959); William E. Gordon, "Toward a
Social Work Frame of Reference," *Journal of Education for Social Work,* 1, No. 2
(Fall 1965), 19–26; Margaret S. Schubert, "Curriculum Policy Dilemma in Field
Instruction," *Journal of Education for Social Work,* 1, No. 2 (Fall 1965), 35–46;
Rachel B. Marks, "Education for Social Work," *Encyclopedia 1965,* pp. 277–83;
Boehm, "Education for Social Work," pp. 259–63.

7 See Martin Bloom, "Behavioral Science Theory and Social Work Practice,"
Social Service Review, 39, No. 1 (March 1965), 11–22; Charlotte Towle, "Social
Work: Cause and Function," *Social Casework,* 42, No. 8 (October 1961), 385–97;

These qualities, furthermore, encompass conceptual thinking, open-mindedness, clarity of purpose, accuracy, courtesy in professional relationships, and a belief in the value of citizen participation and in the right of the individual, the group, and the community to make decisions within the framework of a democratic society.

It is easy to understand that these areas of professional competence can be fully developed only if academic classwork and clinical supervised field instruction are integrated. Field work requires, as a rule, two full days weekly for the first graduate year and three days weekly for the second year. Supervisors are either members of the university faculty or staff members of the social agency where the student receives his field work training. In both instances an intensive cooperation between the teaching faculty and the field supervisor in observing the student's professional development and learning must be maintained. Field work is designed to integrate the academic knowledge, practical understanding, and professional skill of the student by personal contact and direct work with clients.

A number of schools of social work have set up an advanced program beyond the level of the master's degree. This has been classified either as "the third year" with the aim of strengthening the professional skills of the student or as "the doctoral program," leading to a Doctor of Social Work or a Doctor of Philosophy degree. The latter program, as a rule, requires two more years of postgraduate studies, which offer a deepening and refinement of knowledge and skill, new knowledge directed toward definition and solution of professional problems (with the evaluation and testing of social work methods and hypotheses), and the broadening of professional perspective. The doctoral program integrates social work knowledge and methodology with those of other scientific disciplines; develops independent critical professional thought and interprofessional relationships; and prepares primarily for teaching social work, for the administration of social welfare programs, and for social work research.[8]

Alfred Kadushin, "The Knowledge Base of Social Work," in Kahn, *Issues in American Social Work*, pp. 39–79; Henry J. Meyer, "Professionalization and Social Work," ibid., pp. 319–40; Norman A. Polansky, "The Professional Identity in Social Work," ibid., pp. 293–318; Donald Feldstein, "Professionalization versus Consumerism," *Social Work*, 16, No. 4, (October 1971), 5–11; and Anatole Shaffer, "Community Organization and the Oppressed," *Education for Social Work*, 8, No. 3 (Fall 1972), 65–75.

[8] Charlotte Towle, Eveline Burns, and Eleanor Cockerill, *Social Work Education in the Post Master's Program (Guiding Principles)* (New York: Council on Social Work Education, 1953), pp. 9–11, 23–29; Charles Frankel, "Professional Education as University Education," *Social Service Review*, 32, No. 3 (September 1958), 234–46; Witte, "Education for Social Work," 225–31. See also Arnold Brecht, *Political Theory* (Princeton, N.J.: Princeton University Press, 1959); Gerhard Colm and Theodore Geiger, *The Economy of The American People* (Washington, D.C.: National Planning Association, 1961); Herman D. Stein, "Issues in the Relationship of Social Science to Social Work Education," *International Social Work*, 4, No. 1 (January 1961), 10–18; and Boehm, "Education for Social Work," p. 265.

For many years, the graduate schools of social work were organized as the American Association of Schools of Social Work (AASSW); colleges which offered undergraduate programs formed the National Association of Schools of Social Administration (NASSA). In 1952, the Council on Social Work Education absorbed both associations. The functions of the Council on Social Work Education are to establish standards and to accredit schools of social work, to aid in better selection and education of students and social workers, to improve social work education, to interpret social work to the public, and to help in continuing professional growth of employed social workers. The organizational structure is based in a council consisting of a House of Delegates, a Board of Directors, and standing committees. Some changes in this organization are under consideration.

REGISTRATION OR LICENSING OF SOCIAL WORKERS?

Professionals in medicine, teaching, law, and nursing are recognized by an official license, certificate, or registration which is required before they can perform professional service. In France, Germany, Austria, and Sweden, social workers need a license to practice their profession. In the United States, however, no license has yet been introduced, but suggestions have been made that licensing should be required or that the practice of social work should be restricted. In 1933 the California Conference of Social Welfare organized registration on a voluntary basis, requiring the passing of a carefully prepared examination. In 1945 a statutory system of official registration and certification for social workers replaced the voluntary program in California. Applicants who have completed successfully one year at an accredited graduate school of social work and who pass a written examination receive a certificate authorizing them to use the title "Registered Social Worker" (RSW). The Board maintains a register of social workers, conducts research, prescribes qualifications, gives examinations, and issues certificates. A certificate is suspended or revoked if a registered social worker is convicted of an offense involving moral turpitude; is a habitual drug addict; is declared insane or incompetent; advocates the overthrow of government by force, violence or other unlawful means; or has committed a dishonest or faudulent act as a social worker resulting in substantial injury to others. The National Association of Social Workers introduced in 1961 a voluntary system of registration as "certified social workers" for persons with a master's degree and two years experience under competent supervision. Social Workers are accepted under these conditions in the Academy of Certified Social Workers (ACSW).

The value of the registration for the protection of the public and for the self-respect of professional workers depends partly on the personnel practices of social agencies. Another decisive factor for the value of registration is the continuing and increasing interest in the measure on the part of the public, the employing social agencies, and social workers themselves.[9]

There is no doubt that present social services must be maintained and extended according to the changing needs of the people. The number of adequately trained social workers must be increased. The public will gradually come to recognize its stake in competent social work practice.

PROFESSIONAL ORGANIZATIONS IN SOCIAL WORK

Professional organizations of social workers have been in existence since 1918, when the American Association of Hospital Social Workers was founded, which later became the American Association of Medical Social Workers. It was followed by the National Association of School Social Workers in 1919. In 1921 the American Association of Social Workers, which succeeded the National Social Workers Exchange, became the largest organization in the field of social work. In 1926 the American Association of Psychiatric Social Workers was set up, and in 1946 the American Association of Group Workers. Two study groups, the Association for the Study of Community Organization, beginning in 1946, and the Social Work Research Group, in 1949, pursued the special interest in these fields.

Since 1949, however, the professional representatives have attempted to emphasize the common elements in social work and to coordinate all professional organizations of social work in the United States. This aim was accomplished by the merger of all seven organizations into the National Association of Social Workers on October 1, 1955. It now represents the united social work profession in the United States. The purpose of the Association is the promotion of high quality and effectiveness in social work practice and the improvement of social conditions in society. The organization and activities are designed to further a sound unification of objectives and action in social work, but with flexible diversification in line with the particular interests of the members of the Association and with the changing needs of a growing profession. The Association publishes a quarterly professional journal, *Social Work,* and the *Social Work Year Book,* now *Encyclopedia of Social Work.* Among the objectives of the Association are constructive social legislation,

---

[9] Susan Pettis, *Licensing and Registration of Social Workers* (New York: American Association of Social Workers, 1953); Arnulf M. Pins, "Implications for Social Work Education," *Public Welfare,* 25, No. 1 (January 1967), 21–28. Utah established certification of social workers in 1971, Michigan in January 1973. The National Association of Social Workers prepares suggestions for nationwide licensing of social workers.

adequate working conditions and salary, recruitment of able persons for the profession, and cooperation with other professional and civic organizations.[10]

The Association accepts as members persons holding a degree from a graduate school of social work which is accredited by the Council on Social Work Education and persons holding a baccalaureate degree from an accredited program of undergraduate social work studies. Student members may join the Association in their second year of graduate studies. Special interests can be served through the organization of committees or commissions. There are about 52,000 members organized in 150 chapters in all states and in Puerto Rico.

STANDARDS OF PROFESSIONAL PRACTICE

The principles of American social work arise from the beliefs in a democratic society. Foremost among them are the following:

1. Firm faith in the dignity, worth, and creative power of the individual.
2. Complete belief in his right to hold and express his opinions and to act on them, so long as by so doing he does not infringe on the rights of others.
3. Unswerving conviction of the inherent, inalienable right of each human being to choose and achieve his destiny in the framework of a progressive, yet stable, society.

Professional social work is built on an integrated body of knowledge distilled from physical, medical, psychological, and social science, and on technical methods derived from both this scientific knowledge and the tested experience of skilled practitioners.

Principles of ethical conduct of the social worker direct his relationship with the clients, the social agency, his colleagues, the community, and the profession of social work. These principles are embodied in a code of ethics, which together with standards for professional practice was adopted by the Delegate Assembly of the American Association of Social Workers in 1951.[11]

10 Nathan E. Cohen, "Social Work as a Profession," *Social Work Year Book* (1957), 560–62; John C. Kidneigh, ibid. (1960), 568–71; Greenwood, "The Elements of Professionalization;" David G. French, "Professional Organization," *Encyclopedia 1965*, pp. 574–79; Arnulf M. Pins, "Changes in Social Work Education," *Social Work*, 16, No. 2 (April 1971), 5–15.

11 Harriet M. Bartlett, "Social Work Practice," *Encyclopedia 1965*, pp. 755–63; Alfred J. Kahn, "The Societal Context of Social Work Practice," *Social Work*, 10, No. 4 (October 1965), 145–55; Margaret Schubert, "Curriculum Policy Dilemmas in Field Instruction," *Journal of Education for Social Work*, 1, No. 2 (Fall 1965), 35–46; Walter L. Walker, "Changing Thought and Action Styles of Students and Faculty," *Journal of Education for Social Work*, 8, No. 1 (Winter 1972), 56–63.

Because social work is founded on belief in the value of the individual, it has a special responsibility to protect civil rights based on democratic principles. Only by following this belief can social work discharge its professional obligations with intellectual integrity. The professional social worker has the moral responsibility to work toward the abridgement of discrimination for any reason. The civil rights of clients served by social workers and those of social workers themselves have to be protected to preserve human dignity and self-respect. Under these conditions social work will combine its concern with clients with support of action for social change.

SOCIAL WORKERS AND LABOR UNIONS

During the Depression years of the 1930s, social workers and clerical and technical employees of social agencies began to join labor unions which were interested in organizing staffs of social agencies into their membership. When many workers, without graduate social work education and degrees, were employed in public welfare agencies, but were not eligible to become members of the professional social work organizations, they began to identify with the trade unions and felt that their work with unemployed families was strengthened by their participation in the labor movement. They felt the same insecurity in their jobs which their clients experienced when they were fired as production decreased or business went down.

The political climate under the New Deal was favorable to trade unions. The *Norris-LaGuardia Act of 1932* and the *National Recovery Act of 1933* strengthened the bargaining rights of trade unions; those rights were maintained by the *National Labor Relations Act of 1935* after the National Recovery Act was ruled unconstitutional by the Supreme Court. Thus, the right of labor unions to organize workers was legally established and employers were prohibited to interfere through unfair labor practices.

The aim of the so-called "rank-and-file movement" was to improve working conditions and wages, to gain influence in the professional organizations, and to stimulate social action. Both AFL and CIO unions were included, but none of them consisted entirely of social workers and social agency personnel. In the AFL, two unions recruited social workers as members—the American Federation of Government Employees and the American Federation of State, County, and Municipal Employees. Some social workers in public welfare agencies were organized also in the United Public Workers of America, a CIO union.

Under the auspices of the CIO, workers in voluntary social agencies organized in the United Office and Professional Workers, which established a National Social Service Division that coordinated the local chapters of the Social Service Employees Union. Together with United Public Workers of

America, they formed a Joint Committee of Trade Unions in Social Work which arranged conferences and meetings at the time of national and state conferences of social work. There were conflicts among the organized social workers over whether the typical trade union methods, such as striking, picketing, and demonstrations, were appropriate means to fight for better wages and conditions, because their employers were either government agencies or private welfare boards, not industries, and because there was danger that their clients would suffer most from such measures.[12]

During the Second World War, social workers in trade unions split on the issues of participation in the war, Nazi Germany, and the Soviet Union. After the war, in 1948, when the large labor unions united in the AFL-CIO, several groups of social workers left the United Public Workers of America and the United Office and Professional Workers of America, which had many social workers as members, and joined the Industrial Union of Marine and Shipbuilding Workers. This split weakened the activity of social workers in labor unions and led to the demise of the two large social work unions.

At present, the largest number of social workers employed in public welfare agencies is organized in the American Federation of State, County, and Municipal Employees (about 12,000). Some social workers in federal agencies are in the American Federation of Government Employees, both affiliated with the AFL-CIO. Social workers in private agencies are organized in the Community and Social Agency Employees (AFL-CIO), but their number is much smaller than that in public agencies. Recently, there has been new interest among social workers in joining a labor union.

Unions of social workers have not limited their activities to collective bargaining, negotiations over salaries and working conditions, sick and vacation leave, and participation of union members in boards of agencies, but have concerned themselves as well with the policies of social agencies regarding other union–labor relations, the client groups, and the development of social legislation and services.[13]

These aspects of union activities have resulted in a number of conflicts between unions and the boards of directors of private and public welfare

12 Nathan E. Cohen, *Social Work in the American Tradition* (New York: Dryden, 1959), pp. 203–6, 279–80; John A. Fitch, "Professional Workers as Trade Unionists," *Social Work in the Current Scene* (New York: National Conference of Social Work, 1950); Hilda Siff, "Labor Unions in Health and Welfare Agencies," *Encyclopedia 1965*, pp. 443–47; Alvin Zander, et al., "Relations among Occupational Groups," in Vollmer and Mills, *Professionalization*, pp. 237–43; Walter A. Friedlander, "Labor Unions and Social Workers," *International Social Work*, 13, No. 4 (1970), 28–36; Elma P. Cole, "Unions in Social Work," *Encyclopedia 1971*, p. 1510.

13 Wilbert E. Moore, "Unions in Social Work," *Social Work Year Book* (1949), 519–20; Wayne McMillen, "Unions in Social Work," *The Compass* (July 1947), 6–8; Harold L. Wilensky, *Intellectuals in Labor Unions* (New York: Free Press, 1956); Hilda Siff, "Labor Unions in Health and Welfare Agencies," *Encyclopedia 1965*, pp. 443–47; Cole, "Unions in Social Work," pp. 1507–11.

agencies. There have been questions raised over whether certain aspects of union membership, particularly political postulates, are compatible with professional concepts and ideals. The professional organizations in social work, as well as in several other professions, do not oppose membership in labor unions with respect to improvement of salary and working conditions and collective bargaining. The 1946 Delegate Conference of the American Association of Social Workers recognized the right of social agency employees to bargain collectively and to be represented by a union of their choice. One particular difficulty in these negotiations is that a strike in a hospital or a social agency involves serious dangers for patients and clients. Therefore, strikes should not be applied except as a means of last resort. Special emergency activities must be executed without causing irreparable damage to human beings.

Except among social workers in government agencies, collective bargaining, including social security provisions, is regarded as a proper form of union participation in presenting desirable working conditions to boards of social agencies. But not all boards have agreed to accept these suggestions, and the proportion of staff members organized in one or the other labor union at present varies greatly in the different states and regions. The activities of unions in social work have contributed to the recognition of the value of staff participation in policy formulation and in the development of new methods of practice in social agencies.

THE NATIONAL WELFARE RIGHTS ORGANIZATION

Although in other countries clients of public welfare agencies have joined in self-help groups for some time, and in the United States similar powerful organizations have been established among war veterans and their survivors, particularly after wars, clients of public relief have only recently formed an organization to fight for their rights as citizens and for humane treatment. The National Welfare Rights Organization (NWRO) was founded in connection with the black power movement by a young black Ph.D. in chemistry, George Wiley, in 1966, after the failure of the "poor people's campaign" and its march on Washington.[14] Wiley established in Washington, D. C. a Poverty/Rights Action Center to give the poor a voice at the grass-roots level; organized a march of welfare clients, mainly AFDC mothers, from Cleveland to the Ohio state capitol in Columbus; and staged similar demonstrations throughout the country. Northern California AFDC mothers were

---

[14] Gilbert Y. Steiner, *The State of Welfare* (Washington, D.C.: Brookings Institution, 1971), pp. 280–313; David A. Hardcastle, "The Indigenous Nonprofessional in the Social Service Bureaucracy," *Social Work*, 16, No. 2 (April 1971), 56–63.

inspired to form their welfare rights organization by a University of California School of Social Welfare student engaged in field practice in the Oakland slums. NWRO is effectively coordinating public relief clients, mostly mothers on AFDC, giving them for the first time a feeling of being able to fight bureaucratic policies without having to depend on social workers. It has also brought them the support of lawyers, politicians, social workers, and professional organizations, enabling them to participate in social welfare policy negotiations with federal, state, and local authorities and to be heard in conferences and conventions throughout the United States. In some of its actions, demonstrations, and sit-ins, the NWRO has been joined by other militant groups, such as the "brown berets" of the NAACP, Catholic activists, and the Chicano farm laborers union.[15]

Although NWRO began without prominent leadership, without funds, and with only a few small local groups unaccustomed to organization and effective cooperation, it has become an efficient, independent organization with significant goals which has had an important influence on federal, state, and local welfare agencies and their policies.

VOLUNTEERS IN SOCIAL WORK

Volunteers have been the pioneers in all fields of social work, not only in group work, but also in casework, health services, and community organization (preceding professional, paid social workers). They started out by assisting people in financial stress who did not want to ask for poor relief; they founded relief societies, health organizations, schools for the blind and deaf, children's homes, day nurseries, recreation services, settlement houses, family welfare agencies, and the charity organization societies. They laid the foundations for modern social work, and they recognized the need for professional training of social workers in a complex society.[16]

The first paid employees in social agencies were volunteers who had formerly served without compensation. With the increase in the number of trained, paid staff workers, volunteers began to play a less important role in social agencies, particularly in casework and health agencies. During a later phase, professional social workers questioned the need for volunteers on their

15 Frank Riessman and Hermione L. Popper, eds., *Up from Poverty: New Career Ladders for Non-Professionals* (New York: Harper & Row, 1971); Philip Kramer, "The Indigenous Worker," *Social Work*, 17, No. 1 (January 1972), 43–49; Gilbert Y. Steiner, *Social Insecurity: The Politics of Welfare* (Chicago: Rand McNally, 1966), pp. 153ff, 282–310.

16 Robert F. Fenley, "Volunteers in Social Work Welfare," *Social Work Year Book* (1957), 592–98; Eugene Shenefield, "Citizen and Volunteer Participation," *Social Work Year Book* (1960), 157–62; Wilfred M. Calnan, "Differential Use of Manpower," *Public Welfare*, 25, No. 1 (January 1967), 45–55.

boards and committees and were afraid that they might interfere with their professional operations. More recently, however, this skeptical opinion has changed, and the genuine, intrinsic contribution of volunteers serving on the board of a social agency, to interpreting its work to the public and to carrying out its program, has been recognized again. A partnership between volunteers and professional workers is developing. This partnership has proved essential in the field of public relations (explaining the agency's work to the people), in the collection of money at fund-raising campaigns, in establishing policies on boards and committees, and in direct services to people with whom the agency deals.

The new relationship between volunteers and professional workers is based on mutual respect and on a sharing of responsibility between both. To do an efficient job, the volunteer needs to be sincerely interested in the work; must be willing to accept guidance, training, and supervision; and must feel responsible for carrying out the assignment given to him, so that he is no less dependable than a paid worker. However, the professional staff should express recognition of the value of the volunteer's work—respect for his desire to contribute his time and effort without demanding monetary compensation.

In large cities, volunteer bureaus under the auspices of the local community welfare council, and special committees in smaller communities, examine those agencies in which volunteers are needed. They encourage the application of volunteers at the bureau and promote their recruitment and training. They recommend the volunteers to social agencies for which they are best suited.

Women, men, and an increasing number of young people, individually and in groups, serve as volunteers in private and public social agencies. These people can perform many types of service such as being child care and hospital aides, group leaders, arts and crafts instructors, clerical or typist help, automobile drivers, receptionists, entertainers, and librarians. They are especially important in civil defense planning for emergencies because services cannot be staffed with trained, professional workers alone.

The participation of volunteers in the field of recreation is particularly essential. Recreation agencies have to meet such a broad demand for leadership and guidance that they are never able to engage sufficient paid personnel. The executives in recreation also are willing to use services of volunteers on a broader scale than health and casework agencies are. Finally, recreational activities are such that the participation of volunteers in games, sports, gymnastics, arts and crafts, camping, and discussion groups is convenient. In leisure-time work, the large number of volunteers available makes their effective selection, training, and supervision an increasingly important task for the trained professional worker.

Volunteers in Service to America (VISTA) was a new type of volunteer service in connection with the war against poverty (see Chapter 10). Unlike volunteers who work with social agencies, VISTA volunteers lived and worked with the poor in slums and crowded tenements, in decaying mill and mine towns, in migratory work camps, and on Indian reservations. They helped the poor as friends and advocates in all fifty of the United States, the Virgin Islands, and Puerto Rico, after six weeks of training in home economics, teaching children and adults, child care, and methods of improving living conditions of the poor.[17] Their functions resembled those of the Peace Corps overseas. VISTA volunteers had to be American citizens over eighteen years of age; they received only subsistence allowance, medical care, and $50 each month set aside to be paid at the end of the assignment, usually after one year of service. Even retired people were eligible for VISTA service. In July 1971 VISTA, the Peace Corps, and several smaller programs such as "foster grandparents" and the Office of Voluntary Action were combined into ACTION.

OUTLOOK

Social work, as a dynamic profession, is subject to changes influenced by the development of society, our religious, cultural and sociological values, and by scientific progress. Certain trends illustrated in this book indicate important phases of the present situation, briefly summarized here.

(1) Social work is still in need of a clarification of its purpose and philosophy. It has made progress toward agreement among social workers in this respect and is developing a program of interpreting its aims so that the public may be made aware of what social services mean for society. The development of codes of ethics, personnel practice, and civil rights provides significant proof of the strength of professional ideas in social work. In addition to traditional social work methods, advocacy and social action are now accepted as legitimate social work functions.

(2) With the increasing recognition of social work and its contribution in solving social problems of society, not only public and private social agencies, but also industry, labor unions, commercial firms, hospitals, health agencies, churches, and the courts employ social workers and take advantage of their skill. Individual social workers operate in private practice as family or marriage counselors, in cooperation with psychiatrists or psychologists, and even serve as "ombudsmen."

[17] Frank Riessman, "The Revolution in Social Work: The Non-Professional," *Trans-action*, 2, No. 1 (November–December 1964), 12–17; Howard C. McClary, "Volunteer Aides for Problem-Ridden Families," *Children*, 8, No. 5 (September–October 1961), 175–78; Nelson C. Jackson, "The Use of Indigenous Volunteers," *Social Work Practice* (New York: Columbia University Press, 1964), pp. 74–87; George Brager, "The Indigenous Worker: A New Approach to the Social Work Technician," *Social Work*, 10, No. 2 (April 1965), 33–40.

(3) Characteristic of present-day social work is its commitment to teamwork with other professions. Because social workers derive their knowledge from the sociologist's concept of the social process, the political scientist's knowledge of government and administration, the psychologist's comprehension of human behavior and mental functions, the anthropologist's understanding of cultural factors and personality differences, the geneticist's knowledge of hereditary influences, the economist's insight into the process of our economy, the psychiatrist's cognition of emotional illness and health, and the physiologist's observation of physical and nervous functions, they integrate their work with that of other professions. The interdisciplinary approach, the cooperation of several professions in the prevention of pathological conditions in individuals and groups and in the treatment process, promises further progress in the results of diagnosis, cure, and preventive services.

(4) Social workers are on the way to coordinating their professional activities. They are attempting to clarify the common generic basis of the various types of social work, and they have unified their professional organizations and strengthened a comprehensive system of social work education and accreditation of its institutions.[18] There is a trend toward evaluating the success of social services by critical research and social indicators.

(5) Nonprofessional "indigenous workers," usually former clients, are used as assistant or auxiliary social workers and are beginning to play a significant role, particularly in the antipoverty program, but also in many private and public agencies. The cooperation of these paraprofessional workers improves relations with client groups and thus increases the effectiveness of social work operations.

(6) Social work is giving increasing attention to social work research. It no longer relies solely on research done by the social sciences, medicine, psychology, and anthropology but assumes responsibility for developing its own critical research, testing its methods and the results of its operations. The multidiscipline idea, accepted in social work, requires social workers to draw from the social and biological sciences basic data on human beings, their nature and behavior, on our society and economic structure. However, social workers are contributing to this research their own concepts, observations, and experiences. This contribution includes an examination of the potentials and dynamic forces in the social group and in the community, the willingness to measure social needs and trends, and the effect of social work practice with an application of methods and knowledge of related scientific fields.

(7) The international scene has been opened to social work, which is developing worldwide concepts, has begun to recognize the impact of social problems in faraway countries, and is assuming responsibility for contributing

[18] Norman V. Lourie, "The Question of Advocacy," *Public Welfare*, 30, No. 2 (Spring 1972), 12–15.

its professional ideas, knowledge, and skills to the well-being of people everywhere. Social work is aware that in such an international climate, and under cultural, social, economic, and health conditions often very different from our own, new concepts and new approaches are necessary. From the observation of foreign nations by members of the Peace Corps and by social welfare consultants sent to foreign countries by the federal government through the Agency for International Development, and from visitors to our country and social work students, social workers are learning other ways of meeting human problems and are reevaluating our methods and philosophy of social work. Social work has, through its international experiences, strengthened its conviction that the most effective and satisfactory way of helping people is to assist them to help themselves.[19]

SELECTED BIBLIOGRAPHY

ABBOTT, EDITH, *Social Welfare and Professional Education,* rev. ed. Chicago: University of Chicago Press, 1942.

BECK, BERNARD, "Welfare as a Moral Category," *Social Problems,* 14, No. 3 (Winter 1967), 258–77.

BISNO, HERBERT, *The Place of the Undergraduate Curriculum in Social Work Education.* New York: Council on Social Work Education, 1959.

BOEHM, WERNER W., "Education for Social Work," *Encyclopedia of Social Work 1971,* pp. 257–73.

————, *Objectives of the Social Work Curriculum of the Future.* New York: Council on Social Work Education, 1959.

BUTLER, RUTH M., *An Orientation to Knowledge of Human Growth and Behavior in Social Work Education.* New York: Council on Social Work Education, 1959.

ETZIONI, AMITAI, *The Semiprofessionals.* New York: Free Press, 1969.

GROSSER, CHARLES, WILLIAM HENRY, and JAMES KELLY, *Nonprofessionals in the Human Services.* San Francisco: Jossey-Bass, 1969.

GURIN, ARNOLD, and ROBERT PERLMAN, "Community Organization Curriculum," *Journal of Education for Social Work,* 5, No. 1 (Spring 1969), 37–48.

HAMILTON, GORDON, "Helping People—the Growth of a Profession," *Social Work as Human Relations.* New York: Columbia University Press, 1949, pp. 3–18.

HOLLIS, ERNEST V., and ALICE L. TAYLOR, *Social Work Education in the United States.* New York: Columbia University Press, 1951.

JOHNSON, ARLIEN, *School Social Work: Its Contribution to Professional Education.* New York: National Association of Social Workers, 1962.

KAHN, ALFRED J., ed., *Issues in American Social Work.* New York: Columbia University Press, 1959.

KIDNEIGH, JOHN C., "Social Work as a Profession," *Social Work Year Book* (1960), 563–73.

KLENK, ROBERT W., and ROBERT M. RYAN, *The Practice of Social Work.* Belmont, Calif.: Wadsworth, 1970.

19 For a more detailed discussion of international social services, see Walter Friedlander, *International Aspects of Social Welfare* (Englewood Cliffs, N.J.: Prentice-Hall, in Press).

LEE, PORTER R., *Social Work as Cause and Function*. New York: Columbia University Press, 1937.

LUBOVE, ROY, *The Professional Altruist: The Emergence of Social Work as a Career*. Cambridge, Mass.: Harvard University Press, 1965.

LUNDBERG, HORACE, ed., *School Social Work*. Washington, D.C.: U.S. Office of Education, 1964.

LURIE, HARRY L., *The Community Organization Method in Social Work Education*. New York: Council on Social Work Education, 1959.

MENCHER, SAMUEL, *The Research Method in Social Work Education*. New York: Council on Social Work Education, 1959.

MOORE, WILBERT E., *The Professions: Roles and Rules*. New York: Russell Sage Foundation, 1970.

MORGAN, JOHN S., *Welfare and Wisdom*. Toronto: University of Toronto Press, 1966.

MURPHY, MARJORIE, *The Social Group Work Method in Social Work Education*. New York: Council on Social Work Education, 1959.

PAYNE, JAMES E., "Ombudsman Roles for Social Workers," *Social Work*, 17, No. 1 (January 1972), 94–100.

PINS, ARNULF M., "Changes in Social Work Education," *Social Work*, 16, No. 2 (April 1971), 5–15.

PUMPHREY, MURIEL W., *The Teaching of Values and Ethics in Social Work Education*. New York: Council on Social Work Education, 1959.

REYNOLDS, BERTHA C., *Learning and Teaching the Practice of Social Work*, 2nd ed. New York: Farrar & Rinehart, 1953.

RIPPLE, LILLIAN, ed., *Innovations in Teaching Social Work Practice*. New York: Council on Social Work Education, 1970.

STEIN, HERMAN D., "Competence and Ideology in Social Work Education," *Journal of Education for Social Work*, 5, No. 1 (Spring 1969), 81–90.

STUDT, ELLIOT, *Education for Social Workers in the Correctional Field*. New York: Council on Social Work Education, 1959.

TOWLE, CHARLOTTE, *The Learner in Education for the Professions*. Chicago: University of Chicago Press, 1954.

WEISSMAN, IRVING, *Social Welfare Policy and Services in Social Work Education*. New York: Council on Social Work Education, 1959.

———, and MARY A. BAKER, *Education for Social Workers in the Public Social Services*. New York: Council on Social Work Education, 1959.

WILENSKY, HAROLD L., and CHARLES N. LEBEAUX, *Industrial Society and Social Welfare*, rev. ed. New York: The Free Press, 1965.

WITMER, HELEN LELAND, *Social Work: An Analysis of a Social Institution*. New York: Farrar & Rinehart, 1942.

name index

subject
index

Action, 537
Administration, of social services
  budget, 187, 188
  definition, 177
  functions, 178–83
  organization, 178
  personnel, 183–86
  trends, 188–90
Adoption, 365–69
Adult offender, 508ff.
Aged and aging, 151, 345ff., 419ff.
  environmental factors, 421

  family services, 345ff.
  housing needs, 345ff.
  medical care, 419ff., 425
American Friends Service, 214
American Group Therapy Association,
  154
American Junior Red Cross, 89
American Revolution, 63
Ancient charities, 9
Assistance. *See* Public assistance
Association for Improving Conditions of
  the Poor, 82–84

362.973
F 913 i

120 179